This Other Eden

The Unauthorised History of
Wishaw High School

By the same author

Wishaw High School

The Glory Years – and Some Earlier Rubbish

This Other Eden

The Unauthorised History of
Wishaw High School

A. McMahon

Les vrais paradis sont les paradis qu'on a perdus.

Marcel Proust, *Le Temps retrouvé*

First published in the United Kingdom in 1999 by

A. McMahon,

26 Strathlachlan Avenue,

Carluke,

South Lanarkshire ML8 4DX

Amended, enlarged, and retitled version published in 2016

ISBN 978-0-9535109-1-7

Cui dono lepidum novum libellum
arida modo pumice expolitum?
Elissa, tibi: namque tu solebas
meas esse aliquid putare nugas...

Catullus, *Carmina (adapted)*

I am what is called a principal teacher emeritus - from the Latin 'e'
meaning 'out' and 'meritus' meaning 'so he should be'.

Stephen Leacock, Here are my Lectures (adapted)

Once given the chance, Noodles had never disappointed anyone who
expected the worst of him.

Joseph Heller, Closing Time

The masters went upstairs.
    'That's your little mob in there,' said Grimes; 'you let them out at
eleven.'
    'But what am I to teach them?' said Paul in sudden panic.
    'Oh, I shouldn't try to teach them anything, not just yet, anyway.
Just keep them quiet.'

Evelyn Waugh, Decline and Fall

May I not write in such a stile as this?
In such a method too, and yet not miss
Mine end, thy good? why may it not be done?
Dark Clouds bring Waters, when the bright bring none;
Yea, dark, or bright, if they their silver drops
Cause to descend, the Earth, by yielding Crops,
Gives praise to both, and carpeth not at either,
But treasures up the Fruit they yield together:
Yea, so commixes both, that in her Fruit
None can distinguish this from that, they suit
Her well, when hungry: but if she be full,
She spues out both, and makes their blessings null.

John Bunyan, The Pilgrim's Progress (Preface)

Cum tener uxorem ducat spado, Maevia Tuscum
figat aprum et nuda teneat venabula mamma;
patricios omnes opibus cum provocet unus,
quo tondente gravis iuveni mihi barba sonabat;

cum pars Niliacae plebis, cum verna Canopi
Crispinus, Tyrias umero revocante lacernas,
ventilet aestivum digitis sudantibus aurum,
nec sufferre queat maioris pondera gemmae:
difficile est saturam non scribere.

Juvenal, Satires

'Very well,' said this gentleman, briskly smiling and folding his arms. 'That's a horse. Now, let me ask you girls and boys, Would you paper a room with representations of horses?'

After a pause, one half of the children cried in chorus, 'Yes, Sir!' Upon which the other half, seeing in the gentleman's face that Yes was wrong, cried out in chorus, 'No, Sir!' - as the custom is, in these examinations.

'Of course, No. Why wouldn't you?'

A pause. One corpulent slow boy, with a wheezy manner of breathing, ventured the answer, Because he wouldn't paper a room at all, but would paint it.

'You must paper it,' said the gentleman, rather warmly.

'You must paper it,' said Thomas Gradgrind, 'whether you like it or not. Don't tell us you wouldn't paper it. What do you mean, boy?'

'I'll explain to you, then,' said the gentleman, after another and a dismal pause, 'why you wouldn't paper a room with representations of horses. Do you ever see horses walking up and down the sides of a room in reality - in fact? Do you?'

'Yes, Sir!' from one half. 'No, Sir!' from the other. 'Of course, No,' said the gentleman, with an indignant look at the wrong half. 'Why, then, you are not to see anywhere, what you don't see in fact; you are not to have anywhere, what you don't have in fact. What is called Taste, is only another name for Fact.'

Charles Dickens, Hard Times

'Men,' Colonel Cargill began in Yossarian's squadron, measuring his pauses carefully. 'You're American officers. The officers in no other army in the world can make that statement. Think about it'.

Sergeant Knight thought about it and then politely informed Colonel Cargill that he was addressing the enlisted men and that the officers were to be found waiting for him on the other side of the squadron. Colonel Cargill thanked him crisply and glowed with self-satisfaction as he strode across the area. It made him proud to observe that twenty-nine months in the service had not blunted his genius for ineptitude.

Joseph Heller, *Catch 22*

'Let's see now,' said Welch, 'what's the exact title you've given it?'

Dixon looked out of the window at the fields wheeling past, bright green after a wet April. It wasn't the double-exposure effect of the last half-minute's talk that had dumbfounded him, for such incidents formed the staple material of Welch colloquies; it was the prospect of reciting the title of the article he'd written. It was a perfect title, in that it crystallized the article's niggling mindlessness, its funereal parade of yawn-enforcing facts, the pseudo-light it threw on non-problems. Dixon had read, or begun to read, dozens like it, but his own seemed worse than most in its air of being convinced of its usefulness and significance.

'In considering this strangely neglected topic,' it began. This what neglected topic? This strangely what topic? This strangely neglected what? His thinking all this without having defiled and set fire to the typescript only made him appear to himself as more of a hypocrite and fool.

'Let's see,' he echoed Welch in a pretended effort of memory; 'oh yes: The Economic Influence of the Developments in Shipbuilding Techniques 1450 to 1485.'

Kingsley Amis, *Lucky Jim*

Contents

Acknowledgements

On several occasions, I have had a letter published in the *Wishaw Press* inviting former pupils of Wishaw High School to get in touch with me if they had any photographs, newspaper cuttings, or copies of *The Octagon* that might assist me in the writing of this book - or even if they just wanted to talk about any memories they might have of their alma mater. Apart from Miss Mary Jessimer, who was kind enough to send me some school magazines, the response has been pitiful to the point of being almost non-existent.

I have also written to a considerable number of former pupils and former members of staff, suggesting that they might possibly provide me with a written account of their time at the High School. None of them has bothered to reply.

Even more disappointingly (I can think of several, more scathing adverbs that would be more appropriate), an equally large number of people have promised me material - photographs, memoirs, etc. - and failed to keep their promise. The two honourable exceptions from this troop of defaulters have been Ian Megahy and Miss Sheila Sprot: 'utrique igitur gratias ago maximas.'

My thanks are also due to Mrs Margaret Harvie, who undertook the bulk of the proofreading; Mrs Lynn Kerr, who provided me with a number of photographs; Mrs Jennifer Carty, Miss Jennifer Kelly, and Miss Lori McCallum, who did most of the basic research; Mrs Liz Clarke, whose scrapbooks have proved to be invaluable; and the editor of the *Wishaw Press*, who kindly gave me permission to reproduce various articles and reports.

I apologise in advance to anybody whose name has been misspelt. This book is based largely on secondary sources, and if a person's Christian name appears in the *Wishaw Press* or the school magazine as 'Alan' (when it should be 'Allan'), or his surname is recorded as 'McDonald' (when it should be 'Macdonald'), I have, of necessity, followed suit - and thus made the same mistake.

People's memories (including my own) are not always infallible. I accept responsibility for all *lapsus memoriae*, but I am only prepared to accept censure for those that appear under my 'by-line'.

At the end of John Ford's classic western, *The Man Who Shot Liberty Valance*, the newspaper editor declares: 'When the legend becomes fact, print the legend.' I have followed his advice and included several stories that are probably apocryphal. In defence of such a questionable course of action, I can only quote, with respect to each of the stories in question, a very old Italian proverb: 'se non è vero, è molto ben trovato.'

Preface to *This Other Eden*

First of all, I have a message for those people to whom I sent a copy of *Wishaw High School* and from whom I did not receive so much as a word of thanks: Abite in malam maximam crucem, impudici, scelesti, verberones, bustirapi, furciferi …..cunni.

Secondly, I would like to thank most sincerely all the FPs who took the trouble to write to me after they had read *Wishaw High School*, some of whom supplied me with material that I have been only too glad to include in certain chapters.

However, the main reason why I decided to publish this book is that I am a perfectionist - and *Wishaw High School* falls far short of perfection. It contains too many factual errors, too many instances of questionable punctuation, too many infelicitous expressions, and too many passages verging on the twee, a trait that is anathema to a satirist like myself.

Like Lloyd George, I can't see a belt without hitting below it - so it also contains one or two scathing and supercilious comments that might be regarded as offensive. In short, it is a shoddy piece of work, the product of an irrational and totally inexcusable rush to get it published as quickly as possible. Throw it into the nearest dustbin if and when you acquire a copy of this book.

My warmest thanks are due to Mrs Margaret Watson, who converted *Wishaw High School* into digital text; Mrs Joyce Hefferman, whose reminiscences provided the basis of Chapter 47; Dr Iain Stevenson, who gave me some valuable insights into the publishing business; Stuart Rattray, whose autobiographical sketches were the inspiration for Chapter 40; and Pauline McMichael (née Anderson), Scott Price and Sarah-Jane Rodger who helped to type the many additions and corrections to the text.

Finally, I owe a huge debt of gratitude to George Price, without whose artistic, technical and logistic input this book would never have been published.

Prolegomenon

At the beginning of the twentieth century, there were three main types of school in Scotland: elementary, higher grade, and higher class. Elementary schools were basically the equivalent of today's primary schools, but they also provided supplementary courses of a practical and vocational nature for those pupils who had passed the Qualifying Examination, but who intended to leave school at the statutory leaving age of 14 without embarking on any form of post- elementary education; higher grade schools offered a three-year course of general education leading to the award of the Intermediate Certificate; higher class schools, which soon came to be known as secondary schools, were relatively few in number (the nearest one to Wishaw was probably Hamilton Academy), and tended to be regarded as rather elitist, since in addition to charging fees they prepared pupils for the Leaving Certificate, the sine qua non of admission to a university and a career in one of the professions.

The demarcation lines between these three types of school were not always clear-cut. Many elementary schools created a higher grade department; many higher grade schools were staffed and equipped on a scale that enabled them to provide the full range of post-elementary courses, and in due course they were accorded secondary status. Such were the processes by which secondary education was established in Wishaw.

fons et origo

In 1905 there were five elementary schools in Wishaw: Berryhill, Cambusnethan, Wishaw RC., Wishaw Public, and Wishaw Academy; there was no higher grade school and no higher class school in the town. Higher grade education was available, however, in the higher grade department at Wishaw Public, and so it could be argued that the embryo from which Wishaw High School evolved began life in the annexe of Wishaw Public (which, oddly enough, became an annexe of the High School eighty years later).

There were more than 150 pupils in the higher grade department (it was housed in the old Public School building) at Wishaw Public, and the demand for post-elementary education was beginning to outstrip the existing accommodation. 'The headmaster of the Public School,' wrote the Reverend Walter Stott, 'deserves all credit for the inception of the idea of a higher grade department and the help he has given in its development, but the thing has assumed such proportions that it should of necessity be separated from the elementary school.'

Quot homines tot sententiae...

Terence, *Phormio*

The organisation and day-to-day management of education in the Wishaw area were the responsibility of the Cambusnethan School Board, a democratically elected body that met once a month – very often to procrastinate or make a spectacular U-turn, a happy medium being (apparently) outwith its grasp, as it lurched from almost criminal torpidity on one issue to rash, ill-considered initiatives on another. Depending on which members of the Board turned up, a decision could be taken one month and reversed the next; and there was rarely a clear-cut majority, let alone unanimity, on any issue. Like the Baldwin government of the mid-1930s, the Board was 'decided only to be undecided, resolved to be irresolute, adamant for drift, and solid for fluidity'.

The Board normally included a priest, a 'representative of labour', and two or three ministers. The priests, surprisingly, never contributed very much to the monthly altercations; the 'representatives of labour' were idealistic voices in the wilderness; when the ministers, crusty old reactionaries to a man, were not interrupting other members of the Board or raising points of order, they were propounding their opinions on every aspect of education from homework to janitors' uniforms with unshakeable conviction. More often than not, as the following extract from the minutes of a lively meeting demonstrates, they were at each other's throats:

> *Reverend Mr Dean: Will Mr Harper withdraw that statement?*
> *Reverend Mr Harper: I will not.*
> *Reverend Mr Dean: I must ask Mr Harper to withdraw the statement 'in toto'. We have had enough of these innuendoes from Mr Harper. He is a master of innuendo, but of nothing else that I know.*

Bluff, outspoken characters like the Reverend Alexander Harper (who favoured hiring female teachers - because they were paid less than their male counterparts; and, on the question of travelling expenses, declared that it was far more healthful for a girl to walk a mile or so to school than to have her tramcar fare paid by the Board) could have stepped straight out of *Hard Times*.

Collectively, the Board tended to be parsimonious in the extreme (an admirable tendency, one might argue, since almost half its income was derived from the rates), and to regard teachers - even head teachers - as its 'servants'.

In its dealings with the Scotch (as it was entitled in the early 1900s) Education Department, the Board could be very awkward: on one occasion, after it had received a letter from the Department informing it that due to a miscalculation of its annual grant it had been paid £24 too much, and requesting the repayment of this sum, it decided, initially, to ignore the letter; and if the Department didn't drop the said request, to notify it that the money couldn't be repaid - as it had been spent. Moreover, insofar as some members of the Board were self-designated experts on the curriculum and pedagogic technique, 'the stream of memoranda issuing from the Department and its inconsiderate dashing into new subjects and new ways of teaching' were a constant source of irritation.

Over the years, some of the Board's actions could be described as rather high-handed: in 1905, for instance, it summarily lopped one hour off the time allocated to French on the timetable operated by the higher grade department at Wishaw Public ('We flatter ourselves,' explained the inimitable Reverend Harper, 'that we know better than the headmaster'). However, the Board never advanced as far along the road to outright capriciousness as its counterpart in Carluke, whose members played pitch and toss to decide which of several candidates should be appointed to a teaching post that had fallen vacant.

1

1906 – 1914: Primordium

Tantae molis erat Romanam condere gentem.

Virgil, *Aeneid*

In January 1906, faced with the urgent need to cater for the rapidly increasing number of pupils who wanted post-elementary education of an academic nature and doubtless aware that the most obvious means of satisfying this need - the creation of a higher grade school - had been given the official seal of approval some months earlier by His Majesty's Chief Inspector for the West of Scotland ('There is room,' he had declared, 'in a populous locality like Wishaw for a higher grade school, and if a higher grade school is to be constituted, such a project should be initiated as soon as possible'), the Cambusnethan School Board set up an ad hoc committee to look into the various ways in which a higher grade school might be 'constituted'. This committee submitted a recommendation that 'the work of the higher grade department at Wishaw Public School should be conducted in Beltanefoot School as soon as satisfactory arrangements could be made'.

The school at Beltanefoot had been built a few years earlier to ease the overcrowding in Wishaw's elementary schools, but although it housed the infant department of Wishaw Academy, six of its nine rooms were lying empty. However, changing the status of a school overnight from elementary to higher grade smacked of expediency, which in turn invited criticism - or even ridicule. Such anyway was the view expressed by W. B. Thomson when the Board met to discuss the recommendations of the ad hoc committee: 'We will be a laughing stock to our constituents, if we alter a school a year or two after it was erected'; and William Wight raised three further objections of a more practical nature: extensive - and costly - reconstruction would be necessary at Beltanefoot, since the rooms had been designed to accommodate sixty to seventy pupils, and the maximum permissible size of a class in a secondary school was thirty; the fact that Beltanefoot was almost half a mile from the centre of

Wishaw would have an adverse effect on the efforts of the Board to recruit pupils for any school that was located there; and elementary pupils would have to be moved from Beltanefoot.

Taking his cue from the rather lukewarm reaction to the ad hoc committee's proposal, Father Van Hecke suggested an even bolder solution to the problem posed by the overcrowding in the higher grade department - the erection of a new school. Whereupon, the following exchange took place:

Reverend Mr Kennedy: Well, that will cost you nine or ten thousand.
Father Van Hecke: You don't need to build a palace.

In the event, the Board was not disposed to make up its mind between a reconstituted Beltanefoot and a new school (palatial or otherwise), opting instead to set up another ad hoc committee to investigate the cost of the two possible courses of action.

There seems to have been a similar divergence of opinion among the general public. At a meeting of the Wishaw and District Trades and Labour Council, there was unanimous support for the erection of a new school; whereas the following extract from a letter (signed simply 'A Ratepayer') that appeared in the *Wishaw Press* on 16 February 1906 probably summed up the feelings of many ratepayers: 'If economy is wanted, Beltanefoot is empty, and to the plain man it seems strange that the Board should hesitate to use it.'

In March, the second ad hoc committee submitted the result of its inquiries (a new school would cost £9,000, reconstruction work at Beltanefoot £1,400), and a unanimous recommendation that Beltanefoot should be converted into a higher grade school.

Nothing, however, was done to implement this recommendation until the end of July (by which time a new board had been elected), when it was agreed (but only by five votes to four) that tenders for various sections of the reconstruction work should be accepted; that the contractors should make an immediate start to the work; that the higher grade department should be transferred from Wishaw Public to Beltanefoot at the beginning of the new session in September; and that the post of headmaster at the 'new' school should be advertised at a salary of £300 per annum.

Parsimony and the Board's desire to keep up with the educational Joneses had won the day: no excessive demands were to be made on the ratepayers; and now that Wishaw was to have a higher grade school, the Board could disregard (with a clear conscience) the attempts of the

County Council to pressurise it into sending the most promising pupils in the town to the blackest of its bêtes noires - Hamilton Academy.

Three are called, one is chosen

There were sixty-six applicants for the post of headmaster at Wishaw's first higher grade school. On 26 July, after a long and acrimonious discussion about whether certain applicants were 'first or second class men', the Board drew up a shortlist of three: J. Boyd Robertson from Edinburgh; A.J.C. Kerr (throughout his teaching career people referred to him by his surname, preceded by the initial letters of his forenames), Rector of Golspie Higher Grade School; and Alexander Symon, Science and Mathematical Master in the higher grade department at Wishaw Public. Wires were sent to this trio, requesting them to attend a special meeting of the Board at 4 o'clock on 28 July (a Saturday, incidentally).

'I received the wire in Paris,' wrote Kerr, 'where I was taking a refresher course in French at the Sorbonne. I caught the first express to Calais on Friday morning, and expected that on arrival at Waterloo there would still be an hour and a quarter in which to catch the midnight train from Euston to Glasgow. But fog in the Channel held up the steamer, so on arrival at Victoria I had only twelve minutes to get to Euston.

Calling a hansom, I told the man to drive like Jehu, which he did. The porter at Euston took me and my luggage and literally threw us into a 1st Class compartment as the train was moving out of the station.

So I arrived in Glasgow at 8 o'clock on Saturday morning, bought a *Wishaw Press*, and found that I was indeed on a reduced short leet of three. My wife had reported to the Clerk of the Board that I was in Paris, but that I would arrive in time for the interview.

This telegram, to the great amusement of the Board, arrived with the words: "Mr Kerr in parts." The Board, however, was pleased to discover that I was "all there" for the interview.'

After the three candidates had been interviewed, it soon became apparent that Robertson was out of the running, and in a straight fight between Kerr and Symon, Kerr emerged victorious by six votes to three. Any doubts the Board might have entertained about the soundness of their decision were quickly dispelled, when the Clerk informed them after the meeting that Kerr had claimed travelling expenses (to Wishaw) from Golspie - not St. Ouen-sur-Seine.

A Lad o' Pairts

A.J.C. Kerr was born in Glasgow in 1876. As a young boy, he attended Abbotsford Public School; thereafter, he trained as a pupil teacher at Gorbals Public School. In the course of a distinguished academic career, he came fourth in the whole of Scotland in the entrance examination for the Normal (sic) Training College, and passed out from that college second on the list, after gaining certificates in Art, Music, French, Chemistry, Dynamics and Physiography. His teaching qualifications were augmented by the Honours degree (in Classics) he gained at Glasgow University, where he won prizes in Latin, Greek, Mathematics, Education, and Natural Philosophy. He began his teaching career as Classical Master at the Gordon Schools in Huntly, then returned to his native Glasgow to take up the post of Language Master at Hutcheson's Girls Grammar School. Two years later, he was appointed First Master at Alloa Academy, and his meteoric rise culminated in 1904 with the rectorship at Golspie Higher Grade School.

Saturday Night and Monday Morning

Beltanefoot Higher Grade School was formally opened on Monday, 3 September 1906 - almost minus its headmaster. 'As there was no schoolhouse in Wishaw,' Kerr explained, 'I had to sell our furniture on Saturday, the 1st of September, and travel the long journey south on the Sunday, leaving Golspie at 5.40 a.m. Our minister's wife kindly offered to put me up on the Saturday night, and she assured me that the maid would waken me in good time in the morning. She let me down. When I awoke, I had only five minutes in which to dress and catch the train. Luckily, the house was only a field's breadth from the station, so I put collar, tie and boots in my bag and rushed over the dewy field in my slippers. The train was just about to leave the station, so I sought the nearest compartment - where Providence again came to my aid, insofar as my one companion on the 5-hour journey to Inverness turned out to be a traveller for McFarlane Lang. He opened a box of biscuits and two bottles of lemonade to allay our hunger and thirst. So I duly arrived on the Monday morning at the school, where I was introduced to the staff and pupils by the Reverend Alexander Harper, a member of the School Board.'

Nomenclature

On 4 September, since both Kerr and the Scotch Education Department had objected to the original name, the Board agreed to change the name of the 'new' school to 'Wishaw High School'. A month later, Kerr was designated Rector, as opposed to headmaster, of Wishaw High School.

Large streams from little fountains flow,
Tall oaks from little acorns grow.

David Everett, *Lines written for a School Declamation*

If we accept the figure quoted by Kerr himself on many occasions, there were 135 pupils on the roll of the nascent High School. There was also a considerable number of Junior Students i.e. prospective teachers who had opted to combine secondary education with practical training in the art of teaching. This training was supervised by the Master of Method, a post that was invariably filled by one of the more experienced members of staff.

The teachers were eight in number: A.J.C. Kerr himself, who in addition to his duties as Rector was Classics Master and Master of Method; Alexander Symon (First Assistant and Mathematics Master); Alexander Auchinachie (English Master); John Jackson (Assistant Master of Method); Mr Loudon (Art, Music, and Science Master), whose Christian name I have been unable to ascertain; Lizzie Gow (Modern Languages Mistress); Annie Gow (Mathematics Mistress); and Susan Duguid (General Assistant). The janitor was Adam 'Daddy' Allan.

The School Day

The school day consisted of 8 forty-minute periods. There were two assemblies every day: 9 – 9.05am and 1 – 1.05pm; and at the former there was a reading from the Bible and a prayer. There were also 2 'registration' intervals: 9.45 – 9.50am and 1.45 – 1.50pm. The main morning and afternoon intervals lasted for ten minutes (10.30 – 10.40am and 2.30 – 2.40pm) and the 'dinner' interval for one hour (12 noon – 1.00pm)

An Auspicious Start

At the end of the first full week of session 1906—07, Father Van Hecke, Convener of the sub-committee of the School Board that had specific responsibility for the High School (and, interestingly, a Belgian by nationality), reported to the Board that 'things seemed to be in every way very bright and very cheery'. Though the *Wishaw Press* was also impressed, it did have one slight reservation:

The High School has made a very promising start in its new quarters. Everything necessary in the matter of equipment and accommodation has been provided, and if only the complaint as to the situation of the school were removed, there could be absolutely no excuse for any want of success in the future.

It seems, however, that in Kerr's judgment not quite 'everything in the matter of equipment' had been provided, for in November he applied to the Board for a donation of £25 towards 'the completion of the present very incomplete library' (it had only 96 books, most of which were French or German textbooks). Nine months later, the school library contained 400 books.

Two months into the first term of the first session, the Reverend Alexander Harper delivered his verdict on the 'new' school and its rector:

There is a very excellent tone in the school, and already Mr Kerr has both the teachers and the pupils at his beck. Mr Kerr seems to me to be a born teacher, a disciplinarian - and yet a man of judgment. He will not be over-tyrannising in any way, and he will treat his teachers as colleagues.

Aims and Objectives

'Our aim,' Kerr declared at the prize-giving in 1910, 'is to give our students - no matter what profession or business they may follow - the education of a cultured gentleman, an education fitting them, in the best sense, for university or a technical institution.' However, such an elevated aim had to be modified, as he later admitted, by more practical considerations:

Since Wishaw not only lies on the fringe of the industrial belt of Lanarkshire, but is also close to an area given over to fruit-farming and general agriculture, we kept as our fixed ideal the extension of the number and grade of subjects that could be taken in a course leading to the award of the Leaving Certificate (in 1912, for instance, the High School became the first school in Scotland to present pupils for Higher

6

Domestic Science); in other words, long before this concept found favour with the SED, we aimed at a 'comprehensive' or 'multilateral' school, even though we were hindered by the predominance given by the Department - and parents - to the 'academic' curriculum, which prepared all secondary pupils as if they were aiming to gain admittance to a university.

When Kerr entered on his rectorship, he was advised by Dr Andrew, the HMI who was responsible for monitoring the progress of the High School, that in addition to enlarging the number of subjects in the curriculum he should aim to provide 'special tuition' for those pupils who had the academic potential to take part in the Glasgow University Bursary Competition. Kerr needed little encouragement to follow such advice, for he was well aware that success in the Bursary Competition would confer on his fledgling establishment the sort of prestige that was likely to enhance its prospects of attracting pupils who would otherwise have enrolled at such schools as Hamilton Academy and Glasgow High School.

Secondary Status 'de iure'

In November 1906, the Scotch Education Department recognised the High School as a centre for the training of pupil teachers, a status it retained until the Junior Student System was abolished in 1927. According to Father Van Hecke, the School Convener:

Only a few of the many schools that submitted applications have gained such recognition, and the Board is therefore entitled to congratulate itself on having obtained this recognition, and to make its success public by means of an advertisement in the local press. Some people may even be persuaded by such an advertisement to come and try the High School's wares.

Two years later, the High School was accorded secondary status 'in view of its general standing and the qualifications of its staff'. The Board now had (or believed it had) a school that was a match for Hamilton Academy in every respect, a state of affairs that inspired the following paragraph in the *Wishaw Press*:

If their headgear has been worn at an angle these last few days, High School students may quite easily be pardoned their little 'side' [sic], insofar as My Lords of the Education Department have been graciously pleased to acknowledge that Seminary as a Secondary School within the definition of the Department. This means that in future neither the County Council nor any other body will be able to draw an unfavourable distinction between the Beltanefoot establishment and Hamilton Academy (or any other high-class school), the status of both being equal.

In 1910 the Board were rather surprised to learn that 'the Hamilton people' on the County Secondary Education Committee were claiming that Hamilton Academy was the only secondary school in Lanarkshire - presumably on the grounds that it was the only one that charged fees. The Reverend J.A.F. Dean, an irascible man at the best of times, gave this nonsensical claim - and Hamilton Academy - short shrift:

Schools like Hamilton Academy no longer occupy a unique position; and some of them are likely to close, since the vast majority of parents have no desire to pay for an education that is no better than that which they can get for nothing. An attempt is being made to show that the teaching at Hamilton Academy is different from that being given at other schools, something which is contrary to fact. Wishaw High School compares favourably in staffing, curriculum, and results with Hamilton Academy, and it is mere humbug for them to say that a better education is given in that school.

In spite of these strictures, twenty-three pupils from the parish of Cambusnethan opted to attend Hamilton Academy, which charged annual fees of between £4 and £6.

'Staffing'

'The School Board,' according to Kerr, 'did nobly by the school in providing more and more teachers of high scholarship and great teaching ability.' The quality of some of these teachers can be gauged from the distinction they achieved in their later careers: for instance, William McKinlay (Mathematics Master) was a member of the ill-fated Stefannson expedition to the North Pole; Dr William Miller (Science Master), a man of 'outstanding scholarship and inventive power', became Chief Inspector of Schools in Ireland; Miss Ethel Stevenson (Cookery Mistress) was appointed Mistress of Method in Domestic Science at the Glasgow Training College; and Alexander Symon (First Assistant) wrote or co-wrote several mathematical textbooks, one of which, Symon and Milliken's *Arithmetic*, was still in use in the 1950s.

'Curriculum'

The following advert appeared in the *Wishaw Press* on 16 August 1907:

Wishaw High School
This school is open to all pupils who have passed the Qualifying Examination and desire to enter on a 3 or 5-Year Secondary Course, or train as Junior Students for the Teaching Profession. The Staff and Equipment are such that besides a General Course of Instruction, a Curriculum may be followed that is predominantly Classical, or Scientific, or Commercial; or directed (for the benefit of girls) towards Domestic Subjects. For practical work there are Physical and Chemical Laboratories, a Workshop, a Cookery Kitchen, and a Laundry. The Drill Hall and adjoining Recreation Field are utilised for systematic Physical Training. Copies of the prospectus may be had from Local Booksellers or on application to the Rector.

For pupils taking the 3-year course, which led to the award of the Intermediate Certificate, the following subjects were compulsory: English, Mathematics, Science, Drawing, and one language. Though French was prescribed ('partly because of its utilitarian purpose, and partly because the average child - and even a dull child - manages to understand sufficient French in a year or so to read a fairly easy book'), Latin was also available, but only for those 'who could make good use of it in later life'; for those who couldn't, there was Woodwork (a qualified joiner was appointed in 1907 at a salary of £104 per annum) or Domestic Science. PE and Music completed the timetable.

Not surprisingly, permutations of the same six subjects - English, Mathematics, Science, Drawing, French, and Latin - at Higher or Lower Grade formed the basis of the curriculum followed by those pupils who intended to complete the full 5-year secondary course and, hopefully, gain the Leaving Certificate. Greek and German could be taken by 'the cream of the students'.

'Results'

The number of pupils presented for the Intermediate Certificate remained fairly stable during the first eight years of the school's existence: 26 in 1908, 21 of whom were successful; and 26 in 1913, with 23 gaining the certificate.

There was a significant increase in the number of pupils who obtained the Leaving Certificate: 15 in 1912, as opposed to 4 (Mary Paterson, Matilda McLean, Robertson Millar and James McAlpin, the High School's first dux) in 1907.

In 1907 a 3rd Year pupil, J. Allan Steele, gained passes in Higher English, Lower Maths, Lower Latin, and Lower French; in 1913 there was a 95% pass rate in Higher English; in 1911 eleven senior pupils went on to university and the school's academic standing was given a further boost when James T. Wilson gained 19th place in the Glasgow University Bursary Competition in 1910.

His Majesty's Inspectors could hardly fail to be impressed:

This school is organised and conducted with energy and ability. The staff is most capable and hard-working. (HMI Report 1909).

All the work of the 1st Year English class is of good quality. In History and Geography the oral answering shows intelligent knowledge of the work professed. (HMI Report 1907).

In the Lower French classes, the pupils were alert and responsive. Mathematical Studies have followed sound and effective lines, and the efforts of earnest and painstaking teachers have been attended by well-merited success. In Science, the pupils showed reasonable facility and skill in the experimental operations, and a creditable appreciation of the principles underlying their work. As for Art, very careful work has been done in pencil. (HMI Report 1909).

The system of practical training is producing good results, and the out-going students showed, as a rule, very creditable proficiency in handling a class. (HMI Report 1910).

Kerr himself, who combined his duties as Rector with teaching Latin and Greek, earned the following commendation in 1907:

Mr Kerr's work is exceptionally zealous, thorough, and competent.

Orandum est ut sit mens sana in corpore sano.

Juvenal, *Satires*

There was one department, however, that did not gain the unqualified approval of the inspectorate. In January 1908, Captain Foster, Inspector of Drill, intimated to the Board that there was 'great room for improvement in the present physical training of the pupils at the High School'; and that even though the physique of the pupils was good, 'much could be done, especially in the case of the girls, to improve their gait, courage, and alertness'. This was a rather grandiose claim (especially since the girls did their drill in a shed constructed primarily for the painting and decorating class at the night school), but with a view to substantiating it Captain Foster made three recommendations:

There should be short periods of exercise in the classroom at appropriate breaks in the lesson; the boys should remove their coats and waistcoats when taking PE; and the girls should be taught PE by a thoroughly trained lady instructor.

With the withering contempt that Classics scholars have traditionally shown towards the beanbag-tossing fraternity, the Reverend J.A.F. Dean dismissed Captain Foster's report as 'neither sense nor grammar'. Six months later, however, the Board hired a physical training instructress on a joint basis with its counterpart in Motherwell.

The instructress in question (her name was Frood) was not impressed with the facilities that existed at the High School for PE ('The gymnasium is too small and the apparatus is not up to requirements'), and she wrote a letter of complaint to the Board.

However, the only response evoked by her letter was an unsympathetic outburst by Robert Martin to the effect that Miss Frood should have had better things to do than bring to the Board's attention a state of affairs it had known about for some considerable time (and had done nothing to rectify, it should be added).

Less than a month after the opening of the school, an 'athletic club' (an umbrella term that covered a number of sporting activities) was established by the pupils. Such a club, according to a letter in the *Wishaw Press*, was 'the most effective means of creating a good spirit in a school'.

For the first two months of session 1906-07, a local grazier called Rodger allowed the pupils to make use of a field behind the school for recreational purposes; he charged the school ten shillings, which he later donated to the Athletic Club. In November, Lord Belhaven granted the school a lease (for not less than three years) on another field (Birkhill Field) behind the school at a cost of £3 per annum. A gate was constructed to provide access to this field from the playground, and the field itself was surrounded by a 'substantial' fence costing £11.

In 1909 a park in Stewarton Street was leased from Mr J.H. Houldsworth. It was used primarily for cricket and hockey, 'a new pastime' in the Wishaw area, for which 'a complete set of clubs [sic] had to be procured'.

The first two hockey matches of which there is any record were against Kent Road in 1911 and Airdrie Academy in 1912, the former resulting in victory (4-0), the latter in defeat (1-2).

Every year, in an effort to encourage aspiring cricketers, Councillor Scott presented a cricket bat and a cricket bag to the boys who topped the batting and bowling averages respectively. The first recipients of these prizes were R.K. Hinshelwood and James Paterson.

In 1908 (and this is the only occasion on which school cricket is mentioned in the columns of the *Wishaw Press*), the High School defeated Newmains by 9 runs.

In April 1908, a cake and candy sale was held in the school hall to raise money for a tennis court. According to Kerr:
Since the school is a centre for the training of pupil teachers, we hope - nay, expect - to enrol between forty and fifty Junior Students (mostly, girls) in the years to come; and these young ladies (who are in their late teens) will doubtless wish to develop their physical, as well as their mental, faculties.

Boys' and girls' singles championships were held annually, and the winners were presented with tennis rackets by Police Judge Nimmo. In 1913 the championships were won by Alexander Robert and Annie Hunter.

First Trophy

In 1909 the High School won the Schools' Cup Competition, defeating Waterloo 1-0 in the final. Young, the captain of the winning team and the scorer of the winning goal, 'was placed on the shoulders of enthusiasts and, carrying the trophy, was borne in this fashion from Belhaven Park through the streets of the town, the enthusiastic procession of youths attracting attention all along the route'.

Interestingly enough, it was also in 1909 that the High School played what may very well have been its first football match against 'the auld enemy', Dalziel High School - a match it won 3-1.

At a national level, the school was taking part in the Scottish Secondary Shield from as early as 1910.

First Sports

The first schools' sports to be held in the parish of Cambusnethan took place in Belhaven Park on Saturday, 25 June 1910. Each of the eight local schools had its own distinctive colours, and was represented in every event. The High School provided the winners of six track and field events - and the winner of the Highland fling; and came second to Wishaw Public in the overall classification.

Cultural Activities

At the school concert in December 1909, Kerr contrasted 'the education, so called, of ten or twenty years ago, when children were all reduced to one type, with the modern efforts to develop the individuality of each scholar'. 'These efforts,' he continued, 'are directed in the High School to the formation and upkeep of literary and athletic clubs, a literary magazine, and such entertainment as you have witnessed this evening.' The 'entertainment' that evening included violin, pianoforte, and vocal solos; Dutch, Spanish, and gymnastic dances; Swedish exercises; recitations; and performances of scenes from various plays and novels.

Operettas were staged in 1912 (*In the Days of Good Queen Bess*) and 1913 (*Bohemian Girl*). The *Wishaw Press* was full of praise for all aspects of the latter production:

There are few organisations which have at their command talent so outstanding as that displayed by the leading female characters. No better Arline could have been desired than that of Miss Nettie Hamilton, who showed a fine conception of the part, acted with ease and grace, and did full justice to the exacting music, for which her clear, fresh, soprano voice is well suited.

Unstinted praise is due to the chorus for the manner in which they rendered the concerted music, their hearty and harmonious singing being a perfect treat.

At suitable periods in the performance dances were introduced, and these contributed in no small measure to the enjoyment of the entertainment.

Mr Robert Booth, who was responsible for the orchestral score, conducted the performance with his customary ability.

A 'literary' magazine (costing threepence) was published twice per session. One of the 1908 editions was fully illustrated, and included several humorous contributions ('How Johnny Took Home His Report', for instance, and 'A Message from Mars'), the first in a series of articles on 'Old Wishaw Celebrities', a more utilitarian item entitled 'A Plan for the Establishment of Scientific Instruction in Schools', and a fair number of poems.

In 1907 the magazine contained the following - surprisingly daring - poem:

A Novelette in Two Chapters by Eros

Chapter One

A second's touch
Of hands - not much,
But listen!
A maiden sighs,
And see! Her eyes,
They glisten.
A twilight shade,
Where plans are made-
Delightful!
A soft embrace,
Pa's prying face –
How spiteful!

A parent's room,
A daughter's gloom –
Conjecture.
A father's sneer,
A mother's tear –
A lecture.

Chapter Two

A moonlight night,
A hurried flight –
A carriage.

A little church,
With ivied porch –
A marriage.

A baffled sire
Sets forth in ire
To capture.
What can be done?
The two are one –
Oh, rapture!

The 1912 edition of the magazine featured an essay on 'Athleticism' by B. Trotwood:

In this age of progress, we have seen what exercise has done for the nation, and we have recognised the need for it. Athletics, however, should be only a recreation - a relaxation after some hard study or some difficult task has been completed - and ought not to enter into one's mind, except at the right time. It is a fine thing as a relaxation, but it goes too far when it becomes a profession.

There is always a certain amount of danger - and laziness - attached to the practice of sports. Athletes certainly have hard enough work, for sport demands much of them; but they are lazy, inasmuch as they do not care to take up any trade or study. Their life is all play and no real work. They have nothing to show for their labours, so surely such a profession is not worth having.

A great athlete is not necessarily a great man, for he leaves the world as he finds it. No man is truly great who is great only in his lifetime - and an athlete's fame dies with him.

Sufficient recreation can be got after the day's work is over, and men should esteem themselves more highly than to deign to become professionals and be kept by the nation.

Does this system of paid professionals not remind us of Spanish bullfights and the circuses at Rome, which, without doubt, helped to cause that "mother of the world's" downfall? The Romans cared not what happened to them, as long as their 'panem et circenses' were forthcoming. There, those who had to suffer were the conquered slaves, who were victims of the gladiatorial fights. These slaves were rewarded with freedom only in the event of their being victorious; but nowadays men are paid merely for playing, and if they win, an extra reward is theirs.

Let us hope that our enthusiasm for athletics may not grow too great, lest we learn to forget both their real place in men's lives and, more importantly, the higher, nobler subjects with which we ought to acquaint ourselves.

High Society

A literary society, open to both pupils and FPs, was established in 1907, and at its first meeting Kerr delivered a paper on 'Burns: The Man and His Songs'. A Hat Night, a Magazine Night, and a debate on 'Female Suffrage' also featured among the society's activities.

On the social side, the staff dance and the quaintly entitled 'At Home' became annual events. At the latter function (a sort of social), Intermediate and Leaving Certificates were presented to successful candidates, and teachers, pupils and former pupils were afforded an opportunity to meet in a less formal setting. The entertainment might include such items as a pianoforte duet, a sword dance, a tambourine dance, solo and choral songs, a skipping rope dance, bowls, a recitation, clock golf, ping-pong, a violin solo, and a three-act charade. In the course of the 'At Home' in 1908, the 'speech' of Father Van Hecke, the School Convener, won great acclaim. 'You have asked for a short speech,' he said. 'I will be very short. I have nothing to say and I beg to say so.'

The Welfare School

Enshrined in the Education Act of 1908 (and this is what made the act particularly significant) was the belief that schools should focus less on the inculcation of facts and more on the social and physical welfare of the pupils, and this belief translated into several benefits for the pupils of the High School. There were regular medical inspections, an innovation that threw up some comforting (for both the staff and the pupils) statistics: for instance, none of the 96 pupils examined by a doctor in December 1911 was found to be suffering from pediculosis or 'contagious skin disease'.

A dentist was hired by the Board (at a salary of £50 per annum) to visit all the schools in the parish and provide dental treatment wherever it was found to be necessary. The children of parents whose weekly income was less than 25 shillings received this treatment free of charge;

children whose parents earned between 25 shillings and £2 were charged 2d for an extraction and 6d for a filling.

On his own initiative, Kerr set up an 'employment bureau' in the school. Employers, apparently, 'often wrote to him for lads'; and he hoped parents would keep in touch with him, so that he could advise them "about the best subjects for their children's curriculum, and the nature of the employment likely to be found".

Kerr was undoubtedly in favour of involving parents as much as possible in the education of their children. At the prize-giving in 1909, he expressed the hope that parents would make frequent visits to the school and ask to be shown round the premises; in June 1910, the public were given the opportunity to inspect the work of the 'practical classes', which included woodwork, PE (in the gym, where 'a group of girls went through a series of advanced exercises'), experimental science, practical geography, baking, nursing, and housewifery (in a model cottage; and in the laundry, where 'a score of girls were extremely busy - some of them at the washtub, others ironing and goffering the articles that had been washed'); and by 1911, a system of quarterly reports was operative, which enabled Kerr "to furnish parents with a note of their children's progress".

Ludi magister, parce simplici turbae...

Martial, *Epigrams*

Certain members of the School Board were opposed to what were known in 1909 as 'home lessons'. John Fell maintained that school was 'the place for the subjects being taught', and that 'children should be allowed perfect freedom after coming out of school, in order to recreate the powers that had been used there'; Archibald McAllister was even more outspoken, describing homework as 'an evil' and 'a refinement of cruelty'. In May 1911, therefore, at a joint meeting of the School Board and the headmasters of the various schools in the parish, he proposed that 'the system of home lessons be abolished in all the schools under the Board'. Kerr spoke against the motion, arguing that "a carefully graded amount of home lessons developed the individuality and independence of the child and preserved the interest of the parents, a very important factor in a child's progress". McAllister altered his motion in such a way as to make it inapplicable to the High School; but since it (the motion) was defeated, this gesture proved to be unnecessary.

Miscellanea

By the time the first prize-giving was held in June 1907, Provost Thomson had presented the school with a gold medal for the dux; silver medals had been acquired by the Reverend J.A.F. Dean for the pupils who came first in Maths, English, Classics, Science, Drawing, and Modern Languages; and prizes were available for general excellence, thanks to the generosity of the Board (which contributed £3 every year to the prize fund) and several private donors. Unfortunately, since there was no platform in the school hall, the presentation of all these medals and prizes was not visible to many members of the large audience that was present at the ceremony.

In 1912 a savings bank was set up in the school, the Board being of the opinion that it was "an essential part of a child's education to learn the value of saving".

Caps were worn by the boys and cowls by the girls. Both forms of headgear were dark blue in colour, and they were both decorated with a badge designed jointly by Kerr and the school captain. The badge, which was shaped like a shield, had an open book in the top left hand corner, a pen and an ink bottle in the bottom right hand corner, and the name of the school along the bottom edge.

Early in 1907, the walls of the drill hall were 'embellished with two beautiful engravings' - one depicting the Circus Maximus in Rome, the other the dead body of Elaine being brought before King Arthur. That same year, on 18 April, forty pupils visited Jacob's Ladder and 'received a practical lesson on the subject of trees in Garriongill'.

In December 1910, 'due to coal workings', there was 'a serious subsidence of the ground in close proximity to the High School on its west side'. However, the Board was given an assurance, that 'there would be no further threat from this source, as the workings were finished'.

In June 1911, a 'large number' of pupils spent an afternoon at Lanark Loch; and the school choir took part in the Juvenile Choral Competition held in conjunction with the Glasgow Exhibition ('It made a good impression, but failed to get among the prizes').

In February 1914, the Board agreed to purchase a house for the Rector of the High School.

The Staff

In August 1907, Miss Lizzie Finlay, the Cookery teacher, resigned 'in indignation' when she learned that, unbeknown to her, the Board had invited applications for the post of Principal Teacher of Domestic Science.

In September of the same year, the Scotch Education Department issued a memorandum stating: 'A teacher of French must now be able to converse in French.' Father Van Hecke, the School Convener, informed the rest of the Board that 'such a one' could not be 'got' for under £90. He was proved right when Miss Mary Black was eventually appointed at a salary of £100 per annum.

Dux femina facti

Virgil, *Aeneid*

In 1910 Miss Esther Legge was promoted to the post of Principal Teacher of English and History. 'The innovation of having a lady as Principal Teacher of English,' wrote Kerr, 'was not carried through without some demur and hesitation, but it is interesting and enlightening to record that from that year till 1947 the head of the English Department was always a lady.'

A Stitch in Time Saves a Fine

In February 1913, as a result of a complaint from the SED that some girls were not receiving instruction in needlework, the Board decided to ask Miss Rankin to rectify this deficiency between the hours of 4 and 5 every afternoon. Her remuneration for undertaking this task was an extra £20 per annum.

In January 1912, the following eulogy, composed by an anonymous former pupil, appeared in the *Wishaw Press*:
We realized that as pupils we needed in our teacher much more than talent - namely the power to make this talent respected and trusted. Miss Gow possessed talents that are granted only to a favoured few, and she knew how to impart the fruits of her knowledge to our young, untutored minds. In class, she was ever willing to help us in our struggles with the

rudiments of Latin and Mathematics. What patience and perseverance she showed can be understood by us only now, when we realize how crude was the material given to her to mould into shape. How often she must have felt discouraged, when she found our response lagging behind her teaching of these difficult subjects. But ever she smiled and greeted each and all with that gracious word of encouragement peculiar to herself. No one was ever repelled when she was approached concerning some mathematical difficulty. Rather, Miss Annie encouraged us to go to her, and by skilful questioning she would lead us to the right solution. She inspired respect as an able and resourceful teacher, a mistress who gave of her energy unsparingly in the work of teaching. Such energy demanded a return of the same kind from her pupils, but we could not grudge our best to Miss Annie, for she was ever ready to give the due meed of praise to honest effort.

A Cause Celèbre

The sister of that paragon, Miss Lizzie Gow, was in no danger of receiving such a fulsome testimonial from the School Board - with which she was embroiled in a long and acrimonious dispute about the circumstances of her departure from the High School. The Board were under the impression that they had dispensed with her services; Miss Gow was adamant that she had resigned.

Matters came to a head when a letter was sent to the Board by Miss Gow's solicitors threatening to initiate proceedings in the Court of Session unless any entry in the minutes of the Board's deliberations which implied that their client had been dismissed was rescinded, and a public apology proffered. The Board, pig-headed as ever, dug in their heels; so too did Cameron and Christie Cowan (Solicitors), Miss Gow's legal advisers. Eventually, with bad grace, the Board agreed to rescind the offending minute - but not to apologise; nor did they allow any of Miss Gow's legal representatives to inspect the records with a view to verifying the rescissions.

Home of (far from) Lost Causes

Other members of staff were more interested in the two topics that have occupied the minds of most teachers for the last ninety years - salaries and holidays. In June 1910, a petition, signed by all the teachers, was submitted to the Board requesting it to bring the High School into line with the majority of secondary schools in Scotland by lengthening the summer holidays. Kerr himself endorsed the petition, pointing out that several members of staff wished 'to supplement their knowledge by attending summer classes held in August'. The Board, surprisingly, agreed to extend the summer holidays to seven weeks.

Three years later, another petition was submitted. This one called on the Board to review teachers' salary scales (male and female graduates started at £110 and £80 respectively per annum, non-graduates at £100), 'in view of the depreciation of money'. The petition was rejected, but six months later, following a similar request from a deputation of teachers, the Board raised the maximum by £10.

The Roll

In November 1906, there were 151 pupils on the roll of the High School (it is interesting to note, in passing, that the roll of Wishaw Public comfortably exceeded 1,000); this number included one local apostate from Hamilton Academy, who had obviously been impressed by the Reverend J.A.F. Dean's confident assertion that no pupil could 'compete successfully in life' - if he travelled by train - 'with the pupil on the spot'.

Although the roll had climbed above 200 by the following January (this necessitated the addition of two classrooms, a workshop, and a 'cookery kitchen'), the School Convener, Father Van Hecke, expressed disappointment at the number of new pupils (only 32 of the 202 who had passed the Qualifying Examination) admitted to the High School from the elementary schools under the Board's jurisdiction. This reluctance to partake of the benefits of secondary education can be attributed, in part, to the fact that for the first five years of the High School's existence pupils had to pay for their own books and stationery. According to Archibald McAllister, who successfully proposed (in 1911) that the Board should provide such materials free of cost in all the schools in the parish of Cambusnethan, 'It is a well-known fact that it was the prohibitive cost of books at the High School which debarred many a clever working-class student from going there.'

The results of a survey conducted by local headmasters and 'compulsory officers' reinforced McAllister's uneasiness about the 'privileged' social background of the High School's clientele: not a single 'necessitous' pupil was unearthed at Beltanefoot, as opposed, for example, to 36 in Cambusnethan Elementary School and 140 in Newmains R.C. Elementary School.

'The prohibitive cost of books' was estimated (by Kerr himself) to be £1 and 25 shillings for 1st and 2nd Year pupils respectively, and at least 30 shillings for 3rd, 4th, 5th and 6thYear students. One parent was faced with an additional outlay of 28 shillings per session for such items as 'rubber shoes', a cricket shirt, a belt, and two school caps (which were compulsory).

Rather surprisingly, Kerr seems to have adopted a somewhat reactionary attitude with regard to the provision of free books. In a letter to the *Wishaw Press*, he pointed out to parents that care would be taken to ensure that books were not used 'promiscuously', and that there was nothing to hinder them from buying their children's books if they so desired.

From its earliest days, the High School attracted pupils from outwith the parish: ten from Cleland and one from Law in 1908, for instance. By 1911, there were 35 'outsiders' ('Their ability,' said Kerr, 'arouses competition and adds greatly to the efficiency and reputation of the school'), and the total roll had climbed above 300. In October 1913, there were 324 pupils on the roll - 119 in SI, 92 in S2, 51 in S3, 20 in S4, 24 in S5 and 18 in S6; and 'secondary' pupils (i.e. pupils who were likely to be presented for the Leaving Certificate) outnumbered Junior Students, a statistic that was warmly welcomed by the new School Convener, Dr Thomas Brodie, who believed that it was 'the large number of secondary pupils going forward to university that fortified the existence of a secondary school'.

Statements like that make it easy to understand why there was a feeling in some sections of the local community that the High School was a rather elitist institution. It was also perceived as being something of an expensive luxury, a perception that was bolstered by statistics indicating that the cost of providing free books and stationery for the pupils in attendance there during session 1911-12 worked out at £1 and 2s 7½d per head respectively, compared with an average of just over four shillings and just under one shilling per head in the other ten schools in the parish; and that £100 out of every £600 raised from the rates was spent on the High School.

With typical forthrightness, the Reverend J.A.F. Dean insisted that disenchantment with the High School was based on the mistaken notion that 'those who were down at Beltanefoot belonged to the privileged classes in Wishaw'. A less superficial explanation of the prevailing climate of opinion was included in an article written for the *Wishaw Press* in 1913 by Father Van Hecke, who seven years earlier had been the High School's first Convener:

By every test that can be applied, the nature of higher education in a district such as Cambusnethan should be technical and scientific, not professional and classical. The parish and district owe their rise and prosperity to industry, and their further rise and continued prosperity must depend on further industrial development; moreover, the bulk of the revenue contributed through local taxation is derived from industry either directly or indirectly. And so, on the principle that a district's educational system should be designed to confer the greatest good on the greatest number, there is no doubt that a great blunder was made when the then Board decided on the scheme we have at present. The High School should be converted into a technical school, and local pupils who wish to become teachers, lawyers, or doctors should be sent to Hamilton Academy.

312 into 270 won't go.

Less than five years after the opening of the High School, His Majesty's Inspector noted that 'in several classes the number in attendance was larger than could be approved under Article 138 of the Code'; and that 'in one class (1st Year Mathematics) the number reached 44'.

Later that same year (1911), Kerr submitted the following report to the Board:

The roll of the school exceeds its capacity by 42; the Science laboratories are too small and congested; a new Art room is required, since the one in use is an ordinary classroom with inappropriate desks and poor lighting; and the cloakrooms, book presses, and cupboards are totally inadequate for the demands being made on them.

The reaction of one member of the Board to the report was somewhat caustic: 'An Art room? Considering the state of trade, a soup kitchen would be more suitable.'

In 1913 a folding partition (part wood, part glass) was set up in the hall, so that academic subjects could be taught in one half, while the other half was being used for drill; and the Mission Hall opposite the school was used to provide extra accommodation. Despite these measures, classes in different years had to be combined for instruction in drawing, and the total complement of one such group was 62.

As far as having to use the Mission Hall was concerned, John Weir, Principal Teacher of Geography, seems to have drawn the short straw on a fairly regular basis. 'In travelling to and from this building, clad in his MA gown, he had,' according to an anecdote Kerr recounted, 'to pass some cottages on the road. As he did so one morning, a matron came to her door, and on seeing him, she shouted excitedly, "My God! Who made you a minister?"'

The High School Question

For three years, the full term of office of the School Board elected in 1911, meetings of the Board were dominated by the question of what should be done about the overcrowding at the High School. Some members of the Board (particularly Robert Martin, who conducted a one-man campaign against alterations and additions to the High School - on the rather bizarre principle that Kerr 'had no right to fill up the rooms and make a mess of the school') were convinced that too much space was being taken up by too many pupils of dubious perseverance (in 1911, for instance, only 46 pupils from an original intake of 85 in 1908 completed the 3-year course; the other 39 had dropped out at some point during the preceding three years), and that overcrowding could be averted if the school only admitted those pupils who were firmly resolved to complete a 3 or 5-year course leading to the award of the Intermediate or Leaving Certificate respectively.

This issue, as the following exchange demonstrates, caused a certain amount of friction between individual members of the Board:

G.S. Sloan: I would like to ask Mr Pomphrey if it is true that a boy is employed in his office who was less than three years at the High School.

G.N. Pomphrey: I am really surprised that you are so anxious about the number of pupils who have left the High School. It is the first time you have shown any interest in the matter, and it is perfectly obvious why you have asked me such a question. I have nothing else to say.

G.S. Sloan: No member of the Board has been more anxious than you to find out why pupils leave the school prematurely, and I do not think it is appropriate for any member of the Board to employ pupils who have not completed their course.

James Roy: If a satisfactory reason was given for the boy not staying on at school for three years, it is no concern of us who employs him.

G.S. Sloan: Was a satisfactory reason given?

G.N. Pomphrey: I was perfectly satisfied with the reason the boy's father gave for his son leaving school. If the boy was not employed by me, he would be employed by some other body.

In the event, the Board decided (with effect from the start of the new session in August 1913) to vet all applications for admission to the High School; and with a view to facilitating this procedure, the headmasters of the elementary schools were instructed to provide the Board with a record of how potential High School pupils performed in the Qualifying Examination. In addition, the parents of prospective entrants had to sign a form stating that it was their intention to keep their son or daughter in regular attendance at the High School for three consecutive years (unless he or she was incapacitated by illness or prevented by a 'necessary cause'), and that they were prepared to forfeit the sum of twenty shillings if they failed to fulfil this commitment.

This attempt by the Board to alleviate the overcrowding at the High School by regulating the number of new entrants was not a great success. Firstly, the vetting process was virtually a formality: the first time it was implemented, 32 of the 34 applicants were admitted; and Kerr himself was accused by the Reverend Walter Stott of 'allowing parents to send their children to the High School for no better reason than that their neighbours' children had gone there'. Indeed, on several occasions the process developed into something of a farce: in January 1914, for instance, when the High School reopened after the Christmas holidays, more than thirty pupils presented themselves for admission - and were actually admitted provisionally on the authority of the School Convener and the Chairman of the Board - even though their applications had not been approved by the Board (since it had not been notified of the marks the pupils had scored in the Qualifying Examination).

The minutes of a special meeting of the Board convened on the 13th of the same month to vet the aforementioned applications record Robert Martin's impatience with the laxity of the admission system:

Robert Martin (rising): I have another important meeting, so you must excuse me.

Clerk: This is not fair to the pupils who are waiting to have their applications granted.

Robert Martin (who by this time had donned his hat and coat): They are not waiting, Mr Smith, they are all in.

Mr Martin left the boardroom.

After a few minutes Mr Martin re-entered the boardroom, and remarking, 'The more hurry, the less speed', picked up his walking stick, which he had forgotten.

Chairman: Will you not withdraw your objection, so that common sense may prevail in this matter?

Mr Martin: Not at all. We are just being made fools of, absolute fools. The Board passed a resolution to keep the pupils out of the High School until we admitted them. They are only laughing at us.

Mr Martin then withdrew, and the meeting ended.

When the applications were finally approved at a full meeting of the Board in February, Martin was still muttering darkly about Kerr's "insubordination" and "the flouting of the Board's authority".

The impact of the new system was further weakened by the rather cavalier attitude adopted by the general public towards its mandatory elements. At every meeting of the Board, there were 'intimations from eight or ten parents' that they wished to be relieved of the obligation to keep their children at the High School for three years ('We have been humbugged a great deal over this thing,' admitted the Reverend Pollock); and the Clerk of the Board was kept busy writing to the parents of pupils who had left school - without offering any explanation - before they had completed three years, to inform them that they had incurred a fine of £1.

In August 1913, the *Wishaw Press* published the following unsigned letter (to the Clerk of the Board) from an even more uncooperative parent:

Dear Sir,

I beg to acknowledge receipt of your letter of the 7th inst., but I regret that I cannot comply with the Board's requirements. I will, however, be sending my daughter to the High School when it opens on Tuesday next.

A House Divided against Itself

Other schemes mooted by the Board with a view to solving the problem of the overcrowding at the High School never got off the ground - thanks to the endless bickering between the different factions ('Occasionally, irreconcilable elements are thrown together and the results are calamitous,' wrote one commentator on the local educational scene), and a chronic dilatoriness that bordered on dereliction of duty: in February 1912, for example, the Board decided 'to provide at Beltanefoot such further accommodation as the High School might require', but absolutely nothing was done to implement this decision.

That same year, on 1 October, a motion to transfer the pupils on the roll of the High School to Wishaw Public (after it had been 'reconstructed') was carried by five votes to four. This 'rash and ill-considered scheme' (as it was described in a letter to the *Wishaw Press* from a disgusted ratepayer) attracted widespread criticism, and at an 'indignation meeting' convened by Provost Thomson, a resolution urging the Board to rescind its decision and provide additional accommodation at the High School was carried 'with great acclamation'.

On 29 October, after meeting a delegation of ratepayers, the Board decided to accede to their demands. However, the motion which was the precursor of this decision had been deemed to be 'out of order' (since standing orders had not been suspended) by two of the five members of the Board who had been in favour of transferring the pupils on the roll of the High School to Wishaw Public, and they had withdrawn from the boardroom before the vote was taken. So the scene was set for further internecine wrangling.

In December, three members of the Board (three of the 'Infamous Five' who had voted for 'the big flitting' to Wishaw Public on 1 October) took out an injunction against the Board to prevent it from implementing the resolution passed on 29 October (since the Board normally acted with the speed of a tortoise on crutches, such an injunction was as otiose as one prohibiting the committee of Larkhall Thistle's Social Club from hiring a Jesuit as a cloakroom attendant); and a copy of the Note of Suspension and Interdict was served on each member of the Board (including those who had activated this procedure) by a messenger-at-arms from Hamilton.

Initially, the Board decided to contest the injunction in the Court of Session; but in January 1913, after a meeting in the Conservative Club in Edinburgh attended by the Chairman of the Board and lawyers representing the two warring factions, the injunction was withdrawn (I suspect that the litigants were concerned about the cost of allowing the dispute to run its full legal course), and it was agreed that 'with regard to solving the problem of the overcrowding at the High School they would clean the slate and start anew'.

A year later, at the end of the Board's term of office, the slate was still clean - as they had failed to chalk up anything that could be construed as a breakthrough. Plans had certainly been drawn up by a local architect to alter and extend the building at Beltanefoot, but the plans had become the subject of a long-running dispute between the Board and the Scotch

Education Department, and nothing had been done to put them into effect. Not even the deduction by the Department of one tenth of the High School's grant - due to its failure to provide sufficient accommodation - provoked the Board into meaningful action.

You have sat too long here for any good you have been doing.

Oliver Cromwell

For three years then, as the overcrowding at the High School became more and more severe, the Board had vacillated, procrastinated, and bickered among themselves. 'This game of cross purposes,' according to an editorial in the *Wishaw Press*, 'is not calculated to promote the best interests of education in the parish, and we could wish that the long, continual feud (we could give it a stronger name) were ended for ever. Only by the infusion of new blood is there any prospect of a satisfactory improvement being effected in the existing condition of affairs.'

Three members of the Board did not stand for re-election in 1914, so at least an 'infusion of new blood' was guaranteed. The actual election campaign, however, was dominated by 'the High School question', and the differing views of the candidates as to how this question should be resolved did not augur well for a cessation of 'the long, continual feud'.

'The High School Party' (as Dr Brodie and Messrs Roy and Sloan came to be known) favoured the erection of a new high school; other candidates felt that higher (i.e. secondary) education should not dominate the Board's thinking, and that a new school should be built to accommodate all the supplementary pupils in the elementary schools. 'Wishaw,' declared the Reverend G.A. Kennedy, 'is to a great extent an industrial community, and the needs of industry should be paramount in the question of education.' John Taylor was even more dismissive of the High School and secondary education: 'Is this factory for the production of ministers, doctors, teachers, and lawyers (there is no scarcity of them) the most needed form of education in Wishaw?'

Vox populi...

It is not clear from the election results what the priorities of the ratepayers were with regard to post-elementary education in Wishaw: John Taylor polled the fewest votes, and failed to secure a place on the

Board; but G.N. Pomphrey, who was also opposed to the erection of a new high school, topped the poll. Whether or not the electorate had definite views about what they wanted in the way of educational provision, nine hundred of them failed to give expression to these views - as they failed to fill in their ballot forms properly, a failure that prompted the *Wishaw Press* to describe them as 'illiterates'. The local paper did, however, welcome the new Board with a much less abrasive (but nevertheless ironic) comment: 'With all the data it will have at hand, the solution of the High School problem should prove a less difficult task than the previous Board found it to be.'

2

1914 – 1918: Paradise Postponed

The new Board met for the first time on 7 April 1914. Dr Thomas Brodie, the most articulate member of 'the High School Party' and very much an elitist as far as secondary education was concerned ('It is not slow children,' he declared on one occasion, 'that are wanted at the High School, but the smarter ones who will do credit to - and be benefited by - an advanced education'), was elected Chairman.

At a special meeting the following month, the Board decided to commission an architect to draw up plans for two new schools - a high school and a school that would cater for supplementary (i.e. non-certificate) pupils; and to have these plans - and also possible alterations at Beltanefoot – costed by surveyors.

In September (and in camera), the Board decided to proceed with the erection - at a cost of between thirteen and fifteen thousand pounds - of a new high school on a new site and, once it was built, to congregate all the supplementary pupils in the parish at Beltanefoot.

The British and German armies, however, had already congregated at Mons (in direct opposition to each other), and some members of the Board felt that it would be inappropriate to proceed with such an expensive project in wartime. In a letter to the *Wishaw Press*, Robert Martin, arch-antagonist of the High School and champion of the supplementary pupils, lent his support:

The High School may very well be the apex of the local educational system, but you would not expect a mason or an architect to build the chimney on a house or the spire on a church when the walls were only halfway up. The children in the parish between twelve and fourteen years of age should be provided for first; after that the apex can be considered. Any other policy would be for the benefit of the few at the expense of the many. In any case, it is inadvisable to contemplate the erection of a new high school when our national existence is at stake.

Faced, for once, with a moral dilemma of some magnitude, the Board sought advice from the Chancellor of the Exchequer (no less) and the Scotch Education Department. The Chancellor merely acknowledged receipt of the letter sent by the Board to inquire about 'the propriety or otherwise of spending money on a new high school'; he offered no advice.

The response of the SED was much less reticent. After a barbed reference to the Board's 'prolonged deliberations' with regard to the overcrowding at the High School, the Department made it crystal clear that the advent of war was not an acceptable reason for postponing the erection of a new school. The Department also informed the Board that for the third successive year it was withholding 10% of the High School's grant - because it had failed to provide sufficient accommodation.

Nothing concentrated the collective mind of the Board like the maximisation of the annual grant, and there was general agreement that they should make inquiries about possible sites for a new high school. 'Ports have been reached,' the *Wishaw Press* commented (somewhat wryly), 'by the educational ship of the parish which in periods of greater storm and stress were found to be unapproachable.'

In January 1915, a site was chosen on the Coltness Estate, just off Kirk Road; in February, the site was approved by the SED, and this encouraged the Board to commission John Steel, a local architect, to draw up plans for a new high school. By September, the plans had been approved by the Department, and in recognition of the fact that it was finally trying to do something about the overcrowding at the High School, the Board was informed that for the first time in four years no deduction would be made from its annual grant.

At its next meeting in October, the Board decided to delay the implementation of its plan to build a new high school until after the war. In the minutes of this meeting (as recorded in the *Wishaw Press*), it is simply stated that the Board reached the decision in question; there is no mention of any debate, and no mention of any motion being put to a vote. If a vote was taken, it might have been significant that two members of 'the High School Party' - Dr Brodie and a Mr H. Lightbody - were not present at the meeting. On the other hand, there may simply have been a general disinclination among the members of the Board to initiate such a costly project in wartime - especially since they had just been informed that they would receive no financial assistance from the SED.

Back to Square One

Irrespective of how or why it had been reached, the Board's decision was bad news for the High School, since the roll was destined to climb remorselessly from 345 to well over 400 between 1914 and 1918.Theoretically, there was accommodation for only 240 pupils, so the school, of necessity, continued to make use of both the Mission Hall and

31

Thornlie Church Hall; and in 1915 the Board applied for permission to use one of the halls in the new YMCA Institute as a classroom.

In January 1918, due to the shortage of accommodation, only the top 14 of 49 applicants could be granted admission. The remaining 35 were admitted provisionally, formed into a single class, and taught by Miss Nimmo (who was paid an extra £10 per annum for undertaking this responsibility) in a vacant room at Berryhill Elementary School, under the general supervision of Kerr himself.

Not long after this, in an effort to reduce the number of prospective entrants, the Board decided that all applicants for admission to the High School would be required to pay a deposit of £1; and that they would forfeit this deposit if they did not remain on the roll for three years.

Some village-Hampden, that with dauntless breast...

Thomas Gray, *Elegy Written in a Country Churchyard*

The aforementioned deposit was denounced by one local mother as 'an obnoxious penalty'. Another disgruntled parent composed an open letter to the Board:

Gentlemen,
I fully intended sending my child to Wishaw Higher Grade School to complete her education, but I am informed that I must lodge £1 ere she is admitted. The reason given me is 'to secure the child completing her three-year course'. Why should parents, mostly drawn from the industrial classes, bind themselves to any term? My employers will give me no such surety. Is this 'free' education? Further, may I ask if it is legal? It appears to me as putting a halter round our neck - or, to use a police court phrase, 'putting us on probation'. I have made enquiries elsewhere, and Wishaw stands alone in this enactment. I would ask parents at the opening to withhold their money, and I will willingly be a party to 'forcing the situation'. I trust, ere friction arises, you will at your earliest give the matter the attention that is now overdue.

Yours etc.
A Ratepayer

Though he did not publicise his views at the time, Kerr believed that it was 'impracticable' - as well as 'illegal' - to compel parents to pay the £1 deposit, since Wishaw 'consisted mostly of a working-class population, whose wages fluctuated according to the state of the local industries'; and that 'parents, who obviously wanted the best possible education for their children and, rightly or wrongly, thought it was to be found in secondary schools with their up-to-date equipment and specialist teachers, should not be discouraged from sending those same children to the High School'.

High-Flyers

Despite the cramped and depressing environment, the chronic shortage of teachers in certain departments, and frequent changes in the teaching staff due to the exigencies of war, the High School was still able to consolidate its reputation for academic excellence.

Every year between 1914 and 1918, more than thirty pupils gained the Intermediate Certificate; every year, at least one senior pupil gained a place in the first hundred in the Glasgow University Bursary Competition, and in 1916 all four candidates achieved this distinction.

Eighteen pupils gained the Leaving Certificate in 1915; and nineteen in 1917, in which year a High School pupil, Janet Hamilton, was the first candidate from Lanarkshire to achieve a pass in Higher Music.

In 1916, 95% of the candidates presented for the Intermediate or Leaving Certificate were successful; and a similar level of success was regularly attained in the Civil Service Examinations (in 1915, for instance, William Greig was placed 31st out of more than 1,100 candidates).

One can gauge how much progress the High School had made as an academic institution from three interesting statistics: in August 1914, there were nine teachers with an Honours degree on the staff, one of whom was the first specialist teacher of Science to be appointed on a permanent basis; the number of pupils taking Higher Science was the second highest in the West of Scotland; and of the senior pupils who left the school in 1917, eleven gained admission to a university, eleven enrolled at a teachers' training college, and one continued his studies at the School of Art.

High standards were also maintained on the football field, the High School being victorious in the Schools' Cup Competition in 1916 and 1917. Newmains provided the opposition in both finals (played over two legs, and watched by crowds in excess of 3,000), and the day after each final Kerr declared a half holiday. The winning teams lined up as follows: (in 1916) James Henry; John Gibb and John Dobbie; Andrew Girdwood, John Watson, and David Aitken; William Sharpe, Henry Nimmo (captain), Robert Waddell, James Watt, and James Price; (in 1917) John Reid; Daniel Baird and George Phillips; William Rennie, Andrew Girdwood, and Charles Gowans; James Melville, James Baxter, Robert Liddell, Alistair McGregor, and David Muircroft.

In 1918 the Harthill Schools' Football Cup became the third trophy to be won in the space of three years.

In 1914 the school cricket team reached the final of the Newmains Works' Tournament, and the tennis team (made up of pupils and members of staff) was strong enough to defeat Wishaw Tennis Club by four matches to two. Among the pupils who distinguished themselves on the tennis court were Alexander Robert, Sam Allan, Lizzie Hunter, and Jeanie Broadfoot.

In the course of session 1915-16, netball was introduced into the sporting curriculum; in February 1917, swimming clubs were inaugurated for both boys and girls, and the two clubs met for an hour each week at Hamilton Baths.

Nights at the Opera

'A Christmas week without its High School entertainment,' enthused the *Wishaw Press* on 24 December 1915, 'would be rather odd, to say the least of it, because of late years it has come to be regarded as one of the events of the festive season.' The 'High School entertainment' took the form of an operetta (*The Rajah of Rajahpore* in 1915 and *Sisters Three* or *Britannia's Heroes* in 1917) and of a concert in 1914, 1916 and 1918. An orchestra, which included in its ranks both pupils and members of staff, took part in all five productions.

The concert held in 1914 was entitled 'A Patriotic National Concert', and all Britain's wartime allies were represented by a specific item in the programme. The choir sang the national anthems of France Japan, Belgium, and Russia; an Irish jig and the Highland fling were performed; there was a recitation ("Drake's Drum"), followed by a piano duet ('Marche Militaire'), an exhibition of drill, a selection on the bagpipes, and solo and choral renditions of such patriotic airs as 'Land of Hope and Glory'.

How to win friends and (sometimes) influence people

Dale Carnegie (adapted)

As the reputation of the High School burgeoned, so too did the professional standing of its rector. In 1915 Kerr was elected President of the Glasgow Branch of the Secondary Education Association of Scotland, and in 1916 he became a member of that same association's General Council.

Although he was - by virtue of his status as Rector of the High School - an establishment figure, Kerr was not afraid to run the risk of annoying the educational establishment (i.e. the Board), if he felt that his intervention would benefit the school, or his staff, or even his pupils. 'I have no doubt,' he admitted, 'that I provoked everyone concerned by almost continually applying for more staff and more accommodation.'

In June 1914, Kerr submitted to the Board, 'with his cordial support', a petition (signed by seventeen members of his staff) that appealed for a revision of their salary scales, an appeal that was based on the fact that their salaries were 'conspicuously below' those of the teachers in the schools cited in the list that accompanied the petition.

The Board tended to get rather tetchy about claims for an increase in teachers' salaries (especially in wartime), and their displeasure intensified when they learned that at a school function to mark the departure of David Tait, Principal Teacher of Classics, Kerr had remarked that in his new post Tait would be earning £50 more than he would have been likely to receive if the new salary scales proposed by the Board (in response to the aforementioned petition) were implemented.

In January 1917, thanks largely to the representations Kerr made to the Railway Company on behalf of the substantial number of pupils who travelled to the High School from Law and Carluke, the 4.23 service from Wishaw Central to these two destinations was reinstated in the timetable less than a month after it had been discontinued.

Fiat lux.

In July 1915, the Board decided that the High School should have electric light. It was eventually installed at a cost of £116.12s.

An Unusual Presentation

In December 1916, Nettie Hamilton, a pupil at the High School (and 'a talented young vocalist'), was presented with a gold bracelet as a token of Kerr's - and his pupils' - appreciation of 'the willingness with which she gave her services in the interests of the school and the ungrudging manner in which she used her fine gift for the sake of others'. 'The spirit,' said Nan Dunlop, a fellow pupil, 'that has prompted the pupils to show a zealous girl their deep appreciation in this tangible form is very characteristic of the pupils at the High School.'

In the midst of life...

On 19 February 1917, 'as she was walking arm-in-arm with two companions towards the auxiliary classroom in the U.F. Mission Hall in Alexander Street, Marion Telfer (13) suddenly complained of feeling giddy, and fell unconscious to the ground. She was carried into an adjacent house, and every possible means was used to bring her round; but Dr Macfarlane, who had been passing and was called in, pronounced life to be extinct. The sympathy of her classmates found expression in a beautiful wreath of natural flowers, while a little, white cross over her last resting-place will form the permanent tribute of the pupils and staff at the High School.'

We never (well, almost never) close.

The school was closed on two occasions: on 3 April 1917, when, due to a snowstorm, only a hundred pupils turned up; and for two weeks in October 1918 during a flu epidemic.

Frederick the Great (Attender)

In November 1917, having completed five years' perfect attendance, Fred Symon was presented by the Board with a certificate and a five-volume gazetteer of Scotland.

Soupe du Jour

It was mentioned at a meeting of the Board that during the winter of 1917-18 about ninety children at Newmains Primary had been provided with a bowl of soup every day at lunchtime (for which they were charged a halfpenny). This service was intended primarily for those pupils who were unable to go home at the lunch interval, but many others brought 'a piece' and took the soup along with it. Mr Roy suggested that a similar system might be instituted at the High School, since many of the pupils in attendance there were faced with a long journey if they went home for their lunch.

And finally...

The Board was informed by His Majesty's Inspector of Physical Education that the heating in the gymnasium was inadequate. The reaction of one member of the Board to this (implied) reprimand was simply to assert that the pupils got sufficient exercise in the gymnasium to keep them from feeling the cold. However, when it was pointed out that sometimes the pupils had to hang about (with the risk, consequently, that they might catch a chill) waiting their turn to take part in a particular exercise, and that some classes received anatomy lessons (during which they were not engaged in physical exercise) in the gymnasium, the Board agreed to install a 'slow combustion' stove at a cost of £10 15s.

3

Wishaw High School and the First World War

Keep the Home-fires burning,
While your hearts are yearning,
Though your lads are far away
They dream of Home.

Lena Guilbert Ford, *Till the Boys Come Home (1914 song)*

Four members of staff - John Telford (Royal Scots Fusiliers), John Gerrard (Royal Artillery), James Lawrie (HLI), and a Mr McRoberts (Royal Flying Corps) - served in the armed forces during the First World War; others devoted their summer holidays to 'work of national importance' (e.g. in the munitions factories). Kerr himself held the post of Superintendent of the YMCA hut in the military camp at Ladybank in Fifeshire.

Kerr also assumed command of the High School's Cadet Corps - with the rank of lieutenant. This corps was founded in September 1914, but it did not become fully operational until 1916, when its fifty or so members (the membership fee was one shilling per quarter) met regularly once a week, in full khaki uniform, for instruction in drill, signalling, shooting, and skirmishing. By the spring of 1916, the corps had taken part in two route marches, and according to the *Wishaw Press* 'the lads were very enthusiastic'; and in 1917 some of the cadets, supervised by Kerr and Thomas Hyslop (a member of the Science Department), helped out on farms at Lesmahagow and East Kilbride. Senior girls from the High School also worked on the land during the summer holidays.

Knit for Victory

In November 1916, parcels were sent to former pupils on active service. They were accompanied by a letter from Kerr:
Our lady teachers and our girls have been busy knitting socks as a Christmas gift for you all, and both staff and pupils have combined to send you a parcel, as a remembrance, which will cheer you with the thought that your work and service for us are cherished as the noblest

work of your life. That the victory may be speedy and your return safe is the deep desire of all your friends here, who join me in wishing you a happy Christmastide.

Some of the wool used to knit the socks mentioned above was purchased (thanks to the generosity of Miss Frood, the drill instructress) with money collected for the presentation she was due to receive on the occasion of her departure to take up a similar post at Glasgow High School.

Meanwhile, the boys in the Woodwork classes made an equally praiseworthy contribution to the war effort by making crutches and periscopes for the front-line troops.

Letters acknowledging receipt of the Christmas parcels were sent to the High School from as far afield as Palestine and East Africa. One former pupil who served with the expeditionary force in the latter theatre of war wrote:

I was greatly surprised, buried as we are in the heart of Africa (where one acquires a feeling of being cut off from the world), to receive this token of appreciation and your best wishes. The gift arrived at a most opportune moment - and was very welcome, as my kit had become very much reduced through the exigencies of war and enemy action. To begin with, all my kit had been destroyed by fire except what I was wearing at the time - and that was very little, marching as we did during the heat of the tropical day. I managed to partially re-equip, but during an engagement with the enemy two months later my kit was lost in the bush. At that time we were busy on the track of the main German forces, and it was impossible to get kit up from base, as it taxed L. of C. [sic] to their utmost to supply us with food to keep us alive: so perforce I had to brush along on the minimum.

I have been with the Kilwa forces since July 1917, and I have taken part in all their campaigns. It was our column (known as 'the fighting column') which forced and accepted the unconditional surrender of the German forces under Tafel, a force as strong as our own. May I mention, in passing, that at this time we trekked 110 miles in 6 days, and the whole of this forced march was done during the heat of the day (as it was impossible to advance through bush and jungle at night when the enemy were in the vicinity), and after more than a month of constant marching and fighting without a single day's rest?

From the 20th of September 1917 to the 3rd of December 1917, we trekked over 500 miles, fought eight big engagements and numerous skirmishes, and had to contend with many rearguard actions on the part of the enemy. By 'trekking' 1 mean 'footslogging': we had no wheeled transport with the column, and baggage and equipment were carried by natives. And yet people at home say that warfare in East Africa is a picnic.

Kerr also received a letter from an FP in a prisoner-of-war camp in Germany, informing him that his erstwhile pupil had started to learn German and would be grateful for any old German readers and textbooks.

Many commendable financial contributions were made to the war effort by both the pupils and the members of staff at the High School. In May 1915, the pupils decided (unanimously) to organise a monthly collection among themselves in aid of the War Relief Fund, and to forgo the medals and books that were provided as prizes every year by various donors (prizewinners simply received a War Certificate indicating that they had 'won a prize, 'but had voluntarily waived their claim to it owing to the European War'); in December 1916, a War Savings Association was formed, and more than £12 was invested by the 21 pupils who joined it; in June 1918, during War Savings Week, pupils and teachers invested more than £776 in War Savings Certificates, and a fancy dress parade through the town (involving about 150 pupils) raised almost £94 for the Red Cross, an achievement that persuaded the School Convener to declare: 'I am sure the rest of the Board will be as gratified as I am by this expression of patriotic sentiment by the rising generation.'

> **What candles may be held to speed them all?**
> **Not in the hands of boys, but in their eyes**
> **Shall shine the holy glimmers of good-byes.**
> **The pallor of girls' brows shall be their pall;**
> **Their flowers the tenderness of silent minds,**
> **And each slow dusk a drawing-down of blinds.**

Wilfred Owen, *Anthem for Doomed Youth*

In April 1915, the names of former pupils and members of staff serving in the armed forces were inscribed on a roll of honour. By the end of the war, the roll of honour (which was displayed in the school hall) contained more than two hundred names, including those of John Telford and Oliver Wassell (who were awarded the DCM and the Military Medal respectively) and, more poignantly, those of two former duxes killed in action - James McAlpin and John Hunter.

40

In September 1917, both Telford and Wassell were presented - by way of a tribute from the staff and pupils - with 'a handsome volume, suitably inscribed on the front page, in recognition of their gallant service in France and the honour they had brought to the school'. After the presentation, 'both gentlemen gave an interesting and amusing account of some of their experiences in France'.

James McAlpin was the first dux of the High School. When war broke out, he enlisted as a private, but less than two years later he gained a commission as a 2nd Lieutenant. In October 1915, he wrote to his mother:

By this time you will have heard how both Alec [his brother] and myself have emerged safely from the great battle in which our division took part last weekend. We have reason to thank God from the depth of our hearts that we have been spared - when so many of our brave comrades fell.

The action began on Saturday morning after a terrific bombardment by hundreds of our guns, during which the German positions were deluged with shells and their trenches reduced to a heap of rubble. The two leading brigades of our division - Alec's brigade and another - advanced and took the first line of German trenches without much opposition. They continued to advance, and drove the enemy before them for two miles, clearing the village and a hill, at which point the Germans rallied and advanced against our lads in force. They resisted gallantly till ammunition ran short, then retired over the hill. Our brigade advanced and reinforced them, and then the whole division made a stand there, resisting attack after attack for the rest of the day, all through the night, and up to midday on Sunday. The enemy now brought up strong reinforcements of picked troops (Prussian Guards), and the odds being too great, we had to give ground. Many of my friends and comrades went down as they retreated. It literally rained shot and shell upon us. Several times we rallied, but in spite of our best efforts we had to give way, sadly broken and decimated. It almost seemed as if the day was lost and our brave lads had given up their lives in vain. Just in time, however, strong reinforcements of cavalry and artillery arrived. They were followed by the Guards' division, and these fresh troops took up the assault, allowing our broken division to withdraw. The hill and the village that we had won were taken by them, so the day ended in victory.

Since then our troops have continued to push forward. The Germans are giving way, and our French neighbours on the right are also pushing forward with might and main. The rank and file of the German army seem to be demoralised: they surrender to us in droves, many of them making no show of resistance whatsoever. There will be stiff fighting yet before the war is over, but of the final issue there can be no doubt: we shall win through and bring this terrible war to an end before long.

Our division - a Scotch division entirely, thank God for that - has earned the highest praise from Sir John French, and from Kitchener himself. We have done our bit to the best of our ability, and though we are saddened by the loss of many gallant comrades, we feel that Scotland has no reason to be ashamed of us.

We are now at the rear, endeavouring to obtain a little rest and to have ourselves strengthened by new men and officers. In a little while, we expect to be called into the field again to assist in the good work of driving a broken and dispirited enemy out of France.

In April 1917, Mrs McAlpin received official word that her son had been killed in action. She also received a letter of sympathy from Sergeant T. Hunter, in which he wrote:

James fell while leading his men over to the attack, and his last words were a command to advance. I had a long conversation with him the evening before he went into action, and he was cheerful as usual. He was held in the highest esteem by his men, and his loss is keenly felt.

At an assembly in the hall, Kerr (who, as it happened, had invited McAlpin and his wife to supper on the eve of his former pupil's departure for France) paid the following tribute:

I hear that Lieutenant James McAlpin has been killed leading a charge. He was our first dux pupil, took a bursary in open competition on entering university, and had a distinguished academic career. He contributed for several years to the school magazine. He was one of the most brilliant pupils here, and his personality and character had a great and enduring influence.

Mr Booth, the Music Master, then played the "Dead March" from *Saul*, pupils and staff upstanding'.

4

The Great War - Epilogue

The sacrifice which they made collectively was repaid to them individually, for they received, each one for himself, a praise which grows not old and the noblest of all sepulchres: I speak not of that in which their remains are laid, but of that in which their glory survives and is eternally celebrated on every fitting occasion both in word and deed. For the whole earth is the sepulchre of heroes: not only are they commemorated by columns and inscriptions in their own country, but in foreign lands there also dwells an unwritten memorial of them, graven not on stone but in the hearts of men.

Thucydides, *The History of the Peloponnesian War*

The First World War came to an end in November 1918. In the preceding four years, 233 former pupils of the High School had served in the armed forces, and of that number the following 30 had fallen in the line of duty:

James Boyes	Archibald Campbell	Nisbet Cunningham
John Douglas	Alexander Fisher	Samuel H. Forrest
James Forsyth	James Gibson	George Gilchrist
James Girdwood	John Henderson	John Hunter
John Hyslop	William Kenmure	Gilbert Kennedy
Robert Lindsay	William Martin	David Morton
James McAlpin	James Nettleship	Robert Nimmo
Arthur Rogers	Thomas Ross	Richard Scott
George Simpson	Thomas Small	Allan Steele
James Steele	Thomas Strain	Richard T. Tart

'When one remembers,' wrote Kerr, 'the brilliant promise of these lads, one is terribly saddened by reflections on the savagery of our times. Man's advance in Christian ethics has fallen far behind the discoveries of science - or, to put it in another form of words, man has prostituted the scientific discoveries of this century to advance his own bestial purposes.'

Towards the end of 1918, a committee made up of pupils, former pupils, and members of staff was entrusted with the responsibility of raising money for the Burgh's Hero Memorial Fund. A few months later, however, when that project fell through, the committee decided that whatever money they raised from then on - plus the amount that had already been accumulated - should be used to set up 'a tablet in memory of the FPs who had fallen' and institute 'a war memorial bursary' that would be awarded every year to the High School pupil who was ranked highest in the Glasgow University Bursary Competition.

The first winner of the War Memorial Bursary was Mary Brownlie. The 'memorial tablet', which occupied a prominent position on the wall at one end of the hall, was unveiled by the Reverend J.A.F. Dean on 24 June 1920. Described by the *Wishaw Press* as 'massive' (it was 6 feet long and 3 feet wide), it had been designed - in a 'chaste and appropriate manner' - by John Telford, Principal Teacher of Art, and carved out of oak by John Crawford and Company (Glasgow), Woodcarvers and Craftsmen. The pediment featured, in low relief, two handsomely carved figures and the school badge. The former were surrounded by the symbols of the two creative arts (Art and Literature) they represented; the latter was wreathed in laurel leaves 'to indicate honour and respect'. The school motto ('Qui Non Proficit Deficit') was depicted on a scroll underneath the badge; the main panel contained the names, arranged in four columns, of the thirty former pupils who lost their lives on active service during the First World War; and underneath these names the following words were inscribed: 'Their Name Liveth for Evermore'.

Prior to the unveiling of the 'memorial tablet', the Reverend Dean said:

If these boys were here tonight, they would wonder at our gathering; they would say: 'We have done nothing worth speaking about. It was our simple duty, and we could not have done otherwise. I sing but as the linnet sings, I sing because I must.'

However, we must pay respect to the training and environment that made their noble decision inevitable. Decisions have their genesis in the years that precede them. The occasion, it is said, produces the man; but the occasion only produces the man who has been prepared for the occasion.

5

1918 - 1928: Paradise Attained – Eventually

At a meeting of the Cambusnethan School Board in January 1919, the Chairman, G.N. Pomphrey, declared, somewhat fatalistically: 'The sword of Damocles is suspended above our heads - and may fall at any moment, bringing to an end our energies as members of the Board. Consequently, it will be difficult for us to launch out with any new schemes.' 'The sword of Damocles' referred to the imminent abolition of school boards and their replacement, as prescribed by the Education Act of 1918, by ad hoc education authorities.

For the last few months of its existence, the Board was, to all intents and purposes, what Americans would call 'a lame duck administration', and it would have been unrealistic to expect any significant initiatives with regard to the erection of a new high school. Symptomatic of the Board's de facto powerlessness - and its consequent inaction - is the following extract from the minutes of a meeting in February 1919, at which a letter was submitted by the factor of the Coltness Estate asking what action the Board proposed to take in respect of the site it had purchased in Kirk Road for a new high school:

G.S. Sloan: I do not think it is incumbent on us to say anything definite on this subject. We do not know where we stand. The new authority will come and push us out.

Reverend Mr Pollock: I second that. It is futile for us to proceed, now that we are faced with this new situation.

The Board eventually decided that the site in Kirk Road should 'be secured and left as a legacy to the new Education Authority'.

Gone and Soon Forgotten

The elections for the nascent Lanarkshire Education Authority were held on 11 April 1919, and the School Board met for the last time four weeks later. Kerr had this to say about the changeover:

There are arguments both for and against the transfer of powers of educational administration from people living in one parish to those drawn from a whole county. With a school board, the community in a parish takes a more lively interest in both education and finance; but under a county authority, chosen for its members' interest in education, there is usually more opportunity for better buildings and the employment of men and women teachers of higher scholarship - at a salary approximating to their true worth. As far as Wishaw High School was concerned, however, I am bound to say that Cambusnethan School Board never grudged the money that would attract men and women of the highest scholarship, nor the number of teachers needed to cope with the ever increasing number of pupils on the roll.

Responsibility without Power

The Lanarkshire Education Authority set up schools' management committees in all the parishes in the county. These committees comprised parents, teachers (Kerr himself was a member of the Cambusnethan Schools' Management Committee, which met for the first time on 16 October 1919), and members of the Town Council, the Parish Council, and the Education Authority itself; but although the heterogeneous nature of their composition looked very impressive on paper, they had no executive powers and they could only make recommendations to the Authority. Consequently, they spent most of their time dealing with the problem of irregular attendance and vetting applications for free boots and clothing from the parents of 'necessitous' children.

It is interesting to note, in passing, that the local Management Committee refused to entertain requests for free boots during the summer. 'The healthiest children up my way,' declared David Gibson, 'run around with their feet bare. We only create disease when we begin to coddle them.'

As far as irregular attendance was concerned, it was a Herculean task for the Committee to disabuse parents of the notion that they were entitled to keep their children off school on washing days.

Some members of the Management Committee found their 'enforced helplessness' increasingly unacceptable. In 1922 one of these malcontents, G.S. Sloan, resigned in disgust: 'I cannot see the force of sixteen men being called month after month for the purpose of doing little or nothing.'

Two years later, G.N. Pomphrey, the Chairman of the Committee, expressed similarly iconoclastic views: "Either Schools' Management Committees should be granted more power, or they should be done away with altogether." Neither of these stark alternatives materialised: despite remaining powerless, schools' management committees did remain in existence throughout the 1920s and 1930s.

It was not just the Schools' Management Committee that was disenchanted with the new administrative set-up. Local headmasters (including Kerr) complained that the new Authority had burdened them with several 'new duties' which involved 'a large amount of correspondence with Hamilton'; and that while they were perfectly willing to carry out these duties, they were being 'taken away from what was the main end and purpose of their being, i.e. looking after the education of their pupils'.

Unnatural Selection

In 1919 the newly created Schools' Management Committee made no recommendation - and the newly elected Education Authority took no action - regarding the erection of a new high school on the site bequeathed to it by the newly defunct School Board. The pressure on the accommodation at the High School seems to have eased ('There is ample room now,' Kerr reported in June 1920), partly because of the mandatory £ 1 deposit, which had been 'successful in keeping back the natural increase in numbers to such an extent that the school had been able to cope with new entrants', and partly because Kerr had been operating a selection process that disregarded the legal entitlement of every pupil who passed the Qualifying Examination to secondary education. 'I wish parents to understand,' he explained, 'that it does not follow that because a child reaches the standard necessary for a supplementary course in any of the primary schools, he is therefore a suitable pupil to enrol in a secondary school. He must satisfy his present headmaster and myself that he is somewhat better than a mere 'pass', and that he is both clever enough and eager enough to take at least a three-year course at this school.'

To tax and to please...is not given to men.

Edmund Burke, *On American Taxation*

Despite its 'success', the imposition of a £1 deposit was still proving to be controversial, especially since the High School was the only school under the sway of the Education Authority to operate such a system. The following letter was dispatched to the Authority on 18 June 1919:

Dear Sir,

A pupil, in order to gain admission to Wishaw Higher Grade School, has to lodge £1, returnable on condition that he or she completes a three-year course. Widespread dissatisfaction prevails. Is this impost legal? A ruling will be much esteemed.

Yours faithfully,

Geo. Morrison

In August, the Education Authority's Teaching and Staffing Committee recommended that the 'impost' should continue to be levied. The erection of an annexe (completed in January 1921) also helped to obviate any overcrowding in such practical subjects as Art, Science, and Woodwork.

The pressure begins to tell.

The respite was temporary. Boosted by a large contingent of pupils from Carluke Higher Grade School who had opted to embark on the Junior Students' Course, the roll surged over the 500 mark, and Kerr began to sound as if he was being devitalised by the unrelenting pressure on the school's limited accommodation:

I am tired of it, and I want peace. Today, I had three ordinary classes and a drill class going on at the same time in the hall - four teachers, that is, shouting against each other. For the last eight years, both the physique and the mental equilibrium of all my teachers have been under intense pressure. I am not out for any particular plan to deal with the overcrowding; I am out for more accommodation for my classes.

A Devastating Fire

The Authority's plan to alleviate the overcrowding at the High School envisaged structural alterations to the main building and the erection (at a cost of £12,000) of a 'semi-permanent [sic] construction' to house the Domestic Science and Manual Instruction Departments. This plan, which by a strange coincidence had been unanimously rejected by the Schools' Management Committee the previous day, went up in smoke - both literally and metaphorically - in the early hours of Wednesday, 18 January 1922, when a fire (thought to have been caused by an electrical fault) broke out in the 'cookery kitchen', destroying the kitchen itself, two classrooms, the laundry, one of the staffrooms, the Rector's room, a storeroom, a cloakroom, large sections of the roof, the school logbook, the registers, and ('horresco referens') the schemes of work. John Weir, Principal Teacher of Geography, was the first member of staff on the scene, and 'at considerable risk to his life', he saved some of the registers and other school records that were located in Kerr's room. Kerr himself had been confined to bed with the flu, and when he learned about this calamitous depletion of accommodation that was already stretched to the limit, he must have felt like staying there 'semi-permanently'.

Amazingly, the school reopened on the Monday of the following week - the Works Department having cleared the debris, boarded up the broken windows, modified the heating system to suit the changed conditions, and constructed a covered corridor in the hall to provide the pupils with safe access to the classrooms that had not been affected by the fire.

'On that morning,' wrote Kerr, 'the Chairman, Vice-Chairman, and Clerk of the Education Authority visited the school, and from the way they looked at me, I still wonder if they thought I was guilty of arson, for at an earlier meeting of the Schools' Management Committee, exasperated by the cramped conditions at Beltanefoot, I had expressed the wish that Providence would burn down the entire building.

In an effort to implant the idea of a new high school in their minds, I marched my visitors up the Coltness Road to the site on which the School Board had proposed to build such a school. On the way, the Clerk suggested to me that my school should be reduced to intermediate status, that 4th and 5th Year pupils should be transferred to Dalziel High School, and that, in the event of such a transferral, the existing school, duly repaired and partly rebuilt, would suffice. Fortunately, the strong wind prevented the other two gentlemen from hearing him - and I did not encourage him to repeat his suggestion, for it might, in the circumstances, have been accepted as a temporary palliative. Had that happened, senior secondary pupils from our district might still be travelling to the other end of Motherwell for their education.'

When the going gets tough.....

As he now demonstrated, Kerr's political skills were matched by his great organisational ability. Woodwork and Domestic Science classes were discontinued, then later farmed out to two local primary schools; Science classes were combined, so as to form larger teaching groups; the lecture room in the YMCA Institute was utilised as a classroom; a section of the hall was partitioned off for use by the PE Department; and by reducing the number of classes (even though this meant increasing class sizes beyond the legal maximum), Kerr ensured that it was business as usual as far as the academic subjects in the curriculum were concerned.

These 'makeshift arrangements' produced considerable congestion in the corridors and cloakrooms, and Kerr, as he later admitted, had to take 'stern measures' to maintain discipline. He became known as 'the small man with the big voice' - or worse, as the following anecdote illustrates:

It was the last period in the afternoon, and my Latin class was engaged in translating a passage from Caesar's "Invasion of Britain". I asked the pupils what sort of status they would ascribe to Caesar. The answer was 'dictator'. I wrote 'Caesar' on the blackboard, and asked the class to tell me what modern words came from 'Caesar' with a meaning similar to 'dictator'. The pupils answered, 'Czar' and 'Kaiser', and I wrote these words underneath 'Caesar'. Very carelessly, I forgot to rub the three words off the board when we left the room at 4 p.m. Next morning, the incoming teacher found another name added – 'Kerr'.

When things are at their worst they begin to mend.

By the middle of September 1922, despite the fact that the refurbishment of the hall and the Rector's room was nearing completion, Kerr had just about reached the end of his tether. 'I have carried on under difficulties,' he told the Schools' Management Committee, 'and, I think, surmounted these difficulties up till now with the aid of a very fine staff, but the position is now so bad, as a result of congestion, that I am afraid I cannot go on for more than two years without seriously impairing the efficiency of the school. I want permanent and generous accommodation - I do not care where - in order to stave off that evil day.'

This *cri de coeur* received unanimous support from the other members of the Committee ('For the health of the children,' said the Reverend J. A. Nicholls, 'and for the uplift of their minds, there ought to be a High School worthy of the name'), and the Clerk was instructed 'to convey to the Education Authority the desire of the Committee that the building of a new high school should be expedited as rapidly as possible'. Six years later, almost exactly to the day, the new High School was opened... but unlike the Authority, I am 'expediting' the course of events too 'rapidly'.

Initially, it has to be admitted, the Authority did act with surprising rapidity. In October 1922, Sir Thomas Munro, Clerk of the Authority, was instructed by the Authority's Property Committee to offer the Town Council the site in Kirk Road that had been purchased in 1914 by the Cambusnethan School Board - in exchange for a plot of land (earmarked for a housing estate and described by a local councillor as 'the most valuable site in Wishaw') in Kenilworth Avenue, just off the Main Street. Sir Thomas also wrote to the Schools' Management Committee, to inform it that as soon as negotiations had been completed steps would be taken 'to provide the necessary accommodation for the High School'.

In the light of previous fiascos, the *Wishaw Press* gave this pronouncement a cautious welcome: 'The prospect of the Education Authority providing a new high school for Wishaw seems now not to be so remote.' Unfortunately, the Town Council turned down the proposed exchange of sites.

In April 1923, however, after three months of negotiations, the Town Council adopted a recommendation from its Housing Committee that it should accept the Authority's offer of the site in Kirk Road in exchange for eleven acres of land (formerly the location of the 'distillery ponds') in Park Street, which had already been levelled as a possible site for a small housing estate. An understanding was also reached with Lord Belhaven, the original owner of part of the site, that 'in future there should be no coal workings underneath'.

Though hope now triumphed briefly over bitter experience in the columns of the *Wishaw Press* ('In the near future, our local educational establishments will be augmented by the erection of a new high school.'), two years were to elapse before work began on the foundations of the new school; and in the course of the speech he made at the prize-giving in 1925, R.T.C. Mair, Clerk of the Authority and Director of Education, warned the audience rather bluntly that events were likely to continue moving with glacier-like slowness: 'The foundations of the new high school in Wishaw are being commenced, but you need not expect that your next distribution of prizes will take place in the new school.'

Even so, at a special sitting of Motherwell and Wishaw Dean of Guild Court a month after the prize-giving, the plans of the new high school that the Education Authority intended to erect in Wishaw were formally approved: it was to cost an estimated £54,000 and provide accommodation for more than 700 pupils.

No Expense Spared

The Education Authority had originally intended to restrict the capacity of the new school to 550 by providing each ordinary classroom with 'mono' desks (although there were more than 600 pupils on the roll of the High School, it expected this number to decrease when the building at Beltanefoot was converted into an Advanced Division Centre, since such an establishment 'would attract those who would be better suited by a less academic education', and whose parents could not guarantee that their children would remain at school beyond the age of 14); but Kerr had opposed such a pessimistic forecast with characteristic forcefulness, and the Authority eventually agreed with him that the new school should be furnished with 'dual' desks.

More worryingly, the Scottish (as it was now designated) Education Department expressed reservations about certain aspects of the new school's design:

The provision of laboratories and other special rooms - and, still more, the size and character of the assembly hall to be provided in addition to ample gymnasium accommodation - is obviously on an exceedingly handsome scale, and it is apparent that, if desired, a considerable saving could be made in these respects without materially affecting the efficiency of the school.

However, the Department also indicated that it would not 'offer any objection' to the erection of the new school, provided that 'the additional financial burden under which the Authority proposed to place itself in respect of the Wishaw school was not used as an excuse to postpone any other part of the building programme'.

Slow, Slow, Quick, Slow, Slow

There was another long delay (the warning delivered by the Director of Education at the previous year's prize-giving was proving to be fully justified) before the different sections of the construction work were eventually put out to tender at the beginning of 1926. Among the local firms whose tenders were accepted was D. and W. Nimmo Ltd., which won the contract for the carpentry and ironwork.

Much greater urgency was shown by the Authority with regard to the provision of football pitches in the vicinity of the new High School. By February 1926, Kenilworth Park (described by 'Schola' in his column in *The Citizen* as 'very rough, with plenty of ashes and stones about, and in

52

a very dangerous condition') was in constant use as a venue for inter-school football matches; and work had started on another pitch (Waverley, I assume) for the exclusive use of High School pupils.

The Cherries on the Cake

As the work on the High School Mark 2 neared completion, Kerr 'was summoned several times to Glasgow Technical College to inspect and help to improve the plans, and also to advise on the furnishings and equipment'. The outcome of these consultations was that Kerr suggested - and the Authority agreed to implement - several additions to the original design: a weathervane on the 'main school tower', a pond for aquatic plants, a rockery to serve the needs of the Botany classes, and a tarmacadamed area near the school gates that was to be used as a playground.

Kerr had also decided to establish a 'House system' in the new High School, and four prominent landowners - Sir Douglas Seton-Stewart of Allanton, Lord Belhaven, J. Hamilton Houldsworth of Coltness, and Sir R.K. Stewart of Murdostoun - gave permission for their coats of arms to be depicted in stained glass on the windows of the assembly hall.

The sea! the sea!

Xenophon, *Anabasis*

Though some work had still to be done on the dining room, the assembly hall and the Domestic Science rooms, the new High School was finally ready to admit pupils through its portals in August 1928. It was fortunate enough to have not only a well- founded reputation for academic and sporting excellence, but also an energetic and innovative rector who was beginning to carve out a name for himself in the field of education.

6

'A Man for All Seasons'

Robert Whittington

In his capacity as Rector of the High School, Kerr ran a very tight ship - especially from 1921 onwards, when he ceased to have any teaching commitments in the Classics Department; and as the following extracts from the school log illustrate, he expected the highest professional standards from his staff:

30.11.22: Reproved Miss Scott for failing to keep her register up to date.

24.9.24: Found the majority of 4G with work unprepared; warned Miss Sheriff about the consequences, if her disciplinary power did not improve.

19.3.26: Spoke to Misses Carle, Scott, and A. Loudon on punctuality in the morning.

Every so often, slightly more serious incidents occurred:

'You stupid boy!'

14.1.25: Twice have had to deal with Maurice Thomson: in the first instance for an insolent reply, and secondly for absence and lateness.

Three strikes and you're (not) out.

16.2.28: Complaint received from Mr Maxwell, parent of Jenny Maxwell, whom Mr Hyslop struck on the head this week. This is the second instance of such behaviour since he came here.

5.3.30: Another case reported of Mr Hyslop striking a girl on the head; had to convey girl home to Overtown.

'The Chancer'

8.1.23: School resumed; Mr J. Kelman absent.
9.1.23: Mr Kelman has returned. Reason given for his absence is that he was not aware school resumed on January 8th.

'How Late It Was, How Late'

4.11.24: Have written to Mr Mair, Clerk of the Authority, pointing out that Mr Kelman is coming to school a few minutes late each morning.
10.11.24: Mr Donald visited the school today and dealt with Mr Kelman.

'A Disaffection'

31.4.25: HMIs have commented adversely on Mr Kelman's work with Class 5.
19.10.25: Messrs Donald, Mair, and Andrew visited the school today re case of Mr J. Kelman.
7.12.25: Mr Donald and Mr Andrew called today to interview Mr Kelman.
24.12.25: Mr Kelman has been transferred.

Dulce est desipere in loco.

Horace, *Odes*

Though the disciplinary code that obtained at the High School was rather draconian, Kerr was prepared, on occasion, to tolerate 'playful pranks':
There was a gong in the corridor outside my room that was struck by the janitor at the end of each period and at the end of the school day; and on the mantelpiece in my room there was a clock which indicated to me how time was going. One day, during the last period, when I had two lads of the 6th Year taking Greek in my room, I was called out for some act of supervision and left them with a piece of translation to do. On my return, I found that the clock pointed to 4 o'clock, and thinking that the janitor had failed to notice the time, I went out and rang the gong. The boys left my room, and the school 'skailed' - but two minutes later, the janitor

came in and expressed his surprise that I was dismissing the school at 3.45. I need not tell you what the boys had done. Next time they came to me for instruction, all I said was, 'See you leave at the right time, boys', and we all three smiled.

Freedom of Speech

In November 1922, the *Wishaw Press* reported that Kerr was not averse to the pupils 'talking Scotch' in the playground, as long as they were able to speak English with equal, or greater, proficiency; but that he objected to their using 'broken or slang' words, such as 'bob' for shilling and 'jaw' for cheek.

...a most dear lover, and a frequent practiser, of the art of angling

Izaak Walton, *The Compleat Angler*

Kerr had a reputation among his fellow headmasters 'for being fond of giving his pupils half holidays'. 'The reason they gave for this,' he explained in a later speech, 'was that I wanted to go fishing; and the same reason was ascribed to my attempt to get the autumn holiday extended to a full week.'

Sport for All

Kerr was an enthusiastic proponent of the benefits of physical activity, and in the summer months he arranged for every pupil in the school to have regular sports periods - during which they could, under supervision, play hockey, football, rounders or netball, or simply take part in such athletic pursuits as running, jumping, and 'putting the ball'.

The Educational Philosopher

Kerr had strong views on many aspects of the educational process, and both his privileged status as Rector of the High School and his active involvement in the activities of the EIS provided him with many opportunities to express these views:
What my staff and I earnestly plead for is a greater desire on the part of parents to cooperate with us in counteracting the debasing temptations

of the time and the district. Too many children are the real masters at home, and the absence of home-training and supervision after school hours nullifies many of our efforts to train them to be good citizens. (So say all teachers and politicians in 2016)

Pupils are leaving school at the age of 14. Many of them do not find employment, others go to work in factories and workshops; and both groups meet the temptations of gambling, sexual vice, and intemperance, all of which are rampant. I want to see these thousands of boys and girls being brought compulsorily into schools by the provision of obligatory day continuation classes (i.e. evening classes during the day).

I am in favour of religious education in schools, but not just for two periods a week. Teachers should be so imbued with the spirit of Christianity that they teach religion the whole day, every day, in every subject.

Is it not a confession of low ideals that very few pupils embark on a Divinity course when they leave school, thus passing up the opportunity to study for one of the highest, if not the highest, of all professions?

Taken in large doses dogmatically administered without other attractive ingredients, this subject [thrift], like the other branches of moral instruction, becomes nauseous to the pupils and thus loses much of its efficacy. It should be introduced naturally and incidentally in connection with subjects like Arithmetic, which should deal, 'inter alia', with problems of income tax, treasury bonds, N.S.A. certificates, etc., all of which have the practical outcome of inducing the child, and later on the man or woman, to save money.

As far as the pupils at the High School were concerned, Kerr was preaching to the converted. In 1922 the school's Savings Bank was responsible for 523 transactions (an average of 26 a day), and the balance stood at £162 14s 10d; in 1928 there were 2,101 transactions (an average of 55 a day), and the balance amounted to £1461 18s 7d.

In 1922 the proceeds from a jumble sale and a cake and candy stall were used to establish the High School Prize Fund Trust. 'It is a noble and worthy ambition,' Bailie Loudon commented approvingly, 'to be independent and not lean upon the State for something you yourselves can provide.'

The Philanthropist

Though he was clearly a man of strong moral and religious convictions, Kerr also had an equally strong social conscience. During his six years as a member of the Schools' Management Committee, he frequently spoke out in favour of proper provision being made for 'necessitous' children: in 1921, therefore, children in this category from Wishaw and Netherton were supplied with a midday meal at the High School; and in November 1926, High School pupils organised a collection of boots and clothing that were later distributed at Berryhill. He also let it be known that 'with a view to developing a proper spirit of unselfishness on the part of his pupils he allowed a collection to be taken about once a year on behalf of some national appeal'.

The Political Animal

As we have seen, Kerr served on the Schools' Management Committee for six years (1919-1925); and in 1925 he was elected to the Joint Council of Education Authorities and Teachers.

The Union Man

Kerr was Vice-President of the Lanarkshire Association of the EIS in session 1919-20 and President of the Lanarkshire Teachers' Association in session 1921-22. In 1925 he was nominated for the presidency of the EIS, but he was defeated - by 11,296 votes to 5,574 - by Dr J.H. Steel. He was a member of the EIS Council for ten years and an EIS representative for 33 years, the longest continuous period of service in that capacity of any Scottish teacher; and at different times, he was also President of the Cambusnethan Teachers' Association and Convener of the West of Scotland Section of the Secondary Teachers' Association.

The Football Buff

Kerr was a great believer in the character-forming aspects of football:
If football is not to degenerate altogether into mere spectacular bouts of professionalism with all its attendant vices, then our lads must continue to show by their example that football is inherently a clean and manly game, with abundant scope for the exercise of such solid virtues as self-restraint, clean impulses, unselfishness, and true comradeship.
In 1926 he was elected Honorary Vice-President of the Scottish Schools' Football Association.

7

End of Decade Report

'As a staff,' Kerr declared at the prize-giving in 1923, 'we shall be judged in the long run not by Leaving Certificate results, hockey badges, or football cups, but by the type of man or woman, taken as a whole, that we turn out to fill, as we expect, the most important positions in commerce - or in the professions - in our locality. Qualities of the heart are as important as, if not more important than, qualities of the head.' Whichever of these criteria we use to evaluate the High School in the 1920s, there is no doubt that it was outstandingly successful.

'Qualities of the Heart'

HMIs commented more than once on 'the fine atmosphere prevailing not only between teachers and pupils but also among the pupils themselves'; and in his speech at the prize-giving in June 1924, Kerr mentioned 'the evident reluctance of pupils who were leaving to break away entirely from the influence and activities of the school'.

During the Miners' Strike in 1921, train services could be rather erratic, and some pupils from Shotts and Carluke walked six miles to and from school if their usual train failed to materialise. In May 1926, when, as a result of the General Strike, no trains and few buses were running, one pupil cycled to school from Glasgow every day; and large numbers of pupils walked or cycled to Beltanefoot from the surrounding towns and villages.

Not surprisingly, the average attendance rate throughout the 1920s was well over 90%; and in January 1922, the High School had the highest average attendance rate (5% and 13% higher, incidentally, than those of Hamilton Academy and Dalziel High School) of all the secondary and intermediate schools in Lanarkshire. 'These figures,' the *Wishaw Press* proclaimed, 'show that the Schools' Management Committee, the compulsory officers, and the teachers are fully alive to the need, financial and otherwise, to ensure regular attendance.' This is a reference to the fact that the size of the grant (for a particular school) which the Authority received from the SED was based on the average attendance rate of the school in question: the higher the average attendance rate, the bigger the grant.

Leaving Certificate - and Other - Results

The following table shows how many pupils were presented for the Leaving Certificate at the High School, Hamilton Academy, and Dalziel High School; and, in juxtaposition, how many of these candidates were successful:

	1921	1922	1923	1924	1925	1926	1927
W.H.S.	13/11	13/12	10/9	19/17	23/20	18/18	33/28
Ham. Ac.	50/38	38/34	41/38	48/37	54/39	70/40	79/55
Dal. H.S.	18/11	11/10	16/10	37/16	35/23	39/29	35/19

Over a seven-year period, the High School achieved a success rate of 90%, whereas the success rates of Dalziel High School and Hamilton Academy (regarded as the premier school in Lanarkshire) were 62% and 74% respectively, and the average success rate of all the secondary schools in Lanarkshire was 69%. In 1924 Kerr suggested that 'further perfection of the machinery of instruction' was 'hardly possible'; but he was proved wrong in 1926 when, as a perusal of the above table confirms, the success rate was 100% (a feat previously accomplished in 1920).

In order to gain the Leaving Certificate, which was a group certificate, a pupil had to pass in four subjects at Higher level (or in three subjects at Higher level and two at Lower level), and at the High School he could attempt to achieve these passes not only in the stock subjects (English, Latin, French, and Mathematics) of the secondary curriculum, but also - at least at Higher level - in History, Geography, Music, German, Drawing, Dynamics, and Domestic Science. In fact, the High School was one of the few schools in Scotland to present pupils for Higher History and Higher Domestic Science; the first school in the West of Scotland to present pupils for Higher Geography; and the first school in Scotland to present pupils for Higher Music.

In 1923 a record number of pupils (fifty in all) gained the Intermediate Certificate. In 1924, however, the Intermediate Certificate was replaced by the Day School Certificate (Higher), the award of which was dependent on a pupil's performance in a written examination and his teachers' "opinion marks, attested and verified in an oral examination by His Majesty's Inspector of Schools"; and since only those pupils who intended to leave school after three or four years of secondary education were given the opportunity to gain this new certificate, there were very

60

few presentations (three in 1925, for instance, and two in 1927). Such a paucity of candidates indicates very clearly that the number of pupils staying on at the High School for a fifth and sixth year - and possible presentation for the Leaving Certificate - was on the increase.

Every year, at least one pupil from the High School featured in the first hundred in the Glasgow University Bursary Competition. Three pupils achieved this distinction in 1919 and 1928; four in 1921; and five (including John Heugh and Wilson Chambers, who gained tenth and twelfth place respectively) in 1927. Many years later, interestingly enough, John Heugh returned to the scene of his academic triumphs at Beltanefoot as headmaster of Wishaw Central.

In 1926 William Wilson outperformed all the other entrants from Lanarkshire in the Marshall Trust Junior Bursary Competition.

Between 1906 and 1922, more than one hundred High School pupils continued their studies at university, and more than two hundred took the Junior Students' Course with a view to becoming teachers; between 1906 and 1928, twenty-three former pupils gained an MA (Honours) degree at Glasgow University.

'Hockey Badges'

In 1922 the school hockey team, which was coached by Abigail Loudon, won the Lanarkshire Secondary Schools' Hockey League.

'Football Cups'

In 1919 the High School's Elementary (i.e. under-14) team (Murdoch; Craig and Harris; Cullen, Lawrie, and Halliday; Rankine, Watt, Steele, Turner, and Robert) won the Schools' Cup Competition organised by the YMCA. In the course of the speech he made after receiving the trophy, Kerr magnanimously ascribed this success to the fact that the High School had 'larger numbers to draw on'.

In 1923 the Cambusnethan District Schools' Football Association was formed, and Thomas Hyslop, a Science teacher at the High School, became its first secretary. The newly formed association took over the running of the Schools' Cup Competition from the YMCA, and also set up the Cambusnethan Schools' League. A team from the High School (J. Falloon; T. Peebles and W. Nimmo; A. Young, W. Millar, and W. French; A Struthers, W. Semple, G. Heron, J. McEwan, and J. Hamilton) were the first winners of the league championship, and the same team completed a cup and league double with a victory over Newmains Public in the Schools' Cup Competition.

By 1924, the High School was running an Intermediate (under-15) and a Senior (under-18) team in addition to its highly successful Elementary side. That same year, the High School was one of the founder members of the Lanarkshire Secondary Schools' Football Association, under whose auspices an Intermediate and, some time later, a Senior League were instituted.

1926 was an *annus mirabilis* for the High School's football teams. The Elementary team (P. Paterson, G. Harvie, R. Russell, J. Percy, J. Yates, S. Curran, J. Kelly, R. McGeorge, T. Liddell, K. Weir, D. McDermid, J. Yuill, J. Laurie, W. Sorbie, T. Paterson, A McMillan, and W. Wands) were league champions and winners of the Cambusnethan Teachers' Cup; and the Intermediate team won the Scottish Shield by defeating Dumbarton Academy 3-2 in a replay at Hampden Park. The *Wishaw Press's* report on the match was as follows:

If ever a school has had to fight for a shield, that team is Wishaw High School. They had to play two games with Whitehill and three with Larkhall; and then, after being two goals down against Dumbarton Academy last Wednesday, they forced a replay; and last night, on the same field, the same grit and determination and singleness of purpose were crowned with well-deserved success.

Dumbarton Academy had flashes of brilliance which at times threatened to overwhelm the opposition, but they occasionally beat themselves by trying to beat too many opponents. The Wishaw boys made no mistakes of that sort, their chief weakness being a tendency to get flustered when too closely pressed. The Dumbarton boys, however, deserve every praise for their plucky attempt to pull the match out of the fire after being two goals down.

With wind and sun behind them, Dumbarton took the lead after twelve minutes play, when a cross by Thomson was smartly converted by McSkimming; but Crockett scored a grand equaliser seven minutes later, and within ten minutes Reid put Wishaw ahead. A penalty kick by Crockett after the interval put Wishaw two goals up; and then Dumbarton gave of their very best, as McSkimming reduced Wishaw's lead. The remaining twenty minutes were most exhilarating, the Dumbarton boys forcing a corner in the last minute of the game.

Paterson and Crockett were predominant in the winning team; and Miller, Reid, and Hamilton also did well. Dumbarton's standard was more uniform: all their boys could play football, but the cleverest were too fond of the ball.

The High School team was: Quinton; Yates and Miller; McDonald, Paterson, and Dewar; Reid, Hamilton, Crockett, Laurie, and Meldrum.

Peter Paterson, centre half in the above team, was later selected to play for Scotland against Wales and England. He thus became the first High School pupil to represent his country.

In 1927 an Intermediate team from the High School again reached the final of the Scottish Shield, but lost (1-5) to Clydebank High School; it did, however, have the consolation of winning the Lanarkshire League. The Senior team were also (joint) County champions.

Football was now so popular among the younger boys that the school was able to field a second team at under-14 level. It is also worth noting that in the 1920s school football matches were very popular with the general public. On occasion, they attracted crowds of between two and three thousand, and it was even possible to purchase (for 1s 6d) a season ticket that enabled the holder to attend fourteen cup ties.

8

Ten Years in the Life of the High School

1919

Music Makers

By now, the school had an orchestra with more than thirty members, and this orchestra played a prominent part in the succession of Christmas concerts that took place during the 1920s.

Alumni of the High School, unite!

The first AGM of the Wishaw High School Former Pupils' Club was held on 15 April, and A.J.C. Kerr was elected Honorary President; the first event to be organised by the newly formed club was a ramble (attended by forty FPs) to the Falls of Clyde one month later.

By April of the following year, the club had more than 140 members and five different subsections: tennis (cheap tennis was available to the members, since the club could normally secure the use of the two courts at the High School during the summer holidays); literary (in December 1924, this section arranged an 'elocutionary recital' by Miss Marjorie Gullan, which, according to the *Wishaw Press*, 'was not patronised by the general public as it deserved to be'); social (a dance and, from 1926 onwards, a concert were held every year; and in 1925 there was a reunion of former pupils in Chalmers U.F. Church Hall, at which the FP Jazz Band played various 'lively numbers'); football (by 1921, the FP football team was playing in the Scottish Amateur League); and cycling.

In May 1922, in an effort to strengthen the link between the school and the FP Club, all teachers on the staff of the High School and all former teachers living in the district were granted honorary membership of the club.

An FP remembers.

I have only been able to speak to one former pupil (Mrs Isabella Martin) who attended the High School in the early 1920s. Mrs Martin remembers seeing the Great Fire of 1922 from the station steps - and setting off back home to Newmains *tout de suite*.

Her registration teacher was Mr Ramsay, and her 1st Year class remained in the same room all day - except for Science and PE, which seems to have consisted largely of climbing wall bars and jumping over a buck.

At lunchtime and during the intervals, she played hockey in the playground, while two of her classmates, Sarah McLean and Martha Jones, preferred to get on with their studies in the 'shed'.

Mrs Martin did her homework by candlelight - until the curtain caught fire one night, after which she was provided with an oil lamp.

Once a week, she went to the offices of Burgess and Smith, a local law firm, to collect a bundle of free bus tickets that could be used on any of the many available bus services. She preferred to travel by bus, since the trams were far too slow.

1920

Integer vitae scelerisque purus...

Horace, *Odes*

In March, Alexander Symon, First Assistant and Principal Teacher of Mathematics, retired after 25 years in the teaching profession. At a public ceremony in Thornlie U.F. Church Hall, he was presented with a gold watch and a cheque for £217, and after the presentation Kerr delivered the following encomium:

Mothers and fathers could entrust to him the keeping of their children during school hours without the slightest fear that they would hear anything but the finest advice, or see anything but the finest example of how a life should be lived.

Geography is about Maps...

E.C. Bentley, *Biography for Beginners*

The Schools' Management Committee agreed to purchase several wall atlases for the High School.

Ready, Steady, Choke

At a meeting of the Schools' Management Committee, Mr A. Lindsay intimated that on a visit to the High School he had almost been choked by gas fumes emanating from the Domestic Science Department. According to Kerr, this was 'a habitual thing', an admission that persuaded the Committee to 'inquire into the possibility of using electricity in that department'.

Secondary Colours

The (redesigned) school badge now featured part of the motif of the school war memorial, the letters WHS, and the Latin motto: *Qui non proficit deficit*. Girls were required to wear the new badge on the front of their hats.

Un Succès d'Estime

In December, the school staged an operetta (*The Maid of Castlecary*) instead of the traditional concert. Among the pupils who took part in this production were Arthur Roberts, Susan Wilson, Thomas S. Scott, Willie Nicol, Robert Thomson, Molly Young, Ian Shirley, and Joan McNeil. The *Wishaw Press* was lavish with its praise:
The various characters represented were all admirably portrayed, and the acting was excellent all through - as was the music written and arranged by Robert Booth, the school's gifted music master.

1921

Anyone for tennis?

A new tennis court was constructed in the boys' playground, and in subsequent years matches were arranged with such local schools as Dalziel High School and Lanark Grammar - and, further afield, with Hyndland High School. Swimming was also very popular, the girls' swimming club having sixty members.

Refurbishment

During the summer holidays, both the interior and the exterior of the High School were repainted, and the playground was 'laid with tarmacadam and rolled'. Kerr was delighted: 'They have made the place a real treat.'

If a school is repainted, its closure is usually imminent. Unfortunately, this did not prove to be the case as far as the High School was concerned, and Kerr and his staff had to soldier on in cramped conditions at Beltanefoot for another seven years.

All because the young lady loves...

At the Christmas concert, Nellie Young, who had featured in two items on the programme, was presented with a box of chocolates by a member of the audience.

Calendar Girls...and Boys...and Teachers

The High School produced a calendar (the original idea was Kerr's) that was described in the Gossip and Grumbles column of the *Evening Times* as 'unique', insofar as each day of the year contained a 'sage saw' contributed by an FP, a senior pupil, or a member of staff. The month of January, for instance, included the following:

1st Tom S. Craig
May the best of the days of the year that is gone be worse than the worst of the years still to come.

8th Helen McAllister
To confess ignorance is the first step to knowledge.

15th James D. Reid
I only wish that fortune send
A little more than I can spend.

30th Georgina Jackson
There's aye some water where the stirkie droons.

The calendar cost 1/3d.

There was a break-in at the High School during the summer holidays: burglars ransacked every desk in the school, and after forcing open a cupboard in the Geography room, they vandalised a prismatic compass and stole a football. This was not the first time such a break-in had occurred, and at a meeting of the Schools' Management Committee Kerr declared that he would not 'rest' until the perpetrators were 'pretty severely dealt with'. Five Wishaw youths were eventually convicted of the offence at Hamilton Sheriff Court, but their sentence was deferred in order to give their parents time to pay for the damage.

Test Case

There were thirty teachers on the staff, three of whom had been at Beltanefoot since 1906. One of the thirty, John Weir, Principal Teacher of Geography, instituted an action in the Court of Session against Lanarkshire Education Authority in pursuance of a claim for £243 15s, the basis of his claim being that he was entitled to this extra money in view of his added responsibilities as a principal teacher. He was unsuccessful.

1923

Adam 'Daddy' Allan, janitor at the High School since it was opened in 1906 (and described by Kerr as 'a faithful and conscientious worker, who was liked by everybody at the school'), died in May. On the day of his funeral, which was attended by male members of staff and a group of senior pupils, the school closed at 1.15 as a mark of respect. Mr Allan's successor was Matthew Bain, a man who was destined to become one of the demigods in the folklore of Wishaw High School.

Ars Gratia Artis

A Junior Art Club was established under the supervision of two members of the Art Department, John Telford and Henry Nimmo. The club met on Saturdays, and was open to any pupil at any of the local schools who was interested in art.

The Athletics Committee, which supervised all the school's sporting activities, sanctioned the following expenditure:

Travelling Expenses of High School Teams - 12/-
Entertainment of Visiting Teams - 6/-
Re-engagement of a Groundsman - 7/6 (three visits per week, at 2/6 per visit)
Purchase of Hockey Sticks - to be sold to the pupils at half price, and to be retained by them, if they so desired, when they left school.
Purchase of Eleven Pairs of Leg-Guards.

A Hard Slog, 'Hard Times', and Hard Sell

6th Year pupils went on a ramble to Wallhead Farm, Cleghorn; the distinguished elocutionist, John Stelling, performed extracts from the works of Dickens and Shakespeare in the hall; and a Cake and Candy Stall raised £81 for the school's Athletics Fund. There were prizes for the best sultana cake and the best sponge cake, and these were won by Emily Stark and Ina Coleman respectively.

1925

The High School held its first sports on Saturday, 13 June in the YMCA's Recreation Park (in succeeding years, the sports were held in the Recreation Ground of the Miners' Welfare Institute in Alexander Street). According to the *Wishaw Press*, there was 'a large and keenly appreciative crowd of spectators in attendance'; and 'a long and interesting programme was carried on with a smoothness and regularity that spoke well for its organisers'. In addition to the traditional athletic and novelty events, there were invitation relays, five-a-side football, and an exhibition netball match featuring the senior girls. Sergeant Major Arnott from Hamilton acted as starter, and David Anderson, Rector of Dalziel High School, was one of the judges for the boys' track events. The winners of the various championships were:

Senior Boys - Joseph Morrison
Senior Girls - Margaret Grierson
Junior Boys - Andrew Roberts
Junior Girls - Margaret Baxter

Gold medals were presented to the first three champions in the above list by Provost McLees, ex-Provost Loudon, and M. McLean of the

Crown Hotel respectively; a special prize was awarded to the winner of the Junior Girls' Championship by the Sportsman's Emporium in Glasgow.

'The Ascent of Man'

A 'museum of technical engineering and manufacturing' was set up in the school; and a group of pupils, accompanied by John Weir and several other teachers, went on a 'botanical and geographical excursion' to Tinto.

Wishaw Ladies 1 Wishaw High School 1 Wishaw Rovers 0

In the first half of the annual match between the High School girls and Wishaw Ladies' Hockey Club, 'a dog,' to quote the *Wishaw Press*, 'created a lively diversion. He put in more running than the combined efforts of the 22 players, but he distributed his favours so evenly that the teams crossed over with a goal each to their credit. In the event, he was removed before the second half began.'

This match, like most of the High School's hockey matches during the 1920s, was played at Belhaven Park.

1926

In June, Kenilworth Park was the venue of the first sports meeting arranged by the Cambusnethan Schools' Football Association. The High School won the Schools' Championship, and a High School pupil, Peter Paterson, won the Boys' Championship.

A Talented Trio

Three members of the family of Mr and Mrs Robert Gilchrist topped the prize list in their respective years: Pearl was dux of the school, Robert dux of the 3rd Year, and Nancy dux of the 1st Year.

The Epidiascope
Wonderful Invention at the High School

Such was the headline that appeared in the *Wishaw Press* on 12 November. The device in question was the first of its type to be introduced into any of the schools in Lanarkshire, and 'it was found to be very effective in teaching History, Botany, Geography, and allied subjects'.

Small earthquake in Wishaw. Not much damage.

One afternoon, an incident occurred that not only 'produced in Kerr the sensation of seasickness, but also made him more desirous than ever of new premises'. "As I was looking out of the window of the boys' cloakroom," he wrote in a later article, "I noticed that the field next to the playground was undulating like the surface of the sea, after which it settled down in hillocks with deep cavities between them. Part of the adjacent street subsided, and the walls of a neighbouring lodging house ended up on the slant. What had happened? Under the field, seemingly, there was an old coal mine from which the props had been dislodged, and when the ground subsided large cavities became apparent. Fortunately, we were informed that the school building was on a 'dyke' (i.e. solid rock) in the middle of the coal workings."

1927

John Heugh, the school dux, was awarded a Miners' Welfare Scholarship that entitled him 'to take a degree with honours in Classics at Balliol College, Oxford'. Lord Chelmsford, Chairman of the Scholarship Selection Committee, wrote the following letter to Kerr:

I am writing to congratulate you on your handiwork. It is delightful to find that the old traditions of Classics still survive in some schools in Scotland, and I can only hope that Heugh will prove worthy of your recommendation, and of the opportunity we are giving him.

The Secretary of the Scholarship Committee is in communication with the Master of Balliol, and Heugh will presently be informed of everything he is expected to do. I am frequently down at Oxford myself and I shall try to see Heugh from time to time. Tell him we expect much of him.

November saw the retiral of Robert Booth, Principal Teacher of Music. During his tenure of that post, the High School was the only school in Lanarkshire that regularly presented pupils for Higher Music at the Leaving Certificate Examinations. Also worthy of note is the fact that he wrote the music for three of the operettas staged by the school.

9

1928- 1937: 'Saturnia regna'

On 27 June 1928, Kerr sent the following letter to the headmasters of the local primary schools:

Dear Sir,
I am taking my present pupils on a tour of inspection through the new High School, Park Street, Wishaw, from 1.15 to 2.15 p.m. on Friday first. It would be of great service to all concerned with the opening day (21st of August) at the new school if you would allow those who intend to enrol from your school to be present at the new High School gates at 2.15 p.m. on Friday first, when I shall hand over to them plans of both storeys of the school and personally conduct them through the building.
Trusting you will find it convenient to agree to my request, and with best wishes for the holiday season,
I am,
Yours truly,
A. J.C. Kerr

O fortunatos nimium, sua si bona norint.

Virgil, *Georgics*

The new High School, the first completely new secondary school to be erected under the auspices of the Lanarkshire Education Authority (and also one of the last, since education authorities were abolished by the Local Government Act of 1929 and their powers transferred to the councils of the 33 counties, which in turn were required to appoint education committees to exercise these powers), opened its gates to 585 pupils at 10 a.m. on Tuesday, 21 August 1928. One of these 585 pupils, Andrew Brown, has this to say about that first morning:
There was some delay in taking us into the school - probably due to a staff meeting - and a group of senior boys (who looked like teachers to us) took it upon themselves to assemble the newcomers in the playground. Then they marched us into the school (I can still recall the strong smell

of fresh varnish that pervaded the whole building), round all the downstairs corridors, round all the upstairs corridors and, finally, back out to the playground where they left us - in a state of complete bewilderment. In the event, the greater part of the first day was spent transferring books and equipment from Beltanefoot to the new school.

On Wednesday, instruction recommenced in all subjects except Science and Domestic Science: some of the practical rooms (as well as the hall and the luncheon room) were not ready for immediate use. At 3 p.m., in the lecture room, and before an audience comprising senior pupils and members of staff, the previous session's prizewinners were presented with the books they had won, their medals being withheld until the formal opening of the new school in September.

Pergama recidiva

Virgil, *Aeneid*

Though it was built mainly of roughcast brick, Wishaw High School Mark 2 had a stone facade of 'severe simplicity', a point that was developed by the distinguished academic who was to perform the opening ceremony:

The simple solidity of its exterior blends with the somewhat austere lines of the environment, but it veils, rather than displays, the complexity and ingenious commodity of the inward parts.

The new High School was quadrangular in design, three of its four sides being taken up by classrooms (20), laboratories (5), art rooms (2) and a 'manual' room, the fourth by the gymnasium, the luncheon room, and the cookery, laundry, housewifery, and needlework rooms; also incorporated in the design were the Rector's room, the secretary's room, the medical inspection room, and 'retiring rooms' for the staff and the senior pupils. Most of the rooms opened on to outside corridors, as in a sanatorium.

In two corners of the quadrangle there were small ponds, in which it was hoped that various aquatic plants would be grown; in the centre of the quadrangle stood the most distinctive architectural feature of the new school - the octagonally shaped assembly hall.

The lighting in the hall consisted of a large ornamental lantern (with smaller lights attached), suspended from the top of the dome; standard lamps (donated by seven private individuals) at each end of the rostrum; and, on the walls, small, artistically designed 'lantern lights'.

Two flags - the Union Jack and the St. Andrew's Cross - had been presented to the school by ex-Provost Nimmo and Bairds the Drapers respectively, and these were hung on the wall behind the rostrum. On the rostrum itself, the front of which incorporated the war memorial, there was an ormolu lectern, a gift from the staff.

The coats of arms (borrowed from four local landowners) of the four Houses - Allanton, Belhaven, Coltness, and Murdostoun - were depicted in stained glass on the windows, and the decor of the hall was completed by a quotation (from a classical source) inscribed, in large letters, round the walls: "If a man's soul be educated, such a man is to be called happy. A man is not to be called happy if he be splendidly furnished with external things." Among the 'external things' with which the new school was furnished were several 'garden plots', two tennis courts (at the front of the school), and a hockey field and two football pitches (at the back).

At a more utilitarian level, the school had been provided with hot and cold 'sprays', a 'low pressure hot water heating system', and a 'synchronome' electric clock that controlled the clocks in all the classrooms.

The colour scheme in the classrooms was cream and purple; in the hall it was gold, blue, and grey. According to Kerr: 'The staff feel that the colouring is such that it will keep everybody alive and happy, and that there will be no sleeping at work.'

The architect responsible for the design of the new High School was John Stewart MBE, 'a man as modest and retiring as he was gifted and practical' (to quote ex-Bailie Ingram), whose 'conceptions' (and in the opinion of the journalist who wrote up his architectural achievements in the *Wishaw Press* in January 1932, this was a more important consideration) 'saved the ratepayers of Lanarkshire many thousands of pounds'. It would have been more difficult to reach such a conclusion in 1928 when the final cost (£60,000) of his ambitious project in Park Street became apparent.

A Day to Remember

Mr Stewart's 'handsome and palatial creation' (as Kerr described the 'new' school) was formally opened on Friday, 28 September 1928 by Sir Donald MacAlister, Principal of Glasgow University:

Today we are opening the new building of Wishaw High School; we are not opening the school itself. That has existed for many years - growing in wisdom and stature to sturdy adulthood, since it was born as the Higher Grade Department of your own Public School in 1895. It has indeed long outgrown its old garments, and we are today merely clothing it with a new suit ample enough to give free play to its still growing limbs, and seemly enough to mark the station in life which it has won among its peers. Like other youngsters in Wishaw and elsewhere, it has hitherto had to put up with the made-down or made-up garments of its seniors in the educational family. Now that it is big and buirdly, living its own life and valiantly making its own name in the world, it rightly claims, and rightly dons, a "suit o' braws", measured and made for itself. And you, its parents and foster- parents, and we, its neighbours and friends, can but admire and applaud both the handsome show it makes and the proper pride and modest confidence in itself and in its career with which it carries off its well-designed accoutrements.

After the medals had been presented to the various duxes of session 1927-28 by Lady Keith, wife of the Chairman of the Education Authority, the war memorial was rededicated: Lord Belhaven read a passage from the Bible, a prayer was delivered by the Reverend J.A. Nicholls, and a wreath was laid on the memorial by the girls' captain, Jenny Balmain.

In the course of a wide-ranging vote of thanks, Kerr declared that he had 'a profound sense of gratitude to the Authority and all in their employment for doing everything possible to make the school the beautiful structure it was'.

Prior to the opening ceremony, the most important guests had been shown round the new school; and later in the day, members of the public were afforded an opportunity to carry out a similar inspection. In fact, the High School seemed to become 'the cynosure' of more than just 'neighbouring eyes': Kerr himself claimed that for a year or two much of his time was taken up showing Scottish educationalists - and, on occasion, 'representatives' from England and America - over the new building; and in April 1936, an even more distinguished visitor, Field Marshal Sir William Birdwood, declared that 'the cleanliness and brightness of the surroundings appealed' to him, and that he was 'greatly impressed by the beauty of the hall'.

A few days after the new school was opened, Kerr received the following letter from Lord Belhaven:

Dear Mr Kerr,
My wife and I enjoyed the proceedings on Friday, and looking back on the event, I would not have missed taking a part in it for worlds.
Yours sincerely,
Belhaven

The Comprehensive Ideal......and Reality

In November 1928, the 'old' High School became a centre for Protestant pupils in the local primary schools' Advanced Divisions (these were formerly known as the Supplementary Classes, and comprised those pupils who had passed the Qualifying Examination, but who intended to leave school at the statutory leaving age of 14 without embarking on any form of secondary education). Its name was changed: initially, to Beltanefoot Advanced Division School; and then, in the 1930s, to Wishaw Central.

Kerr was opposed to this development. "I said then, and I say now," he wrote twenty years later, "that the Education Authority should not have opened an Advanced Division Centre in Wishaw. There should have been two 'comprehensive' schools (one of them our new school in Wishaw; and the other one in Newmains, to cater for pupils in Shotts, Newmains, Cambusnethan, and Morningside), each of them providing academic, scientific, technical, commercial, and so-called 'modern' education, and each of them giving every pupil the type of education to which he was suited. This would have avoided producing in the pupils of the Advanced Division Centre - and also in the misnamed 'duds' of secondary schools - an inferiority complex."

Kerr was well aware that there were some 'duds' on the roll of the new High School, and he reacted in a typically radical manner:
Even though we raised the standard for entrance, many had to be enrolled who, though they did well in primary school, made little progress in foreign languages and abstract mathematics - and thus developed an inferiority complex and became disheartened. The only remedy for this that I could obtain - for neither they nor their parents wished that they should transfer to an advanced division centre - was the unofficial sanction of the HMI to drop foreign language study almost completely with a very small number who were known to me as certain to leave school at the end of their third year, and who were likely to succeed in technical subjects.

L'école c'est moi.

The new school soon became synonymous with its dynamic rector: 'Mr Kerr is known among his professional brethren,' to quote Dr Morgan, ex-Principal of the Provisional Training College in Edinburgh, 'as "Kerr of Wishaw", and it is a great compliment to him that he is connected in such an intimate way with his school.'

L'éducation nous faisait ce que nous sommes.

Helvetius, *De l'esprit*

Like all great educators, Kerr was a great advocate of the beneficial effects of a good education:
Children should spend as many years as possible of their adolescence in a school environment - not so much for the money and the position it may bring them in later life, as for the enormous assistance this gives teachers in developing, along sane and proper lines, the character, the manners, and even the speech of these young people. The period between 14 and 16 years of age is a most critical one in the formation of character, and it should be spent in the best moral and cultural atmosphere that can be obtained.
In the 1930s, however, even those who had impressive academic qualifications quickly discovered that jobs were not easy to come by (in 1931, for instance, the number of people in the parish of Cambusnethan who were out of work exceeded 4,000), and by 1936 Kerr was advising 4th and 5th Year pupils to leave school without too much hesitation if they were offered a suitable post.

Jobs for the Boys...and the Girls

Kerr regarded himself as the High School's 'careers master' (a responsibility that in his judgment 'should lie with the headmaster, wherever this is possible'), and he took a great deal of trouble to ensure that as many of his pupils as possible obtained appropriate employment (he believed, rather harshly, that the unemployed 'rapidly deteriorated into the unemployable for any responsible calling'). In August 1932, for example, he asked the *Wishaw Press* 'to intimate to all local employers of labour' that there was a large number of boys and girls at the High

School who had 'received at least three years' training in either industrial or commercial subjects', and that he was 'prepared at any time to recommend a certain individual, or furnish an employer with a leet from which to make his choice'; and on 22 February 1934 the following announcement appeared in the *Wishaw Press*:

The Rector of the High School wishes to state that there are at present in his school several well-educated youths who, either because they are the sons of widows or for some other reason, are in very poor financial circumstances and have no friends to help them by their influence to gain a situation. They are highly recommended for local posts, and the Rector will be pleased to answer inquiries about them.

The High School was affiliated to the Secondary Schools' Agency in Glasgow, which acted as an employment bureau for secondary school pupils in the West of Scotland. Moreover, Kerr himself kept in direct touch with both the local Labour Exchange and the Careers Council (which had been set up by the Education Committee in conjunction with Glasgow Labour Exchange), and by virtue of these contacts he was able in June 1934, to take a case in point, to place six boys in situations with excellent prospects in or near London.

Kerr also made use of his many contacts in the business world to find employment for his pupils. John Parton, who was a pupil at the High School in the early 1930s, can recall one of his friends, Jack Hay, being asked by Kerr if he intended to continue his studies at university. "No," replied Hay, "my father isn't keeping too well, and I'll have to try and find a job that offers some security for the future." Kerr suggested a career in banking; but Hay said that since he didn't know anybody in banking circles he wasn't optimistic about his prospects of finding employment in that line of work. Whereupon, Kerr phoned a bank in Edinburgh and informed the manager that he would be sending a senior pupil for an interview the following day.

The Great Innovator

The Triennial Report issued by His Majesty's Inspector in 1937 contained the following observation: 'In many of the recent developments in education, Mr Kerr has tended to lead rather than to follow.' This observation can be substantiated, initially, by one simple example of Kerr's innovative bent: from as early as June 1934, the High School started to operate the timetable for the coming session in the final month of the preceding one, an arrangement that has, of course, become very popular in recent years.

Even more radical - in view of the somewhat restrictive guidelines laid down by the Scottish Education Department (for instance, English, History, Science or Mathematics, and a foreign language were compulsory for the first five years of a secondary course) - were Kerr's efforts to provide the variety of curricula that enabled pupils to take the subjects which best suited their abilities and were most likely to be of some use to them in their chosen occupation. In order to achieve this curricular variety, he introduced several new courses: Zoology in 1928 (this innovation prompted Sir Donald MacAlister, who had declared at the formal opening of the new school that there was a need for more trained biologists, to send a letter to Kerr congratulating him on 'the pioneer work' being done in the biological sciences at the High School); Arts and Crafts, and Applied Science (Woodwork, Metalwork, and Technical and Mechanical Drawing) in 1929; and Commercial (Shorthand, Typing, Bookkeeping, and Commercial Arithmetic) in 1930.

With the exception of Zoology and the addition of Domestic Science, all these courses were available to pupils from second year onwards; and they could all, without exception, lead to presentation at Lower or Higher level in the Leaving Certificate Examinations.

The Arts and Crafts course was particularly popular, and in 1932 the Medical Inspection Room had to be converted into an Arts and Crafts room. The popularity of the Arts and Crafts course encouraged Kerr to seek the approval of the SED for the introduction (the following year) of another new course - Domestic Science and Allied Art - comprising Design, Needlework, Dressmaking, and Embroidery. He also planned courses in Engineering Drawing and Agricultural Science, but he was unable to implement these plans due to a shortage of accommodation.

There is no doubt that Kerr would also have liked to make sweeping changes in the standard secondary curriculum:

I would have given every pupil in his or her first year at secondary school the same general education - with little or no foreign language study and no theoretical mathematics, but with more history, geography, civics, music, art, technical subjects, and science than are given even at the present time [1949]. The academic type of education would have begun in earnest only in the second year; and the other types would have evolved then as well, with the classes named and numbered according to type.

Mais revenons à ces moutons. In 1934, in his Triennial Report, His Majesty's Chief Inspector for the West of Scotland commented on 'the unusually wide variety of courses' on offer at the High School. Kerr, for his part, claimed that as a result of 'the introduction of this great variety into the school curriculum', the pupils 'not only liked school ever so much better but were keener than ever on work rather than idle play and more alive to coming to a decision about their future career'; but since most of the new courses had a predominantly vocational content, he felt it was essential that they should be underpinned by a sound general education:

If you parents decide to make your boy or girl a clerk, don't imagine that can be done by giving them mainly commercial subjects from their first or second year at the school. Even a good typist must, above all, be able to spell and punctuate, and this ability can only be gained by a thorough knowledge of English. Happy the child whose parent is long-sighted enough to see that the surest road to promotion in any career is founded upon a good general education.

Special Relationships

Kerr was well ahead of his time in believing that there should be a close relationship between a headmaster and the parents of his pupils, and that every opportunity should be taken to bring 'the human touch' into this relationship:

It is essential for the true well-being of the pupil, physically, mentally, and morally, that the parents and myself should have an exchange of views and come into close personal touch with each other. I have always welcomed, therefore, the visits of parents to the school for such purposes, and I am never too busy to grant an interview.

'The human touch' was also an important ingredient in Kerr's relationship with his pupils. Although he was a strict disciplinarian, he believed that the best way 'to get to the hearts' of the pupils, boys and girls alike, was to address them by their Christian name; and at the prize-giving in 1934, he declared that he could envisage a time when rigid discipline would be a thing of the past - and corporal punishment would be 'unheard of'.

Visiting Hours

In June 1934, acting on a suggestion of the Secretary of State for Scotland, Sir Godfrey Collins, Kerr set aside an afternoon for parents to see 'the work of the school being carried out in the classroom and, for half an hour, on the sportsfield and playgrounds (in the form of organised games)'. Parents could also consult him about the curriculum that would best suit their children.

The following year, the Open Day was designated as a Parents' Day, and from then on Parents' Days featured regularly on the school calendar. In September 1935, the *Wishaw Press* contained the following report:

Over 300 parents and friends turned out on Wednesday afternoon to see how the work is carried out in the various departments and consult the Rector about the courses of their respective children. After inspecting the art, commercial, laundry, cookery and housewifery rooms, and then the workshop, gymnasia, conservatory and science laboratories, they assembled in batches in the geography room, where they saw the epidiascope and the cinema projector. Music and tea were provided in the assembly hall, the main features of which were explained by the Rector.

The First Picture Show

The 'cinema projector' had been purchased in 1933, 'in order to show' (as the School Convener, G.N. Pomphrey, was quick to reassure parents) 'not pictures of amusement, but pictures of education'. By the end of that same year, the *Wishaw Press* was able to report:

The projector is in full use, and the Geography lessons are much enhanced in value by this visual training - while the pupils thoroughly enjoy the change from general school routine.

In 1934 the school received a grant of £5 from the Education Committee to help pay for the hire of films, on condition that Kerr submitted a report on 'the efficiency of the projector for instructional purposes'.

Radio Days

In 1931 the school purchased an 'all-electric wireless set' with two loudspeakers and 'connections' to four classrooms and the assembly hall; and these were put to good use in November 1932, when several classes listened to their rector giving a talk on 'The Central Coalfields of Scotland'. A second, more powerful set was acquired in 1935, and in November of that year more than 600 pupils were able to enjoy the transmission of a concert featuring the Scottish Orchestra.

A Song Is Born

In 1937 Daisy Macdonald, Principal Teacher of Modern Languages, suggested - and Kerr agreed - that the High School should have its own song. The words and music for such a song were composed by Eleanor Haddow and Jean McCartney respectively, and the song itself was sung publicly for the first time at the prize-giving - by a 'double quartet'. It goes as follows:

> We talk of happy days to come,
> When we have left our school;
> But ever in our hearts we'll keep
> Its great, inspiring rule.
> In climbing learning's pathway steep
> No Royal Road we find:
> Who makes not progress day by day
> Will soon be left behind.
>
> In sport and play we all are keen
> To win that shining shield,
> Naught can surpass those happy hours
> Of contest in the field.
> Our patrons we remember them,
> Each bears an honoured name;
> And mottoes gleam before our eyes
> And teach to play the game.
>
> In Allanton we have to learn
> That hardships help the brave;
> Belhaven's teams full oft ride through
> And paths to glory pave;
> 'Bent but not broken', legend proud,
> On Coltness' banner flies;
> Undaunted by the sternest tasks
> Will Murdostoun arise.

To some the years ahead will bring
Success with fame and praise;
To some the harder path to walk
Life's humble, patient ways.
Whate'er our lot in future years,
One noble aim have we:
With loyal hearts and helping hands
Good citizens to be.

E Pluribus Unum

'I observe,' declared Sir Donald MacAlister at the formal opening of the 'new' High School, 'that the Rector has astutely subdivided his pupils into four Houses, like the four nations of Glasgow University, in order that they may marshal themselves for the honour of Wishaw under the banners of Allanton, Belhaven, Coltness, and Murdostoun respectively. These banners are blazoned on the windows of the central hall, to mark simultaneously their separate individuality and their corporate unity. I congratulate the Rector on his happy thought, and I am confident that by this device of applied psychology he has set in motion forces that will make the life and vigour of every unit - and of the organism as a whole - more fruitful. He has divided, so that he may unite into one living and conscious body, the institution he so wisely sways.' Such praise was fully justified, since the creation of the House System was probably Kerr's most durable innovation.

'Every pupil, boy or girl,' he explained in 1929, 'must belong to one of four Houses, and these Houses compete against each other at football, hockey, tennis, netball, and general athletics, the prize being a beautiful shield, the gift of ex-Provost Archibald. The winner this year is Belhaven House, which holds the shield for one year and has the name of its captain inscribed on the Belhaven panel.

We have found that the House System works excellently in stimulating healthy rivalry and "esprit de corps", and I am certain that it is the team spirit thus evoked which has led to our winning football trophies. Moreover, the committees of each House thoroughly deserve my thanks and congratulations for so successfully controlling the movements of the pupils as they pass in and out of the school and the classrooms therein.'

Kerr often eulogised the House System in his annual reports: he believed, without ever producing any evidence to support this belief, that it generated self-discipline in the pupils, and thus made the task of the staff much easier. Consequently, with a view to consolidating the system, every pupil was required to wear a badge indicating to which House he or she belonged.

In June 1936, H.G. Smith, Managing Director of The Picture House in Wishaw Main Street, presented a silver cup to the school for the winners of the inter-House athletics championship; in 1937, another silver cup (for the winners of the inter-House swimming championship) and a statuette of Mercury on a marble pedestal (for the winners of the inter-House rugby championship) were presented to the school by ex-Provost Nimmo and Dr Oliver Gray, Hon. President of Wishaw Rugby Club, respectively. Allanton was the first House to win the inter-House athletics championship; and also the first House to win the inter-House swimming championship, which was held at the Corporation Baths in Motherwell.

Glittering Prizes

F. E. Smith

Prizewinners in academic subjects also benefited from the generosity of private individuals: for 25 years, ex-Provost William B. Thomson supplied the dux medal; in 1931, medals for excellence in individual subjects were provided by Provost Anderson, William Archibald, Colin Baird, Robert Freeland, and Dr Campbell; and in the same year, Lord Belhaven presented the school with twenty bronze medallions, one of which was awarded each year to the most distinguished Latin scholar in the 6th Year. The medallions, which were replicas of the one struck at Mantua in 1930 to commemorate the 2,000th anniversary of the birth of the Roman poet Virgil in that same town, were deposited in the safe of one of the town's banks.

A Great Benefactor

Kerr had a very high regard for Lord Belhaven, whom he described as "one of Nature's gentlemen":

He took a great interest in the school, and never failed to assist pupils who scored very high marks in the Glasgow University Bursary Competition. This he did by bringing them before the notice of the Duchess of Hamilton, in whose hands lay the bestowal of the Dundonald Bursary. He always accepted my recommendations, and these pupils never let us down. He often visited the school, and he often invited me up to Wishaw House to discuss its progress. I admired his gentle manner, courtesy, true friendship, and general kindness, which gave no indication that he was of exalted rank.

Aide-toi, le ciel t'aidera.

Jean de la Fontaine, *Fables*

'As a school,' Kerr admitted in 1932, 'we do make great demands upon the finances of the country, but we show our appreciation by doing as much as we possibly can for ourselves.' This claim is substantiated by the fact that by the beginning of session 1931-32 four different funds had been established at the High School: the Sports Fund, which was replenished annually by the pupils' subscriptions; the Educational Fund, which enabled the school to purchase such items as a wireless and gramophone records; the General Purposes Fund, under whose auspices help was given to 'necessitous cases' among the pupils; and the Prize Fund, which was sustained by the profit made by the luncheon room. Indeed, the luncheon room proved to be so profitable (after the £58 borrowed from the Education Authority to purchase equipment had been repaid) that in September 1935 a deputation of governors and members of staff from Marr College, Troon, interviewed Kerr and the manageress, Mrs McLean, 'with regard to the provision of food and the keeping of accounts'.

Big is not always beautiful.

When the new High School was formally opened in September 1928, there were 585 pupils on the roll, a total which included a sufficiently large contingent from Shotts and Cleland to make it economically viable for the Railway Company to put on a special train that left Shotts at 8.20 every morning. In his speech at the opening ceremony, Sir Donald MacAlister made it clear that he did not expect the roll to remain static:

Wishaw people are less shrewd, less eager to do the best for their children, than I take them to be, if they do not from now onward press more and more on the school's accommodation, and so raise soon the question not of the solidity of the walls but of their elasticity.

As for Kerr, though he was pleased - after '22 years of trying to fit two pupils into the accommodation for only one' - to have moved to a building that not only accommodated 750 pupils 'quite easily' but could also 'be made to accommodate 800 or 900 with careful organisation', he would have been quite content if the roll had been frozen at 600. 'That,' he said, 'is the maximum number which a headmaster can effectively supervise, and which will allow him to keep in personal touch with each pupil and help him frame his school career according to his talents and his future calling.'

Despite Kerr's misgivings, the increase in the school population so confidently predicted by Sir Donald was not slow to materialise, for on several occasions during the 1930s the roll exceeded 800, thus becoming the largest of all the secondary schools in Lanarkshire. There were two main reasons for such an upsurge: as a result of the recession and the consequent shortage of jobs, many more pupils were staying on at school for more than three years; and there were large intakes of new pupils (a record-breaking 180, for example, in August 1930, and 171 in 1933), even though applicants from the primary schools had to score 70% or more in the Qualifying Examination to gain entry.

Origins of the Species

As far as the family background of the vast majority of High School pupils is concerned, the following statistic is very revealing: in session 1932-33, only three pupils on the roll were supplied with free boots - compared with 113 at Berryhill, 174 at Wishaw R.C., and 448 at Craigneuk R.C.

...creeping like snail
Willingly to school.

Shakespeare, *As You Like It (adapted)*

The attendance rate rarely, if ever, dipped below 90%, and in the course of session 1934-35 twelve High School pupils completed five years' perfect attendance, in recognition of which they were presented with watches by the Schools' Management Committee. Kerr attributed the school's exemplary attendance rate to the positive and harmonious atmosphere that prevailed therein:

The school is run on such lines - and there is such a fine mutual understanding between teachers and pupils - that everyone hates to be absent from school, and everyone finds great pleasure in the varying work and play that go on here.

and to the importance that was attached to the physical well-being of the pupils:

The nature of the school building (it is built on the sanatorium principle), the frequent changing from room to room, expert physical training in the gymnasia, sports periods (two each week, on average, for half the year), organised games, the self-control inculcated by the House System, attention to deportment in marching, and frequent medical inspections have all combined to raise the general standard of physique and improve the pupils' health.

Kerr also claimed that after the move from Beltanefoot the attendance rate improved by 2%, because the new school was situated on higher ground and had more spacious playing fields.

As far as 'sports periods' were concerned, Sir Donald MacAlister expressed the hope (rather optimistically, it must be said) that the teachers would derive as much benefit from them as the pupils:
The zest of the youngsters will enliven and stimulate their seniors, who often need to be induced and encouraged to keep their bodies in vigour and soundness, if the vitality of their teaching is to be maintained at its freshest.

summi vagae moderatores iuventae

Martial, *Epigrams (adapted)*

By 1935, there were forty teachers on the staff. Included in that number were David Lees, who was destined to become Rector of Glasgow High

School; Alf Dubber and Sam Forrest, who wrote standard textbooks for students of English and Mathematics respectively; and Elsa Syme and Archie Leitch, who 'served' the school virtually 'all their days'.

'They also serve...'

The non-teaching personnel comprised a secretary, two janitors, eight cleaners, two 'maids', and the manageress of the luncheon room. The Rector's secretary, Miss Mitchell, was described by Kerr in 1936 as 'having admirable discrimination and foresight'; the head janitor was the inimitable Matthew Bain, who formed a formidable duumvirate with Kerr on the disciplinary front; the first assistant janitor to be appointed was James McIlwain, and he was followed, in quick succession, by J. Black and George Jarvie, 'an ex-Regular Army man'.

Madame, si c'est possible, c'est fait...

Charles Alexandre de Calonne

A week after the 'new' High School was opened, the *Wishaw Press* declared: "It is safe to assume that in such a congenial environment the staff and pupils will maintain, and possibly surpass, the school's notable achievements in the past." The word 'possibly' proved to be unnecessarily cautious, for in three successive years (1929, 1930, and 1931) the High School achieved a pass rate of 100% in the Leaving Certificate Examinations; every pupil, in other words, passed in every subject in which he or she was presented at either Higher or Lower Grade.

Though it is obvious from all his speeches that Kerr set great store by success in external examinations, he did claim in 1933 that he was 'not out for 100% success rates every time' in these exams: "I always like to give a chance to the lame dog, to the candidate, that is, who is likely to fail, but who has a slight chance of doing better than the school's expectations."

In 1929 two 'lame dogs' who were not 'given a chance' rejected Kerr's advice and, at the instigation of their parents, presented themselves for the Leaving Certificate Examinations; and one pupil adopted a similarly rebellious course of action the following year. All three failed to gain the Leaving Certificate.

Very few pupils (never more than four per session) were presented for the Day School Certificate (Higher), and only one failure was recorded throughout the 1930s.

In the space of ten years, High School pupils gained 5th, 6th, 7th (twice), 8th, and 9th place in the Glasgow University Bursary Competition; and in 1931 and 1936 the school had six scholars in the first hundred. The crowning glory of the High School's participation in the Bursary Competition was announced by Kerr at a morning assembly in June 1937:

I have now to make what is perhaps the most important intimation ever made in this school; at any rate, it gives me the greatest pleasure. Robert Dalziel, this year's dux, is first in the university bursaries competition. Special occasions must be specially marked, so I am asking the Director of Education and the School Convener to grant a whole holiday.

The High School's own examinations took place twice per session - in October and April; the Leaving Certificate Examinations (known as the 'Leavings') were held in March. Just after the 'Leavings' in 1936, the following paragraph appeared in one of the evening papers:

When Master Tammie MacTucker wishes to go to the university, and has to pass the higher leaving examinations at a Scottish secondary school today, he uses the abilities which previously earned him his supper to charm the heart of His Majesty's Inspectors of Schools. That at any rate is the suggestion underlying remarks made by the Inspector of German when he visited a West of Scotland High School for the German orals the other day. The Inspector said that nowadays, instead of pupils reading a prose passage to him or reciting a poem, sometimes a pupil - or even a choir - would sing a song. He had recently heard, he said, a song charmingly sung in German by a candidate who is a pupil at Wishaw High School.

Throughout the 1930s, the High School continued to earn high praise from His Majesty's Inspectors:

Classics: The highest classes are in the hands of a scholarly and experienced teacher.

Modern Languages: The department is in a high state of general efficiency, a state of affairs that bears witness to the ability and devotion of the principal teacher and the loyalty of her staff.

Botany: The work is very satisfactory, full use being made of the excellent botanical opportunities in the surrounding countryside.

Needlework: Good methods of work, neatness, cleanliness, and thoroughness are developed, and the girls are encouraged to be practical, economical, and thorough.
English: The teaching is very systematic and thorough.
Mathematics: Throughout the department, instruction is given with marked skill.
Art: Conscientious work is done by the teachers in this department.
Technical: The principles are well grasped, and the drawings accurate.
Commercial Subjects: The classes as a whole gave evidence of sound instruction, earnest application, and solid achievement.
Staff: The teachers are devoted to their labours, and the Rector brings to the task of supervision an alert understanding and the fruits of a ripe experience.

In his speech at the prize-giving in 1932, Kerr suggested another way in which the success or otherwise of his school could be gauged:
The best test of the nature of the education provided here is to be found in the manner in which our students comport themselves in the universities and other colleges when they are no longer spoon-fed and have to reach out independently for their intellectual sustenance.

If such a test is used, it confirms - unequivocally - the success of the High School as an academic institution, for throughout the 1930s the columns of the *Wishaw Press* were full of references to former pupils who distinguished themselves at Glasgow University. Considerations of time and space permit me to mention no more than three: Samuel Curran, in later years Principal and Vice-Chancellor of the University of Strathclyde; Walker Chambers, who eventually became Professor of German at Glasgow University; and Isobel Haddow, the most distinguished female graduate of her year in Arts.

Return to Hampden

Success in the examination room was replicated on the football field in April 1932, when the High School's under-15 team won the Scottish Intermediate Shield, a triumph that was described as follows by the *Wishaw Press*:
Last Thursday night, the final of the Intermediate Shield was played at Hampden Park, Glasgow. There was a good attendance, and the local team took with them a big following and the 'will to win'.

The final was of great local interest due to the fact that the "High's" opponents were Dalziel. On their way to the final, Wishaw had accounted

90

for some of the 'fancied sides', while Dalziel had met and defeated teams which offered them stiff opposition.

The enthusiasm on each side was on a par, but the difference between the teams on the field was decidedly marked.

Right from the start, Wishaw made use of the axiom that the best method of defence lies in attack; and so well did they keep this up, that for practically the whole game they had the balance of play in their favour.

The fast movements and superior weight of the Wishaw forwards told against the Dalziel defence, and Crossley's charge was frequently in danger. However, over-anxiety to get the ball into the net was the big fault of the Wishaw five, and a little steadiness might have brought the opening goal before the eighteen minutes mark.

At this point, Dalziel conceded a corner, and from the flag kick by Laurie a scramble followed in the goalmouth. This put the Dalziel defence in difficulties, and McNay gave Wishaw the goal that was overdue.

With a goal lead, Wishaw continued to press strongly, and Dalziel had difficulty in keeping their goal intact until half-time.

Wishaw resumed as they had left off at the interval - on the attack - and continually harassed the Dalziel defence. Smart play left Don with the ball, and his nice slip to McNay gave the latter an opening to put Wishaw two in the lead.

Wishaw eased off a little near the close, and Dalziel came more into the play - though their forwards failed to overcome the Wishaw defence. Thirty seconds from the final whistle, however, Summers slipped the ball into the net for Dalziel's only goal.

Throughout the game, the Wishaw eleven showed excellent teamwork. Their forwards were clever and their rear division masters of the opposition.

The Dalziel forwards didn't get moving properly due to the 'breaking' methods of the Wishaw half-back line, while their defenders were never comfortable under the Wishaw attack.

The teams were:

Wishaw High School: *Tyrrell; Gardiner and Gentleman; Dougall, Dykes, and Kirk; McNay, Don, Freeland, Hunter, and Laurie*

Dalziel High School: *Crossley; Anderson and Bonomy; Sneddon, Porter, and Dick; McFetteridge, Summers, McLean, Main, and Thomson*

Referee; Mr Rankin (Glasgow).

The High School team was trained by Alex Anderson, who twenty years later became the Labour MP for the Burgh of Motherwell and Wishaw. A future rector of the High School, Neil McKellar, was in charge of the Dalziel team, which included John Bonomy, a stalwart in the High School's PE Department from the late 1940s onwards.

At the presentation ceremony in Miss Buick's Restaurant in Glasgow, the President of the Scottish Secondary Schools' Football Association said he was sure that the Intermediate Shield would be 'housed for a year in a building than which there was none more beautiful in Scotland'. Kerr declared that he regarded 'the victory that evening not so much as a victory for his school as a victory for the united burgh of Motherwell and Wishaw', since it was 'exceptional to find - out of all the schools in Scotland - two teams from one small burgh contesting the final'.

In addition to the Scottish Intermediate Shield, the under-15 team won the Anderson Cup - by virtue of a 2-1 victory over Airdrie Academy (a repetition of the school's success in that competition a year earlier, when Hamilton Academy were defeated 4-1) - and the Lanarkshire Intermediate League. In the course of the speech he delivered after the presentation of these trophies, Kerr mentioned 'a section of hooligans who crept into football grounds to incite players to kick and maul each other about'. 'I urge all schoolboy footballers,' he continued, 'to play the game and pay no heed to that element.'

In 1933 Willie Gentleman, left back in the all-conquering under-15 team of the previous year, was selected to play for the Rest of Scotland against Glasgow. Four years later, the High School again reached the final of the Scottish Intermediate Shield, but lost 0 - 3 to Queen's Park Secondary.

At under-14 level, the High School won the Cambusnethan and District League in 1934 and 1937; and the Cambusnethan and District Schools' Cup (formerly the Cambusnethan Teachers' Cup) in 1929, 1933, and 1934. In the latter two years, the victorious teams were: J. Philipps (who was later reserve goalkeeper for the Scottish under-15 team); T. McSpadyen and J. McMillan; J. Laurie, J. Ross, and D. Taylor; R. Bunce, J. Craig, D. Steventon, A. McNay, and R. Finlayson; and Skillen; McSpadyen and Fowler; Henderson, Finlayson, and McKerrigan; Brown, McNay, Steventon, Nicol, and Gray.

At under-18 level, the High School won the Lanarkshire Secondary League in 1933; and the Keith Cup in 1929 (the inaugural year of that competition), 1933, and 1935 (with the following eleven: Don; Gardiner and Morrison; Tyrrell, W. Laurie, and McKerrigan; McNay, G. Laurie, Dumbreck, Kirk, and Marshall). In 1929 the cup and medals were presented to the winning team in Austin's Tearooms in Hamilton, the first formal presentation ceremony to be organised by the Lanarkshire Secondary Schools' Football Association; and Kerr expressed his delight at the prospect of the new High School being 'graced in its first year by so beautiful a trophy'.

In 1930 the under-18 team were losing finalists in the Keith Cup. The *Wishaw Press* reported, with glorious understatement, that 'in the first half Nelson (Wishaw High School) and McMenemy (Motherwell Higher Grade R.C. School) had a difference and were both ordered to the pavilion by Referee Braidwood'. At the presentation ceremony, Kerr again expressed strong views about the behaviour of spectators at football matches:

I would dearly like to see a better crowd at matches. I do not like to hear the filthy language used in football grounds, and I think something could be arranged so that we can have a fair and gentlemanly crowd, similar to the ones that attend rugger - although I am not advocating any snobbery.

Football is a gentleman's game watched by hooligans, rugby is...

Kerr was doubtless highly delighted, therefore, when rugby began to feature among the High School's extra-curricular activities. The first fixture of which I can find any record was against Whitehill in November 1932; and a month later, Hamilton Academy provided the opposition. The rugby team was coached by William Ferguson, a member of the Science Department, and played its matches at the Welfare Park in Alexander Street. Within a year, several High School pupils had turned out for Wishaw Rugby Club.

A golf section was formed in March 1933, and the first winner of the school golf championship was John Kirk. The following year, two inter-school matches and two handicap stroke competitions were arranged.

Hockey continued to be very popular with the girls, and by 1933 the school was able to field both a 1st and a 2nd XI; John Telford and Frank Dickson coached the cricket enthusiasts among the boys; on occasion, Kerr sanctioned a half holiday for skating; and during the spring and summer terms, 'running practice' was organised after school.

In 1929 the school sports were held on Waverley (a first) and included such events as the hockey dribble, 'netball shooting', 'putting the weight' and throwing the cricket ball. According to Kerr, 'the sports field was in the very pink of order, the weather was delightful and there was a fine attendance of pupils, teachers, parents and friends'. In 1934 by way of a novelty, music and announcements were relayed to the spectators by Murdoch and McKillop's 'sound equipment van'; and in 1935 an intermediate boys' championship was contested for the first time.

In 1935 the Lanarkshire Schools' Athletics Association was formed (its first Vice-President was Robert Frame, a PE teacher at the High School), with the twofold aim of encouraging athletics in Lanarkshire schools and organising an inter-schools athletics meeting; and that same year, the inaugural County Sports (at which the High School came second in the overall classification) were held at Fir Park. In 1936 these same sports took place in the grounds of the High School.

At the Inter-Scholastic Sports (i.e. the Scottish Schools' Athletics Championships) in 1932, Andrew Lawrence won the under-16 long jump.

The swimming gala was still a regular feature on the school calendar, and in 1937 it included exhibitions (by pupils) of graceful swimming, diving, life-saving, and 'trick swimming'.

> **But pardon, gentles all,**
> **The flat unraised spirits that hath dar'd**
> **On this unworthy scaffold to bring forth**
> **So great an object...**

Shakespeare, *Henry V*

In December 1928, at the end of the school's Christmas production (an operetta entitled '*The Magic Key*'), Kerr bemoaned 'the totally

94

inadequate nature of the stages, dressing rooms, and auditoria at the Wishaw end of the Burgh', which was 'an insuperable obstacle to anything more ambitious in dramatic production.' This may have been one of the reasons why concerts and/or 'dramatic sketches' became the favourite forms of Christmas entertainment; but another (more positive) reason was that Kerr wanted 'to give as many of the pupils as possible some training in dramatic and elocution work' (in 1935, for example, more than 130 pupils were involved in the concert).

There was certainly no lack of talent among the staff and the pupils. *The Wrong Dog*, a one-act play written by John Telford, Principal Teacher of Art and founder of a 'dramatic club' in 1934, was performed at the concert in 1935; a jazz band made up of senior boys added a touch of novelty to the show in 1932; and in 1936 another senior boy, James Freeland, wrote a skit on school life in the style of Will Hay.

In 1937 the concert was held in March - before an audience made up exclusively of pupils from the school. After praising various aspects of this concert (especially another 'completely original' skit of James Freeland's on advertisements), the drama critic of the *Wishaw Press* wrote:

Can I suggest that next session a High School concert be given to the public? There is a wealth of real talent at the school, and it has been given a chance to blossom. It is such a pity that parents and other interested parties are not given a chance to fully appreciate what is being done.

The High School was a regular port of call for travelling companies of actors - mostly, but not exclusively, Shakespearean: in May 1935, for instance, in the hall, the actor- manager Roger Williams staged Sheridan's *She Stoops to Conquer*, a production that lasted 2½ hours. Not surprisingly, the audiences at such lengthy performances could become somewhat restive, and John Parton remembers one occasion when there was so much fidgeting that one of the actors halted in mid-soliloquy to read the riot act to the pupils.

Senior pupils were normally more appreciative of Shakespearean drama, and bus trips were arranged to the Theatre Royal in Glasgow, so that they could attend performances of *Hamlet, Macbeth*, and *The Merchant of Venice*. At a slightly less elevated level, in October 1936 staff and pupils attended a matinee (featuring *The Mutiny on the Bounty*) at The Cinema in Kirk Road.

The Two Rs

By 1937, the school library contained 2,000 books; and in 1932 the school magazine made a welcome reappearance. Entitled 'The Wishawtonic', and described in the *Wishaw Press* as 'a pleasing and palatable tonic', it included the following:

Sam Pepys at Hampden

At noon dined at home, and mightily pleased to hear my wife say how her maid did tell her that nigh every person of importance goes to Hampden to see the High School Intermediates in the Shield final.

By seven, when we leave the town for Hampden, it is much depopulated, and none but the non-accounters do walk in the streets. To Hampden, where a mighty concourse of scholars of both schools with many favours in the colours do make a mighty noise, both weird and awe-inspiring.

The teams do take the field, and do look most wondrous fit: my wife doth mention that the mighty Dykes would dwarf the very Guardsmen in The Mall. The game is most fierce, and both teams do play exceeding football. Now a corner, and the tiny Laurie doth place the ball as neatly as the most brilliant effort of the famous Morton; a scramble, and McNay, with a mighty fine shot, has beaten the redoubtable Crossley. The very Heads of Wishaw School do cheer like a group of saucy schoolboys.

Now, after much hard play, the whistle has given half-time. The teams do have their photos taken, and soon the game is on again. Kirk is hurt, but doth pass it over most pluckily. The end approaches, and now McNay hath beaten the goalie - a neat word that, and my neighbour doth whisper it to me huskily, having shouted all his voice away. Such shouting is being done that the Great Fire of London did not occasion more.

But Dalziel are not yet beaten: the great Summers hath got through and scored with a fine shot. Then, all is over - a great game lost and won. Some merry blades do essay to carry the victors off shoulder-high, but none do try this venture with the great Dykes and the two most hefty of backs.

Home again, and the whole town is much delighted with the school's success. To supper without our maid, who doth celebrate the triumph most thoroughly. The game played o'er again, and so to bed. (D.F.M.)

96

Although the school magazine seems to have appeared at irregular intervals during the 1930s, the social (attended by staff, senior pupils from Class 3E upwards, and former pupils who had left school since the previous year's social and had attended the High School for at least five years) and the Armistice service continued to feature on the school calendar every year.

We've got a barrel of money.

The school savings bank went from strength to strength. Indeed, in 1931 it boasted the highest total of deposits (£1309 19s 7d) in the county.

Charity begins at school.

Kerr took an active interest in many charities (one of them was the Royal National Lifeboat Institution, and in May 1933, at the half-yearly meeting of the Scottish Council of that organisation, he was presented with a special award by the Duke of Montrose in recognition of his thirteen years' service); and he must, therefore, have been proud to announce that during session 1932-33 the staff and pupils collected more than £150 for such institutions as the Royal Hospital for Sick Children, the Glasgow Eye Infirmary, the British Legion, and the Scottish Association for Mental Welfare.

Sic itur ad avenue

In May 1934, the Schools' Management Committee (it was now known as the Motherwell and Wishaw Schools' Management Committee) submitted a recommendation to the Education Committee (which had taken over from the Education Authority, and which made up in numbers - 103 - what it sometimes lacked in wisdom) that 'a footpath should be laid' between the High School and Kenilworth Avenue, where two thirds of the pupils 'got their buses'.

The Grand Tour

In July 1935, a group of High School pupils, accompanied by two members of staff, embarked on the troopship *Neuralia* for a 15-day cruise to Norway, Sweden, Finland, Denmark, and Germany. This may have been the first occasion on which pupils from the High School went abroad on a school trip.

The FPs come together - and branch out.

In February 1930, the FPs held a reunion (the first of several during the 1930s) in the new High School. It was attended by more than 160 FPs and took the form of a conversazione, followed by dancing and military whist.

In 1936 the range of activities available to FPs was extended by the addition of swimming, badminton, and debating. In November of that year, the first debate (on the motion that "The National Government has justified the nation's confidence") took place in the Geography room. Three months later, following the example of their contemporaries at Oxford, the FPs joined forces with the Youth Section of the Wishaw League of Nations to debate the motion that 'This House will in no circumstances fight for king and country'. The motion was defeated by 48 votes to 31.

In March 1937, the FPs formed an athletics club. At the inaugural meeting, R.G. Whitelaw was elected captain; the annual subscription was fixed at 2/6d; a coach (R.S.B. McDougall) and a masseur (A. Williams) were appointed; and a motion proposing that there should be no ladies' section was passed unanimously.

The new club had its own distinctive colours: a white singlet with three bands (blue, gold, and blue) across the middle, surmounted by a slightly altered version of the school badge (the letters FP being added to WHS); and training sessions were arranged on Monday and Wednesday evenings (from 7.30 till 9), and on Saturday afternoons (from 2.30 till 4.30).

Among the events organised by the club during the first year of its existence were the club championship, a series of handicap meetings, and an inter-club meeting at the Wishaw Greyhound and Sports Track, which attracted four FP clubs from Glasgow.

In May 1937, the President and Secretary of the Scottish Athletics Association, the President of the EIS, and the Director of Education attended one of the club's training sessions, 'to see how much could be accomplished by an athletics club in a very short time'. A month later, an article in the EIS Journal entitled 'Towards an AI Nation' described the athletics set-up in Wishaw as 'one of the most encouraging sights the Scottish Athletics Association have yet seen'.

(Non) latet anguis in herba.

Virgil, *Eclogues (adapted)*

In September 1934, a full-grown adder, two feet in length, was spotted by passers-by in Kerr's front garden. It was killed - and later exhibited in one of the Science laboratories at the High School.

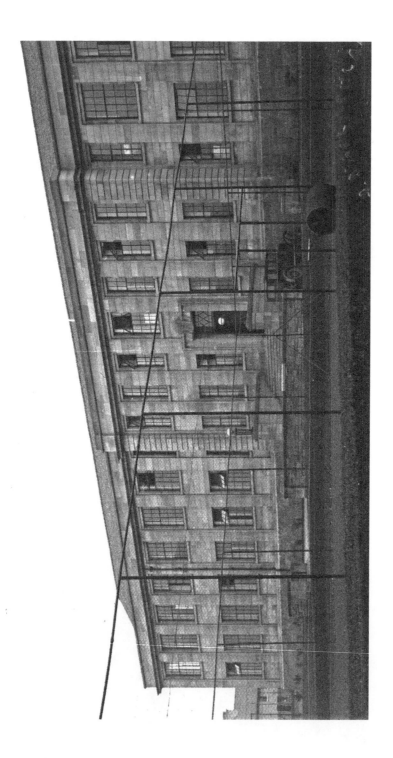

Front of School (circa 1928)

School Hall (circa 1928)

VIP Guests at the Formal Opening of New Building

(September 1928)

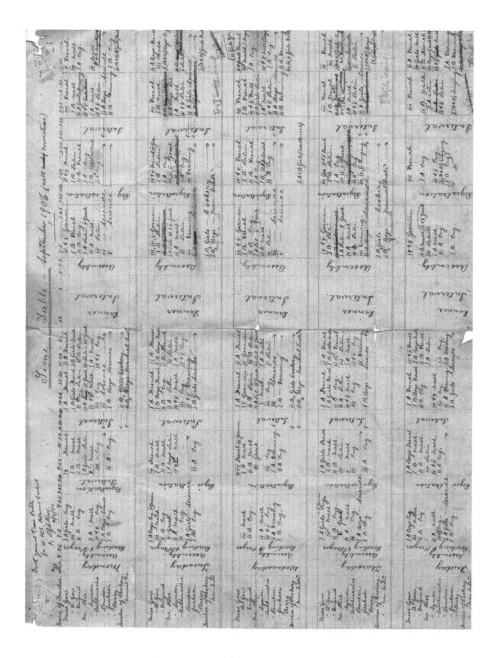

Master Timetable (September 1906)

Science Lab (circa 1928)

Luncheon Room (circa 1928)

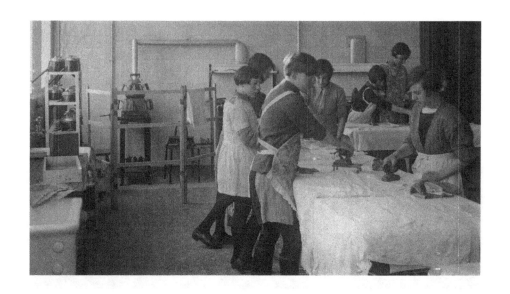

Laundry (circa 1928)

Gymnasium (circa 1928)

Sports Champions (1931)

Agnes Glover, Pearl Leggate, Robert Gardiner, Robert Freeland.

Senior Football Team (1948)

S. Bruce (Reserve)	D. Brown (Right Back)	T. Prentice~ (Left Back)	J. Allan (Goalkepper)	T. Scoular (Right-half)	N. Muat (Centre-half)	C. Small (Left-half)	Mr Ross
C. Laurie (Outside-right)		J. Rodger (Inside-right)	P. Hill (Centre-forward)		W. Westwood (Inside-right)	J. Allan (Outside-left)	

Prize Winners (1948)

Jean Lawson (VI.Maths: 1st Equal, (School Dux)	**John Gilfillan** (VI. Latin, Greek, History)	**Chrissie Smellie** (III. 1st (equal)	**I. Steven** (VI.Maths: 1st Equal, Science, Dynamics)	**Clara Cray** (VI. English, French, German)	**C. Black** (V.)	**June Clelland** (III. 1st (equal)

T. Russell (IV.)	**Sarah Lawson** (1st, 1p, q)	**D. Marks** (1st, II.p, q, r)	**E. Scoular** (1st, 1a, b, c, d)	**W. Wilson** (1st, II.a, b, c, d, e)	**Sheena Howat** (1st, III.p, q)

Wishaw High School pupils who took part in the
Glasgow University Bursary Competition in 1930:

Ebenezer Loudon (39th),   Archibald Nelson (46th),   Walter Jackson (11th),
Robert Russell (71st),   Nellie Preston (103rd).

1922.

18th Jan. N.W. wing of school and school hall both
destroyed by fire about 5 a.m. School
dismissed. Rector off owing to ill-health,
& Mr Symon acting as Interim Rector.

23rd Jan. School re-opened to-day. All classes
accommodated except those in Cook
Dom. Science & Woodwork. Rector on duty
again; has re-organised the classes,
combining two sets of two classes in
order to suit the restricted accommodation provided. Lecture Room of V.M.I.
again being used; also one of the science
laboratories is used as an ordinary
class-room.

Conference in Rectors' room to-day.
Present :- Sir Henry Keith Rev. G. Andrew
Messrs G. N. Pomphrey, J. Taylor, Wm
Malcolm, J. Stewart + Rector.

30th Jan. Arrangements completed for carrying
on a certain amount of Dom. Science
& Woodwork of High School classes
at Waterloo P. School.

4th & 5th Feb. Miss Forbes absent - ill.

A page from the original School Log (18 Jan – 4 Feb 1922)

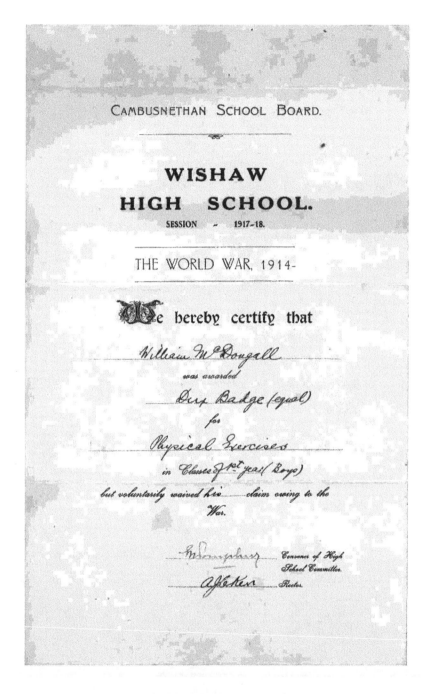

**Dux Certificate for Physical Exercises
awarded to William McDougall (1917-18)**

10

Memories

I have spoken to a fair number of FPs who attended the High School in the 1930s. They all have many fond memories of their alma mater:

Kerr was a typical old-style dominie. He parked his car (a streamlined American model) in the girls' bicycle shed.

Films were very often shown during Geography lessons. If any of the pupils made a comment about the film being shown, John Weir, the Principal Teacher of Geography, would immediately issue the command, 'Put up the blinds.'

It required very little mental effort to visualise 'Papa' Wilson, the Principal Teacher of Classics, decked out in a toga. (Morton Cadzow)

Kerr was a great disciplinarian, but he was very fair: if we got the belt, we deserved it. He could give people quite a severe belting, but nobody resented it; indeed, most FPs remember him with affection.

He took a keen interest in the football team, and also in athletics.

The teachers seemed to be very conscious of his capabilities as an administrator, and he for his part was proud of his school and his staff.

Kerr and Matthew Bain, the janitor, made a great team: Bain, for instance, was forever impressing on us that we were still representing the school when we were outside its confines. However, the smokers at 'the burning bush' could see him coming a mile away, and this enabled them to take evasive action.

The teachers took their work very seriously, and they were obsessive about examination results: Maggie Coutts (English), for instance, was a dedicated crammer, with no sense of humour.

Homework had to be signed by a pupil's parents, and there were snap checks on homework diaries.

Hymns had to be learned at home for the morning assemblies, which also included a reading from the Bible - by a teacher or the school captain - and a prayer delivered by Kerr or Sam Forrest, the First Assistant.

Tom Hamilton of the Science Department was very popular with the pupils. In the course of his first year on the staff, the senior boys painted his feet red in the girls' bicycle shed.

Another member of the Science Department, Tom Hyslop, was nicknamed 'Hopping Tommy'. He had a club foot and a stick - and he used to spit in the sink.

The senior pupils' common room was situated opposite the Rector's room. Chess and shove-ha'penny were very popular there.

Three-course lunches (costing 3d) were provided in the luncheon room, and pupils were required to present a token at the serving hatch.

In June 1933, the prizes were presented by Willie McFadyen, centre forward of Motherwell F.C. and top scorer in the Scottish First Division in seasons 1931-32 and 1932-33. (William Gentleman)

Primary school pupils who wished to enrol at the High School were interviewed by Kerr. He inspected their jotters and questioned them about the work they had done at primary school, in order to test their grasp of it. If an interviewee performed satisfactorily, Kerr would tell him or her on the spot, "You're in." To those who didn't come up to scratch he would say, "I'm sorry, you'll have to go to Wishaw Central."

The school was overcrowded (some classes were taught in the corridor, or in the luncheon room), but Kerr didn't use the shortage of accommodation as an excuse to turn prospective entrants away.

Kerr sometimes called upon senior pupils to assist him with his administrative duties. On one occasion, I was given the master timetable for the coming session and instructed to make sure that two classes were not scheduled to occupy the same room at the same time.

Maggie Burns (French and Latin) threw bits of chalk at individual pupils - who then had to retrieve them.

Peter Johnston (Music), who was a very pawky character, had played the piano in various cinemas before entering the teaching profession.

John Weir (Geography) had a rubicund complexion (he liked a tipple), and he always had his classes lined up early at the end of the last period in the afternoon - to make sure that he never missed the 3.55 bus to Hamilton.

John Telford (Art) was keen on fishing, and he sometimes left early to catch the train to Lanark. So too did Kerr, but with supreme diplomacy they never 'saw' each other.

The Loudon sisters, Abigail (PE) and Mamie (Maths), didn't speak to each other.

When Sam Forrest (Maths) smiled, only one side of his face moved.

Alex Anderson (History) taught with the aid of a chamois leather belt. He would walk round the room inspecting pupils' jotters, and

112

anyone who had made a mistake was sent out to the floor. When a line had formed, he would work his way along it with his belt; but he never hurt anybody.

Frank Dickson (Science) would set up an experiment and then ask his pupils, 'What do you think would happen if we did this or added that?' After the inevitable series of unlikely - or just plain silly - answers, he would declare with Socratean humility, "We'll try and find out."

When it came to writing up experiments, he was a stickler for correct usage with regard to the definite and indefinite articles.

If a pupil touched the doorknob as he went past his room, Frank would chase him along the corridor.

On one occasion, he told Ian Sandilands, who was very tall for his age, to sit down - as he had no intention of looking up to a pupil.

Frank's version of the Greek motto that was inscribed on the walls of the hall was as follows:

> If, to training, the mind
> Of a man be inclined,
> Send the town crier round and make it snappy:
> 'Such a mind, such a man,
> Accords with God's plan,
> For every "good devil" is happy.'
>
> Twixt him and the man
> Whose mind 'also ran'
> The gap becomes wider and wider;
> For the innards of one
> May shine like the sun,
> Whilst the other's a polished outsider.

My final memory is of an American negro (whose father had been born into slavery) enthralling the pupils with a talk on his early upbringing. (John Parton)

At morning assembly, Willie Gentleman would look up pointedly at the ceiling (though there was nothing there), and soon everybody else in the hall would be doing likewise.

When we played football at the intervals, school caps were sometimes used as goalposts.

A tuck shop was set up in the luncheon room. It sold sweets and bottles of Barr's lemonade.

Kerr was nicknamed 'Toosh'. Nobody seemed to know why.

Since they felt the cold very badly, two South African boys (the Gardiners) wore salmon pink drawers when they turned out for the football team. (Robert Russell)

Pupils walked along the main corridor in fear and trepidation of Kerr.

At morning assemblies, when the top of his mortarboard became visible above the back of the rostrum, there was absolute silence - though he still hadn't entered the hall. (Ian Sandilands)

Maggie Coutts (English) and Daisy Macdonald (Modern Languages) were regarded as the High School's SS.

Kerr was also a rather 'Hitlerite' figure, and he was both feared and respected.

Peter Johnston took the 5th Year for Music last period on Friday afternoon, and still managed to engender a real feeling for music in his pupils. (Alexander Wallace)

After a fall of snow, Major Bain would line up the pupils on Waverley: those in Allanton and Belhaven at one end, those in Coltness and Murdostoun at the other end. When he blew his whistle, they charged at each other. (Eddie Tweedlie Snr.)

We were very fond of our 'open plan' building and Kerr was forever pointing out the advantages of a 'blow' of fresh air between classes. (Wilma Gilchrist)

I travelled to the High School from Carluke, and I was very often late. The excuse I invariably proffered was, 'The bus was late.'

In my final year, I sometimes had Kerr for Latin and Greek. He wasn't as good a classical scholar as my regular Classics teacher, James Wilson: he kept a translation beside him, and he didn't go into the same detail.

I was pally with Sam (later, Sir Samuel) Curran, who as well as having the ability to grasp the essence of mathematical problems very quickly could turn his hand to a wide range of activities, both academic and sporting: in the space of a year, for example, he became very competent at golf, which, in the event, he gave up, in order to devote more time to his studies. (George Gilchrist)

The building was cold and draughty compared with Carluke Higher Grade.

Maggie Burns (French) was very sarcastic and censorious towards any pupil from Carluke who didn't come up to her high academic expectations.

The janitor, Major Bain, was a bit of a show-off who liked people to know that he had been in the army. He wore his medals, and obviously regarded himself as being on a par with the teachers.

In the course of a football match between the High School and its deadliest rival, Hamilton Academy, an incident took place that caused considerable acrimony between two opposing players not only for the rest of the game but also in the pavilion afterwards. The Rector of Hamilton Academy reported the matter to Kerr, who immediately suspended the High School player from school football for a month. Though he was a very imposing figure, Kerr was also approachable, and in my capacity as school captain I appealed to him - on behalf of the rest of the team - to revoke the suspension. He would have none of it.

On another occasion, the senior team was travelling back to Wishaw after a Scottish Shield tie at Bo'ness. As the team bus (a blue Rio, hired from Smith of Bogside) raced towards a particularly sharp corner at the foot of Wilderness Brae in Cumbernauld, the driver shouted out: 'When we get to the corner, everybody lean over to my side of the bus.'

I also remember being badly spiked at the school sports, and Bob Frame (PE) taking me down to the doctor's surgery in Glen Road. I lay down on my chest, and two of my pals held me in this position while the doctor poured a bottle of iodine on my leg prior to stitching it.

Alex Anderson (History), who coached the football team, seemed to have a soft spot for Heart of Midlothian F.C. He wouldn't allow me to have a trial with Motherwell; and Jim Dykes, one of the most influential members of the High School team which won the Scottish Intermediate Shield in 1932 (another team that was trained by Anderson), signed for the 'Jam Tarts'. (John Young)

11

The Final Curtain

At the annual FP reunion in February 1931, Kerr was presented with a fishing rod and a wallet of notes to mark his 25 years as Rector of the High School. In the course of thanking the FPs for their kindness, he said that it was 'just the sort of thing needed to brace a man for new endeavours'. 'I am still a long way from the age for retiring,' he continued, 'and I have not reached the stage of living simply on memories.'

One of Kerr's 'new endeavours' was to represent the EIS on the Council of the International Committee on Mental Hygiene; and in 1936, while attending a conference on that same topic, he visited child guidance clinics in Islington and the East End of London, visits that encouraged him to campaign for the provision of such a service in every county in Scotland.

From the middle of March 1936, however, Kerr seems to have been plagued by indifferent health (he was absent from the school for spells of varying length that year, and for four weeks at the beginning of 1937), and it was on these grounds that he retired on 22 October 1937: 'I am not short of ideas, but I lack the energy to put them into effect.'

When Kerr's retiral was brought to the notice of the Motherwell and Wishaw Schools' Management Committee, G.N, Pomphrey, the School Convener, had this to say:

I was present here fully thirty years ago when Mr Kerr was appointed, and since then I have been in more or less constant touch with him and the High School. Events have shown that the appointment was fully justified, since under his guidance it is now one of the most successful schools in the county. I think, therefore, that it is quite in order that I should move formally that we record in the minutes our appreciation of the faithful service which Mr Kerr has rendered to the school, express our regret that through ill health he has had to give up his duties, and convey to him the wish that with improving health he will enjoy a long retirement.

On the final day of Kerr's rectorship, the pupils assembled in the hall at 2.20 to say their last farewells. The school captain, George Cowan, read out a valedictory poem written by Mrs Haddow, Principal Teacher of English:

116

There's a sob in this wind of October,
The leaves fall down with a sigh;
Our hearts are heavy, our eyes are dim,
For we're met to say 'goodbye'
To you who so long have laboured
Within this town and school
To guide the feet and to mould the thought
Of those beneath your rule.

And now at this bend of a long, long road,
Look back with rare content,
For the lives you've shaped, the careers you've built,
Are a marvellous monument.
We want you to know that for many a day
Our thoughts to the southward will bend,
With a fond recollection of you who have been
Our rector, our teacher, our friend.

In your evening of days, as with rod and line
You walk by some moorland stream,
May you know by the grace
Of the Fisher of Men
The fulfilment of every dream.

Kerr revealed his hopes and dreams - at least as far as the High School was concerned - at the presentation ceremony arranged by the staff:

I have visions of even higher heights to which Wishaw High School may rise, of a time when post-primary pupils of all types will be taught according to their tastes and abilities - and not forced to take subjects for which they have no aptitude.

I hope that one day all the rooms for the practical subjects will be scrapped as such, and turned into classrooms; that an additional building will be erected in the grounds, which will contain workshops devoted to technical and engineering subjects, physical exercises, arts and crafts, music, and commercial subjects; and that there will also be a sports pavilion (fitted up with dressing rooms) for our present and former pupils, a dining hall, and, dare I mention it, a swimming pool.

In an article he wrote for the *Wishaw Press* in 1955, Kerr described his retiral in the following terms:

From 1920 onwards, angling was my chief pastime - a fact that on one occasion caused the Science master, Mr Frank Dickson, to burst forth into verse, one line of which pictured me declaring, 'My rod and staff me comfort still.' In October 1937, I laid down my rod of office and sought to wield regularly on the rivers of the South the rod beloved of anglers.

However, since he had decided to stand for the Town Council in the town (Lockerbie) where he was destined to spend the first years of his retirement, there is no doubt that Kerr had every intention of continuing to play a vigorous part in the political life of his local community. Indeed, by a strange coincidence, he became a town councillor on the same day as he ceased to be Rector of the High School.

12

A.J.C. Kerr - as others saw him

He saw visions and dreamed dreams, and as all dreamers are at times, so was he a bit of a thorn in the flesh of prosaic folk.

G. N. Pomphrey, School Convener

By 'prosaic folk', Mr Pomphrey probably meant inspectors, councillors and members of school boards, education authorities, and schools' management committees - individuals and administrative bodies, that is, which were interested primarily in attendance rates and examination results (in respect of which, it should be stressed, the High School had an exemplary record during Kerr's rectorship), and which, more importantly, had to 'pick up the tab' for a headmaster's "dreams and visions". One thing is certain: nobody could have been more 'prosaic' than an inspector who was 'very particular about sanitation', and Kerr was fond of telling the story of a visit to the school by a certain Dr Wattie, who had just been appointed to the post of His Majesty's Chief Inspector of Schools:

One morning, Mr Bain the janitor brought to my room an old man with a shabby coat and a well-worn hat, and angrily asserted that he had found him in the boys' latrine and brought him to me to deal with. Luckily, I spotted who it was, and I held out my hand saying, 'How are you, Dr Wattie?' Exit - hastily - Mr Bain.

Despite this contretemps, Kerr claimed (in 1931) that the school had never had a bad report from His Majesty's Inspectors:

Indeed, my personal relationship with these gentlemen - and ladies – has been very pleasant, and they have helped me in no small way to secure better equipment and accommodation for my staff. Moreover, I am particularly indebted to Mr T.B.M. Lamb and Mr William Robb, whose cheery presence, stimulating views, and expert teaching ability have been an inspiration to everybody at the school.

During the early years of his rectorship, Kerr, by his own admission, 'gave the School Board many a headache with his requests for more accommodation and additions to the teaching staff' (it has to be pointed out, however, that all requests - from Kerr or anyone else - gave the Board a headache, since a request, if granted, was not only likely to cost money but also - to their equally intense chagrin - implied that they had failed to provide something they should have provided); 'but they always acceded to his wishes in the end'.

Kerr also had a good word for his other political masters:
I have been let alone and trusted by the Education Committee. When it finds a man who is doing his work, it leaves him alone; there is no pettifogging criticism, and no interference.

Throughout the whole period of my rectorship, I was blessed with a series of intelligent and helpful Conveners, from Dean Van Hecke (cultured, pawky, far-seeing, and a staunch friend of well-doers) at the outset, to Mr G.N. Pomphrey in the 1930s.

It is clear, then, that Kerr was particularly adept at forming working relationships with the educational powers that be, and although his importunity must, on occasion, have exasperated them, I think they realised that it was fuelled by a laudable desire to make the High School a first-rate establishment in every possible respect.

Supremely confident in organisation and mindful of every detail, he seemed to become immediately conscious of any hitch in the working of the complicated machine he controlled. He never spared himself, and his example in this respect set a high standard for all. He was always ready, even in his busiest hours, to discuss difficulties and suggest solutions; he would size up a situation immediately and make a quick and wise decision.

Sam Forrest, First Assistant

Kerr undoubtedly performed 'miracles of organisation' at Beltanefoot - especially after the fire in 1922, when there was a horrendous shortage of accommodation and the High School's secondary status was in the balance. However, he wasn't just an efficient administrator; he was also a hands-on rector, making his presence known - and felt - in every section of school life. Indeed, his energy seemed to be inexhaustible.

No snob can live in Wishaw. Wishawtonians value a man for his honesty and his grit, and they have no use for a man who parades his dress or his manners.

ipse dixit

Kerr had an affinity with the working classes and their aspirations; and he also had a passionate belief that education was the key to the fulfilment of those aspirations. People sensed that he wanted the best for, and from, their children: consequently, 'his best friends and his most encouraging supporters in a school context (i.e. among parents and former pupils) were the working-class men and women of Wishaw'.

Refusing to lock himself up in an ivory tower, Kerr played an active part in the social, religious, and sporting life of the town. He was a director of the local YMCA and an elder of Chalmers Church; he was regarded as 'a special friend' by the Wishaw and District Branch of the British Legion, having been present at its inaugural meeting, and having always encouraged High School pupils to contribute generously to the annual Armistice Appeal; he played golf, tennis and bowls, and he was captain of Wishaw Draughts Club for more than twenty years.

Brilliant traditions have been founded on your purposeful and resourceful efforts.

Ex-Provost Anderson

Among the 'traditions' established by Kerr were the school sports, the House System, the Christmas concert, operettas, the magazine, and the school song. Most of them survived for the greater part of the school's existence; some were still going strong in 1992.

Wishaw High School was a creation of Mr Kerr's vision and energy.

James T. Wilson, Principal Teacher of Classics

Starting almost from scratch in an environment that was to remain very dispiriting for more than twenty years, Kerr created - by sheer will power - not only a viable secondary school (an achievement in its own right), but also a secondary school that by the 1930s was challenging (or even surpassing, it could be argued) the most highly regarded schools in the West of Scotland.

Mr Kerr was the builder of the great edifice of higher education that was reared in Wishaw.

James T. Wilson, Principal Teacher of Classics

Though he did not dig the foundations or lay the first brick, Kerr developed - and eventually completed – Wishaw's 'great edifice of higher education', and during his rectorship thousands of pupils received secondary education at the High School.

Mr Kerr has similar balance (we never see him flurried or flustered), resilience (he always comes up smiling), and steel centre.

William Robb, HMI (at an FP reunion, in the course of which Kerr was presented with a fishing rod)

If Kerr was resilient, his resilience must have been really taxed during the twenty-two years the High School was situated at Beltanefoot, when hopes of a new building (or at least of increased accommodation) were raised on a regular basis - only to be dashed just as regularly.

There was much good fellowship between Mr Kerr and his staff.

Sam Forrest, First Assistant

Kerr never missed the annual social, which was also attended by most of his staff; nor, from 1934 (its inaugural year) onwards, the staff whist drive and dance. As far as his professional relationship with the staff was concerned, Kerr believed 'in trusting a teacher until he made himself untrustworthy', for in that way 'you got the best work out of a man'.

To the older pupils he was a sympathetic and helpful counsellor.

Sam Forrest, First Assistant

Kerr went out of his way not only to advise senior pupils about their future careers (academic or otherwise), but also to find suitable employment for them.

It will be difficult to think of anyone else in his place.

Chrissie Morrison, Girls' Captain

'Impossible' would have been closer to the truth, for who could replace a man who had energised Wishaw High School for more than thirty years?

13

1931-1939

A Safe Pair of Hands

For the vacant post of Rector, the Staffing Committee drew up a short leet of eight that included two members of staff at the High School - Samuel Forrest, First Assistant, and Francis Dickson, Principal Teacher of Science. Neither of them featured in the decisive vote, which was between Alexander D. Robertson, Headmaster of West Coats Higher Grade School, and the committee's eventual choice, Dr Duncan K. Wilson, Principal Teacher of Science and First Assistant at Rutherglen Academy.

An Officer, a Scholar, and a Gentleman

Duncan Kippen Wilson was a native of Glenfarg, a small village twelve miles south of Perth, and received his early education at Arngask Public School and Perth Academy, where he was dux medallist in 1905.

In the course of a distinguished academic career at Edinburgh University, he won a succession of bursaries, medals, and class prizes, and he eventually graduated MA (with 1st Class Honours in Mathematics and Natural Philosophy), BSc.

His first teaching appointment took him to India as Professor of Chemistry at Madras Christian College. On his return to Scotland, he had a brief spell as Mathematical Master at Dalkeith High School, and an even briefer spell (until the outbreak of the First World War in 1914) as Mathematical and Science Master at his alma mater, Perth Academy.

During the early years of the war, he served as a private in the 15th Royal Scots and as a corporal in the Royal Engineers (Gas Section). In 1916 he was promoted to the rank of 2nd Lieutenant in the R.G.A. He was present at the battles of Loos, Arras, and the Somme, and he was wounded at the third battle of Ypres in 1917.

After the war, he resumed his teaching career at George Heriot's School, where he was also Scoutmaster of the school troop. He left George Heriot's in 1925 to become Principal Teacher of Science - and (eventually) First Assistant - at Rutherglen Academy.

In June 1932, his thesis on the teaching of Mathematics in Scotland earned him a PhD from Glasgow University. This thesis (it was entitled 'The History of Mathematical Education in Scotland to the End of the 18th Century') was later published under the auspices of the Scottish Council for Research in Education.

Doctor in the School

Dr Wilson entered on his duties as Rector of the High School on 16 November 1937. Four days earlier, Sam Forrest, who had been Acting Rector since A.J.C. Kerr's retiral in October, was presented with a walnut table as a token of the staff's 'esteem and affection' - a gesture whose spontaneity was unprecedented in the annals of staff presentations.

The new rector was introduced to the staff and pupils ('a fearful ordeal', he later admitted) by the School Convener, G.N. Pomphrey, at a special assembly in the hall. 'You have here,' Dr Wilson told his audience, 'a magnificent building, erected by the Education Committee for your benefit. You are attending a school which has gained a great reputation as a centre of learning, and I would ask you to remember always that every one of you can do a great deal to make or mar that reputation. Every time you prove yourselves lazy, untrustworthy, ungallant, or discourteous, you are dragging the name of your school in the mire; every time you show yourselves faithful to a trust, chivalrous, and manly or womanly, you are increasing the fame of your school. The eyes of the public are always upon you, and the reputation of Wishaw High School is in your keeping.

Some of you have talents for academic work, some for sport, some for music, art, drama, or literary work. Whatever your talent, I hope you will always endeavour to make the most of it. No one who does his best will ever get a raw deal from me.

On the football or hockey field, some are cast for the part of centre forward; others have to play out on the wing. In school work, I should like to see you all being busy, bustling centre forwards, for these are the fellows who score most of the goals.

I, like you, have taken on a tremendous responsibility. I am following in the footsteps of a great headmaster, Mr Kerr, who served this school with brilliant success for nearly half a lifetime; you are following in the footsteps of the many famous men and women who have earned for Wishaw High School a reputation second to none in Lanarkshire. You and I must see to it that there is no falling off, and that Wishaw High School advances till it becomes known as one of the finest schools in Scotland.'

No advance was possible that particular day, however, since the school closed at 1 p.m.

If it ain't broke, don't fix it.

Bert Lance

Dr Wilson had the good fortune to take command of a school that was in a 'very healthy and flourishing' condition, and the good sense to appreciate that a new rector is not always obliged to institute a new regime. He neither needed - nor indeed wanted - to make radical changes: *When I took over the reins of office, I had acquired, from a wide experience of teaching, certain ideas as to the management of a large secondary school. It was with pleasure, tempered by some feeling of exasperation, that I discovered that most of my pet theories had here been translated into practice. The post-intermediate classes were organised on a four-subject basis; the pupils therein were given a wide choice of curricula, and the individual aptitudes of scholars were consulted; the House System, teaching the elements of self-control and self-government, was in operation; above all, there was an elaborate system by which boys and girls were provided with guidance as to their future career, with the Rector as careers master. After ten days' study of the organisation of Wishaw High School, I was inclined to describe Mr Kerr as one of the greatest headmasters in Scotland.*

Imitation is an even sincerer form of flattery.

Following Kerr's example, Dr Wilson extended "a cordial invitation" to all parents (but especially to those whose children were in the 3rd and 4th Year) "to come and talk with him about their son or daughter's choice of course and future career".

The Two Cultures

In the course of session 1937-38, the Scottish Education Department issued Circular III, the object of which was to widen the range of subjects that pupils could take as part of their Leaving Certificate course; this made it possible for pupils with no aptitude for Science and Mathematics to drop both these subjects at the end of their third year, and for poor linguists to drop French and German at the same stage.

At the prize-giving in 1938, Dr Wilson declared that, 'thanks to the foresight of A.J.C. Kerr in establishing Commercial and Domestic Science courses, the High School was well placed to take full advantage of those relaxations of the rigid secondary curriculum'. However, when - in response to a 'considerable demand', particularly on the part of 3rd Year girls, for a special course in Commerce - he devised a curricular option that combined Commercial Subjects with English, French and Arithmetic, it failed to secure the approval of the SED.

Summa Repetita

In November 1937, as he freely acknowledged, Dr Wilson took charge of a school 'with a fine record in scholarship as well as in sport'. After eighteen months in command, he would have been justified in claiming that the highest standards were still being maintained in the examination room and on the sports field.

In 1938 thirty-five of the thirty-seven candidates from the High School gained the Leaving Certificate, five of them with five passes at Higher Grade and four of them with four; Robert Curran was sixth in the Glasgow University Bursary Competition; and the boys' captain, George Cowan, won a mining scholarship worth £150 per annum for the duration of his degree course.

In 1939 there were 167 individual passes at Higher or Lower Grade - an all-time high for the High School; there was also a record number of passes in Higher Mathematics; and Margaret Chapman gained the Leaving Certificate at the age of fourteen. That same year, Robert Deans was placed fourth in the Bursary Competition, and he was joined in the first hundred by another three High School pupils.

During session 1939-40, the Day School Certificate (Higher) was replaced by the Junior Leaving Certificate. The new certificate was awarded - after "the successful completion of at least three years' secondary education" - on the recommendation of His Majesty's

Inspector, who based his recommendations on "teachers' estimates and the pupils' school record". Very few High School pupils were presented for the Day School Certificate (Higher); and I have found no record of any pupil gaining the Junior Leaving Certificate.

In 1938 the under-18 football team (Maxwell; Naismith and Hardie; Noble, Marshall, and Denholm; Bankier, Vincent, Sinclair, Steele, and Armstrong) defeated Dalziel High School 3-0 in the final of the Keith Cup. The captain of this team, David Denholm, wrote in the school magazine:

Our stentorian supporters are a source of envy and wonder to all the teams we have met this season, while Mr Paterson has impressed us as a true sportsman and friend by his interest in our welfare, physical and otherwise.

In the same year, John Archibald won the under-14 high jump at the Scottish Schools' Athletics Championships; and David Hutchison and Alexander Jamieson became the first members of the school's thriving swimming club to gain the Bronze Medallion Award for life-saving.

By 1939, the High School was running two rugby teams (matches were arranged for the Senior XV with schools as far afield as Eastwood, while the Juniors played several games against Dalziel High School), and thanks to the 'enthusiasm and dedication' of William Ferguson (ably assisted by another member of the Science Department, Bill Clark), it was now 'stronger in rugby', according to the *Wishaw Press*, 'than at any other time in its history'; indeed, many of the school's most promising players were recruited into the ranks of Wishaw Rugby Club, which, incidentally, presented caps to two pupils nominated by the Athletics Committee - William Morton and Alex Wallace. The excellence of the school's rugby teams was a by-product of a fiercely contested inter-House rugby championship (in 1938 it was won by Murdostoun, who defeated Coltness 11-0 in the final), all the games in this championship being played on Waverley.

At an American tournament for under-15 girls organised by the Scottish Women's Hockey Association and held in the grounds of Glasgow Girls High School, the High School won three and drew one of its four games, but failed to make the final stage on number of goals scored.

Not Competing on a Level Playing Field

The High School may have been as capable as ever of producing excellent athletes and footballers, but Dr Wilson was far from impressed by the facilities it provided for certain games and their participants. The tennis courts, 'derelict places where the only sets that grew were sets of dandelions', were 'quite unplayable'; Waverley was also unplayable for half the football season due to 'insufficient drainage'; 'above all, the school was handicapped by a lack of stripping accommodation, this deficiency being especially felt by the FP sections'.

Ask, and it shall (sometimes) be given you.

In the course of the speech he made at his retiral dinner, Dr Wilson suggested that 'a successful headmaster should be able to get the Education Committee to do things for his school'. If we accept his definition of success (i.e. 'getting things done for the school'), Dr Wilson undoubtedly chalked up his fair share of successes – at least with regard to the provision of better sports facilities.

In September 1938, the Schools and Schemes Sub-Committee of the Education Committee recommended the 'complete reconstruction' of the school's tennis courts at a projected cost of £215; and the new courts were formally opened by Mrs John Craig of Cambusnethan Priory in April 1939. That same year, Waverley was drained, and with the aid of a loan (amounting to £550) from Lanarkshire County Council, a sports pavilion was erected in the school grounds.

To raise money with a view to repaying the aforementioned loan, a Garden Fête was held in June 1939. 'On this red-letter day for Wishaw High School,' to quote Dr Wilson, 'the school was transformed from a seat of learning to a centre of industry and amusements. In the main hall, the charming young ladies in charge of the stalls engaged prospective buyers in earnest conversation regarding their wares, and effected practically a complete clearance.' The fête raised £130.

It was not only in the matter of sports facilities that Dr Wilson tried 'to get the Education Committee to do things for his school'. In March 1938, he submitted a request that an electric bell should be attached to the clock on the back wall of the school; in April, after he had written a letter of complaint regarding the 'inadequate heating system' in the conservatory, an electric immersion heater was installed; and in October, he put in a requisition (unsuccessfully) for a gross of single desks - which he planned to use in the hall when examinations and certain Music classes were being held there.

When one gate shuts.....

Since the school gate had to be kept open at all times (it alone provided access to the janitor's house), it was used by 'some very undesirable people' - especially at the weekend. In February 1939, therefore, Dr Wilson suggested to the Schools' Management Committee that a small gate should be constructed at the front of the 'gatehouse'.

The Wrong Kind of Snow

The winter of 1937-38 was particularly severe. On 24 December, under the heading 'Wishaw High School Notes', the following report appeared in the *Wishaw Press*:

Last week, every other event, even the change of classes, was dwarfed by the snowstorm. Each morning, at prayers, the hall was empty-looking and the country pupils arrived at various times, late but cheerful, full of tales of buses that did not run and trains that could, of long walks through the snow, of drifts six feet deep, and of helpful motorists. The attendance suffered, but oh the fun with snow fights and skating.

Despite these problems with the weather, the High School still managed to maintain its customary high level of attendance: the average attendance rate for session 1937-38 was 93.9%; and, at an individual level, Sadie McIlwain had completed nine years' perfect attendance by the end of the following session.

Floreant alumni.

There was one feature of life at the High School that disappointed its new rector. 'Knowing how valuable a strong Former Pupils' Club can be to a school,' he wrote in the 1956 edition of the school magazine, 'I had expected a much stronger growth than I found at Wishaw, even allowing for the difficulties confronting such an organisation in a provincial centre.' Dr Wilson's initial disappointment was reinforced by the outcome of the first meeting of the FP Club he attended in his capacity as Rector: no business could be transacted, due to the lack of a quorum.

It was not all doom and gloom, however, on the FP front. Both the Debating Society and the Athletics Club were thriving, and the Hockey

Club was holding its own despite a shortage of members (this deficiency prompted Dr Wilson to make an annual appeal to any girls who were leaving school to consider joining that particular section).

Every year, the Debating Society arranged a series of debates (on such social and political issues as 'Home Rule for Scotland') that 'attracted the general public of Wishaw in considerable numbers' (more than 140, on one occasion). New ground was broken in January 1938 with a Ladies' Public Speaking Competition; it was won by Isobel Haddow.

In February 1939, a full-scale parliamentary debate was held in the hall. The Speaker was R.G. Whitelaw, and the motion before the House was that "This House expresses its approval of the foreign policy of His Majesty's Government in effecting the signing of the Anglo-Italian Pact". Among those taking part was a certain John Junor from Glasgow, and I have a hunch that this gentleman may have been the John (later Sir John) Junor who became editor of the *Sunday Express*. If this was the case, I think you should be told.

In addition to organising regular training sessions and its own club championship, the Athletics Club took part in several triangular meetings with other FP Athletics Clubs; and in June 1939, the High School FPs won the Duke of Hamilton Trophy at the FP Athletic Union Championships.

Dr Wilson was both 'anxious to see the FPs extend their activities' and keen to encourage closer ties between them and the High School. Dr Wilson's wish was the FPs' command, and the FP Football Club was formed early in 1938; a series of friendly fixtures was arranged, the first of which resulted in a 7-0 victory over Motherwell Central FPs; and to provide further encouragement, both John Laurie and Jim Dykes (who, having played with distinction for the school, signed for Dundee and Heart of Midlothian respectively) presented the club with a new ball. The newly formed club (its first captain was T.B. Gardiner) had a large enough membership to enable it to field two teams, and later in the year it was admitted into the Glasgow and District FP League. Its first league game resulted in a 2 - 2 draw with Eastbank Amateurs.

In April 1938, two teams of eight, representing the High School staff and the FP Club respectively, took part in a spelling bee; Dr Wilson 'presided and was entrusted with the duties of "gonger"'. The following year, a general knowledge bee was arranged.

In an effort to boost the membership of the FP Club, the annual subscription was reduced to 2/6d; and having been elected Honorary Vice-President at the AGM in 1939, Dr Wilson immediately announced that it was his intention to try and enrol at least 200 associate members.

School life 'carried on as usual during alterations on the map of Europe'.

Sir Winston Churchill (adapted)

During the first two years of Dr Wilson's rectorship, the traditional events on the school calendar were as popular as ever. Indeed, in March 1938, if we are to believe the *Wishaw Press*, 'probably the largest ever function in the history of the High School was held': 77 tables were set up in the hall for a whist drive (in aid of the Prize Fund) that attracted more than 300 participants.

At the prize-giving in June, the medal presented for excellence in Geography and Botany (the first such presentation) had been donated by A. J. C. Kerr. Later in the proceedings, when 'the great man' rose to speak, he was greeted with 'a spontaneous outbreak of clapping and cheering'.

In November, both Kerr and Dr Wilson attended the school social, the first occasion on which the pupils had the opportunity to meet their new rector informally; 'but those who had any fears were soon to realise that they had anything but a spoilsport in their midst'. More than 160 pupils (from the 3rd, 4th, 5th, and 6th Year), former pupils (provided that - and this was an innovation of Dr Wilson's - they had left school since the beginning of the session), and teachers attended the social, in the course of which Dr Wilson expressed his 'indebtedness to the ladies and gentlemen of the staff who had devoted so much time to teaching the pupils dancing steps beforehand'. However, according to an article in the school magazine by Eleanor Haddow, the pupils were caught on the hop by the introduction of a novelty dance entitled 'Oranges and Lemons':
Several oranges and lemons were distributed, and then the dance began like an ordinary 'double novelty' - before developing into a version of 'hot poker', the fruit being handed on at each change of partner. When the music stopped, the 'victims' (i.e. those who were left with the fruit) were obliged to stand in the centre of the hall and sing the school song.

132

The Christmas Concert was held in the YMCA Hall, with the proceeds going towards the repayment of the loan the school had received from the County Council to finance the erection of the new sports pavilion.

In 1938, after a lapse of several years, the school magazine was successfully resurrected - more than a thousand copies being sold in the space of a week. The magazine itself is a very impressive production (Kerr described it as 'the best magazine the school had ever produced'), with articles on a wide range of serious topics: looking after pets in hot weather, Scottish Youth Hostels, tennis, cooking, stamp collecting, the Royal George Coal Washery at Newmains, splitting the atom, the Post Office, budgerigars, the RAF, hints for bathers and the internal combustion engine. It also contains poems, photographs, a short play entitled 'The Capture of Wallace', and the following parody of the school song by Jessie Rafferty, Bessie Forrest, and Gowans Archibald:

I used to talk of happy days,
When I should go to school,
But when I went, I soon found out
That I had been a fool.
In climbing learning's pathway steep
Home lessons must be done,
And pictures must be sacrificed
For prizes to be won.

In all the classrooms I am keen
To show a waving palm,
Nought can surpass that happy time
Of sitting an exam.
My teachers they are wrathful then,
When my poor best they see,
And father swears at my report,
And puts me o'er his knee.

In algebra I have to learn
That y squared's 'y' times 'y'.
In French 'I go' is 'Je vais',
But 'I might go' is 'Que j'aille'.
History's dates fill leisure hours,

Of which I have not many.
An arithmetic formula
Finds interest on a penny.

I hope the years ahead will bring
Success with fame and praise;
But I'm afraid that if they do,
I'll need to mend my ways.
But even if I don't succeed,
I trust that I will be
As happy as I've always been
Since I was in IC.

The 1939 edition of the magazine contains a marvellous advert listing twelve reasons why Newmains and Cambusnethan Co-operative Society's sliced bread was the housewife's favourite, a poem by Isobel Halliday:

How Sweet this Life ...

How sweet this life and free from care
Had we no lessons to prepare.

No history dates to sit and swot
Which are alas too soon forgot.

No grammar dull, no weary prose
No verse to scan till eyelids close.

No dreadful sums to spoil the day
We'll never need them anyway.

No science, Latin, maths or French
Our thirst for knowledge soon to quench.

No maps of places far from home
But then, we don't intend to roam.

How sweet this life and free from care
Had we no lessons to prepare.

And the following (unintentionally) ominous extract from an account of a trip to Germany:

Saturday evening provided the most thrilling experience of the entire trip - a visit to the local headquarters of the Hitler Youth Movement at Konigswinter Hotel. Here we were entertained by stirring marching songs - the English boys replying with Masefield's *Cargoes*; and the evening ended with the singing of the national anthems of both countries. I for one will never forget the stirring strains of 'Deutschland, Deutschland uber alles' followed by the vigorous Nazi salute – 'Kampf heil, Sieg heil, Hitler heil'.

During session 1937-38, in response to a request from a number of junior pupils, a Stamp Club was formed, and James Wilson, Principal Teacher of Classics, kindly agreed to supervise its activities.

That same session, the Debating Society organised an interesting series of events that included debates (on such topics as nationalisation), a Hat Night, a Balloon Night, a Spelling Bee, and an amusing discourse (*Mathematics for Alice*) written and presented by Sam Forrest, Principal Teacher of Mathematics and First Assistant.

Salmagundi

February 1938

A 'large and enthusiastic' audience gave Miss Edna Turner and Mr Charles Blake three cheers after they had performed scenes from *Julius Caesar*, *Twelfth Night*, and *The Taming of the Shrew* in the hall.

Abigail Loudon was appointed Senior Woman Assistant, and thus became the first woman to hold such a post at the High School. The school log states:

The Rector explained to Miss Loudon that her duties would be to attend to the physical welfare of the girls and give them help and advice in cases of illness at school. Miss Loudon promised to act as coach and secretary of the girls' hockey club, in addition to supervising swimming, running, and netball.

March 1938

The whole school was treated to a showing of *Captains Courageous* at The Plaza cinema. According to Gordon McNay, some of the boys were in tears - even though they tried very hard to hide it.

Trips were arranged to the Empire Exhibition and a gymnastic display by the Swedish Olympic Team at the Kelvin Hall. At the latter, 'it was noted with some satisfaction that the national colours of Sweden were those of Wishaw High School, and everyone warmed to the flag as well as to the performers'. The former trip inspired the following poem - written in the style of McGonagall, but of unknown authorship:

One day we pupils and teachers three
Went the Empire Exhibition for to see.
We travelled in a private bus,
Because trams and trains would have been an awful fuss.

The Exhibition is most beautiful to behold
In any weather, whether warm or cold,
And if you should go up the Tower,
You'll get a nasty dunt if you fall ower.

The Canadian Mounties are very fine to be seen,
With their scarlet coats and their eyes of blue and green.
The Pavilions too are well worth going into,
You see more there than from the top of Tinto.

Then, if you go into the Amusement Park,
You can hear shouts of great enjoyment - hark!
There are so many amusements in the Exhibition,
You really don't know which one to go on.

For the Scenic Railway provides you with many thrills,
And it's safe so long as you don't have any spills.
Then there's the Clachan and Victoria Falls,
And a great scarcity of cheap food stalls.

Yes, that was the only bit of beastly luck,
For in our throats our dry sandwiches had stuck.
Oh yes we did enjoy our day indeed,
And we'll go back with all haste and speed.

May 1938

A group of teachers from the Colonies visited the school, and pronounced themselves impressed by the work of the Technical and Domestic Science Departments.

June 1938

Major Bain, the head janitor, was awarded the MBE in the King's Birthday Honours List; and to mark the occasion, he received a presentation from the male members of staff. Dr Wilson praised his 'fine spirit'; and Alex Anderson described him as 'most efficient in his school duties, and always cheerful, willing, and capable'.

April 1939

'Great excitement,' the *Wishaw Press* reported, 'has arisen over the hatching of some Loch Leven trout in the High School's conservatory. The eggs were obtained a month ago by Mr James Hamilton of the Art Department.'

Still alive, and still well, and still living in Lockerbie

The 1938 edition of the school magazine contained the following update about A.J.C. Kerr:
As might be expected of a man of such overflowing energy, not by any means exhausted, he has not been content to restrict his external life, like many others, to a daily walk and gossip.

This is a reference to the fact that in addition to serving on the Schools' Management Committee in Lockerbie Kerr represented the Town Council of that same town on Dumfries County Council (which later elected him Convener of the Roads Committee). He was also busy on the literary front: in 1939 he wrote a booklet entitled 'Angling in Southern Scotland - a Guide'; and 'his pleasant and discursive essays on the art of fishing in the Border streams were making him known to the readers of the *Glasgow Herald* and the *Annandale Herald*'.

14

1939-1945: War and (Relative) Peace

At the prize-giving in June 1939, Dr Wilson presented his report on a session that had been 'overshadowed by the clouds on the political horizon'. He said that his aims had been 'to carry on the traditions of Wishaw High School and keep pessimism out of the hearts of the pupils, to whom belonged the future'. 'In this building,' he added, 'we work hard during working hours and play hard during play hours, so we have no time for gloomy thoughts and forebodings.'

At the beginning of September, immediately after war was declared on Germany, the High School was closed for a fortnight. School life was further disrupted, when the school reopened, by the introduction - due to the shortage of air raid shelters - of a 'shift system': 'Classes 3, 2D, 2F, IB, ID, and IF,' according to the school log, 'attended school in the morning, the other classes in the afternoon.' 'The other classes', it should be noted, did not include certificate classes, the pupils in which followed their normal timetable.

In Dr Wilson's opinion, 'the half-day system had a disastrous effect, not merely by reason of the loss of time, but also by discouraging the habits of steady application to work without which none can hope to climb the hard road to learning'. At a meeting of the Schools' Management Committee in March 1940, Bailie Charles Donnelly was equally scathing:

The present voluntary method of either sending a child to school or keeping him away from school is simply playing into the hands of those careless parents who have no regard for their children's education. We do not know how long the war will last; but if it lasts for two years, a boy about the age of twelve will have lost the best part of his education if his parents are careless.

These strictures persuaded the Committee to suggest to the Education Committee that the 'shift system' should be abolished. Two months later, 'compulsory education' was re-established.

The only other significant disruptions of life at the High School during the Second World War were several evacuations of the school (but only for practice) and the cancellation of the prize-giving in 1940 (books and medals were 'distributed quietly' in the relevant classrooms). It is also worth noting that a number of Roman Catholic pupils from the

138

Wishaw area and thirty Protestant pupils from Glasgow and Edinburgh were enrolled temporarily at the school.

In 1942 Dr Wilson commented as follows on the relative immunity of the High School from the side effects of the war:

It has always been my desire that the pupils who pass through the school during wartime should enjoy a school life as nearly normal as possible. In session 1941-42, thanks to the absence of overhead disturbances, that ideal has been possible of realisation.

Wishaw High School and the War Effort

930 former pupils, nine members of staff and the school janitor, Matthew Bain, served in the armed forces during the Second World War.

On the home front, many members of staff undertook Civil Defence duties: Dr Wilson, for instance, did his share of fire- watching, 'which was carried out in the comfortable rooms of the Domestic Science Department' - where 'he was fortunate to have as a fellow-watcher another chess addict like himself'.

Some senior pupils also volunteered to undertake a spell of fire-watching; and after they had finished their shift (which they did in groups of four, supervised by two teachers) at 8 a.m., they were excused classes for the rest of the morning. Others assisted with the registration of evacuees.

In 1941 many High School pupils - and a fair number of former pupils - joined the 498th (Wishaw) Squadron of the Air Training Corps, 'a very lively and flourishing organisation', two of whose officers, Tom Hamilton and David Hair, were members of staff at the school.

In 1943 Dr Alexander Logan started an Ambulance Class at the school, the outcome of which was that twenty-two pupils were presented for the St Andrew's Ambulance Certificate. Two years later, fifteen girls attended a Sick Nursing Class arranged by Mrs Freeland. Both these classes were destined to feature regularly on the school calendar, even after the war had ended.

Dig for victory...

In January 1940, the High School secured allotments on Wishaw Estate for the nominal rent of 1/- per annum; and the following month, a series of four lectures on gardening was given to 1st and 2nd Year boys by Miss Copeland of the Agricultural College. These lectures must have been very enlightening, for eighteen months later '7 cwt. of good quality spuds were lifted for use in the luncheon room', and fifty cabbages were sent to the County Infectious Diseases Hospital.

...and gather potatoes...

In the later stages of the war, mixed groups of High School pupils 'lifted' potatoes in such distant locations as Cupar and St Andrews (the girls being billeted in the Westerlea Hotel, the boys in the Grand).

...and pick berries...

In 1943 and 1944, parties of girls from the High School spent part of the summer holidays berry-picking at Essendy near Blairgowrie. One of the girls provided the *Wishaw Press* with the following account of her stint as a berry-picker:

When we arrived at Essendy and viewed the huts that were to be our homes for the next two weeks, there were certainly a few groans; but after a splendid dinner the girls set to, and when it was discovered that there really were mattresses and pillows, faces brightened a bit. An hour later, the dormitories were unrecognisable. Boxes had been transformed into dressing tables, mirrors decorated the walls, flowers adorned the tables, and the beds had assumed a most inviting aspect. Pin-up boys, such as Bing Crosby, Frank Sinatra and Victor Mature, were much in evidence, and we spent the evening discussing the various merits and demerits of those heroes.

Next morning, having discarded the feminine garb for the more convenient uniform of slacks or dungarees, the girls made their way to the first field; and soon the competitive spirit was at work, reckoning being always in £sd and not in lbs.

For two days, the working hours were 8.15 a.m. to 4.15 p.m.; and then we had the weekend free. Cluny Loch was the favourite resort for the bathing belles, but at this early date we had not exhausted all Blairgowrie's possibilities - and the cafe proprietors soon knew that High School pupils were in the vicinity.

On Sunday, the girls joined the pupils of several other schools in a visit to Cluny Church; and the rest of the day was spent sunbathing or, in the case of the more energetic, visiting the Beech Hedges, a local beauty spot.

During the weekend, the berries had ripened considerably, a fact that caused a great deal of pleasure, since it meant that they would now 'weigh heavier', and those three halfpennies would be more easily come by. Little encouragement was needed to make the girls 'pick clean': every rasp counted.

A great deal of interest was aroused in the camp by the arrival of some Belgian schoolchildren, who were also able to help with the fruit harvest. The junior girls decided to give them a proper welcome; and after hoarding all the precious parcels that arrived from home - and after many visits to Blairgowrie to spend their well-earned wages - they issued the invitations, and the party was held on Saturday night. Music was provided by the guests, who had brought with them mandolins and banjos. The rafters rang to the sound of lively Scotch songs and the strains of the more romantic French airs, but when it came to 'Mares eat oats', language was no barrier - and the building threatened to collapse. When the time for tea arrived, the table was so loaded with good things inveigled from Blairgowrie shopkeepers and the folks at home that there was no room for the cups. For dessert, the best that could be provided was that much-despised (in conversation, at least) fruit - raspberries; but even these, tastefully served with cream, were voted delicious and second helpings asked for.

By Tuesday, there were a few sad faces when the time came to say goodbye. No one felt that a holiday had been sacrificed to the war effort. On the contrary, everyone expressed themselves willing - determined, in fact - to return to the fruit harvest next year.

...and be a lumberjack.

In July 1940, thirty-two boys, four girls, and two teachers took part in a scheme initiated by the Forestry Commission (in conjunction with the EIS) at Newton Stewart. The *Wishaw Press* described the scheme as follows:

It will combine an attractive, healthy holiday with the opportunity to perform voluntary work in the forests during the summer holidays. The work to be done will consist of measuring, stacking, brush burning, etc., while the forest management side will include bracken cutting and nursery weeding.

Facilities for recreation will be provided, as it is not intended that the pupils will be kept with their noses to the grindstone for long periods. Another welcome piece of news for volunteers is that all expenses - travelling, subsistence, and insurance - will be met, and the pupils will also be provided with a limited amount of pocket money.

Each pupil will be required to take his or her personal equipment, including blankets. Camping gear will be supplied where necessary, though it would be of assistance if parties took their own.

Nervos belli, pecuniam infinitam

Cicero, *Fifth Philippic*

Throughout the war, High School pupils were as generous with their money - as instanced by their purchase of Defence Bonds and Saving Certificates in aid of national appeals - as with their time and labour:

War Weapons Week (June 1941) - £588
Warship Week (May 1942) - £880
Wings for Victory Week - £1,917
Salute the Soldier Week - £2,724

Towards the end of 1940, a Comfort Fund was set up with a view to boosting the morale of FPs serving in the armed forces, the merchant navy, and the W.A.S.A. collection was taken every Friday; greetings cards were printed by the Art Department; Miss Stewart and Mrs Stewart 'knitted comforts'; Mr Dickson obtained the relevant addresses; and, eventually, parcels were sent to more than 250 FPs (and to 332, the following Christmas). Parcels containing books and cigarettes were also sent to serving FPs on a regular basis.

In April 1942, Class 1C raised £8 for the Aid of Russia Fund by holding a mini -concert in the hall.

In 1943 part of the proceeds from the annual concert, which was held (for the first time) in June, was donated to the Red Cross. The concert featured three choirs - 1st Year (Boys and Girls), Intermediate (Girls), and Senior (Boys and Girls); solos by Marion Russell and Doris Watson; a display of Highland dancing by Annie Craw; a masurka, performed by B. Cassels, J. McClelland, M. Steele, and I. Young; two scenes from *A Midsummer Night's Dream*; a shorter scene from *The Tempest*; and a comedy sketch involving Mary E. Smith, Margaret Adams, James Green, Douglas Harvie, Robert Young, and James Sommerville.

Two years later, the Red Cross benefited financially from a match between the High School's under-18 football team and its counterpart at Dalziel High School.

Not What the Doctor Ordered

Between December 1939 and August 1941, the school roll dipped from 743 to 680. Dr. Wilson's explanation of this decrease - and his reaction to it - was contained in the speech he made at the prize-giving in 1941:

A very unsatisfactory feature of the school in wartime is the tendency on the part of parents to take their children away from school immediately they reach the age of 14, even though they have signed a solemn undertaking to keep their children in a secondary school for five years - and even though, in many cases, those same children are entering blind alley occupations. In some instances, where the child has shown himself or herself to be incapable of benefiting from a scholastic education, the action is understandable; but in other cases it is a criminal waste of talents that for the country's sake, as well as for the sake of the child, should be given a chance to develop.

A year later, Dr Wilson was still complaining:

Despite a series of appeals to their parents, too many pupils who should have gone on to gain the Leaving Certificate have left during their third year to accept posts which in many cases are not worthy of their abilities.

If that was the case, it certainly couldn't be laid at Dr Wilson's door, for he made every effort to find suitable posts for his pupils:

May I say how pleased I am to have visits from parents who wish to consult me with regard to the careers of their children. I grudge no trouble that it may cost me to get them the information they desire, and I appreciate the friendly relations which we have established with one another. My employment bureau has been active, and local employers have kept me busy finding suitable boys and girls for them.

According to Morton Cadzow, a former pupil of the High School, Dr Wilson would also talk to senior pupils individually, and encourage them to continue their studies at college or university.

As the military situation began to improve (in which connection, it is worth mentioning that in 1943 a former dux of the High School, Walker Chambers, acted as interpreter between General Montgomery and various German and Italian generals who had been captured in Tunisia; and that in December 1944 Walker Chambers and another former pupil, Eddie Tweedlie - in his capacity as a shorthand writer - were present at the interrogation of General Hasso Von Manteuffel, Commander-in-Chief of the 5th Panzer Division during the Battle of the Bulge), and outright victory became an increasingly likely prospect, the roll started to rise again; and by January 1944, it had reached the 750 mark.

In August of that same year, Dr Wilson was delighted to report that a record number of pupils had enrolled in the 4th, 5th, and 6th Year, and that for the first time in his rectorship the numbers in the 6th Year justified the formation of a 'Sixth Form'. However, there was 'one drawback':

With a hundred more pupils and three fewer teachers than in 1939, the strain on the staff is a severe one, and it is sincerely to be hoped that the position as regards staffing will soon be eased.

Success Story

High levels of attendance were maintained throughout the Second World War: in the third week of November 1942, for example, an all-time record of 97.3% was established. In addition, the Report of His Majesty's Inspector in 1943 pointed out that 'the normal class work of the school continued to progress in a very satisfactory manner'; and that the amount of ground covered 'did not differ noticeably from what would have been expected in normal conditions', an achievement that 'reflected great credit on the headmaster and his staff'.

These official plaudits were supplemented by a letter Dr Wilson received in December 1941:

Dear Sir,

I have had it in mind for some time to write to you to express the appreciation of Mrs McClelland and myself of the progress which Alastair made during the three years he was under your charge. I should be obliged if you would convey our thanks to all the members of staff under whom he studied and from whom he received so much benefit.

I should be pleased if you would accept the enclosed cheque, to be utilised at your discretion, as a donation from us to one of the school funds or schemes that are currently operative.

Yours faithfully,
A. McClelland

Inconvenient Exams, Exceptional Pupils

Dr Wilson was not overly impressed by the administrative procedures that preceded the Leaving Certificate examinations during the war years: *They have proved to be a very poor substitute for the real thing, for they have involved the attendance of the most highly qualified and experienced members of staff at meetings of the Subject Panels for two weeks at critical times in the school session, thus seriously aggravating staffing problems.*

Even so, High School pupils continued to excel themselves in those same examinations: in 1941 there was a record number of presentations, and the number of successful candidates (35) was the second highest on record.

In the Glasgow University Bursary Competition, Robert Lannigan was 17th in 1940 and Robert Barrie 16th in 1945; in 1943 - and also in 1945 - four High School pupils gained a place in the first hundred. One of the successful four in 1943, Peter Nardone, had a particularly impressive academic and sporting record during his years at the High School: he was first in his class in 1st and 2nd Year, Intermediate Dux in 1940, Dux of the 4th Year in 1941, Dux and Captain of the school in 1943, captain of the under-18 football team, runner-up in the senior championship at the school sports, and a member of the Rest of Scotland team that was selected to play in the annual match against Glasgow.

There can be no daily democracy without daily citizenship.

Ralph Nader

'A common charge against schools,' Dr Wilson acknowledged, 'is that they do too little to fit young people for the duties that lie before them as citizens in a free, democratic society.' Consequently, in an effort 'to train senior pupils for their future responsibilities', he organised a Brains Trust, a series of debates, and visits to the law courts. He also made arrangements for them to attend meetings of the Town Council.

A course in citizenship was added to the curriculum of 1st and 2nd Year pupils during session 1944-45. Dr Wilson explained why:

It is clear that younger pupils have little knowledge of the workings of democracy in our land, and some of the gaps in their knowledge can be filled by instruction in citizenship.

In the summer term of that same session, the Higher English class formed itself into a debating society, with a view to 'acquiring knowledge of the rules of debate and facility in public speaking'.

It should be emphasised, finally, that Dr Wilson's efforts to cultivate a sense of civic responsibility in his pupils must have received a boost from the good example he set by serving on the Schools' Management Committee from June 1943 onwards.

Valete

In the early 1940s, several long-serving members of staff retired, died (in one instance), or resigned (in another instance):

David Roberts was a member of the Technical Department for 37½ years, almost the entire span of the High School's existence.

Catherine MacLean 'succeeded - by a superhuman effort - in conquering the worst disability that a teacher can have [deafness, I think], and did extraordinarily good work inspiring her pupils to overcome the difficulties of Mathematics'.

John Telford, Principal Teacher of Art, 'stage-managed plays, constructed scenery and footlights, coached pupils in acting technique, and designed two of the hall's most prominent features - the war memorial and the coats of arms (in stained glass) of the four Houses'.

Daisy MacDonald, Principal Teacher of Modern Languages since 1919, was blessed with 'great musical and literary gifts, which were revealed by the use she made of music and drama in her classes - an approach that goes a long way to producing "French without tears"; and she was always on the lookout for new methods and devices that would commend the subject to the average pupil'.

Francis Dickson, Principal Teacher of Science, who died in 1942, was credited with 'playing a major part in building up the high reputation of the school for scholarship'.

William Ferguson, who organised the Christmas party every year and was largely responsible for establishing rugby in the sporting curriculum of the High School, left to take up a teaching post in England.

Sam Forrest, First Assistant and Principal Teacher of Mathematics, was 'not only a mathematician but also a classical scholar and poet, a kind of "Admirable Crichton", with a personality so big that one felt like a schoolboy beside him'. He was treasurer of both the Athletic Fund and the Education Fund; exercised sole responsibility for the Milk Account; and was a member of the committee that ran the luncheon room. Among the textbooks he wrote were *Mining Mathematics*, *Mathematics for Technical Students*, and *A First Trigonometry*. As far as his pupils were concerned, 'even a reproof (such as, "Dear me, Robert, I thought you would have known better.") was an implied compliment, and hence an incentive'.

Another Famous Victory

In April 1942, the High School (represented by the following team: Paton; Barrie and Graham; Bryce, Simpson, and Harris; Cameron, Jack, Rae, Dick, and Ellarby) won the Scottish Intermediate Shield for the third time by virtue of a 2-1 victory over Alva Academy. According to the *Wishaw Press*:

There was no weak spot in the Wishaw team. Their forward play was particularly pleasing to watch, Jack at inside right being the inspiration of the line, and the others responding well. Bryce, Harris, and Simpson were a strong trio at half-back, while the backs, Barrie and Graham, dealt adequately with the spasmodic attacks of the Alva forwards. Paton, who had no chance with the goal against him, had one splendid save in the second half. Alva fought pluckily, but the High School team was stronger and cleverer.

On Thursday morning, at prayers, Dr Wilson, the Rector, congratulated the team on their success, and on the very sporting way in which they had played. He then awarded the traditional 'double' that is customary on such occasions. The team this year was in the charge of Mr Frame, the sports master, and to his enthusiasm and training much of the success is due.

The senior team also won a trophy - the Keith Cup - in 1942; and the following year, it won the Lanarkshire League.

In the early 1940s, the High School was still able to field two hockey teams; however, neither team played many games, a state of affairs that Dr Wilson described as 'regrettable'. In November 1942, the 1st XI, strengthened by the inclusion of several FPs, played a team made up of members of the W.A.A.F.; in the course of session 1941-42, the High School girls defeated their counterparts from Peebles High School for the first time in the history of that biennial fixture; and in 1943 and 1945, the school took part in under-14 and under-15 hockey tournaments at Anniesland and Scotstounhill respectively.

The school also fielded two rugby teams. In session 1941-42, the 1st XV, according to Dr Wilson, was 'the finest rugby team in the history of the school, and had also proved to be the best in Lanarkshire'; and in November of that same session, new ground was broken with a fixture against Jordanhill College. Even so, rugby had to be discontinued in 1943, mainly because of the lack of a field.

The school golf championship was held every year, and in 1944 the golf team played a match against Hamilton Academy; tennis was so popular (on the newly 'reconstructed' courts) that in 1943 the season was extended well into November; and during session 1944-45, the school ran a netball team.

Other extra-curricular activities included a Model Aeroplane Club (inaugurated in 1939, with a membership of thirty); a Stamp Club (founder and secretary: Harry Smith); and three choirs: Junior Boys, Intermediate Girls, and Senior (comprising boys and girls in the 4th, 5th, and 6th Year).

On the debit side, 'the difficulties imposed by the blackout and travelling restrictions' made it 'impractical' for the Debating Society to remain in existence; and the sports were held 'on a smaller scale than usual' (in 1940, for instance, there were no invitation events).

A Whiter Shade of Pale

In February 1940, a representative of Lever Brothers delivered an 'interesting and educative' lecture to 2nd and 3rd Year girls on the washability of modern fabrics.

Nouvelle Cuisine

At the prize-giving in 1942, Dr Wilson announced that although the luncheon room continued to provide satisfactory meals for those pupils who were unable to get home at lunchtime, the Education Committee would be taking control of it in the near future. In fact, the takeover occurred in April 1945.

Two Yanks at Wishaw

In September 1942, two American soldiers were shown round the school by Dr Wilson.

Junior Masterchefs

In February 1943, a cooking competition was organised as part of the Secretary of State's campaign to popularise the use of potatoes and oatmeal. The winner of the Senior Section (Classes 4, 5, and 6) was Isabella Girdwood, a future Principal Teacher of Domestic Science at the High School.

The following year, Martha Simpson triumphed in the Lanarkshire final of the Scottish Primary Products Competition, the participants in which were required to prepare three dishes - each of which used either potatoes, or oatmeal, or two fresh herring as its main ingredient.

ferulae tristes, sceptra paedagogorum

Martial, *Epigrams*

According to an entry in the school log on 30 March 1943, the mother of Margaret Adam informed Dr Wilson that Miss Mamie Loudon had 'injured' her daughter on the wrist with a strap, and that she had reported the matter to the police.

A play's the thing.

Excursions were rare during the Second World War, but in November 1943 three teachers and 120 pupils attended a performance (in Glasgow) of *The Merchant of Venice* by the Wolfit Company.

Stars and Slides

In the summer term of session 1944-45, Professor Smart of Glasgow University delivered a lecture on astronomy with the aid of 'lantern slides'.

'Dies Laetissimi'

The High School was closed on VE and VE+ I Day, i.e. 8 and 9 May 1945.

Consumebatur tamen.

According to Dr Wilson's foreword in the 1946 edition of the school magazine, 'The famous and historic "Burning Bush" was a war casualty.' Whether the 'Burning Bush' still existed in part after the War, or had been totally obliterated (it is not clear what exactly Dr Wilson meant by the phrase 'a war casualty'), its location remained the haunt of smokers.

Nadir

Most FP activities came to a halt at the start of the Second World War. In March 1940, however, the committee of the Athletics Club were still expressing a desire 'to see every FP in the district making use of the facilities offered to those who enjoyed physical fitness', a high degree of which, they argued, 'would be specially beneficial to those who would shortly be called to the colours, as it would help to soften the change from civilian life to the hard physical training of the army'; and that same month, boxing was added to the club's more conventional activities. The Football Club managed to keep going (by playing a series of friendly fixtures) till 1941; thereafter, all FP activities were suspended for three years.

In April 1944, in an effort to resurrect the FP Club, a meeting was held in the school hall and an interim committee formed. A full year had elapsed, however, before the first social event was organised - an outing to the theatre to attend a performance of *The Skin of Our Teeth,* starring Vivien Leigh.

At the prize-giving in 1945, Dr Wilson claimed that a strong FP club would be 'an asset of incalculable value to the school'. Unfortunately, several factors militated against the emergence of 'a strong FP club', and these factors were enumerated in a letter (from the retiring President, William Clelland) that was read out at the AGM of the FP Club in October 1945: the discouragingly small membership (only seventy-two); the lack of interest shown by most of the members, and the disheartening effect this had on some of the committee; the lack of co-operation from the school; the fact that it was necessary to apply to the County Council for the use of the school hall for various social functions - and the delays this could cause; and the paper shortage, which prevented the publication of an FP column in the local paper.

Nobody was particularly surprised, therefore, when the FP Club was formally disbanded at an extraordinary general meeting (attended by only eight members) in June 1946. The *Wishaw Press* observed caustically: '*The former pupils of Wishaw High School are seemingly incapable of the effort needed to build a really successful club.*'

A Red-Letter Day

Soon after this, ironically, the (defunct) FP Club received a letter addressed to 'My Unknown Friend' and signed by Alexander Khalamaizar of Neglinna Street, Moscow - the simple explanation of which was that a year earlier, under the auspices of the Anglo-Soviet Youth Fellowship Alliance, the FPs had formed a Soviet Club, with the aim of providing every member with a Russian friend who had a similar job, interest, or hobby.

15

In Memoriam Aeternam

A memorial edition of the school magazine was published in 1947. 'In this Memorial Number of the Wishaw High School Magazine,' Dr Wilson wrote in the foreword, 'we seek to pay our meed of homage and gratitude to all the men and women who, after spending their early years of adolescence in our school, went out to serve their country in the armed forces during the fateful years 1939 to 1945. We record the names of those who have returned safely from far-off Burma and India, from the desert battlefields of Africa, from Italy, France, Germany, Holland, Belgium and Norway, and from the wide seas of the Arctic, Atlantic, Indian and Pacific Oceans; of those who endured the loneliness, privations and horrors of the prisoner-of-war camps; and of those who were wounded or maimed.'

The list in question (it was headed 'Those Who Served') contained the names of 930 former pupils, several of whom contributed articles about their wartime experiences:

Last Signal

Suddenly, a blinding flash burst upon the Arctic night, accentuating the blackness of the sea and throwing into relief the snow-covered hills of Russia. Seconds later came the dull roar of an underwater explosion, as a torpedo struck home. The First Lieutenant raised his binoculars and said the one word, 'Goodall'. I looked with horror at what had been - only minutes earlier - the proud, trim figure of a 'Captain' class frigate. For'ard of the bridge, she was a shapeless mass of distorted metal; amidships, a fire had broken out; further aft, one could detect figures still moving about on the quarterdeck. I shivered, as I glanced for a moment at the ice-cold sea and realised the dilemma of those tiny figures - death in the blazing inferno that had been their home, or a sudden plunge to freezing extinction in the black depths. As we drew nearer, a ring of flame began to spread in ever-widening circles round the stricken ship, whose damaged fuel tanks were obviously discharging oil on the sea; and we watched with bated breath the desperate attempts of our fellow sailors to battle against the current that was carrying them straight towards the burning ship.

Robert S. Whitelaw, Surgeon/Lieutenant, R.N.V.R.

Burma Vista

While obstacles of climate, disease, accident, and the ever-present danger from enemy action are the natural accompaniments of daily life for the soldier in wartime (and it is perhaps no overstatement to say that in the Burma theatre all of these were there in the highest degree), one remembers from that campaign not so much the intense, humid heat and the personal discomfort as the morale-sapping feeling of isolation - of being in this world, but not of it.

Robert S. Gilchrist, Captain, Royal Signals

Per Ardua ad Astra

From behind the door came the voices of the pilots of a Lancaster bomber squadron, all speaking English - yet in different accents; for they belonged to young men from Australia, New Zealand, Canada, and the United Kingdom. A bell rang twice, and the chatter ceased. Then a nasal drawl from the land of the Southern Cross broke the silence with the one word, 'Twitch'. The occurrence was not unusual, and the pilots were soon in another room - listening to their Flight Commander, as he read from his typewritten notes. When I heard my name called, I felt an increase of interest as the emotionless voice proceeded: 'Meal 17.45 hours, specialist briefing 18.45 hours, transport to aircraft 19.30 hours, take off 20.30 hours. Round up your crews now and give your aircraft a thorough check.'

I gathered my crew together, and soon we were all out at our proud Lancaster, 'E' for 'Easy'. While I ran up all four engines, checking their performance, each crew member was engaged in testing his own particular part of the aircraft. At last, we were satisfied that she was in perfect order; and when we had stretched ourselves out on the grass, the conversation turned upon the probable target that evening. 'Full tanks, skip, and eight two- thousand pounders,' said an overalled sergeant, 'must be a long trip.' And so it went on, suggestion following suggestion, until I ordered my crew to bed to rest till evening.

Thomas McC. Rae, Flight Lieutenant, RAF

Out of the Shadows

It was the afternoon of Monday, 25 September 1944, our last attempt to escape across the Lower Rhine had failed and, utterly worn out, we were being marched under German escort along a sheltered road. We passed through a residential suburb, its lovely villas shattered, its gardens full of wrecked S.P. guns, burnt-out panzers, and broken-down anti-tank guns, their crews still lying unburied, their faces blackened. The smell of death was everywhere. German soldiers emerged from cover to throw us apples from the trees and cigarettes from our own lost air supplies. We met Dutch civilian refugees with handcarts and prams, complete with white flags. So this was Arnhem.

A smart staff car stopped alongside us to discharge a dapper German press photographer, grinning broadly as he prepared to take propaganda shots. Until that moment most of us had been dog-tired, dazed, and depressed: we had expected death or wounds, but never capture. At the sight of that smug, gloating face, however, the old paratroop spirit reasserted itself, and we greeted him with grins, 'V' signs, and hoots of derision. He flew into a fit of rage, dancing and gesticulating until even the other Germans were amused; but his shots were spoiled, and he had to be satisfied with a helpless party of wounded behind us.

After being searched and interrogated on the outskirts of Arnhem, we were visited by a medical orderly equipped with only paper bandages and aspirins for even the most seriously wounded; then we were herded into a box-car (all fifty-seven of us), and the doors were locked. Ten days later, they were opened at Frankfurt-on-Main, our water supply during that period consisting of rain caught in our steel helmets, or passed to us through the slats by slave workers. Here again the treatment for wounds and starvation was the standard one - aspirins. We resumed our journey under similar conditions, and eventually I reached Stalag VIII C at Sagan in Lower Silesia.

Robert B. Syme, Captain, Intelligence Corps

The Tumult Dies

It is the morning of Victory Day, and I am wedged tightly among the London crowd waiting for the Marching Column of the Victory Parade to appear. All morning, the excitement has been mounting, mounting, mounting, and the passage of the Royal Family, the great war leaders, and the Mechanised Column has merely served to whet the crowd's appetite. No one is very interested in the last of the Mechanised Column now passing: there is a sameness about machines which does not thrill you, and which is vaguely depressing. The crowd is quiet as the trucks clatter by - and now we can hear the cheering swelling in the distance, then nearer and nearer. Heads turn, eyes strain, and here they come - the ordinary people, marching row upon row, row upon row, with steadfast step, the people who won the most ghastly war humanity has ever known.

Margaret S. Anderson, Petty Officer, W.R.N.S.

These reminiscences were followed by a tribute to 'The Fallen' from the boys' captain, Jack Shields, and a brief dedication of the magazine by its editor, Percy Quinn:

The School Pays Tribute

Their renown is clear and bright, and we remember many of them proudly as our former companions and adored leaders. If only we can emulate them and carry on the work they left undone, they will not have died in vain. The present generation of Wishaw High School pupils honours them, and hopes to bear itself as worthily in the years to come.

Dedication

The purpose of these pages is not to pay vainglorious and boastful lip-service to 'The Fallen', but to set before ourselves a standard of achievement that will inspire us in a world seething with unrest, a world over which the threat of war still hangs - as a backdrop to every peace conference. The best memorial we can erect to these our comrades of yesteryear is that of applying to the task of creating permanent peace the spirit of self-sacrifice and dogged endurance which they so liberally poured out.

The largest - and most poignant - part of the magazine is taken up by photographs and short obituaries of all eighty-three of 'The Fallen'; it concludes with the following lines by Rupert Brooke:

These laid the world away; poured out the red
Sweet wine of youth; gave up the years to be
Of work and joy, and that unhoped serene,
That men call age; and those that would have been,
Their sons, they gave, their immortality.

The Fallen

Royal Navy

George Bell	James G. Duncan	Duncan McC. Harris
William S. McCall	Alexander McI. McNay	James B. Paterson
Alasdair L.H. Polson		

The Army

George E. Allan	David S. Allardice	Donald F. Armit
William Black	James G. Boughey	Matthew P. Christie
David Denholm	Adam C, Gibb	Andrew M, Hamilton
Gavin R. Harvie	William J. Johnston	William Laurie
Robert Lindsay	John Linning	Arthur Lyall
William Millar	William McI. Poole	Robert Russell
Robert Scott	Richard Steventon	Thomas P. Watson
Samuel Westwood	William Wheelan	William S. Yates

Royal Air Force

Andrew N. Adams	John Beattie	Robert J. Blake
Arthur S. Carson	John S. Clyde	James Craig
Ernest Edward Dennis	Walter E Dennis	Robert McF. Don
John B. Eyre	James K.G. Freeland	James M. Gibb
Norman I. Gill	Bertram S.W. Grieve	Donald Gunn
James S. Gunn	Z. Rankin Hamilton	George Harvie
Tom W. Hunter	William S. Hutchison	Robert Inglis
William B. Jamieson	Thomas Kelly	William Lannigan
W. Stuart Marshall	James S. Mathison	Samuel McAlonan
Vallance McCall	James McCartney	AndrewY.M. McCombe
James McLean	David McNeilly	John C. Millar

William Murphy   Alexander A. Murray   Harold A. Paterson
Robert M. Paton   Peter W. Rattray   Douglas J. Reid
Thomas M. Reid   James C.D. Riddell   John F.S. Ritchie
Arthur C. Roberts   James McD. McL. Smith   James Stanners
Adam G.M. Watson   John Whyte   David G. Wood
James A. Wynn   Robert W. Yuill

Merchant Navy
William Millar   James W.K. Mitchell

16

Wishaw High School 1939-1944: A Portrait and Some Sketches

The portrait was supplied by Sheila Sprot, who writes:

But for the war I might never have been a pupil at Wishaw High School, and I suspect that the same is true of many of my contemporaries. It was customary at that time for 'bright' primary pupils to go to Hamilton Academy - or even, if they were really 'bright' and their parents could afford it, to one of the Glasgow schools.

I would probably have gone to Hamilton Academy (since my mother was a former pupil), but with war obviously looming it was decided that I should go to Wishaw High School, as it was nearer home - and in 1939 no one knew what privations we might have to face.

I never regretted that decision. Wishaw High was a good school, and it gave its pupils a sound academic grounding. It also had the advantage of giving people the chance to get to know all their contemporaries in the Wishaw area; and in the course of time, local doctors, nurses, lawyers, accountants, teachers, and shopkeepers were people I had known at school. This network of friendships and acquaintanceships has many benefits, one of which is that it makes you feel part of a community.

There were probably disadvantages as well. Being a fairly small school, Wishaw High tended to operate a rather restricted and academic timetable. I never set foot in the Domestic Science Department, so I never learned anything about cooking, running a home, looking after babies - or sex education, come to that. I never set foot in the Business Studies Department either, and I had to learn typing and shorthand at an age when it was much more difficult to learn such skills.

I was never a member of any club: for me there was no drama or stamp collecting, no chess or table tennis. I never took part in any organised games (like hockey), but that I did not regret. I never had any real musical education (I certainly wasn't given the chance to play an instrument), nor did I receive lessons in art appreciation. Although no child leaves school nowadays without being exposed to all these experiences, it could be argued that a no-frills curriculum concentrated our minds on what was important for us at that stage in our lives and at that period in the country's history.

I went to the High School in January 1939. I don't remember much about my first day there, but I do remember being very impressed by the building (it was so square and white - and stylish, with its open corridors and octagonal hall), and by the hockey pitch, two football fields, and two tennis courts. It was all very different from my primary school. I also remember being very impressed by a fussy lady who accompanied Dr Wilson into the hall. I thought she was some 'high heid yin', but she turned out to be Miss Mitchell, the Rector's secretary. Nothing changes much.

When the war began in September 1939, the school was blacked out, a difficult operation with all these big windows (especially in the hall) and the open corridors; and netting was put on the windows to prevent the glass from shattering. Previously, the windows had purple curtains to keep out the sun, the Maths corridor in particular having a permanent problem with the glare. Purple, for some reason, seemed to be the predominant colour in the school's decor.

Arrangements were made for us to disperse in the event of daytime air raids. We were all given houses near the school to go to; and when the siren went, I made my way to a house in Kenilworth Avenue, whose occupants were complete strangers to me. I regarded this as great fun. I only remember going there twice, as, fortunately, there were very few daytime air raids. The nocturnal ones didn't cause much excitement and, as far as I know, no damage was done to the school - even though several bombs (jettisoned, I think) did land in the wood behind the bungalow at the corner of Waverley Drive, quite close to the school.

The most disruptive thing that happened was that we were put on part-time education: one week the boys went to school in the morning and the girls in the afternoon, the following week vice versa. How long this went on I don't know. It had something to do with the number of people that could safely be evacuated from the school in the event of an air raid; and it may also have had something to do with shortage of staff. I don't think the shift system went on for any length of time, as our education didn't seem to suffer.

There were a number of evacuees on the roll, most of whom came from Glasgow. In my year there were two - Jean Torrance and Margaret McPhail - both of whom stayed on for the duration. Most evacuees left after a few weeks, as nothing much happened in the first year of the war.

I was in a 'good' year, i.e. one that contained a lot of clever people. Most of them went on to have distinguished careers in one field or another. Some of the names come to mind, in no particular order: Robert Barrie, Robert Bankier, John Prentice, 'Tudge' Baird, Orry Stewart, Isobel Hogg, Olive Parton, Edith Carlin, Mary Clark, Anne Young, Willie Archibald, Mary Chapman, and Jessie Whitehouse.

Unlike most of my classmates, I left school in 1944 at the end of fifth year. By then, I'd had enough regimentation, and I was ready to move on.

The staff all seemed very old to me (there were no young ones at all), but I realise now, of course, that they couldn't have been all that old.

Some whom I remember are 'Bunny' Hair, my Maths teacher; 'Stotter' Brown (also Maths); Meg Coutts (English); Daisy MacDonald (French); 'Sanny' Anderson, who later became an MP; 'Sammy' Forrest; Mr Clark (Science); 'Papa' Wilson, who attempted to teach me Latin; Mamie Loudon; Abby Loudon (PE); and Archie Leitch (Geography).

My schooldays I recollect as being very happy days. I liked school, I liked the other pupils, and I liked the teachers. To me the school was the people, not the place.

We didn't wear school uniform (as clothes were rationed), and after our first blazer, blouse, and gym tunic were past their sell-by date, we could wear what we liked. For PE we had shorts made out of blackout material. I had one precious square-necked blouse that I only wore for PE, and it did me until I left school - even though it was very frayed and fragile.

Fortunately, my gym tunic had been bought to accommodate the natural growth process, and it lasted me until I left; but I outgrew my blazer very quickly. House badges were handed down from one generation to the next.

I remember the double desks in the classrooms (some of which survived almost to the end of the school's existence), the high teachers' desks, the pointers, and the dusters. Our education was all talk and chalk, but it did us no harm.

The Art Department had single desks (that doubled as easels) in semicircles - very avant-garde. Mr Smith and Mrs Stalker (she wasn't Mrs Stalker then, but I can't remember her maiden name) reigned supreme there; and Higher Art pupils were treated as very special people (for instance, they had access to the storeroom), a state of affairs that still obtains today.

The Science labs had big benches (with Bunsen burners in the centre of them), and glass-fronted cupboards containing sets of scales. The first practical lesson I ever had was learning how to use the scales; this involved picking up the weights (in grams and milligrams) with little tongs from immaculate, varnished boxes with green felt lining.

We had a canteen under the gym. There 'Ma' McLean dished up the same menu every week: if it was Friday, it was pie and beans, and lovely baked rice pudding. The lentil soup lasted right through the week. It had a sort of metallic flavour that I can still taste today.

The Geography rooms had folding partitions between them, probably so that films could be shown; however, I can't recollect this actually happening.

The hall, which had a podium, was a magical place for school dances, with a real band and slipperene on the floor; a cold prison for such exams as the dreaded Highers; and a warm, sunny haven on prize-giving day, when the sun always seemed to shine. With the addition of a makeshift stage, it was used for school concerts, a difficult undertaking with a blackout in force.

The stone stairs resounded with different noises; and there was a prefect on every landing. The staff stair was 'verboten', as was the staffroom. I had never even been at the door of this holy of holies, till I returned as a teacher twenty years later.

One unique feature of the architecture was the open corridors. They were designed to provide plenty of healthful fresh air; but when the snow was swirling through them, health was the last thing they engendered.

The cloakroom, with its rows of iron pegs and its stone floor, was the only place where we could shelter from the weather.

Then there were the 'lines', when we all marched into the school with the House captains, very superior young ladies in 'costumes' in those days. We had a House System even then.

We were a kind of elite, I suppose, but we did get a good education - an inspiring education - in spite of the war.

We had nicknames (not invented by us, I may say, but passed down to us) for all the teachers, but we certainly never used them to their faces. We admired and respected most of them. They tended to be intellectuals, and they taught us far more than their professed subjects. People like Meg Coutts and 'Sanny' Anderson were liable to go off at tangents. They stretched our imagination by introducing things like mythology, astronomy, knots, the intricacies of a ship's rigging, bits of Scottish history and folklore, and even the Stock Exchange, none of which were on the syllabus.

On one occasion, I even remember Dr Wilson taking our Maths class (an unheard of occurrence), and I remember his lesson to this day - the history of Mathematics, something which I knew nothing about, but which I have never forgotten.

Dr Wilson was a remote, godlike figure in a gown, to whom nobody (neither teachers nor pupils) seemed to talk. I was only in his room once: it must have been at the end of third year, when we had to decide whether to do Highers in Science or languages. I walked into his room absolutely terrified. He looked at me, then at my report, and said, "You'll be doing Science." End of interview. My whole life was decided by that one sentence. I wasted years after that studying Physics (which I hated), which meant that I had to give up Latin, which in turn meant that I couldn't take English at university - because I didn't have Lower Latin.

My one regret about my time at the High School was this bad advice. I would have loved to study English at university. What a pity we didn't have Guidance or careers advice in those days.

The one piece of careers advice I did get was from Meg Coutts. After the Highers, she went round the class asking us what we were going to do when we left school. I said I didn't know, but that I had thought about the Civil Service. She looked at me, aghast, and said, "Why aren't you going to university?" I said I'd never thought about it. She said, 'Go right now and get an application form.'

There must have been shortages of staff and materials during the war, but none of them seemed to impinge on us as pupils. I always seemed to be in smallish classes; and the only thing I remember about shortage of materials is having to use every inch of my jotter in the Maths class (this meant halving the pages and going right to the bottom of each column). We were also asked to buy our home readers for English, not because they weren't available at the school, but to encourage us to start a library for ourselves. I remember my aunt having to comb the second-hand bookshops in Glasgow to get me a copy of 'Guy Mannering'.

The High School was a progressive school in some ways: for one thing, it was co-educational. For every subject (except PE), we were in mixed groups, and we learned to form natural friendships with both sexes. We grew up together as it were.

Corporal punishment was almost non-existent; indeed, I can't remember any forms of punishment being meted out on a large scale. Occasionally, we were given lines, but we treated them as a joke, priding ourselves in the originality of what we wrote.

The original building was probably ideal for the number of pupils and the kind of academic education for which it was built, but even by my time it had started to burst at the seams. The library was used as an English classroom, the hall for Music classes. The gym (divided by a partition) was always inadequate, but at least showers were available after PE. Incidentally, we were made to wear hairnets in the gym - not a pretty sight.

On hot, sunny afternoons there was very often a sports period: all lessons ceased, and we spilled out on to the playing fields for netball, rounders, hockey dribbling, long jump, etc. I don't know why this was ever done away with. We get so little good weather that it seems a pity not to enjoy it.

In really inclement weather, we used to be sent home at lunchtime. This happened quite frequently, and even in the 1940s, with so many mothers working, it caused problems.

I don't remember ever being overburdened with homework, though I know this did occur in some other schools of the academic type. On ordinary school days, I probably did about an hour a night; at weekends, nothing. Before exams, I worked every night for three weeks - except for a Friday, which was always my night off. I enjoyed my school work, and I never regarded homework as a chore. If I was lazy in class, I made up for it at home.

Because of the war, there weren't many social activities. We were, however, taught to dance, and there was always a Christmas dance, the highlight of the year. We learned to dance in the gym, boys and girls together, with the partition opened up. How the boys loved the Scottish country dances and the Viennese Waltz! What excitement there was! One, two, three, One, two, three. We may have been a 'good' year, but we didn't shine on the dance floor. We danced to an old-fashioned wind-up gramophone that had frequent hiccups.

We also had much more sophisticated dance practices - taken usually by Mr Frame, the PE teacher, or Arthur Naismith, a very superior senior pupil, allegedly in his seventh (some said eighth) year. We learned the modern waltz and the quickstep, and we even attempted the slow foxtrot. We also learned peculiar things like the Highland Schottisch, St Bernard's Waltz, etc. We got to know pupils from other classes and other years, so it was all very exciting. These hour-long practices were held at 4 o'clock on Friday afternoons in the weeks leading up to the dance.

Pre-war, the school dances had been very posh affairs, with the staff in evening dress; but during the war, getting any kind of dress for a dance was a problem. To this day, I can remember what I wore to each dance, as getting something new to wear was a great challenge.

Pupils came to the High School from quite far afield (from Shotts, Carluke, Cleland, and Hartwood), and they all travelled by bus. There was a good bus service even during the war; there were no 'specials', just the ordinary service. The attendance rate seemed to be high; and the further away from the school one lived, the more it was a point of honour to be there every day.

I don't remember any truancy. Well, that's not strictly true. One afternoon after the Highers, we bunked off to the school allotment, which was down near the golf course, on Wishaw Estate. We were, of course, found out, but all I can remember in the way of punishment was a mild reproof from Mr Clark, our Science teacher. We did spend occasional periods 'working' on the allotment officially, but we did very little work. The staff and some of the boys worked, the girls sunbathed.

When I was at the High School, great efforts were being made to raise money for the erection of a sports pavilion. Every class had a target, and every pupil had to make some sort of effort. I got my mother to bake empire biscuits, which I sold during the intervals. I can't remember when the sports pavilion was actually built. Indeed, it seems absurd that we had such a preoccupation at such a time.

You might think my memories of wartime at the High School would include sad moments like Dunkirk or the fall of Paris; but although I remember these events taking place, I don't remember them in relation to the school. Nor do I remember any tragedies - like pupils losing parents or other close relatives. I suppose we lived in our own little world, and to a youngster these events seemed infinitely remote.

The sketches are based on the recollections of James Dyer:

John Weir - nicknamed 'Boozy John'

Mary Mitchell - the Rector's secretary and a good friend to every lost or despondent pupil

'Tossy' Hyslop used to spit into a sink several yards from where he was standing, then order some unfortunate pupil to turn on the tap.

Ella Reddick – fast on her feet and quite a talker

Elsa Syme – blessed with a very friendly and supportive personality

Mamie and Abby Loudon had a long-standing feud with each other, which came to blows more than once on the school premises. Rumour had it that Mamie came out on top in the scratching and hair pulling duels, possibly because Abby was a much nicer person.

Sam Forrest – surprisingly courteous for a teacher of that era

Margaret Burns – congenial, as long as you didn't forget your homework

Dan Martin returned to the school after serving in the war. He was much respected by the boys because of his war service and, more trivially, because of the stylish manner in which he swung his briefcase.

Bobby Frame – distant and bored with the job

Maggie Coutts – demanding but very fair

Archie Nelson – very friendly, but not in the best of health

Dr Wilson – 'The Boss' with a strong physical resemblance, we all thought, to Hitler

Archie Leitch, aka 'Oscar' (for no apparent reason), had a tendency to become irritable (again, nobody knew why), if a boy appeared in his class wearing a kilt.

James Wilson was known as 'The Parson' by the younger pupils and as 'Papa' Wilson by the more mature students. During the 5 years I was taught by him, abject terror was gradually replaced by an appreciation of what a friendly man he was.

Johnnie Gass only remained a member of the English Department for a short time, possibly because he didn't get on very well with the principal teacher in that department, Maggie Coutts. On one occasion, she actually gave him a dressing-down in front of our English class for his failure to mark exam papers in what she considered to be a satisfactory manner.

Wishaw High School Staff (circa 1906)

166

Wishaw High School Staff (circa 1920)

Wishaw High School Staff (circa 1930)

Wishaw High School Staff (1940s)

Wishaw High School Staff (1950s)

Wishaw High School Staff (1971)

Wishaw High School Staff (1978-79)

Wishaw High School Staff (June 1992)

17

The Memorial Trust

By the beginning of 1946, both the High School and the FP Club had established funds to honour the memory of the eighty-seven former pupils who lost their lives in the service of their country during the Second World War. In May of that same year, a merger of the two funds (which amounted to almost £400) led to the creation of the Wishaw High School War Memorial Fund. Dr Wilson suggested that part of this fund should be used 'to erect an Honours List in the school hall in keeping with the one for the former pupils who fell in the First World War'; and that, 'as an additional memorial', the fund might also be used 'to purchase and equip new playing fields, of which the school and the FPs stood badly in need'.

The 'Honours List' took the form of a brass plaque, and was unveiled on 11 January 1948 by Mrs Linning, mother of one of the two former captains of the school who made the supreme sacrifice during the Second World War. A memorial service was conducted by the school chaplain, the Reverend D.C. Whitelaw, assisted by a former pupil of the school, the Reverend T.M. Philipps.

Various events were organised with a view to raising money for the War Memorial Fund: a school concert, an FP concert, a match between the school's under-18 football team and its counterpart at Our Lady's High School, an FP Bridge Drive and, in June 1949, a fête cum carnival. This featured a 'mini-museum' (compiled by Sam Curran and Derek Winton), in which there were not only models of ships, planes, and locomotives, but also miniature and period furniture; an 'Art Gallery'; 'Wonders of the World'; a marionette show; a film show; a shooting range; a wide range of stalls and sideshows (e.g. 'Snip It', 'Beat the Goalie', and 'Try Your Strength'); an ice cream stall; an American Tournament on the tennis courts; piano solos and duets (by Stanley Bruce and John Allan), which were broadcast from the hall; and an outdoor concert that included a Highland fling, a recitation, and various choral items. 'Teamwork was the key,' according to the *Wishaw Press*, 'and the team consisted of the pupils, the FPs, and the weather.'

Teamwork was also the theme of Dr Wilson's foreword in the 1949 edition of the school magazine:

This summer we have achieved a real unity. Teachers, parents, pupils, and former pupils all have one aim in view - and that is to raise a substantial sum to add to what we already have in the War Memorial Fund, so that we may acquire new playing fields for the school. It is a really delightful feeling that is engendered by the knowledge that everyone is working wholeheartedly for one very desirable object.

In February 1950, the executive committee of the War Memorial Fund was replaced by the Memorial Trust (such a change was required by law if land was to be purchased for new playing fields), and it was decided that the trust should comprise the Rector of the High School and his First Assistant, the School Convener, and the Convener of the FP Club. These four trustees were charged with the responsibility of purchasing a site for the new playing fields, the management of which was to be devolved to an executive committee consisting of six members of staff at the High School, six members of the FP Club, three members of the Education committee, and four members of the public with an interest in the playing fields.

In March 1950, the trustees purchased twenty acres of land on Wishaw Estate; the area in question was situated on one side of the low road to Cleland (between the Calder Bridge and Collyshot Mine), and was known locally as Deer Park. The trust planned to take possession of the site in May, but for some unspecified reason (or reasons) it didn't (or couldn't), and the Deer Park project came to nothing.

However, fund-raising in aid of the trust was still a priority for both the school and the FP Club: a Summer Fair (opened by Kathleen Garscadden, 'Aunt Kathleen' of *Children's Hour*) was held in August 1950 and a Garden Fête in June of the following year. The fête, which was declared open by Alec Finlay, featured country dancing, a military band, a mannequin parade, a display of matchbox covers by Tom Scoular, and a personal appearance by Comish Hunter (with his 'latest racing car'). The *Wishaw Press* reported the afternoon's activities under the headline: 'All Wishaw at the Fête - And the Sun Was There Too'. Almost £500 was raised for the Memorial Trust, an outcome that inspired Dr Wilson to declare: 'One of the finest things in life is to get a whole community working together for one object.'

In January 1952, thanks largely to the efforts of the School Convener, Edward Lawson, the Town Council agreed to 'transfer' (I take it this means 'lease') to the Memorial Trust 26 acres of land situated on the left hand side of the main road from Wishaw to Waterloo, and bounded on its other three sides by Greenhead Road, the Tinto housing scheme, and the new road leading from the A73 to the Wishaw Co-operative Society's creamery. This plot of land, according to the Director of Housing, was 'unstable and unfit for building thereon, as a consequence of mineral workings'.

The acquisition of a site was real progress, and it encouraged Dr Wilson to issue (in the foreword of the 1952 edition of the school magazine) 'a clarion call' to all pupils, former pupils, and friends of the High School 'to rally round and give their support to the Memorial Trust, so that the new playing fields would become not merely an ornament to Wishaw - by providing a handsome approach from the east - but also a credit to a grand old school that would soon be celebrating its jubilee'.

Later in the year, eighty pupils from the High School took part in a tree planting operation at the site of the new playing fields; and the Memorial Fund ('a chance for local patriotism to assert itself') was boosted by a Christmas Fair and the generosity of the trustees of Wishaw Cricket Club (defunct since 1913), who donated the funds of the club on condition that they were used by the Cricket Section of the FP Club, 'as and when the opportunity arose' at the Stewarton Street site.

In May 1952, the new playing fields - and the hall on the other side of the road, which was also part of the lease - were officially opened by Dr Wilson. Two minutes' silence was observed before the inaugural match between the FP Football Club and the school's under-18 team.

18

1946-1953: A Second Golden Age

In the 1946 edition of the school magazine, Dr Wilson enumerated the ways in which the Second World War had impacted on the physical surroundings of the High School - and also expressed some of his hopes for the future:

For the community housed by day in Dryburgh Road - as for the nation at large - reconstruction is a slow, wearisome, and (at times) depressing business. True, our staff is already back to pre-war strength; true, we have revived our swimming clubs. As we write, wire netting is being erected round the tennis courts, so this summer tennis will be less like the parlour game 'Hunt the Slipper'; and more light can now reach the eyes - if not the brains - of our pupils in the classrooms. But if we ask when our spray baths, which were spirited away on the 4th of September 1939, are returning, or when we are to get rid of the dangerous, decayed, and unsightly stairs at the back of the school (stairs that were never climbed purposefully save by unpunctual fire- watchers), A.R.P. answers, 'Manana'; if we ask when the dreary and depressing black paint with which our walls were adorned twelve years ago is to be replaced by something brighter and cleaner, Lanarkshire County Council says, 'Cras'.

Some day, we may find a plumber who can contrive to fill our dear lily pond with water that will not run away; some day, we may have a hockey pitch that is once again fit for playing hockey on; some day (to look to the more distant future), we may have a new tuck shop; some day, we may be able to deck our captains and prefects with badges of office; some day, also, that elusive Secondary Shield may adorn the hall where its younger Intermediate brother has been a familiar visitor - and if we can then add a flourishing rugby club to our extra-curricular activities, reconstruction will be well under way.

Meantime, we welcome the revival of the magazine as a portent of better and more spacious times than the last six years, and we hope that this edition will be the first of a lengthy new series.

The Sweet Smell of Success

Despite a brief renaissance in 1946, rugby never 'flourished' (due to the lack of a suitable field), and the problem of the disappearing water in the lily pond was never solved. However, some of Dr Wilson's other hopes were realised after varying lengths of time.

Between 1946 and 1953, the school magazine appeared at least once every year. In 1947 and 1948, two editions of the magazine were published - one in June and one in December.

When the resurrection of the school magazine was first mooted in 1946, 'the project,' according to the editor, 'languished and was in danger of dying from sheer inanition, when two young and enthusiastic members of staff, Messrs McBride and Quinn, came to the rescue, gingering up tardy contributors and undertaking the hunt for advertisements and the collection of orders from the pupils. The success of the magazine (1200 copies were sold within 24 hours of its becoming available) was due very largely to the spadework done by these two gentlemen.'

The foreword in the 1953 edition contained a significant announcement:

In the magazine itself, 1953 is the year of the New Deal. The pupils of a senior secondary school are destined to occupy positions of responsibility when their schooldays are over, and it is well that they should gain - at school - some experience in using their powers of initiative and invention. This magazine has been produced by a committee of pupils, with only a benevolent guiding hand from one or two of their elders. The production itself speaks for the success of the experiment.

The members of the committee were: from the 6th Year - D. Marks, A. Hepburn, and J. Cunningham; from the 5th Year - June Newlands, C. Wood, and W. Tannahill; from the 4th Year - J. Henry, Moira Stewart, B. McAlister, L. Graham, M. McPherson, J. Murdoch, and D. Cullens; and from the 3rdYear - J. McAlister and J. Arthur.

The school was 'redecorated' in 1948. A newly painted school is odds-on to be closed in the not too distant future, and in 1950 the High School did close...two weeks earlier than usual... for the summer holidays, which meant there was no concert.

In March 1950, the luncheon room, which was 'overtaxed' (450 meals were served every day, and since this necessitated three sittings, it was almost impossible to serve everybody in the hour-long lunch interval), was converted into an additional classroom; and the new canteen (with seating accommodation for 375 pupils) was opened. The following year, the new canteen served 14,000 meals in the space of six weeks.

Another conversion to be completed in 1950 was that of Kenilworth Park (on which football had been played for more than twenty years) into a hockey field for the High School.

In 1951 the school's under-18 football team won the Scottish Secondary Shield, a triumph that was the subject of the following report in the *Wishaw Press*:

On Monday evening, Wishaw High School played Albert Secondary, Coatbridge, in the final of the Secondary Shield at Broomfield Park, Airdrie. The teams lined up as follows:

Wishaw High School - J. Train; W. Shearer and W. Smith; G. Hunter, J. Robertson (captain), and J. Ross; D. Moffat, W. Brown, I. Hunter, J. Rodger, and J. Lumsden.

Albert Secondary - H. Mitchell; W. Findlay and A. Lammond; S. Price, I. Dow, and J. Roberts; J. Whitelaw, A. MacPherson, J. Dickie, F, Morrow, and J. McMaster.

It took the players some time to find their feet, and neither side was allowed to settle. Each appeared to have the same idea, and that was to keep their goal intact by getting rid of the ball whenever a difficulty arose.

Goalward thrusts by the shortest route were the main features of the play, but a steady Wishaw defence prevented anything of a really dangerous nature reaching their keeper.

Albert also stood up well to Wishaw's best efforts, and Mitchell gave every indication of being a reliable keeper: he held a fast drive from Rodger on the goal line, the best attempt at a goal in the first 20 minutes of the game. Soon afterwards, at the Wishaw end, MacPherson hit the side netting with a snap shot.

Then came the goal that won the match: Brown got possession from Shearer, and Albert were forced to concede a corner; the flag kick was taken by Moffat; an Albert defender misjudged his headed clearance and the ball fell at Rodger's feet; he had a clear opening and he scored from close in.

Wishaw fully deserved their first half lead, as they had done most of the pressing; but although they were strong and forceful, their left wing were inclined to hold on to the ball for too long.

There were no goals in the second half. Even so, Wishaw were again the more aggressive side, and on two occasions the Albert goal had a narrow escape.

Only once did Albert look like levelling the score; this was when McMaster, from well out, sent the ball past the far corner of the upright.

In the closing ten minutes, Wishaw were well in control, but they were unlucky with their finishing: I. Hunter shot just past the upright, and Moffat missed by the narrowest of margins - with a weak shot that the keeper failed to reach.

The final whistle said the Shield was Wishaw's, and the more enthusiastic of their supporters ran on to the field to congratulate the players.

Each side has played more impressively than they did on Monday night, and constructive play was at a premium. However, Wishaw, with their fast, forceful style, were the better side. All their forwards played well; G. Hunter, Robertson, and Ross had a tight grip on the opposition forwards; the full backs, Shearer and Smith, were steady, even though the former had the fastest player on the field to contend with on the occasions he eluded G. Hunter; Train in goal was reliable, but he had little to handle that was really dangerous.

The respective team managers - Mr J. Bonomy (Wishaw High School) and Mr W.S. MacDonald (Albert Secondary) - are both former Queen's Park players.

During the first half, a photographer took his stance behind the Wishaw goal; and he was also at the rear of the Wishaw net in the second half. He was an optimist.

The High School's supporters were conveyed to Airdrie in two double-deck buses, four single-deckers, and a fleet of private cars.

After the game, James A. Scott, President of the Scottish Secondary Schools' Football Association, presented the Secondary Shield to Dr Wilson in the pavilion. Dr Wilson said that his school had fought for it for many years, and that it was a great honour to finally win it. He thanked his team for the way in which they had played, and Mr Bonomy for his attention to their training and his valuable advice. "If Wishaw High School doesn't win the shield next year," he continued, "I hope Albert Secondary win it."

A big crowd gathered at the Fountain in Kenilworth Avenue to await the arrival of the shield and the High School team. The players were given an enthusiastic reception, and Robertson, the team's captain, had to comply with shouts of 'Speech'. Dr Wilson, who also made a short speech, expressed regret that A.J.C. Kerr, former Rector of the High School, had been prevented at the last minute from attending the match.

The victorious team, accompanied by a happy crowd of supporters, marched down the Main Street and up Dryburgh Road to the school. The following morning, pupils were given an opportunity to admire the shield when it was paraded round the classrooms.

In connection with the Secondary Shield Final, it is worth mentioning that Jim Rodger, inside left in the High School team, was a member of the St Mirren side that won the Scottish Cup in 1959; and that Archie MacPherson, the football pundit and commentator, played inside right for Albert.

It is evident from poems and articles in the school magazine during the 1940s that winning the Scottish Secondary Shield had assumed the same importance in the collective psyche of the High School as winning the SPL ten consecutive times assumed in the minds (for want of a more appropriate word) of the cretins who support Rangers. In 1951, when the school finally secured the Holy Grail, Eric Allan wrote the following poem for the magazine:

Not on the Shield But with It

The fortunes of the gallant one and ten,
Those strong and valiant High School men,
I sing, oh Muse, and so I humbly ask
For strength to carry out this mighty task.

From victory to victory they've proceeded,
To conquer Albert now is all that's needed.
On Broomfield's sward the battle will be fought,
To see if they will have the Shield or not.

Each warrior with the greatest care puts on
His blue and yellow armour, which has known
Fierce contests where was raised the battle-cry,
As when they struggled 'gainst Our Lady's High.

Boots for Achilles fit are girded on
The modern Achilles, Mrs Waddell's son.
I can't say whence they came: I realise
That I am not allowed to advertise.

And now the cry 'Fags out' they all await,
Which summons all the heroes to their fate.
Now out on the green turf the warriors run,
And Jove looks down and says, 'Now for some fun.'

Up in the grandstand, perched above the crowd,
Sphaeropode, guardian spirit, shouts aloud,
"Come oan, pit the heid oan 'em, ye lazy louts",
And for our heroes lustily she shouts.

Our gallants play 'mid shouts and clamour till
They notch a goal: the score is one to nil.
What things do Wishaw's heroes do this night,
Before they merge victorious from the fight.

And to the Fountain back they bring the booty,
Each warrior this night has done his duty.
Each hero's heart beats quickly in his breast,
As with delight upon ice cream they feast.

And none do suffer 'mid the joyful sounds:
The gentle Sphaeropode has healed their wounds.
I only wish the school had won it sooner,
Congratulations all, yours truly, Homer.

A Tight Situation

In the years immediately after the end of the Second World War, as more
and more pupils stayed on at school to complete the full five-year
secondary course (a development that was expedited by the Education
Committee's decision to provide free transport - to and from school - for
all pupils who resided more than three miles from the nearest appropriate
school), there was a steady increase in the roll of the High School. As
early as January 1946, 'the problem of accommodation became acute',
and Dr Wilson 'was forced to use every nook and corner in the building
to get sufficient classrooms'.

'The problem of accommodation' was exacerbated by the raising of
the school leaving age on 1 April 1947, and by January 1949 the roll had
shot up to a record-breaking 858. 'Every available corner,' Dr Wilson

reported, 'had to be utilised in the main building, and such places as the senior boys' room, the study, the darkroom, the Metalwork rooms, and the Science storeroom were in continual use. Even the sports pavilion had its turn - and there was a rumour that the furnace room had housed a class. With too many classes chasing after too few rooms, life was difficult.'

Horsas for Classes

Fortunately, the number of classrooms was increased by six with the erection (behind the main building) of two new prefabricated huts in the autumn of 1948. 'Although they are hardly artistic masterpieces,' Dr Wilson commented, 'they have almost solved the problem of accommodation, and in the depths of a Wishaw winter there are many less comfortable places around the school than the prefabs.'

In 1950 there were 878 pupils on the roll. Since there wasn't room for all of them in the hall, four classes assembled in the luncheon room every morning, and the hymns, prayers, readings, and announcements were relayed to them by means of the school's 'loudspeaker equipment'. Three years earlier, by the way, a microphone and an amplifier had been installed in the hall; and 'while these solved the problem of inaudibility,' to quote from an article by Percy Quinn in the school magazine, 'they raised a fresh difficulty, in that verbal errors, lack of preparation on the part of those reading the lessons, and the deep sighs of an overwrought heart were now painfully audible in all parts of the hall'.

In the early 1950s, as the demand for labour (especially in the thriving armaments sector) increased, "many of the school's promising pupils were absorbed into industry" when they reached the statutory school leaving age (which was now fifteen), and the school roll dropped well below 800. 'Full employment,' said Dr Wilson, 'means empty places in the classroom.'

Educational Priorities

This decrease in the roll (which obviously mitigated 'the problem of accommodation') was counterbalanced by the fact that additional rooms were needed in the Science, Technical, and Domestic Science Departments to cope with the expansion in the teaching of practical subjects, an expansion that was the inevitable consequence of a recommendation in the Report of the Advisory Council on Secondary

Education that pupils of average ability should be offered a much less academic curriculum.

Dr Wilson had reservations about this change of emphasis in the curriculum:

In concentrating on the needs of the many, there may be a danger of neglecting the few gifted ones who will be our future leaders in every sphere of life. However, we feel that so long as senior secondary schools are staffed with highly qualified teachers there is little danger that outstanding pupils will not get as good a chance as they have had hitherto.

One of Dr Wilson's 'outstanding pupils', David Eaton of Class 4, did not share his rector's rather elitist views:

At present, the course of study in most schools is designed to suit the minority of pupils - so the many are sacrificed for the few. Many lives are wasted so that a few lives may be successful. This is not 'the greatest good of the greatest number', but the greatest good for the minority - which is all wrong. Why should the majority of pupils be given a liberal education (which suits the requirements of a few), when they need a utilitarian education? What use is French to an engineer, or Latin to a sailor?

Selection Procedures

From 1951 onwards, the decision about whether or not a particular pupil should be admitted to the High School was made not by Dr Wilson (in conjunction with the headmaster of the relevant primary school), but by 'a judicial body known as the Promotions Board that operated from the neighbourhood of Glasgow' (as the good doctor rather sniffily described the new set-up). Continuing, uncharacteristically, in the same vein, he indicated that he would refrain from commenting on the new body until it had time 'to get over the errors of youth and inexperience'.

In an article he wrote for the *Wishaw Press* in July 1955, A.J.C. Kerr expressed an even stronger preference for the old selection system:

The method of promotion from primary to senior secondary schools was in my opinion superior to that now followed. The primary school headmasters sent in to the Director of Education lists of those recommended for a five-year course of secondary education. These lists were sent on to the headmasters of the senior secondary schools, who then conferred with the primary school headmasters and, in our case at any rate, agreed upon admissions without having to refer back to the

Director of Education. Nowadays, the headmasters of senior secondary schools have little or no say in the matter, and the decisions are made by a promotions committee that is influenced largely by the marks scored in intelligence tests, for which, unfortunately, many children are crammed by tutors - with the result that both they and their parents suffer from undue strain on their nerves in their final years at primary school.

The Staff

After the war, there was a significant improvement in the staffing situation (which, in the words of Dr Wilson, "brought about a reduction of the pressure on individual teachers, and an all-round improvement in the pupils' work"), and by 1950 the staff numbered fifty. One of those fifty was Pearl Gilchrist, a member of the English Department, who used to tell other teachers not to interrupt her in her room unless she was busy.

According to John Parton, who taught at the High School from 1945 onwards, Miss Mitchell, the Rector's secretary, was always very obliging, even though she did not enjoy very good health: 'She would break off from what she was working at to type out a reference for a teacher, or help him to balance the totals in his register.'

To Serve Them All My Days

The post-war years saw the retiral or departure (to fresh desks and blackboards new) of several long-serving members of staff:

Mrs McLean (who was replaced by Mrs Thomson) presided over the luncheon room and, latterly, the canteen. Pies seem to have featured pretty regularly on her menus, a fact that inspired the following rhyme:

> *Chapman's pies are the best,*
> *Cos in your belly they do rest.*
> *Chapman's pies are the worst,*
> *Cos in your belly they do burst.*

David Hair served in the Mathematics Department for nineteen years.

Peter Johnston (Principal Teacher of Music) 'produced delightful concerts that were certain to be remembered for a very long time'.

Rattray Ash (English) 'was largely responsible for the successful resuscitation of the FP Club'.

Maggie Coutts (English) was 'a strong personality, who made a lasting impression on the lives and thoughts of both her pupils and her professional colleagues'.

Tom Hamilton (Science) 'gave splendid service' to the school both academically and in the field of extra-curricular activities: he looked after the Junior football team and organised the school concert. He also carved his initials on one of the windows in the gents' staffroom.

John Weir (Principal Teacher of Geography) spent the whole of his teaching career (spanning forty years) at the High School. He was one of the first teachers in Scotland to present pupils for Higher and Lower Geography; and also one of the first to make use of such visual aids as the epidiascope and the film projector.

Jean Lawson's 'services were not confined to the Maths classroom. In that little room which will always be known as "Miss Lawson's room", she acted as school banker, looking after deposits in the local schools' savings bank and the sale of Savings Certificates - thus helping to inculcate in her pupils the peculiarly Scottish virtue of thrift.'

A New Certificate

In 1950 the Leaving Certificate was replaced by the Scottish Leaving Certificate. Dr Wilson was not impressed by this new certificate, which was awarded to all pupils who completed the five-year secondary course and achieved a pass in at least one subject at Lower Grade:

Session 1949-50 has seen the devaluation of the pound and the devaluation of the old leaving certificate. Whether the final devaluation of the former has now been completed we cannot say, but the Group Leaving Certificate, as we have known it for forty years, has gone for ever, and in future the criterion of a satisfactory secondary education will be not so much the possession of a leaving certificate as the possession of a good leaving certificate. We are glad to say that our senior pupils are, on their own initiative, adopting this new criterion.

Since it is impossible to establish with any accuracy how many pupils acquired 'a good leaving certificate', we must content ourselves with a few more accessible statistics: in 1950 fifty-seven pupils gained the Scottish Leaving Certificate; in 1951 pupils were presented (for the first time) in a new combination of subjects - Botany and Zoology - for Higher Science; in 1952 five departments achieved a pass rate of 100%; and in 1953 the school dux gained seven Highers and one Lower.

In the Glasgow University Bursary Competition, the most distinguished performances were:

1949: Charles Black (11th)
1953: Francis Gardner (12th)
1952: William Wilson (17th)
1948: Clara Gray (19th)

In a similar competition organised by St Andrews University, Ishbel Wilson came 36th in 1946.

In 1951 Sheena Howat was 44th (out of a total of 3,700 candidates) in the Civil Service (Clerical Classes) Examination.

In 1947 twenty High School pupils took part in an essay competition initiated by the Dickens Society: one of them (John Dickson) won a Certificate of Merit.

In 1950, to further encourage academic excellence, Colonel Hamilton, Master of Belhaven, presented the school with twenty-two medallions, one of which was awarded every year to the top pupil in History; and that same year, the trustees of the fund established to commemorate the services of John Lockhart to music in Wishaw provided a prize for distinction in Music.

Rain stops play.

In September 1945, a violent rainstorm washed away the surface of the hockey field, exposing the stones underneath and leaving such deep ruts that it was too dangerous to continue using it; for the rest of the season, therefore, the hockey teams had to play most of their matches away from home. However, this (far from) little local difficulty did not prevent the 1st XI from taking part in a tournament at Westerlands.

Another innovation was a match between the 1st XI and the staff 'in the presence of a record gallery. The staff team, consisting of five ladies and six gentlemen, played a surprisingly good game, and made the 1st XI fight hard for their narrow 2-1 win.'

In the course of session 1946-47, work began on the H.O.R.S.A. huts - on the site, unfortunately, of the hockey field. No hockey was played that season or during the three that succeeded it, with the exception of a match against Dalziel High School at Cleland Estate in December 1949.

Writing in the 1947 edition of the school magazine, Margaret Cranston, the 1st XI captain, claimed that pupils were beginning to lose interest in hockey - and that some of the younger ones hardly knew what the word 'hockey' meant. Rounders was actually provided as a substitute, but 'interest in this game proved to be not so great as people had expected'.

Lorries stop play.

The netball court became the second victim of the H.O.R.S.A huts project when its surface was torn up by the heavy lorries of the building contractors.

All (building) work and no play(ing fields) makes Jack an inactive boy.

The paucity of playing fields was targeted by Percy Quinn in the editorial he wrote for the 1947 edition of the school magazine:

With a school population of 800, it seems to us little short of farcical that one football field should be expected to suffice for our physical needs. We look cynically at the half-finished prefabs cluttering our erstwhile hockey pitch and wonder if some far-sighted official could not have forecast the present state of stagnation there - and delayed the start of building operations until enough material had been collected to finish the job within a reasonable time.

Trespassers stop play.

The shortage of playing fields worsened in the late autumn of 1948: Waverley was rendered unplayable ('unauthorised persons' trespassed on it when it was unfit for play, with the result that 'its surface was almost ruined') and, in the event, remained so for four years. School football matches had to be played at such venues as Waterloo, Houldsworth Park, Recreation Park (Wishaw Juniors' ground), and Victoria Park, Newmains; and in 1950, 1951, and 1952 the sports were held at Recreation Park.

Despite the problems arising from the non-availability of Waverley, football continued to flourish at the High School: Juvenile (under-13), Junior (under-14), and Post-Intermediate (under-16) teams were fielded for the first time in the school's history; and for brief spells during sessions 1949-50 and 1951-52, the school was able to run six teams.

At Intermediate level, the High School reached the final of the Anderson Cup in 1946 and the final of the Scottish Intermediate Shield in 1953, losing 0 - 3 in the latter to Our Lady's High School with the following team: J. O'Hara; W. McDougall and R. Carr; T. Lawson, W. Hunter, and H. Stevenson; H. Rattray, W. Reid (captain), D. Leiper, S. Reid, and A. Barr; and won the Lanarkshire League and the Larkhall Charity Cup in 1951.

The Post-Intermediate team (James Lumsden, Tom Muir, Charles Broadley, Ian Prentice, Bill Shearer, James Robertson, James Ross, Willie Brown, Ian Hunter, David Moffat, James Rodger, James Adams, Tom Prentice, and Billy Westwood) won the Lanarkshire League in season 1949-50 without losing a game.

In 1948 James Robertson, who was destined to captain the school's shield-winning team three years later, was capped for Scotland against England; and in 1953 Billy Reid represented his country against Wales and England.

Fresh Fields

In July 1948, the Schools and Schemes Sub-Committee of the Education Committee approved plans for a new hockey field, the drainage and returfing of Waverley, and the provision of a footpath from Kenilworth Avenue to the High School. It was 1949, however, before the new footpath (and access road) materialised; and 1950 before the new hockey field (formerly Kenilworth Park) was ready for use, and hockey reappeared on the sporting menu. By this time, 'the playing fields situation' (to quote Dr Wilson) 'had become almost desperate', and the new hockey field had to be used for netball, athletics, cricket, and football.

In October 1952, the 1st XI took part in a tournament organised by the West of Scotland Senior Hockey Association; in March 1953, an under-15 XI participated in a similar tournament held under the auspices of the West of Scotland Junior Hockey Association; and that same year, Murdostoun became the first winners of a cup presented to the school for inter-House competition at hockey.

Waverley was officially reopened in October 1952 with a match between the staff and the under-18 football team; and the sports returned to Waverley the following June.

Cricket, Lovely Cricket

'For the first time since 1937,' Dr Wilson announced at the prize- giving in 1950, 'cricket has been played at Wishaw High School. A wicket of sorts has been improvised on the new hockey pitch, and House matches (which aroused remarkable interest and enthusiasm) have been carried through. The rebirth of cricket at the school has stirred the blood of many former Wishaw cricketers, and help has been offered most generously: for instance, a most pleasing gesture was the gift from Mr Oliver Wassell of a silver-mounted cricket ball (won by Wishaw Cricket Club in 1890) for inter-House competition.' For the record, Allanton were the first winners of this unusual trophy.

The following year, according to Dr Wilson, 'cricket took a firm hold and a considerable list of fixtures was carried through'; one of them was a 22-overs match between the school team and an FP XI that resulted in a win for the former by 5 runs. At an individual level, W. Shearer, W. Gibb, and W. Court were awarded their colours.

In 1952 Angus Dick and C. Weir topped the batting and bowling averages respectively. The standard of play was described in the school magazine as 'high', and 'this happy state of affairs was in no small measure due to the coaching of Mr Angus McIntosh, though it should be noted that Messrs Clark and Benwick also took an interest in the fortunes of the cricket team'. Cricket at the High School received another boost when an anonymous donor presented the school with a cup for inter-House competition at junior level.

At the District Sports, the High School won the Brownlee Cup in 1950 and 1951, and the Fortissat Cup in 1952 (these cups were awarded for the best team performance at intermediate and senior level respectively); at the County Sports, Ian Hunter won the under-16 880yds in 1948; and at the Scottish Schools' Athletics Championships, the intermediate relay team gained bronze medals in 1951.

The swimming gala and the school golf championship continued to be held every year. The gala was split into two sections: boys' events one week, girls' events a week later. Murdostoun won the inter-House swimming championship (and with it the Nimmo Cup) in 1946 and 1947. Kenneth Mackenzie, who won the Rusk Cup in the inter-schools event at a gala organised by Motherwell Swimming Club in June 1946, was the most outstanding swimmer produced by the High School in the post-war years.

In 1947 a golf match was arranged (at Bellshill Golf Club) between the staff and the pupils, the result of which was a narrow victory for the staff; in 1949 G.N. Pomphrey, the School Convener, presented the school with a medal for the winner of the golf championship (the first recipient of this medal was James Haig); and in 1953 Martin Shaw won the County Golf Championship.

Silence is become their mother tongue.

Oliver Goldsmith, *The Good-Natured Man (adapted)*

The Literary and Debating Society was revived in 1946. Dr Wilson was delighted, and he explained why:

Wishaw High School has produced many fine scholars and has had classes with numbers of very distinguished pupils in them; yet, visiting inspectors have all had the same tale to tell of how difficult it was to get even the best of them to express themselves in a 'viva voce' examination. Perhaps it is the strong cult of Mathematics in the school that has produced the hesitation to express an answer in words unless the answerer is absolutely certain of his accuracy. More probably, it is due to the lack of experience in public speaking, experience that may be acquired in a debating society.

In 1948 the Literary and Debating Society's calendar included a talk on carols by Peter Johnston, ex-Principal Teacher of Music at the High School; a Hat Night; two inter-school debates (with Dalziel High School providing the opposition); an analysis of the National Health Service by Dr Peacock; and a debate on the respective merits of liberal and vocational education.

First-aid and nursing classes were held every year until the late 1940s. In June 1946, the nursing class was treated to a lecture and a film, both of which had been arranged by the Ministry of Labour and Information as part of its campaign to attract girls into the nursing profession.

In 1950 an Arts Club and a Film Society were established. Talks on 'Educational Psychology' and 'A Trip to Denmark' were given to the members of the Arts Club, who also attended two concerts in the St Andrew's Halls featuring the Scottish Orchestra. The Film Society (membership cost 2/6) met six times per session, and among the films shown were *Goodbye Mr Chips* and *Mr Deeds Goes to Town*. During session 1952-53, Wishaw Film Society transferred its surplus funds (amounting to more than £27) to the High School's Film Society.

In the late 1940s, Henry Cocozza, a former pupil of the High School (and a talented film director in his own right, who won the premier award at the Scottish Amateur Film Festival for his surrealist film, *Phantasmagoria*), arranged special showings of such films as *Henry V* and *Pride and Prejudice* for the senior pupils.

In May 1951, a branch of the Scripture Union was formed at the High School; and by 1953, there were 125 members, with the juniors (Classes 1-3) meeting on Tuesdays and the seniors (classes 4- 6) on Thursdays. Miss McPhail 'capably and willingly conducted the meetings' and Dr Wilson himself took a keen interest.

In January 1952, a Philatelic Society (the first meeting of which attracted twenty pupils) was added to the list of extra-curricular activities; and the following year, 'the merry piping of the newly formed Recorder Society could be heard after 4 o'clock most Friday afternoons'.

The Dancing Years

The Christmas parties and dances were still two of the most popular events in the school year. According to the school magazine:
At the 1st and 2nd Year parties, the unrestrained fervour and uninhibited behaviour at "ladies' choice" dances were in marked contrast to the demure conduct of the would-be sophisticates of the upper school. The standard of performance on the floor was eloquent tribute to the painstaking coaching of Mr Frame and Miss Loudon, although an occasional 'butterfly' or 'eel' made manifest the subversive teachings of Mr Victor Sylvester; and in certain sets of eightsome reels strong local patriotism and 'colloquialisms' crept into the renderings, in spite of Mr Frame's stern eye upon the 'heretics'.

Salve, regina...

1953 was Coronation Year. In the course of the year, a Coronation Staff Dance was held in the school hall; the school captains, Agnes Hepburn and Derrick Marks, took part in a Coronation Tree Planting ceremony at King George V field; the pupils attended special showings of *A Queen is Crowned* at The Cinema; and (in June) there was a Coronation Year Concert. The *Wishaw Press's* report on this 'unique show' was as follows:

The concert, in which more than 150 pupils and a third of the staff were directly involved, fell into two main parts - a one-act play, 'Dark Brown', by Philip Johnson and a historical pageant ('Qui Non Proficit Deficit') composed and written by members of the History Department.

In the latter, there was scope for high drama and broad humour, for tragedy and light comedy - all artistically produced by the English and History Departments. The verse-speaking of the girl commentator who linked the items deserves special mention.

The Music Department provided sixteenth-century French songs, eighteenth-century pastorals and magnificent choral items - together with a varied collection of such instruments as bagpipes, pianos, trumpets, mandolins, accordions, and recorders.

The PE and Commercial Departments arranged Scottish country dances, English folk dances, and tap dances with precision and gaiety.

Pupils from the Art Department, supervised by their teachers, produced scenery and costumes in immense profusion - and with fine skill.

Other departments tackled the problems of more than adequately staging the show in a hall inadequate for such a production, and of dealing with all the administrative matters that accompany such a venture.

Altogether, it was a concert to be enjoyed, a concert in which a great deal of hard work had been deftly concealed in order to produce an air of sparkling spontaneity.

Capital Excursions

In July 1952, forty pupils from the 4th, 5th, and 6th Year spent a week in Paris; a week in Clermont Ferrand, during which they gave displays of Highland and country dancing; and two days in London, during which they visited the House of Commons. In the course of this visit, they met the two local MPs, one of whom, Alex Anderson, taught at the High School in the 1940s.

Nearer home, a wide variety of trips was arranged in the late 1940s and early 1950s: Classes IB, 1C, and 2Q climbed Tinto in June 1947; and different groups of pupils attended performances or showings of *The Barber of Seville* (Theatre Royal), *Hamlet* (The Cosmo), *Macbeth* (The Citizens), *The Thrie Estaits* (St Andrews Halls), and *Ivanhoe* (The Picture House).

Oh I get by with a little help from my friends...

Lennon and McCartney

'Nowadays,' Dr Wilson wrote in the foreword of the 1952 edition of the school magazine, 'most secondary schools have a Parent-Teacher Association that helps to further mutual understanding. We take the opportunity, through the pages of this magazine, to suggest that if there is any desire on the part of parents and friends to form a closer partnership with the staff, it will be warmly welcomed as an aid not only towards the solution of the financial problem of equipping the new playing fields in a way that will be worthy of the school, but also towards cementing friendship between parents and teaching staff and enlisting all possible agencies to further the interests of the pupils.'

Six months later, the Memorial Trust called a meeting of the parents of all the pupils at the High School in order to enlist their support for the new playing fields project; and to enable them to provide this support the parents formed an association at the same meeting.

The first event (a whist drive) to be organised by the Parents' Association took place in November 1952 and was attended by 200 parents and friends; the first ordinary meeting of the Association (at which a certain Mr Shepherd was elected president) was also held in November, and was addressed by two members of the Dalziel High School Parents' Association.

The following year, the committee of the Parents' Association expended a lot of time and effort drumming up support for the association, especially from the parents of new entrants. On the social side, a whist drive was held every week in Dimsdale Hall.

Risorgimento

At a committee meeting in January 1948 - since there was unanimous agreement that the first concern of the FP Club should be to ensure that it was run efficiently ('By building a firm foundation,' Dr Wilson proclaimed, 'we shall in time reach heights that will make Mount Everest, or at least Tinto, look like molehills') - the committee authorised the printing of membership cards (the cards, which had to be produced at all FP functions, were eventually distributed in April). Members of the club were also urged to ask all the former pupils they knew (or met by chance),

194

'Have you joined the FP Club yet?'; and if the answer was, 'No', to inquire, 'Why not?' By the end of the year, 340 former pupils had joined the FP Club.

As far as recruiting new members was concerned, it was obviously in the interests of the FP Club to establish close ties with the High School: so the club welcomed the chance to provide a supplement to the April edition of the school magazine. The supplement began with a statement to the effect that the FPs were 'proud' to have been accepted as part of the school, and that 'Thank goodness he or she has left' was not their epitaph. This was followed by articles from FPs in Canada, Japan, and Palestine - and a News Column:

Back from South Africa is Willie Grant. After a year when rain fell on only three occasions, he still thinks Wishaw is the best place in the world.
Jimmy (Ramoo) Kerr is in China, where he is an Inspecting Officer with Chinese Customs. Chasing pirates is a far cry from chasing a football on Waverley Field, but we hope Jimmy shows the same skill nowadays.
Maurice Thomson, married and a Surgeon Commander in the Royal Navy, specialises in tropical diseases, and he will be going to Singapore to continue his study of the effects of various bug- bites. Why not Arran, Maurice?
Peter Paterson, the school's first schoolboy international, is Controller at St Helier Airport, Jersey.
Our good wishes go to Joe Hardie in his new charge at Trinity Church, Irvine.

At a Special General Meeting in May, a new constitution (one clause in which gave an assurance that members would receive a free copy of the school magazine) was ratified; and it was also decided that life membership of the club should be available at a cost of one guinea (the annual membership fee was 2/6).

The school captains acted as unofficial liaison officers between the school and the FP Club, and at the end of session 1949-50 Jeanette Taylor and Tom Prentice received the following accolade: "They have not only shown much interest in the club's functions but have also been responsible for ensuring that pupils leaving school are aware of the opportunities provided by the club to renew the friendships they established at school."

Success Story

The FP Club reached its zenith during the late 1940s and early 1950s, and a tremendously wide range of social and sporting activities was organised under its auspices: dances, rambles, quizzes (FPs v members of staff at the High School; or one section of the club pitted against another), debates, Brains Trusts (before 'small but appreciative audiences'), bus runs, theatre outings, tennis, netball, badminton, table tennis, chess, bridge (in 1953 the FPs topped the 2nd Division of the Lanarkshire Bridge League), choral practices, carol singing, gramophone nights, keep-fit classes, and country dancing ('usually, the only male member in attendance was the pianist').

There was also an FP orchestra, the first public appearance of which was at Hamilton Town Hall in February 1949, when it provided the incidental music for a performance of *Tobias and the Angel* by the Little Theatre Group.

In March 1948, a meeting was held with a view to forming an FP hockey team; consequent on this meeting a friendly match was arranged against Dalziel High School FPs. The following year, the High School FPs played on a full-size field for the first time - at Hamilton against the Academy FPs' 2nd XI; and in November 1950, they played their first game in the Scottish Women's Hockey League (a game that ended in a 5-0 victory over Barr and Stroud). By 1951, the FP hockey club was strong enough to run two teams - and, more significantly, it had already won the league championship.

The FP football club was also strong enough to field two teams in the FP leagues. One of the club's matches (against Neilstonians) inspired the following headline in the *Wishaw Press*: 'Twelve Saw High School Win' Every Saturday, in addition to putting at least one of its pitches at Cleland Estate at the FPs' disposal, Dalziel High School provided transport from Carfin Cross and post-match teas.

Surprisingly, the athletics club (arguably the most dynamic section of the FP Club before the War) was not resurrected during this golden age of FP activity.

There was regular coverage of all the activities of the FP Club in the *Wishaw Press*; there was even a series of short articles on 'Club Personalities'. These included 'Big Davie' McAinsh, the club's secretary; Margaret Anderson ('the "General Factotum", but not by any means "Largo"'); and the convener, Walter Moonie, whose 'smiling and bespectacled face was in evidence at such varying activities as hockey matches and quiz nights, and whose good nature ensured that discussion at committee meetings did not descend to argument and quarrel'.

We, at the height, are ready to decline.

Shakespeare, *Julius Caesar*

By 1953, for some inexplicable reason (or reasons), the FP Club was on the wane: the tennis, netball, and badminton sections had either been temporarily or permanently disbanded; and at the AGM in April, the convener announced 'a substantial decrease in general membership' (there were only thirty-three life members and fifty-five ordinary members). In an effort to boost these numbers, the constitution of the Club was amended in such a way as to allow former members to retain their membership.

The Beautiful Game

In November 1947, in the gym, Wilson Humphries of Motherwell FC gave a talk on football.

Alive and Well and Living (Now) in Girvan

By the end of 1947, A.J.C. Kerr was living in Girvan. His energy and sense of civic duty were undiminished: he was Convener of the Attraction Committee (Children's Section), President of the Old Men's Club, and the After Care Officer for ex-members of the armed forces in the South West of Scotland.

Masterclass

In October 1949, Class 2A took part in a demonstration lesson staged by Peter Johnston (back at the High School as Principal Teacher of Music after a spell as Organiser of Music for the County of Lanark) at Motherwell Central School. The aim of the lesson was to teach the pupils, with the aid of slides and a film, how to identify the instruments of a conventional orchestra by sight and sound.

You Ain't Heard Nothing Yet

In session 1949-50, with assistance from the Education Committee, the school purchased a gramophone (for the Modern Languages Department) and a Bell and Howell sound projector.

Top of the Form

In October 1952, at Motherwell Town Hall, the High School and Dalziel High School took part in two quizzes (one for senior pupils, one for juniors) sponsored by the *Evening Citizen*. The High School teams included Anne Donnelly and Derrick Marks (who went on to have a distinguished career in local government - and who is currently Commissioner for Local Administration in Scotland), but Dalziel were victorious in both contests.

Boundary Changes

During session 1952-53, a slight alteration was made in the alphabetical boundary between Coltness and Murdostoun, so that pupils would be more evenly divided between these two Houses.

Chimney on Fire Stops Match

Such was the headline in the *Wishaw Press* on 16 January 1953. The match in question took place at the Welfare Park in Motherwell and involved the under-18 teams of the High School and Our Lady's High School. 'With ten minutes to go, Our Lady's were winning 7-1. Suddenly, as the wind changed direction, volumes of smoke were carried across the pitch, and at one point not a single one of the 22 players could be seen.'

> **Immortales mortales si foret fas flere,**
> **Flerent divae Camenae Naevium poetam...**
>
> Naevius

In the article he wrote about the High School for the SSTA Magazine in 1953, Alf Dubber, Principal Teacher of English, drew his readers' attention to the premature death (in 1946) of William Jeffrey, a former pupil of the school, whom he described as 'a brilliant journalist on the staff of the *Glasgow Herald*, and a poet whose genius is only now beginning to be viewed in proper perspective'.

19

The School Magazine (1946-1953)

On Being Late One Day for School

On being late, one day, for school
The teacher said, "You silly fool,
Hold out your hand and make it snappy,
You'll soon be feeling far from happy."

Mary Finlay (3C)

Just Imagine

Just imagine that Scottish Shield,
Won by our team on Hampden Field,
Displayed in hall for all to see –
And oh how happy I would be!
Just imagine if this poor ode,
Though not by Pope, nor yet by Joad,
Is printed here where all may see —
And oh how happy I would be!

David Nardone (4C)

The Stranger

He came one dark, cold, wintry night. He had no teeth, was practically bald, and had a wrinkled countenance. Every time he called, mother hastened to attend to him - and I felt utterly neglected. When I entered the room, he stared at me with small, curious eyes, and I realised that I was bitterly jealous of him. Before he came to stay with us, mother would buy me all that I wanted; but this has changed, and now she does everything possible to please him - not me.

Now I love him as much as mother. Why? Because he is my baby brother.

Andrew Gavin (2Q)

The Hall

The hall is such a spacious place
That every pupil has to face.
We may all sing and pray in there,
But talk we must not dare.
The special notes are given there,
But little do we care
About the hockey and football.
Played solely by seniors all.

Jean Smith (1Q)

Pedagogues on Trial

An ideal teacher, then, should be one who can discipline his pupils
without Orbilian severity and elicit the best work from them all - not
merely from the intellectual ones. He should also have a sense of humour,
know his subject extremely well, and be able to inspire his pupils to like
it and wish to excel in it. Another mark of a good teacher is that his pupils
acquire without effort the ability to use their intelligence - and to think
for themselves when tackling the problems, mathematical or otherwise,
that occur during their school career - and retain this ability in later life.
Also, no teacher who is not just, conscientious, and fair can ever be
wholly successful.

M. Wilson (Class 6)

Homework Palace

Whatever the faults of our teachers, we must give them credit for their
generosity - in dishing out homework. No matter how much or how little
is given to any class, many pupils prefer the cloakroom to the table at
home when it comes to doing homework. Whether this is due to crying
babies or steady girlfriends I do not know, but doubtless there are reasons.

A Patron (3C)

The Burning Bush

When cigarettes went up a shilling,
To pay this price boys were not willing.
The burning bush went out that day,
The reason was boys could not pay.
To Mr Dalton they did write,
To tell him of their awful plight.
The burning bush is still quite black,
Because they got no answer back.

Willie Stewart (3D)

The School's Super Senior Soccer Side

Heartbroken, back-broken Allan plays in goal,
Each week the crowd threatens to dig him a hole;
But game after game he comes out again,
The best in the team but for just other ten.

With 'Piggie' and 'Prof' the defence is complete,
Both of them need a hard kick in the seat.
Their breathtaking dribbles and beautiful swerves
Have made our poor goalie a bundle of nerves.

The halfbacks are 'Scootsie', 'Norrie', and 'Joe',
Who prove every week that a snail isn't slow.
They play in defence as they play in attack –
No wonder poor Allan has such a sore back.

The forwards, however, are equally bad,
They cannot score goals and their efforts are sad.
They kick the ball hard and they kick the ball far,
But it always comes back after hitting the bar.

Out on the right wing play 'Stan' and 'Rodge',
Past all opponents they know how to dodge;
But they have a fault, although very small:
They always forget to remember the ball.

Our star centre forward's not Lawton, just 'Pete',
He would be quite good, but he can't keep his feet.
When 'Pete' and the back are both in a race,
The back hits the ball, and the ground hits "Pete's" face.

The left wing consists of 'Jimmy' and 'Kit',
Their teamwork is clever, one must admit;
But however nifty their tactics may seem,
We always see better in some other teams.

Our loyal supporters must be insane:
Both turn out to see us in hail, snow, and rain.
One is big 'Baxy', the other wee 'Andy',
Who often as linesman has made himself handy.

In the league we're the strongest, though out of the cup,
For the team at the bottom holds all the rest up;
But this team, on the whole, is quite a dead loss,
In spite of the efforts of W.L. Ross.

Goalkeeper, Net-Boy, and Critic

A Seasonal Complaint

A new disease has broken out in Wishaw High School. Everyone, in consequence, is walking about with a strained look on their face.

In the corridor, I hear such sentences as, 'Oh dear, 20 for Maths, 20 for History, 30 for Geography...' 'Strange,' I muse, staring after the retreating figure. 'Perhaps she is going to buy some Christmas cards for her Maths teachers...but twenty's rather many.'

Just then a teacher comes out of the staffroom with a bundle of papers under his arm and a frown on his usually pleasant face. I hear him mutter under his breath, 'Disgusting...atrocious.'

I turn round to see my best friend rushing towards me. Her hair is very dishevelled, and she has a strange look on her face. 'Oh dear,' she says, 'Maths, nothing; Bookkeeping, nothing. No marks...no marks.' Then she stops, with a hysterical laugh. I rush her off to the washbasins, where I make certain she has a long drink of water.

When she has fully recovered, I lead her into the classroom and sit her down on my case. "There, there," I say, "you'll soon be all right." A group of girls is standing quite near us and I hear one of them say, "We got our English back this morning. I've passed, I've actually passed. I got 51."

Enlightenment dawns on me at last. It is not St Vitus's dance that is making everybody jump in the air or pull out their hair by the roots. It is just a trifling disease known to quite a few schools at present, and its name is examinitis.

Joan Adam (4P)

Autres Temps, Autres Moeurs

This modern age has perhaps the greatest claim to the title 'The Age of Reason'. It is a practical age; we are a practical people, ruled by practical statesmen striving for a practical objective - efficiency in the running of an exceedingly complex community. Such undiluted materialism is reflected in all aspects of modern life, and nowhere is its influence greater than in the field of education.

The state has for some time past deemed it necessary to control, to some extent, the provision of education and the type of subjects to be taught in schools. This has resulted in a radical change in the nature and content of the school curriculum. The leisurely life of study, the quiet search for truth that was the basis of the aristocratic student tradition in the days before the Industrial Revolution...both have become as antiquated as the life led by Miss Austen's characters. The Grand Tour has gone, along with sailing ships and horse-drawn carriages; the humanities have been replaced by the study of the sciences for practical purposes. In the studies of the modern youth, there is no searching after truth for truth's sake.

There has been no attempt in modern educational policy to restore the balance between our knowledge of science and our moral capacity to control it. Rather, the modern system aggravates the imbalance, and if things continue as they are, we may see the swamping of all our ethical standards.

The modern mind can be regimented to a high degree of efficiency for the complex scientific life, but it cannot be invested with individuality by an educational system that favours the practical subjects in the curriculum. The altruistic motives of earlier times, which resulted in free education, have been abandoned, and today education is used, even by the representatives of the people, to increase the productivity and efficiency of the proletariat. Education is being used by them to organise - and improve - the civilised community for practical ends.

So far, the outcome of this policy has been disappointing; its future implications are terrifying. The age of materialism is doomed before it becomes fully operative, and General Omar Bradley has explained why:

'We have too many men of science, too few men of God. We have grasped the mystery of the atom and rejected the Sermon on the Mount. Man is stumbling blindly through spiritual darkness, while toying with the precarious secrets of life and death. The world has achieved brilliance without wisdom, power without conscience. Ours is a world of nuclear giants and ethical infants.'

The education of today produces the philosophy of tomorrow, and that philosophy will continue to be materialism. It is only by radical changes of policy in the field of education that a fuller life can be assured in the future.

John Dickson (Class 6)

If winter comes...

The snowdrop lifts its head
And shyly looks around,
A crocus smiles nearby and says,
"It's pleasant above ground."
A rabbit runs across the grass,
A bird begins to sing,
A butterfly comes fluttering past —
And suddenly it's spring.

Margaret Gibb (2R)

Abandon hope...

So you're new to Wishaw High School, are you? Like me to show you around? You would? Splendid!

I'm sorry, dear, I didn't mean to frighten you. Did it really look like a frightening leer? It was meant to be a smile of welcome.

205

This object is the top gate, and it is an obstacle designed to prevent you from playing hockey on Saturdays. However, it does open sometimes: I went through it – rather than over it - once myself.

The spikes aren't really very sharp. Excuse my limp, won't you. Here, I'll help you down. Notice the marvellous vista of two counties. The far one is the football field.

This one, dear? No, it's not our private beach; it's the hockey pitch. Here, we daren't tell each other to go and eat coke.

Are you a good runner? You are? Good! You'll be able to run round the pitches three times a day. And when you're really fit, you'll have the privilege of gaining a few bruises.

This is our private forest. Not many trees, I admit, but the teachers say there's plenty of wood in the school. I really don't know what they mean by that.

No, you silly child, that isn't a housing scheme. These are our prefabs. Good things too: they give you a break between lessons. I'm always hoping I'll have a brainstorm one day and end up at home instead of in Room 40.

What's this for? For posting letters? Of course not! That's for our waste paper. Remember, we don't really need a trail of orange peel to your home. Your name, address, and all the details of your murky past are safely in the administration block.

What's that? The office, of course.

Here we are inside the noble edifice itself. Don't let the air of cleanliness upset you. These are the Domestic Science rooms, where the girls bake their cake and eat it - at their own risk.

This is where you hang your clothes - if you're clever enough to reach fourth year, when you're allowed in as a special privilege. Now, up the marble staircase.

On this floor, ladies and gentlemen, we find test tubes and T- squares and skeletons. What's that, dear? Those people? No, they aren't the skeletons I meant. They're in Coltness.

Down the other marble staircase. Pay no attention to that deafening noise, dear: the animals are being fed.

You say you want to go home? You aren't coming back? But it's not as bad as that. Honestly, it isn't.

No, it's not a frightening leer; it's a sympathetic smile.

Hey, come back...come back...

Berra McAlister (Class 4)

The Still of the Night

It is evening. A gentle breeze fans the topmost branches of the trees. In the distance a dog barks, but silence reigns in the woods and the sleepy village until an owl hoots suddenly from the ivy-covered clock tower. Then silence is restored.

Having changed imperceptibly from a delicate pink to a pale red, the sky now turns orange as the sun sinks to rest behind the misty hills. Nothing can be heard in the clear air save the faint, gentle bleating of sheep high up on the slopes of the hill. The sky has now become dark blue, like a sable cloak studded with myriad, glittering precious stones.

Down by the river a partridge stirs, calling to its mate as the gentle zephyr dies away and the moon creeps out in all her silver splendour from behind the treetops. Everything is bathed in a clear, cold light.

The river babbles on through the reeds, over the shingle and under the old wooden bridge. Down through the drowsy valley it flows, whispering to the bulrushes and laughing at the mayflies hovering just above its surface.

Up in the marsh, a frog croaks and an answering croak comes from the fens.

Now the moon is high in the heavens. A slight breeze ruffles the tall blades of grass in the fields. Again a dog barks sharply in the distance. It is night.

E Simpson (2B)

Evening Falls

Softly across the summ'ry woods and fields
The dim, diaphanous veil of evening falls
Lightly – the throats of all the songbirds sealed
In slumber, save the curlew's plaintive calls.

Only the upper reaches of the wooded heights,
Mottled with fresh green beech and sombre pine,

Are bathed in pools of aureate light,
Suffusèd with a radiance quite divine.

The tranquil beauty of the darkening sky
Is flecked with clouds of roseate hue,
Long, trailing wisps of opalescent fire,
Glinting with pink and sapphire blue.

The dew lies dank on all the orchard slopes,
Large diamond drops on blossom misty white;
Beneath the branches flit the ghostly moths,
The dusky landscape wrapt in velvet night.

Thelma C. Paterson (6th Year)

AUGEANTICS

Bring blocks of ice to cool their fevered brow,
Brew cups of tea, and don't disturb them now.
Their mien is grim and fraught with care,
Their fingers intertwined with straggling hair.
All the house in fear and trembling goes,
And family pets proceed on careful toes.
Demented groans disturb the silent house,
Affrighting most the timid, creeping mouse,
Who, setting out to leave his shelt'ring hole,
Now stops and trembles in his inmost soul.
An anguished cry disturbs the placid air;
The night departs; the rosy dawn doth break;
The world is fresh, and Nature's now awake.
But still their frantic effort they prolong,
No heed is paid to rising sun or young birds' song.
What horrid torment makes them cry out so?
Why must their frantic hands be on the go?
Have they committed some appalling crime,
And now must suffer till the end of time?
What is the mystery that surrounds them there?
What inward anguish makes them stoop with care?
Draw near, my friends, while I confide in you:
These are no criminals with aught to rue,

But harmless creatures knowing not disgrace,
Though wild of eye, distraught, and pale of face.
Their woes have been imposed by brutal rule,
Whose strict enforcement agitates their school.
The reason why their weary fingers lag?
Their task? They must write something for the mag.

Sally Lawson (4A)

Open Letter to Bus Companies

Dear Sirs,

As a member of the long-suffering travelling public, I would like to bring to your attention a few suggestions that might lead to an improvement in the design of your buses.

First of all, the bus must be capable of getting from A to B in a reasonable time without undue lateral or vertical movement.

Secondly, it should have seats that can accommodate two persons of average size - as opposed to one and a half, the number currently prescribed. Moreover, the seats should be designed in such a way that they do not corrugate the passengers.

With regards to descending from the upper to the lower deck, I would like someone to devise a means of carrying out this simple action that did not necessitate a nosedive with pike and spiral.

Still on the subject of the upper deck: there should be enough headroom to enable a person of average height to walk upright along it without running the risk of denting the roof, or his cranium, or both.

I hope that these few suggestions will be implemented in the buses of the future.

Yours faithfully
W.M. Brown (3A)

'...a well-graced actor leaves the stage...'

Shakespeare, *Richard II*

Dr Wilson retired on 15 October 1953. To mark his retiral, he received a crystal vase from the Parents' Association, golf balls from the canteen staff, a golf bag, two golf clubs and a caddie car from the pupils, and a cheque from the FPs that enabled him to purchase a nest of tables and a fireside chair; and at his retiral dinner in the Crown Hotel, the staff presented him with a television set.

What manner of man was he?

In the course of his speech at the aforementioned retiral dinner, J.T. Wilson, First Assistant at the High School, enumerated Dr Wilson's personal qualities: trustworthiness ('His word is truly his bond and his promise is sure of fulfilment'); a strong sense of honour ('A man of honour himself, he treats others as honourable men, a line of conduct that prompts them to give of their best and fosters harmony and cooperation'); innate modesty ('While he is ever ready to recognise the merits of others, he is never heard making claims for himself; and although I have known him for nearly thirty years, I have never heard him refer to his own splendid career, with the result that it is only in the last month or two that I have learned how notable it was'); unfailing courtesy ('He is willing to listen to everybody's point of view, and insofar as he has shown the patience of Job in his rectorship here, he may be said to have suffered fools gladly'). To this list one could justifiably add thoughtfulness, a quality that manifested itself in the invitations he extended to A.J.C. Kerr to attend various school events. 'These have really invigorated me,' said the great man.

Speaking at the same function, Edward Lawson, the School Convener, highlighted Dr Wilson's 'high Christian principles': 'Throughout his career in public life, he has endeavoured to help those who are in most need of help.'

Sheila Sprot, who attended the High School in the 1940s, describes Dr Wilson as 'tall and thin, and rather hawklike'. 'Shy and remote,' she continues, 'he was the kind of person I suspect no one knew very well.

He had a charming wife (she was a very good pianist), and a daughter who was a bit younger than me. He went to the same church as I did, and he sat in the pew immediately in front of the one where I normally sat; he always sat side-on (as though he was deaf in one ear), so I was always in his line of vision - and therefore had to be on my best behaviour all the time.'

Neil McKellar, Dr Wilson's successor as Rector of the High School, paid the following tribute to him in *The Octagon*:

He was a simple, kindly man of unbounded sympathy and understanding. Though he rejoiced at the material successes gained by the school during his period of office, nothing gave him greater pleasure than the opportunities that office gave him to help any boy or girl, or any professional colleague, in any way in his power; and the help was given quietly and unobtrusively, without fuss and without thought of self.

John Archibald, who served under Dr Wilson as boys' captain in 1942 and as a member of staff in the 1950s, says that he was 'quiet, honest, and not at all devious', and that he had 'no great sense of humour'. Actually, there are one or two flashes of dry humour in Dr Wilson's speeches: for instance, speaking about his decision to retire (which was not voluntary), he suggested that the Education committee had more or less asked him, "Must you stay? Can't you go?"

What manner of rector?

Like A.J.C. Kerr, his distinguished predecessor, Dr Wilson had great organisational skills, and these enabled him 'to arrange intricate timetables with seeming ease and fit in not only classes and portions of classes but also individual pupils'. It was fortunate that he was blessed with such administrative expertise, for it was one of his 'cardinal principles that every boy and girl should be able to take the curriculum most suited to their requirements and capabilities, and that practically no combination of subjects, consequently, should be unobtainable because it was difficult to timetable'.

According to J.T. Wilson (in his capacity as First Assistant, he worked in tandem with the Rector on administrative matters, so he was ideally placed to reach this conclusion), Dr Wilson 'paid great attention to detail, and showed complete imperturbability' in dealing with the multiplicity of problems that beset the headmaster of a large school - from the filling up of forms and schedules to the finding of lost books and other missing property'.

Dr Wilson had a firm belief in the value of extra-curricular activities. Consequently, he not only gave the various clubs and societies at the High School 'verbal encouragement', but also 'fostered them (particularly athletics and the Scripture Union) by his attendance'.

He was also convinced that the playing of games "aided the pupils' physical development" and, more importantly, 'trained their character': so he did his utmost to improve and augment the sports facilities that were available to the school and the FP Club. However, his efforts were not entirely successful; for although the school, for example, gained a pavilion and a hockey field during his rectorship, the second of these gains was balanced by the loss of a football field (Kenilworth).

There is no doubt that Dr Wilson had great intellectual presence and commanded great respect from both the inspectorate and his staff. In 1952 the 'supervision' of the school was described in the Triennial Report as 'kindly and effective'; and the following year, A.S. Kelly, one of Her Majesty's Inspectors, assured him that 'he would go into retirement with the respect of those members of the Scottish Education Department who had had the privilege of meeting him at the High School'. Alex Anderson, who taught at the school in the 1940s before becoming the local MP, declared that 'no finer gentleman was ever his chief', and that 'he was sure later generations of teachers could say the same'.

For his part, Dr Wilson 'endeavoured to treat his colleagues as he always liked to be treated himself - as specialists, that is, who knew their jobs and could be trusted to do them without unnecessary interference'. He certainly kept a very low profile; and he wasn't seen around the school as much as A.J.C. Kerr. 'He always wore a gown,' according to Sheila Sprot, 'and he tended to hang about between the front door and the downstairs corridor. As pupils, we hardly ever spoke to him, and my main impression of him was that he seemed to be a very clever man who was on an entirely different intellectual plane from the rest of us, as if his mind was always on higher things.'

Morton Cadzow, on the other hand, can still recall the occasion when he and other two High School pupils were selected to play for Lanarkshire against Glasgow at Hampden Park, and Dr Wilson offered to take the three of them - and the red Belhaven House strips, which were to be worn by the Lanarkshire team - in his car to the match. They arrived at Dr Wilson's house in Kirk Road to find that his car wouldn't start: so he hired a taxi for them.

'When I came to Wishaw,' Dr Wilson declared at his retiral dinner, 'I set myself the task of making the school as happy a place for teachers and pupils as was consistent with the maintenance of that standard of hard work which is essential if a school is to fulfil its purpose.' There was undoubtedly a much more relaxed atmosphere in the school during Dr Wilson's rectorship than in the relentlessly dynamic Kerr era. One gets the impression that the school was very much at ease with itself; that Dr Wilson felt it had nothing to prove; and that he had no great desire, consequently, to go looking for something new to prove. One might almost say that like 'the House of Peers, throughout the war', he

> 'did nothing in particular,
> and did it very well.'

But, on reflection, such a suggestion is far too harsh.

Though the atmosphere in the school was relaxed, it was also (in the words of Russell Rodger) 'very disciplined. There was a tight, but unobtrusive, code of discipline, and fights and bullying were so rare as to be almost unimaginable.' If a disciplinary problem did arise, Dr Wilson was disinclined to overreact. One afternoon, to take a case in point, George Westwood and two of his friends absented themselves from school in order to attend a showing of *National Velvet* at The Plaza. When they came out of the cinema, they walked straight into the arms of Dr Wilson, who 'invited' them to come and see him in his study the following morning. In the event, they were given a gentle reprimand.

Achievements

'I came to a big school,' Dr Wilson claimed, 'which had a fine reputation for scholarship and sporting excellence, and provided an unusually wide and varied curriculum for its pupils. To my successor I hand over an even larger school - with as fine a reputation scholastically as ever it had, a much bigger staff, an even more varied curriculum, and an enhanced reputation for sportsmanship and athletic accomplishment.'

Without a doubt, the High School's reputation, both academically and on the football field, remained as high during Dr Wilson's rectorship as it had ever been. However, I find it strange that he should expect to be given credit for an increase in the school roll and the number of teachers on the staff; and as far as the curriculum is concerned, some FPs have told me that one of the in-jokes among the senior pupils in the early 1950s was that the master timetable on the wall opposite Dr Wilson's room remained in situ - and unchanged - from session to session. It is impossible to either substantiate or disprove Dr Wilson's claim that members of the various school teams were more sporting than in earlier times.

Dr Wilson was positive that a flourishing FP Club would be a great asset to the school. He took a keen interest in the running of the club, and its miraculous revival after the Second World War was 'to no small extent due to him'.

Dr Wilson continued the process (it had been started by A.J.C. Kerr) of turning the High School into a 'comprehensive' school: as Kerr himself said, 'He has taken up that work, and he has done it well.' Alex Anderson was a trifle more lavish with his praise: 'The High School is continually extending the variety of its courses, and it more nearly approaches the 'comprehensive' school than anything I have seen.'

Dr Wilson's greatest achievement was the formation of the Memorial Trust; and his 'big idea' was the plan to provide - under the auspices of that trust - new playing fields for the High School and the FP Club. A sound enough start was made with a view to implementing this ambitious scheme, a plot of land and a hall having been acquired in Stewarton Street and Dimsdale Road respectively; and if Dr Wilson had not retired, it is possible - given that he was so strongly committed to it - that the playing fields project would not have run into the sand.

Failures

Dr Wilson himself suggested that he had not acquired one or two of the traits of a good headmaster:
In my younger days, the head of a school was known irreverently as 'The Bully'. The qualities that inspired such a nickname must, I fear, be inborn, for I have never been able to acquire them.
Dr Wilson did belt pupils, but it was a very rare occurrence.

A successful headmaster, in his opinion, was one who was able 'to get the Education Committee to do things for his school'. In the early stages of his rectorship, he did succeed in getting 'some essential improvements' carried out, but later 'he seemed to lose the knack of moving the powers that be'. Though he managed to 'screw' *(ipse dixit)* a new hockey field out of the Education Committee, he received no offers

214

of financial help in respect of the new playing fields, or a library, or a stage in the hall.

'I did it my way.'

Dr Wilson arrived at the High School with no experience as a headmaster, and in succession to 'one whose shoes were not easy to fill'. Even after he retired, A.J.C. Kerr's personality and managerial style must have continued to permeate the High School; but Dr Wilson did not allow himself to be fazed by the former or railroaded by the latter into establishing a similar regime. He had the self-assurance to carry out his duties in his own - completely different - way, and he soon 'showed himself to be not only capable, but more than capable, of being rector of a large secondary school'.

At Dr Wilson's retiral dinner, J.T. Wilson, the author of the above observation, declared:

The crucial test for a headmaster is the kind of spirit or atmosphere that pervades his school. This more than anything else that a school can offer determines the quality of the boys and girls who pass through it, and the impress they will make when they leave school to go out into the world.

Mr Wilson had no doubt that Dr Wilson 'passed this test with honour', even though he did not specify what sort of 'spirit or atmosphere' should obtain in a school if it is to produce young men and women who will make their mark in a socially acceptable manner. There is every likelihood, however, that the calm, civilised, and respectful atmosphere that pervaded the High School was conducive to that outcome. There is no statistical evidence to support this supposition; I can only cite the following generalisation by a former pupil who attended the school in the 1940s: 'None of my contemporaries wasted their lives.'

Final Farewells

Towards the end of Dr Wilson's retiral dinner, the chairman for the evening read out a telegram from John Weir, formerly Principal Teacher of Geography at the High School: 'Best wishes to Dr and Mrs Wilson. Strongly recommend, sir, a spade for your trump card now.'

The School Convener, Edward Lawson, a man noted for his bizarre turn of phrase, ushered Dr Wilson into retirement with a triple benediction: 'Goodnight, good luck, and God bless you.'

Dr Wilson's parting words were: 'Good luck and prosperity to Wishaw High School.'

21

1953-1955

Big Mac

Dr Wilson was succeeded by Neil B. McKellar, Principal Teacher of English at Uddingston Grammar School.

Curriculum Vitae

Neil McKellar was a native of Tarbert in Argyllshire, and he was educated at the local higher grade school, North Kelvinside Secondary School and Glasgow University, where he graduated in 1928 with 2nd Class Honours in English Language and Literature.

He trained as a teacher at Jordanhill College of Education, and began his teaching career as an assistant in the English Department at Dalziel High School.

After eighteen years (four of them as Acting Principal Teacher) at Dalziel High School, he was appointed Principal Teacher of English at Uddingston Grammar School. His academic standing was further enhanced by his appointment as External Examiner in English for the Ministry of Education in Northern Ireland.

During the war, he served for 4½ years as a commissioned officer with 497 (Motherwell) Squadron of the Air Training Corps, and as sole instructor in Air Navigation he successfully presented more than 100 cadets for the Air Ministry Proficiency Certificate. He also served as a voluntary ambulance driver with Glasgow Civil Defence.

Throughout his teaching career, he took a keen interest in extra-curricular activities, especially football. At Uddingston Grammar School, he played a major part in the resurrection of the FP Club and the publication (for the first time) of a school magazine.

As well as being Honorary Vice-President of the local battalion of the Boys' Brigade, he was in great demand as a speaker at Burns Suppers.

Ave

The High School's new rector was introduced to the staff and pupils by the School Convener, Edward Lawson, on 20 October 1953. Having been assured by the convener that he would have 'one of the finest staffs of any school in Lanarkshire', McKellar assured those same teachers that they would have his 'confidence', and that he would work with them 'to keep the school always at the forefront'. As for the pupils, he expected them 'to work hard and play hard' - and 'to be punctual'.

Having announced his intention to close the school at 2.30 (as an expression of his thanks for the warm welcome he had received), he shook hands with the school captains, Gordon Hunter and Lalla Weir.

A Good Omen?

Ten days later, the High School's Junior team (D. Whiteford; R. Rodger and D. Leiper; I. Wilson, A. Russell, and J. Bennett; R. Duncan, S. Reid, I. Johnstone, H. Rattray, and T. Earl; Sub: G. Gillespie) defeated Hamilton Academy 3-1 in the final of the Watt Cup at Recreation Field, Wishaw. 'As an old football player,' said McKellar at the presentation ceremony, 'it is a happy augury that my first trophy should be a football cup.' The Junior team, it should be noted, had also won the Motherwell and Wishaw League the previous season.

He had a dream.

In January 1954, eighty new pupils were admitted to the High School. Although the school (whose roll was now approximately 750) was still some way short of reaching saturation point, McKellar felt that there was a 'pressing need' for a new science laboratory, a metalwork room, and an additional room for homecraft. He therefore submitted plans to the Director of Education, 'which, with the maximum economy of space and finance, would not only have met these needs, but would also have ensured that the Art, Music, and Technical Departments were housed in compact units, a much more satisfactory arrangement than the status quo'. 'Dis aliter visum.'

Parent Power

The Parents' Association was founded in 1952 'to assist the Memorial Trust in its efforts to provide playing fields for the school'. By the spring of 1954, it had raised more than £100 for the Memorial Trust and purchased sixty chairs and a supply of dishes for Dimsdale Hall, the 'headquarters' of the FP Club; it had also organised such varied events as social evenings, country dancing, a Theatre Night, trips to the Edinburgh Tattoo and the Daer Reservoir, and a succession of whist drives - not to raise money, but to 'rope in' more parents (an objective it failed to attain, since the majority of parents, to quote one committee member, 'were as apathetic to the scheme of things as voters in the local elections, with the result that even house to house canvassing had little effect in increasing membership').

McKellar was invited to present the prizes at one of the aforementioned whist drives, and in the course of the evening he said 'many nice things about his new post and his new friends in Wishaw'. He also extended an open invitation to all parents to visit him at the school 'if they wanted advice or assistance on any scholastic matter that affected their children'.

Atque in perpetuum...ave atque vale.

Catullus, *Carmina*

In February 1954, a memorial service was held in the hall for Alex Anderson, the local MP, who prior to going into politics had taught English at the High School for more than twenty years. McKellar spoke of Anderson's 'breadth of mind and scholarly demeanour, his lucidity of exposition, his services to school football, and his charming Caithness lilt that had endeared him to a host of pupils'. Two minutes' silence was observed, and the service ended with the staff and pupils singing the 23rd Psalm and saying the Lord's Prayer in unison.

Pond(s)-Life(less)

Once again there were lily ponds ('not only decorative in themselves, but also of great practical use in the teaching of Botany and Zoology') in the quadrangles; unfortunately, there was no specialist teacher of Botany or Zoology to make use of them. Even so, McKellar had plans to develop the conservatory in such a way that it would eventually have provided a supply of fish and aquatic plants for the ponds.

Reading maketh a full man; conference a ready man...

Francis Bacon, *Essays*

McKellar wasted no time in informing the authorities that the school required a library, 'an essential feature of every school in these days of the decline of reading before the onslaught of the cinema, the radio, and the television set'. Although the Education Committee was equally quick to approve a proposal that Room 17 should be converted into a library, it was 1958 before the pupils were able to make use of this new facility (which contained 2,000 books, and was under the general supervision of James Forrest, a member of the English Department).

With a view to improving the pupils' diction and communication skills, a record player and a tape recorder were purchased by the school; and Dai Davies of the History Department held classes in public speaking.

Seven teachers left the school in the course of session 1953-54; and as a result of 'the serious shortage of adequate teachers and the makeshift policy of replacement' (two issues on which McKellar waxed indignant throughout the full span of his rectorship), only one of the vacancies was filled on a permanent basis. If, for any reason, the Principal Teacher of Maths or Science happened to be absent, there was nobody else in these departments with the qualifications to take the advanced classes.

In May 1954, the Intermediate team (H. Wheelan; R. Rodger and P. MacIntyre; J. Bennett, D. Leiper, and I. Wilson; J. Finlay, H. Rattray, I. Johnstone, S. Reid, and R. Duncan) defeated Wishaw Central in the final of the Anderson Cup. The *Wishaw Press*'s report on this match contained the following:

A small portion of the crowd consisted of some irresponsible juveniles who got a bit out of hand. It was evident that their teachers were not present, else the throwing of tufts of grass at each other would not have occurred.

In the final week of June 1954 (and June 1955), the school staged both a revue and a potpourri of plays. The revues (*Say Please* and *Then and There*) featured such items as the Boys' Glee Club, *The Foiling of Sir Jasper* (a parody of silent films), an accordion solo, the Harmonica Hoboes, *Whimsey in the Wood* (a venture into puppetry), and *Buroo Buffoonery* (a lesson on how to get a job in three different languages - Russian, English, and American); the plays included A.A. Milne's *Oliver*

Island, Meet Mrs Beeton, a comedy by L. Du Garde Peach, and a mime entitled *The Wife of Bath's Tale*.

'Dies Irae'

The prize-giving in June 1954 was doubly unique: it was the first occasion on which the school's first three rectors - Kerr, Wilson, and McKellar - appeared together on the same platform; and the first occasion on which a rector of the High School said anything remotely critical in public about the pupils on its roll. In fact, McKellar made some extremely disparaging comments about the pupils in 5th and 6th Year:

Too many of them are deficient in real effort; too many of them, consequently, are taking six years, instead of five, to gain a respectable Leaving Certificate, a practice which is having such a disastrous effect on the level of scholarship in Class 6 that fewer and fewer High School pupils are taking part in the Glasgow University Bursary Competition.

McKellar's remedy for this unsatisfactory state of affairs was to suggest that both the Group Leaving Certificate and the Intermediate Certificate should be resurrected; and that pupils should be required to gain the latter before they were allowed to embark on a course leading to presentation for the former.

In October, the Parents' Association held a Music Night in the school hall. In the course of welcoming the large number of parents who attended this event, McKellar declared that 'three forces' made an impact on pupils' lives - the home, the school, and 'the world outside'; and that a headmaster was 'the hub and connecting link between these three forces'. He therefore thanked the Parents' Association for helping him to get to know the parents, who in turn had a right to know what was going on in the school.

Peter Johnston, Principal Teacher of Music, then explained to the audience that his aim was not to stage a concert, but to give them the opportunity to learn at first hand what went on every day in the Music Department. Demonstration lessons were given by Mr Johnston with the help of groups of 1st and 4th Year pupils; and the evening's proceedings ended with performances by a recorder group and several solo instrumentalists.

The American - and the High School - Way

In February 1955, an exchange of tape recordings (covering the whole gamut of daily life in their respective schools) was arranged by James Forrest, an assistant teacher of English at the High School, and B.A. Quigg, formerly Superintendent of Schools in Rome City, Georgia (the two men had been in regular correspondence with each other since a chance meeting in Glasgow during the War).

The High School tape (which was accompanied by photographs of different aspects of school life) included an introductory talk about Wishaw and its connection with the Covenanters; morning assembly (McKellar later remarked, 'jocularly', that 'the amount of coughing in the hall would reveal to the people in Georgia the rigours of a Scottish winter'); the Senior Choir singing Psalm 124 ('Now Israel may say...'); the Junior Choir singing 'Bonnie Dundee'; a tour of various classes; an interview with the janitor, Major Matthew Bain; excerpts from a play (*The House with the Twisty Windows*) and one of the Debating Society's debates; a skit (*Bacon Omelette*) on the Shakespeare-Bacon controversy written by J. Lockhart Whiteford, assistant teacher of History; an explanation of the House and Prefect Systems; a senior pupil reading a passage of ancient Greek; the school song; a short message of good will from McKellar; three cheers for Rome High School, the destination of the tape; and, interspersed throughout the three-hour-long recording, a commentary by Messrs Forrest and Whiteford on the High School and its immediate neighbourhood.

Pupils and their parents were given an opportunity to listen to the tape at a meeting (in the hall) arranged by the Parents' Association. During the interval, McKellar gave a short talk on the various courses available at the High School.

Cultural Experiences

During the Easter holidays, 108 pupils and 14 members of staff took part in a three-day excursion ('the first trip of its kind in the annals of the school') to Stratford-on-Avon. On the way south, the pupils 'saw some of the glories of the Lake District, about which they had read in verse or been instructed in Geography' - and the bus in which the boys were travelling broke down as it tried to negotiate the Kirkton Pass; in Stratford, they visited many places of literary and historical interest (including the birthplaces of Shakespeare and Anne Hathaway) and

222

attended a performance of *Twelfth Night* at the Shakespeare Memorial Theatre. The return journey took in 'the glories of the Scott country'.

Three trophies won...

At the Motherwell and Wishaw Schools' Swimming Gala, Bobby Watt, a 2nd Year pupil, won three trophies: the Kerr Trophy (50yds freestyle), the Taggart Cup (50yds breaststroke), and the Morgan Trophy (50yds backstroke).

...and two caps.

David Leiper and Sammy Reid played for Scotland against England at Goodison Park, Liverpool.

....and one certificate

William Smith was awarded a Certificate of Merit (for distinction in Scottish literature) by the Burns Federation.

O, farewell, honest soldier,
A tried and valiant soldier.

Shakespeare, *Hamlet*

Major Matthew L. Bain MBE, DCM, TD, school janitor tor 32 years, retired at the end of session 1954-55. At a presentation ceremony in the Crown Hotel, McKellar described him as 'a janitor extraordinary, a remarkable man who had served his country in the armed forces in two world wars - and in the Territorial Army in peacetime - for as many years as he had served Wishaw High School'; Dr Wilson said that he was 'indebted to him for his attention to discipline outside the classroom'; and A.J.C. Kerr, who made the actual presentation, praised his 'industry and conscientiousness'.

John Parton, who served under Major Bain in France during the Second World War (after which he joined the Technical Department at the High School), can still recall the following incident:
Our camp depended on tanker lorries for its water supply, an inconvenient arrangement. It was brought to the Major's notice that the

village water main ran through the camp. Although the pipe was covered by an almost impenetrable layer of red tape, his solution was obvious and immediate - find a plumber and don't worry about the formalities:

Deil tak' them, if they canny thole
A pipe wi' but one extra hole.

Major Bain's successor as senior janitor was James Harkness. 'We did not need three guesses,' commented the school magazine, 'to discover in which regiment he did his soldiering; already we see echoes of his Guards' training.' However, a few months after he entered on his duties the school log states:

School heating quite unsatisfactory for the second day running. Several pupils complained to Miss Henderson, and several members of staff complained to me. A frank discussion took place between the Clerk of Works, the Rector and Mr Harkness, and the latter was clearly given to understand that efficient heating, lighting, and cleanliness are his responsibility.

The Old Groaner

At the prize-giving, McKellar pronounced himself dissatisfied with the shortage of qualified staff (vacancies in several departments had been filled by 'uncertificated or improperly trained teachers'), but pleased that more 5th Year pupils than at any other time during the previous ten years had achieved a 'very good' Leaving Certificate. 'This is as it should be,' he insisted, 'since it leads to higher levels of scholarship in Class 6, which has been adversely affected by pupils in the 6th Year making a second attempt at the Leaving Certificate.' It is obvious from these, and similar, comments that the calibre of the 6th Year and the content of the curriculum they followed were two of the many bees in McKellar's educational bonnet:

A sixth year provides the only satisfactory conclusion to a full course of academic study at a senior secondary school. It puts the coping stone on the whole educational edifice, and without it a pupil frequently fails when competing with other sixth-formers at college or university.

224

'Custos Morum'

Abigail Loudon, the High School's first Woman Adviser and a member of the PE Department for more than 34 years, retired on 31 August 1955. Throughout her career, 'she guarded and nurtured the physical well-being of legions of girls, and endeavoured to instil into them something of her own high idealism of conduct and morality; she helped out at a wide range of extra-curricular activities - parties, concerts, excursions, and sports meetings; and although she had the broad vision required by modern educational theory, she still retained that insistence on high standards of behaviour and morality without which liberty degenerates into licence.'

In September, McKellar addressed a meeting of the parents (numbering more than a hundred) of new entrants to the school. Among the subjects he touched upon were courses, bursaries, school meals, bus tickets, and school regulations.

A Christmas Service (the first of which I can find any record) was held in the hall. The girls' captain, Mary Beattie, read a passage from the Bible; a short address was given by the school chaplain, the Reverend D.C. Whitelaw; a solo was sung by Mary Swanson, with the whole school joining in for the refrain; and the service ended with the pupils saying the Lord's Prayer in unison.

Everything You Always Wanted to Know about Part-Time Jobs But Were Afraid to Ask

In the 1955 edition of the school magazine (which was now entitled *The Octagon*), McKellar penned the following on the "Rector's Page":

Did you know that if you want to do part-time work, such as delivering milk or newspapers, you must (a) be at least 13 years old (b) get your father to complete an application form issued by me, on which I have to verify your date of birth and report on your attendance, conduct, and progress at school (c) be medically examined by the school doctor (d) not be late for school, fall behind in your lessons, or injure your health because of your employment (e) carry your permit with you while working (the police have the right to examine it) and (f) not work in any place likely to affect your health adversely, e.g. places of entertainment, fairgrounds, cafes, even barbers' shops are taboo...

A.J.C. Kerr, Rector from 1906 till 1937

Dr Wilson, Rector from 1937 till 1953

Neil McKellar, Rector from 1953 till 1966

Sam Barnard, Rector from 1966 till 1988

Jimmy Cleland, Acting Rector from 1988 till 1989

Iain Murray Rector from 1988 to 1992

22

1956: Jubilee Year

On five successive evenings in May, a dramatised version of John Bunyan's allegorical masterpiece, *The Pilgrim's Progress*, was performed by High School pupils in Wishaw Old Parish Church. In an article he wrote for the *Wishaw Press*, McKellar explained why it was appropriate that such a production - at such a venue - should be part of the jubilee celebrations:

A commemorative function (especially one associated with a school) cannot be more fittingly housed than in a church, and the perilous journey of Christian, beset as he is at every turn by trials and temptations, is analogous to the struggle of the school down through the years.

Wishaw High School, like Bunyan's hero, has known its good companions like Faithful, its fair-weather friends like Pliable, and its arch-enemies like Envy and Lord Hategood. How often, too, have its work and its staff been misjudged by Mr Blindman and his fellow jurors, Mr Malice, Mr No-good, Mr Enmity, and the rest; and how frequently have the staff wrestled with Ignorance - to no avail.

At one time, we have seemed to be in sight of the Delectable Mountains; at another, sunk in the Slough of Despond. Like Christian, the school struggled manfully onward; but, unlike him, it has not achieved its goal. Certainly, there are Hopefuls among us and we are in good heart; but in this Vanity Fair world of ours, surrounded as we are by all the tinselled allurements of a materialistic age, we can be sure of only one thing, and that is that the way ahead is as difficult and challenging as at any time in the past.

The prime mover of the production in question ('a cultural experiment, in which both staff and pupils were eager to participate') was James Forrest, a member of the English Department, who was also responsible for writing the script; the action was performed on a platform in front of the pulpit - and also in the aisles, which were used to represent the pilgrim's way; and a mixed choir seated in the gallery gave renditions of such hymns as 'Who would true valour see', accompanied by a professional orchestra.

The leading roles were played by the following pupils, all of whom won universal acclaim: William Tennant (Bunyan), Livingstone Russell (Christian), Alisdair Macdonald (Appollyon), Margaret Gilchrist (The

Evangelist), Stewart Smith (Pliable), Ian Shirlaw (Wordly Wiseman), Lamond Laing (Faithful), Clark Armit (Lord Hategood), Alexander Mackie (Hopeful), and Neil Megahy (Ignorance).

Several parts of the production were later recorded in the BBC studios in Glasgow - for transmission in the autumn.

I hate Paris in the springtime.

During the Easter holidays, a group of High School pupils visited Paris. The (rather harsh) observations of one of them were recorded in the *Wishaw Press*:

The food, which was typically French, was palatable to at least a certain percentage of the party; the Metro was very stuffy; the Paris Corporation buses were antique; and the Eiffel Tower resembled a seaside resort at the Glasgow Fair. The police, however, who were of comparatively small stature, were most polite and helpful.

On 3 September (the date on which the High School had been opened at Beltanefoot fifty years earlier) a service of dedication, conducted by the school chaplain, the Reverend D.C. Whitelaw, was held in Wishaw Old Parish Church. After the opening prayer, McKellar asked the Reverend Whitelaw 'to dedicate to the praise and glory of God' the new Bible that A.J.C. Kerr had presented to the school some time previously (with the provisos that his gift was kept secret, and the fiftieth anniversary celebrations were the first occasion on which the lesson was read from it). The Reverend Whitelaw said that the gift was accepted as 'a most sacred trust', and would be 'guarded reverently' in the days to come. He then delivered the prayer of dedication.

McKellar read the lesson from the new Bible, after which a short address (on 'The Complete Life') was delivered by the Reverend Whitelaw, who took as his text 2nd Timothy, Chapter 4, Verse 13: 'The cloke that I left at Troas with Carpus, when thou comest, bring with thee, and the books, but especially the parchments.'

Later in the day, a golden jubilee dinner was held in the Crown Hotel. After the meal, McKellar spoke of the school's scholastic achievements, past and present, and paid tribute to 'the two men of vision' who had preceded him as Rector. Thereafter, various (increasingly irrelevant) toasts were proposed, or replied to, by A.S. Kelly, Her Majesty's Chief Inspector of Schools: 'A happy relationship has always existed between myself and the rectors of Wishaw High School'; A.J.C. Kerr: 'It is not stone and lime that make a school, nor success at university or any other institution - but corporate spirit'; Dr Wilson: 'The FPs have a strong and flourishing club, and I hope that they will soon be in the position of having not only quarters of their own but also playing fields'; Professor Walker Chambers: "Scotland's tradition of liberal education must be maintained - not supplanted by specialisation"; George Lawson MP: 'A higher minimum standard of education is required for every pupil in the land'; W.H. Bell, Chairman of the Education Committee: 'The committee always tries to use its financial resources to the best advantage of a school population in Lanarkshire of more than 95,000'; Thomas Henderson, Assistant Director of Education: 'The burgh needs a theatre'; and Edward Lawson, the School Convener: 'The burgh leads the way in Scotland as far as housing is concerned.'

A vote of thanks was proposed by John Gibb, Assistant Principal of Jordanhill College of Education and a former pupil of the High School: *As a schoolboy, I never believed it possible that one day I would be called upon to deputise for the Reverend J.A.F. Dean, an Olympian of his time, a god who occasionally came down from Mount Olympus to visit the school at the prize-giving.*

Cash from Kids

During Jubilee Year, every class in the school was encouraged to make a contribution to the Memorial Trust Playing Fields Fund. The pupils 'brought amazing zest, enthusiasm, and ingenuity to the task', and more than £300 was raised in many 'unorthodox' ways. One orthodox way in which money (£9, to be exact) was raised was a Sports Evening, in the course of which the school cricket team defeated a doctors' XI by two runs.

This was the noblest Roman of them all...

Shakespeare, *Julius Caesar*

James T. Wilson, Principal Teacher of Classics since 1926 and Depute Rector since 1943, retired at the end of October. At an informal function in the hall (Mr Wilson insisted on a function of this nature, 'so that the younger members of staff might enjoy themselves'), McKellar waxed lyrical about his depute:

He has taught Latin and Greek to legions of Wishaw boys and girls with matchless skill, painstaking care, and patient understanding; and he has been Depute Rector with universal acceptance, meeting the fads and personal idiosyncrasies of three successive rectors with the same equanimity and the same calm and unruffled demeanour.

It is difficult to imagine any committee meeting without the guidance of his lucid intellect and ripe wisdom, and he will be especially missed in the deliberations of the Memorial Trust, of which he has been a member since its inception.

He has been my counsellor and friend, and he has guided my feeble steps in the paths of wise and tolerant government.

One by one the golden threads joining us to the past have parted, and tonight, as we bid farewell to Mr Wilson, we are profoundly aware that the last of these threads - bright, gleaming, strong, and untarnished through the years - is being severed, and that we are witnessing the close of a great era teaching-wise in the history of Wishaw High School.

In the course of his characteristically muted tribute, Dr Wilson likened his namesake to "that somewhat fabulous character, the Scottish dominie, who sacrifices most of his leisure time in a quiet country village in order to help the lad o' pairts".

Not surprisingly, Mr Wilson confessed to being 'overwhelmed' by such panegyrics - and by 'the beautiful instrument' (a television set) he had received from the staff. Earlier in the day, the boys' captain, William Tennant, had presented him with a vase and a nest of tables.

Soldier, rest. Thy warfare o'er,
Sleep the sleep that knows not breaking.

Sir Walter Scott, *The Lady of the Lake*

Major Bain, school janitor for thirty-two years, died in November. The Matthew L. Bain Junior Endeavour Prize was instituted in his memory; and the prize itself was awarded every year to the 1st, 2nd, or 3rd Year pupil not included in the Prize List who 'had worked hard, played hard, and always tried to uphold the good name of the school'. In the course of time, a senior version of the prize was established.

Gloom and Doom

Even in the school's jubilee year, McKellar devoted most of his annual report to one of his favourite complaints - the failure of the teaching profession to attract an adequate number of Honours graduates:

Recruitment from the High School is typical of Scotland as a whole: in a Sixth Year of some thirty pupils, only one, in my opinion, will take an Honours degree and become a teacher. Unless there is a statesmanlike review of the status and salaries of teachers - not next year, but now - secondary education in Scotland will collapse in irretrievable ruin.

Still on the subject of teachers: in 1956 there were, by a curious coincidence, fifty-six teachers on the staff. As for the Parents' Association, the other half of the 'partnership', it broke new ground by holding a joint meeting with its counterpart at Wishaw Public.

Cap Winners, Wicket Takers, and Record Breakers

John McCulloch played for the Scottish under-15 football team against England, Ireland and Wales.

Having won the senior championship at the school sports with the loss of only one point, Willie Hunter went on to represent Scotland in an athletics match against Northumberland and Durham. It is worth noting that five years later Sandy Robertson equalled Hunter's feat at the school sports; and that after setting a new record for the 200yds low hurdles at the Scottish Schools' Athletics Championships, he also ran for his country - against England and Wales at Cardiff.

William Cringean took 90 wickets and averaged 14.2 with the bat for the 1st XI, while two members of the Junior XI, Tom Dobbie and John McCulloch, took 34 and 35 wickets respectively. Dobbie actually developed into a fine batsman, and three seasons later he and Bryce Cassels formed a consistently sound opening partnership in the 1st XI. Two other cricketers of note in the mid-1950s were S. Murdoch and J. Ritchie, who scored 89 (average 11.1) and 97 (average 12.1) runs respectively in 1955.

As far as field events are concerned, the following pupils are worthy of a mention: Betty Rodger (long jump), who bettered the previous record by almost 1½ feet at the Inter-Counties Youth Sports; Andrew Hepburn (high jump), who cleared 5ft 7in; Ian Johnstone (short putt); William Tennant (discus), whose best throw was 95ft 11in; David Leiper (also discus); W. Fyfe (javelin); Kenneth McFadyen (also javelin); and J. McPhail (javelin, yet again), who threw his spear 113ft 11in.

23

1957

Sunt hic etiam sua praemia laudi.

Virgil, *Aeneid*

In February, Wishaw Toastmasters' Club presented two prizes to the High School for excellence in public speaking - the first winners of which were William H. Smith and Christine Brownlee. Later in the year, Miss J.D. Ronald, a member of the English Department, and several members of the Debating Society broke new ground by attending one of the club's meetings.

In June, to mark the Golden Jubilee of the Rotary movement, the Motherwell and Wishaw Rotary Prize was inaugurated. The first recipient of this prize (awarded annually for 'meritorious work or service by a young person either in the local community or at the school he or she attended') was William Tennant, 'an outstandingly good student and school captain' (according to Peter Morrison, President of the Rotary Club), who 'had shown inspiring qualities of energy, resource, and leadership in all aspects of school life'.

HMS WHS

Later that month, 'Wishaw High School pupils set foot on the deck of HMS Pinafore and cast off for their first voyage to the enchanted domain of Gilbert and Sullivan; in doing so, they dealt successfully with the rocks and whirlpools that claim so many amateur productions.'

The *Wishaw Press* also commented on 'the really fine male chorus and - despite the smallness of the stage - the high standard of stagecraft'; and among the individual members of the cast it singled out for praise were Elizabeth Buttery (Little Buttercup), Lamond Laing (Captain Corcoran), Robert Reid (Rt. Hon. Sir Joseph Porter), Stewart Topping (Ralph), Mary Swanson (Josephine), David Torrance (Dick Deadeye), Livingston Russell (Bill), William Ritchie (Bob Becket), Ian

Sommerville (Tom Tucker), William Tennant (Sergeant of Marines), and Margaret Glover (Sir Joseph's First Cousin).

McKellar himself directed the operetta, and with his active encouragement a Gilbert and Sullivan production became a regular feature on the school calendar.

Dismay

There were now 840 pupils on the roll, and it was becoming more and more difficult to accommodate them all. At the prize-giving, Councillor John Johnston, the newly appointed School Convener, expressed 'great alarm'; but he could see 'no solution', since no sooner were new schools opened in the district than they were 'reported to be overcrowded'.

Disenchantment

Despite 'a very good year in the Leaving Certificate Examinations', McKellar was still far from happy:

Good pupils continue to leave school for unworthy vocations offering high wages, and far too many girls are avoiding the arduous university courses altogether in favour of the shorter non-graduate course at Jordanhill for primary teachers.

Of course, the latter were not the sort of teachers McKellar was always crying out for; he wanted Honours graduates.

Distinction

John Hamilton won the high jump at the Scottish Schools' Athletics Championships.

Disport

During June, the girls' relay team was victorious at the Lanimers, the Motherwell and Wishaw Police Sports and the school sports held by Dalziel High School and Coatbridge Junior Secondary School.

The High School was now able to field eight football teams. In addition, a league was started on Saturday mornings for the benefit of 1st and 2nd year classes, and matches in this league served as trials for the Junior and Juvenile teams.

Discoveries

During the summer holidays, a group of senior pupils, supervised by Miss Watt, Miss MacFarlane and Mr Mitchell, spent a fortnight on the Norfolk Broads:

Botanical and zoological points of interest were numerous, birdlife being abundant and flowers and shrubs unlike those in our area being common; and James Duncan almost caught a pheasant with a 20ft pole.

> **Yet once more, O ye laurels, and once more**
> **Ye myrtles brown, with ivy never sere,**
> **I come to pluck your berries harsh and crude.**

Milton, *Lycidas*

A.J.C. Kerr died on 21 September at the age of 81. Throughout the entire period of his retirement, he had taken 'the liveliest interest in the affairs of the school; and there was no event on the school calendar, no academic or athletic distinction, and no extra-mural project of which he had not been aware - and to which he had not responded either by his presence or, when that was not physically possible, by letter to McKellar'. He had also made a speech at the prize-giving in 1956, and 'up to a short time before his death he was still reading reports about the school and dictating letters (he could no longer hold a pen) to many of his old friends and former pupils'.

At a memorial service in the hall, McKellar described A.J.C. Kerr as 'the real architect of Wishaw High School, a wise counsellor and a good friend, a man who would need no memorial in Cambusnethan Cemetery, since there was a great human memorial in the form of the legions of former pupils who openly acknowledged their debt to him and would always cherish his memory'. Miss Henderson, Woman Adviser, read one of Kerr's favourite passages - the death of Mr Valiant-for-Truth - from Bunyan's *The Pilgrim's Progress*; it ended with the words: 'So he passed over, and all the trumpets sounded for him on the other side.'

The funeral was attended by many of Kerr's former pupils and colleagues; senior pupils from the High School lined the entrance to the cemetery; the service at the graveside was conducted by the school chaplain, the Reverend D.C. Whitelaw; and McKellar himself was one of the pall-bearers.

The parties are over.

By 1957, four Christmas parties - 1st Year, 2nd Year, 3rd Year, and Senior - were arranged every year, and McKellar was present at all four that year. The hall was 'exceptionally well-decorated, the motif being nursery rhymes, and a beautiful Christmas tree, gifted (as in previous years) by WG. Gibb, added the final touch.' 'These are joyous occasions,' McKellar told a reporter from the *Wishaw Press*, 'when lessons are forgotten and staff and pupils join together in gay abandon. Such has been the enthusiasm of the younger pupils that many of the staff have been danced off their feet - and will thus doubly welcome the Christmas break.'

No Room at the Bottom

In the week before Christmas, McKellar announced that there would be no preparatory class at the school when it reopened for the new year. 'Not only has the school reached saturation point,' he explained, 'but so many pupils in the 4th, 5th, and 6th Year are staying on at school (an excellent tribute to the foresight of their parents) that it would be quite unfair to them - and the newcomers - to devise a make-do-and-mend system of accommodation which would make conditions, already difficult, almost chaotic.' Pupils who were ready to embark on the secondary stage of their education remained at their respective primary schools until June 1958, and enrolled at the High School in August of that same year.

Postscript

A former pupil of the High School, John Prentice, was captain of the Falkirk team that won the Scottish Cup. Prentice went on to have a distinguished career in football management.

24

1958

O tempora, O mores.

Cicero, *In Catilinam*

In May, at the Industrial Life Office's annual luncheon, McKellar limbered up for his customary tirade at the prize-giving by deprecating the decline in academic standards ('Primary pupils are woefully deficient in the 3Rs, and their secondary counterparts now achieve a poorer Leaving Certificate in six years than they used to achieve in five') and the prevalence of equally low standards of 'conduct, culture, and morality'. In his opinion, the main reason for the latter decline was that the 1950s were 'the golden age of diminished responsibility and passing the buck': so if 'people just faced up to all their responsibilities - accepting not only credit for doing good but also liability for any wrongdoing - many of society's ills would be cured'. He went on to say that he was trying to cultivate such a sense of responsibility among the pupils at the High School; and that while this policy might not produce all the specialists industry was calling for, it would undoubtedly produce what he felt was more important - good citizens.

Any colour - so long as it's blue.

In the "Rector's Page" in *The Octagon*, McKellar fired a verbal torpedo at a more specific target:
There ought to be more ties, scarves, and blazers in evidence - especially among the senior boys. Many who advance arguments of expense or the difficulty of getting suitable sizes seem to experience no trouble in obtaining much less appropriate (less 'fitting' would perhaps be a better way of putting it) garments of the most garish hues, all of them adorned with nondescript badges. I am growing less tolerant of such sartorial subversion. The only valid reason for not wearing a school blazer is the economic one, and that is the only reason I intend to listen to next session.

Wha's like us?

At the prize-giving, McKellar claimed a number of records and firsts for the school – not always convincingly, as the following examples demonstrate; 130 candidates, compared with 82 at Dalziel High School and 101 at Our Lady's High School, were presented at the Leaving Certificate Examinations (incontrovertible); the pass rate in individual subjects at Higher level was 92% (it's very doubtful if this is a record); and fifty pupils gained certificates of university entrance standard or better (likely).

However, pessimistic as ever, he proceeded to suggest that 1958 might be 'the last year Wishaw High School achieved academic success'. "If that proves to be the case," he declared, "I will lay the blame fairly and squarely where it belongs - on an apathetic public. People who will draw up petitions to have the position of a bus stop shifted seem to acquiesce with complete indifference in a state of affairs that vitally affects their children's future." Once again there are no prizes for guessing that he was back on board his favourite hobby horse - the chronic shortage of teachers.

On the subject of firsts, McKellar announced that, to the best of his knowledge, 1958 was the first year in which the staff and pupils had, of necessity, become 'displaced persons' for two important school events: for the school's 'second venture into the realms of comic opera', accommodation had to be sought outwith the campus, but as a result of 'the wonderful cooperation of Mr Whiteside (the headmaster) and Mr Ross (the janitor), the temporary sojourn of 'The Mikado' and his people in Lammermoor Primary School proved to be as enjoyable as it was popular'; and thanks to the school chaplain and the Church Session of Wishaw Old Parish Church, the prize-giving was held in 'a beautiful place of worship' that imbued the ceremony with 'significance and impressiveness'.

By September, the roll exceeded 900, another record. Having to provide accommodation for such a large number of pupils was, as McKellar himself admitted, 'an outsize headache'; and even though all 900 were 'fitted in', this was only made possible by 'makeshift arrangements that were quite unsatisfactory', and 'made an extension of the school building quite imperative'.

Since he must have suspected that such an extension was unlikely to materialise in the prevailing economic and educational climate (although a considerable number of new schools had been erected in Lanarkshire, most of them were primary or junior secondary schools; meanwhile, the older high schools were 'the victims of almost complete neglect'), McKellar urged the Education Committee not 'to become intoxicated with novelty' - and 'to reconsider its building programme, so that without denying the just claims for new schools in many areas some adjustment in outlay could be made to meet the long-overdue claims of senior secondary schools'.

As far as the quality of its library (formerly Room 17, and opened in February) was concerned, the High School lagged behind not only the new schools with their 'luxurious fittings', but also many senior secondary schools - even though the proceeds from a quiz organised by George Brown, Principal Teacher of English, had been used to produce 'quite considerable improvements', and several benefactors (including Mr and Mrs Mackie of Mossneuk Crescent) had donated 'suitable books', the total number of which now exceeded two thousand.

One of the pupils who served as librarians wrote the following article for *The Octagon*:

An Epic of Courage

Who would be a librarian? I am, and there are other twenty poor fish in the same (mucky) pond, four of whom are genuine(?) 5th Year girls. We are the few, the stalwart few, who run the library. Then there are the many, the horrible many, the hooliganly many pupils of Wishaw High School who use and misuse the library.

Every day, at lunchtime, three of the few stroll round to the library, ostensibly very cool, calm and collected, but inwardly quaking like .....'s Strawberry Jellies (to identify....., watch ITV on Wednesdays at 8.40 p.m.). We set out the file and stamp our feet: it's cold in Room 17. Immediately, a howl is heard, like coyotes with sore tails. 'Let us in,' yells a scruffy little fellow in a raucous voice and a faded blazer - as if we in our exalted posts and faded blazers would condescend to acquiesce in such an outrageous request. Instead, we politely tell Charles to go and jump into the nearest large puddle.

Finally, however, as the hands of the clock move relentlessly on to 12.30, we don our tin helmets and load up the machine gun, and feeling more or less protected, we open the door. Five minutes later, we pick ourselves out of the dust, rescue the stamp from amidst the hordes of screaming feet (they aren't really screaming, but as librarians we had to have a transferred epithet somewhere), and restore something like order. This means putting everybody outside again.

Torment cannot last for ever, and as the harsh clangour of the bell is heard above the ruckus, we are saved, in the last stages of mental paralysis, by our hero (fresh from the primitive American jungles), who clears - with a few kind words - the room, his throat, and a pile of bodies. We then put all the books on the floor back on the shelves, remove garbage and wreckage, and put the casualties [sic] in the box in the janitor's room to await claimants.

There are, of course, a few compensations for such a hazardous occupation: there is great joy, for instance, in hearing some miserable Charlie explain that his book is overdue - and depriving him of a few shekels, denarii or talents, according to his age, financial position, and alleged political allegiance. So it goes on, day after day, and still we survive the onslaughts with courage and determination. We will never surrender - at least not until we have enough boodle on which to retire from office.

Stop Press

W. Anderson took eight wickets against Woodside without conceding a run; and T. Dobbie took seven wickets, at a cost of eight runs, against Airdrie Academy.

25

1959

Sunt lacrimae rerum.

Virgil, *Aeneid*

Early in the year, William Tennant, boys' captain in session 1956—57, was killed in a road accident. Thanks to the generosity of Mr and Mrs A. Tennant, the William Tennant Memorial Trophy was instituted in his memory, the first (joint) winners being Mabel Paterson and Bryce Cassels.

1959 also saw the premature death (from some form of kidney disease) of John Cranston, one of the most popular pupils at the High School in the mid-1950s. When his cortege made its way up the Main Street, many local shopkeepers stood outside their shops as a mark of respect.

The FP Football Club commissioned a special trophy (the John Cranston Memorial Trophy) in recognition of his services to the club as its first secretary, and this trophy is still presented at the end of every season to the Player of the Year.

Sicelides Musae, paulo minora canamus.

Virgil, *Eclogues (adapted)*

A skipping group from the High School was included in the Motherwell and Wishaw team that took part in the BBC's *Top Town* entertainment contest. It was suggested in *The Octagon* that 'they deserved a better fate than the judges saw fit to award'.

At the Scottish Schools' Athletics Championships, Ruby Nicol won the under-17 100 yards; the girl's relay team (Mary Watson, Isobel McNab, Rona Baird, Margaret Simpson, and Ruby Nicol) won the under-

15 event in record time, and were awarded the Mildred Storrar Cup for the most meritorious performance in the relay races at the championships.

One innovative feature of session 1958—59 was the formation of a junior basketball team, the members of which were 'much indebted to Yves de Saintdo, the French 'assistant', for introducing the game to the High School and coaching them with such enthusiasm'.

Rector McKellar Criticises Bulldozer Approach to New Education Set-Up

Earlier in the year, the Scottish Education Department had announced its intention to introduce O-Grades in place of Lowers at the Leaving Certificate Examinations in 1962, the new grades being designed primarily for those pupils who were likely to complete no more than four years at a senior secondary school, and who (in view of the length and arduousness of the courses that led to presentation in one or more subjects at Lower level) were equally likely to leave school without a certificate of any kind. In Lanarkshire, the authorities decided that it would be in the best interests of such pupils to begin their secondary careers in schools that provided only four-year secondary courses; and that diverting pupils to these new 'high schools' (as they were designated) would lessen the pressure on senior secondary schools, many of which were afflicted by severe shortages of staff and accommodation. In line with this policy, sixty potential recruits to the (blue and yellow) colours were instructed to report to Brandon High School in Motherwell after the summer holidays.

McKellar felt that the dividing line between 'O-Grade and Higher pupils' had been drawn in far too uncompromising a manner (hence the headline quoted above); and he also expressed disquiet at the fact that parents - as well as primary and secondary headmasters - were excluded from the process of deciding which secondary school a pupil should attend:

I fully understand the distress in many homes in the Wishaw area when it was learned, almost like a bolt from the blue, that a child whose elder brother or sister - of no better attainment - had passed through Wishaw High School successfully was to report to a school which was unfamiliar to him by virtue of its new appellation, and attendance at which involved considerable travel.

Despite the 'loss' of those primary pupils who had been assigned to O-Grade courses, the High School's roll still exceeded 900 - thanks to a big increase in the number of pupils in 4th, 5th, and 6th Year, which 'astonishingly' (to quote McKellar) had climbed above the 300 mark.

The old order changeth...

Tennyson, *Idylls of the King*

In October, Margaret Burns retired after 36 years' 'devoted service' in the Classics Department. 'Characteristically', she declined any form of public presentation; but she did accept (in private, from McKellar) a pearl necklace, as a token of her colleagues' esteem. McKellar also took the trouble to pen the following encomium for publication in the *Wishaw Press*:

Miss Burns's retiral means that another of the few remaining links with our past is broken, that another pillar of the school is removed, and that we are approaching the end of an era in the school's illustrious history.

Her standards, both of work and conduct, were exacting, but she asked no more of her pupils than of herself. The unclouded mind, the stern application, the dissatisfaction with the second- rate, and the high code of morality were as characteristic of her as her neat penmanship; and legions of High School pupils down the years readily acknowledge their debt to her teaching skills and personal example.

And yet, perhaps not surprisingly, she is essentially a simple person of simple tastes, embodying the poet's ideal of 'plain living and high thinking' - and modest almost to the point of self- effacement.

Another four long-serving stalwarts were not long in following Miss Burns into retirement:

Jemima Reekie (Principal Teacher of Commercial Subjects) 'built up the department from humble beginnings by her own hard work and inspirational qualities'.

Isobel Stewart (Principal Teacher of Domestic Science) was a 'dainty little lady who made every festive function more gracious with her floral decorations and 'melting moments', and the teacups she had filled would have stretched from the High School to Walter Street and back again'.

Isabella Henderson (Woman Adviser) deserved the highest praise for 'the kindly way in which she treated the girls who seemed to arrive in countless numbers complaining of feeling unwell, the quietly shocked but highly effective tone she adopted when some misdemeanour required her attention, and the perfect organisation of the girl prefects, who, without exception, adored her'.

Elizabeth McKenzie of the Modern Languages Department was credited with "dogged perseverance and an inexhaustible faculty of resource"; and "with the advent of each session her enthusiasm flowed anew, manifesting itself in a deep interest in each pupil's progress".

26

The High School in the 1950s - A Pupil's View

'Among the teachers I remember,' writes Neil Megahy, 'were 'Jock' Bonomy (PE), who placed great emphasis on 'playing the game'; 'Oscar' Leitch (Geography), a man with a short fuse, whose blackboard work was the epitome of neatness; 'Luggy' Weir (History); Mamie Loudon (Maths), who dressed in black and did the *Glasgow Herald* crossword in the presence of her classes; 'Dodo' Johnston (Music);Alf Dubber (English), who wore paper collars; 'Papa' Wilson (Latin and Depute Rector); Millar 'the killer' (Maths); and 'Dai' Davies (History), who supervised the Debating Society and wrote sketches for the school concert.

Very few members of staff had cars, and most of them travelled by bus.

There were inter-House competitions (junior and senior) every year in football, hockey, cricket, netball, athletics, and swimming. Prior to the gala, which included an event known as 'the long plunge' for senior pupils, a half or full point could be earned by swimming a breadth or length of the pool respectively.

Murdostoun was the most successful House and Coltness the least successful. This led to a readjustment in the number of pupils in these two Houses, with those pupils whose surnames began with the letters Ra and Re being transferred from Murdostoun to Coltness.

In 1951 the Scottish Secondary Shield was put on display in the hall.

Waverley was set out for the sports by the Technical Department; and a surveyor's chain was used to measure the distance between the starting and finishing lines.

All the large sports equipment (shots, javelins, hurdles, and football and cricket nets) was kept in a wooden hut at the back of the school.

Visiting football and hockey teams changed in the pavilion.

A coaching camp was held every year at Helensburgh. Budding athletes were given tuition, by experienced coaches, in putting the shot and throwing the discus and javelin, or helped to improve their starting and baton-changing technique; aspiring golfers also received individual coaching. Football, hockey, and rugby were played in the afternoon.

In the early 1950s, the school staged several concerts, and these included sketches, short plays, and choral items. The school hall was octagonal in shape, and this made it very difficult to accommodate a stage and seating.

The stage that eventually materialised was prefabricated by the Technical Department, and was simple to erect and dismantle; curtains and drapes were provided by certain Domestic Science classes; and make-up was always the responsibility of the Art Department.

When the director required a dimming light, it was made by the Technical Department. It consisted of a fireclay pipe sealed at one end, then filled with salt water; an electric current was passed through the water from the bottom of the pipe and the resistance changed by raising and lowering the other wire. It sounds dangerous, but it worked.

One vivid memory I have is of the sketch produced by 'Dai' Davies and 'acted' by Class 3C in 1952. I was a sergeant drilling three privates; there was a captain as well, and we were all in army uniforms. The sketch was so funny that in spite of all our valiant efforts we couldn't stop laughing - and this brought the house down.

The whole school assembled in the hall once a week. Sometimes we had to learn a hymn (e.g. 'Far round the world') off by heart, at other times we had to bring a hymn book. The Rector sat in the centre of the dais, flanked by the school captains; the teachers had seats to the left and right of the dais; 1st Year pupils (boys on the left, girls on the right) were seated at the front, 6th Year at the back. Announcements were made about important school events (such as the sports), and there was usually a hymn, a prayer, and a short address by the Rector. In 1956 the House captains were asked to take the service, including the address.

Discipline was strict, and the pupils were generally well- behaved.

The Film Club met in Rooms 19 and 20 (the Geography rooms), which were separated by a folding wooden partition. Room 19 had a long, raised desk, behind which there was a roller blackboard and a pull-down screen. Films tended to be either educational or popular classics. I can still remember *Metatetranicus Ulmi* (*Red Spider*) and *The 39 Steps*, which contained a shocking (to us) scene that involved the girl to whom Richard Hannay was handcuffed taking off her stockings in a hotel bedroom.

For a short time, we had a Jazz Club. It met in the hall and was tolerated by the Rector.

The Debating Society met in the Geography rooms after school every Friday. Alf Dubber and 'Dai' Davies introduced us to the various techniques of debating, e.g. humour, points of order, and building an argument. On one occasion, two teachers staged a mock debate on the motion that 'This House says that a banana is a better fruit than a tomato'; some pupils were asked to speak for or against the motion, others were encouraged to speak from the floor. I myself was threatened with expulsion for telling a joke (introducing humour, as I thought), at which nobody would raise an eyebrow today.

A group of senior boys used to meet in a secluded area behind the canteen for a quick drag; juniors were not encouraged to venture into this enclave. In wet weather, the toilets were used as a smokers' den, and they were raided from time to time. In my final year, there were no smokers among the senior pupils.

The prefabs were fine up to a point: it wasn't pleasant crossing over from them to the main building - and vice versa - in the winter rain and snow.

Many pupils and teachers used the canteen at lunchtime. Meals were cooked on the premises and, to the best of my knowledge, they were good value. The girls sat at the end of the canteen nearer the school, the boys at the far end; the teachers were seated in the middle and undertook supervisory duties on a rota basis.

About 1955, a new system was introduced that involved each table of eight being treated as a family, with a prefect in charge. Someone was allocated the task of going to the hatch to collect the food in large containers; the prefect then served the food on to the plates, ensuring that everybody got a fair share. It was a system that worked well.

At the beginning of session 1955-56, John Bonomy, the PE teacher, asked me - and another four senior boys - to start a fitness programme (called circuit training) that had been pioneered by Gordon Pirie, a world-class long-distance runner. A series of exercises was set up in the gym; we performed three 'circuits' of these exercises, and our times were recorded; and over a period of time, the number of 'circuits' was gradually increased. In the spring, when we started outdoor training, we were very fit.

Only the juniors were entitled to free milk. This was distributed, under the supervision of a janitor or a teacher, in the girls' quadrangle outside the Domestic Science rooms.

Towards the end of each session, classes would discuss - with the help of a teacher - a suitable destination (e.g. Ayr or Largs) for the class trip and arrange for a coach to take them there.

During the last week of the session, the staff normally played the pupils at football and hockey.

The senior boys usually got up to some prank on the last day.

In my last year (1956), we arranged for all the 5th and 6th Year boys to cram into the Chemistry storeroom, and about twenty minutes into the period we marched out in single file through all the Science classes (in those days, that was quite daring). We also climbed over the roof and hoisted a Jolly Roger on the flagpole.

At the school dances, the boys used the classrooms to the left of the main door as a cloakroom, the girls the ones to the right. We were brought out in single file and paired off at random; we then paraded over to the canteen for sandwiches, cakes, and lemonade; afterwards we came back to the hall, where the normal procedure was for the boys to congregate at one side and the girls at the other.

On one occasion, my partner happened to be wearing a strapless evening dress. She was taken aside by Abby Loudon, the Woman Adviser, and severely reprimanded. It ruined her evening.

The only problems with alcohol were confined to the teachers, and these always provided a good talking point for several days.

Special buses, leaving from Kenilworth Avenue, were available for pupils from Shotts and Allanton. Every now and then, there was a clampdown on boisterous behaviour on these buses.

Some pupils used the regular bus services to Law, Cleland, Overtown, etc.; a few cycled to school, and they deposited their bikes in the bicycle shed. There was very little interference with them.

The school uniform consisted of a royal blue blazer (with the school badge), combined with either short, grey trousers (junior boys), or long, grey trousers (senior boys), or a grey skirt (girls).

About 1953, the girls started to wear coloured stockings, which were all the fashion. This caused a panic among the staff until a compromise was reached: girls were allowed to wear blue or yellow stockings, since these matched the school colours.

In the winter, pupils wore long, waterproof coats and a school scarf. The coats were hung up in the unlocked cloakrooms - and they were safe there, even though everybody had access to them.

Schoolbags were also deposited in the cloakrooms at lunchtime.

People's property - even items left in coat pockets - was respected. I can only remember one occasion when pilfering took place, and that caused a major scandal until the culprit was caught.

The belt was used by all the teachers, but girls were not belted very often. Lines and detention were also meted out, even though detention was a particularly harsh punishment for those pupils who had bus passes. Serious misdemeanours were dealt with by the Rector, but indiscipline was not a major problem.

TB had become more of a worry, and a mass X-ray programme was organised that involved mobile units visiting the school. There were mass inoculations as well - the Salk vaccine, for instance, a breakthrough in the fight against polio, being administered in a sugar cube.

In 1956 eight 6th Year pupils from each of the senior secondary schools in Lanarkshire were invited to a conference at Coatbridge Technical College. We attended talks and short films about the future of Northern and Southern Rhodesia, and then we broke up into study groups; democratically elected group leaders reported back later to a plenary session. The conclusions we reached were obviously not what the organisers wanted to hear, but although the government didn't act on our advice at the time, what we had decided was the best option for the countries in question eventually came to pass.

On the day King George VI died, a teacher came into the classroom around noon to give us the news, and we were sent home. My mother did not believe my explanation for being home so early, but when we switched on the radio, there was only solemn music. I think the school was closed for the funeral.

The coronation of Queen Elizabeth took place in June 1953. Only a few people had television sets, and they were small black and white ones. I myself went down to the YMCA Institute, where a number of sets were set up round the hall.

About 1955, the Queen and Duke of Edinburgh drove through Wishaw in an open limousine. Uniformed organisations and schools were allocated a section of Stewarton Street or the Main Street. As a memento of the Coronation, pupils were given a lapel badge.'

27

The Octagon (1954-1960)

Reviews

Read What They Said about *The Octagon*

The Times: If it succeeds, then English literature is doomed.
Mr R.A. Butler: The best school magazine they have
Mr Kruschev: Niet
Reveille: Too highbrow
Daily Worker: Bourgeois imperialist propaganda
Colonel Nasser: There will have to be considerable alterations before the text can be accepted.
Pravda: An unprovoked attack on the U.S.S.R.
Mr Hammarskjold: A UN force will be sent in at once.
President Eisenhower: What's the editor's handicap?
Truth: Support this magazine: it needs it.
Daily Mirror: School Mag Hits 3Rs for Six.
Wastepaper and Refuse Collectors Gazette: Worth buying
Nyoo Spelirs Leeg: A lodibl produkshun
YZ (Class 1): Can I have my money back?
Editor: No!
J. Arthur Rank: The End

Rector's Page

Gladly, I turn now to talk of other things - not 'ships and shoes', etc., but milestones. Interesting things, milestones, don't you think? They are the silent ready reckoners of the roadway; they tell you how far you've gone, and how far you have to go; from them you can learn your speed of walking or cycling, or your petrol consumption. They glower at you with expressionless faces as you tramp homeward through the rain after a long hike; they seem to smile benignantly upon you when you're in sight of home.

The nicest milestone I know is at the top of the hilly road through Glencoe. It says simply - perhaps unnecessarily - 'Rest and Be Thankful'. And that advice, in the words of the radio comedian, is 'a good idea, son'.

Rest is necessary, but so is thankfulness, an expression of your gratitude that you've been blessed with the health and strength to achieve your objective. As our school passed the fiftieth milestone in its history at the beginning of this session, we tried to do just that. We paused to give thanks for the devoted service of all the good people - headmasters, teachers, pupils, and friends - who have taken this school so far along the road of progress.

Soon we will be in sight of the fifty-first milestone. Let us all resolve that we will derive increased devotion to our task from the shining example of our predecessors; let us resolve that each successive milestone will mark our progress both forward and upward, so that at our sixtieth anniversary we may have cause once again to 'Rest and Be Thankful'.

Summer

The waters wide and wondrous deep,
The glinting waves and scorching heat,
The gulls that with their careless cry
Betray their everlasting joy,
The sun, whose rays make bright the world,
Show summer's sail has been unfurled.

The ice has gone, the rapids roar,
Cold and dark preside no more,
The children play with heavenly glee,
The leaves are now upon the tree.
The flowers dressed in tinted hue
Show summer is here for me and you.

Mary Haggart (2B)

Guess Who?

Lurking on the stairway,
Guarding every line,
Oh, how much we love them! (???)
The truth you can divine.

Hoping to delay us
Every single day,
First they shout, "Stop running",
Then yell, "Don't delay."

In the hall on Mondays,
And on Fridays too,
They disturb our gossip,
And yell, "Split up, you two."

When we take our dinner,
Hoping for some peace,
They disturb our pleasure,
And shout, "Let talking cease."

But still we have to suffer
Under their tyrant rule...
But what's to be done about it,
Except destroy the school?

W. McK. and A.F. (2A)

A Corsican's Impression of Scotland

Hello. Yes, it's the wee yin. First of all, I would like to thank all the pupils of Wishaw High School for realising right from the first day that I was the French 'assistant' - and not a girl from Wishaw Public who had strayed into the wrong school by mistake. No doubt you will now appreciate the truth of the old Scots saying: 'Gude gear gangs into little bouk.'

The highlight of my year here was Hogmanay. As you say, it was great. I had never realised that Scotch whisky could be so good. Of course, I am not implying that this was the only thing I liked about your New Year festivities; in fact, what I enjoyed most about this time of year was meeting lots of people and making new friends. Among these new friends were even some of my pupils.

Later in the month, I acquired a taste for yet another of your Scottish delicacies - haggis. You know, in France there are many funny jokes about this 'creature', so I must admit that I was very pleasantly surprised.

Coming from the Riviera, I found the weather a bit different; but it was not quite as bad as I had been led to believe by my friends in Nice, who told me that Scotland was at the North Pole - and that I would need to wear layers of woollen sweaters and a fur coat. That would have been very embarrassing, as my wardrobe does not include a fur coat.

I was more impressed by the beautiful scenery than I had expected to be, because the Highlands remind me of Corsica with its huge forests and multitudes of sheep running about.

The Scots may have the reputation of being mean, but I will put your minds at rest and say that during my stay here I always experienced warm hospitality.

I want to thank everybody for the great time I had at Wishaw High School: my first experience of 'teaching' was not too bad after all. I don't know if your French has improved very much, but I am sure that you can now understand my English.

Now the holidays are coming, and I am going home. But I think that "ce n'est qu'un au revoir", for I hope to come back some time next year. So 'bonnes vacances' to everybody, enjoy yourselves very much, and be real angels when the next 'assistant' comes in August.

Josèphe Arrighi

A Christmas Rose

Sweet, beauteous flower of snowy winter days,
When once I've seen thee dressed in purest white,
The memory forever with me stays...
'Tis in my mind a scene of pure delight.

Again I see the petals soft and smooth,
The dark and dainty leaves of glossy green,
The flowers which Winter's icy gardens soothe,
And joy and gladness bring where'er they're seen.

Far sweeter thou, O fair and fragile rose,
Than any flower of sun and Summer's heat.
In Winter's frost, in wild wind, rain, or snows,
No Summer's flowers I'll find, but thee I'll meet.

The seasons quickly pass and winters fly,
But memories of sweet flowers - they never die.

Margaret Graham (3A)

Fire Drill

A jangling bell,
A pupil's yell,
O, what a thrill!
What can it be?
Strange mystery?
No, fire drill.

The pupils rise,
They can't disguise
An inward glow.
Release from French
Is such a wrench,
As you must know.

They race outside,
They try to hide
Their joyous glee;
For, after all,
To have roll call
Means they are free.

Each one awaits,
Anticipates
Some games and fun,
But hopes are dashed
And dreams are smashed:
The drill is done.

A swaying mass
Returns to class,
Moves on its way.

No more fire drill —
At least until
Next practice day.

Mary Hepburn (Class 4)

The Getaway

I crouched on the ground, waiting my chance for a getaway. Every fibre in my body was tensed. If I had moved a muscle, I would have been detected. I had to get away quickly. There were hundreds of people standing round about, but none of them could help me. I was on my own.

I lifted my head to get my direction. Suddenly, I was looking into the black muzzle of a revolver. In just over ten seconds it would be over. But I could not stand it. I rose to my feet and ran. I had only gone two yards - when there was a loud report, then another. It was no use running. You see, I had false-started in the 100 yards at the school sports.

S.R. (Class 5)

The Pupil's Handbook

Each year in August, as a rule,
We welcome new boys to our school,
And though they're somewhat rough and crude,
They always seem a happy brood.
Let us some hints to them express,
(Though 'tis not our purpose to depress),
To keep them on the narrow path,
Avoiding some dread prefect's wrath.

Rule 1, dear friends: on the left side stay
In corridor or on stairway;
And if you dare walk two-abreast
To hear some joke, repeat some jest,
A voice will bellow loud and clear,
"Hey there, you fool, come straight back here,

260

And from your face remove that smile —
You're meant to walk in single file."

Four other rules should be observed,
If high esteem you wish preserved:
You must not talk or chat in school,
Or throw things in the goldfish pool;
Down banisters you must not slide,
Lest into prefects' arms you glide;
And at your teachers never swear,
E'en though your temper thin might wear.

Please do not smoke - though it's provoking
To see some seniors slyly smoking,
While you this pleasure must forgo,
Because "he's only twelve, you know".
Likewise, with maidens be discreet;
And don't go careering up the street
In cafes and such like to tarry —
But rather join the school library.

These simple rules will get you there,
Provided they're observed with care:
You'll be the prefects' pride and joy,
A super-duper High School boy.
But would the school be much improved,
With rough and tough youths all removed?
For then, when all is said and done,
A prefect's lot wouldn't be such fun.

M.H. (Class 5)

Hidden Treasure

Yonder on the mountain top
Gentle beauty hidden lies,
Unmatched in splendour by the peaks
That raise their towers to the skies.

Lovely as she is today,
Lovely she will ever reign,
Aloof, unseen, by man unspoilt,
Queen of her broad domain.

Eternal, proud, through winter snows,
Through summer heat and storm-winds' power,
Nature's elect in that vast world –
The simple alpine flower.

W.T. (4A)

My First Day at Wishaw High School

The sun was streaming through my bedroom window, as I awoke to the thought that it would be my first day at Wishaw High School. I was so excited that I was hardly dressed when my friend called for me.

Quick as I was, we missed the bus; but Mr Currie, my friend's father, took us to the junction of Ryde Road and Kirk Road.

My first impression of the school was of a huge, whitewashed building surrounded by sundry smaller buildings, two of which were the prefabs and the janitor's house.

It was amazing to find a crowd of curious 2nd Year girls looking at you as if your hair was standing on end, or as if you'd lost a button off a new blazer, or something like that.

After going into the hall and being told which class I was in, I was led - with my new classmates - by a prefect to Room 30 to meet our registration teacher. We spent the morning in this room copying our timetable.

In the afternoon, however, we went to different classes. I enjoyed this very much, and when it was time to go home, I discovered that I had one jotter.

I found it hard to go in single file. Also, all the prefects kept shouting, 'Keep to the left'; and since I was used to keeping to the right, this was the absolute limit. I was warned not to go up the wrong stairs and meet some of the staff.

When I arrived at the school, I realised that it was entirely different from what I had expected. I had thought that all the teachers would walk about in robes and mortarboards, that the Rector would be an old, wrinkled, bad-tempered man, and that the school would be built like an old-fashioned mansion, with a huge staircase for the staff in the middle of the house and a smaller one at each side for the boys and girls.

One thing I was glad to find out was that the dinners were much better than the ones at my old school.

I was left breathless when I saw the gym, because I had never expected it to be so large.

To crown my happiness, I was told when I went home that I could go wherever I wanted to go. That was to the baths.

Margaret Boyd (IB)

Surprise Attack

Silence lay upon the air – the calm before the storm. Then the announcement was made. It was the signal for the attacking forces to advance, but for a long time they seemed to be paralysed with fear. Nobody moved, everybody just looked at each other. Finally one solitary figure began to cross no-man's land, its echoing footsteps seeming to give courage to the others. There was a noise like the sound of a thousand drums as their feet thundered towards their target. The poor, beleaguered enemy hadn't a chance. Their mouths went dry, their tongues stuck to the roofs of their mouths, their knees began to knock and their hands became clammy. No wonder. Before they could escape, we were in among them and the boys were left cursing whoever had the bright idea of having a ......ladies' choice.

Phyllis Wright (Class 4)

28

1960-1966

The Times They Are A-Changing

Bob Dylan

By the end of the 1950s, the High School, like many other senior secondary schools in Lanarkshire, was bulging at the seams. There were two reasons for this: more primary pupils were achieving the standards required for admission to a senior secondary school; and more secondary pupils were staying on at school after they reached the statutory leaving age of fifteen, partly because there was a shortage of good jobs, and partly because parents realised that a respectable leaving certificate (at the very least) was essential if their sons and daughters were to have any chance of getting one of the few good jobs that were available.

In June 1960, in response to the mounting difficulties accommodation-wise, the Education Committee announced its plans for an extension to the High School: the prefabs were to be demolished and 'new buildings' erected between Waverley and the main building. Unfortunately, these plans were never implemented.

G&S at WHS

During that same month, the school staged *The Yeoman of the Guard*. This was followed by *The Gondoliers* and *The Pirates of Penzance* in 1961 and 1963 respectively.

All-Rounder Par Excellence

He parked his six-feet high frame and eleven stones of healthy muscle on the edge of an easy chair, bowed his head to hide just the hint of an embarrassed smile, and said: "I'd like to run in the Olympics some day, but I don't think I'll ever manage that."

The speaker was certainly being level-headed - but also, perhaps, a little too modest, since of all the millions who daily dream of Olympic fame, Andrew Hepburn, an eighteen-year-old Shottsonian, a pupil at

Wishaw High School, a scholar, an athlete and an extraordinary footballer, has a better chance than most of realising his dream.

Such were the first two paragraphs of an article that appeared in the *Wishaw Press* on 24 June. Its protagonist was boys' captain in session 1959-60, won the senior championship at the sports in 1960 (setting four new school records in the process), played for the Scottish under-18 football team against England at Burnley, and represented his country (in the 440 yards) in an athletics international against Wales.

Bluestockings in Blue Blazers

At the prize-giving, McKellar drew the audience's attention to 'an unusual fact':

All the first prizes from Class 1 to Class 6 have been won outright by girls - except in Class 4, where a boy had the temerity to challenge for first place. I can only suggest that the boys should either look to their laurels, or accept that the appellation 'weaker sex' applies, intellectually at least, to them and not to the girls.

Having also mentioned the fact that the school's 'tennis devotees had lost their playing-ground in the cause of improving the school frontage', he gave those same aficionados an assurance that they would be provided with 'suitable accommodation very soon behind the main building'. Sadly, though McKellar willed the end with regard to new tennis courts, the Education Committee did not will the financial means.

In December, a Christmas Fair was held in aid of the Memorial Trust Playing Fields Project; it was opened by John Gibb, Assistant Principal of Jordanhill College of Education and a former pupil of the High School. 'One of the most pleasing features of the day,' the *Wishaw Press* commented, 'was the crèche, where a very happy band of young children, supervised by senior pupils, amused themselves with a great variety of toys, while their parents toured the stalls.' The sum raised by the fair exceeded £800, and in praising this 'wonderful effort' McKellar declared that a school which could achieve 'such an outcome in such difficult times and in such weather conditions' had every reason 'to be at once proud and humbly grateful'.

1961

His life was gentle ..

Shakespeare, *Julius Caesar*

Dr Wilson died at his home in St Andrews on 18 January. At a short memorial service in the hall, McKellar described him as 'a simple, modest man of unfailing kindness and great humanity'. 'The criterion of a headmaster's success,' he added, 'is the spirit of his school, and when he retired in 1953, Dr Wilson left a happy and united school, a fitting tribute to his benevolent rule.'

Bible Studies

During the Easter holidays, five senior boys attended a six-day conference organised by the YMCA at Bonskied House near Pitlochry. The highlight of the conference, which included a discussion on the relevance of the Bible to everyday life, was a visit from Sir John Hunt.

Workloads

In November, Robert Liddell, Principal Teacher of Modern Languages and Depute Rector, resigned due to ill health. In the course of an interview with a reporter from the *Wishaw Press*, McKellar said that "Mr Liddell's case was another example of the consequences of the intolerable burden that was being placed upon experienced teachers". 'With vastly increased numbers in the advanced classes,' he went on, 'at least twice as much work is being asked of fewer and fewer qualified staff, and the menace to the health of devoted teachers like Mr Liddell is becoming more obvious every day. This is a situation that has to be viewed with alarm by all those interested in the future of education in Scotland.'

Still on the subject of teachers' health: Jim Fleming, a new recruit to the Modern Languages Department, broke his collarbone in two places during the Staff v Pupils football match.

The Fickle Fingers of Fate

The school had a new janitor - 'Tommy' Miller. 'Tommy' was a hard-bitten 'wee droll', who occasionally helped me to umpire the inter-House cricket matches. He knew nothing about the rules of the game (but neither did the vast majority of the participants), and the gesture he employed to indicate that a batsman was out (I really should have told him that only one finger was required) would not have found favour with the more fastidious members of the MCC, especially since he was in the habit of confirming his decisions by growling, "Fuckin' out".

Finders (Not Always) Keepers, Losers (Usually) Weepers

A lost property office was set up in the pavilion, which ended up 'housing mountains of unclaimed articles'. Pupils were required to pay a small fine if they wished to regain any item they had lost.

1962

In January, the Senior Debating Society organised the High School's first Burns Supper, an event that was destined to become a regular feature on the school calendar. Such an outcome may have had something to do with the fact that McKellar was a devotee of the national bard and chairman of the local Burns Club.

The Opium of the Pupils

As far as ordinary meetings of the Debating Society were concerned, McKellar said he was particularly pleased to learn that the senior pupils had included 'religious and Christian topics' in their discussions; and that at the Christian Youth Movement Conference in Hamilton they had not only "contributed much of value to the debates" but had also been "stimulated by the vigour and enthusiasm of the Church's representatives". 'In these days of falling moral standards,' he asserted, 'it is a fine thing that intelligent young people and the Church should get together to meet the challenge.'

The Superlativeness of the Long-Distance Runners

In April, the under-15 cross country team (Allan Carson, James Finlay, Fraser Organ, and William Smith) became the first winners of the Alec Barrie Trophy, a trophy that had been donated by Shettleston Harriers for competition among schools in Glasgow and Lanarkshire.

The under-18 football team won the Keith Cup. This was the first of three consecutive appearances by teams from the High School in the final of that competition, the second ending in victory (1-0) over Coatbridge St Pat's and the third in defeat (1- 2) at the hands of Dalziel High School.

A rector's lot is not a happy one.

In May and June, 332 pupils were presented at the remodelled Scottish Certificate of Education examinations, the results of which were not made known until early in August. According to McKellar, the new set-up had 'disturbing consequences':

As a result of the vast increase in the number of candidates, the amount of clerical work devolving on the school has been doubled; and while the Scottish Education Department has had to recruit a great deal of extra help to attend to its side of the business, no such additional assistance has been available to headmasters, who, it must be remembered, have to look after the rest of the school at the same time.

Timetabling for next session can only be, at best, a piece of guesswork. Not knowing the results of the SCE Examinations, we have little idea of how many post-intermediate pupils will be returning to school next session - and even less idea of what subjects they will be studying: consequently, we have no idea at all of how many teachers will be required.

A further consequence of the late declaration of examination results is that Higher candidates have applied for admission not to one, but to nearly every university and college in Scotland; or else they have applied for jobs with half a dozen prospective employers. I have had to deal, therefore, with hundreds of questionnaires and enquiries - a further heavy burden, and one that involves a lot of sheer guesswork.

Finally, although the introduction of the less demanding O-Grades means that there will be a huge increase in the number of pupils who acquire a leaving certificate, many pupils who acquire a certificate will not, contrary to their expectations, acquire a job - since employment prospects are bleak.

One other consequence of the new-style examinations was the cancellation of the annual operetta.

Permanent Secretaries

By now, Helen Costley had joined Pearl Davies on the clerical staff, and McKellar praised 'their efficiency and acceptance, with the utmost cheerfulness, of an excessively heavy workload at this trying time' (another reference to the SCE Examinations Mark 2). It is worth noting, en passant, that Pearl Davies' period of service lasted till 1985, and Helen Costley's till the High School was closed in 1992.

Parent's Nights were held on successive Tuesdays in June. The headmasters of several primary schools were present at the first of these events; representatives from local industry, further education, and the Youth Employment Service attended the second. On both occasions, after McKellar had spoken about the new Scottish Certificate of Education (touching on its implications vis-a-vis the curriculum and the opportunities it could open up on the job front), parents (numbering more than 900 over the two nights) were given the chance to consult the staff and the special guests. "The closest cooperation," McKellar explained, "between those concerned with a child's education - the home, the school, the college, and the workshop - cannot fail to be mutually profitable, and the success of the two meetings is at once a consequence of the parents' interest and a great encouragement to myself and my staff."

Also in June, as part of the Scottish Week organised by the National Union of Farmers, sixty High School pupils were given the opportunity to observe modern farming methods at a nursery in Lanark and a farm near Lesmahagow.

The German Connection

During the summer holidays, a party of fifty-seven pupils from Wishaw High School, Dalziel High School, and Our Lady's High School visited Schweinfurt, the Burgh's twin town in Germany. During their sojourn in Schweinfurt, the pupils took part in a sports meeting and a football match (the opposition being provided by their hosts), and paid visits to local schools and ballbearing factories, the town hall (where they were accorded an official reception), a monastery, and the East German border.

A reciprocal visit was arranged in 1963, after which Provost Lawson declared:

What Schweinfurt and the Burgh of Motherwell and Wishaw are doing is an example not only to their two countries but also to the whole wide world.

Visits to Schweinfurt continued to be arranged throughout the 1960s and 1970s; and, in a modified version, they were still taking place in the 1990s.

Another party of High School pupils ventured even further afield - to Lake Constance in Austria, as part of a tour of seven European countries.

1963

Mary L. Mitchell, the Rector's secretary and the last member of staff whose period of service (39 years, in her case) bridged the gap between the old and the new High School, died in hospital on 14 March. At a short service in the hall, McKellar paid tribute to 'her tireless energy and general efficiency, her loyalty and devotion, her great sympathy and understanding, her tact and discretion, and her sense of humour'. 'Moreover,' he continued, less tautologically, 'Miss Mitchell was held in great esteem and affection by teachers, pupils, janitors, cleaners, and school meals personnel.' Tangible confirmation of her universally high standing was immediately provided by the many donations that were instrumental in creating the Mary L. Mitchell Memorial Prize for excellence in Commercial Subjects - the first winner of which was Ina Clark.

The race IS to the swift.

1963 was an outstandingly successful year for the school's athletes. Fifteen 'gold' and eight 'silver' medals were won at the County Sports; and at the Scottish Schools' Athletics Championships, Eric Warren won the under-15 100 yards, and both the boys' (Eric Warren, John McAra, Ian Kidd, and David Murray) and the girls' (Jean Rae, Sadie Miller, Christine Sloan, and Marjory Johnstone) under-15 relay teams were crowned as Scottish champions.

The 1st XI cricket team won the Sneddon Trophy for the first time.

An Autumn Fayre raised more than £80 for old age pensioners; and the Junior Choir made its first public appearance - at the Christmas service.

1964

As a result of the acute shortage of qualified teachers that was highlighted so persistently by McKellar in his annual speech at the prize-giving, the school had to call on the services of five uncertificated teachers at different times during the year, even though McKellar himself was anxious to have the employment of such stopgaps terminated as quickly as possible and a fully-trained, graduate profession created.

Pull the Finger Out

Record numbers of pupils were presented at both Ordinary and Higher Grade in the SCE Examinations. According to McKellar, however, too many pupils who were capable of sitting Highers in their fifth year were forced to wait until their sixth year to do so, because they had concentrated on taking O-Grades in their fourth year. 'The 6th Year,' he said, 'is becoming increasingly cluttered up with pupils who have set their sights too low and are extending to six years a course they should have completed - at least in their best subjects - in their fifth year.'

More and more pupils were also trying 'to wangle a leisurely time and an abundance of free periods' by dropping subjects in which they had gained an O-Grade. McKellar therefore made it compulsory for these pupils to take up other subjects in place of the ones they had dropped. 'In a school like ours,' he declared, 'we must make sure that standards are maintained, and that no pupil avoids a hurdle just because he is too lazy to train in order to clear it.'

Once more unto the beach, dear friends, once more . . .

During the summer holidays, a party of thirty-two boys spent a fortnight at Finale Ligure on the Italian Riviera. This was the first in a series of similar trips arranged and supervised by Derek Winton, Tom Forsyth, and Willie Hunter.

A second Autumn Fayre, organised by the Senior Debating Society, raised over £100 for the Wishaw Old Age Pensioners' Association - and the money was eventually spent on providing local pensioners with a food parcel at their annual Christmas treat in December. A group of High School pupils attended this event and helped to distribute the parcels.

Obituaries

Bill Clark, who died on 3 September, was Principal Teacher of Science at the High School for sixteen years. However, 'his enthusiasm for teaching Science was not confined to Wishaw; for he also served on the Advisory Panel responsible for drawing up the new Science syllabus. In the staffroom, he loved to express his views (and on all subjects these were worth hearing), and he will long be remembered for his boyish enjoyment of any humorous situation that arose. Above all, he was a highly conscientious teacher, one instance of this conscientiousness being the extra tuition he gave his Higher Chemistry classes - from 8.15 till 9 o'clock, two or three times a week - prior to the Leaving Certificate examinations.'

The Reverend Donald C. Whitelaw, who died in the course of the same session, was school chaplain for more than twenty years. 'He chose to be a guide, philosopher, and friend to the school, not merely an examiner in biblical knowledge. Even so, nothing pleased him more than to hear a beautiful passage from the Bible (the longer the better) repeated from memory by a High School pupil, an exercise he rightly regarded as a good antidote for some of the slovenly speaking and writing of modern times. His Christmas addresses to the assembled school were models of their kind.'

1965

Two Honorary Dicks

In February, two High School pupils, David Watson and Willie McFadyen, who were largely responsible for the arrest and conviction of a local man who had broken into a car in the Main Street and stolen a radio, were interviewed by Bill Tennent on STV's popular magazine programme, *Here and Now*; they also received a letter of commendation from the Chief Constable, and a set of private investigator's credentials from the Association of Private Investigators.

It should be noted that Willie McFadyen was also a fine cricketer: I can remember umpiring a match in which he achieved a hat-trick.

J'accuse (1)

The following month, in the course of opening an Exhibition of Arts and Crafts at Wishaw Community Centre, McKellar said that it was a pleasure to meet people who knew how to make use of their leisure time - particularly in an era when there were more 'onlookers' than ever before. 'I find it both surprising and disappointing,' he complained, 'that the children at Wishaw High School spend the bulk of their leisure time at the school playing shove-halfpenny. Parents should ask themselves just how much their children ape them when it comes to spending their leisure time.'

J'accuse (2)

A week later, the *Wishaw Press* published a letter (signed 'Typical Parents') that expressed both disbelief and resentment at McKellar's 'pessimistic' views regarding his pupils. The letter also contained a disparaging reference to 'the low standards of dress and behaviour' at the High School - a state of affairs that was deemed by the parents in question to be 'most disturbing', in view of 'the high standards which clearly obtained in many other schools in the Burgh'. This is the first occasion on which criticism was levelled publicly at the High School, and such lese-majesty is surprising enough to suggest (I put it no more strongly) that some sort of decline may have begun to set in at the school. In the event, McKellar made no effort to answer his critics.

The annual swimming gala was held (and this was a first) in the newly opened Wishaw Baths. The highlight of the afternoon's proceedings was the Staff v Pupils relay race.

The French Connection

At the invitation of Pierre Valette, a former French 'assistant', a party of boys from the High School and Dalziel High School spent part of the Easter holidays in Vézénobres, a small town just north of Nîmes; and similar trips (confined to High School pupils) were arranged in 1967, 1971, and 1974. All four trips involved sightseeing, several football matches, at least one civic reception - and lavish hospitality.

I myself took part in two of these trips, and it was a pleasant change - from some highly embarrassing experiences in various parts of Great Britain - to be the only member of the group whose name was always pronounced correctly by our French hosts and spelt correctly in the local newspapers (I think this may have had something to do with the fact that the first President of the Third Republic was a certain Patrice Mac-Mahon). Derek Winton's name, on the other hand, appeared in one of the newspapers as 'Winston Berk'.

One of the lab technicians (his Christian name was Alec; I can't remember his surname) acted as trainer for the duration of the various football matches we played, and all the medical paraphernalia (plasters, painkilling sprays, etc.) was kept in one of the players' toilet bags. On one memorable occasion, after he had run on to the field to minister to an injured player, Alec mistook a tube of toothpaste for a tube of analgesic cream and started to massage the player's leg with the contents.

It should be recorded, finally, that reciprocal trips were arranged in 1966 and 1972.

Back on the home front: the Juvenile football team reached the final of the Cameronian Shield for the first time; various groups of pupils visited the Livingstone Memorial at Blantyre, Pitlochry Theatre, Faskally, Hadrian's Wall, and the Marine Biological Station at Millport; Peter Hughes, "the burly youngster from the Law with the up an'-at-'em style", played for the Scottish Youth team against England, Ireland and Wales, and for the Scottish under-18 team against England and Wales; and in the National Travel Scholarships Competition organised by Brooke Bond, Joyce McLean's essay (in the form of a newspaper report on the Scottish Christian Youth Assembly in Edinburgh) won the prize for the best essay submitted by a senior pupil on the roll of a school in Lanarkshire.

The High School's roll (roughly 800) continued to be augmented by pupils from 'O-Grade schools' like Brandon High School and Carluke High School, 'with which there was close, amicable, and fruitful cooperation'.

Of the pupils who left school in June, seventy-four (an all-time high) continued their studies at university or such colleges as Art School and Jordanhill College of Education; only forty went into industry or commerce.

Who steals my purse steals cash.

The school log for 15 September reads as follows:
There were two cases of theft today in the school: one case a petty theft from the blazer of a girl in the gym; the other very serious, in which Miss Yuill had a sum of more than £60 stolen from her handbag, which she had left in the storeroom. The police were called in, but made little progress in their investigation.

1966

In May, the 6th Year presented the school with the new trophy they had purchased with the proceeds from an athletics match against Dalziel High School. The trophy was awarded every year to the winners of the Senior Girls' Invitation Relay at the school sports.

Goodbye, Mrs Chips.

The retiral was announced of Mary ('Polly') Mackie, who for twenty years had 'helped to satisfy the appetites of thousands of pupils in the school canteen and tuck shop'.

Après Neil le déluge?

McKellar himself retired at the end of June. One of the considerations (indeed, the only one he mentioned explicitly) that prompted his decision to retire was 'the great upheaval' (basically, the creation of comprehensive schools) that was about to take place in the provision of secondary education in the Burgh. 'In the trying days ahead,' he explained, 'it is essential for the school to be led by a younger man full of drive, resource, and foresight.'

In reality, there was no 'great upheaval' - at least not immediately. What happened was that some certificate pupils from Newmains and the south side of Wishaw were instructed to enrol at Coltness High School - not, as in the past, at the High School. The High School ceased, therefore, to be the only senior secondary school in Wishaw, since it lost its 'monopoly' with regard to presenting secondary pupils for Highers at the SCE examinations.

A much more ominous feature of the Director of Education's blueprint for the development of secondary education in the Wishaw area was that it envisaged a time when the High School would be required to 'combine' with Coltness High School, so that these two schools could 'provide for the educational needs of the north side of Wishaw'.

McKellar's retiral was marked by a dinner at the Crown Hotel, Carluke, attended by J.S. McEwan (Director of Education), William Bell (Chairman of the Education Committee), Alex McIntosh (Town Clerk), and A.S. Kelly (Her Majesty's Chief Inspector of Schools). After a witty tribute ('the highlight of the evening', according to the *Wishaw Press*) from George Brown, Principal Teacher of English at the High School, and a speech by the Director of Education in which he stressed how much McKellar's services to the teaching profession were appreciated by the authorities, McKellar was presented - by way of a gift from the staff - with two Parker Knoll chairs. Earlier in the day, it should be added, he had received six crystal glasses from the janitors and cleaners, a golf club and a caddie cart from the pupils, and an ornamental cigarette lighter from the secretarial staff.

McKellar's memories of his time at the High School are recorded in the 1966 edition of *The Octagon*:

You've often heard me say that when you leave school the things you remember best have little to do with examinations, or prizes, or classroom instruction. A good school is a little community, and it is the unusual, the unexpected, the amusing incidents affecting you as a member of that community that stand out in your memory as you bid farewell to your old school. Your first day at the High School, your first Christmas party, the day when you won the sack race or dropped the baton at the last changeover in the relay race, the day when things did not go according to plan on a school excursion, the day when you dropped a plate in the canteen - these moments, and perhaps a few others that are more painful to recollect, are likely to be remembered.

On the eve of my own departure, I find that this truth also holds good for me. The academic and athletic distinctions of High School pupils, past and present, bulk large in my memory; but as I write, it is rather a series of ill-defined, half-forgotten images that flit across my mind's eye like identikit pictures, unreal, nameless, fragmentary. I see a stage that quivered beneath the feet of the sailors who hailed their 'right good captain' in our first, and in some ways our happiest, production of comic opera – 'HMS Pinafore'; I see a High School boy - groaning under his load of hiker's equipment - sinking into a chair in a French cafe with the memorable remark, "Ah'm fair bate."

I recall the evening of an inter-schools Burns Supper, when a group of High School girls had to pipe in the haggis vocally - because the piper was late; a superb KoKo in our production of 'The Mikado', *the little flower in his cap swaying in time to the music of 'Willow, titwillow, titwillow'; a memorable Christian in Bunyan's* "The Pilgrim's Progress", *which we staged in Wishaw Old Parish Church; a nightmare journey in a bus holding a football cup in my lap, while joyous High School pupils made the 'Hampden Roar' seem like a whisper; fainting cases in the hall at the morning service; 'Artful Dodgers' at clocking-in; the sad fate of the 'Burning Bush'... I could fill a book with such reminiscences. That it is time I retired, however, was made quite clear recently, when a small boy stopped me in the corridor with the salutation, 'Please sir, ma grannie was asking for you.' I have never felt so old.*

Under-14 Football Team (1917)
Winners of Cambusnethan Schools Cup

Under-18 Football Team (1929)
Winners of Sir Henry Keith Secondary Trophy

Under 15 Football Team (1932)
Scottish Intermediate Shield Winners

Senior Hockey Team (mid-1940s)
Back: Jenny Barrie, Elsa Allan, Helen Hall
Middle: Ann Chapman, Jean Morrison, Betty Rae
Front: Jean Smith, Margaret Murray, Ann Hunter, Ishbel Young, Miss Gallacher

Intermediate Team (1949)

R. Haston, I. Prentice, Mr. Bonomy, C. Broadley, A. Orr, J. Ross
R. Gavin, Jim Rodger, R. Shearer (Capt.), J. Lumsden, R. Hannah
R. Barr, J, Barrie.

Senior Football Team (1949)
Mr. Ross, E. Anderson, T. Prentice, J. Robertson, J. Rodger, P. Hill.
W. Westwood, W. Brown, D. Bruce, J. Allan, S. Bruce, T. Scoular.

Junior Football Team (1952)

J. Hislop, H. Smith, W. McDougall, J. O'Hara, R. Duncan, R. Rodger, D. MacIntyre, I. O'Connell.

J. Finlay, S. Reid, W. Thomson, H. Stevenson, H. Rattray.

Intermediate Football Team (1953)

T. Noble, W. Laing, J. O'Hara, I. Bryden, R. Barr, T. Lawson, N. Hyslop.

W. McDougall, W. Hunter, W. Reid, H. Stevenson, B. McIntyre.

1st XI Hockey Team (1952)
B. Rodger, E. Anderson, H. Scott, A. Stewart, N. Wassell. E. Scott.
I. Scott, B. Sloan, L. Weir, H. Lyon, J. O'Neill.

2nd XI Hockey Team (1953)
R. Watson, B. McAlister, J. Henry, B. Paterson, J. Herbert, M. Spicer.
M. Stewart, C. Shaw, F. Dinwoodie, M. McPherson, C. Scott

1st XI Cricket Team (1951)

1st XI Hockey Team (1953)
B. Ritchie, M. Swanson, H. Scott, E. Kerr, J. Montgomery, M. Spicer.
F. Hunter, B. Sloan, L. Weir, B. Rodger, A. Stark.

Winners of Scottish Secondary Shield (1951)

Girls' Relay Team (1960)

Intermediate Football Team (mid-1960s)

Senior Cricket Team (mid-1960s)

288

Juvenile Football Team (late 1960s)

Tennis Enthusiasts (late 1960s)

Under 16½ Football Team (1968)
Winners of Waddell Cup

Senior Football Team (1968)

Senior Hockey Team (early 1970s)

Senior Rugby Team (early 1970s)

My Favourite Team

29

The High School under McKellar

The roll remained fairly stable (at around 800) between 1953 and 1966, and since the capacity of the school continued to be no more than 650 (though plans were drawn up for an extension on several occasions, they were never, as we have seen, implemented), the accommodation available at the school was under constant pressure.

From the standpoint of both pupils and members of staff, the physical conditions were rather unprepossessing. Six teachers had no room of their own (I was one of these peripatetics - in my case, peripathetic would have been a more fitting description - and it was a real burden, in every sense of the word, having to lug books and jotters from one room to another at the end of virtually every period); there was no proper library (every year, in *The Octagon*, the librarians complained about 'the awkward working conditions'), no medical or 'rest' rooms, and no common rooms for the senior pupils; and the staffrooms and toilet facilities were grossly inadequate.

Though the overall roll did not fluctuate to any great extent, there were several significant changes in its composition: there were fewer pupils in 1st Year, since only those who were reckoned to be capable of eventually 'sitting their Highers' gained admittance; but as a result of the introduction of the Scottish Certificate of Education, more and more pupils were staying on at school beyond the statutory leaving age, and the numbers in 4th, 5th, and 6th Year almost trebled in McKellar's time. Indeed, there were almost as many pupils in the senior school as in the 1st, 2nd, and 3rd Year.

More and more pupils gained three or more Highers (the minimum required for admission to a university), and the number of university entrants doubled in the space of ten years.

The High School maintained its impressive success rate in what McKellar called 'the supreme test of scholarship in schools' - the Glasgow University Bursary Competition. At least one pupil from the school was placed in the first hundred in every year of McKellar's rectorship (four pupils achieved this distinction in 1966); and John Watt gained tenth place in 1964.

According to McKellar, teams from the High School 'continued to be a force to be reckoned with not only at the traditional games of football, hockey, cricket, netball and golf, but also on the athletics track'. The following list of sporting successes confirms this claim in respect of football, cricket, and athletics:

Football

1954 - Motherwell and Wishaw Intermediate League
1955 - Motherwell and Wishaw Intermediate League (jointly with Our Lady's High School)
1956 - Motherwell and Wishaw Intermediate League
1957 - McGowan Cup
1959 - Motherwell and Wishaw Intermediate League
Anderson Cup (Vicerunt: J. Cooper, W. Kilpatrick, I. Baillie, B. McKnight, A. Kerr, J. Fraser, S. Robertson, J. Moore, S. Francis, S. Mauchline, and P. Austin)
1962 - Lanarkshire League Division 2
Keith Cup (Vicerunt: E. Ross, T. Johnstone, A. Mauchline, W. Duncan, A. Kerr, T. Bowden, S. Francis, J. Moore, D. Gilchrist, A. Walker, and I. Bill)
1963 - Keith Cup (Vicerunt: N. Telfer, W. Turner, E. Barr, G. McGuffie, W. Duncan, J. Duncan, D. McVicar, T. Rae, P. Hughes, D. Gilchrist, and J. Fyfe)
Watt Cup (Vicerunt: J. Ferrier, J. Rattray, R. Wright, R. Wilson, C. Waddell, J. Taylor, E. Shaw, J. Bissett, R. Train, J. McAra, and A. Fleming)
1964 - Motherwell and Wishaw Intermediate League
Anderson Cup (Vicerunt: A. Johnston, J. Rattray, R. Wright, R. Wilson, C. Waddell, J. Gillon, J. McLaughlin, J. McAra, A. Fleming, G. White, J. Bissett, and J. Ferrier)
Lanarkshire League Division 1
1966 - Lanarkshire League Division 2

Cricket

1963 - Sneddon Cup

Athletics

Area Sports
1956 - Meek Cup (Senior Boys' Team Championship)
1959 - Brownlee Cup (Senior Girls' Team Championship)
    Intermediate Girls' Team Championship
    Intermediate Boys' Team was victorious in cross-country race
    sponsored by Shotts Welfare AAC.
1960 - Meek Cup
    Brownlee Cup
1961 - Brownlee Cup

County Sports
1954 - Gordon Hunter (880 yards)
1956 - Willie Hunter; Donald McIntyre
1960 - Ruby Nicol (100 yards); Margaret Simpson (100 yards);
    Andrew Hepburn (100 yards); Alex Robertson (100 yards)
1964 - Eddie Tweedlie (440 yards)
1965 - Eddie Tweedlie (440 yards)

As far as other games are concerned, the records are not detailed enough to enable me to either confirm or refute McKellar's aforementioned claim. Hockey was certainly played with great enthusiasm, and the number of teams fielded by the school increased gradually over the years: in session 1959-60, there were no fewer than seven. In the course of that same session, the 1st XI reached the quarter-final of the Glasgow and West of Scotland Senior Secondary Schools' Hockey Tournament; while in session 1963-64, the record of the 1st XI was: Played 16, Won 11, Drawn 2, Lost 3, and that of the 2nd XI: Played 16, Won 9, Drawn 2, Lost 5.

Though a senior golf championship was contested every year (and a junior version on occasion), there is only one reference in the archives to matches against other schools in Lanarkshire: in 1961 the golf team won five matches and drew one.

In 1958 the girls' tennis team reached the final of the West of Scotland Schools' Tennis Cup; two years later, the under-15 netball team won all its matches at the Youth Panel Sports, but lost in the County final to St Mary's; and in session 1964-65, the badminton team defeated both Hamilton Academy and Bellshill Academy.

In the mid-1950s, the High School produced several outstanding swimmers: Betty Rodger and Bobby Watt, who were chosen (in Watt's case, on more than one occasion) to swim for Lanarkshire at the Scottish Schools' Swimming Championships; Rita Brown, who was second in the 50 yards freestyle at those same championships; David Torrance, who won the 50 yards backstroke and the 50 yards breaststroke at the Motherwell and Wishaw Schools' Swimming Gala in 1956; and Fay Kennedy, who won the 50 yards breaststroke at the same gala.

In 1961 Mary Nicol won the 100 yards backstroke at the Scottish Schools' Swimming Championships; and at the Motherwell and Wishaw Schools' Swimming Gala, George Barr, Ann Torrance, and Elizabeth Rankin won the Morgan Trophy, the Mann Cup, and the Majury Cup respectively, by virtue of their victories in the 50 yards backstroke, 50 yards breaststroke, and 50 yards backstroke.

'In extra-curricular activities of the cultural variety,' McKellar declared at the prize-giving in 1966, 'the school has continued to expand and prosper.' This was no empty claim, for during the 1950s and early 1960s extra-curricular activities of a non-sporting nature really took off, a development for which McKellar himself deserves a lot of credit. Not only did he take an active interest in such social and cultural events as the Christmas parties, the Gilbert and Sullivan operettas, and the Burns Supper organised by the Senior Debating Society, but in session 1955-56 he launched a Junior Arts Club (there already was a Senior Arts Club, the quondam Literary and Debating Society) that attracted more than 250 1st and 2nd Year pupils to the wide range of sections it sponsored; these included Arts and Crafts, Country Dancing, Nature Study, Embroidery, Drama, Public Speaking, Model Making, Stamp Collecting, Chess, and Film Appreciation, a list to which Puppetry, Model Railways, and Photography were added in later years. Every year, the work of the different sections was put on display at a Parent's Night.

'There were chemical gardens and fossils,' the *Wishaw Press* reported, 'microscopic marvels, a profusion of fish, and other intriguing items in the room occupied by the Nature Study group; in the Photography and Stamp Collecting room, we were transported, in imagination at least, to all corners of the world; the Model Club gave us miniatures in plaster, cardboard, Meccano and wood, and also a demonstration of model aircraft in flight; the hall resounded to the strains of Scottish country dance music, as the Dancing Section went through their nimble paces; young enthusiasts in the Debating Society pled for, and against, an increase in pocket money; colour, charm, gaiety, and grief were mingled skilfully in the Drama Group's production of *The White Widow*, and this year, for the first time, pupils both produced and performed an excerpt from *Fly Away Peter*!'

The Senior Arts Club was much more limited in scope, its activities being confined to debates and visits to the opera, the theatre, and the cinema. In the event, the umbrella terms 'Senior Arts Club' and 'Junior Arts Club' were discontinued in the early 1960s, and from then on many extra-curricular groups simply had separate sections for junior and senior pupils.

The Last Picture Show

It was perhaps a sign of the times that by 1960 both the Junior and the Senior Film Society had folded. The 1958 edition of *The Octagon* contained the following explanation:

Not only the commercial cinema seems to be affected by the lure of the telly. It is evident from attendances at meetings of the Film Society that other forms of entertainment are exercising their pull. It is to be hoped, however, that the repetitive joys of the Lone Ranger will fade, and that it will be realised, as it has been by the more sensible of our pupils, that there is more to entertainment that idling one's time away. There is more worthwhile material in a single well-chosen film than in many hours of cacophonic melodrama in an electronic Dodge City.

In 1959 the Senior Choir made its first appearance at the Lanarkshire Music Festival, and three years later it gained first place in its section. The Junior Choir (with which Tom Aitken and Pat McCue were associated in its formative years) achieved a similar success in 1965, by which time it was conducted by George Annand.

Both the boys' and the girls' sections of the Scripture Union flourished throughout the 1950s and 1960s: in 1959, for example, sixty-five High School pupils submitted entries in an essay competition run by the National Bible Society of Scotland; and during session 1965-66, the girls' section had more than a hundred members. Among the teachers who took a keen interest in the Scripture Union were Elizabeth McKinnon, David Cook, Elma Paton, Colin Rankin, Isobel Hogg, Tom Neil, Elspeth Nelson, and Elsa Syme.

In 1964 the Senior Drama Club took part in the Schools' Drama Contest that was held every year at the Citizens Theatre in Glasgow, and Margaret McDougall was commended by the adjudicators for her 'outstanding' performance as St Joan in an excerpt from the play of the same name; the following year, the Junior Drama Group performed an excerpt from *Pygmalion* before an audience of senior pupils; and Colin Menzies' portrayal of Puck in the Dramatic Verse Competition was widely praised. This revival of drama at the High School was largely inspired by Maurice Bonnar.

In 1964 the chess team were joint winners (with Hamilton Academy) of the Lanarkshire Schools' Chess League; Norman Lindsay won the Lanarkshire Championship and the Glasgow Reserve Championship; and James Findlay won the Premier B Tournament at the Lanarkshire Easter Congress. That same year, the Stamp Club published the first edition of its own magazine, *The Posthorn*.

The Senior Debating Society produced many fine public speakers. In 1965 the boys' team (Lamont Baillie, David Baillie, and Ronald Cullen) and the girls' team (Christine Wilson, Christine Tait, and Joyce McLean) won the YMCA Trophy and the James Anderson Memorial Shield respectively; a year later, the A.R. Dalziel Trophy was won by James Dibdin, and the Motherwell Gavel Club Trophy by Joyce McLean. Also in 1966, more than a hundred pupils participated in a mock election arranged by the newly formed Junior Debating Society.

Finally, the mid-1960s saw the creation of a Folk Club by Bill Brodie and Maurice Bonnar. The Club composed additional verses for such songs as *Johnnie Lad* and *Cosher Baillie*, introduced theatrical lighting, and arranged a series of guest singers.

30

'A man severe he was and stern to view...'

Oliver Goldsmith, *The Deserted Village*

Few occasions generate as much ingratiating bullshit as somebody's retiral, so it's hardly surprising that most of the formal tributes to McKellar which appeared in *The Octagon* are of little or no value. Jimmy Mason, for instance, mentioned McKellar's "imposing appearance and sweeping stride" (nobody could quarrel with such a description), but then he ascribed to him "a warm humanity that embraced both the staff and the pupils", an ascription which is as ludicrous as the contention of Lockhart Whiteford that "he took over the rectorship at a time when the shell of tradition had not yet been hardened, and the school's place on the educational scene was chosen but not yet established". McKellar exhibited as much warmth and humanity as an ice pick; and the High School had been one of the top schools in the county for more than twenty years before he became rector.

**non amo te, Sabidi, nec possum dicere quare;
hoc tantum dicere possum, non amo te.**

Martial, *Epigrams*

I joined the teaching staff at the High School in 1963. In the course of the ensuing three years (the final three years of his rectorship), McKellar probably spoke to me no more than three or four times: so it is virtually impossible for me to make a detailed assessment of his personal qualities. All I can say is this: although 'he done me no wrong', there was something about him that was slightly off-putting.

McKellar did not impress Sheila Sprot, who describes him as 'not a very charismatic individual'; and 'more like a modest businessman than the head of a large academic institution'.

When she arrived at the school for the first time, McKellar was waiting on the front steps - not to welcome her, however, but to show her where she should park her car.

If the weather was inclement, Sheila would give McKellar a lift home. He never really had very much to say on such occasions, and she couldn't help thinking that he should have been giving her a lift (this, of course, was in the days when women didn't think it was demeaning to be treated in a courteous manner).

According to John Parton, McKellar had a habit of blurting out unpleasant truths (or what he perceived as truths): soon after he became Rector, for instance, he is supposed to have remarked that he had been 'sent up to Wishaw to instil some discipline into the High School', a remark that did not go down too well with the staff; and on another occasion, he suggested that teachers who had an Ordinary degree were 'not fully qualified'.

Both Eddie Tweedlie Snr., Principal Teacher of Business Studies from 1961 till 1979, and Eddie Tweedlie Jnr., boys' captain in session 1964-65, got on very well with McKellar. Eddie Snr., who was SSA representative at the time and, as it happened, the sole member of that union on the teaching staff at the High School, recalls being faced with the somewhat unnerving prospect of having to inform McKellar that he would be withdrawing his labour for a day. In the event, McKellar's reaction (amazingly) was: "You're quite right to be taking strike action, Mr Tweedlie, and the rest of the staff should be joining you." Moreover, he refused to sanction any changes in the arrangements for the prelims (Eddie was due to supervise an exam in the hall on the day in question) that could have been construed as strike-breaking.

Eddie Snr. also told me that McKellar didn't get about the school very much; and that to some members of staff (especially those based in the huts) he was known as 'the Livingstone Daisy', since he only ventured out of his room when the sun was shining. Even so, he had several unofficial 'spies' (Don Weir, Archie Leitch, and John Smith, a former crony at Dalziel High School), and they probably kept him au fait with all the minor scandals, mishaps, and indiscretions of everyday life in a secondary school.

Eddie Tweedlie Jnr. remembers very clearly McKellar's dignified presence, long stride, ramrod-like bearing, and brightly polished shoes - and also his habit of rattling a set of keys in one of his pockets, as he delivered his learned sermons at morning assemblies.

Sometimes, since Eddie was a pretty nippy runner, McKellar would send him up the Main Street to round up doggers; and this suggests that, contrary to received opinion, he may indeed have had a sense of humour - albeit a rather whimsical one.

Russell Rodger, on the other hand, describes McKellar as 'a hard man who rarely smiled and had a very abrupt way of talking'. Even when he was informing pupils, on a one-to-one basis, how they had fared in the SCE examinations, he displayed little or no warmth.

According to Miss M.E.M. Christie, who served under McKellar both as a member of his department and as a member of his teaching staff, he was much more relaxed and gregarious ('madcap gambols at school parties' is one of the phrases she uses in an article she wrote for the 1966 edition of *The Octagon*) during his years at Uddingston Grammar School; but having become Rector of the High School, he seems to have made a conscious decision to assume a stern and forbidding persona, and to keep both the staff and the pupils at arm's length.

Sometimes, but only outwith the confines of the High School, the mask was discarded. Harvie Stark lived across the road from McKellar (who frequently dropped in for a dram and a chat with his father), and he still has a vivid recollection of the occasion when he and some of his friends paid their rector a call early on New Year's Day. Astonishingly, McKellar, who clearly had already had a few, offered his pupils large whiskies.

However, to most High School pupils - especially if they read his contributions to *The Octagon* - McKellar must have seemed a rather dry old stick. Over the years, he made use of the "Rector's Page" to give a detailed account of the new SCE examinations; to offer the following portentous advice on choosing a career: 'Undoubtedly, the decision you make in this matter has a vital bearing on your future happiness. Sometimes, the mistakes you make can be rectified, but too often a hurried, foolish choice results in a life of disappointment, frustration, and even misery'; and to answer such questions as: 'How can I enter the civil service?', 'How and when can I apply for an educational grant or bursary?', and 'Can I leave school at fifteen?', to which he gave the following answer:

You are eligible to leave school only if you attain the school- leaving age of 15 before a fixed leaving date (usually the first day of a school holiday period). If you 'miss' a leaving date, you are not allowed to leave school until the next fixed leaving date. The only exception to the rule is that if you become fifteen during a holiday period of which the first day was a fixed leaving date, you can leave on the first day of the holidays, but you cannot commence work until your fifteenth birthday.

difficilis, querulus, laudator temporis acti
se puero, castigator censorque iuvenum

Horace, *Ars Poetica*

The Swinging Sixties, which 'regarded discipline, culture, and morality as Victorian anachronisms' (*ipse dixit*), and which 'decorated the Beatles and desecrated the Beatitudes', did not appeal to McKellar: he talked about his pupils being 'exposed to the onslaught of the evil forces of a materialistic age', and he regarded schools as 'the last bastions of stern application and responsible discipline'. Unfortunately, it was also his contention that in the matter of discipline schools received 'no support from some parents, and little encouragement from either the press or the law courts'; and that although schools could demand 'stern application' from their pupils, such demands were very often ignored.

McKellar was one of the first educationalists to identify lack of parental support for schools and their disciplinary code as a serious problem, a problem that in his judgment (and how astute that judgment has proved to be) would have grave repercussions for both schools and society as a whole; he was also the first rector of the High School to criticise his pupils publicly - and consistently - for lack of application:

The most alarming and discouraging symptoms of this age's educational malaise are the increasing unwillingness of secondary pupils to make the maximum effort, the eager acceptance of the easier route to riches, and the aversion to discipline, particularly rigorous mental discipline.

There are as many able pupils today as ever there were, but even they do not take the Leaving Certificate examinations in their stride, as their predecessors did. Part of the explanation for this disappointing state of affairs is to be found in the last-minute preparation that goes on. For a week or two prior to the exams - and even up to the very start of each examination - senior pupils cram themselves with half-digested mental food that should have been masticated thoroughly years before; and no one in this condition is fit for a searching test on any subject. Training by fits and starts never yet produced a champion; continuous application and high endeavour alone succeed.

McKellar was something of a reactionary as far as educational reforms were concerned. During his stint as a classroom teacher, he had been the archetypal 'chalk and talk' dominie, and he was wary of 'the new teaching machines of every sort and dimension' (whatever they may

303

have been). As for changes in the SCE examinations, he did not seem to have a very high regard for O-Grades in the context of a senior secondary school: for one thing, he frequently referred to them, mistakenly, as 'O-Levels'.

The days of the authoritarian (in the best sense of that word) teacher and the authoritarian rector were numbered, and I don't think McKellar viewed this development with any great enthusiasm. However, I am fairly certain that his decision to retire was instigated primarily by the prospect of secondary education being organised on comprehensive lines. 'A school is not made on a drawing board,' he declared at the prize-giving in 1966, 'nor is it created by shifting children about to satisfy an educational theory.'

McKellar was not afraid to speak his mind about flaws in the educational system. Virtually every year, at the prize-giving, he complained vigorously about the shortage of qualified teachers, prophesying the imminent destruction of the school's academic reputation, Scottish education, and civilisation as he knew it, unless some action was taken to alleviate that shortage; and he spoke out against the employment of uncertificated teachers, even though he had to make use of their services on numerous occasions. I have a feeling, however, that the apocalyptic tenor of his views - especially with regard to the shortage of teachers - may have led to their being taken less seriously than they should have been.

McKellar's rectorship was characterised by an almost puritanical seriousness of attitude and an unrelenting insistence on the highest standards not only of diligence and behaviour (from the pupils) but also of training, scholarship, and professional commitment (from the staff). When he became Rector, the High School - like Airdrie Academy, Dalziel High School and several other schools in the larger towns throughout Lanarkshire - was a solid, respectable senior secondary school, providing academic pupils with a sound, basically academic education; when he retired, this description was still valid, but storm clouds were massing just over the horizon.

31

The FP Club and the Memorial Trust (1953-1966)

The FP Football Club was virtually the only section of the parent organisation to remain in existence for the duration of these thirteen years; indeed, it went on to celebrate its silver jubilee in 1984, and it still (in 2016) fields a team in the Central Scottish Premier League. In April 1981, the club won the Glasgow and District President's Shield by virtue of a 3-1 victory over Xaverians; the LFA Premier League and the J. C. Wilson Shield in 2003; and most notably, the Scottish Amateur Cup in 2011.

There is no mention of the hockey section in the columns of the Wishaw Press after 1962; however, after changing its nom de guerre to Wishaw (plausible) Ladies (highly implausible), it seems to have played on till 1989.

The bridge section won the Lanarkshire and District Cup in 1957, but two years later, apparently, it folded; from 1959 to 1961 (when the cost of membership was five shillings) the FPs had a large - and thriving - choir that fulfilled many local engagements; the drama, jazz, golf, cricket, and table tennis sections were blessed with only an ephemeral existence; the rugby section that was formed in February 1967 was even more short-lived, for although the FPs applied for membership of the Glasgow and District League, there is no record of their actually playing any games.

On the social side, regular dances and occasional outings were arranged; and a lot of time and effort was expended on the lighting, heating, and redecoration of Dimsdale Hall, the 'headquarters' of the FP Club.

The Charter of the Land

In April 1955, the Housing Committee of the Town Council offered - and the Memorial Trust agreed to accept - an extension (for five years) of the lease it already held on 26 acres of land at the junction of Greenhead Road and Stewarton Street. Though a start was made to levelling off another section of this area with refuse from local building sites (a second football pitch had been mooted), for the next ten years (the lease having been extended for a further five years in 1960), most of the land was sublet to a local farmer for grazing purposes.

Stirrers

Eventually (in April 1965, to be exact), some FPs expressed their dissatisfaction with the lack of any significant development of the site in a letter to the *Wishaw Press*:

Dear Sir,

It is with considerable annoyance that we pass the Wishaw High School Memorial Trust Playing Fields these days.

Since 1947, several thousands of pounds have been raised by pupils and former pupils, but the net result of these efforts is one miserable football pitch and several acres of wasteland. Some of the money has also been used to purchase and equip an FP hall in a dilapidated building that we believe is shortly to be demolished.

What has happened to the rest of the money? How much money is in the fund? When will Wishaw High be able to boast about having playing fields on a par with those of Dalziel High School?

Eighteen Interested FPs

The Impossible Dream

Joe Darion

The answer to the last question posed in the FPs' letter was, 'Never'. Less than a year after the letter was published, the Memorial Trust terminated the lease on the Greenhead Road- Stewarton Street site; and at the same time, it declined the Town Council's offer of an alternative location for a new hall (Dimsdale Hall, as the disgruntled FPs had suggested, was to be demolished as part of the burgh's redevelopment plan). Speaking on behalf of the Memorial Trust, McKellar explained why: 'The construction of a new hall and new playing fields is quite impracticable, and beyond the financial resources of any school.' Oddly enough, the site of the projected new playing fields is still, apart from a few clumps of trees, open grassland today.

We were not with the Woolwich ...
or the Halifax ... or the Abbey National...

The money in the Memorial Trust lay in two or three ordinary bank accounts for almost thirty years (an oversight that led to the school and its FPs being deprived of a potentially considerable amount of interest); in 1990 it was transferred to an account with the Leeds Permanent Building Society; in 1992, when the High School was closed, it was 'passed on to the Former Pupils' Association' (the FP Football Club, I assume), and a separate fund was established 'to help former pupils and staff in any educational and recreational activities they might take up'. 'People who have talents,' Iain Murray explained, 'will be able to get small grants from the fund, so there will be a little bit of Wishaw High School that continues to live on.'

32

The Octagon in the 1960s

The Greedy Wasp

One day we had a picnic,
With bread and jam for tea.
We thought that there were two of us,
But found that there were three.

For Mister Wasp had joined us,
He buzzed, "Oh, what a treat!
If there's one thing I do enjoy,
It's bread and jam to eat."

I shooed him off politely,
Because I feared that he
Would soon grow tired of bread and jam,
And take a bite of ME.

But Mister Wasp grew greedy,
And in the jam he fell.
What happened to him after that,
I do not care to tell.

June Smith (1C)

Hail and Farewell

Enjoy your schooldays while you have the chance, because they are, as
everyone will tell you, the happiest time of your life. Sometimes, I admit,
in the last six years I have been depressed - and have threatened to leave
school at the first possible opportunity; but now that 'my time is nearly
up', I don't wanna go.

I will take with me - and cherish - many happy memories of my schooldays. In order to enjoy school life to the full, you must, I think, combine study with sporting activities. I have tried to do this, and I am sure that if you follow my lead you will succeed in enjoying the best of both worlds.

It is only natural that the sporting side of school life remains clearer in your memory. In my first year, I didn't take too active a part in sport, and I look back on that fact with regret; by second year, however, I had realised my mistake, and I took up hockey seriously. Playing this game has provided me with more happy moments than I ever dreamt possible, and I like it so much that I hope to continue playing with the former pupils in future years. I have met many girls and made countless 'friendly enemies' from other schools; and the game itself produces team spirit of the best kind - as well as the joys of victory and valuable lessons in defeat. I encourage all of you to take up this wonderful game: it has much to recommend it, as you will learn from the members of the 1st XI in another article.

I also remember the school sports, the Area Sports, and the County Sports with unalloyed joy. Although you can pass from success to failure so quickly, the enjoyment you take from athletics makes it all worthwhile.

One fact is plain: school life should never stop at 4 o'clock. Every night of the week, at least one branch of the Arts Club meets - whether it be the Debating Society, the Scripture Union, the Chess Club, or some other club - and I strongly recommend at least one of these clubs to you.

Then there are the annual events like the school dances, the gala, the Burns Supper, and the Commonwealth Conference, all of which are equally enjoyable, and all of which I will remember in later life.

We must never forget that the High School could not exist without the help and support of the teachers - though many of you will no doubt disagree. You tend to take them for granted: so you don't realise how fortunate you are to have such a happy and hard-working staff. One teacher told me last week that he enjoyed teaching very much because he liked people, and that he would never change his vocation. I think that he expressed the views of the whole staff.

My most treasured memory will be of the family atmosphere in the school. This is a factor I am sure we do not fully understand at the time, but it is brought home to us when we face the world outside. There is a friendly atmosphere surrounding the school all day and every day, and this will be hard to find anywhere else.

It is with regret, therefore, that I think about leaving school, and I know it will be with equal regret that I enter in my diary: 'My last day at school.'

Jan Cameron

Dash

Jump out of bed - dreadfully late;
Look at clock - half past eight;
Gulp down breakfast - briefcase to pack;
Rush downstairs - land on back;
Grab my blazer; run for bus.
Oh, I've missed it - such a fuss!
Dad gets car out; go to school.
No one in playground. I am a fool.
If only I'd listen instead of play,
I'd have known today was a holiday.

Margaret Cringles (4A)

The Ages of Man

Since the dawn of history, women have been saying to themselves - and others: "Aren't men peculiar?" Perhaps it would also be true to say that men have continually expressed a similar opinion about women, but that, at present, is beside the point.

Shakespeare believed in the 'seven ages' of man. Let us deal firstly then with the first of these ages – "the infant mewling and puking in the nurse's arms". At this tender age, no child - in view of its puckered, tear-stained face - could by any stretch of the imagination be said to be attractive, and it would perhaps be true to say that 'only a mother could love him'. And she does love him; not only that, she positively dotes on him. We have only to look at some popular songs, past and present (such as "My son, my son, you're everything to me"), to realise the truth of this.

At the toddling stage, a small boy craves a great deal of attention, and delights in creating havoc. When he insists on sharing his midday meal with the dining room carpet, his father is delighted that his son is so unselfish; however, when he throws a handful of pebbles which scratch the paintwork of daddy's car, that is quite a different tale.

All too soon, however, toddler becomes schoolboy. At this stage, hero worship is predominant and, strange as it may seem, his father's word is law. One eight-year-old boy, on being asked why he should always keep his feet clean, replied in reverent tones: "My daddy says it's in case you have an accident." The small boy invariably has great ideals and ambitions. I myself asked twenty of the species what they would like to be when they grew up. Sixteen of the twenty chose the admirable vocation of a football player.

Soon adolescence sets in. Hero worship is still very apparent, but father is no longer the hero. 'My daddy' has now become 'the old man', someone to whom, by some trick of heredity, he is related. His hero is now some worthy like Cliff Richard or that renowned and distinguished artist, Elvis - both of whom, it must be conceded, have done much for the general welfare of mankind. Most of his attention is now centred on the young lady of his choice. How often do we see gallant Casanovas leaving school at 4 p.m., carrying books in one hand and leading their sweetheart with the other. How touching it is to see a youth forsaking five of his accustomed fifteen cigarettes a day in order to take his latest young lady(?) to the pictures.

A very mature character is the young man entering his twenties. He has one ideal - his ideal woman; and one ambition - to find her. Sooner or later, he embarks on the sea of marital bliss, and from this point onwards his life changes. He is a little more considerate towards other people, a little happier, a little meaner than he was in his carefree bachelor days. His happiness is complete when he is, at length, able to survey life through a screen of wet nappies and tins of baby food.

Thus the ritual begins all over again with his own children. He himself, unfortunately, is, to use a popular phrase, 'not getting any younger'. He is approaching the age of the 'lean and slippered pantaloon'. He has for a long time been 'sans teeth', and his handsome, manly face is now creased with furrows of age and care.

Second childhood sets in when he reaches the fair age of forty, and once more he delights in creating havoc and having his favourite womanservants dance attendance on him. Once more, songs like 'Oh, my papa' are dedicated to him, and he basks in the glory of his own self-importance. Nor is he immune from ambition and hero worship. He worships the woman next door - her looks, her cooking, her intelligence. And his ambition? He is still trying to find his ideal woman, of course.

A.N. (Class 6)

Thoughts on the School Dance

At least we get away early. Wonder what the sandwiches will be like. Same as last year's, I suppose. Dash it, missed the bus! Have to walk. Here at last. Everyone's masticating cream cakes and last year's sandwiches. Here comes a cream cake. Duck! Back to the hall. First dance. Stampede by the boys towards the girls. Caught in the rush. Pity. Corns are a nuisance. So are boys. Wonder what's on television. He's nice. But he can't dance. Not him again! He can't dance either. Neither can the teachers. No offence. Him again! Fed up. Still hungry. Him again! Ouch! Last dance. Relief. Do I see some talent at last? He's gorgeous. Coming towards me. Swoon. Pity. Didn't ask me. Never mind. Him again!

3rd Year Girls

From the Sunny Spanish Shore

Motherwell Station is a pretty prosaic part of the world from which to set out on vacation for exotic lands, but at 10.30 on a Sunday evening the Royal Scot (perhaps the most inaptly named train in the world) drew out of the station, bearing its load of enthusiastically singing High School pupils.

London, at 7 a.m., is a particularly dreary place, and the attempts of some of our party to locate Carnaby Street proved fruitless - although the profusion of miniskirts did bring a contemplative gleam to the eyes of those who study the wonders of nature.

At Dover, we caught the cross-Channel ferry; and under the soporific influence of British Rail sandwiches and a peculiarly neutral-tasting orange squash, most of us tried to catch up on the sleep we had missed the previous night.

At Boulogne, we were shuttled aboard the Paris Express with the minimum of fuss. That's my story, and I'm sticking to it.

The bus tour of Paris was a mistake, for most of the party disregarded the imposing facade of the Place de la Revolution and concentrated on waving to the Parisiennes taking their evening constitutional along the boulevards.

French Railways couchettes are not the most pleasant way to get from Point A to Point B, but we did manage to survive the experience; and the following morning, we arrived in Perpignan. From there, we crossed the border into Spain by coach.

Our first experience of the Spanish way of life was in the town of Gerona, where we sampled the delights of brandy (at fourpence a glass) and those horrible concoctions the Spaniards laughingly call cakes.

To chronicle everything we did at our holiday destination of Calella would require a book - and, very probably, a blue pencil. The routine of beach, meal, beach, meal, nightclub never seemed to drag, due, no doubt, to the presence of (as one of the party whose command of colourful English is greater than mine remarked) 'them rerr Spanish dollies'.

The local habit of drinking wine from a glass spout four feet or so from one's mouth was often attempted, but never mastered - as many a soaked shirt testified. It was also the one and only time the inhabitants of Calella saw one of their straw hats decked with an SNP badge. Bemused Spaniards who asked who or what SNP was were mischievously informed that it stood for 'Shotts Nazi Party'.

The 'educational' excursions were popular; and although the trip to the monastery at Montserrat did raise a few hackles, it was redeemed by the fact that the return journey took in a champagne factory and an establishment where all the local liqueurs were provided free. Our visit to a nightclub was also thoroughly enjoyable, and the exuberant display of flamenco dancing left the party with such a tremendous collective thirst that they just had to take advantage of the nightclub's generous offer of free champagne.

On our return to Paris, we had more time to sample its culinary delights. But why does French bread always taste like rejects from the Michelin factory? And who else but the French would dream of putting cork stoppers in bottles of Coca Cola?

Speaking of culinary delights reminds me of a certain member of the party who decided that a disgustingly odoriferous stick of salami would make the perfect present for the folks back home. For this reason, he was banished to the corridor by his philistine bunkmates, there to meditate in solitary grandeur over his prized possession.

And so it was that we arrived back at Motherwell Station at 4.21 in the morning, exactly - and incredibly - fifteen days after we had left, thanks to those three stalwart guardians of the innocents abroad - Messrs Winton, Forsyth, and Brodie.

Iain Stevenson (Class 6)

Shopping List

Jeans and jumpers,
Shifts and suits,
Leather jackets,
Knee-length boots,
Fancy blouses,
Short, straight skirts,
Beatles sweaters,
Dave Clark shirts,
Bri-nylon macs,
Gloves and rings,
Scarves and handbags,
Modern things,
Low-heeled shoes,
With rounded toes:
All my money
Goes on clothes.

Anonymous (Class 5)

The First Year - a Report

In this session's 1st Year there are approximately 100 boys and 120 girls. Some have no pet hates of any kind; others expressed a dislike of cats, spiders, and mice. The boys don't seem to like the girls very much, but at the same time they themselves are not altogether popular with the girls. While the boys dislike school, doing the dishes and getting up early, the girls don't like Latin, Music and - believe it or not - washing their hair.

Both the boys and the girls are fond of swimming; and the boys also expressed a preference for fishing, football, and stamp collecting.

On the subject of food, most like fish and chips; a few like soup; and only one pupil really likes ice cream.

The most popular types of book are those concerned with mystery and adventure; other preferences include horror stories, football annuals, science fiction, and Greek mythology. One girl even mentioned Pinky and Perky. Everyone to his or her own taste.

The majority of pupils in 1st Year have at least one brother and one sister.

While wages seem to have been frozen, pocket money has certainly increased. The boys now receive an average of ten shillings a week (as opposed to five shillings in 1965), and the girls receive an average of between eight and nine shillings (as opposed to five shillings in 1965). Pupils today have so much more money to waste, something I'm sure they do very well.

Most pupils keep reasonable hours, with the majority going to bed between 9.30 and 10.30 p.m., and the remainder going later than 11 p.m.

Homework, as always, doesn't seem to be very popular, since the average pupil spends three hours per night watching television. Some even spend five hours in this way, the result being that there is very little time left for homework.

The pupils spend their weekly pocket money on sweets, dances, riding lessons, and other forms of amusement. Most of them, however, manage to save a certain amount.

French and PE are the most popular subjects, with Art following closely behind; Music and Science are not generally enjoyed.

Smoking is not popular: only a very small number have indulged, and most of them have not repeated the experience.

Most of our 1st Year pupils are well informed about politics. Everyone stated that Harold Wilson was Prime Minister - except one girl, who was rather doubtful, and several boys who seem to be under the impression that he is a Russian spy.

To sum up: the average 1st year pupil was born in May 1956; he spends most of his money on sweets, and swimming is his favourite hobby; he watches TV far too much, and prefers to hurry home and watch it instead of concentrating on his homework and taking an interest in after-school organisations.

So, boys and girls of the 1st Year, you are not the angels you think you are. Your good and bad points have been highlighted by this survey: so BEWARE.

M.M. and E.M. (Class 5A)

The School Alphabet

A's for Mr Annand,
He's really a hit.

B's for Mr Bonomy,
He keeps us fit.

C's for the canteen,
Wherein we do eat.

D's for Miss Donnelly,
She's really quite sweet.

E is for every
Poor pupil within.

F's for Miss Fraser,
She makes quite a din.

G's for the gala,
It's held once a year.

H is for holidays,
Everyone cheer.

I is for imports,
The 1st Year, we mean.

J's for the janitors,
They keep the place clean.

K is for something,
Of which we kan't think.

L is for lessons,
They really do stink.

M's for Mr McKellar,
He's really a good chap.

N is for nonsense,
Which gets us the strap.

O's for Mr Orr,
He's really a toff.

P's for the pupils,
Who like the day off.

Q is for questions,
We're asked all the time.

R is for ruler,
To draw a straight line.

S is for smokers,
They do love to puff.

T is for teachers,
Sometimes they get tough.

U, V, and W,
X, Y, and Z-
We've written enough now,
We're off home to bed.

Colin Menzies and James Forrest (2A1)

Almost a Scot

'Would you like to write a few lines for the school magazine?' This question, asked a few days ago, made me realise how soon my year in Scotland would come to an end. It is anything but easy to describe a whole year's experiences in a few words, but let me try anyway.

As with anybody who plans to stay abroad for some time, I was aware of my preconceptions regarding Britain in general, and Scotland in particular. Time and again, I had read that Scots and Bavarians have one thing in common - an inclination to roll up their sleeves and enjoy themselves. However, I have now had the opportunity to meet Scots who are as averse to this as Bavarian teachers are to drinking lemonade with their dinner.

The most enlightening experience I have had, therefore, has been watching my preconceptions, good and bad ones, collapse. You have no idea how very similar we are. But if somebody were to ask me to state an obvious difference between our two nations, I would say that the general public in Germany are not quite so helpful and hospitable as their counterparts in Scotland, and that with regard to increasing one's German / English vocabulary, attending a football match in Germany is less productive than being in the crowd at Fir Park (*experto credite*).

I must admit that I had tremendous difficulty getting used to the Scottish accent. I remember a weekend in Leicester, when my friends and I were to represent Glasgow University at a folk song concert. As our car broke down at Gretna Green (just fancy that), we were late; in fact, we arrived only ten minutes before the concert finished: so all we managed to sing was 'Come to the Barrowland'. Singing one or two verses of this song was my first attempt to tackle the Scottish accent in public, and to every genuine Scottish ear this must have been nothing short of disastrous.

However, now that I have spent my lunch break in the staffroom for the last ten months, I might as well admit that I have picked up a lot of indispensable Scoticisms. A special thanks, therefore, to my 'tutors'.

A skiing Christmas at the Devil's Elbow and my first ever Hogmanay were easily the highlights of the year. During both of these, I experienced what a Scot means by hospitality. Top marks must also go to the school dances. Wearing a kilt may not have enabled me to master the Highland fling, but I have kept trying ever since.

As far as the German Department is concerned, I sincerely hope that the help I gave you was as great as the pleasure I took from being with you.

As for the staff badminton club, thanks to all of you who gave me some good advice about a game I had never played before. I only hope I was as good a loser as I was bad as a player.

318

A special thanks also to my Junior football team. I know it took us a while to get used to each other, but I enjoyed every minute of those Tuesday nights and Saturday mornings.

Let me finish by thanking all the pupils and members of staff who helped to make this last year a most memorable and unforgettable one for me.

Auf Wiedersehen to you all.

Helmut Sauermann (German Assistant)

Classic Characters

Archimedes: a Greek ancestor of Archieandrews who had very high principles
Atalanta: an odds-on favourite doped by apples
Achilles: the biggest heel of all
Bacchus: the most notorious of Roman bookmakers
Hebe: first sufferer of the jeebies
Hercules: first boy scout to do twelve good turns
Mars: Roman god who retired to his own planet and founded a chocolate factory
Homer: a Greek pigeon fancier
Pan: an ancient Greek tinker
Priam: inventor of the baby carriage

Anonymous (4B)

Cycling Circumlocutionist

As I was travelling down a steep declivity at a remarkable velocity, the front wheel of my velocopede came into violent contact with a bump on the macadamised highway, precipitating me onto the front part of my cranium and causing me to see certain parts of the solar and galactic systems.

On regaining my visual capacity, I proceeded to elevate myself to a perpendicular position; and after retrieving my capricious contraption, I endeavoured - by performing some acrobatic contortions - to replace my posterior on that part of it which was upholstered. In a state of disorientation (induced by the shock of my unfortunate unseating and not by alcohol), I decamped from the scene of my utter humiliation.

When I arrived at the residence of my mater, she ejaculated in her beautiful Oxford accent: "Aw hen, did ye fa' aff yer bike an' hurt yer heid?"

Sandra Moorehead (2A)

My Brilliant Career

I arrived at the High School six years ago - a sweet, innocent little boy with short trousers, a new blazer and briefcase, and hair that got cut regularly. Look at me now. 'Nuff said.

I spent my first year wondering where all the smoke was coming from as I wandered along the cloisters. I thought "pon's snash" was a Latin quotation; and when the 'coffee house' was mentioned, I took it to be the senior boys' tearoom.

Come second year, I joined the Film Society and amused myself by trying to trace the squeals that did not come from the soundtracks of the films. One night, I sat in the back row and quickly came to the conclusion that it definitely had something.

In third year, I learned that chasing girls around the playground was better than chasing boys, especially if you were lucky enough to catch one. Temptation beckoned and I followed without hesitation.

With the advent of fourth year, I had to work much harder, especially in the evenings, so I rationed myself to five dates a week, which gave me more time to concentrate on my homework / telly.

Fifth year meant the Highers and more hard work, but after they were over, I had a whale of a time till the end of term.

The jazz dances (cool and swinging, man) and the happy-go-lucky attitude of everybody in sixth year made my final year at the High School the most memorable.

It would appear therefore that there's some truth in the belief that your schooldays are among the happiest days of your life. I certainly had a ball.

PS: Anyone for "pon's snash" in the 'coffee house'?

Deadbeat (Class 6)

33

1966-1973

Slammin' Sam

McKellar's successor at the helm of the High School was Sam Barnard, a former dux and captain of Dalziel High School, and a graduate (with 2nd Class Honours in English Language and Literature) of Glasgow University.

In the course of his wartime service in the RAF, he was trained as a navigator and wireless operator, and after receiving his commission, he flew with 107 and 613 Squadrons. In 1945 he was awarded the Distinguished Flying Cross.

His teaching career mirrored that of his predecessor: nine years as an assistant teacher of English at Dalziel High School, and eight years as Principal Teacher of English at Uddingston Grammar School.

As cold waters to a thirsty soul, so is good news from a far country.

Proverbs ch.25, v.25

When Sam's appointment as Rector was confirmed, we were all very relieved: the favourite for the post, according to the rumour sweeping the school, had been some martinet from Larkhall who was kicked out of the Tonton Macoute for alleged brutality.

Omne ignotum pro magnifico est.

Tacitus, *Agricola*

Sam took over as Rector in August 1966. In the course of a later interview for *The Octagon*, he was asked: 'What was your first impression of Wishaw High School?' His answer was: 'A physical impression of a very imposing building.'

High Teas

One of Sam's first initiatives was to set up a catering corps à la Dalziel High School. This 'new organisation', made up of 5th and 6th Year girls and supervised by Anne Donnelly, served visiting football and hockey teams with refreshments on Saturday mornings in the school canteen.

In connection with hockey, it is also worth noting that in the mid-1960s the High School was able to field seven teams. Among the members of staff who helped to coach these teams and umpire their games were Margaret Park, Hazel Morrison, Barbara Miller, Jenny Barrie, Moira Brown, Elizabeth Robison, and Elizabeth Fraser.

Keeping up Appearances

In October, Sam attended his first school event - the Autumn Fayre held in aid of the British Empire Cancer Research Fund. The *Wishaw Press* reported, rather enigmatically, that 'in the thick of the activities at the fayre was Mr Sam Barnard, the Rector, an experienced fund-raiser, but having his first experience of the methods used at Wishaw High School'. In the event, 'Wishaw methods' raised £275, and seeing May Young, Woman Adviser and one of the organisers of the fayre, in action (she was the Hyacinth Bucket of the ladies' staffroom) must have been a novel experience for Sam. Two-facedness was as common among the teachers at the High School as it has always been in society as a whole, but countenance-wise she invited comparison with a heptahedron.

Rude Mechanicals

'For weeks on end during session 1966-67,' according to a purple passage in Sam's annual report, "joiners, bricklayers, plumbers, and plasterers ambled along the school's windy corridors, or paused to watch the classes going by. Slowly and painfully out of this easy-paced chaos emerged new staffrooms and toilet accommodation for the staff."

And not before time. There wasn't room to swing a gerbil in the gents' staffroom; and what made matters worse was the fact that some Principal Teachers (Bob Craig and John Smith, for instance) had 'their own' chairs, and it   was regarded as beyond the pale for anybody else to sit on them - the chairs, that is.

Electricians were also at work (during the night), their aim being to make the school 'better illuminated, adequately powered, and considerably less likely to catch fire'.

Let us now praise famous men...

Ecclesiasticus ch.44, v. 1

On the academic front, the High School's most distinguished former pupil is Sir Samuel Curran. The entry for Sir Samuel in the 1997 edition of "Who's Who" reads as follows:

Curran, Sir Samuel (Crowe), Kt 1970; FRS 1953; FRSE 1947; F Eng 1983; Principal and Vice-Chancellor, University of Strathclyde, 1964-80, Fellow, since 1990; b 23 May 1912; s of John Curran, Kinghorn, Fife, and Sarah Owen Crowe, Ballymena, Ulster; m 1940, Joan Elizabeth yr d of Charles William Strothers and Margaret Beatrice (née Millington); three s and one d. Educ: Glasgow Univ. (MA, BSc; PhD 1937; DSc 1950); St John's Coll., Cambridge (PhD Cantab, 1941; Hon. Fellow, 1971). Cavendish Laboratory, 1937-39; RAE, 1939-40; Min. of Aircraft Production and Min. of Supply, 1940-44; Manhattan Project (Min. of Supply), Univ. of California, 1944-45 (Invention of Scintillation Counter, 1944). Natural Philosophy, Glasgow Univ., 1945-55 (Invention of Proportional Counter, 1948); UK Atomic Energy Authority, 1955-58; Chief Scientist, AWRE, Aldermaston, Berks, 1958-59; Principal, Royal Coll. of Science and Technology, Glasgow, 1959-64;Vis. Prof. in Energy Studies, Univ. of Glasgow, 1980-88. Pres., Scottish Soc. for the Mentally Handicapped, 1954-. Member: Council for Scientific and Industrial Research, 1962-65; Science Research Council, 1965-68; Adv. Council on Technology, 1965- 70; Chairman: Adv. Cttee on Med. Research , 1962-75; Adv. Bd. on Relations with Univs, 1966-70; Electricity Supply Res. Council, 1978-80 (Dep. Chm., 1980-82); Dep. Chm., Electricity Council, 1977-79; Chief Scientific Adviser to the Sec. of State for Scotland, 1967-77; Member: Oil Develt Council for Scotland, 1973-78; Adv. Cttee on Safety of Nuclear Installations, 1977-80; Radioactive Waste Management Adv. Cttee, 1978-81; Adv. Council of Atomic Power for Good (APG), 1978-; UK Nat. Commn for Unesco, and Educn Adv. Cttee, 1978-; Standing Commn on Scottish Economy, 1987-; Director: Scottish Television, 1964-82; Hall Thermotank Ltd, 1969-76; Cetec Systems Ltd, 1965-77; Internat. Res. And Develt Co Ltd, 1970-78; Gen.

Steels Div., BSC, 1970-73; Nuclear Structures (Protection) Ltd, 1981-. Hon. Pres., Scottish Polish Cultural Assoc., 1972-; President: St Andrews Soc., Glasgow, 1982-88; Inst. Of Envmtl Safety, 1992. FRCPS (Hon), 1964; FIEE (Hon), 1989; Hon. LLD: Glasgow, 1968; Aberdeen, 1971; Hon. ScD, Lodz, 1973; Hon. DSc, Strathclyde, 1980; Hon. D Eng, Nova Scotia, 1982. Freeman: Motherwell and Wishaw, 1967; City of Glasgow, 1980. DL, Glasgow, 1969. St Mungo's Prize, 1976; Comdr., St Olvav (Norway), 1966; Comdr, Order Polish People's Republic, 1976. Publications: (with J. D. Craggs) Counting Tubes, 1949; Luminescence and the Scintillation Counter, 1953; Alpha, Beta and Gamma Ray Spectroscopy, 1964; (jt) Energy Resources and the Environment, 1976; (with J.S. Curran) Energy and Human Needs, 1979; Issues in Science and Education, 1988; papers on nuclear research and education in Proc. Royal Society. Recreations: horology, golf.

In April 1967, Sir Samuel was presented with the freedom of the Burgh of Motherwell and Wishaw. The citation reads as follows:

At Motherwell and Wishaw, the Twenty fifth day of April in the year One Thousand, Nine Hundred and Sixty-Seven.

Which day, the Provost, Magistrates and Councillors of the Burgh of Motherwell and Wishaw, being assembled, admitted and received and do hereby admit and receive Doctor Samuel Crowe Curran, MA, PhD, DSc, FRS, Principal and Vice-Chancellor of the University of Strathclyde, as an Honorary Burgess of the Burgh with all the rights, privileges and immunities thereto belonging. In recognition and appreciation of his valuable contribution towards the advancement of knowledge through research work and in the field of nuclear science, and of his distinguished services to education and to Scottish industrial and economic affairs; and as an expression of the high esteem in which he is held by the citizens of the Burgh.

Incidentally, the High School can take pride in having a second vice-chancellor in the ranks of its former pupils – William Ritchie of Lancaster University.

The High School's most famous FP (if a person's fame is to be gauged solely by the number of people who have heard of him) is Tommy Gemmell. In May 1967, Tommy scored the first of Celtic's two goals in the final of the European Cup:

Craig pushed intae the box, the defenders moved tae block him - but he cut the ba back intae the path o' the charging Gemmell. Aa the big shots that Gemmell had fired intae the net in earlier games wer like rehearsals for this ane. The contact had tae be perfect tae beat Sarti. It was. It was a thunderbolt. Its speed defeats the ee - ye see a defender turning awa and the ba in the net. A perfect moment - Wallace tae Craig tae Gemmell tae the net. It was only a kick and a goal - but whit a goal! But there is nae question that Gemmell met mair than the ba when he struck it perfectly; he met his destiny. Tae ken Gemmell, even frae pictures, is tae ken that he was made for that moment. (from *Jock Stein - A Scots Life* by Glenn Telfer).

Up till 1997, Tommy could be heard, in his capacity as a part-time football reporter and pundit, on Radio Clyde on Saturday afternoons. He had absolutely nothing of any substance or originality to say, but at least he managed to steer clear of the intermittent solecisms that deface the comments of other ex-players like Willie Miller and Charlie Nicholas.

If we move forward to 1998, and continue to measure a person's fame by the number of people who have seen, or heard of, him, we must conclude that the High School's most famous alumni are Stuart Dougal, a Grade I referee (with FIFA status in season 1998 - 99), who has officiated at a fair number of televised matches (including the Old Firm game in September 1998); and John Cleland, who as one of the main contenders for the Auto Trader RAC Touring Car Championship features regularly on *Grandstand*, and has been interviewed by Steve Ryder on many occasions.

A Better Way to Get Away

'Few schools,' Sam declared at the prize-giving in 1967, 'can send so many pupils abroad as we do.' During the Christmas holidays in 1966, for example, ten pupils and five teachers had participated in what was possibly the first skiing holiday arranged by the High School - at Colle Isarco in Italy. Lesley Jesson wrote an article about the trip for *The Octagon*:
Off we all went on the first morning to display our remarkable ability on the beginners' slopes. I doubt if the sight of us and our performance persuaded anyone to invite the Olympic selectors along, but we did get a grounding in the art of skiing (perhaps snowing would be a better word than grounding, since we were more often on the snow than on our feet). I was amazed at the adaptability of the human frame: some of the

326

positions into which we (teachers included) got our bodies had to be seen to be believed.

Then came the search for souvenirs. I am sure that never in the field of the Italian tourist trade have so many searched for so much with so little. While we were shopping, we were afforded many opportunities to utilise our knowledge of German and Italian. Take, for example, the case of the young lady who, having been told to ask for 'drei Coca Colas' (for the uninitiated, 'drei' is the German word for three and is pronounced 'dry'), wanted to know the difference between dry and wet ones.

The highlight of every evening was our sing-song in the lounge. Mr Brodie accompanied us on the guitar, much to the amusement of the other guests and the hotel staff.

Angus Dick, Barbara Miller, and a certain Miss Melville organised similar skiing trips in 1968 and 1967, to which year we now return.

The Swinging Sixties

With the encouragement of their rector (a keen and proficient golfer), sixty pupils signed up for golf lessons with the professional at Wishaw Golf Club.

Sam was also a Gilbert and Sullivan enthusiast, and for the first time in five years the school staged (in Coltness Primary School) a comic opera - *The Gondoliers*. The leading characters were played by Eoin Stafford, Mary Tait, June Lambie, Harry Watson, Gordon Walker, Jim Reid, Elizabeth Gilchrist, Eleanor Cumming, and Gavin White; and *The Octagon* reported that 'a fine (?) chorus was just about held together by Tom Young of the PE Department'.

In October, Archie Leitch, Principal Teacher of Geography, whose entire teaching career (spanning 32 years) was spent at the High School, died in a Glasgow hospital after a long and painful struggle against ill health. According to a tribute in *The Octagon*:

He organised many of the social activities of the school, such as dances and Christmas parties; he was also the founder of the original Film Society, and the success of this enjoyable and financially sound enterprise owed much to his confidence and foresight in purchasing the necessary equipment and arranging suitably varied programmes. However, his unique contribution to the life of the school can best be measured by the remarkable number of pupils who were inspired by him to study Geography at university.

A fund was established to commemorate his service to the school, and this made it possible for a prize to be awarded every year for excellence in Geography. The first (joint) winners of this prize were Gordon Walker and Iain Stevenson, who many years later appeared on *Mastermind* and *Brain of Britain*, in the latter of which he won one of the regional rounds and was only pipped by one point for a place in the final. He also founded a successful publishing house (Belhaven Press), which he named after one of the four houses at the High School - even though as a pupil he was a member of Murdostoun House.

In session 1967-68, the roll was not far short of 900, partly because the 6thYear was much larger than usual. However, most of the pupils who had decided to stay on at school for a sixth year had done so in order to sit the Highers they missed out on in fifth year - and not with the intention of attempting more advanced work.

Five new rooms - four classrooms and a Technical room with facilities for both woodwork and metalwork - were erected at the back of the school. Sam had reservations about this development:
Hutted classrooms provide accommodation, but they create administrative and disciplinary problems, and constitute, to some extent, a divisive element at a time when it is more than ever important that the school should be a cohesive unit. A school has a central core, and the nearer that core our pupils can be educated the better. I do not envy the pupils or the staff whose school has a main building and an annexe, and if we get many more classrooms added at the back of the main building, that is what we will have.

In the main building itself, the corridors were bricked in at a cost of £4,310. The *Wishaw Press* commented as follows:
While the central courts may have lost some of their scholastic character and architectural dignity, the corridors have also lost some of their gale force draughts.

Abesto omen.

The school was painted (never a good omen) during the summer holidays.

Apocalypse Soon

With effect from August 1968, several changes were made in the catchment areas and academic status of the secondary schools in Wishaw. Firstly, whereas all senior secondary pupils (i.e. those who were reckoned to be capable of eventually gaining one or more Highers) residing to the north of a line drawn along Stewarton Street and the full length of the Main Street continued to enrol at the High School, those residing to the south of this line now began their secondary career at Coltness High School (from 1970 onwards, however, pupils in this category were to attend the new secondary school - Garrion Academy - that was going to be built on the south side of the town). Consequently, many pupils who were set on "following father's footsteps" into the High School were 'diverted' to Coltness High School - a turn of events that caused 'a mild furore' among their parents, since 'the idea that no other local high school could provide the education given at Wishaw High School died hard, especially when it was bolstered by that same school's long-standing traditions'.

Secondly (and much more ominously), pupils from the north side of the town who had been assigned to courses designated (euphemistically) as 'Standard Secondary' (i.e. those who were not expected to gain O-Grades or Highers) now found themselves on the roll of the High School. This was the first stage of the process that led to the school becoming a comprehensive, and it proved to be a real culture shock for many of the staff - including Sam, who summed up the situation as follows:

We have certainly had some novel disciplinary problems; however, in my judgment, the real difficulties lie in the curricular field, where answers must be found to such questions as: 'What are we to teach?' and 'How are we to teach it?' New methods and techniques will have to be evolved, and new standards accepted; as for teachers (and this is the most testing challenge), they will have to adjust rapidly from, say, a class in advanced mathematics at five to ten to one doing the most elementary calculations at ten o'clock.

One of the factors in the High School's decline was its failure to deal vigorously enough with the challenges posed by the change in the composition of its roll. Brian Smith, one of the two Americans who joined the English Department in the 1970s, explained this failure in the following passage:

I think I arrived at Wishaw High School about four years after the onset of the comprehensive education caper. To my mind (and this is perhaps a jaundiced view), the old junior/senior secondary system must have been superior, given the situation I discovered at the High School. The early days of comprehensive education (in my judgment, a euphemism for adolescent penal servitude) were pure hell for the non-academic pupils. It was murder on the teachers as well, and I am sure that many of them were driven from the classroom into early retirement, nervous breakdowns.. .or worse.

Our pedagogical training was at university in a scholarly, academic environment, where theory and intellect held sway. The skills necessary for working with youngsters of a more technical bent, who like to dismantle engines or work with wood, bricks and mortar, or who have an interest in agriculture... ...these skills are quite different from the skills required to work with pupils following an academic curriculum

We of the Western democracies have had to come to terms with the political correctness that is now driving our legislators - and has produced such schemes as comprehensive education. The interface between academic education and what is now called 'Tech-Prep' (Technological Preparedness in Education) in America has almost always been problematical; it was especially problematical in the case of Wishaw High School at the time I was there, when a senior secondary school had been forced to take large numbers of junior secondary pupils - even though the staff had been given no special training, and no appropriate curriculum adjustment had been made for the non-academic students. Twenty years later, it still makes me angry; in the parlance of psychologists, it was a lose-lose situation. Everybody lost: the academic kids lost, because the climate of the school was destroyed; the teachers lost, because they were forced to deal with a new 'clientele' they were ill-equipped to work with; and the non-academic pupils lost, because they were demoralized by course work they couldn't handle, a demoralization that profoundly - and adversely - affected their self-esteem.

A Departure from Tradition...

In June 1969, the prize-giving was held in the evening, admission by ticket only.

...and a Departure

John Smith, Principal Teacher of Art for 26 years and 'a popular and valued member of staff', retired. John was a member of the solo school in the gents' staffroom, and every morning he and Bob Craig, Principal Teacher of Classics, rattled through the crossword in *The Scotsman*.

During session 1969-70, three new prefabricated huts were erected behind the school. Since the roll now exceeded 1,000 for the first time in the history of the school, this additional accommodation (it took the form of a Music room, a Sewing room, and a well-equipped and self-contained base for the Geography Department) was 'manna from heaven'.

Sam foresaw problems arising from the one thousand strong complement of pupils:

When we reach the stage of having more than a thousand pupils in a school, there is a danger that the whole educational system may be dehumanised and pupils may feel like the inmates of a factory. We now have a situation in which it is impossible for a headmaster to make himself personally responsible for the full development of every pupil in the school; indeed, it is even impossible to know all your pupils by name. There must therefore be some delegation of function.

More Chiefs than Indians

In Lanarkshire, the Director of Education devised a twofold strategy to alleviate the interpersonal and administrative problems that were likely to arise in large comprehensive schools: the creation of a new structure of promoted posts (the first member of staff at the High School to occupy one of the new posts was Don Weir, who was appointed Head of the Upper School with special responsibility for the 5th and 6th Year); and the expansion and formalisation of the House System, with each House being allocated a Senior Housemaster/Housemistress, a Housemaster/Housemistress, and two Assistant Housemasters/Housemistresses.

All these posts (and there was an enormous number of them) involved a responsibility payment, and some cynics suggested that the whole point of the exercise was to attract teachers to Lanarkshire from other parts of Scotland. In the event, the Director of Education, the Assistant Directors, and the members of the Education Committee were kept busy for several months interviewing thousands of applicants; and the County Buildings were in a state of such turmoil and hyperactivity that a young fellow cleaning the windows of the council chamber was (allegedly) appointed Head of the Middle School at Claremont High School.

Si Fortuna volet, fies de rhetore consul.

Juvenal, *Satires*

On the subject, specifically, of the new House posts, Sheila Sprot has this to say:

There was a great scramble for them, and since teachers without an Honours degree had, up to this point, been kept off the promotion ladder (except in the non-academic disciplines), everybody was in there grabbing. No particular qualifications were deemed necessary, except, I suppose, a good reference from your head teacher. There were some very unlikely appointments and, of course, some very good ones. I myself applied for about twenty posts at Wishaw High School and various other schools, but I didn't even get an interview. This was very galling, as I had more than twenty years' experience - and young teachers more or less just out of college were being appointed. I went on the trip to Schweinfurt in 1971, and in the course of organising it I met many members of the Education Committee, something which I suppose must have helped me when I applied for the next vacancy to come up at the High School.

Sam had high hopes for the House System Mark 2:

We hope that our Housemasters and Housemistresses will get to know their pupils really well, correlate reports from their subject teachers, and learn about their difficulties in class, in the playground - and even, perhaps, at home; in short, we hope that they will convince every pupil that there is someone who cares about him as a person and can give him a sense of security.

It is difficult for some pupils to feel part of a school with a roll of over a thousand, and so we hope that they will think of their House as a home. This is a great challenge, but it is also a great opportunity, and in our Housemasters and Housemistresses we have the right teachers for the job. A new age will not dawn dramatically, but I am convinced that in the long run the lives of all our pupils will be enriched.

Sam's observations give a clear indication of the direction in which the House system was heading, and in the course of time it came to be known as the Guidance system: Senior Housemasters/Housemistresses became Principal Teachers of Guidance and the post of Assistant Head Teacher (Guidance) was instituted.

There are few more impressive sights in the world than a Scottish Guidance teacher on the make.

Sir J.M. Barrie, *What Every Woman Knows (adapted)*

The House/Guidance system was - and indeed still is - a perfect example of what Kingsley Amis called 'the inverted pyramid of piss', i.e. 'a great parcel of attitudes, rules, and catchwords resting on one tiny (if you looked long and hard enough) point'; it was also - since Guidance teachers conjured up more and more specious and unnecessary tasks on which to spend the increasing amount of time they were allocated for their Guidance duties - a perfect illustration of the validity of Parkinson's Law: 'Work expands so as to fill the time available for its completion.' Sheila Sprot tends to agree:

The whole thing was a bit over the top; it could all have been done by four Guidance teachers with the cooperation of the rest of the staff. Because the Guidance people were there, jobs had to be found for them to do; however, some of the jobs (like checking on absentees and truants, issuing reports, and making announcements about what was going on in the school) could have been done by a good register teacher. It was, in many ways, a wasteful system, and it must have cost a fortune to run - money that in my judgment would have been better spent on other aspects of education. In the event, I think we made a reasonable success of the Guidance system at the High School; at least we didn't totally alienate the rest of the staff, who mucked in at Wiston, for instance, when they might well not have done.

BBC Cameras at Wishaw High School

In February 1970, four 6th Year pupils - Elizabeth Bell, Martha Waddell, Gavin Bridges, and Rankin Cutler - who took part in a Young Enterprise Scheme designed to give them practical experience of the world of industry and commerce were featured in *The Money Programme* on BBC2. A camera crew visited the school to film some background material on the prospective entrepreneurs.

In April, a High School team, supervised by Colin Craig of the Biology Department, participated in a conservation contest arranged by Shell Retail in association with Nature Conservancy. The team's project was a survey of Allanton Woods, with a view to determining the impact of man and nature on the environment.

The Senior hockey team (Lesley Denholm, Catriona Gavin, Ann Crockett, Lisbeth Johnstone, Janet Girdwood, Helen Dunsmuir, Marion Parker, Margaret Sim, June Lister, Anne McLure, Kitty Walker, Moira McFadyen, and Grace Russell) won the Lanarkshire Schools' Hockey Competition, and thus became the first recipients of the Tait Trophy.

There may be trouble ahead...

It was also in April that the Education Committee finalised its plans for the reorganization - on comprehensive lines - of secondary education in Wishaw and surrounding districts: all prospective secondary pupils living south of Glasgow Road, the Main Street, Stewarton Street, and Wishaw Road were to be enrolled at Garrion Academy, which was due to be opened by the end of the year; and all those from the north of the town were to attend Coltness High School for two years, and then transfer to the High School for the rest of their secondary careers. The High School, therefore, was destined to have no 1st Year in session 1970-71, and that session's 2nd Year would be the school's last; in effect, the High School was to become a 'senior comprehensive' school.

Sam expressed several reservations about the proposed new set-up: *It is difficult to conceive of a school without a First Year, and we will miss the bright and eager faces, the new blazers, and the open-eyed innocence of a new intake; more seriously, we will be deprived of the opportunity to mould our pupils when they are at their most impressionable. Conversely, we view with some apprehension the arrival in 1971 of large numbers of 3rd Year pupils whose attitudes will have already been largely determined.*

One other aspect of the new arrangements gives cause for regret: in future years, pupils from Shotts will be educated at Garrion Academy, and so the long-established link between Wishaw High School and that community perched on the edge of the wild moorland will be broken. Shotts may not have the best bus service in the world, but it produces sturdy, independent sons and daughters whose academic and sporting feats have been a strong thread in the life of our school.

June 1970 saw the retiral of Donald Stalker, Principal Teacher of Technical Subjects, who 'established standards of skill and accuracy in technical drawing that became legendary'. Seemingly, he was also a mine of information about former pupils' university results and occupations – and he even knew where most of them had taken up residence.

But...let's face the music and - play table tennis.

In June 1971, after the reconstituted House system had been in operation for a session, Sam claimed that the link between home and school was being 'forged stronger every day', and that parents were reassured by the knowledge that 'a sincere and personal interest' was being taken 'in the total development of their sons and daughters'.

He also detected the emergence of 'a new spirit of friendly cooperation', one manifestation of which was the most 'astonishing' Staff v Pupils match he had ever seen:

There were table tennis tables in every corner of the hall, men's and women's matches taking place simultaneously, and perhaps as many as a hundred spectators occupying the few square inches of space that were left.

That same month, as part of an exchange programme sponsored by the English Speaking Union, four pupils - and Anne Donnelly - spent three weeks in New Jersey; and the retiral was announced of May Young, Woman Adviser since 1959, and Jimmy Dickson, Principal Teacher of Mathematics since 1942 and Depute Rector since 1962.

Jimmy Dickson, "one of nature's gentlemen", was "blessed with a quiet, gentle personality and a delightful sense of humour". His favourite aphorism was: "Those who can't count don't count."

'Whoever has opened the window has opened it too wide,' said Miss Brodie. 'Six inches is perfectly adequate. More is vulgar.'

In some respects, May Young reminded me of the protagonist of Muriel Spark's most celebrated novel. She was also, with her gimlet eye and Victorian prudishness, the duenna from hell, and her principal mission in life was to make sure that the skirts of her pubescent charges remained decorously long - and their knickers decorously *in situ*.

Later in the year, a party of High School pupils spent a fortnight in Greece, their itinerary including a week in Crete, four days' sightseeing in Athens, a tour of the Peloponnese, and a cruise to several of the Greek Islands. A similar trip was arranged in 1973.

The traditional Autumn Fayre became a Christmas Fayre - which, thanks to the hard work of the 6th Year, raised £210 for Cleland Hospital.

The Misfits

In session 1971-72, for the first time in its history, the High School had no First or Second Year; it did, however, have a huge Third Year - well over 400 pupils, in fact, for most of whom the High School was their third school in as many years. 'Not surprisingly,' Sam reported, 'settling down proved to be a difficult process. A few never settled down at all, and from the earliest days these pupils claimed a freedom to which they were not legally entitled until the end of the session.' Others were bored ('for them life at school became a tedious round of keeping out of sight and out of trouble'), and 'their very boredom led them into the trouble they were so anxious to avoid'.

The absence of 1st and 2nd Year pupils seems to have had an adverse effect on the school's efforts to recruit teaching staff. According to Sam: *Young teachers coming out of college prefer to come into contact with as wide a range of pupils as possible, and some of them - since they do not wish to miss out on the freshness and enthusiasm of younger pupils - have declined teaching appointments at the High School because it is a senior school.*

By now, the House system had taken root, and Sam felt that it was working well - 'in spite of the frustrations caused by the total lack of suitable accommodation and the staff's failure to get through to some pupils':

More and more pupils are receiving the guidance they need - and, in some cases, need desperately. They are learning that their teachers care, and they are developing a healthy and fruitful trust in them, a process of mutual discovery that I hope will continue over the months and years ahead.

A wide range of activities was also arranged under the auspices of the four Houses. In 1972, for example, the captains of Belhaven House submitted the following report:

The various clubs held after school have been extremely successful, enjoyable, and well-attended. Our Folk Club visited Wishaw Hospital at

336

Christmas to entertain the old people, and our Arts and Crafts Club made some Christmas decorations which were donated to that same hospital. The most popular lunchtime activities have been table tennis (a tournament was organised), netball, and volleyball. We also held a Games Evening and a Social Evening, both of which were very successful; and we intend to arrange a House trip to St Andrews.

Panem et Circenses

I myself was an Assistant Housemaster for several years in the early 1970s. I spent most of my time selling Mars bars and organising table tennis matches, and my one significant 'contribution' to the House System (for which all Guidance teachers should have been eternally grateful) was to propose, successfully, that all lunchtime House activities should cease forthwith.

In May 1972, ten boys from the High School embarked on the three-masted schooner *Captain Scott* for a three-week adventure cruise in northern waters.

We are not amused.

As part of the celebrations to mark the centenary of the Education Act, an Open Day was arranged - at which, according to Sam, "parents and friends had an intriguing glimpse of the more dramatic aspects of the school's work". These parents and friends also got a glimpse (some got more than a glimpse) of a bucket of water, when David Wilson (who was playing one of the characters in the trio of extracts from the comedies of Plautus that was staged by the Classics Department) decided to enliven the proceedings with a little slapstick.

In June, an operetta (*Barbarian*) based on Mozart's *The Marriage of Figaro* was staged in the hall. The musical director of this production was John Dobbie, Principal Teacher of Music, who later in the year was invited by the Secretary of State for Scotland to become a member of the working party that had been set up 'to consider the place of music in the school curriculum'.

Apocalypse Now

In 1973 the school-leaving age was raised to sixteen. This development obviously led to a large increase in the number of pupils on the roll, which in turn imposed 'additional stresses' on accommodation that was already inadequate - and on the staff, as Sam was quick to concede:

Some pupils who either totally reject the idea of school or are close to doing so feel resentful and cheated at having to spend another year at school, and many disciplinary problems arise as a consequence of this.

These problems were compounded by another consideration: although it was 'all too easy and tempting', as a result of the new regulations that governed the award of the Leaving Certificate, to present almost everybody for an O-Grade in one or more subjects, 'the best needs of some pupils were not being met by either the syllabuses for the O-Grade examinations or the examinations themselves'. Sam was convinced, therefore, that 'an entirely new form of assessment' was urgently required.

So much they talked, so very little said.

Charles Churchill, *The Rosciad*

Lanarkshire appointed Advisers in all the subjects that normally feature in the curricula of secondary schools. On the whole, Sam welcomed these new appointments:

Their visits to schools have ended the feeling of isolation that many teachers experience; they have opened up lines of communication between different schools; and, hopefully, they will eventually eliminate the inequalities in the distribution of equipment that exist between one school and another. At their instigation, teachers are also becoming more deeply involved in curricular development; and while this is exciting and desirable, it invariably means additional work and loss of free time for staff who are already under pressure.

In my experience, the visits of Advisers to the school were as welcome as a shoal of piranha in a bidet.

During Disabled Week, a group of High School pupils, led by Allan Henderson and Victor Topping, won a trophy for their project on 'Accessibility for the Disabled'.

The senior girls' choir (under the baton of David Carson) gave a recital of traditional and contemporary church music in St Giles Cathedral. The choir was formed in 1971, and in the space of two years it took part in more than thirty concerts and recitals

In June, the senior pupils presented *An Evening of Music and Drama* in the small hall of Wishaw Public (the site of the High School in its embryonic form). The programme for the evening included three short plays (a light comedy, a tragedy, and a farce), and a cantata entitled "Daniel '73".

34

Extra-Curricular Matters (1967-1973)

In 1967 the under-15 football team won the Anderson Cup and the Motherwell and Wishaw Intermediate League. Norman Stevenson, the captain of this team, was capped for Scotland against England, Ireland, and Wales.

Wishaw Lawn Tennis Club offered the school the use of its courts, and as a result of this offer a tennis club was formed - with an initial membership of just over fifty.

Elizabeth Tweedlie won the Lanarkshire Girls' Tennis Championship for the second year in succession.

Netball reappeared on the extra-curricular menu, and the under-16 team competed in the Lanarkshire Schools' Netball League.

The girls' public speaking team (Joyce McLean, Kay Morrison, and Ruth Robson) won the Motherwell YMCA Trophy.

The Scottish country dance team (it had been formed by Elizabeth Robison) gained second place at the Festival of Country Dancing in Hamilton Town Hall; the following year, the team topped the senior secondary section at the Lanarkshire Music Festival.

The Drama Club staged two one-act plays - *The Proposal* by Anton Chekhov and *The Devil His Due* by Seamus Fail - at Coltness Primary School. The evening's entertainment also included a selection of folk songs and war poems.

The Junior cricket XI won the Home Park Trophy, a success that was destined to be repeated on another four occasions in the 1970s and 1980s.

The Film Society was resurrected by Mr and Mrs Morrison. Educational films were shown at lunchtime; evening meetings of the Society featured such films as *The Ipcress File* and *The Pure Hell of St Trinian's* (sic).

The activities of the Natural History Society included studies of pond life and wild flowers, bird recognition, and several field outings.

Attendance at both the Boys' and Girls' Scripture Union plummeted (a sign of the times, perhaps), and several joint meetings were held.

In 1968 the 1st Seniors were joint winners - with Coatbridge St Pat's - of the Lanarkshire League and losing finalists in the Keith Cup; the under 16½ team, which included David Main, Alex Hinshaw, Keith

Gillon, Irvine Swan, Houston Brown, Derek McLeod, John Forrest, and George Walker, won the Waddell Cup.

The High School entered a team in the newly formed Lanarkshire Schools' Badminton League.

A senior netball team was formed by Helen Young. Isobel Johnston continued the good work in the early 1970s.

Among the excellent public speakers produced by the Senior Debating Society were Catherine Brownlee, Yvonne Davis, Donald Lithgow, and John Dempster, who won the A.R. Dalziel Memorial Trophy.

The Junior Choir, conducted by Miss S.L. Hamilton, performed a two-act operetta - *The Bells of Bruges* - at Coltness Primary School.

Several members of the Physics Club joined the local branch of the Radio Society of Great Britain.

In 1969 the 1st Seniors (Alex Hinshaw, Keith Gillon, Alan Mauchline, Robert Thom, Gordon Kennedy, David Main, Steven McCabe, Ronnie Balmer, Norman Stevenson, John Boal, and William Hill) won the Keith Cup.

As a result of the great upsurge of interest in golf, prizes were instituted for the most promising players (male and female) in the junior school; the first recipients of these prizes were Anne Cuthbertson and Jim Hamilton, the latter of whom certainly fulfilled his early promise (he has been captain of Shotts Golf Club, and he still takes part in the more prestigious local events). Another two pupils from this era, Kenny Harrison and Johnny Johnston, developed into low handicap golfers, and both of them (especially Harrison, who has won the club championship on numerous occasions) have achieved a fair amount of success in competitions at their home courses (Carluke and Wishaw respectively).

Elizabeth Tweedlie won the Scottish Schools' Under-18 Singles Championship and, by virtue of her success, £100 for the school funds; she also represented Scotland in a tennis international against England, and played at Wimbledon in the British Junior Championships. In later years, she won the Lanarkshire Ladies' Singles Championship, and gained blues for tennis in three consecutive years at Edinburgh University.

The Folk Club had a new MC – Douglas Hope

In 1970 David Main played for the Scottish under-18 football team against England and Wales. Soon afterwards, his football career suffered a considerable setback: he signed for Motherwell.

Robert Tweedlie won the South of Scotland Under-16 Tennis Championship and the Lanarkshire Boys' Championship, a success he was destined to repeat in 1971.

In 1971 volleyball featured on the sporting calendar for the first time, and both the boys' and the girls' team joined the Lanarkshire League.

Ian McLelland was selected for the Lanarkshire under-16 volleyball team.

Kitty Walker played in goal for the West of Scotland junior hockey team.

William Cross won the Motherwell Gavel Club Trophy.

The under-17 relay team (Allan Henderson, Victor Topping, Ian Phillip, and Ian Thomson) was victorious at the Scottish Schools' Athletics Championships, equalling the championship record in the process.

The school choirs and instrumentalists 'took music to the community' by giving twelve concerts in various local churches; and a brass group was formed under the supervision of its visiting tutor, Mr McLeavey.

In 1972 the under-15 football team, coached by Douglas Hope, won the Motherwell and Wishaw League without losing a game.

Jim Thomson won the 1500 metres at the Scottish Schools' Athletics Championships; he was also a member of the Scottish Schools' team that competed against England and Wales in an international athletics match.

At the County Sports, John Paul and Victor Topping won the shot and the 200 metres respectively.

On the tennis court, Robert Tweedlie replicated the successes of his sister, Elizabeth, by winning the Scottish Under-18 Singles Championship and representing Scotland in international competition.

Under the 'able guidance' of Ronnie Hamilton, members of the Photography Club (which had begun life as the Murdostoun Camera Club) photographed 'models on location', staged exhibitions, provided a developing and printing service, and mounted a display of the photos they had taken of a wide range of school activities. John McQueen eventually took over from Ronnie Hamilton, by which time the club was also providing any photographs that were required for *The Octagon*.

Old books were discarded from the school library, and 'new books, new furniture, and new equipment helped to increase the number of borrowers'. Moira Brown undertook supervisory duties in the late 1960s, as did Richard Blackburn and Eddie Tweedlie Jnr. in the early 1970s.

In 1973, for the first time in more than 25 years, there was a teacher - Fraser Gracie - on the staff who was keen enough on rugby to run a school team. Gracie's pioneering work with the Senior XV was consolidated in subsequent years by John Arton and Peter Boa.

David Wright, Iain McGillivray, and John McLaren played for the Lanarkshire Schools' rugby team. Wright was also selected for the Glasgow and District team.

The Music Club aimed to broaden pupils' musical interests by giving them the chance to play and talk about their favourite pieces of music. In the course of the following year, arrangements were made for pupils to attend performances of *La Sylphide* and *Carmen* at the King's Theatre.

35

Recollections of the 1960s and Early 1970s

Nan Murray, Janette Scott and I were in the Higher Music class. When we were playing the piano, Sid Laird would sit beside us with a ruler in his hand; and every time we made a mistake, he would rap our knuckles - so they were permanently bruised.
(Maureen Anderson)

Neil McKellar reminded me that brown shoes did not go with the school colours.
(Sandy Anderson)

If 'Luggy' Weir stood in front of the window on a bright, sunny day, his ears positively glowed.
(Sandra Brown)

In my sixth year, I spend many an afternoon in the Carlton Café hoping I wouldn't be caught.
(Ronald Dick)

'Granny' Young took great delight in announcing to my class that Sir Alex Douglas-Home had just become leader of the Conservative Party and PM.
(Adam Park)

Some of my pals and I used to speed up the hymns at the morning assembly, so that we could finish ahead of the pianist.
(Ian Rae)

If someone in the Woodwork class made a pig's ear of a joint and asked for another piece of wood, John Parton would say to him, in a voice loud enough to be heard by the rest of the class, 'Do you think wood grows on trees?' Whereupon, he would bubble over with laughter.
(Robin Smith)

I remember 'Paw' Brown being very impressed when I told him that I was the proud possessor of more than a hundred books.

Enunciating every word in her own unique style, 'Granny' Young once asked me to explain the difference (in meaning) between the words 'villain' and 'villein', and when I was unable to do so, she informed me that Hitler was a 'villain', whereas 'villeins' were poor, but respectable peasants.

The teacher who had the greatest influence on me was Archie Leitch: his graphic approach really brought the subject (geography) to life. I still keep on my desk the battered old prismatic compass he gave me as a keepsake on virtually the last occasion I was present in his classroom. It's ex-army issue, but I don't know for sure if it dates from his war service.

The other memorable member of the geography department was David Mackay aka 'Boko' (a character – a magician, to be exact – in a popular comic). The connection was his habit of swinging a blackboard pointer round his head (like a magic wand), and thrusting it in the direction of badly behaved pupils.
(Iain Stevenson)

I was particularly impressed by the *esprit de corps* that was prevalent throughout the school: for instance, virtually all the pupils were keen to run for their House at the sports (provided you took part in certain events, you could earn a point for your House); and it was unheard of for a member of any of the football teams not to turn up on Saturday morning.

Dalziel High School were our greatest rivals on the football field, and they beat us in the final of the Keith Cup in 1972. A few months after that game, I got a job in Hamilton - and every morning, as I went past Dalziel High School in the bus, I felt physically sick.

In 1971, in the 3rd Round of the Secondary Shield, we had an away game against Elgin Academy, and I remember attending an extremely boring Burns Supper on the Friday night prior to the game.

In the next round we were drawn at home against Buckie High School, but we could only manage a draw. Sam Barnard was not overjoyed, since it meant another expensive bus trip to Teuchterland. After the replay, which we won 2-1, our departure from Buckie was delayed while John Higgins bade some girl a lengthy and emotional farewell.

In a school context, I have a vivid memory of Isobel Hogg setting fire to a lump of potassium permanganate (because it burns in air, it is normally kept in a jar filled with oil, and she had removed it from the jar with a pair of tongs), and James Maule throwing a beaker of water over her.

(George Brownlie)

At the beginning of my year as girls' captain, I was summoned to Sam's room by 'Granny' Young, the Woman Adviser, and told to kneel down. Having produced a ruler, she proceeded to measure the distance between the hem of my skirt and the floor. After it had been established that my skirt - and that of the vice-captain, who had been subjected to the same procedure - were of an acceptable length, we were sent round the school to demonstrate to the girls what was required of them vis-a-vis the length of their skirts.

'Granny' Young spent most of her time dispensing sanitary towels and glasses of hot water mixed with salt - her remedy for every malady from nausea to a broken leg. The one beneficial effect of this treatment was that once it had been administered even the malingerers felt really sick.

Bob Craig used to go purple with rage; Don Weir must have covered miles, as he paced up and down in front of his classes; Margaret Park had a very sharp tongue, and she made good use of it when commenting on some girls' attempts to perform certain exercises; a certain Mr Hood, who took over from Tom Forsyth as our English teacher, dressed - and taught - in a very trendy manner, and also played the guitar.

John Smith could be very supercilious towards those pupils who did not have much artistic ability. On one occasion, as he cast a rather disdainful eye over one of my mediocre canvases, I couldn't resist remarking, "Good, isn't it?"

Some of the boys (especially Ian Reid) made Archie Leitch's life hell. "You're not nice," he told them one day, "I'm a sick man." On the other hand, if 'Agatha' Christie was having a bad day, her reaction was: "I'm in no mood to be tampered with."

'Paw' Brown was not the greatest disciplinarian in the world: a mini-riot would be taking place under his nose, but all he would say was: "I get the impression there's an element of unrest in the room." On occasion, we had to memorise a passage from some literary masterpiece; and after George had asked somebody to recite it, he would look up at the ceiling in incipient rapture: so the reciter simply used the book he had under his desk as an aide-memoire.

There was a ledge outside Isobel Hogg's science lab, and some classes used to have a competition to see how many pupils could climb out of the window and sit on it without her noticing.

Sid Laird was forever grabbing girls by the hair. He got a shock one day, when Linda Howieson's hair came away in his hand: she was wearing a wig.

We learned bugger all French from Derek Winton (for one thing, he was forever disappearing into the storeroom for a fag), but we did learn how to make the perfect chocolate mousse, and every last detail of the bridesmaids' dresses his nieces were going to be wearing at a forthcoming wedding.

I remember Derek telling us that when he got back home after school he put on a pair of slacks and had a martini topped with a cherry. This was the cue for one of the boys to announce that when he arrived home in the afternoon he usually put on a pair of dungarees and had a cup of tea and an iced bun.

Derek had very eloquent eyebrows, a trait that was a big help to us during the Aural Comprehension section of the Higher French examination (this was in the days before a standard version of the French passage on which pupils had to answer questions was played on a cassette recorder). As he read the passage to us, he would raise his eyebrows when he came to a word or phrase that formed the answer to one of the questions.

(Elizabeth Sommerville)

Among the teachers I particularly remember are 'Agatha' Christie, 'Perry' Mason, 'Paw' Brown, Sid Laird, Bob Craig, and Derek Winton.

'Paw' Brown always wore a gown, and if a wasp found its way into his room, he would pursue it with a table tennis bat in his hand - all in all, a rather bizarre spectacle.

Sid Laird was forever punching people, but he had a masterly touch when it came to deciding who would play the principal characters in the school's production of *The Gondoliers*.

Bob Craig took the top class in each year group. Occasionally, he would promote one or two pupils from 3B or 4B, but he then subjected them to such a grilling (to make sure their knowledge of Latin grammar and syntax came up to his very high standards) that within a few days they were almost invariably relegated to the teaching group from whence they had come.

I went back to the High School a year or so after I left, and Derek Winton was one of the teachers I looked in on. He was wearing a green suit, and for some reason or other he fired several questions at me in French, which I did my best to answer (also in French). One of the questions he asked was: 'What subjects are you studying at university?' When I said, 'French', his amusement knew no bounds.

One Saturday morning in the mid-1960s, the Intermediate team had to make the long journey to Dundee for a shield tie. To loosen our leg muscles, Tom Forsyth, who was in charge of the team, made us get off the bus and walk the last part of the journey.

On one of the school's trips to the south of France, I was standing in a cafe one day beside Bobby Wright; ten seconds later I was standing beside an empty space - as he had collapsed with what was later diagnosed as a perforated stomach ulcer.

On the final night of *The Gondoliers* (in which I was playing Don Alhambra), I decided to make my entrance with two roses - one red, one white - protruding from my wig. 99.9% of the audience were highly amused, but I could tell from his face that Sam Barnard (who was sitting in the front row) did not appreciate my little drollery.

(Gavin White)

Most of my memories pertain to the various football teams I played in.

After the Junior team won the Watt Cup in 1963, McKellar put the trophy (which was minute) in his pocket and left with barely a word of congratulation for the team.

The following year, a photograph of the Intermediate team was published in one of the comics that were popular at the time - either *The Tiger* or *The Lion*. When we played St Michael's in the Scottish Shield, Lou Macari was a member of the St Michael's team; the referee had only one arm, and it could only point one way - in favour of St Michael's; and Alan Ferrier, our goalkeeper, decided to wear a Rangers scarf.

As the High School and Dalziel teams were limbering up in the tunnel prior to the Keith Cup final in 1964, the Dalziel captain (I think his name was Mathieson) tossed the match ball to the notoriously uncompromising 'Fodie' Duncan and suggested that it would be advisable for him to get a few kicks at it before the game started - as he wouldn't get a kick at it during the game. Dalziel won the toss and kicked off; the ball was played back to Mathieson, who barely had time to control it before he was 'taken out of the play' (as Arthur Montford would have said) in spectacular - and extremely painful - style by a vengeful 'Fodie'.

It was the same 'Fodie' Duncan who, having decided to play centre forward for the pupils in their annual match against the teachers, gave John Bonomy a really torrid time.

John Bonomy was loath to provide the football teams with new equipment: we had to play in short-sleeved jerseys in the middle of winter; and getting a new ball (especially a white, laceless one) from him was like drawing teeth.

Still on the subject of whiteness: Peter Hughes, centre forward in the ˥ior team had white boots - a real novelty in the 1960s.

˥he last game at which Hugh Phillips, one of Scotland's most ˙shed referees, officiated may very well have been a Scottish Shield tie between the High School and Coatbridge St Pat's.

Bonnar, a member of the History Department, played in goal ˥eam when they went 'on tour' in the south of France - ˥ wasn't always 100% sober and his eyesight was pretty po˥ ˥at became patently obvious two minutes into the first gam˥ w˥ ˥failed to see the ball flashing past him for the first goal.

On ˥ same trip, the boys threw Maurice into the pool at the agricultural college where they were billeted: they were fed up listening to him lauding the merits of Celtic FC. As Maurice couldn't swim, Jack Gillon had to jump in and do the needful.

(Bobby Wright)

I remember when the corridors were open to the elements; in the winter, the snow would pile up outside the classroom doors. I also seem to remember the corridors being warmer in those days - because the cold inside fused with the cold outside, instead of forming a wind tunnel.

I remember how Room 11 terrorised those of us who wore miniskirts. Why? Miss Young. She was a History teacher, and a mini-tyrant. We would try to sneak past her room, but her inbuilt radar always picked us up - and we would have to kneel on the stone corridor, so that she could measure the distance between the hem of our skirts and the ground. Any more than six inches and we were in trouble. Then we had to stagger up on to our platform soles and listen to a lecture about what we were doing to our feet.

I remember Mr Weir who taught in Room 12. He spent the entire period walking up and down, and we worked out that he walked about six miles every week.

I remember the 'silent zone', the area where the offices and staffrooms are today; we were not allowed to speak in that area, in case we disturbed the teachers. It was also a school rule that you had to carry your schoolbag in your right hand - so that you didn't scrape the paint as you went along the corridors.

I remember the prefects; they were 6th Year pupils, and they were allowed to give us lines if we misbehaved in the corridors. We never questioned their authority.

I remember the day John McLung threw a snowball at Mr Lindsay - who completely lost his temper. My friend Sandra and I were reduced to tears, because we had thought that Mr Lindsay was a really gentle man.

I remember what seemed to be longer, hotter summers - when we would go up to the football pitch to sunbathe.

I remember how frightened we were of Mr Craig, the Latin teacher. We used to line up outside Room 7 in trepidation, knowing that he was bound to catch us out when he quizzed us about our homework. On one occasion, I nearly got the belt for saying 'Uh-huh' instead of 'Yes, sir'.

I can't remember ever using what to me will always be the boys' stairs (the ones nearer the library). I used the staff stairs once when I was in the 6th Year.

(Janey Mauchline)

On my first day as a pupil at the High School, some of my pals and I came into the school grounds via the main gate, and as we were making our way up the steps towards the front door, we were accosted by the janitor, Major Bain. He took our names, told us that he intended to report our 'misdemeanour' to McKellar, and warned us that if we repeated it he would make sure we were all belted.

The Art Department were remarkably lazy: John Smith and Mary McBride would give the class something to do at the beginning of the period, disappear, reappear 1 hour 15 minutes later, and collect the product of our artistic labours - which we never saw again.

'The fall of the Roman Empire' was Bob Craig's wry comment when he dropped the map he was planning to hang up on the wall. Bob was rarely in such good humour; indeed, the only time he had a smile on his face was when Labour won the General Election in 1964.

George Brown kept a tube of toothpaste and a tin of shoe polish in his cupboard, and he cleaned his teeth and polished his shoes every morning.

During the Second World War, George served with the RAF in Norway. There are many references to Norway in *Hamlet*, and whenever he came across one of them, he was in the habit of reminiscing about his wartime experiences. Just in case he needed a gentle nudge to go off at a tangent, George McNeil, a member of his Higher English class, would remark: "You were in Norway during the war, weren't you, sir?"

When I returned to the High School as a member of the English Department, I soon discovered that George could be very diplomatic in the way he carried out his duties as the Principal Teacher in that department. Having come into my room one day to find me reading the riot act to a 3rd Year class, he tiptoed back out, closing the door quietly behind him.

On another occasion, George was taking 4C (by mistake, I suppose), and he decided to read a traditional Scottish short story (*Rab and His Friends*) to them. He was mystified by the mutinous reaction of the punters to this 'jolly good tale'.

After telling a joke, Stanley White (his nickname was Polonius) would tap the nearest member of his audience on the shoulder, thereby unbalancing him. This set off a chain reaction: and so, as he glided away, there were cups and bodies everywhere.

One particularly rainy morning, Sid Laird flagged down my father and me twenty yards from the foot of the steps at the front of the school, and dived into the back of our car. "You've got an umbrella," he explained.

Members of staff usually collected their salary cheques from Pearl Davies, the Rector's secretary. One day, she remarked to me that another young teacher who had started in the profession at the same time as myself was receiving a larger monthly salary: so the following month I asked for my cheque in a brown envelope. She was not a happy bunny.

(Eddie Tweedlie Jnr.)

I suppose most of the teachers must have been reasonably competent, but there weren't many skilful or inspiring educators among them. All I can recall about some of them is their name or nickname ('Dr Beaker', for example, who taught chemistry). Others I remember because of the positive or negative experiences I had in their classroom.

My feelings about Andy Kerr were coloured by a comment he made about my ineptitude in the field of music. 'If this was an orchestra,' he said, 'Mr Dempster would only be fit to play the kettledrums.' In my book, this was not only a personal insult but also a gross undervaluation of percussionists' musicianship.

John Parton's idea of punishment was to get you to stand in front of the class and pretend you were perched at the top of a very high ladder – on the point of jumping into a wet towel. When you were in position, he would gently tap your butt with a T-square. He also liked to spice up his lessons with such irrelevances as the fact that "Napier's Bones" was an early calculating device invented by John Napier (1550 – 1617) and had nothing to do with that gentleman's physical remains. The only problem with such information was that we had to listen to it at regular intervals.

'Bum' Dickson never managed to awaken me to the joys of mathematics, though I do remember sitting in the chalk-laden atmosphere of his room, overlooked by the large geometric shapes on the windowsills, while (as an end-of-term diversion) he explained the mysteries of the binary system and basic computing.

Every year, Don Weir declaimed the same material (I know, because I sat through it in both 5th and 6th Year), pacing up and down the classroom while we recorded his words of wisdom. Every year, he salivated over Thomas Carlyle's description of Robespierre as 'the seagreen incorruptible'; and every year, when we reached Palmerston's Conspiracy to Murder Bill, he wondered aloud with mock seriousness what poor William had done to turn people against him

George Brown was undoubtedly erudite, but he seemed to be under the impression that English literature had become extinct about the time of Thomas Hardy. I remember handing in an essay about a trip with my parents to the Scottish National Orchestra Proms in the Kelvin Hall. One of the items on the programme was the Polovtsian Dances from Borodin's *Prince Igor*. Bryden Thomas was conducting, and in my (ludicrously detailed) account of the evening's proceedings I described how he stretched out a foot to straighten the edge of the red carpet on the podium. When my essay was returned to me, the only indication that George had found any fault with it was two comments in red biro at the very end: 'Write a little less and a little larger. Avoid polysyllabic words and phrases.'

One of the teachers I rated very highly was also an English teacher, 'Perry' Mason. He encouraged us to read D.K. Broster's *Flight of the Heron*, and also introduced us to modern poetry by playing a recording of John Betjeman reading some of his poems. He was very firm and addressed the boys by their surname.

Maurice Bonnar was a marvellously flamboyant history teacher. Every period, I was allowed to get away with a fixed number of 'Dempsterisms' – 'Dempsterisms' being inane, immature remarks (such as mistranslating the Magna Carta as 'The Big Cart'), which I thought were very witty. If I exceeded my quota, I got the belt.

Bob Craig, the Principal Teacher of Classics was a very knowledgeable man - also warm-hearted, if a trifle irascible at times. He was in the habit of keeping the most able pupils to himself, and after the preliminary examination in Higher Latin he sent everyone in the class who scored less than 48% down to Jimmy Lindsay's. When I left his class for the last time, he gave me a copy of fellow classicist A. E. Housman's *A Shropshire Lad*, something I have always treasured.

On a less exalted level, I have some happy memories of the school canteen. Most days, there was a main course and a pudding, the pudding being accompanied by custard served from a battered metal jug - and there was always a skin on the custard. I loved the days when there was soup instead of pudding, as it was accompanied by shortbread and the combination of sweet and savoury was irresistible.

The atmosphere in the canteen was noisy and cheerful. There must have been a boy with the surname Cater, for everybody started shouting, 'Cater the Waiter', when it was his turn to go up to the hatch and collect the food for his table.

(John Dempster)

36

Decline and Fall Part I - The Seeds are Sown

In the early 1970s, all post-primary pupils from Cleland, Newmains, Morningside, and the north side of Wishaw attended Coltness High School for the first two years of their secondary careers; thereafter, they transferred to the High School. As far as the teaching staff at the High School were concerned, this was an excellent arrangement: the responsibility element accruing to the salaries of teachers in promoted posts was abnormally large (in fact, it was one of the largest in Scotland), due to the huge number of pupils in 4th, 5th, and 6th Year; and we all enjoyed an extra two months' 'holiday' every year during the prelims and the SCE examinations. Some parents, however, were highly critical of the whole set-up:

Pupils at both schools do not have a feeling of belonging to either; and pupils in the top classes at Coltness High School are not prepared to become virtually 1st Year pupils again when they move down to the High School.

Both schools are understaffed, since few teachers want to teach at a school (the High School) with no 1st or 2nd Year, and few experienced teachers are willing to risk damaging their career prospects by taking a post in a school (Coltness High School) where there are no certificate classes to teach.

At both schools, this shortage of staff has resulted in serious disciplinary problems, and also in part-time education: some 6th Year pupils, for instance, are offered only twenty periods of instruction (out of a possible forty) per week; and where else in the county is there a secondary school whose senior pupils have to plead with teachers to take them into their classes and - since their pleas are usually in vain - have even to attend evening classes before they feel they are getting sufficient instruction to enable them to sit certain Highers? (the school in question was, of course, the High School).

Taking their cue from such critical observations, the Coltness High Parents' Action Group submitted an urgent request to the Director of Education that the High School and Coltness High School should be amalgamated - a request that was turned down with similar rapidity.

By the end of 1973, however, the Director of Education had decided in principle that post-primary pupils from the north side of Wishaw and the surrounding villages should remain in one school for the duration of their secondary careers, and a consultative process was set in motion to establish the best means of achieving that outcome. Parents were asked to vote for one of two basic options - Option A: amalgamate the High School and Coltness High School, and operate them as one school on separate sites; Option B: provide the full range of secondary courses at both the High School and Coltness High School.

With the benefit of hindsight, it is clear that the staff at the High School (or, more realistically, those who acted as the school's mouthpieces in the corridors of power) should have pushed for some sort of amalgamation with Coltness High School. Although that school was - and still is - housed in a tatty building on a tatty site in the back of beyond, it could have served as an annexe for the High School (a similar set-up obtained in Motherwell, where Dalziel High School utilised the former Brandon High School as an annexe); another eminently practicable form of amalgamation (though it was ruled out, at least for the foreseeable future, by the consultative document) would have involved extending the High School - which was, after all, ideally situated in the centre of the town, and had ample room in its grounds for such an extension. Amalgamation might have ensured the High School's eventual survival; the parents of north Wishaw, however, voted for Option B.

Zoning arrangements for the two prospective six-year schools were obviously going to be especially significant, and the Executive Committee of the North Wishaw Parents' Association (which included representatives from the High School, Coltness High School, and their feeder primaries) submitted recommendations (based on statistical information supplied by Sam) to the Director of Education that would have ensured parity between the two high schools in respect of both the size of their overall rolls and the size of their 5th and 6th Years.

The arrangements eventually announced by the Education Committee - in an 'unholy alliance' (to quote Murdo Morrison) with certain parents and teachers - had a mixed reception:

'The Unholy Trinity', as Mr Morrison describes them, are only trying to improve the present hopeless situation.

Artificial zoning arrangements will produce two six-year schools of vastly different sizes and a most unequal distribution of pupils capable of certificate work - with Coltness High School having a much larger senior school. It can readily be seen that this imbalance will result not only in the staffing problems at the High School becoming even more acute, but also in a decline in its academic standards, which have always been among the highest in the county. If the present zoning system remains intact, Coltness High School will go from strength to strength, and parents of a promising pupil who wish him or her to be educated with pupils of a comparable academic calibre will be well advised to move house to the appropriate zone - if they have not already done so.

Under the newly established zoning system, the High School may once more become a school of whose record and reputation people can be proud.

The powers that be, in their infinite wisdom, have decided to destroy Wishaw High School.

We as parents are glad that an effort is being made to rehabilitate the High School by addressing the problem of the unsatisfactory part-time education our children are currently receiving.

The so-called zone for the High School is amateur in conception and impractical in application.

The new Wishaw High School will be a second-rate centre, relegated to the ranks of a holding camp for the local employment exchange.

This last gloomy prophecy was delivered by Murdo Morrison, and it proved to be amazingly accurate. What is equally incontrovertible is that the zoning arrangements instituted in 1974 were, without a doubt, the most significant factor in the decline of the High School. In 1975, for instance, the respective intakes of the High School and Coltness High School were as follows:

	Certificate Pupils	Non-Certificate Pupils	Remedial Pupils
Wishaw High School	89 (39%)	106	36
Coltness High School	97 (58%)	62	9

Senior (?) Boys (1941)

357

Captains and Prefects (1949)

R. Scott, I. Hislop, J. Cathro, T. Scoular, S. Bruce, J. Allan, D. Young, J. Robertson.

C. Hall, G. Prentice, D. Bruce, T. Gray, D. McLean, S. Black, H. Jamieson (Vice-Captain). J. Rodger, T. Prentice.

E. Paton, M. Gibb, B. Gibb, M. Lawson, J. Taylor, M. Mudie, J. Paterson, B. Baxter, H. Allan (School Captain), S. Watson.

A. Adams, M. Pringle, N. Henry, M. Murray (School Captain), Dr. Wilson (Rector), J. Allan (School Captain), S. Watson, I. Wells (Vice-Captain), I. Nimmo.

Captains and Prefects (1952-53)

School Captains and Prefects (1960)

School Captains and Prefects (1965)

Senior Pupils (late 1960s)

Rector and School Prefects (1967)

School Captains and Prefects (1969)

School Prefects (1970)

School Captains and Prefects (1971)

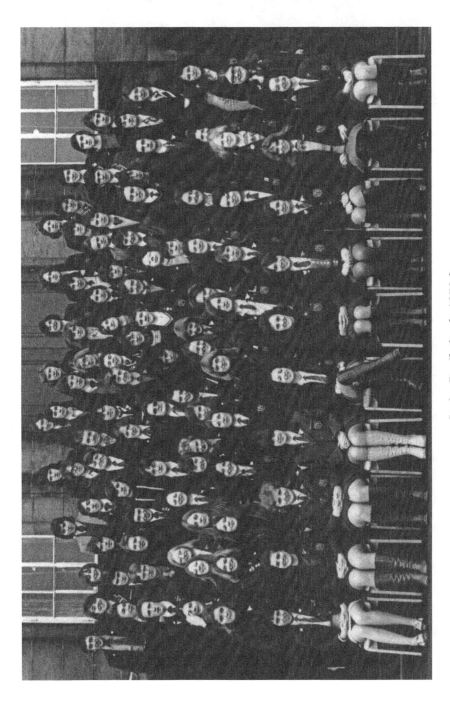

Senior Pupils (early 1970s)

School Captains and Prefects (1974)

School Captains and Prefects (1976)

37

1974 -1976

...it was the spring of hope, it was the winter of despair...

Charles Dickens, *A Tale of Two Cities*

'We must all hold on for one more year,' Sam urged the staff and pupils at the prize-giving in 1973, 'and thereafter there is the promise of much better things to come.' He was wrong. In 1974 a modified system of part-time education continued to obtain at the High School; indeed, it was extended into the following year. If my memory serves me correctly, Sam divided the school day into nine (obviously shorter) periods, as opposed to eight, and the pupils were dismissed at the end of the eighth period every day. By this master stroke, devised in response to complaints from some members of staff that they did not have enough free time, he made sure that every teacher had at least one free period every day.

Another cause for concern (and one that was not so easily remedied) was 'the presence in the school of some boys and girls whose conduct could only be described as disgraceful'.

Grandmasters

The Chess Club, which had about twenty members, was on the up and up; it met three times a week and all its meetings were well attended. The intermediate championship was won by Iain Anderson; in the senior championship, there was a tie between James Talbot and Philip Gilchrist.

We are men more dined against than dining.

Sir Maurice Bowra (adapted)

In June 1974, George Brown, Principal Teacher of English, and Jimmy Lindsay, Special Assistant in the Classics Department, hung up their mortar boards. George Brown, according to an article in *The Octagon*, 'had outstanding knowledge and power of understanding', and also the skills to help pupils not only to learn but also to want to learn'; Jimmy Lindsay 'could astutely discern those who preferred not to work, and he lavished his great erudition exclusively on those who would benefit most from his help'.

The retiral dinner arranged for these 'two exceptionally talented men' at the Garrion Hotel in Motherwell proved to be exceptionally disastrous. One of the waiters had gone off home with the key for the wine cellar, and somebody had to scuttle over to AA Brothers for a few bottles of vino; the dessert (an individual Cadbury's Chocolate Mini Roll) had clearly come straight out of a packet; George Brown attempted a trick with a table tennis ball that failed to work - due, he claimed, to the atmospheric conditions; and Jimmy Lindsay was persuaded by Sam to give an account of his wartime experiences as an intelligence officer with specific responsibility for the translation of Japanese documents - an account, it has to be recorded, that was both extremely long and extremely boring.

At the County Sports, Alistair Blair and Steven Graham were victorious in the 400 metres and high jump respectively.

The summer show was entitled *Fantasy Impromptu*; it featured the Junior Choir, a piano duet, *Up Caesar* (a farce, in every sense), and a miniature jazz opera (*An Operatic Parable*), written by John Dobbie, Principal Teacher of Music. 'This concert,' the *Wishaw Press* concluded, 'must rank as one of the most unusual - if not as one of the most entertaining - in the recent history of the school.'

The Return of the Natives

In August, the High School was blessed, once again, with a 1st Year. The 3rd Year, on the other hand, was only about half the size it had been during the previous three years.

The annexe (formerly Wishaw Public) was opened. It provided accommodation for the Art, Technical, and Business Studies Departments.

Sixteen girls from the 4th, 5th, and 6th Year helped the ladies of the WVS to operate a trolley service in the wards of several local hospitals. Two years later, a similar group raised £120 from a Bottle Stall at the fête arranged by Wishaw Hospital.

In September, the Parents' Association was re-formed, its aims being 'to promote the educational opportunities and welfare of all pupils, and foster a useful relationship between staff and parents by means of a liaison committee'.

A month later, at its first meeting (attended by the office-bearers of the nascent Wishaw High School Parents' Association), the Wishaw Secondary Schools Joint Parents' Committee advocated the speedy ratification of teaching appointments - particularly in those subjects where there was a shortage of teachers - and discussed the implications of the government's intention to set up schools' councils; at its second meeting in November, the Committee agreed that something should be done about the 'deplorable' conditions at the High School.

Dr Jeremy Bray, the local MP, paid a visit to the school to view the 'deplorable' conditions for himself. Having been shown round the school by Sam and the School Convener, Bailie William Irvine, he said that he was appalled by the state of the main building and by the inadequate toilets, library, gymnasium, social areas, and storage accommodation. 'Routine maintenance,' he continued, 'has been neglected, the whole school needs repainting, accommodation is inadequate, the surface of the playground is crumbling, and the extra classrooms erected in 1947 have passed well beyond their useful lifespan - in short, the Education Committee has seemingly neglected the school and its grounds. Mr Barnard, his staff and the pupils are working well in difficult circumstances - and the spirit in the school is admirable - but they should not be required to work in such conditions.'

I myself 'taught' in one of the HORSA huts mentioned by Dr Bray, and in the winter months I was rarely able to discard my coat.

A team from the High School took part in the Capitaliser Competition organised by the Royal Bank of Scotland 'to help pupils in 5th and 6th Year to understand the working of the stock market without running the risk of losing money'.

For the second year in succession, David Wright was selected for the Lanarkshire Schools' rugby XV.

Netball was still popular enough to enable the school to run both a junior and a senior team, the latter of which won its section of the league. Maureen Clemenson, a member of the senior team, was selected to play for Lanarkshire.

Under the supervision of John Arton, 6th Year girls 'took over the gym on Mondays after school to pursue their interest in basketball'.

In 1975 the senior girls' hockey team were runners-up in the Tait Trophy. Fortune, however, did not smile so kindly on the netball team, which was forced to withdraw from the Lanarkshire League: the Lanarkshire Netball Association had decreed that no league games could be played on a court smaller than 65 by 35 feet, and the court at the High School was 5 feet too short and 5 feet too narrow.

Five days shalt thou labour ...

The 1973 Education (Work Experience) Act gave the green light for work experience to be included in the curriculum of those pupils who were in their final year of compulsory education. Two years later - with the permission of the Director of Education and the cooperation of the local Careers Office - David Carmichael, AHT (Guidance), inaugurated a work experience project, the object of which was "to broaden the pupils' outlook and experience by exposing them for a week to the world of work", and thus "facilitate the transition from classroom to workplace". The sixty 4th and 5th Year pupils who took part in the project worked normal working hours, made their own travel arrangements, and received no remuneration.

The day of the fête - and what a day for it,
Blazing with bonhomie and sun.

Anonymous

The Midsummer Fête (it was held on the lawns at the front of the school, and was opened by Councillor Hutchison Sneddon) raised over £2,000. Sam claimed that the fête was 'good for school morale', and that 'a great deal of camaraderie' had been evident among those who 'worked so hard to ensure its success'. Similar fêtes were held in 1976, 1977, 1978 (in which year, the Wishaw High School Fête Queen, Lorna Christie, declared the fête open after driving through the town in an open-top car with her four attendants), and 1979.

Gordon Currie (200 metres), Ruth Fullarton (200 metres), and William Dickson (800 metres) won their respective events at the County Sports.

During the summer holidays, a party of 5th and 6th Year pupils went on a cruise to Russia, Finland, Denmark, and Sweden on the SS Uganda. Sheila Sprot, one of the members of staff who accompanied them, has many pleasant memories of the cruise:
We had a good choir with us, and it contributed hugely to the concert that was held on the final night of the cruise. The passengers were very impressed, and I overheard one old lady saying, "If that's comprehensive education, I'm all for it."

In August, the High School once again became a six-year school - a six-year comprehensive, that is, not a six-year senior secondary.

Two Yanks at Wishaw

Two Americans - Bill Haapa and Brian Smith - joined the English Department. Bill Haapa, who was descended from the chief of the Chippewa Indians, told a reporter from the *Wishaw Press*:
The pupils here are friendly, and those in 4th and 5th Year are more concerned about their future than their American counterparts. Another difference I have noted is that there is much less classroom discussion in Scottish schools.
Brian Smith wrote the following article for *The Octagon*:
1975 was for me the year of the SHIRE - Lanarkshire that is, although by the time I arrived it was no longer Lanarkshire, but Strathclyde Region. One morning in March, a letter arrived in the morning post telling me of a job teaching English in Scotland. Although I was selling gold and silver bullion at that time in Boston, Massachusetts, I had previously (after I graduated from the University of Maine in 1967) been an English teacher, and I had decided to return to teaching in the fall of 1975: so the letter was very welcome that morning in March. In fact, I made up my mind then and there to go to Scotland if the arrangements could be made; and it turned out to be a very wise decision - for I met you.

I can only guess what 1975 was like for you, but let me try. Sometime during the summer, when you were wealthy with time and school was a long way off, you heard that an American was coming to teach English in Wishaw. You probably didn't think much about it at the time, but

374

nevertheless you were aware that it was going to happen, and you were a little curious - perhaps even mildly cynical - about it. An American teaching English to a Scotsman - what next?

Well, the first day of the new session finally arrived - and lo and behold, he was one of your teachers; and what a strange experience it was. Not only did he have a strange accent, but he always mispronounced 'schedule', called a biscuit a 'cookie', and had a weird way of teaching. He didn't believe in the belt, but if you misbehaved in class, he invited you back for 'tea' at 3.55; and if you were unlucky enough to get caught blowing barley, you got to sweep out the classroom after school. Yes, it was really strange having a foreign teacher.

Well, enough of history. Let me just say in closing that I am having a wonderful year. Scotland is a beautiful country, not unlike my beloved New England, and a great place to spend time exchanging ideas and customs. I do hope my presence as your teacher is not too traumatic, and that the rewards outweigh the disadvantages of having a foreigner teaching your mother tongue. As for myself, I can only say that it is the most enjoyable job I have ever had, and I want to thank you for being such good pupils and new friends.

Dog(ger)sbody

In the autumn of 1975, George Dick became the High School's first pupil representative on the newly established Wishaw and Shotts Schools' Council. To the best of my recollection, the council had few, if any, executive powers and spent most of its time chasing up chronic absentees.

John McLaren and Iain McGillivray were selected (again) for the Lanarkshire Schools' rugby XV.

The Biology Club kept the conservatory tidy, fed the animals, and went on a trip to the Marine Biological Station at Millport.

The State of the High School Message (Christmas 1975)

When people ask me, 'Is Wishaw High School slipping? Is it as good as it was?', they are thinking of the days when Wishaw High School was selective, when every pupil was capable of achieving academic excellence, and when the SCE results were the only criterion by which we were required to measure our success.

That school ceased to exist several years ago - by Act of Parliament. For the majority of our pupils the SCE examinations are an irrelevance, and while we must not cease to foster high standards of scholarship and academic discipline among the minority of pupils who are capable of achieving them, we must also remember our obligations to the majority, whose needs are entirely different; and we must achieve these aims without in any way creating the impression that one kind of excellence is better than another (it may be different, but it is certainly not superior). That is the greatest challenge in secondary education today.

At a more personal level, the school has an aura of humanity and friendliness on which all visitors comment; there is also, from visitors who are professionally competent to judge, admiration for the excellent work that is going on, and amazement that it can be produced in such a depressing physical environment.

Finally, although the conduct of some of our pupils brings shame upon us all, I doubt if there is a better staff in any other school. If there is, I would like to meet them. ('Sam Ipse dixit')

Whenever I felt that my reserves of cynicism needed replenishing, I simply read the above 'message'.

'Shock, Horror, Probe, Sensation'

The 'physical environment' remained very 'depressing' in 1976, a state of affairs that was highlighted in an article (by Alison Downie) in the *Glasgow Herald* which compared the High School, unfavourably, with Park Mains, a new, custom-built comprehensive in Erskine:

The main building is a rectangle of grey stone, within which there are long, drab corridors with scarred, blue-painted walls; stone stairs with black, iron balustrades; a series of identical square classrooms with scored wooden desks; and a number of cubby holes, all of them stuffed with educational materials for which no adequate storage accommodation exists.

The Rector, Samuel Barnard, begged me to draw a veil over the boys' toilet facilities: "They've been a major source of complaint for years and years, but now at last they're going to be completely modernised."

376

In a unique collection of hutted classrooms, there are examples of every style of prefabricated hut produced between 1947 and 1975.

The assembly hall is a real monstrosity: for some strange reason, the architect chose to design it as an octagon, thus rather cunningly combining maximum space with minimum usefulness.

According to Mr Barnard, it is the non-academic pupils who suffer most from the lack of facilities for both practical and physical education; the academically inclined pupil suffers less, provided the teaching is good.

He also claimed that the academic record of the school is 'middle of the road and compares favourably with those of other schools of the same type'.

One of the teachers, a former pupil, told me: "Teaching in a place like this is very hard work. We haven't the facilities, so we have to improvise. In any case, a school isn't just a building; there's a good family spirit here."

Alison Downie finished her article with a reference to another kind of spirit - 'the frontier spirit' - which she sensed was prevalent among the staff and the pupils, and which seemed to her to have been engendered by the conditions at the High School.

One 'worried' parent was not impressed by Sam's description of the academic record of the school as 'middle of the road'; and in a letter to the *Wishaw Press*, he claimed that he was just one of many parents who wanted more detailed information (number of individual passes, success rates of different departments etc.) from Sam about the performance of High School pupils in the SCE Examinations. I can find no record of any response from Sam - who did, however, claim in his annual report that the school had managed 'to cope with all the problems of vandalism, truancy, violent behaviour, and staffing shortages without too much [sic] upset to school life'.

Opportunity Knocks

The end of session entertainment took the form of a concert devised and produced by Ronnie Hamilton, and held in the Civic Theatre. Three choirs - Senior, Junior Boys', and Junior Girls' - sang a variety of songs; and there were also contributions from the Brass Group, dancing, verse reading, comedy sketches, a 'virtuoso performance' on the drums, and a series of 'variety items' featuring senior pupils.

In the programme for a similar concert in 1977 (in which nearly 200 pupils took part), Ronnie Hamilton wrote:

The format that has evolved allows us to give a considerable number of our pupils a rare opportunity to appear on a professional stage. We hope that the concert will generate something of a family atmosphere; it is an occasion that needs, if it is to be successful, the cooperation of parents, pupils, and staff— and "that," as they say, "can't be bad."

Another innovation was the Christmas Dinner arranged by the 6thYear and attended by 63 OAPs. The menu for this was: A Glass of Sherry; Vegetable Soup; Steak Pie with Potatoes and Vegetables; Fresh Cream Trifle; Tea or Coffee and Christmas Cake. After the meal, the pensioners played a game of bingo which had been 'fixed' in such a way that they all completed their cards simultaneously, and they all, consequently, won a prize. One of the pensioners, Mrs Elizabeth Brown, expressed her appreciation as follows: "It's really nice to come to the school that all my family attended. They say that the young ones don't bother any more, but they do."

A third (and slightly less noteworthy) innovation was the formation of a basketball team by Bill Haapa, one of the two Americans who had joined the English Department.

Overweight, Overrated, and Over Here

Bill Haapa also featured in the never-to-be-forgotten Staff Superstars Contest that took place in the mid-1970s (I can't remember the exact year). One of the individual events was the 100 metres, and he had installed himself as favourite for this by regaling (and irritating) everybody with accounts of his incomparable prowess as a sprinter; however, when he saw the underfoot conditions (Waverley was pitted with ruts), he refused at first to run, then changed his mind and ran in his bare feet. To his - and nobody else's - chagrin, Big Chief Running Bear (footed) came in last. Ian Maxwell, who prior to the contest had never had a golf club in his hand, won the pitching event; but the overall winner was Ronnie Sutherland, a man who marched (or, in this instance, ran, jumped, threw, and dribbled) to the sound of a very distant drum.

38

Decline and Fall Part II - Threats of Closure

In 1975 the County of Lanark was superseded by Strathclyde Region, and the High School, consequently, came under the administrative sway of the Lanark Division of that region's Department of Education.

In September 1976, the Divisional Education Officer produced a consultative paper in which it was suggested that 'the organisation of secondary education in Wishaw should be based on no more than two schools' (as the number of secondary pupils in the town did not 'warrant' three secondary schools), and that the two schools should be Garrion Academy and Coltness High School.

The finality of the assertion that the number of secondary pupils in Wishaw did not 'warrant' three secondary schools seems to be at variance with Paragraph 6 of the consultative paper, where, after some unconvincing estimates of the prospective aggregate roll of the secondary schools in Wishaw, it is admitted that three viable schools could, arguably, be established from an aggregate roll ranging from 2,850 to 3,050, but that such a set-up 'would require to be supported by a detailed study of the zoning arrangements, to ensure that each school's catchment area contained a sound social blend'. In view of the scandalously unbalanced nature of the catchment areas that had already been established in Wishaw, one can only wonder at the effrontery of the DEO in mentioning - let alone insisting on - such a proviso.

The reasons adduced by the consultative paper to explain why Coltness High School was to be given precedence over the High School were equally debatable: whereas the site of Coltness High School was 'quite adequate' for an extension to - or the 'remodelling' of - that institution, 'mineral reports' indicated that an extension to the High School (to replace the annexes and temporary classrooms that made up 50% of its accommodation) would be 'difficult'. A shifty document, in short, lacked even the courage of its complete lack of conviction.

Right is not might.

The consultative paper met with almost universal rejection; indeed, the only people to support its recommendations were the three members of the Wishaw and Shotts Schools' Council who voted against Sam's submission that there should be no change in the status quo as far as secondary education in Wishaw was concerned.

The opposition to the consultative paper was spearheaded by the Wishaw Secondary Schools Joint Parents' Association, which claimed that a detailed 'mineral report' on the area made it quite clear that the High School could be 'doubled in size' - as the site of its campus was 'completely stable'; and this claim was supported (though he seemed to be contradicting one of the main findings of the 'mineral report') by Regional Councillor James Fyfe, who was confident that an extension 'could be built on the fault' (sic), since 'new methods of building allowed for faults and subsidence'.

The Joint Parents' Association also expressed 'minimal' confidence in the statistics quoted in the consultative paper to justify a reduction in the number of secondary schools in Wishaw. In their judgment, the projected decrease in school rolls was dependent on a complex series of 'ifs' and 'maybes' that involved moving pupils to schools which were not equipped to take them - or had not yet been built; and, more importantly, since Wishaw was recognised as an area of 'high growth potential' (900 new houses were in the pipeline), the school population was liable to increase, or at least remain fairly stable.

Sam ('I am appalled by the idea') and the staff were, of course, totally opposed to any attempt to close the High School, and they marshalled a series of cogent arguments against the contents of the consultative paper: schools, like the two proposed for Wishaw, with more than 1,500 pupils were socially and educationally questionable; if a case could be made for having two schools (each with fewer than 1,000 pupils) in Motherwell, the same line of reasoning could be employed to justify the existence of three schools in Wishaw (moreover, an examination of the proposals relating to the provision of secondary education in other parts of the Division - especially those areas where the erection of new schools was under consideration - suggested a willingness to accept rolls of under 1,000 that could almost be interpreted as official policy); the threat of closure, even though it might not be implemented in the immediate future, would have a harmful effect on the morale of the staff, the pupils, and their parents; the long-established traditions and academic standing of the High School were such that its closure would represent a serious loss to the community; and finally, in view of the fact that Dalziel High School was described in the consultative paper as 'the traditional senior secondary school for Motherwell in years past', the High School surely merited not only a similar description - but also similar consideration, as far as its future was concerned.

These arguments were publicly endorsed at a 'very well- attended' meeting of parents and members of staff on 16 November 1976, at which it was unanimously agreed that 'the number of secondary schools required to serve the educational needs of the Wishaw area was three'. However, Strathclyde Region's Education Committee approved the recommendations contained in the consultative paper - despite the efforts of Regional Councillor James Fyfe ('Why consult the people, and then turn your back on them and do something else?'), who proposed, unsuccessfully, that three secondary schools should be retained in Wishaw.

Iain Macdonald, Vice-Chairman of the Wishaw and Shotts Schools' Council, commented scathingly on the Education Committee's decision: 'This decision makes a mockery of consultation; the wishes of the people have been flouted. However,' he added (more accurately than he probably imagined at the time) 'the matter is not finished.' Sam, meanwhile, remained calm: 'There is no panic or dismay at the school.'

A Spectacular U-Turn

At a meeting of the full Regional Council, it was decided that the proposals rubber-stamped by the Education Committee should be referred back to it for 'further investigation and discussion'. One can only assume that Regional Councillors Fyfe, Burns, and Gibson managed to convince the Labour Group that the closure of the High School and the extension of Coltness High School would be politically inexpedient. Nothing concentrates the minds of local politicians like the suspicion that a particular policy may lose them votes at the next election, and the electorate of North Wishaw would not have been overjoyed at the prospect - if the High School was closed - of the academic tranquillity of Coltness High School being shattered by an influx of Goths and Visigoths from Craigneuk and West Crindledyke.

After 'further investigation and discussion', the Education Committee duly changed its mind - and recommended the retention of three secondary schools in Wishaw. Councillor Burns (somewhat ironically, it must be assumed) praised the Education Committee for its 'wise' decision; Sam declared that pupils and parents would now be 'relieved of their concern about the future of the school', and that he and his staff could now 'get on with the business of education'; Councillor Fyfe, however, with amazing foresight, issued a warning: 'A close watch will have to be kept on the situation, for there is the danger, if population trends alter, that this problem could arise again.'

Early in 1978, there was an unexpected development: the Scottish Education Department expressed reservations about Strathclyde Region's proposals with regard to the provision of secondary education in Lanark Division. In particular, it suggested that if the erection of a new school in Newarthill was not accompanied by the closure of one of the existing secondary schools in the Motherwell and Wishaw area, there would be 'an over-provision of secondary places' in the Division.

In May of the same year, therefore, the Education Committee decided that a second review of 'the arrangements pertaining to the provision of secondary education in the Motherwell and Wishaw area' should be initiated; and in October, a second consultative paper was issued by the Director of Education. Three options were mooted, each of which envisaged two secondary schools in Wishaw; once again there was a reference to 'the mineral workings that would render an extension of the High School highly problematical'; and once again the consultative paper was clearly, if not explicitly, in favour of establishing Garrion Academy and Coltness High School as the only two secondary schools in Wishaw - even though it did suggest, rather unconvincingly, that Coltness High School could change its name to Wishaw High School and serve as the 'core' of a High School Mark 2.

Political reaction was swift - and adverse. Councillor Fyfe described the proposals as 'sheer lunacy', and hinted that 'certain people who felt thwarted' were responsible for putting the closure of the High School back on the agenda. Dr Jeremy Bray MP was slightly more explicit: *Officials of Strathclyde Region, without the Council's authority, seem to have regarded the SED's reservations about the erection of a new school in Newarthill as an opportunity to reopen the Wishaw High School question, a question that was settled six months ago.*

A Pyrrhic Victory

The sub-committee (comprising councillors from the Motherwell and Wishaw area) set up by the Education Committee to review the situation disregarded the consultative paper and recommended (*nem. con.*) that the arrangements approved by the Education Committee in August 1977 with regard to the provision of secondary education in Wishaw should be remitted back to the SED completely unchanged. The basis of these arrangements, as we have seen, was that three secondary schools were to be retained in the town; in addition, both the High School and Coltness High School were to have approximately 700 pupils on their roll, and Garrion Academy double that number; and with a view to achieving 'balanced rolls', existing catchment areas were to be 'adjusted'.

Councillor Fyfe, who had been a member of the sub-committee (and who was rapidly gaining a reputation as the Tiresias of local politics), greeted the salvation of the High School with a prophecy: 'We are in for a period of intense political activity on this issue'; and a warning: 'Many people seem set on having Wishaw High School closed.' In the event, both his warning and his prophecy proved to be well grounded. On more than one occasion, in the course of the next ten years, it did seem as if some people were 'set on closing' the High School; and there was 'a period of intense political activity', which focused, unfortunately, on catchment areas and, even more unfortunately, produced adjustments to the existing catchment areas (which already favoured Coltness High School) that did the High School even fewer favours, as the following statistics demonstrate:

Projected Overall Rolls: Coltness High School - 800; Wishaw High School - 1,050

Projected Number of Pupils in S5 and S6: Coltness High School - 185; Wishaw High School - 150

Projected Percentage of Pupils in Each Annual Intake Likely to Extend Their Secondary Career beyond 4th Year: Coltness High School - 80%; Wishaw High School - 45%

As far as catchment areas were concerned, there was 'no balm in Gilead' for the High School.

NB: In the preceding account, 'secondary' should be taken to mean 'non-denominational secondary'.

39

1977-1980

Bog-Standard Cloakrooms

In March 1977, work began on a £32,000 project to convert the pupils' toilets into storage space, and the cloakrooms into toilets; this, it should be pointed out, was the first time the toilets had been modernised since the school was built. Charles Lindsay, Chairman of the Parents' Association, expressed the hope that 'some kind of supervision would be exercised over the new facilities'.

Vandals Rule OK

In the course of an interview for *The Octagon*, Sam was asked if vandalism was 'a significant problem' at the High School. His answer was: 'Yes, it is a problem, but it is not any more of a problem here than in other schools, or indeed in society at large.'

A full-size netball court was marked out in the girls' playground.

Hilary Mauchline and Linda Watson were selected for the Lanarkshire Girls' hockey team.

Only eighteen months after he took up rugby, Alastair Hill was chosen to play for the Scottish Schools' XV against England at Meadowbank Stadium, Edinburgh - 'a phenomenal achievement', to quote Sam's comment in the *Wishaw Press*. Hill himself told the local paper that his two principal ambitions were to play for the full Scottish team and to be the youngest prop forward to represent his country. He did not fulfil either of these ambitions, but at least two other members of the Scottish squad - David Johnston and Steve Munro - did succeed in becoming full internationals.

The school rugby team, meanwhile, struggled on with the help of Peter Boa.

The Scripture Union, on the other hand, supervised by Ruth Hodgson, experienced something of a revival, the average attendance at meetings being 25.

There were still more than a thousand pupils on the roll, and the numbers in the various year groups were: SI - 241; S2 - 236; S3 - 242; S4 - 192; S5 - 104; S6 - 30.

Please, sir, I want some more.

Charles Dickens, *Oliver Twist*

In the course of her investigation into what schoolchildren had for lunch, Helen Russell of the *Wishaw Press* paid a visit to the school canteen in March 1978. Her report reads as follows:

There was a choice of three main dishes - mince pie, gammon, and fish fingers; all three were served with chips and looked very appetising. Helpings seemed adequate, and many of the pupils came back for 'seconds' - or even 'thirds'. Though the pupils did not give the food their wholehearted approval, they did agree that a school lunch was excellent value at 25 pence; and having sampled the lunch of the day, I would go along with their assessment. Robert Drysdale (12) said: "I love pie and chips, then cake and custard; these are my favourites. But I eat up my dinner every day; it's usually good."

In December, after being shown a film that illustrated - in a very graphic manner - the dangers facing teenage pedestrians on the roads, 1st Year pupils spent three weeks on a project on road safety.

From 1978 onwards, rugby tended to be played by only the younger pupils in the school, and although he was not an aficionado of the game, Tom Young started a 1st and 2nd Year team; Clark Govan provided the technical input.

Up yours, Arthur

As a result of the miners' strike, there were fuel shortages during the winter of 1978-79; unfortunately, these did not affect the High School, where Charlie Scott, the janitor, took a perverse pride in having a superabundance of coal. Every day, a few of us would stand at the window of the gents' staffroom, hoping and praying that the coal lorry would not materialise; but to our great annoyance, it always did. It may have been at this time, therefore, that the phrase 'We never close' became part of the folklore of the High School.

The Candidate

In March 1979, John Ralston, Head of the Upper School, was selected to contest North Lanark for the SNP at the forthcoming general election (one of his fellow candidates, interestingly enough, was John Smith, the future leader of the Labour Party). I remember going up to Shotts to attend a debate featuring the two Johns and the rather nondescript Conservative candidate. Big John was wearing a white shirt that looked new, but unfortunately wasn't spotless - as he had cut himself shaving; having barged into two old age pensioners, he glowered at them for being so stupid as to stand in his direct line of lurch from the back of the hall to the platform; and to crown this *richesse d'embarras*, he came to a grinding halt in the middle of his peroration, having lost or misplaced the last page of his speech.

In May, a group of High School pupils participated in a work experience project at the General Motors plant at Newhouse. The boys worked for a day in each of the following departments: structural, machine shop, assembly, stores, and maintenance; the girls helped out in the commercial and administrative departments.

There was a major change in the format of *The Octagon*: from 'blazer pocket' size to A4 (12" by 8"); there was also 'a dramatic increase' in the number of photographs and drawings (caricatures, for example, of various teachers) it contained. In the foreword, Sam sang the praises of the Sixth Year: 'It is probably the smallest in the history of the school, but it is also the most closely knit; and I doubt if it has ever been surpassed for enterprise and public spirit.'

During the summer holidays, John Bonomy, a member of the PE Department for 31 years, was awarded the Bronze Medal for Youth Sport and Leisure, in recognition of his efforts to forge sporting links between France and Scotland.

Alison Laird gained a distinction in the Brass Section at the Lanarkshire Music Festival; and Sheena Christie joined the ranks of the many fine public speakers produced by the school who won the A.R. Dalziel Memorial Trophy.

Two new clubs were established - the Electronics Club and the Weight Training Club. The aim of the former was 'to give pupils some idea of future technology'; Clark Govan supervised the latter.

Just before Christmas, six different charities (including the RSPCC and Dr Barnado's) benefited from a sponsored Hush In that raised £600.

It should be noted, before we leave the 1970s, that during that decade the number of hockey teams fielded regularly by the High School decreased from six to two. Members of staff who helped out with the hockey teams included Isobel Johnston, Mabel Leslie, Liz Clarke, Aileen Nimmo, Elizabeth Jackson, Joyce Livingstone, and Doreen Howieson.

Schoolgirl Sandra is super at sums.

In February 1980, Sandra McCumisky, a 2nd Year pupil, won a certificate and a cheque for £20 in a nationwide competition (to deduce as many mathematical facts as possible from a given diagram) instituted by Blackie and Chambers, publishers of *Modern Mathematics for Schools*.

The Chess Club attracted large numbers of boys - and girls - from the 1st and 2nd Year, and a junior championship was inaugurated; it was won by James Redfern. The school champion was Andrew Watson.

The Junior Choir (75 strong) presented the cantata *Jerusalem Joy*.

The 2nd Juniors, managed by David Bell and Willie Beck, completed the football season without losing a game.

The Octagon was published for the last time.

During the summer holidays, Kenneth Mathie took part in an expedition to Iceland arranged by the British Schools' Exploring Society. In 1981 Allyson McLung was a member of a similar expedition.

In December, the High School held a Mini Careers Convention for the benefit of 4th and 5th Year pupils. In attendance were representatives from banks, shops, local hospitals, engineering firms, the Careers Service, and Lanarkshire Automobile Training.

40

Uselesses or A Portrait of the Piss Artist as a Young Man

once upon a time and a very good time it was 1975 actually first day at WHS new blazer shoes or Doc Martens decisions decisions will I get a shampoo and rinse in the boys' karzy courtesy of the Loo Ducks Clan the bus from Newmains is packed with school pupils and a few star-crossed members of the general public sitting in front of me are an elderly couple the man has a shiny bald head the woman is wearing the sort of hat favoured by EIIR an arm stretches out over my shoulder grabs the hat and places it at a jaunty angle on the head of the slaphead very short ode on a distant prospect of Wishaw High School ye distant spires ye antique towers ye manky huts I must however boldly go the rector looks like Mr Spock after an ear transplant and the theft of his Grecian 2000 I feel very small and insignificant akin to Tom Brown at Rugby John Brown on his early peregrinations through the southern states of America or Gordon Brown in No 10 how do the teachers manage to remember the names of so many pupils most of them don't particularly the Latin dominie Titus Digito Intento Derisor I try not to but I'm examining my personal timetable every 10 minutes like foreign nationals in Lisbon or Istanbul during the Second World War we are all trying to suss each other out who can I trust who's likely to nick my Curly Wurly I must stop answering teachers in a sing-song voice I sound like a speaking clock with a Swedish accent my timetable is falling apart where's the sellotape flick-talk flick-talk I'm flicking small particles of mercury every which way get a wigging from Graham Johnstone too many books now for one Adidas bag mer(e)cury I start flicking all the scattered particles in the same direction and create a little pool on the bench oh dear Riot Act read défense de toucher le mercure flicken der Quecksilber ist fucken verboten lunch at wee Susie's talk about a greasy spoon there's enough grease on the hamburgers to lubricate the engines on an aircraft carrier bedlam in Kenilworth Avenue as hundreds of pupils from WHS and St Aidan's converge on the same bus-stop at 4 o'clock singing 'Down in the jungle where nobody goes' on the bus home sound the trumpets beat the drums one of the teachers knows my name not the stupid Titus in Room 43 oh to be at Kersewell now that April's there I have removed the mattress from my bed and am using it as a sledge to slide along the shiny floor of the dormitory one of our group climbs out of the window in his pyjamas don't ask me why and surprise surprise we lock him out boys' inhumanity to boys he'll have to rouse one of the teachers from the school I wish him luck they've all OD'd on currant scones orienteering competitive sport in which runners contrive to get themselves lost with the aid of a map and a compass we are not alone my mucker Passepartout and I are being followed by two girls of the opposite sex sadly they are not nymphomaniacs just two run-of-the-mill maniacs who hope to get round the course in eighty minutes or less with the help of yours truly and Passepartout such faith such stupidity we all end up in the middle of nowhere don't panic don't panic on second thoughts panic panic get us out of here phone the police phone the fire brigade phone Bear Grylls a-ferreting we will go a-ferreting we will go with a Scottish Worzel Gummidge final score Ferrets 1 Rabbits 1 after extra time the dead rabbit tinkles on Passepartout now Pissepartout as he carries it back to the college I do not believe it this rabbit is no more it has ceased to be it has expired and gone to the great rabbit hutch in the sky this is a late rabbit it's a stiff bereft of life it rests in peace it has nibbled its last carrot if you hadn't slung it over your shoulder it would be pushing up the daisies it's rung down the curtain and joined the choir invisible this is an ex-rabbit so phone David Attenborough for an explanation we learn a lot of country lore red sky at night shepherd's delight red sky in the morning shepherd's warning red sky in the afternoon some cunt's set fire to the shepherd's hut nemo saltat nisi inebrius at the disco on the final night of our week in the country the boys hide behind the curtains in the main lounge so that they don't have to dance with the girls my blazer is starting to look a bit tatty will it survive a second session boa v python('s flying hors de la fenêtre circus) Peter the snake has a Kaiser Wilhelm moustache and a jacket that billows out around him like Batman's cape he could certainly do with Batman and Robin's help to prevent some Germanophobes from exiting his classroom via the window vorsprung durch Everest in recognition of the constrictor's status as a German teacher the unconstricted give him a Nazi salute as they depart I've started being cheeky to the House prefects don't pull rank on me you ranker good moaning I have a massage from Michelle she asked me to deliver it to you as quickly as pissible Audrey speaks French like a native....of Cambuslang not so much a francophone as a franc(ie and josie)phone the ceiling of Room 2 is splattered with dollops of pulp recipe leesten very carefully I shall say this only wance take a page from any French textbook crumple season to taste chew till soft then use a ruler to flick it upwards on to the ceiling Susie's has lost its Michelin star so I've stopped going there for lunch King's sweetie shop is a possibility so is Greggs the bakers with his long hair and even longer beard Robert Bell looks as if he has just returned from a year in the Brazilian rainforest he prances round the room gesturing melodramatically as he acts out all the parts in Hamlet or Macbeth he uses different voices for the different parts even the women's is there no beginning to this man's talents iacta alea est it's the Carlton Café and piping hot chips for lunch Macavity isn't there Catwoman aka Liz Patrick asks if anyone has seen her pussycat I answer facetiously and get the belt catastrophe my trousers fall down in Frau Logan's German class are my cheeks red already this year is shaping up to be a real anus horribilis you stupid boy dumbkopf schweinhund droopy-drawers why are you exposing your naked knees to all and sundry you stupid woman do you not know that today is the thirty-second anniversary of the assassination of the Fuhrer's pet ostrich and that all trousers must be worn at half-mast the man serving the chips in the Carlton has the biggest eyeballs and the greasiest hair in Western Europe imagine Steve McQueen in a light brown raincoat with John Lennon-type glasses ecce Brian Smith the Connecticut Massachusetts actually Yank at the court of King Samuel Scotland and America two countries divided by a common language I am dishing out King's Oddfellows to my fellow students of English literature I like the red ones best funnily enough it's the same with Rowntree's fruit gums most people seem to have a similar preference remember Hancock in The Blood Donor well anyway the far from quiet American throws a wobbly he even utters the F-word.....fanny down on which I am instructed to sit what's the difference between a brothel and the school tuck shop in the latter you get screwed without having to take your clothes off with their wild hair bulging eyes and histrionic style of teaching half the members of the Science Department remind me of Dr Magnus Pyke I am looking forward pruriently to Section Six of the General Science course the human reproductive system it's known as Section Sex but all it raises is a few titters I(v)an the Terrible holds our maths class spellbound nothing concentrates the mind like his reputation for being the hardest belter on the staff the Toscanini of the tawse poetry in motion the Shelley of the Lochgelly n+1 little girls from school are we the Maths Department seems to be the natural habitat of maiden aunts fluffy grey-haired women in their fifties or sixties who wear frilly dresses and glasses that have definitely not been designed by Calvin Klein you're going to like this not a lot but you'll like it Sheila Sprot gives us some algebraic equations to tackle surely you're having us on

I'm not having you on and don't call me Shirley five or ten minutes later she asks if anyone is having any problems I put my hand up and say yes miss the manager of Patrick Thistle you silly twisted boy we interrupt this party political broadcast on behalf of the WCLO(the West Crindledyke Liberation Organisation) for the following warning from the Met Office Hurricane Hilda is moving rapidly southwards and is expected to reach this page in the next few seconds Helen Young is a world-class shouter the belle of the decibels pack all your wine glasses in cotton wool she scales new vocal heights when unbeknown to her I use my watch to reflect a ray of sunlight onto the blackboard then onto different parts of her person and the rest of the class fall about laughing the more they laugh the more she loses it exit maths teacher pursued by a glare two years before the mast my blazer is now too worn to be worn must decide which subjects I'm going to take in 3rd year small choice in rotten apples one of my choices is geography what a ricket the worst blunder since the charge of the Light Brigade time's winged chariot doesn't hurry past the geography hut I think it must have had a puncture can time really come to a halt I sometimes think so as I stare at the massive clock on the back wall of the main building the big hand is static most of the period what doesn't stop moving is the conveyor belt of pupils being belted by Neil Jardine for failing to do their homework all the PE teachers wear the same sort of clobber dark blue sweaters black trousers and white trainers they look like middle-aged or geriatric naval cadets John Bonomy takes us on long cross-country runs round the perimeter of Wishaw Golf Course that's a bit of a bummer however I have a cunning plan a plan as cunning as a fox who's just been appointed Professor of Cunning at Oxford University JB leads from the front commendable but very unwise he can't see what's going on behind him and what's occurring is this some of us Slo-Mo Farrows peel off from the back of the peloton at the top of Belhaven Park and re-join it half an hour later at the end of the run am I alone in thinking that the girls at St Aidan's are better looking than the demoiselles in blue and yellow John Arton has an uncanny ability to reproduce the sound of a referee's whistle up on Waverley we are staging a reprise of the recent World Cup qualifier between Scotland and the Galapagos Islands le siffleur extraordinaire is refereeing after ten minutes the score is Bravehearts 0 Penguins 2 history is repeating itself the ball goes over the byline the whistle sounds but is it a corner or a goal kick I glance at the referee what's he going to signal Houston we have a problem a three-pipe problem a riddle wrapped in a mystery inside an enigma where's his whistle is it where he's been told to stick it on several occasions is he another Joseph Pujol Le Pétomane redivivus the male pupils at St Aidan's assure me there is much more talent at WHS Tom Young tries to get us interested in cricket no way I don't want to be a 'flannelled fool' some of the teachers will say I'm already halfway along that road the medicine ball surely the most useless object ever invented putting the shot and throwing the discus or javelin equally pointless well the javelin isn't as some unwary punters know from painful experience if you prick us with its tip do we not bleed Sam Graham could stand in for Tom Selleck and the girls fancy him apparelwise PE brings out the worst in people the good grief light blue shorts all the rage in Antibes St Tropez and Morningside the bad khaki shorts à la Bridge on the River Kwai madness madness and the ugly woollen shorts crappy crummy grotty manky poxy yucky naff uncool endsville the pits is this a string vest I see before me similar to the one worn by Cyril Heslop in the first episode of Porridge Fletcher of course wore a singlet for his medical have you ever had crabs no I don't eat seafood any medical problems bad feet any medical problems Bad Feet are you now or have you ever been a practising homosexual what with these feet John Ralston wears a gown but his academic persona is somewhat undermined by the Lochgelly draped over his shoulder he assails the nearest desk with this in order to bring the class to heel I may not have been a 'flannelled fool' but I'm now a 'muddied oaf' and have been picked for the 1st eleven football team Brut or Blue Stratos a no-brainer for a member of the blue army anyway ma I made it top of the world I'm so money super market for I'm also a member of the senior choir during their rendition of 'The Bare Necessities' I play Baloo the Bear and lead a conga line round the stage at the Civic Centre during school hours I spend most of my time in the Annexe the land of the lotus-eaters the land where time and most of the teachers stand still the land of the lost the land where the Art Department have indolence down to a fine art the land that time and Sam Barnard forgot the land where tetchy Techy teachers disappear mysteriously from the room and return fifteen minutes later smelling of cigarette smoke and in a much less tetchy mood in the central hall we budding Monets sketch fruit and old wine bottles sometimes a live model we try to make her laugh by blowing kisses or flicking paint at anybody preferably a teacher who has his back turned the fifth year have the largest common room in the British Isles no surprise there it's the assembly hall a fashion statement my school uniform now comprises a blazer shirt tie with as large a knot as possible white socks Levi jeans and high-lacing

392

Doc Martens boots the pupils' council numbers me among its members as a House prefect I'm getting a taste of my own medicine younger pupils are giving me lip how are the mighty fallen Dr Fagan even addresses me by name say it again Sam that may have been a fluke the rebel is now part of the establishment the sardonic onlooker has become an eager participant indifference or even antipathy towards the school has been replaced by affection fears have been superseded in turn by leers jeers cheers and now tears as with so many pupils and teachers over the years WHS has worked its magic I'm travelling back home from school for what may well be the last time hopefully by car if I can sook up to somebody who's passed his driving test and has the wheels this is the way my scholastic quinquennium ends not with a bang but with a banger and a simper

There are eight million stories in the naked school. This has been one of them.

41

The Octagon in the 1970s and 1980s

Seasons of Love

That summer you were not here
Was endless rain and endless tears.
There were no happy days in the sun –
Nothing, just emptiness.

That autumn you were not here
Was dark and dismal.
For me the days ended before they had begun,
And the nights were long and lonely.

That winter you were not here,
The snow was hard and dirty,
And Christmas was just another day
To spend alone.

You came with spring,
But like spring
You stayed only three months,
Then left me - alone.

M.M. (Class 3)

The Truth, the Whole Truth, and Nothing But the Truth

People are inclined to say that your schooldays are the best days of your life. I for one beg to differ with these hypocrites; for hypocrites they must certainly be.

Who of us who had to, or still have to, travel by bus can say that we enjoyed fighting our way through the horde of blue, black, and green blazers and the bombardment of briefcases (of all shapes, weights, and sizes) swung with great gusto by their owners, so that we could embark safely - though a little battered - on the 8.30 SMT chariot bound for Wishaw?

Some mornings, we actually managed to stagger through the school gate in Kenilworth Avenue at one minute to nine, convinced that we had plenty of time to get into our lines. Then the bell would ring, inspiring a torrent of unrepeatable abuse, and we would have to explain our late arrival by saying, "Sorry, Miss, we couldn't get on a bus."

I dreaded assembly. Imagine asking three or four hundred people dressed for the height of winter (nobody ever told us to take our jackets off) to stand for half an hour in a space big enough to accommodate only two hundred. Windows were only opened if more than six pupils fainted.

After assembly, one's brains were put to work - which was a pity if one didn't happen to have a brain. I always thought it was nice to have a double period of English, or some other relaxing subject, after assembly: at least one could rest one's weary legs for a couple of hours. At any other time, double periods of anything were pure hell. Has anybody invented rubber seats for pupils yet?

In winter, we had to walk along those open corridors (weren't we lucky to have such healthy conditions?), with gentle, little, frozen snowflakes blowing up our regulation, knee-length skirts. Miss Young's regulations were always adhered to - or else.

You may or may not believe this, but I enjoyed Latin the most. Good old Mr Lindsay! He got me through O-Level Latin.

At 4 o'clock, there was a repetition of the morning's stampede - only about five times worse. I often wondered how the British got the reputation of having the most orderly queues in the world - and so would anyone else who tried to board a bus in Wishaw between four and half past four.

Does all this sound as though schooldays were the best days of my life? At least nowadays I can get on a bus in the morning - largely because I'm up an hour earlier than I used to be. No longer do I suffer from sore legs: after being stuck behind a typewriter for a couple of hours, it's certainly not my legs that are sore. No longer do I freeze in open corridors: the office always feels as though it is only a mile from the equator, since the heating usually rises to 80 degrees - and sticks there. No longer do I have to fight to get on a bus at night: by the time I knock off, most people are stuck in front of the television watching *Crossroads*.

Working means being independent, being treated as an adult and an equal, and, best of all, having money in one's pocket. Wait until you have been working for a couple of years, and then, when you look back on your schooldays, you'll agree with everything I've said.

A.W. Wilson (former pupil)

Effects

A Poem Written Just Before the Highers

Sitting here, four days before the exams,
I wonder: Did they really know?
Did Shakespeare and John Keats realise
That they would hold the key to my future?
Could Einstein and Darwin imagine
The effect
That they would have
Not only on the world,
But on me?

I don't suppose I was even considered,
When they decided on the Thirty Years War;
And who cares about the consequences
Of the Peace of Westphalia?
I do.
I must.

Jane Armit (Class 6)

Advertising

One method of making people remember a product is to make them associate it with a particular tune. Not so long ago, 'Morning' from Grieg's *Peer Gynt* was linked with a specific brand of instant coffee; and what is more famous that the tune of "McEwan's is the best buy"?

Another very important method is to persuade young mothers that they are not caring for their children if they do not give them certain things - from a particular kind of baked beans to a specific tube of toothpaste. If an advertisement can make a young mother feel this way, it is almost certain that she will put things right - and become a caring mother by buying the product: thus the objective of the advertisement is achieved.

A lot of advertisements for alcoholic drinks are very amusing - the ones involving the Invergraw grousebeaters, for example; however, just as many annoy me very much. I am referring to the ones that display their product being drunk on a South Sea island or a snow-clad mountain, or in the course of meeting Christopher Reeve or Debbie Harry. They would never show a broken home caused by a parent's or a child's addiction to alcohol; or advertise how expensive their product is - so expensive, in fact, that a heavy drinker's family continually runs short of money. Of course, I do not expect advertisements to show scenes of this nature (they would hardly help to sell the product), but I wonder just how many people have found out the hard way that a South Sea island can only be reached on a package tour - and that an alcoholic drink can't get you there.

Advertisements work by making us wish for things we do not have; for most of us, however, these wishes are unfulfilled, as not everyone is good-looking, rich, and youthful. Advertisements would have us believe that these are the important things in a life worth living. If this is the case, do we end up believing it? Or do we perhaps already believe that these are the things that are necessary in life? This would make advertisements merely a reflection of what we believe; in which case, what we have been laughing at every night may have more in common with ourselves than we would like to think.

Sheena Christie (5A)

This Awful Place

We come here to read and write,
Some folk come just for a fight.
Some folk read and some folk add,
But we all know that they are bad.
They get their dinner in the hall,
Then they go and play football.
We come to school in mist and fog,
But some folk go just for a dog.
I don't think they realise,
How bad it is to vandalise.

They carry on all through the day,
Then they look for a wall to spray.
When asked for an item for this paper,
They said, "So a wull, it's just a caper."

Anon (Class 3)

Modern Studies Trip to London

Last May, a party of thirty of the crème de la crème of Wishaw High
School went to London. Our first port of call was Regent's Park Zoo,
where the staff greeted their relatives in the Monkey House. Mrs Thatcher
was out when we called (so was the Queen); but luck was on our side,
insofar as we managed to see the Changing of the Guard - along with ten
thousand Japanese tourists. For the affluent members of our group, a visit
to the Stock Exchange proved worthwhile, but the mental strain was too
much for Mr Graham. Madame Tussaud's Chamber of Horrors wasn't
too horrific, considering some of the boys we have in the 4th Year. Our
visit to the Planetarium left half of us starry- eyed and the other half fast
asleep. Last but not least, an evening out at a West End theatre for a
performance of *Jesus Christ Superstar* was appreciated by everybody.

Lesley Brown

Rod

I lay on my bed gazing up at the ceiling.
My whole world was complete:
Rod was lying beside me.
I looked tenderly into his big brown eyes,
And kissed him gently on the nose.
Soft music filled the room as I snuggled
Up to him.
I told him my secrets, as I always did
When we were alone like that.
I loved him because he always listened attentively,
Never saying a word.
Now it was getting late.

I decided that I should get some sleep.
Before I did so, I said my prayers:
'God bless mummy, God bless daddy,
And God bless Rod, my teddy bear.'

Anonymous

Captain's Report

As I sit down to write this illuminating (?) report, memories of my six years at Wishaw High School come flooding back. All these memories are coloured by something that will forever remind me of my schooldays - friendship.

However, on my first day at the High School, way back in 1966, this was the furthest thought from my mind as I crept, rather sheepishly, into my registration class. A sea of mostly unknown faces greeted me, but luckily I was able to pick out one or two of my friends from primary school. Soon we all overcame our shyness, and "the secretary in the back office's son" started to make the friendships that I am sure will endure, even after we have gone our separate ways.

I have many memories, some happy, some sad: the disappointment of four defeats in football finals; the joy of triumphs on the cricket field; badminton matches; the choir and the operas; and sports days, even though my athletic ability leaves a lot to be desired and Allanton always seemed to finish last.

Wishaw High School has given me trips to France, Greece, and (shortly) Italy; also the opportunity to meet pupils from other schools through work and sport. Life, however, involves giving as well as receiving, and I hope that in return for all that the school has given me, I have put done my bit it by participating in as many extra-curricular activities as possible and doing my best in any duties assigned to me. In order to gain complete satisfaction from your schooldays, a balance must be struck between work and pleasure, and this balance can be achieved by participation in extra-curricular activities. I would encourage everybody to take as active a part as possible in the affairs of the school, as this benefits both yourselves and the school.

The thought of your last day at school may sound marvellous to a number of people, but I'm afraid that last day is too close for my liking. The teachers, who in my first year seemed to hate everything in a blue blazer, have become people for whom I have great respect; and (dare I say it?) they are human. My thanks go to Mr Barnard and all the members of staff who have struggled to tempt me with some of the fruits of knowledge. On the subject of food, who could forget to mention Mrs Allan and the canteen staff? Thank you, ladies, for six years of lovely food.

As is the custom, I must thank all my fellow officials; it is no more than they deserve. In a year when we have tried to experiment, they have supported everything and worked exceptionally hard; I could not have asked for a better crew (sorry about that one: it's all the braid that does it). My thanks go especially to my fellow captain, Grace, who has overcome the difficulty of living in the wilds of Allanton to become an excellent captain; and to Robert and Norma (I seem to know that girl) for their support and hard work.

I wish those of you who are lucky enough to be returning next session all the best, and I hope that you can keep the High School where it belongs - right at the top. Finally, best wishes to my successor, who I hope will regard being school captain as a great honour. I certainly have regarded it as such.

Tom Costley (Class 6)

The Jannies' Lament

The toilets are all leakin', the girls' sinks are bloaked,
The outside doors are jammin' - we cannae get them loaked;
An' we cannae get nae watter oot the busted main.
Wull ye send a man tae soart it? It's no oafen we complain.

Ye'll huv tae send some men oot tae soart thae broken lights –
It's amazin' how the weans reach tae sich oafy heights;
The windie panes is smashed, thur's a bad smell oaf the drain.
Wull ye send a man tae soart it? It's no oafen we complain.

Ootside oan the hockey pitch they huvnae goat a post –
An oafy bad position when they ur playin' host;
An' as fur the football pitch, we'd be better aff wi' nane.
Wull ye send a man tae soart it? It's no oafen we complain.

The windie coards is broken, there's a few slates aff the roof —
If ye doant believe me, jist come an' see the proof.
Thur's dry rot in the classrooms, an' the Rector wis jist sayin',
"You will have to get it sorted. It's not often we complain."

The plaster's comin' aff the wa's an' fa'in' oan the flair,
The watter's comin' aff the wa's an' runnin' doon the stair —
The men that built this school didnae ken whit they wur doin'.
We'll huv tae get it soarted, afore it a' fa's doon.

Joan Dempsey (Class 6)

Snowbound

The first icy kisses of winter float gently downwards. Carried by the breath of the breeze, they eventually settle on the stark, harsh, and forbidding contours of the surrounding mountains, transforming the steep faces into gentle curves.

Forty feet above the woodland floor, a grey squirrel leaps on to the branch of a magnificent Scots pine. In doing so, it dislodges some of the snow that lies on the spiney branch, and sends it cascading towards the ground.

The snow is deeper now, and the small woodland creatures are held captive by it. Unable to hunt or fetch food, some fall asleep - never to waken again.

A vixen, trapped in her earth, succumbs to hunger; she gnaws at her hind leg, severing muscle and sinew till the white ivory of her femur is clearly visible. A polecat, cautiously nosing its way through the snow, comes upon her, and saves her from a slow and agonising death by sucking the rich, warm blood from her pulsating jugular vein.

Farm animals suffer too. A pregnant ewe lies trapped beneath a drift covering the dry-stone dyke that has offered the only means of protection from the elements. She breathes through blowholes in the snow made by the warmth of her breath; but after spending a day and a half beneath the drift, she wearily gives up her existence, and the unborn lamb freezes slowly to death in her womb.

Lindsay Newell (4A)

The Greatest Art

You'll fail, motley poet, you'll fail,
You'll never find epithets to describe emotion;
You'll try to define joy - and you'll only find despair;
You'll never succeed: your medium is inadequate,
Words can only mean other words.
But he, the great composer —
His medium is sound,
Each note a megaword,
Each note an expression of emotion.
He'll succeed in this hardest of creative arts:
Only music can reproduce emotion.

Ludwig (5B)

Teachers' Films

1 Little Big Man - Mr Fleming
2 The Music Lovers - Mr Dobbie and Mr Carson
3 The French Connection - MrWinton
4 Paint Your Wagon - Mr Harvie
5 Butch Cassidy and the Sundance Kid - 'Dougie' and 'Dinkie'
6 The Go-Between - Mr Weir
7 Up Pompeii - Mr Lindsay
8 When Eight Bells Toll - 'Wee Tommy'
9 M.A.S.H. - Canteen Staff

J.C., C.L., and E.F. (Class 4)

Girls' Six Hits

Ellenore B - 'A daughter of the Gods, divinely tall.'
Favourite Saying - 'Do you think they make my feet look smaller?'
Usual State - Running down Kirk Road at 8.58 a.m.

Dorothy C – "Oh, it's nice to get up in the morning, but it's nicer to stay in bed."

402

Favourite Saying – "I'm starvin'."
Usual State - Sleeping in the French class
Kathleen P - 'Her face, oh, call it fair, not pale.'
Favourite Saying - 'Well, you see . . .'
Favourite Occupation - Doing German and German and German . . .

Kitty W - 'The more I see of men, the better I like dogs.'
Favourite Saying – "Naw, I'm no doin' it."
Favourite Occupation - Walking the dog

Boys' Six Hits

Duncan McK – "Please don't shoot the pianist, he's doing his best."
Favourite Saying – "Aye, I'll play at your wedding."
Favourite Occupation - Arguing with Mr Dobbie

John Paul - 'If there were two birds sitting on a fence, he would bet you which one would fly away first.'
Favourite Saying – "I'm no kiddin', but…..honest…"

Alan M - 'One of us was born a twin.'
Favourite Saying – "No, I'm Alan, he's John."

John M – "It's all the same to me."
Favourite Saying – "No, I'm John, he's Alan."

Scintillating Stickwork

Wishaw High School All Stars 2 Senior Girls XI 1

The All Stars enthralled a capacity crowd of 23 - plus a three- legged, glass-eyed dog - with a superb display of scintillating stickwork. Despite a plucky performance, the girls had no answer to the superior technique and style of the All Stars in a game that was a microcosm of contrasting styles: skill versus character; finesse versus brawn; and tactical genius versus effort. In the final analysis, the All Stars had too much skill, invention, and tactical awareness for the girls to counteract.

From the bully off, the All Stars were superior in all departments: Jardine gave Henderson all sorts of problems with his continual probing; Boa marked Danger Woman Johnston very closely; and Morrice led the forward line with the penetration of a prongless fork. This early superiority brought a quick reward, when Johnstone, the star of *Rising Damp*, opened the scoring from ten yards. The girls fought back - with 'new woman' Neilson a standout - and this gallant effort produced a sensational equaliser before half-time: Mauchline crossed from the right, and the powerful Spankie breenged the lithe Maxwell aside to fire in a glorious drive from all of six inches.

In the second half, the All Stars refused to be rattled, despite some intimidatory tackles from Dempsey and Stewart. Class began to tell, and midway through the half the All Stars restored their lead. The ball sped quickly from Boa to Forrest, from Forrest to Sutherland, and from Sutherland to Nicholson; the 'Maryhill Maestro' sent a glorious, misdirected pass through to the stylish Morrice; and with the grace and elegance of a rice pudding, the centre forward picked his spot. What a move! What a pass! What a goal! What a game!

The senior girls tried desperately to retrieve the situation, hard-hitting defender Torrance ('Just call me Tam Forsyth') being pushed up front in a futile attempt to salvage a draw. Tempers flared as 'Killer' Stevenson perpetrated several hideous fouls, and Boa was badly hurt in the midfield. There was, however, no further scoring, so the All Stars had triumphed yet again.

In an exclusive interview after the match, I talked to 'Grasper' Graham, director, coach, player manager, and lavatory attendant of the All Stars hockey team. The unshaven mother of nine said in his typically forthright manner, 'Well, John, the boys done well.'

'Grasper' has just returned from a fact-finding tour (in the course of which he visited Brazil, Peru, the German Democratic Republic and Forgewood), and I thought it would be appropriate to quiz him about the latest tactical developments. Had the era of zonal defence come to an end? Did he plan to adopt the Peruvian 'catenaccio' system? Did he think the German concept of a 'libero' would revolutionise hockey? Had he cleaned his teeth that week? Puffing pensively on a Capstan Full Strength, the part-time Modern Studies teacher, atrocious speller, and retired ballet dancer said, 'Well, Arthur, the boys done well.'

I then asked him what difference the freedom of expression he allowed his players had made. Was there really room for individualists like 'Bite yer legs' Nicholson? How much would the sudden departure on a free transfer (for disciplinary reasons) of French wizard, Pierre Le Boa, affect the team? Surely the All Stars would miss his powerful lateral runs from deep defence? 'Grasper' shrugged and said, 'Well, Archie, the boys done well.'

'Grasper' is optimistic about the future of the game in Scotland; he sees a glimmer of light at the end of the tunnel of depression that has confronted Scottish hockey for so long. His own team has certainly brought spectators back to Ash Park - by forsaking defensive tactics for open, attractive play. Choosing his four-letter words judiciously, 'Grasper' concluded, 'Well, Alec, amoaffurapint.' With these words, this seemingly inconsequential figure (who has made Grecian 2000 and Wernets Super Strong Fixative Powder household names) slipped quietly out of Wishaw High School. A few lingering fans offered words of advice and encouragement - most of it physically impossible. 'Grasper' rode off on his single seater tandem, his slight body silhouetted against the setting sun and the magnificent panorama of the Craigneuk blast furnace.

Anonymous

Aural (Un)Comprehension

When the Lord gave out ears,
I thought he said beers,
And I ordered two large ones.
When the Lord gave out legs,
I thought he said kegs,
And I ordered two oversized ones.
When the Lord gave out chins,
I thought he said gins,
And I ordered a double.
When the Lord gave out noses,
I thought he said roses,
And I ordered a big red one.
When the Lord gave out brains,
I thought he said drains,
And I said 'no thanks'.
Oh Lord, what a pickle I'm in.

Mark Holloway (3B)

Ce n'est qu'un 'Au Revoir'

Once upon a time when, I was very young and very naive, I left the remote 'country' of Brittany to go and play at being a teacher with my Celtic cousins in Scotland - and how wonderful it was going to be, as I pictured in my mind's eye nice little groups of smiling, well-behaved pupils who all spoke perfect French.

However, when I arrived in Wishaw, my illusions were rudely shattered by my landlady's sons, who regaled me with so many horror stories about the High School that I was rather nervous when I reported for duty. Jim Graham, whom I took to be a teacher, led me to the ladies' staffroom - and for the next ten months I became 'Mademoiselle Garanchet'.

Now my teaching career (at Wishaw, anyway) is coming to an end, and I have been asked to write something for the magazine. First of all, then, let me list some of the things that have made my time at Wishaw so enjoyable: the kind welcome I received from the teachers and secretaries; the excursions my friend Helga and I went on to different parts of your lovely country; the cheery 'Hello, miss', with which pupils greeted me in the street; being addressed as 'tu' by a pupil in 3B, because he 'wanted to be friendly' (I was really touched by that); 'the Kersewell experience', from which I learned that even teachers can be human; and senior pupils doing their best to cheer me up when I was feeling a bit homesick. For this reason, I would like to wish them all the best in sixth year or at university - and maybe in France, if they become Scottish 'assistants' over there.

Scotland is indeed a beautiful country, and I'm going back home with loads of photographs to show to my friends. So when they see me looking sad, they will know what's the matter with me: J'aurai le mal de l'Écosse.

Odile Garanchet

A Trialogue

Son:	Can I switch the telly off?
Mother:	What on earth for?
Son:	There's a play on Radio 4 that sounds very interesting. I'll read out what it says about it in the *Radio Times*.
Mother:	But the telly's on.
Son:	Well, switch it off.
Mother:	You know very well that we never switch the telly off. In any case, I'm watching something.
Son:	No you're not. You're reading the paper. Anyhow, who wants to watch a programme about the civil war in Portuguese West Africa?
Mother:	Your father's watching it.
Son:	Dad, can I put the radio on?
Father:	We never listen to the radio.
Son:	There's a good play on.
Father:	It doesn't say anything about it in the paper: so it can't be all that good.
Son:	It never says anything in the paper about what's on the radio.
Mother:	Let's have a look in the *Radio Times* then. Huh, never heard of him……or him……or her……or him! I can't stand his spotty face.
Son:	You won't see his face, mum.
Mother:	Well, I don't like his voice either.
Father:	Haven't you got any homework to do?
Son:	Not in the middle of the summer holidays.
Mother:	Anyway, you've missed the first five minutes of the play.
Son:	OK, the play's history. I'm going for a walk.

The son's personal revolt against the dictatorship of television has failed, as he knew it would. After years of indoctrination, the mindless followers of the box have formed an impenetrable wall around it.

Trio

42

'The Wiston Experience'

In those vernal seasons of the year, when the air is calm and pleasant, it were an injury and sullenness against Nature not to go out, and see her riches, and partake in her rejoicing with heaven and earth.

John Milton, *Of Education*

Every year, at the beginning of May, 1st Year pupils were given the opportunity to spend a week at Wiston Lodge, a YMCA hostel situated within walking distance of the lower slopes of Tinto; this week became known as 'the Wiston experience', and was arguably Sam Barnard's most noteworthy and durable innovation. Few head teachers would have had the imagination to devise such a project; and even fewer would have been willing to second the members of staff (from their normal teaching duties) and provide the financial resources that were required to ensure its success.

On the Thursday night of the Wiston week, the pupils staged a concert in the larger of the two lounges, and at the end of the concert Sam normally made a speech. In the last of these annual speeches, it would have been entirely fitting - in view of the setting and his own impending retiral - if he had suggested the following epitaph for his rectorship: 'Si monumentum requiritis, circumspicite.'

If his audience *had* looked round about them, they would have seen the happy, tanned faces of thirty or forty of their peers, and the tanned faces of half a dozen teachers they had probably come to know a lot better; through the windows of the lounge, they would have espied the lawns where they had been initiated into the mysteries of toxophily, and the woods they had traversed on nature walks or in the course of the orienteering competitions; they might even have caught a glimpse of the tennis court or the aerial runway. All these, and many other, aspects of the Wiston week and the happy memories they inspired serve as a monument to Sam's years at the High School.

'The Wiston experience' actually originated in 1971 as 'the Kersewell experience', the essence of which was that all 3rd Year pupils spent 2½ days at the former agricultural college on the outskirts of

Carnwath. Sheila Sprot, a member of the Guidance staff for many years, has many vivid memories of Kersewell:

'We took the 3rd Year to Kersewell for two or three days, so that we could get to know them better. To the best of my recollection, the pupils didn't have to pay anything.

Kersewell had many advantages as an outdoor centre: huge, wooded grounds and, within walking distance, several farms, a river, and even a lake. There were classrooms for any formal instruction that might have to be given; there were dormitories, catering facilities *in situ*, and a kind of headmaster.

Kersewell was where we started a new High School tradition: introducing our pupils to life in the country. It was amazing to discover just how little they knew. They didn't even know the names of the most common flowers, such as crocuses and violets, let alone coltsfoot or wood anemones; some of them didn't know what a stile was, or what purpose it served. It astounded me that they should be so ignorant of things I had learnt on walks with my father as a small child, and had never forgotten. To such pupils a bird's nest was a marvellous revelation, and the creepy crawlies under a stone an introduction to another world. Since they couldn't recognise oaks, beeches, pines, or even holly bushes, they had to learn by observing - and that was real education.

I remember going up the hill at the back of the college on a Geography expedition with Ronnie Hamilton. At the top, I enjoyed a glorious panorama of South Lanarkshire as he explained glaciation - something I had previously known nothing about. I never see these smooth hills now without thinking about how they were formed.

On another occasion, I went walking in the woods with the Biology group; we lifted up big stones, looking for centipedes and beetles, and identifying them - detective work on a small scale, and great fun.

And then there was orienteering... and sunny afternoons spent manning the course, so that the little dears would not get lost in the woods.'

The 'kind of headmaster' Sheila Sprot mentions was John More, the Principal of Kersewell College. He ran the place with military precision and demanded very high standards of behaviour from visiting groups: for instance, the boots and cagoules that were issued to pupils and members of staff had to be returned in pristine condition - and he inspected them personally. John was a rather diffident and reserved sort of character; but you knew where you stood with him, and he was always very pleasant and obliging towards the teachers from the High School.

The one predominant memory I have of Kersewell is of the excellent quality of the scones on which we used to gorge ourselves at every meal of the day, especially supper. Even those members of staff who were the epitome of moderation in dietary matters for the other fifty-one weeks in the year offered little resistance to the lure of such an ambrosial combination of flour, fat, and milk.

I also remember the early morning runs to which the boys were subjected (Eddie Tweedlie used to bring up the rear with a baseball bat in his hand); 25-a-side games of football and rugby; lazy afternoons spent lying in the sun at Point 5 of the orienteering course; one of the orienteering groups missing Point 5 altogether and ending up on the Lang Whang - halfway to Edinburgh; a particularly hard-bitten 3rd Year girl being reduced to tears by Eddie Tweedlie's rendition of some soulful melody on the piano; bussing all the pupils over to Thankerton so that they could climb Tinto, an achievement that was rewarded with a certificate (the forerunner of the Wiston Certificate) enrolling the recipient in the Tintock Tap Club.

Climbing Tinto was the origin of the hill walking element of 'the Kersewell/Wiston experience', and from Tinto we graduated to the Pentlands. The walks we attempted in the Pentlands were obviously much longer (even so, I can recall Alan Marshall turning up for one of them in a pair of Hush Puppies), but the groups were smaller, and sometimes we took a primus stove with us and cooked sausages for lunch.

On one of the walks, Robert Robertson and I were pushing on in front with the more energetic members of the group; and Drew Morrice was a few hundred yards behind us, chivvying the stragglers and providing the pastoral (in its literal sense) care that marked him out for a career in Guidance. Suddenly, we were confronted by two stroppy yokels and an extremely unpleasant dog that was virtually out of control. One of the choleric bucolics demanded to know who was in charge of our group and why we were walking along a private road. "It's nothing to do with me," said Robert, "you'd better have a word with the wee fellow back there."

Kersewell College was closed by Strathclyde Region in the mid-1970s, and the High School had to look for somewhere else as a base for its innovative programme of social and outdoor education. Wiston Lodge was chosen. According to Sheila Sprot:

'It had several disadvantages: for one thing, we had to pay; and the grounds were nothing like as spacious and varied as those at Kersewell,

410

so the orienteering was a bit more limited in scope. Nevertheless, we carried on with the same activities (Geography, Biology, orienteering and hill walking), supported by the expertise of several teachers from the High School and one or two members of staff at the Lodge. We also made use of the assault course, which had an aerial runway.

Wiston was less institutionalised than Kersewell; it was more like a hotel than a youth hostel, though I don't suppose the boys who were unfortunate enough to be billeted in the huts at the back of the Lodge would have agreed with this assessment. In the event, these huts were later converted into fairly luxurious chalets.

The pupils loved Wiston; but, unfortunately, the cost of a week at the hostel became progressively steeper, and though some pupils were lucky enough to be subsidised by the school, or private individuals, or even Social Services, others missed out.

The staff also enjoyed their week at Wiston, but it was hard work having to look after the pupils day and night. What I really hated was having to turn out in the evening to play rounders: the weather always seemed to be on the cold side and the evenings interminable. Like the kids, I would rather have been indoors watching television.

I remember the lovely smell of the countryside that greeted us on arrival - a mixture of pine trees and cut grass; and also the daffodils, which were still in season, even though we usually went to Wiston in May.

We had some really dreadful weather - snow on one occasion, rain on many more occasions, and mud, mud, mud.

My happiest memories of Wiston relate to the daily visits we made to a local farm. We would stand in the milk parlour, watching the mechanical milking; or round the huge, refrigerated milk tank, listening to the farmer (a born teacher, if ever there was one) explaining how very scientific modern milk production had become. His wee dog, a Jack Russell, used to follow our pupils back to the Lodge, and they were always very worried in case it got lost. The farmer was quite unconcerned, and told them it would find its own way home; it must have done, I suppose.

There were a few 'casualties' - mainly as a results of blisters and sprained ankles - but remarkably little homesickness. I can remember one occasion on which I had to take a pupil to the Casualty Department at Law Hospital, and she was very annoyed when she was taken home, not back to Wiston, after her ankle had been strapped up.

We had lovely barbecues - with rolls, sizzling sausages, fried onions, brown or tomato sauce, and cups of cocoa - followed by a sing-song round a camp fire under the big tree at the front of the Lodge, with certain members of staff (who shall remain nameless) leading the singing, and generally making fools of themselves.

We also had some dreadful concerts on the final night, when the Rector drove up to Wiston to dish out the certificates.

One of the good features of Wiston was that Tinto was more or less at the back door, and the pupils were always very proud of having climbed it; I think every one of them managed it at some time or other during the week. They regarded this as a great achievement, though they probably walked much further and climbed much higher on the day they went hill walking.

And then there was archery on the front lawn. Some of the pupils became very good at this (but keeping them out of range of the arrows wasn't always easy); the staff, particularly yours truly, were not so proficient.

I can remember cold, wet days at the assault course: although it was situated among the trees, it always seemed to be the coldest spot on the estate. I would urge timid pupils to clamber up rope ladders or along log walkways; just looking at these gave me the shivers. I always felt that the mad scrambles of the boys to see who could complete the course in the fastest time were rather dangerous, and should not really have been encouraged - but then, I wasn't a thirteen-year-old boy.

It astonished me just how pernickety the pupils were about the food, which was usually excellent: I was brought up to eat anything that was put in front of me and clean my plate (but I was a child of the 1930s). I suspect that the variety of foods that makes up a healthy diet was simply outwith their experience, and that they were wary of anything different. As it was, they moaned constantly about the meals, and masses of food were left on the plates - and, consequently, wasted. Healthy eating was one aspect of social education in which we failed miserably; however, as far as table manners were concerned, we did succeed in getting the message across to them that knives and forks were not for playing with, and that they should wait until everyone was served before they began eating.

We tended to forget the deprived background of most of our pupils. These were children who had never been in the country before, children to whom the hoot of an owl was terrifying; and prior to Wiston, many of them had never been entertained by adults, or shown how to enjoy a

412

civilised meal. We had to teach them a great deal more than the 3Rs, and we did our best.

Their sheer enjoyment of the whole experience made it worth all the effort; they loved Wiston, and they talked about it in later years as one of the happiest interludes in their school careers. I can't remember a single pupil who didn't enjoy the week at Wiston. It was very tiring, however, for the staff, who - apart from the Guidance teachers, who regarded it as part of their job - were paid no extra money for their efforts.

Wiston was about pupils getting to know teachers - and vice versa - in a different atmosphere and doing different things in a different setting; it was Wishaw High School's "thing", something special we did that other schools didn't.'

Et in Arcadia ego

My own very happy memories of Wiston are concerned mainly with the hill walking section of the week's activities. Though the various walks were very demanding (I'm sure that 99% of the girls - and a substantial percentage of the boys - were unlikely to be put under such physical pressure in their later lives), the standard of walking achieved by the pupils was very high; indeed, it seemed to get higher every year.

In most groups there were always one or two who trailed behind the others from within a few hundred yards of the start of the walk to the pick-up point five hours later, and one or two who were amazingly adept at not being landed with a full rucksack on any of the uphill sections of the walks; but for the most part, the pupils were pleasant and uncomplaining.

The members of staff (too numerous to mention) who accompanied me on the walks were never less than congenial; the spring weather could be gorgeous, and it was heaven on earth to bask in the sun on the lower slopes of Coulter Fell just above the reservoir, while the pupils paddled in the burn.

Sometimes, however, the weather bordered on the horrendous, and on one occasion, after we had been forced to abandon a walk halfway up Tewsgill, we ended up in the Little Chef Restaurant at Abington eating pancakes and ice cream.

To continue on the hill walking theme: in my mind's eye, I can still picture Drew Morrice struggling through the heather with John Hastie on his shoulders ('Greater love hath no' Guidance teacher 'than this . . .').

Then there was the never-to-be-forgotten- and, thankfully, never-to-be-repeated - race up Tinto that made it necessary for Ian Maxwell and me to hare up to the top of that hill one evening after dinner (even though we had both taken part in a five-hour hill walk earlier in the day), so that we could time the contestants.

All the staff at Wiston Lodge were very helpful, none more so than Brian (I never did find out what his surname was), the Assistant Secretary, who drove the minibus that conveyed the hill walking groups every morning to the starting points of the walks at Coulter and Abington, and brought them back to the Lodge later in the day. He was thoroughly reliable and unfailingly punctual.

During some of the weeks we spent at Wiston Lodge, the weather, the congeniality of the company, the pleasantness of the surrounding countryside, the behaviour and responsiveness of the pupils . . . everything, in short, conspired to create the impression that we had somehow found our way to the Shangri-La of the educational world.

43

'The Wiston Experience' - as Experienced by the Pupils

Sportsmen and sports commentators are forever using the cliché: "It's all about...". Well, Wiston was all about the pupils and the different experiences it provided for them, so it is only right and proper that any analysis of 'the Wiston experience' should include some input from the pupils. The following diary was compiled by Audrey Gracie in May 1982:

Tuesday 5th of May

Went orienteering in the morning and afternoon. Got lost only once in the morning. It was great and it only rained for about five or ten minutes. Climbed over dykes and stiles. I found a cat that belonged to Mr Carnaby. Then we got lunch - chips, corned beef and beans, followed by a cup of tea and a piece of cake.

Then we went up to our dormitories and wrote our diaries for the morning.

In the afternoon we went on a big orienteering course, which was very hard. On the way back we got lost twice, but we got back okay. I collected a lot of things - some sheep's wool, pine cones, pine needles, and a piece of knotted wood.

Then for tea we had a three-course meal that consisted of soup with bread, potatoes, mince pie and peas, and orange pudding. We then wrote our diaries and played at table tennis and pool, and we also played the juke box.

At 9 o'clock we had supper - tea, scones and a cake each. Then we went to the games room until 10.05 p.m., then off to bed. We were a bit noisy and we were carrying on but that was only because we were excited staying with each other. Mr Carnaby also told us the rules of Wiston Lodge. The first day was very tiring but well spent.

Wednesday 6th of May

Today we went on the assault course. Out of five different things there was one I couldn't do properly. Then we came back to draw the things, then we returned to the assault course where three girls were timed. These were Lisa Gavin, Hazel Grierson, and Jane Harkin. Jane came last with

4.26, Hazel was next with 3.57, and Lisa was first with the winning time of 3.40.

For lunch we had sausages, dried egg and beans. After lunch we were practising archery. I was a load of rubbish but I enjoyed it. After this it was the highlight of Wiston Lodge for me. It was the ariel runaway [sic], which was brilliant, of course, but scary at first when you had to jump off the platform. When we went down everybody was shouting and screaming to have some more shots at it.

We relaxed in our room for half an hour and then went down for tea, which was of soup and bread, followed by shepherd's pie, potatoes and peas, then raspberry and vanilla ice cream. At night time we had the potted sports which were held in the games room. In my team were Lisa Gavin...and I can't remember the others but never mind we never won anyway. After the potted sports we had our supper and then we went off to bed. Tonight Diane Lindsay got sent out into the corridor to sleep because she was misbehaving.

Thursday 7th of May

The snow was falling all day. For biology we had Mr Johnstone and for crafts we had Miss Sprot. In biology we had to put big heavy boots on because of the snow. We took a walk around the Wiston grounds. We were talking about plants and animals and in particular we were talking about a single-celled plant called - wait for it - 'pleurococcus'. Mr Johnstone was telling us that these grew at the bottom of trees, walls, houses, fallen logs, twigs, pine cones, almost anything. They live at the bottom because they have more water there. They also need sunlight to make their food. We talked about lichens, fungi, mosses and algae which are non-flowering plants.

In the afternoon we went out into a field to bring up worms. To do this we had to lay down a quadrant, which is a four-sided frame, and then mix some water with a chemical called potassium permanganate. We then sprayed this solution inside the quadrant. This irritates the skin of the worm - aren't we cruel? - and so it comes up. So you rinse it with clean water – there's a heart there somewhere - then throw it away.

After biology we had crafts, which was inside. I made a 'Snoopy' picture. We used material that looked a bit like felt. We were allowed to take our pictures home. After dinner we sat and wrote our diaries and then we had a sing-song. This was very good.

As it was too wet to have a campfire outside we just lit a coal fire inside, but it was like the real thing because we had hot dogs for supper.

Then we went to the games room for a wee while and then to bed. This was our last night sleeping at Wiston Lodge.

Friday 8th of May

Today we had to climb up Tinto Hill with Mr Young. We were lucky because it was a scorcher of a day, but we were terribly exhausted. After we had reached the top we came rolling all the way back down again and we had to get changed as soon as we got back to the lodge. The lunch was good on the last day. It was chicken soup with bread, chips and a sausage roll, and apple crumble to finish off. Then we all packed our bags and put them in the bus. Well, I don't know about you, but my week at Wiston was BRILLIANT.

P. S. I forgot to tell you that we won the prize for having the best-kept bedroom.

Over the years the following comments on different aspects of 'the Wiston experience' appeared in the diaries of individual pupils:

Biology: 'Estimated number of worms in the field - 13.5 million'

Geography: "We met a horse and started feeding it grass, but it liked Emma's T-shirt better."

Orienteering: "I went orienteering today - you know, that competition where you get lost."

Hill walking: 'Hill walking was great except for walking up the hill.'

Assault Course: 'Mr McGeechan attempted it, but he fell off and snapped the rope. He said it was an old rope - what an excuse!'

Farm: "I couldn't squeeze the cow hard enough to get the milk out."

Concert: 'Our act was good when we rehearsed it, but it turned out to be a disaster.'

Disco: "Twenty minutes later I was dancing to my heart's content in the middle of the lounge."

And finally, the following appeared in *High Times*, the school newspaper, in 1971:

Wiston Alphabet

W is for the wandering in the hills each day.
I is for the insects that we found to our dismay.
S is for the staff who catered for our every need.
T is for the teachers to whom we paid much heed.
O is for the ointment rubbed on our blistered toe.
N is for the nature trail along which we did go.
L is for the lambs which we all fed with glee.
O is for the open fields before us we could see.
D is for the disco where we danced the night away.
G is for the games room where we many an hour did play.
E is for the enjoyment felt on each and every day.

Lament for Wiston Lodge

We love you, Wiston, oh yes we do,
And when we left you, we felt so blue,
Say we'll come back again, please do,
Oh, Wiston, we love you!

44

1981

It is more blessed to give than to receive.

Acts of the Apostles ch.20, v.35

Ten pupils took part in a Sponsored Swim (50 lengths per swimmer) in aid of the Italian Earthquake Appeal. During the 1980s and 1990s, staff, pupils, and former pupils of the High School participated in many events designed to raise money for equally worthwhile causes: four members of the FP Football Club took part in the London Marathon, thereby raising £1,000 for the Edward Lawson Centre (May 1982); a Sponsored Silence (involving the 3rd Year) raised £413 for Radio Clyde's *Cash for Kids* appeal (December 1988); a group of 1st and 2nd Year pupils raised £317 for the Sir Malcolm Sargent Cancer Fund for Children by taking part in *Readathon 88* (basically, they had to read six books in a week), an event that was underwritten by Typhoo Tea, and similar contributions were made to the fund in 1989 and 1990; the Smartie Marathon (March 1990) aimed to raise £500 to sponsor an athlete in the Special Olympics (pupils, parents, and teachers were invited to buy a tube of Smarties for 20p, fill it up - once they had eaten its contents – with 1p coins, and bring it back to the school, whereupon they received another tube free); a Bring and Buy Sale in aid of the Blue Peter Appeal for Romanian orphans raised £118 (December 1990); Yorkhill Hospital benefited - to the tune of £100 - from the efforts of two 2nd Year boys, Grant Law and Stuart Hallford, who cycled from Wishaw to Biggar and back (May 1991); and finally, Geraldine MacPhee and her 3rd Year Home Economics class produced and sold 400 'cute little furry bugs, some with natty baseball caps', in aid of the Telethon Appeal (May 1992).

The (Almost) Towering Inferno

Graham Sneddon, who - by a lucky chance - was making his rounds earlier than usual, discovered a fire in the annexe, and after summoning the fire brigade, he fought the blaze single-handedly until they arrived.

An inter-House cross-country championship (based on races at three different age levels) was instituted. There were some years when more than 150 pupils took part in this championship.

Alan Burns won a bronze medal in the 100 metres backstroke at the Scottish Schools' Swimming Championships.

At the Lanarkshire Music Festival, Margaret Graham of 1B1 topped the cornet section; and the Brass Ensemble, conducted by Trevor Laird of the 6th Year (an accomplished soloist, who gained a place in the first three at both the Scottish and the West of Scotland Brass Championships) was third in its section.

Trees were planted round the lawns at the front of the school by a squad of 4th Year boys.

A group of 4th, 5th, and 6th Year pupils from the Art Department, supervised by Ian Kay, spent a weekend in London taking in the sights and an exhibition at the Royal Academy.

Laurie Kain won the under-14 singles at the Carlton Open Badminton Tournament; in 1983 she and her partner won the Ayr Open mixed doubles; and for three consecutive years (1982, 1983 and 1984), she represented Lanarkshire at the Scottish Schools' Badminton Championships. Her doubles partner, Arlene Hill, was similarly honoured in 1984.

The Fourth Protocol

It was decided that attendance at the swimming gala should be restricted to the number of pupils that could be comfortably accommodated at Wishaw Baths (on one memorable occasion, some of the punters actually climbed out of the windows and clambered down drainpipes in order to escape from the noise and the heat); and the restriction was achieved by excluding the 4th Year from the gala. Staff were given the option of undertaking supervisory duties either at the baths or the school (the softest of soft options, since the 4th year simply treated themselves to a half holiday on the day of the gala).

Walking Holidays

One of the recommendations of the newly established Code of Practice on Safety in Outdoor Education was that teachers supervising any form of outdoor education 'should have qualifications and/or experience as specified in the Code'; however, the specified 'qualifications' could be acquired by attending a far-from-rigorous, three-day course on 'Safety on Land' at Caldercruix Outdoor Centre. The first teachers from the High School to attend this course were Tom Young, Clark Govan, Drew Morrice, Robert Bell, and Anne Hood; but in the course of the next few years, practically every member of staff (only the janitor and his dog disclaimed all interest in outdoor education) managed to book in at Caldercruix.

Piste Artistes

Anne Hood organised a skiing trip to La Clusaz in the French Alps - and, two years later, a more prosaic trip to Glenshee. In 1989 and 1990, Clark Govan led expeditions to the same area.

For the first time in many years, a pupil from the High School took part in the Glasgow University Bursary Competition. The pupil in question, Sheena Christie, gained a highly creditable 15th(=) place.

The workforce of Meridian Ltd. donated a trophy in memory of Jimmy Walker, a long-serving employee, who had a family connection with the High School. The first recipient of the Jimmy Walker Trophy (which was awarded annually for service to the community outwith the school) was Lesley Mann, who worked at a club for the mentally handicapped in Newmains, and also at the Edward Lawson Centre.

More than 120 1st, 2nd, and 3rd Year pupils from the High School and St Aidan's participated in an athletics match, the result of which was a victory for St Aidan's by 190 points to 145.

...some achieve greatness...

Shakespeare, *Twelfth Night*

The school staged a production of *Joseph and His Amazing Technicolour Dreamcoat*. According to *The Bulletin*:
The soloists - Una Bence, Donna McArthur, Sheila Green, Lillian Beattie, Robert Shaw, David Gillespie, and Robert Gillespie - all won high praise, but perhaps the real stars were the chorus, whose singing was both a sheer joy and a great credit to Mrs Banks. The accompanist, Sheena Christie, and the backing group (Derek Smith, Douglas Lindsay, Ross Yuill, and Rhona Aitken) added an exciting new dimension to the

421

performance; and the promenade tea provided by Mrs Clarke, the ladies of the staff, and the senior girls was the perfect end to a very happy night.

...and some have greatness thrust upon them.

Shakespeare, *Twelfth Night*

Kenny Nicol succeeded Elspeth Nelson as the High School's representative on the Wishaw and Shotts Schools' Council. He was the sole nominee.

A new electronic photocopier was installed in Room 26.

Carol Gray was selected for the West of Scotland Girls' hockey team.

The Parents' Association presented the school with a small computer system - a computer, a tape recorder, and a television set.

It was established that more than 300 High School pupils lived in Areas for Priority Treatment.

The Intermediate Choir (consisting of girls in the 2nd and 3rd Year) sang at the farewell concert for the Reverend Haisley Moore, the school chaplain. Mr Moore was a charming man, but his prayers and sermons, delivered in a broad Northern Irish accent, were as unintelligible as Linear A.

It was decided that the two prizes gifted by the Motherwell and Wishaw Rotary Club should be awarded to Sheena Christie and Andrea Finlayson, the latter of whom 'continued to show remarkable courage and cheerfulness as she strove to overcome the severe handicaps imposed by her very poor eyesight'.

422

45

The Art of Coarse - and Not So Coarse - Cricket

In the 1960s, 1970s, and early 1980s, the High School achieved a good deal of success on the cricket field - even though it had no proper facilities for the game, and was competing against schools which benefited greatly (in the matter of coaching, for instance) from their association with clubs that were members of the Western Union or the Glasgow League.

Teams from Coatbridge or Uddingston would take the field in immaculate white shirts and flannels; some of their batsmen (especially those who had their own bat) would spend an eternity taking guard and looking sagely round the field; their bowlers would set fields that were reminiscent of the first morning of a five-day test match, and arrange their run-up with the aid of a theodolite and an Ordnance Survey map of North Wishaw. The High School hillbillies, dressed mainly in jeans and T-shirts, would watch all this poncing about with a mixture of contempt and bemusement - and then bowl out the opposition for 23, or hoick their bowlers' best deliveries into the back gardens of the houses on the far side of Waverley.

Although most of the boys who played for the High School's cricket teams were not natural cricketers, they were natural athletes; they had a good eye, and they were fiercely - not to say aggressively - competitive. My own contribution as coach was simply to make sure that they observed one or two basic principles of batting, bowling, and field setting.

During my years as master in charge of cricket, the school produced three outstanding batsmen - Bobby Kerr, Tom Costlev, and Calum Currie; and one magnificent bowler - Amjad Hassan. All three batsmen had a sound defensive technique, a rare, almost non-existent commodity in school cricket, where a good-length ball pitching in line with the stumps either reduces most batsmen to virtual immobility or provokes them into a wild and usually fatal slog; all three could also drive the ball straight back past the bowler or through mid-off and mid-on, the hallmark of a top class player.

Tom Costley and Calum Currie were both very patient batsmen: they were quite content to play defensively and wait for the inevitable bad delivery, which they would then despatch to the boundary. Bobby Kerr's batting was founded on wonderful footwork, and he was never slow to get down the wicket when facing spin or seam bowling.

Amjad Hassan played for the 1st XI while he was still in 1st Year; he could bowl very fast, and facing him, when he played for the 3rd XI, must have been a terrifying experience for his contemporaries. I always thought, however, that he was even more impressive when he bowled at medium pace: he was able to make the ball swing through the air or deviate off the seam, and you could almost hear the ball fizzing as it left his hand.

As far as wicketkeepers are concerned, Alan Johnston was the most proficient technically, David Main the most acrobatic; as for captains, the shrewdest and most tactically aware was Jim Anderson, whose cool, analytical attitude - and predilection for a quick drag - were reminiscent of Douglas Jardine.

46

1982

A Miracle of Rare Device, A Sunny Leisure Dome

A 1st Year pupil, Sui Yin Cheng, was chosen to present the Provost of Motherwell and Wishaw with a commemorative medallion at the opening of Wishaw Sports Centre. The PE Department at the High School wasted no time in booking the centre for several hours at a time on certain days of the week, so that pupils could 'have a go' at such games as squash, badminton, and five-a-side football.

Mrs Eleanor Pearson succeeded Mrs Allan (who had suffered a stroke) as Cook Supervisor in the school canteen.

The Cane Mutiny

Strathclyde Region announced its intention to abolish corporal punishment in schools. The EIS members on the staff reacted to this development with an unanimous assertion that teachers were entitled to conditions that were 'compatible with effective teaching', and that an 'arbitrary removal' of corporal punishment would be unlikely to produce such conditions; that there was 'no compelling case' for the abolition of corporal punishment; that 'many parents' wished schools to retain it; and, finally, that 'legal alternatives (such as suspension) should be investigated' before corporal punishment was phased out.

25 pupils, plus John Boal and Mrs Dickson, spent a weekend in London, during which they took in the Japanese Exhibition at the Royal Academy.

The school received a cheque for £500 from the Urban Renewal Unit to promote extra-curricular activities. The money was spent on strips.

Both the Concert Band and the Orchestral Percussion Ensemble gained a Certificate of Distinction at the Lanarkshire Music Festival. According to the programme for one of its concerts:

Many reasons can be given for the success of the Concert Band - not least the members' hard work and willingness to rehearse for long hours; but they will be the first to give the credit to their conductor, Willie Young, who joined the Music Department in 1981. Anyone who knows the situation will smile at the inadequacy of the word 'conductor' to describe a man who does everything from holding rehearsals every day at lunchtime and most nights after four o'clock to organising sponsored walks, bingo nights and discos - and whose unquenchable energy and enthusiasm have overcome every obstacle in the way of progress. In a sense, the band is Mr Young's family, and you will be aware of this special bond as you listen to them play.

Clocking Off

To mark her retiral, the pupils presented Isobel Johnston, Principal Teacher of Guidance and a member of the PE Department for twelve years, with a quartz clock.

Recollections of a Retiring Person

'When I joined the staff as Senior Housemistress of Murdostoun in August 1970,' wrote that same Mrs Johnston, 'Wishaw High was not a comprehensive school; it was a senior secondary. At that time, we had no 1st or 2nd Year pupils, and it was not until 1975 that 1st Year pupils arrived in full force and with great enthusiasm, something I found very stimulating. Since then, Wishaw High has been fully comprehensive - and comprehensively full.

As some of you will know, I have taught in many Lanarkshire schools during my teaching career; but I had the good fortune to be at Wishaw High longer (almost twelve years) than at any other school. I can't mention all the highlights (there were too many), but I must at least record a most unusual happening in session 1976-77: Murdostoun won both the Shield and the Cup.

As I taught in both the PE and the Guidance Department, I sometimes felt that the girls' PE classes would have benefited from extra Guidance, and that the Guidance staff might have benefited from extra PE - especially before the Wiston week.

One traumatic experience was a visitation by an HMI who was responsible for three different subjects, two of which were PE and Guidance. This particular HMI is well known for her loquacity, and my listening powers improved greatly during that week.

Much of the time Guidance teachers spend in the House rooms is devoted to filling in forms, writing references, and compiling reports. On

426

my retiral, I was the subject of this last procedure - for my "friends" on the Guidance staff assessed me on Form A, Form 7, and Form C.S.11. Here's what they said about me:

Educational Attainment

Geography: Good (Finds her way easily to the staff lounge at Wiston)

History: Good (Seen more of it than most)

Biology: Good (Two children after all)

Reading: Good (At reading…the riot act)

Art: Good (Drawing - for the past 30 years - firstly beer, now a pension)

Physical Coordination: Good (Powerful right arm)

Special Abilities: Beanbag throwing and losing jotters

Further Comment: Has a great future behind her.

You will, of course, realise that no one is expected to believe a word of this.

I thoroughly enjoyed my years at Wishaw High School, and I will remember the school with great affection, especially since I made so many friends among the staff and the pupils. Moreover, I will always remember the kindness and thoughtfulness shown to me over the years by the senior hockey teams and the 6th Year girls.'

An Offer They Couldn't Refuse

Twelve members of staff took up Jean Verth's offer to provide instruction in typing.

The Parents' Association hired a sign writer to bring the honours boards up to date.

Andrew Willis received a voucher worth £20 as a result of his triumph in the Senior Section (ages 14 to 16) of the Bovis Design a Home Competition.

A recording of two songs ('Bridge over Troubled Waters' and 'Daybreak') by the Senior Choir was broadcast on Radio Scotland, as part of a series entitled 'Make Minor Music'.

Two Inter-House rugby sevens competitions were inaugurated. The 1st Year competition was won by Belhaven, the 2nd Year one by Coltness.

The Reverend Robert Mayes ('a young man with a great zest for the outdoor life', according to Sam) succeeded the Reverend Haisley Moore as school chaplain. I only met him once - on one of the hill walks at Wiston. He had a beard, smoked a pipe, and had very little to say.

Elspeth Nelson, a member of the Chemistry Department, was chosen to represent the elders of the Church of Scotland at the General Assembly of the United Reformed Churches of England and Wales.

Enchanting Evening as Young Cast Gives a Great Show

'Audiences at Garrion Academy,' the *Wishaw Press* reported on 25 June, 'had a number of "enchanted evenings" last week, when they attended Wishaw High School's production of *South Pacific*. Thanks to the acting and singing ability of a whole host of lovely girls and handsome boys, a tear-jerking story was portrayed in a warm and sympathetic manner.

Principals were well-cast: Emile De Becque was played by Calum Currie (his singing voice was heard to advantage in such well-known songs as "Some Enchanted Evening" and "This Nearly Was Mine"), and his children by Pamela Clarke and Drew Watson; playing opposite Calum as Nellie Forbush was Ailsa McMillan - in her first major role.

The appearance of the GIs (Boys' Chorus) and Bloody Mary (Lesley Brown) enlivened the plot, and Lesley is to be congratulated for her rendition of "Bali Ha'i" and "Happy Talk".

Comedy is a must in any show, and Drew Smith (playing Luther Billis) nearly brought the house down with his belly dance. He was ably supported by Ian Campbell (as Stewpot) and Iain Weaver (as Professor).

Lt. Joseph Cable, the heart-throb of the girls, was played by John Leighton, and the love scenes with Liat (the lovely Donna McArthur) were performed with great tenderness and sincerity.

Peter MacLean never put a foot wrong as Captain George Brackett: his diction and timing were excellent.

Elspeth Banks, the Musical Director, cleverly adapted the score to allow the chorus to give renditions of several songs that are normally sung as solos.

Make-up was in the capable hands of members of the Motherwell and Wishaw Operatic Society; costumes were uniformly excellent; and a special mention must be made of the props, which, despite their importance, can easily be overlooked. It was obvious that every detail had been considered, especially in the Radio Shack; and the recovery from the Island was most convincing.

428

Months of hard work had clearly gone into the finished production; and Elspeth Banks, Janey Mauchline (Producer/Choreographer), Ruth Hodgson (Accompanist), and David Gardner (Percussionist) can take credit for providing a great show.'

Rodgers and Hammerstein Rule OK(lahoma)

Elspeth Banks, Principal Teacher of Music, favoured a musical as the end of session entertainment: *South Pacific* had been preceded by *Carousel* in 1980 and *Oklahoma* in 1981, and was followed by *Guys and Dolls* in 1984.

Stuart Rattray played the ghost in *Carousel*:
I had to be fitted out with a white kaftan, white trousers and white shoes. To make the kaftan, Janey Mauchline drew a line round my body while I lay on top of a white sheet, cut out this shape and used it as a template to produce a second body-shape. She now had the front and the back of a kaftan, which she proceeded to sew together. Result: one kaftan. It was a perfect fit - for a giant playing card. It had a front and a back but there was no space between them.

I loved playing the ghost. I had a free hand to wander around the stage and do whatever I wanted. I was supposed to be invisible to the rest of the cast and they were told to ignore me. In one scene, I played a little game of 'keek' with the audience, darting out from behind the chorus and waving at them. During the finale ('You'll never walk alone') on the final night, I came forward to the front of the stage and gestured to the audience that they should join in. Not for the first time, we got a standing ovation.

After the show, the cast and crew repaired to Girdwoods in Hill Street. Though I was only seventeen, I had no trouble getting served: I still had the grey hair of my ghostly persona and I looked like a fifty-nine-year-old.

During the summer holidays, forty Modern Studies pupils visited Paris and Brussels, the primary object of their visit being to observe the EEC and UNESCO at work.

Janice Orr, the school librarian, left 'to take on the daunting task of starting a new library in a new school (Taylor High School)'. Sam suggested in the *Bulletin* that she would be 'encouraged by her success in organising the library at the High School'; and that 'after coping with the peculiar problems posed by a library in a converted canteen directly underneath a gym', she would take the challenges arising from her move to Taylor High School in her stride.

Janice Orr was succeeded as librarian by Lesley Kerr.

Elspeth Banks became a member of the Music Panel of the SCE Examination Board. She was the first teacher from Lanarkshire to serve in this capacity, and the first woman ever to do so.

Two carols - 'Bethlehem Blessing', a joint effort on the part of three 1st Year pupils; and 'Spirit of Christmas', composed by Shona Clark - were entered in a carol competition arranged by the BBC's current affairs programme *Nationwide*.

The Parents' Association purchased an oboe for the Concert Band.

The school's ailing heating system was given a thorough overhaul. Three new automatic stoking systems were installed, the entire electrical system was rewired, and a new control panel was fitted.

It's better than magnificent, it's mediocre.

Sam Goldwyn

Treasure Peninsula was the most successful of the pantomimes staged by the staff; indeed, some knowledgeable observers said that it compared favourably with the House assemblies. Sam Graham, Clark Govan, and George Randall were absolutely immense; Derek Winton, the only member of the cast with any pretensions to be described as a thespian, gave a magisterial performance as Squire Trelawney; Liz Clarke confirmed her status as Cambusnethan's leading chanteuse and comedienne; and other members of staff, who were as useless at acting and singing as I was at directing, made invaluable contributions by simply being on stage - something that took a lot of courage, in view of the shambolic nature of the proceedings, the cynicism of the director, and the derisive attitude of the producer, Ian Maxwell, who (like Alfred Hitchcock) believed that 'actors should be treated like cattle'.

Rara avis in terris nigroque simillima cycno.

Juvenal, *Satires*

On 3 December, the following item appeared in the *Bulletin*:
The Social Committee are to be congratulated on their organisation of last week's Cheese and Wine, which was thoroughly enjoyed by all who attended. There is, however, one worrying aspect: some wine was left over, something that has never happened before. Was it a question of over-ordering or, more seriously, does it indicate a reduction in the ability of the staff to consume this liquid refreshment? Perhaps we will find out at the next one.

Wiston Lodge

Hillwalking at Wiston

Archery at Wiston

Orienteering at Wiston

Campfire at Wiston

Assault Course at Wiston

47

Downstairs, Upstairs

Joyce Hefferman was a pupil at the High School in the 1970s and a member of staff in the early 1980s. Here are some of her reminiscences:

The front of the main building was very imposing; less so the side of the building, where the girls lined up and had to go through the nerve-wracking process of marching past 'Granny' Young, who was on the lookout for anybody wearing too short a skirt. If you were late, you had to write out 'Punctuality is the pride of kings' a specified number of times.

One day, during my first year at the High School, there was a continuous ringing of the bell, the signal for a fire drill. Jimmy Lindsay, our Latin teacher, hadn't a clue what was going on, and we had to tell him that we really should be evacuating the building. It's just as well there was no actual fire (we would all have been incinerated), for before he marshalled us out of the room he spent some time looking for various books to put in his case.

Even scarier was the occasion when a rather weird character strolled into our French class out in the huts. Speaking with a very exaggerated German accent, he told our French teacher (Miss Brown, I think) that he was an inspector, and that she should continue with the lesson. Anne Scott was asked a question, which she answered - whereupon the 'inspector' shouted at her, 'Get off your bum when you address a teacher.' We all thought this was hilarious, but we were also rather apprehensive. Eventually, our strange visitor wandered off. Sometime later, I heard that he had also paid a visit to St Aidan's, this time with a replica gun.

In some respects, we were a lot more naïve in those days. If Helen Young, our Maths teacher, ever had to leave her classroom, the first thing she did when she returned was to ask anybody who had been talking during her absence to put up their hand. We always owned up, and as a punishment we had to copy out a large chunk of our Maths textbook.

We could also be very cruel. I remember one occasion when all the members of our Science class hid behind a mobile blackboard, and Miss Hogg was almost reduced to tears as she cried out, "Where are you? I know you're in here somewhere."

I have many happy memories of my time in the Junior Choir, though latterly my chief function was to turn the pages (of the songbook or sheet music) for the pianist - and I only actually sang when really low notes were required. What I especially liked about being a member of the choir was the wonderful teas we were treated to when we gave a performance outwith the school.

The most memorable of these performances took place in St Giles Cathedral. I wasn't even needed as a page turner, since Mr Carson wasn't accompanying the choir on the cathedral organ (he was turning the pages for the organist): so I went for a walk round the cathedral while the choir practised. I bumped into a very large flower arrangement and sent it flying. Absolutely mortified, I reported my clumsiness to the only other person I could see in that part of the cathedral (I thought he was the caretaker). He was really kind and told me not to worry, as there were too many flowers anyway. Later, during the actual service, I saw the man again. He was giving the address.

When we were in sixth year, Lydia Milligan and I decided to activate the fire alarm - just to see if the staff and pupils would respond with greater urgency than was usually the case. We 'borrowed' a spanner to break the glass on the front of the alarm, and when the bell started ringing we ran down the staff stairs - almost straight into the arms of Mr Barnard. Since we were senior pupils, he asked us to try and find out which alarm had been triggered. He then switched off the alarm, having concluded (a mite cavalierly, we thought) that there was no actual fire. Unfortunately, we had to own up in order to save the skin of a younger boy who found himself 'in the frame' for our misdemeanour. Mr Barnard made us feel very small when he questioned us in his office.

Five years later, I was up before him again, this time as a new member of staff. Although I very much enjoyed my time there as a pupil, and although I wanted to teach in a school that wasn't too far from where I lived, I did not wish to start my teaching career at the High School (by 1980, it didn't have a very good reputation). I had very mixed feelings, therefore, when I learned that the only vacancy for a science teacher in Lanark Division was to be found at my old school.

I taught RE, chemistry and general science to 1st and 2nd year pupils. I also had several non-certificate classes on my timetable. The pupils in these classes were not expected to sit any SCE examinations, so I was free to devise my own syllabus. I taught them everything from dental hygiene to simple car mechanics, from surveying a local river to making and testing cement. I even made a foray into the field of sex education - a topic which certainly guaranteed their rapt attention.

The most 'exciting' incident during the two years I spent teaching chemistry centred round a chemical element (phosphorus) which ignites spontaneously in air. Thanks to my own carelessness, a small piece of phosphorus fell onto one of the benches and set it alight. Though I washed the bench thoroughly, it continued to flare up, and I had visions of my never being able to use the lab again. Luckily, an older (and wiser) member of the science department came to my rescue, and on his advice I washed the bench with a copper sulphate solution.

I felt very sad when my teaching career at the High School ended in 1982. In fact, I sat in my lab and cried for more than twenty minutes. I had really loved all the years I spent there as a pupil and a teacher.

48

A Team from All Seasons

Between 1963 and 1991, I refereed or watched (in a coaching capacity) more inter-school and inter-house football matches than anybody else in the history of the school. As far as winning games was concerned, the most impressive team was probably the Intermediate XI that in the course of session 1963 - 64 won the Anderson Cup and the Motherwell and Wishaw League (without dropping a point) - and also, despite a series of away ties, reached the quarter-final of the Scottish Intermediate Shield. Coached by Tom Forsyth, it was a solid, well-organised unit with absolutely no weaknesses, and it just never looked like losing.

Selecting individual players for a composite team is a much more invidious task, but here goes. Judged solely by his achievements in the professional game, Allan Ferguson (who after a long spell with Hamilton Accies signed for St Johnstone in 1998) is clearly the best goalkeeper produced by the High School. However, although there must have been occasions during the 1980s when he turned out for the school, I never actually saw him in action: so I can't comment on his ability.

Alan Merry was endowed with two of the qualities that one associates with a top-class goalkeeper - great physical presence and a tendency to make very few mistakes. Even so, I never felt that he was as commanding as he should have been, especially when he was dealing (or trying to deal) with the schoolboy goalkeeper's nightmare - high crosses.

Another two goalkeepers worthy of a mention are Colin Bird (in later years, on the books of Coltness United), who was a reliable shot-stopper; and Gordon Morris, who showed a lot of promise until he was badly injured.

Most schoolboy defenders are convinced that it is necessary not only to mark forwards very tightly all the time, but also to keep pushing up to the halfway line - in an effort (very often a vain effort) to play the sort of offside game advocated by the high priest of such tactics, Peter Melrose. Andrew MacLean was one of the very few players who had the nous to appreciate that more often than not defenders, especially central defenders, should be more concerned about the space behind them than the forwards in front of them; for this is where the ball, and the forwards, end up nine times out of ten. Who knows what Andrew might have achieved in the game if he had been taller and stronger?

Ian Reid would always feature in my 'dream team' - either at centre half, the position he normally occupied in the school team; or at right back, since I can't recall any outstanding occupants of that position - by virtue of his reliable kicking and intelligent reading of the game: he was always one step ahead of the opposition forwards. As he moved up the school, a ruthless, stop-them-at-any-cost element sometimes crept into his style of play (this was in the days when players were not automatically sent off for certain professional fouls).

Kenny Lutton had that extra yard of pace which all the best players seem to have, and his adaptability (he could also play in the midfield) reminded me of David Hay; Robert Thom was a courageous, wholehearted 'stopper', just the sort of player that was needed on a wet Saturday morning when Waverley was a sea of mud; Eric Bennett, a really classy sweeper, was the only genuinely 'two-footed' defender to play for the High School in the period under review; Ronnie Wilson, a great attacking full back, bombed down the left wing at every opportunity, and was completely immune from the mental block that prevents 99.9% of schoolboy defenders from doing anything - apart from standing around like tailors' dummies - when their team has possession of the ball.

Billy Milligan and George Watters were not flashy players (I'm pretty sure that a lot of their hard work went unnoticed), but no team can be consistently successful without midfielders who are prepared to work their socks off for the duration of every game; Sandy Bryson could run all day, and had a truly magical left foot; Norman Stevenson was a hard, aggressive player, interested only in pushing forward - a real clockwork terrier, in short: wind him up and he would snap away at the ankles of the opposition for eighty minutes.

I first saw Les Dalrymple in a 2nd Intermediate game at Biggar; he was knee-high to a garden gnome and playing out wide on the right wing, but the first time he touched the ball I realised that he was something special. A year or two later, he was playing for the 1st Seniors and scoring just as many goals as his great rival, Willie Pettigrew. It might even be argued that he was a better all-round player than Pettigrew, for he was undoubtedly a better dribbler and, despite his small stature, better in the air. He was also the classiest and most effective forward I came across in my years at the High School.

It always amuses me when people criticise a striker like Romario on the grounds that 'all he does is score goals'. If a striker scores goals on a regular basis, he doesn't have to do anything else to justify the appearance of his name on the team sheet.

Jim Roberts was a striker out of the same mould as Muller and Romario, and although he was a member of a rather mediocre team, he converted (into goals) a huge percentage of the few chances with which he was presented.

David Main was the most versatile footballer in the history of the High School: he was a brilliant goalkeeper; he had the skill and the stamina to play in the midfield or up front; and when he joined the ranks of the professionals, he played at left back most of the time. The only quality he lacked was pace, and for that reason I always thought his best position was goalkeeper: he was confident and very agile, and crosses held no terrors for him. Consequently, he would be in goal for my 'fantasy' XI - but what a substitute he would make!

Actually, my two substitutes are Kenny Mathie and John White. I am well aware that most people will say: 'Kenny Who?'; and 'John Who?' Neither of them, admittedly, won any caps or medals, and neither of them was tough enough to get going when the going got tough. However, they were both endowed with great technical skill - a very fragile skill, it is true, but one that enabled them to turn effortlessly on the ball, or glide past an opponent as if he wasn't there. 'Ars est celare artem.'

Depending on the opposition, there are three different formations (two of which are almost identical) in which my team from all seasons could line up:

Either:

David Main

Eric Bennett

Ian Reid   Robert Thom /   Ronnie Wilson
                      Andrew MacLean

Kenny Lutton   Norman Stevenson   George Watters   Sandy Bryson

Les Dalrymple   Jim Roberts

Or

David Main

Eric Bennett

Ian Reid   Robert Thom /   Ronnie Wilson
                Andrew MacLean

Billy Milligan   Norman Stevenson   Kenny Lutton   George Watters

Les Dalrymple   Jim Roberts

Or

David Main

Ian Reid   Kenny Lutton /   Andrew MacLean   Ronnie Wilson
                Robert Thom

Billy Milligan   Norman Stevenson   George Watters   Sandy Bryson

Les Dalrymple   Jim Roberts

49

1983

The Last Hurrah

Coached by Drew Morrice, the under-12 team (Leigh Dalgleish, Craig Dargavel, Lindsay Shearer, Robert Johnston, Ian Bishop, Scott Anderson, David McLean, Ross Murdoch, Duncan McIntosh, Gary McKay, and James McPherson) became the first winners of the Lanark Challenge Cup. In the event, this was the last football trophy to be won by a team from the High School.

Who Dares Wins (SAS)

Who Cares Who Wins? (WHS)

Tom Young and I (and Jimmy Pringle, latterly) continued to run football teams, but it was a hard row to hoe: very few boys were willing to play for the school, and even fewer could be relied on to turn up on Saturday morning. We did, however, provide a regular game of football for those pupils who were not good enough to get a game with any of the boys' clubs, so our efforts were not a complete waste of time.

Crimes and Punishments

Consequent on the abolition of corporal punishment in August 1982, a disciplinary system based on punishment exercises, exclusion from the classroom, and suspension was inaugurated at the High School. After the new system had been operative for seven months, EIS members on the staff expressed mixed views not only on its effectiveness but also on the way in which it was being implemented:

The biggest threat to the effectiveness of the system is inconsistency among the staff in implementing the disciplinary procedures.

As far as the totally disruptive pupil is concerned, exclusion from the classroom does not work; but it does work in the case of most children.

Strathclyde Region should be devising a policy to deal with those pupils for whom suspension is not a deterrent but an attractive proposition.

It is taking longer for classes to settle down at the beginning of the period, and valuable teaching time is being taken up by disciplinary procedures. The main burden of work arising from the new system is shouldered by the Guidance staff, the AHTs - and even the Depute Rector, since disciplinary problems are reaching that level far more quickly than in the days of corporal punishment.

Give me employment - but not yet.

More than fifty pupils took their formal leave of the school on Tuesday, 31 May (the official leaving date), and as part of the leaving procedure they were interviewed by the Careers Officer. One of the 4th Year boys asked her not to get him a job before Friday, as he was going to Wembley for the Scotland-England game.

The school acquired a National Panasonic VCR and ten VHS cassettes.

The Parents' Association organised a Prize Bingo Session in the hall.

At the prize-giving, Councillor Jim Foley presented the school with a certificate acknowledging the part it had played in the Keep Motherwell District Tidy Campaign (High School pupils had helped to clean up a local gulley). In 1984 sixty 3rd Year pupils took part in a clean-up campaign in Newmains; and four years later, as part of National Environment Week, High School pupils assisted with the campaign to persuade members of the public to 'sign the pledge' not to drop litter.

No-Go Areas

In August, at the beginning of the new session, certain parts of the school were declared out of bounds at the intervals. One of these 'forbidden territories', the upstairs corridors in the main building, was described in the *Bulletin* as 'deserted and uncannily quiet'.

Christopher Glen and Alistair McIntosh were selected for the Lanarkshire under-15 rugby team.

At the National Mod (which was being held in Motherwell), eleven High School pupils manned the computer terminals that formed part of the communications system.

The repainting of the school began: so we all assumed that another attempt to close it was in the offing.

Today's Special: Bombe Surprise

The school log for 4 October reads as follows:
A phone call this morning suggested that a bomb had been planted in the canteen. The canteen staff were evacuated and the premises thoroughly checked by the janitors and the police. Nothing was found, and staff returned in time to serve lunch.

At the Lanark Division Swimming Championships, Alan Burns took part in six finals - with the following outcome: 400 metres freestyle - 2nd; 200 metres individual medley - 1st; 100 metres freestyle - 2nd; 100 metres backstroke - 1st; 100 metres breaststroke - 2nd; 100 metres butterfly - 3rd.

The results of a referendum on smoking were as follows:
Members of staff in favour of a ban on smoking in the presence of pupils - 46
Members of staff against such a ban - 5
Members of staff in favour of a total ban on smoking - 23
Members of staff against such a ban - 28

The Boys from the Blackstuff

'Everyone,' wrote Sam in the *Bulletin*, 'who has bumped over the potholes at the main gate will be happy that the central drive is being repaired - and particularly happy that the work is being done by such an efficient group of workers. They never seem to stop, and every phase of the operation seems to fit neatly into place with no fuss and no loss of time. Indeed, it looks as if the whole operation will be completed in two days.'

Isobel Girdwood, Principal Teacher of Home Economics, retired. According to the *Bulletin*, she found a 'unique' way of expressing her thanks for the cheque she received from the staff (early in 1984) - as a result of which 'everybody spent a week munching their way through marzipan and sugar done up in all sorts of attractive shapes by her skilful hands'.

The death was reported of Margaret Mitchell, a member of the secretarial staff from 1975 till 1979. The *Bulletin* described her as

444

'courteous, helpful, and efficient'; and 'although she never enjoyed the best of health,' it added, 'she always responded to the frequently frantic demands for clerical services with cheerfulness and good humour.'

James Dickson, Principal Teacher of Mathematics from 1943 and Depute Rector from 1960 till 1972, also passed away. According to Sam, "he was one of nature's gentlemen with a quiet, gentle personality and a delightful sense of humour".

The Cold Gradations of Decay

Samuel Johnson

By 1983, the High School was in a state of terminal decline: its roll had begun to fall and its academic reputation was in free fall. On the basis, for instance, of the number of O-Grades and Highers its pupils gained in the SCE examinations, it was placed 28th (out of 35) in the 'league table' of secondary schools in the Lanark Division. Sheila Sprot explains the decline as follows:

The change from High School, with all its implications of academic excellence, to what I would flippantly describe as Craigneuk Academy was not an easy change to make (changing upwards from comprehensive to senior secondary status would have been much easier, with everyone striving to improve standards and show what they could do). A staff that had been trained to teach academic subjects in an academic way was faced with hordes of children whose academic peak was reached at about the age of ten; and the school's problems were compounded by the fact that its catchment area was almost totally an area of great social deprivation.

Parents of bright pupils with academic aspirations became less and less willing to send their children to the High School to mix with the hoi polloi (and who, if he was being realistic, could blame them?). Consequently, the academic top of the school faded, and the school became bottom heavy. This did not make it a bad school, but it made it a very different school; and it took time to adjust. Comprehensive schools require a good social mix to make them work. The High School never had that, so we were on to a loser from the start.

The building was unsuitable, many of the staff were unsuitable (in the beginning, at any rate), and when two new schools - Coltness High

445

School, which took the 'good' part of our catchment area, and Garrion Academy, which had superb facilities - were opened, we were left in an educational backwater. We were the traditional high school without the traditional pupils.

Tapped Untalent

Kingsley Amis

Things did not improve in the late 1980s and early 1990s, as the following statistics demonstrate:

Percentage of School Leavers in Session 1989-90 with Three or More Ordinary/Standard Grades (Grades 1-3):

Wishaw High School	33.3	(the lowest in Lanark Division)
Coltness High School	53.1	
Garrion Academy	40.0	
Calderhead High School	36.9	

Percentage of School Leavers in Session 1989-90 with Three or More Highers (Bands A-C):

Wishaw High School	12.2	(5th lowest in Lanark Division; 136th in Strathclyde)
Coltness High School	27.9	
Garrion Academy	12.5	
Calderhead High School	14.6	

Percentage of School Leavers in Session 1989-90 with Five or More Highers (Bands A-C):

Wishaw High School	1.9	(8th lowest in Lanark Division; 300th - out of 375 - in Scotland as a whole)
Coltness High School	13.6	
Calderhead High School	3.8	

Percentage of 4th Year Pupils Gaining Three or More Standard Grades at Levels 1-2 in 1992:

Wishaw High	8
Coltness High School	26
Garrion Academy	20
Calderhead High School	15
Lanark Division	25
Strathclyde Region	28
Scotland	31

Percentage of 5th Year Pupils Gaining Three or More Highers (Bands A - C) in 1990, 1991, and 1992:

	1990	1991	1992
Wishaw High School	8	8	5
Coltness High School	20	25	21
Garrion Academy	6	12	8
Calderhead High School	8	6	5
Lanark Division	14	14	14
Strathclyde Region	16	16	16
Scotland	17	17	17

In short, the High School developed (metaphorically) the features of a stegosaurus - a brain as small as a walnut and a long, thick tail: so nobody should have been surprised when it eventually suffered the same fate - extinction. There were one or two reasonably able (by the standards of the High School in the 1980s) pupils on the roll, but they were almost invariably sucked into the quicksands of mediocrity - and worse, much worse - that surrounded them.

50

The Guidance System: Its Rationale and Achievements

51

1984

Some things don't go better with coke.

On 31 January, the heating system was shut down, and pupils in the 1st, 2nd, and 3rd Year were sent home at the morning interval. The *Bulletin* explained why:

There was nothing wrong with the boilers or the automatic stokers, but there soon would have been if any of the six tons of coke that were delivered on Monday afternoon had got into the system. The coke, which should have gone to the HORSA huts, was deposited in the boiler house bunker as a result of a unique combination of circumstances: a janitor receiving his first delivery of fuel from a driver who was delivering to the school for the first time. An impressive rescue operation was mounted on Tuesday morning, the coke was shovelled back out again, and the heating was restored by the end of the day.

2nd Year pupils were, in the words of the *Bulletin*, 'dentally examined'. The examination (the second of the three that were conducted at yearly intervals as part of a huge research programme sponsored by Unilever) included X-rays and saliva tests; and all the pupils in the survey - and their close relatives - were supplied with toothbrushes and toothpaste for the duration of the experiment.

Jim Watt, former boxing champion, addressed the 1st and 2nd Year boys as part of the Fitness for Life campaign initiated by STV and the Milk Marketing Board.

Dr Jeremy Bray MP presented the school with a number of bound volumes of Hansard covering the years 1964-65, 1966-69, 1976-77, and 1980-81.

Karen Nelson, Alison Gibb, and Avril Simkin were awarded Certificates of Distinction at the Lanarkshire Music Festival.

Six 4th Year pupils had their first sailing lesson at Strathclyde Park.

The retiral was announced of Mrs Agnes Johnston, who for fifteen years 'cheerfully dispensed sweets and custard' in the canteen.

The Kennedy family presented a trophy to the school in memory of Gordon Kennedy, a former boys' captain, who was killed in a tragic accident in 1983. The trophy was awarded annually for the most distinguished performance by a High School pupil in the field of athletics.

At the County Sports, 'gold' medals were won by Drew Clark (800 metres), Kenneth Morrison (200 metres), Rebecca Murray (200 metres), and the 2nd Year girls' relay team (Marianne Nelson, Tracy Nelson, Tracey McCulloch, and Michelle Allan).

Ten senior pupils and two teachers (George Randall and David Alexander) spent four days touring the Highlands, the object of the exercise being to study the physical landscape and experience at first hand life in the more remote parts of the Scottish mainland.

Primum Mobile

In June, at the AGM of the EIS in Rothesay, the delegates voted overwhelmingly for an independent review of teachers' salaries, a vote that was the prelude to a prolonged campaign against the intransigent refusal of the Secretary of State for Scotland to authorise such a review. By a strange quirk of fate, the opening stages of the national campaign coincided with the climax of the campaign mounted by the Lanarkshire Association of the EIS against consortia.

52

The Great Consortium Carfuffle

consortium: a combination of several banks, business concerns or other bodies; association; fellowship

Chambers Concise Dictionary

In August 1984, as part of Strathclyde Region's 16-18 Action Plan (and despite the 'vehement opposition' of parents, teachers, and the Lanarkshire Association of the EIS, which, earlier in the year, had organised a protest rally in the Civic Centre), the secondary schools in Lanark Division were divided, on a geographical basis, into consortia (pronounced CONsortia, with the stress on the first syllable): the Wishaw-Shotts consortium, for example, comprised the High School, Coltness High School, St Aidan's High School, Garrion Academy, and Calderhead High School. All O-Grade and Higher classes in certain 'minority subjects' (e.g. Latin and German) were hived off to one of the schools in the consortium, and pupils from the other four schools were expected to present themselves at this school for instruction in those subjects: to take a case in point, all the pupils in the Wishaw area who wished to take Higher Latin were required to do so at St Aidan's High School.

There were several practical reasons why the creation of consortia ('the work of zealots in the County Buildings,' according to Fred Forrester, Organising Secretary of the EIS, 'who had ignored developments in other parts of the region') was destined to meet with resistance on the part of the pupils: many of the latter associated a particular subject with a particular teacher (by whom they had been taught for several years), and they were disinclined to continue their studies in that subject with a different teacher in a different school; and having to commute between their base school and other educational establishments made it difficult - or even impossible - for some of them to take part in extra-curricular activities at the former. Moreover, in the context of the Wishaw-Shotts consortium, pupils from Garrion Academy were unlikely to be wildly excited by the prospect of having to find their way to Shotts in the middle of winter, a seven-mile journey that involved changing buses at least once; and in an area where a sizeable percentage of the population are so hostile towards the Roman Catholic Church and its adherents that William of Orange T-shirts are always in fashion, how many pupils from the High School or Coltness High School would have been falling over themselves to make the much shorter journey to St Aidan's High School? As far as consortia were concerned, then, it was always on the cards that pupils would vote with their feet, and the likelihood of such an outcome was confirmed when several pupils from Calderhead High School opted out of Higher German because it was only available at one of the schools in Wishaw.

For their part, the regional authorities claimed that their main objective in setting up consortia was to safeguard 'minority subjects' - and thus preserve as wide a range of curricula as possible at a time when there was a significant decline in the rolls of many secondary schools. In making such a claim, they conveniently (and rather disingenuously, it must be said) overlooked the fact that if certain 'minority subjects' were disappearing from the curricular menu of some schools, it was probably because they had decreed, as part of their version of the 16-18 Action Plan, that any O-Grade or Higher class with fewer than ten pupils should be discontinued - at least as a separate entity in the school where it originally appeared on the timetable.

If a consortium is to be a viable proposition, the timetables of the schools that make up the consortium have to be standardised (likewise, the length of the periods and the lunch interval), and travelling time has to be incorporated in the school day. Since the High School and Coltness High School worked a 40-period week (as opposed to the 25-period version that obtained at Garrion Academy), major changes in the 'configuration of the school day' (to quote the rather portentous phrase that was in vogue at the time) were obviously required if these two schools were to participate in the Wishaw-Shotts consortium in a meaningful way. The EIS, however, advised its members not to accept such changes, if they were imposed without prior consultation and agreement.

Many members of the public must have thought that the EIS was making a mountain out of a molehill (did it really matter, for instance, if the lunch interval at the High School and Coltness High School began at 12.30 p.m. instead of 11.55 a.m.?), but in reality the standardisation of timetables necessitated by the consortium had several more serious disadvantages: pupils studying several subjects at Higher level lost one hour's teaching time in each subject every week; teaching blocks of 110 minutes were created, and since the Higher course in most subjects normally consisted of only two of these blocks per week, pupils lost contact with their teacher in a particular subject for up to four days at a time; in addition, the long, unbroken teaching blocks overtaxed the concentration of younger pupils.

Since the EIS had also advised its members not to accept (in their classes) pupils from other schools in the consortium, teachers in the Wishaw area found themselves at loggerheads with the authorities at the beginning of session 1984-85; indeed, some pupils had only been back at school for a few hours after the summer holidays - when they were sent home.

We're all deemed, deemed ah tell ye.

All head teachers received a letter from the Director of Education advising them of the disciplinary action that was to be taken against any teacher who refused to teach a particular group of pupils: recalcitrant pedagogues were to be warned that they were in breach of contract, and that they would not be paid for the day or days on which they 'refused to work'. This procedure (it was called 'deeming', which sounded like, and in certain respects actually resembled, some obscure 19th Century legal process involving - in the persons of Sam, Ruth Hodgson, and Drew Morrice - a deemster, a clerk of the court, and an advocate) took on an air of absurdity, as forty teachers lined up outside Sam's room waiting their turn to read out the prepared statement handed to them by the EIS's own Joseph Beltrami. Some pupils got wind of this strange-sounding ritual and took to asking various members of staff, with a mixture of wonderment and apprehension, 'Please, sir, have you been deemed?'

After more than a week of disruption, during which the staff, for the most part, loitered with intent (not to accept any changes in the school day or pupils from other schools), and large numbers of pupils had to be sent home (a journey that a hundred of them enlivened, on one occasion, with a fraternal visit to St Aidan's, where they broke a few windows and hurled more than a few obscenities at the papists), a temporary truce was established. A Joint Working Group (comprising three members of the educational establishment and three union representatives) was set up to review the proposed arrangements for the Wishaw - Shotts consortium; timetabling experts were despatched to the High School to try and resolve the problems associated with the standardisation of the timetables of the schools in the consortium; and, for the time being, individual schools were allowed to operate a timetable mutually agreed between themselves and the DEO.

The Joint Working Group was unable to produce joint recommendations, and the timetablers' remit seemed to preclude them from breaking up the 110 minutes-long teaching blocks: consequently, the Director of Education announced his intention to recommend to the ruling Labour Group on Strathclyde Regional Council that the changes originally proposed by the DEO in respect of timetables and the configuration of the school day should be implemented in all the schools in the consortium - including those where they had been rejected by most of the teachers (whether or not they were members of the EIS). So it was back to square one.

EIS members walked out of the High School in protest at 'the continued failure of Strathclyde Regional Council and the Regional Executive of the EIS to solve the timetabling difficulties in the Wishaw - Shotts consortium'. 'Teachers,' they complained 'have been excluded from crucial decisions, and they have been offered no meaningful alternatives to the scenario favoured by the Region.'

Such protests were becoming increasingly irrelevant, however, since the two main participants in the dispute were desperate for a settlement: the Region for obvious reasons; the EIS (at least at national level), because it didn't wish to be distracted from the campaign it had recently initiated to secure an independent review of teachers' salaries.

Further talks were arranged, and eventually a compromise was reached: at the High School and Coltness High School, the 40 - period week was replaced - but not immediately, and not in one fell swoop - by the 25 - period version (this was more or less inevitable, since the 25 - period week was the norm throughout the region); the timing and duration of the lunch interval were changed, there being little likelihood of the EIS taking to the streets in defence of its members' inalienable right to have their pie and chips at five to twelve; schools were allowed to run classes in 'minority subjects', even though they contained fewer than ten pupils; and the Region did not insist on the movement of pupils from their base school to other schools in a consortium, if the consortium in question was 'artificially contrived'.

In the event, the years subsequent to the dispute witnessed hardly any movement of pupils in the Wishaw – Shotts consortium: one or two CSYS Biology and Chemistry students made their way up the yellow brick road to Coltness High School, but there was no brain drain on a large scale. As for the word 'consortium' (which, just like 'referendum' in more recent times, inspired some bizarre pluralisations), it disappeared over the educational horizon as suddenly as it had heaved in sight.

53

1985

Cur non mitto meos tibi, Pontiliane, libellos?
Ne mihi tu mittas, Pontiliane, tuos.

Martial, *Epigrams*

David Alexander, a member of the Geography Department, was one of the authors of a handbook (entitled 'Administering Change in Assessment') that listed the pros and cons of the strategy employed by Lanark Division to introduce the assessment techniques required for the new Standard Grade courses.

As a result of a break-in (the third in nine months), the Music Department lost eleven electronic organs, seven six-string classical guitars, blank cassettes, audio equipment and its only bass guitar, the total value of all these items being £1,500. 'To be deprived of such a large number of instruments,' lamented Elspeth Banks, 'is devastating. Now we will have to change completely the courses of almost every pupil who uses the Music Department.' Three months later, at Hamilton Sheriff Court, James Murdoch pleaded guilty to the offence and was sentenced to three months' imprisonment.

The Concert Band staged its first ever concert (*Music for a Summer Evening*) in the assembly hall at Garrion Academy. Dressed (to "everyone's great delight") in full Highland regalia, Jamie McLaughlin, Lesley Dyer, and Alistair McLaughlin presented an 'invigorating' selection of traditional Scottish bagpipe music; Walter Reid of Scottish Opera, accompanied by Ruth Hodgson, sang a medley of Scottish ballads and love songs; and solo performances by clarinettists Shona Clark and Karen Scott, horn player Gail Moncrieff, vocalist Lisa McIlwraith, and Gillian Kerr (on the euphonium) 'went down well with the audience of parents and friends'.

Senior pupils from the High School helped the attendants at Wishaw Sports Centre to supervise pupils from Newmains Primary who were trying their hand at roller-skating and other sports.

Boiler House Blues

The school log for 5 and 6 November reads as follows:
Overnight flooding in the boiler house led to the complete failure of the heating system in the main building. Pupils in 1st, 2nd, and 3rd Year sent home at 10.30; 4, 5, 6 accommodated in huts. Ditto 6 November.

Teachers of the world, unite. You have nothing to lose but a day's salary.

By now, the EIS campaign to secure an independent review of teachers' salaries was in full swing - its main elements being a work to contract, a withdrawal from all development work, and a series of one-day 'rota' or 'rolling' strikes. On at least one occasion, those teachers at the High School (or most of them) who were members of the SSTA (the second largest teachers' union) lent their support to the EIS campaign by withdrawing their labour for a day.

The Persuaders

George Younger, the Secretary of State for Scotland, responded to EIS demands for an independent review of teachers' salaries by proposing a review of both salaries and working conditions. On the day on which this proposal was due to be discussed by the Council of the EIS, a busload of teachers (including several from the High School) travelled to Edinburgh to lobby the members of the Council and, hopefully, persuade them to reject the said proposal. Their journey was not in vain.

54

Howffs

**Ille terrarum mihi praeter omnes
Angulus ridet.**

Horace, *Carmina*

The Technicians' Room

Box Room

The technicians' room was frequented by the members of the Science Department (who in earlier years had tended to congregate in the Chemistry storeroom at intervals and lunchtime) - and Liz Patrick, who found the atmosphere more congenial than that of the ladies' staffroom. Sometimes, she brought her dogs (in cases) with her, and these included such exotic breeds as the papillon, described by Neil Kerr as 'looking like a hot-water bottle'.

Despite the frequent changes in the personnel of the various branches of the Science Department, the technicians' room was always, as Sam himself remarked, 'a very happy and friendly place'.

Helen Leith 'kept everybody in order' and made sure that tea and coffee were always available.

One or two television sets were also available (they were switched off if Iain Murray appeared on the scene); and in addition to test matches and international football matches, Graham Johnstone can remember watching the Falklands campaign unfold.

Neil Kerr has particularly vivid memories of John McGuire, who seems to have been permanently disgruntled about every aspect of the teaching profession; Bill McGeechan, who used the aftershave he had received at Christmas as windscreen washer fluid; and Helen Leith, who liked to sit on an electric fire - a potentially hazardous habit, since the bolts securing the outer casing of the fire had rusted, and the casing had severed the electric cable.

The Ladies' Staffroom

At ev'ry word a reputation dies.

Alexander Pope, *The Rape of the Lock*

Towards the end of the school's existence, the ladies' staffroom became a mixed staffroom; up till then, my appearances in this sanctum sanct-(imonious) orum were confined to the tea break at meetings of the Staff Badminton Club. However, I have been reliably informed that all the ladies had 'their own' chairs and their own cups; and that once a month there was a Baked Potato Day (the potatoes were baked in the oven, and different people supplied different fillings, e.g. coleslaw and chilli con carne).

The ladies' staffroom was the favourite haunt of a lot of smokers; and there seems to have been a lot of lively discussion about political matters. I also have a feeling that considerably more work (marking, for example) was done there than in the gents' staffroom.

The Gents' Staffroom

Room with a Cue

From time immemorial, there seems to have been a solo school in the gents' staffroom.

In the early 1960s, the solo aficionados were John Smith, Bill Clark, Tom Forsyth, Jim Orr, and Derek Winton. Tom Forsyth liked to attempt very risky misères: hence the phrase 'a Forsyth mis' (pronounced miz); and if other members of the school felt like having a bit of a punt, they would declare: "I think I'll try a Forsyth mis."

For a fairly lengthy spell during the 1970s, pool was all the rage: Belhaven House had purchased a pool table, and since it was stored in the cloakroom adjoining the staffroom, it was all too readily available.

Shove-halfpenny was popular in the early 1980s. Ronnie Hamilton brought in an authentic shove-halfpenny board; and there was a league of sorts and a cup competition - which fortunately (since there was no cup) fizzled out.

Chess was also popular for a brief spell in the early 1970s, when Stanley White was a member of the English Department; among those he played against were Eddie Tweedlie Jnr and John Parton.

In the 1960s, a fair number of teachers used to mark exam papers in the gents' staffroom: Don Weir, for instance, would spend an eternity marking History essays. Jimmy Lindsay was even more punctilious, and every ten seconds he would ask Bob Craig if he should deduct half a mark here or a quarter of a mark there. As Bob grew more and more irritated, his neck grew redder and redder.

Latterly, nobody did any marking in the gents' staffroom; indeed, with the exception of the first day of a new session, the gents' staffroom was never very busy. Most people collected material from their pigeonholes in the morning, and that was the only time they were seen in the place. This may have been one of the reasons why it was converted (in the 1990s) into office accommodation for the secretaries.

The Admin Staffroom

Fun and (Board) Games

Those who hung out in the Admin staffroom - John Ralston, Sam Graham, John Wright, Ian Shedden, Drew Morrice, Clark Govan, and David Leslie - were designated by Helen Young as 'the odd bods'. On the final day of the winter and summer terms, 'the odd bods' organised a special lunch: Graham Sneddon sometimes provided a home-made steak pie, and on one occasion Jimmy Clelland prepared Pork Creole.

From time to time, John Ralston had his lunch (which, like Dick Whittington's, was usually wrapped in a huge, red handkerchief) in the Admin staffroom. However, his was no ordinary packed lunch: he feasted on such delicacies as rollmops and a particularly prestigious brand of gentleman's relish. After he had juggled with, and eventually guzzled, the former, the table - and everything lying on it - was covered in scales and vinegar; indeed, salt and vinegar flavour worksheets became very popular with pupils in the Modern Studies Department.

Big John spent a lot of time joshing John Wright, and he himself was the target of several practical jokes: for example, Sam Graham convinced him that he would not be able to tune in to Channel 4 unless he had a new aerial fitted on the roof of his bungalow.

On another occasion, David Leslie was having great difficulty persuading Big John to return a library book he had (very unwisely) allowed him to borrow. Eventually, he composed a letter (purporting to be from the library), which 'informed' him that he had been fined £100 for failing to return a book that was three weeks overdue. Having shown

460

Big John this letter, he told him that as he had been in possession of the book for most of the period in question he would have to pay the tine. The following day, Big John presented David Leslie with a cheque, signed by his wife, for £100.

Drew Morrice remembers spending a day and a half engrossed (as were his co-participants, the other members of the History and Modern Studies Departments) in a labyrinthine board game based on military strategy and the art of diplomacy, pedagogic duties, in the meantime, going largely by the board (sic) - even though Sam popped his head round the door and asked (somewhat ironically) how the game was going. In fact, the game was eventually brought to a halt when John Wright (whose forces were on the point of being wiped out) threw the board up in the air.

The Maths Storeroom

Moriarty: How are you at Mathematics?
Harry Secombe: I speak it like a native.

The Goon Show

Over the years, the male members of the Maths Department detested the place, characterising it as 'all cigarette smoke and Jenny Barrie rabbiting on about the results of the 3rd Year trigonometry tests'; some of them (David Forrest, for example) tried to change things, but they soon had to admit defeat. Sheila Sprot has more affectionate memories of the storeroom in question:

When people work together day in and day out, they have to get along with one another. They have to have a place where they can moan and let off steam; a place where they feel safe and supported; a place where they can thrash out problems and discuss the nuts and bolts of their craft; a place where they can get away from the job; a place where they can meet people of similar interests and a similar intellectual background; a place where, if they feel like it, they can bring up their concerns about the world, or have their spirits lifted by the latest bit of gossip or scandal - or even by the latest joke; a place where they can have a cup of tea and a biscuit in relative peace; a place where they can occasionally be indiscreet, knowing that because they are with friends and fellow teachers it will go no further. The Maths storeroom was that special place for us.

We met there every interval - not just the Maths Department, but some of our colleagues from other departments as well, notably the PE ladies, who kept us from becoming too incestuous. The head of the Maths Department always sat at the head of the table, but he/she did not take the chair: topics were raised by anyone who felt like talking; and if, as sometimes happened, we were too exhausted to talk, we sipped tea or coffee (both were always on offer), comforting ourselves, if we were not dieting (which we frequently were), by munching chocolate biscuits. It was amazing how that cuppa and that ten-minute break could give you the strength to face the terrors of 3E last two periods on a winter afternoon.

We discussed a wide range of topics: the pros and cons of the teachers' strikes (we all, in varying degrees, had a conscience about striking); dieting (constantly); education, in all its aspects; politics (sometimes, but not often); the minutiae of our personal lives (very often); the problems associated with working mothers, elderly parents, errant teenagers, crying babies, and mortgages; the cost of living; plumbers who didn't turn up; interesting bridge hands; and even crossword clues. We talked a lot, and even though we didn't solve the world's problems - or even our own - at least we aired them, and that is therapeutic. Although we didn't always agree with one another, we never fell out.

Even though the storeroom, due to its smallness, did not lend itself to entertaining visitors, we did entertain a lot of visitors: HMIs, trainee teachers and their tutors, former pupils from distant parts of the world, former colleagues, and other members of staff who happened to be passing. All were welcome, but we never changed our ways of doing things for any of them; we never put on a show, except for big occasions like presentations to colleagues who were getting married, or had been promoted, or were celebrating their 60th birthday. Occasionally, someone would bring in a cake or some home baking, which everyone - especially the men - really appreciated.

We had a big table (for working on, as well as for eating off) and a motley collection of old chairs - and even older stools, from the science labs; we also had a sink, a draining board, and a kettle, which we bought out of our tea fund. I was in charge of this fund for a longish spell, and I had to buy tea, coffee, milk, and biscuits. I was always out of pocket, for in the tradition of all self-respecting Maths teachers I could never balance the books.

462

The storeroom was a very untidy place: there were always piles of papers and books lying about, and the floor always looked dirty - likewise, the sink. The cupboards were used to store exam papers, stationery supplies and the like, and the shelves housed our departmental library - if it could be given such a title. Many of the books were old and out of date (Maths is constantly changing, and Maths books become obsolete more quickly than most), but nobody liked to throw them out, as nobody was quite sure who they belonged to.

The cleaners used the Maths storeroom as a base; they had their tea there, and they kept their mops and brushes outside the door. This didn't exactly add to the ambience of the place; it also meant that they set up shop at quarter to four - so we had to get out.

Some of us worked in the Maths storeroom during our free periods, but there was only room for one person to spread out all his work on the table; and there tended to be constant interruptions: the phone went, or somebody knocked at the door. However, it did have the advantage of being handy if we were displaced from our classrooms. It was also a place where you could smoke; indeed, it always seemed to be wreathed in smoke.

It was one of the many inadequacies of the school that a big and important department like Maths had such an unsuitable base: it didn't contain a photocopier, or a computer, or even a typewriter. For this and other reasons, working conditions were very difficult: so we did a great deal of work at home, e.g. setting and marking exam papers, preparing lessons, and writing reports. Teaching is the kind of job that seems to take over your whole life; but that has always been the case, and probably always will be.

55

1986

A plague o' both your houses.

Shakespeare, *Romeo and Juliet*

The series of one-day strikes continued, as the EIS campaign for an independent review of teachers' salaries entered its third year. In an effort to break the deadlock, various proposals were broached by the EIS, the Secretary of State for Scotland, a coalition of the Church of Scotland and the Roman Catholic Church, and the Scottish Joint Negotiating Committee on Salaries; however, none of the proposals was acceptable to both the EIS and the Scottish Secretary. On one occasion, Raymond Robertson, the prospective Conservative candidate for the parliamentary constituency of Clydesdale, blamed the EIS for blocking a possible solution to the dispute; Drew Morrice, President of the Lanarkshire Association of the EIS, responded with the assertion that it was 'a distortion of reality' to blame the union. That was the intellectual level of the debate.

Here we go, here we go, here we go...

Some local parents, meanwhile, were beginning to express strong reservations about the EIS's tactics: in a letter published in the *Wishaw Press*, one parent complained about 'the disruption of children's education', and suggested that teachers were 'marching along the Scargillesque route' (i.e. 'taking to the streets, carrying placards, picketing and, above all, being stubborn') to what they 'obviously supposed would be victory over the government'. Such outbursts were worrying (if teachers were going to bring their salaries campaign to a successful conclusion, it was absolutely essential that they didn't lose the support of parents - or of the general public, for that matter), and later in the year a public meeting was held in Hamilton, at which Jim Martin, Assistant Secretary of the EIS, explained why the union was urging its members to reject the latest offer (based on the Main Report) from the Secretary of State for Scotland.

Two final points on union activity at the High School: in February 1986, EIS members refused to cross a picket line set up by local janitors at the front gate; and in 1992 those 'same' members received a letter from the Secretary of the Lanarkshire Association of the EIS thanking them for their support over the years. 'During the campaign of 1984-87,' the letter continued, 'yours was known as a strong EIS school, and I am sure this goes back many years before that.'

Potest quia posse videtur.

Virgil, *Aeneid (adapted)*

Calum Currie, a former pupil of the High School, graduated BEd (with 1st Class Honours) at the Scottish School of Physical Education at Jordanhill College. Since he was also awarded the Hugh C. Brown Memorial Prize for excellence in teaching, this was the first time in the history of the Scottish School of Physical Education that the said prize and a 1st Class Honours degree had been gained by the same student. When he was a pupil at the High School, Currie played football for the school at various age levels. He was a fast, aggressive centre forward, and he gained several representative honours: if my memory serves me correctly, he played for the Scottish under-15 team against England at Wembley.

The Axeman Cometh

It was revealed in the *Wishaw Press* that a special subcommittee had been set up by Strathclyde Region to look into the 'dramatic' fall in the rolls of certain primary and secondary schools in Lanark Division; and that there was 'considerable speculation' about the long-term future of the High School. However, Regional Councillor James Gibson, a member of the subcommittee, made it clear that he was totally opposed to the closure of the High School; and Regional Councillor James Fyfe was equally forthright:
We have too many schools in the region for too few children, and some rationalisation will have to take place. But there are areas in which the figures are far worse than they are in Wishaw (where there are 2,436 places and 2,326 pupils), and for that reason I don't believe any of our

465

high schools will have to close. We also have the benefit of having a voice on the committee.

According to Provost John McGhee, the District Council and the Labour Party were prepared to 'fight all the way' to avert any closures. 'The present speculation - and it is no more than speculation - cannot be allowed to continue,' he said, 'since it will have an adverse effect on both the teachers and the children at the schools in question.'

The Judo Kid

Bernadette Christie was selected to represent Great Britain at the World Schools' Judo Championships in Israel; earlier in her career, she won the Lanarkshire under-16 Championship, the Scottish under-16 and under-18 Championships, the British National under-16 Championship, and a team gold at the British YMCA Championships. In 1989 her sister, Helen, won the Scottish Championship and was runner-up in the British Championship.

'Hop On', a robot used by the Central Scottish Bus Company to promote its new range of cheap season tickets, visited the High School.

4th and 6th Year pupils took part in various projects to raise enough money for the residents of Stewarton House to purchase a radio cassette recorder and a television table.

Another group of 4th Year pupils spent the winter months working on a project on local newspapers. The pupils visited the local offices (in Kirk Road) of the *Wishaw Press*, toured the printing works in Hamilton where the paper is produced, and then embarked on a survey of local readers.

56

A Year in the Life of Wishaw High School

Report Forms

Let's have some new clichés.

Sam Goldwyn

It was always a great boon to receive the old-style report forms (which contained a pupil's grades - and comments on his performance - in every subject on his timetable) after they had been completed by several other departments: if you were faced with a series of comments like 'Rarely present', 'Who?', and 'Absolute tosser', you could safely scribble something similar and move on quickly to the next report form. Unfortunately, you had to work 'blind' with the new-style report forms, since they were made up of separate sheets for each subject.

An Aptitude for Platitude

As far as the obligatory comments were concerned, most teachers contented themselves with a single - and invariably meaningless - platitude (like 'Working reasonably well') per pupil; the members of the History Department, however, were blessed with the ability to combine two, or even three, platitudes in the one comment, e.g. 'Reginald is working reasonably well after a somewhat indifferent start, and a modicum of success is a possibility.'

Sam Graham, a member of the Modern Studies Department, included the words 'worker' and 'working' in most of his comments, but he occasionally wrote them in such a way (I don't know whether or not it was deliberate) that the letters 'or' looked like 'an': so comments like 'A real worker' and 'Working enthusiastically' must have raised a few.....eyebrows.

It was also Sam Graham who, having described one of his pupils as 'an apathetic performer', was later accosted by an irate parent and asked: "Whit dae ye mean by callin' ma boy pathetic?"

I myself gave up trying to eschew clichéd comments after being reprimanded for describing a Chinese boy as 'not velly good at Latin'.

'Do you spell it with a 'V' or a 'W'?' inquired the judge. 'That depends upon the taste and fancy of the speller, my Lord,' replied Sam Weller.

Charles Dickens, *Pickwick Papers*

The spelling of certain pupils' names could vary disconcertingly in the report forms submitted by different departments: in December 1988, for example, Jimmy Clelland pointed out (in the *Bulletin*) that Matthew McCreaddie of S3 'did not have a matching pair out of six reports'.

Comic Relief Day

An immense variety of schemes has now been hatched to take money from the unwary. Sponsored events include typing and eating cold baked beans. There are competitions to match photographs of certain teachers' children with their parents and pick the member of staff with the most hideous tie. A 'Spot the Difference' contest for staff should raise a few laughs, as should the paper clowns from Mrs Mauchline's room; and Mrs Cowie's class will be selling 'Fun Day' biscuits at the interval. All in all, it now has the makings of a 'fun day' for everyone - and we will be doing a bit of good as well. (Staff Information Bulletin No 19, March 1989)

Work Experience

Temps

For five days, in February 1992, seventy-nine 4th Year pupils 'ventured beyond the school walls into the adult world of work', temporary situations having been found for them in shops, offices, factories, banks, garages, hospitals, playgrounds, vets' surgeries, primary schools, Wishaw Baths, and Strathclyde Park. In line with Strathclyde Region's policy on Equal Opportunities, one girl entered 'the male-dominated preserve of engineering' at Motherwell Bridge Construction Ltd.; while one of the boys 'excelled in the traditionally female vocation of supervising young children' - at Berryhill Nursery School.

The pupils kept diaries, from which the following extracts are taken:

I watched Mary do some operations on cats and dogs. (Lynn Scott - Newmains Veterinary Centre).

Today I made 41 pairs of knickers. (Carol Williamson - Meridian).

I read some stories to a group of children, and in the afternoon I cleaned the storeroom. (Marilyn Brownlie - Fir Park School).

Today I helped Geoff load and unload parcels on the Inter-City trains. (Lee Jenkins - Motherwell Station).

The Gala

Not Waving But Clowning

On one occasion, George Randall went away (home, if he had any sense) with the keys for the dressing rooms, and the competitors were thus denied access to their clothes. That was the most exciting incident in the history of the gala; the most tedious, plucked from a cornucopia of soporific memories after much deliberation, was a diving display by the Aquagoons that went on for an aeon, boring most of the audience to death and - since the individual divers were dressed in women's clothes - offending the sensibilities of some of the more po-faced matrons on the staff.

The Easter Concert

The Junior Choir (more than a hundred strong, some years) normally took centre stage at this concert. In 1982 it presented *Creation Jazz* and extracts from *Cats*; in 1983, a concert version of the musical *Annie*; and in 1990, songs from *Jerusalem Joy*.

Caldercruix

Everyone who has thought about the success of Wiston has wondered at some time or other, 'Why does it stop at 1st Year? Shouldn't there be a follow-up of some kind?' We may get at least a partial answer to these questions next week, when a party of twenty-six 2nd Year pupils goes to Caldercruix Outdoor Centre for a comprehensive programme of outdoor activities (hillwalking, rock climbing, abseiling, canoeing, orienteering, gorge walking, and dry slope skiing), under the supervision of the instructors permanently based at the centre. If it succeeds, as we hope it will, it may point the way to how we can build on 'the Wiston experience'.

Four members of staff - Ann Dalton, Lynn Roberts, Clark Govan, and George Randall - will accompany the pupils. (*Bulletin*, April 1984)

In 1990 this initiative was developed in such a way as to cater for 3rd and 4th Year pupils.

Fire Drills

Women and Classics Teachers First

Fire drills should have been held at regular intervals, but during Sam's rectorship they were as infrequent as sightings of Halley's Comet in the night sky. Eventually, one was held in June 1988:

We've done it at last. Wishaw High School's long-overdue fire drill took place on Wednesday and was highly successful: not only did we evacuate the buildings speedily and in an orderly fashion, but we also managed to get back into the school quickly enough to gain an early (by ten minutes) stop. Shh...not a word about this.

Clear winners in the speed stakes were Mr Wright and the staff of the main building in the annexe, who evacuated it in 2 minutes 35 seconds flat (a new High School record), and I am pleased to state that there is no truth in the rumour that they had the classes lined up behind the doors from 2.45 onwards.

To Mrs Buchanan and her class in Room 19 we unhesitatingly award the CDM for conduct above and beyond: they worked on steadily throughout the 'conflagration' and were deemed 'lost' by the course steward, Mr Johnstone.

Seriously though, we did identify two serious faults in the warning system, and matters are in hand to have these rectified as soon as possible. We also require painted room numbers in the muster area - if these can be acquired. (*Bulletin*, June 1988)

The Visit of the New Intake

Lasciate Ogni Speranza Voi Ch' Entrate.

Dante, *Divina Commedia*

Up till 1987, these half-day visits were almost entirely taken up by a tour of the school under the supervision of senior pupils. From 1988 onwards, the visits were extended to three days, and in addition to a guided tour arranged by the Guidance (sic) staff, a special timetable was devised to enable the Primary 7 pupils (accompanied by their regular teacher) to sample all the subjects that feature in the curriculum of a secondary school.

The Day of the Jackasses

Visits to the school by primary pupils were not a good idea. Within half an hour, the initiates had become attuned to the relaxed atmosphere that permeated the High School during the final weeks of the summer term; and by the end of the afternoon, they were running around like Millwall supporters on speed.

The Sports

'How's your young hopeful been doing, Lady Circumference?'
'My boy has been injured in the foot,' said Lady Circumference coldly.
'Dear me. Not badly, I hope. Did he twist his ankle in the jumping?'
'No,' said Lady Circumference, 'he was shot by one of the assistant masters. But it is kind of you to inquire.'

Evelyn Waugh, *Decline and Fall*

In my capacity as starter, I never actually managed to shoot any of the pupils (my eyesight has never been particularly good), but on one occasion I did get a lot of black looks from the judges for starting a 200 metres race while the preceding one was still in progress.

Maxwell's Law:
The success of the sports is in inverse proportion to their duration.

After the final event, the competitors and spectators (if there were any) disappeared with record-breaking speed, leaving Tom Young and Clark Govan to collect all the paraphernalia of their latest fiasco - sacks, batons, hurdles and the tatty, bug-infested recorder's tent - and hump it back down to the main building.

Her face, at first...just ghostly
Turned a whiter shade of pale.

The song I will always associate with the sports is 'A Whiter Shade of Pale'. Every year, from the late 1960s onwards, it was one of the first records to be played over the PA system prior to the opening events.

The Prize-Giving

To see him fumbling with our rich and delicate language is to experience all the horror of seeing a Sèvres vase in the hands of a chimpanzee.

Evelyn Waugh

More bromides were dispensed at the prize-giving than at all the branches of Boots the Chemists: so it was a great pity that these ceased to be offset, from the mid-1960s onwards, by the entertainment provided by the presence (as chairman for the evening) of the School Convener, usually a local councillor with a feeble grasp of English grammar and the coherence of John Prescott. The first time I heard Eddie Lawson in full rhetorical flow, I laughed so much that before I left the church I mouthed a silent prayer of thanks to the manufacturers of Pampers: he introduced the guest speaker, Professor Walker Chambers, as Professor Chambers Walker, and referred several times to the men who had 'predeceased' him as School Convener.

Hallowe'en Party (Disco from 1990 onwards)

Anyone looking for a cure for an in-service hangover on Tuesday could have found it in the school hall that same evening, when 1st Year pupils made the rafters ring at their Hallowe'en Party. 6th Year pupils took charge and did an excellent job, not least by turning up in an array of very colourful costumes; in fact, Clelland Sneddon (as Andy Pandy) and Lynn Cowan (as Boy George) won special awards. The conventional prizes for fancy dress went to:
Prettiest - Heather Sharples, who might have stepped daintily straight out of Camelot
Funniest - Gail Little as a very scruffy, Krankie-type schoolboy
Ugliest - Lorraine McLoy as a hideous-looking witch
Most Original - Nancy McArthur as a can of Barr's Irn Bru
(*Bulletin*, November 1983).

472

The Inter-House Quiz

The first Inter-House Quiz was held in the small hall of the annexe, with John Ralston as quizmaster. In the early rounds of the quiz, Big John was at his most genial and avuncular: correct answers were accorded a 'Yes indeed', and wrong ones a sympathetic "No, I'm afraid not". As the afternoon dragged on, however, and the audience became increasingly restive, Big John's good humour began to wear a bit thin; and eventually, in the round devoted to proverbs, he exploded after the following incident:

'What should you do with sleeping dogs?', he asked one of the contestants.

'Give them a kick up the jacksy,' shouted one of the punters from the back of the hall.

In 1981 (by which time the school hall had become the regular venue for the quiz, and Uncle John had been given the chop as quizmaster) Sam made the following - rather snide - comments about the quiz:

It was a very enjoyable, if somewhat lengthy, evening, and the Guidance staff are to be congratulated on a first-rate piece of organisation which saw a bewildering array of gadgetry assembled - and working - for the occasion. (Bulletin, November 1981)

Parents' Evenings

The Unspeakable in Full Pursuit of the Uninterested

Parents' Evenings were normally held in the hall and classrooms of the main building - and as far as some teachers were concerned, they were no picnic: in December 1982, the janitor abruptly terminated the last interviews of two teachers by switching off the lights; and in April 1988, 'the Endurance Award for Guidance was presented to Liz Clarke, who sustained the interest of parents till 10.30.'

I myself, being a 'teacher' of Classics, was never overwhelmed by large numbers of parents, and some of those who did consult me seemed to have a rather hazy grasp of what sort of subject Classics actually was: I remember being asked by one woman if I taught the classical guitar.

Sheila Sprot was also less than enthusiastic about Parents' Evenings:

When I was a pupil at the High School in the 1940s, the last thing we pupils wanted was to have our parents visiting the school; it was always our aim to keep these two areas, school and home, as far apart as possible (I don't know why). I often thought about this as I sat in a cold classroom, in artificial light, usually on the snowiest night of the year, trying to be polite as one anxious parent after another trotted in; and I rejoiced that in my time as a pupil any discussion about your report took place in the privacy of your own home.

In 1990, by which year the turnouts were becoming increasingly meagre (in June 1988, for example, only twelve parents turned up for a 1st Year Parents' Evening), Iain Murray decided to hold Parents' Evenings in the annexe. The first two at that venue took place between 4 and 6 p.m.

The Old Folks' Christmas Lunch

The Old Folks' Lunch on Wednesday was a great success; in fact, it was probably the best we have ever had. There was a marvellous atmosphere in the hall, and the 6th Year are to be congratulated on a first-rate piece of organisation that managed to combine good humour, gentleness, and compassion. The pupils themselves wish to thank Miss Hodgson, Miss Pearson, and Mrs Costley, without whose helpful guidance the event would not have been possible; the PE Department for their patience and understanding; the Art Department for the decorations in the hall and on the tables; the Home Economics Department for the meal; all the teachers who helped to transport the guests to and from the school; and the 4th and 5th Year girls who acted as couriers and helped out in the kitchen. (Bulletin, December 1981)

Over the years, the 6th Year raised money for the Old Folks' Christmas Lunch in a variety of ways. These included a twelve-hour 'Sports Marathon' (1985), a sponsored 'Stay Awake' (1989), and a 'Cyclethon' in 1990, during which pupils pedalled for five hours on an exercise bike outside Scotmid's new store in the Main Street.

Some of the old folk attended several different Christmas lunches every year; and in 1983, as one old lady was ushered out of the hall, she was heard to remark to her companion: "The St Aidan's wan wis better."

The Christmas Dances

Music is drifting out of the gym as Mr Young and his staff initiate 1st and 2nd Year pupils into the mysteries of 'social dancing'. Yet another generation of High School pupils are mastering the intricacies of the Gay Gordons, the Military Two Step, the Dashing White Sergeant, and the

474

good old St Bernard's Waltz in preparation for their dances. (*Wishaw Press*, December 1991)

Over the years, the number of Christmas dances decreased from four or five to two - a dance for 1st, 2nd and 3rd Year pupils and a senior disco - in 1991.

The final dance in the history of the High School (in December 1991) was described as follows in the *Wishaw Press*:

If I were to say that the hall was more like the studio of 'The Clothes Show', you will get the general idea. Dancing was a mixture of the traditional and anything else. Staff and pupils had the opportunity to meet each other in an informal setting.

Here are some comments from 1st Year pupils:
'I liked being kissed by the girls under the mistletoe.'
'I was dead shy dancing with the teachers.'
'The country dancing was a good laugh.'
'The disco was the best bit.'

The Carol Concert

Many people regarded the Carol Concert as the jewel in the crown of the school year. Sam had this to say about it in 1981:

The Carol Concert in Wishaw Old Parish Church on Wednesday night surpassed the high standards already established for this event, and regulars are unanimous in the view that this year's concert was the best yet. More pupils seem to take part every year, and the range of musical talents is ever-widening. The whole complex operation is orchestrated by Mrs Banks with inspirational efficiency and, this year, with an air of relaxed self- confidence that seemed to transmit itself to both the performers and the audience. The church was packed, and a feature of the evening was the number of former pupils who attended. Tea was provided afterwards in the annexe, where the Art Department had mounted an impressive exhibition of pupils' work; and the atmosphere there was warm, friendly, festive, and celebratory - as well as taking on the characteristics of a very happy reunion.

The mainstays of the Carol Concert were the Concert Band and the Junior and Senior Choirs. In the 1990s, guest appearances were made by choirs from the High School's feeder primaries.

57

1987

Winged Words

A team from the High School, comprising Pamela Clarke and Aonghas Morrison, won the public speaking competition sponsored by Motherwell District Home Safety Committee; according to the judges, 'the youngsters injected a great deal of humour into their ten-minute spot, and their content and delivery were excellent'. The same team was victorious in 1988.

Westminster-orientated Words

A Mock Election was arranged by the Modern Studies Department, as part of a project ('Newsround Extra Election') organised by John Craven under the auspices of the BBC. One school in each of the 650 parliamentary constituencies (the High School represented Motherwell South) sent the result of its poll to the BBC.

Weasel Words

In line with one of the recommendations of a report it had commissioned on 'Adapting to Change', Strathclyde Region decided to set up Local Review Groups (composed of parents, teachers, non-teaching staff, and local regional councillors; and chaired by a regional councillor from outwith the area under review), 'to examine the whole range of educational provision' in forty-seven different districts throughout Strathclyde.

Council officials 'vehemently' rejected suggestions that the sole object of the exercise was to make cuts, and a spokesman was quoted as saying: 'We are not in the business of closing or merging schools simply to make financial savings.' For his part, Regional Councillor James Gibson claimed that the review would provide 'a wonderful opportunity to enrich the standard of education'. Once again, the vultures were circling round the High School.

Music Makers

During the summer holidays, the Concert Band toured Picardy; in the course of this tour, they visited a cemetery near Amiens in which the members of a Scottish military band are buried. To raise money to finance the tour, the band took part in three concerts - one at the Civic Centre with the CWS (Glasgow) Band, one at Garrion Academy with an American swing band, and one (the annual summer concert) at the High School.

Literary Liaison

The English Department joined forces with P7 at Newmains Primary School to work on a project based on the novel *Ash Road*. The outcome was 'a remarkable variety of art and craft work, as well as a comprehensive display and video of the entire project'.

58

'Ex Africa semper aliquid novi'

The Bulletin

All the news that's fit to print.

Adolph S. Ochs

The *Bulletin* was one of Sam's more successful innovations. From 1980 till 1984, it was published every Thursday afternoon, and most members of staff collected it from their pigeonholes the following morning; it was discontinued during 'The Troubles' (as the salaries campaign and its attendant strikes, walkouts, etc. came to be known), but reappeared in April 1988 as the *Staff Bulletin*.

The *Bulletin/Staff Bulletin* was basically 'a means of keeping staff informed about what was going on in the school'. It contained official announcements about the latest developments at divisional, regional, and national level; information from such external agencies as the Scottish Examination Board; staff news of all kinds; news of forthcoming events in the life of the school, and reports on those that had already taken place; news of pupils who had distinguished themselves in some way; appeals (e.g. for catalogues that could be used in the Business Studies Department); and news of the EIS.

You've got to ac-cent-tchu-ate the positive
Elim-my-nate the negative....

Johnny Mercer

The tone of the *Bulletin/Staff Bulletin* was consistently upbeat and laudatory to the nth degree. New members of staff, for instance, were invariably invested with heroic qualities:

Miss Ann Dalton showed remarkable resilience and good humour in coping with the transition from Corfu to Wishaw High School in less than 24 hours. (23.10.81)

Miss Mary McDougall, the new Principal Teacher of Business Studies, will take up her appointment on Monday. She has already spent a day with us, and promises to get into top gear straight away. (9.3.84)

De mortuis - et emeritis - nil nisi bunkum.

Harold Laski (adapted)

If their faces fitted, teachers who retired or were promoted could instantly achieve the status of a demigod/demigoddess:
She has shown herself to be a talented and enthusiastic teacher of English; intensely caring towards all the pupils in her charge, she has demonstrated that all-too-rare ability to bring out the best in even the worst of them. With the loss of such a teacher, I am concerned that Wishaw High School is slowly bleeding to death. (24.6.88)

Of course, if you died, you were canonised on the spot - not by papal bull, but by pap and bullshit.

Along the electric wire the message came:
He is not better - he is much the same.

Alfred Austin (attributed)

From a medical standpoint, the title of the *Bulletin/Staff Bulletin* was an accurate description of a substantial part of its contents:
Mr McQueen's back seized up on him on the last day of the Spring Term, and he has not been able to return after the holidays. (27.4.84)
Miss Girdwood is on a strictly controlled low calorie diet, and the problem is how to build up her strength. (17.12.82)
Mr Morrice has been absent all week with what is officially described as a 'juicy' sprain of the ankle. (26.2.82)
It was nice to see Mr Nicol back on Monday. He is looking well, and he has found the first week back less of a trial than he had expected after such a long lay [sic]-off. (13.1.84)

> **Reality goes bounding past the satirist like a cheetah laughing as it lopes ahead of the greyhound.**
>
> Claud Cockburn, *Crossing the Line*

Occasionally, items appeared that were, unintentionally, evocative of *M*A*S*H*, or *Catch-22*, or *Decline and Fall*:

The Good News...

A new Banda spirit duplicator has been delivered and is now operational in Room 26.

...and the Bad

Someone has borrowed the instruction booklet for the said Banda. Please return it to Mrs Leith. (6.3.81)

Lost and Found

The instruction booklet for the new Banda has been found - but not as a result of last week's plea in the Bulletin. No one had borrowed it; it had merely been caught up in the fold of its plastic cover. (13.3.81)

I can just imagine Radar announcing these three items of information over the PA system.

Silly Season

The spell of hot weather leads inevitably to pupils arriving in school after the lunch interval soaked to the skin, after falling or being pushed into the paddling pool in Belhaven Park. Clothes that have been soaked in this way will not, repeat not, be dried in the tumble-dryer in the Home Economics Department. (4.6.82)

This could be a directive from General P.P. Peckem.

Absence Cover

Miss Catriona MacPhee arrived on Monday to provide cover during Mr Anderson's absence from the Technical Department. She is qualified to teach Spanish, but she has undertaken the task of supervising Technical classes with such efficiency that Mr Baird is completely bowled over. (23.3.84)

Miss Catriona MacPhee, who substituted for Mr Anderson - and then for Mrs Banks (handling the Music classes with the same aplomb she had shown in the Technical Department) - left on Wednesday afternoon. She is due to start in the Chemistry Department at Larkhall Academy on Monday. (30.3.84)

These two paragraphs would not be out of place in a conversation between Paul Pennyfeather and either Dr Fagan or Mr Levy of Church and Gargoyle, Scholastic Agents.

In one or two items, if we give Sam the benefit of the doubt, there may even have been a soupçon of intentional irony:

The demonstration-recital by Mrs Lesley Walker that was to have taken place at lunchtime today has had to be postponed until after Christmas because of a family illness. The delay should give us time to adjust to the idea that Mrs Walker is a bassoonist - not a flautist, as was stated in last week's Bulletin. (11.11.84)

Pass the sick-bag, Alice.

The *Bulletin/Staff Bulletin* also contained a lot of tosh. Some of it was schmaltzy tosh:

Our feelings for Mr Young and the PE staff were a mixture of sympathy that they had had such rotten luck and admiration for the resolute way in which they struggled to overcome the difficulties. (3.6.83)

Some of it was portentous tosh:

All news in this or any other Bulletin pales into insignificance by comparison with Mr Stirling's promotion to the post of Rector of Lesmahagow High School. No one is more deserving of success than Mr Stirling, and the delight of all members of staff at the news is equalled only by their dismay at the thought of life at Wishaw High School without him. Everyone will want to offer personal congratulations and good wishes, and to reflect privately and soberly on the implications of his departure. (25.6.82)

...nil posse creari de nilo.

Lucretius, *De Rerum Natura*

One final extract - from the *Bulletin* published on 2 February 1981 - is worthy of note:
There was no issue of the Bulletin last Friday because there was no news.

Le style est l'homme même.

Compte de Buffon

Surprisingly, in view of the genre to which it belonged, the *Bulletin/Staff Bulletin* was written (by Sam and, latterly, Jimmy Clelland) in a fairly literary style, and although its tone was a bit too cloying for my taste, I always regarded it as compulsive reading.

The same could not be said about its successor, the *Staff Information Bulletin*, the first issue of which appeared during session 1988-89 (I have been unable to ascertain the exact date). The difference in style and content between the *Bulletin/Staff Bulletin* and the *Staff Information Bulletin* was as dramatic as that between *Nostromo* and the owner's manual for a Nissan Micra, as the following extracts demonstrate:
The Scottish Joint Negotiating Committee for Teaching Staff recently revised the car allowance payable to teachers in day schools under the provisions of Appendix 4 of the Conditions of Service, and the mileage rates applicable from 1 January 1989 in the case of teachers using their cars on official business (for example, travelling between a school's main building and a distant annexe, attending meetings called by the Director of Education or the Divisional Education Officer, and attending meetings of curricular development committees or working parties whose members are nominated by the Divisional Education Officer etc.) are detailed below... (Staff Information Bulletin No 23, April 1989)

FIFA - any teacher interested in taking part in a competition for this event should see me as soon as possible.

Caldercruix Outdoor Pursuits Centre - should now be addressed as Caldercruix Outdoor Education Centre.

Job Sheet - can be found in the Main Staffroom.

Advertisement - for a Project Manager has been placed in each staffroom.

HASAW - Standard Circular No 33 (Revised): Amendment to Safety in Outdoor Pursuits /Education. Certain pages have been revised in the above Code of Practice.

Multiblocks - Any departments ordering multiblocks from their per capita allowance are asked to contact Mrs Leith and/or Mr Woods (AV Technician) so that a bulk order may be placed. (Staff Information Bulletin No 26, May 1989)

Teetering as they did on the edge of incoherence, many of the *Staff Information Bulletins* read like the English version of the emergency fire regulations in a 2-star hotel on the Costa Blanca:

Tea will be provided at the end of the ceremony, to allow everyone the chance to mingle. (25.6.92)

Would all register teachers please remind their pupils that they are not allowed above ground level in the main building during the intervals or at lunch time. (14.4.89)

Pupils, it seems, should neither be heard nor seen.

The Staff Forum

There was a meeting of this brainchild of Ronnie Hamilton's on 18 January 1983. Having finalised its constitution and discussed 'discipline in the corridors' at this meeting, the Staff Forum did not meet again until the beginning of March, when a president and secretary were appointed. Nine years later, the staff were still waiting for the third meeting of the forum.

The Conference for Christmas Leavers

In December 1983, short talks were given by the works manager of a local firm (who spoke about the process of applying for a job from an employer's point of view), a panel of former pupils with recent experience of both having a job and being unemployed, two trade unionists from USDAW, and the Careers Officer. Refreshments were provided by the Home Economics Department, and Ruth Hodgson orchestrated the whole shooting match.

Scottish World Citizens Award Scheme

In May 1984, Lorna-Jane Currie and Jacqueline McNeilly, who had previously been awarded certificates at Foundation and Intermediate level, gained the Gold Award. The High School thus became the first school in Scotland to present candidates successfully at all three levels of the scheme, which was financed by the United Nations Association.

Strathclyde Park

During session 1983-84, all the 1st Year Geography classes visited the park as part of a project they were doing on Motherwell and Wishaw District. They were taken on a guided walk by the Park Rangers, and then spent some time in the Visitors' Centre examining the various flora and fauna that are found in the park.

Wishaw High School: This Week

Dans ce meilleur des mondes possibles... tout est au mieux.

Voltaire, *Candide*

The High School was the first school in Lanark Division to provide material for a weekly column in the local paper. The first of these columns appeared in the *Wishaw Press* on 9 June 1989 and began as follows:

Welcome to 'Wishaw High School: This Week', a new column put together by the following pupils: Raymond Connor, Claire Dunlay, Shalani Raghavan, Richard Wolseley, Eleanor Cowan, Pamela Clarke, Aonghas Morrison, and Alistair Colthart. We hope you'll become regular readers.

Janey Mauchline (initially) and Pat McGowan (latterly) supervised the newshounds and edited their copy.

The High School thus started a trend that spread, regrettably, like chlamydia in a cathouse - with the result that all local newspapers are now full of paeans in honour of dynamic teachers, odes to highly motivated and superbly behaved pupils (all of them in school uniform), and encomia for football teams that 'never' lose - for the simple reason that their defeats are never reported. Every week, the *Wishaw Press* contains reports from Clyde Valley High School, Dalziel High School, Coltness High School, Braidhurst High School, Our Lady's High School, Carluke High School, and St Aidan's High School, where everybody from the head teacher to the janitor's cat seems to have been invested with a quasi-papal infallibility; and this conglomeration of relentlessly upbeat material is now proving to be almost as effective in combating insomnia as the pages of photographs marking the opening of every bowling club in North Lanarkshire. Somebody at the High School has a lot to answer for.

High Times

The High School's own newspaper was first published in 1989. The four members of staff responsible for getting this project off the ground were Liz Clarke, Janey Mauchline, John Wright, and Ian Shedden; but by 1992 Liz Clarke, aided by her husband's desktop publishing skills, had shouldered the burden of editing and publishing *High Times*.

The format and design of *High Times* were very attractive, and in three successive years (1990, 1991, and 1992) it gained a Certificate of Merit in the Schools' Newspaper Competition organised by the *Daily Telegraph*.

Issue Number 6, published in February 1991, contained the following: News Items re Wiston, the School Board, various members of staff (Anne Donnelly had broken her wrist), the Parents' Association, the Carol Concert, the Christmas Dances, and the Inter-House and Inter-Primary School Quizzes; Head Teacher's Comments; Gossip ('Does GM love DG?'; 'Which female teacher travelled for over 100 miles while searching for Stirling University?'); letters to, and replies from, an Agony Aunt; Fun and Games; Sport; and poems, such as the following, by pupils from the High School and its feeder primaries:

> W inter is come and it is cold.
> I t makes my fingers numb.
> N ow it is snowing.
> T he sky is grey.
> E veryone is cold.
> R obins fly away.

Elaine Warnock (Lammermoor Primary School)

One or two very striking poems appeared in later issues of *High Times*:

Hi Mummy

Hi mummy, it's me.
Is that your name?
It's my name for you anyway.
I love you, mummy.
You're my best friend.
I'm glad that you're the one who protects me.
I can't wait until I'm born – so that I can see your face,
When you hold me in your warm embrace.
I can't wait to see the trees and the grass.
Where are you going today, mummy?
The shops? The park?
Yes, it must be the park.
I love the park.
Although I can't see it yet, I can feel it's there, just like you.
I have feelings too.
Wait!
We're not going to the park.
The shops?
Are you going to buy me new clothes, mummy?
I'll need to snuggle deep inside them, when I'm born,
So they keep me warm.
We're on the bus now: I can hear it with my tiny ears.
We've stopped.
Where are we going now?
It's not the shops either.
Where do these big white doors lead?
I'm scared, mummy.
Can we go home?
Mummy, why are you lying down?
Mummy! A needle!
Stop them, mummy! Stop them!
It's coming closer, it's touching me.
Oh mummy, the pain is shooting through me,
Tearing me apart.
It's shooting through my arms, my legs,
486

It's shooting through my heart.
Help me, mummy, please!
I don't want to die.
I want to see the trees and the grass,
I want to feel the wind in my face,
I want to walk and race with the new friends that I'd make,
I want to taste and touch —
I want to do a lot of things out there.
Why, mummy? Why?
Why are you killing me?
I love you, mummy,
I really do.
I wanted you to love me too.
Why couldn't you let me be?
Why, mummy?
Why me?

Angela Fleming (S4)

Halfway House

Pupils readmitted to the school after a period of suspension did not follow their normal timetable *in toto*: for as long as was deemed necessary, they spent some time every day in Halfway House, a special unit set up during session 1989-90 in response to the 'Young People in Trouble' report. Jimmy Pringle was in charge of the unit.

'Keep on Colour'

Session 1989-90 also witnessed the implementation of 'Keep on Colour', a system whose provenance could be traced to Braidfield High School, where Iain Murray had been Depute Rector. The behaviour of every pupil in 1st and 2nd Year was monitored period by period, and the results of this process were recorded on a chart in each class's registration room: a broad band of colour opposite a pupil's name signified consistently good behaviour; a distinct lack of colour indicated that the pupil in question had been guilty of various misdemeanours. Time was spent at Guidance periods on a review of each pupil's performance during the preceding week, and those pupils who had failed to 'keep on colour' were helped to understand the reasons for this and encouraged to improve matters; parental help could also be enlisted by the school. At the end of each term, pupils who had no blank spots on their escutcheon received a letter, or a certificate, of commendation.

In session 1990-91, as the following report in the *Wishaw Press* indicates, the system seems to have been refined:

'Keep on Colour' has started again. This is a points system which monitors pupils' behaviour in class. At the beginning of the week, every pupil in S1 and S2 has 25 points. If you do particularly well, the teacher can award you a bonus point; however, if your behaviour is poor for any reason, points are deducted, e.g. one point for late coming. The system has had a positive effect, and we are sure that things will continue to improve.

The Games People Play

In March 1991, the Parents' Association and several members of staff helped to pilot a new game called 'Dialog'; devised in Denmark, it was being tested in the High School with a view to its being used eventually by parents and teachers in secondary schools throughout Scotland.

Shot at Jobs Day

In June 1991, in the annexe, members of the Careers Service and representatives from various colleges and such firms as Daiwa, Meridian, Safeway, Anne Rodger and William Low offered 3rd Year pupils 'hands on' experience in a wide range of occupations and skills (these included welding, plumbing, painting, bricklaying, and hairdressing); pupils were also given a chance to undergo a mock interview with some of the employers in attendance. A bonus for many of the pupils was that they were able to take home with them the end products (e.g. bookshelves and ironwork) of their efforts.

New Image Rugby

In June 1991, Iain Murray sent the following letter to the parents of P6 and P7 pupils in the High School's feeder primaries:

Dear Parents,

488

I am delighted to invite you to come along and watch the exciting new game to which P6 and 7 pupils at Wishaw Academy, Newmains Primary, and Berryhill Primary are being introduced. The game is called 'New Image Rugby', and has just been imported into this country from New Zealand. It is played in mixed teams by both boys and girls; no tackling is allowed, and the game concentrates on teamwork and passing skills. Wishaw High School is one of the first schools in Scotland to be involved in introducing this new game to pupils from its catchment area.

The programme is as follows:

9.30 - 12.30 - Primary 6 Competition
1.00 - 3.00 - Primary 7 Competition

The two competitions, which are sponsored by Digital, will be supervised by the PE Department at Wishaw High School. Mr Clark Govan, a member of that department, and a representative of the Scottish Rugby Union have been involved in coaching pupils on a regular basis at the three primary schools in question.

Wishaw High School will be awarding a cup to the winners of the Primary 7 Competition.

Up to 250 pupils from the three primary schools will be taking part, and the school canteen will be open all day to provide snacks and drinks for all those in attendance.

This will be an exciting new example of the close links that exist between Wishaw High School and its feeder primaries, and also of the adaptability of teachers in pioneering new activities. It is especially important in this age of equal opportunity that we expand the range of sports that are suitable for both sexes.

Do come along and support your child - and see the birth of a new game. It is hoped that Roy Laidlaw, a former member of the Scottish rugby team, will be present to open the event and present the prizes. This will be a fun day. Do come along and support it.
Yours faithfully,
Iain Murray

The New Image Rugby Tournament described above was featured in the *Daily Record* and the *Evening Times* - and also on the front page of the *Glasgow Herald*.

New Image Hockey

In session 1991-92, the High School fielded an S1/S2 mixed hockey team and, for the first time in its history, a boys' hockey team. The latter team's first game was against Dalziel High School on the astroturf pitch in Houldsworth Park - under floodlights.

Season's Greetings

In December 1991 (and this was another first), the school produced a Christmas card. It was designed by Ian White of SI and went on sale for 30p.

Support your local...teacher

In February 1992, a Schools' Support Project involving the Education and Social Works Departments of Strathclyde Region was based in the High School. Its main aim was to improve the attendance records of persistent truants by offering them, and their parents, support (sic).

59

1988

Quidquid delirant reges plectuntur Achivi.

Horace, *Epistles*

The Board of Studies was renamed the Senior Management Team, and thenceforth accounts of its deliberations were published in the *Staff Bulletin*. Overnight, it was rumoured, millions of pounds were wiped off the market value of SmithKline Beecham, the company that produces Mogadon.

The change of name gave rise to several jokes:

Question: What's the difference between the SMT and the Senior Management Team?

Answer: There's no difference: they both carry a lot of passengers.

A team of twelve 2nd and 3rd Year pupils took part in the Heinz Relay Marathon at Meadowbank Stadium. They returned with a cheque for £100, which was divided equally between the High School and Christian Aid.

The school acquired a stencil-cutting machine.

Scott Dickson was placed 67th= in the Glasgow University Bursary Competition; in 1989 he was 44th and the only pupil in the Wishaw area to gain a place in the first hundred.

Elizabeth Young retired after 34 years' service as a cleaner.

Room 44

The concrete floor, grey, cold, unyielding, jackboot loud;
The walls of crumbling brick, enhanced by 'Anglo-Saxon Blue'
Graffiti, superscribed on 'Institutional Cream';
Steel window frames, by vandals twisted into non-alignment,
Clutching plastic, plywood, polythene against the cold.
This is the so-called olive grove of Academe?

Asbestos-riddled Horsa Hut (post-war, pro tem!),
A den of dark decay, despair and disaffection,
With leg-loose chairs, ripped roller-board, boor-battered books,
Speaks volumes to young minds of the value and esteem
Giv'n to the Classics by this Mammon-driven world.
This is the so-called olive grove of Academe?

The ghosts of sages past, recorders of ancient life,
Philosophers, playwrights, scribes of wisdom, wit and woe
Let out in disbelief a suffering, silent scream.
The glory that was Greece, the grandeur that was Rome
Now huddle here - two empires in a Horsa Hut.
This is the so-called olive grove of Academe?

A dish of polished stones, the lapidary's art,
Shoots fulgent shafts to pierce th' environmental gloom;
And bold, defiant hyacinths release a stream
Of spirit-lifting scents into this barren place,
Where bust of Homer, sightless seer (now noseless), nods,
In this, our so-called olive grove of Academe.

But there were times within that festering, scabrous cell
When spirits of the ancients breathed into our souls,
Their voices softly urging, 'Think! Reflect! Dream!'
And, lifted on these timeless wings to higher planes,
We shook off the shackles and in breathless chorus joined:
'This IS the hallowed olive grove of Academe.'

This poem, which was written by Margaret Harvie, highlights the squalid working conditions in the huts and the ability of some teachers (I wasn't one of them) to transcend these conditions and fire their pupils' imagination.

Custard's Last Stand

The school canteen was transmogrified into a cafeteria that provided a wide range of food from cold beef burgers to lukewarm beef burgers. When it was eventually privatised (by Catering Direct), the food and service plumbed new depths of atrociousness; and I dread to think, in the light of all the revelations about BSE and CJD, how much damage I may have done to my health by eating so many canteen/cafeteria beef burgers. I am also reminded of a line from Juvenal's *Satires* that has, in its literal sense, a ring of truth about it:

Occidit miseros crambe repetita magistros.

The Concert Band took part in a joint concert with its counterpart from St Aidan's High School; it also provided a programme of music prior to one of the SNO's promenade concerts in the Kelvin Hall.

Worth going to see? Yes (it's a day off school); worth seeing?....who cares?

Arrangements were made to enable as many pupils as possible to visit the Glasgow Garden Festival - 'a day out of this world', according to the *Staff Bulletin*. Three members of staff braved the roller coaster.

Six senior pupils from the High School were part of a local team of young entrepreneurs that won the prize awarded for the most successful enterprise (it was entitled 'Gold Royce') in Strathclyde and the South West.

With a view to promoting *Cartoon Aid* (a cartoon book compiled by various well-known artists and cartoonists to raise money for the Band Aid Trust), the Art Department decorated the windows of Arnott's store in the Main Street with 'a colourful display'.

Derek Winton ('We will miss his skill as a raconteur') and Sheila Sprot ('mentor, counsellor, and, on many occasions, surrogate mother to countless pupils in Belhaven House') retired after 31 and 24 years' service respectively.

Donkeys Led by Donkeys

The horrendous PAT was introduced as part of the agreement that led to the end of the salaries campaign. I've forgotten what the acronym stood for (it should have been Pollock Added Time), but I remember what it entailed: sitting in my room for an extra two hours every bloody Monday afternoon. The EIS must be the only union in the history of the trade union movement to have negotiated a longer working week for its members.

Lynsey Simkin and Amanda Murray raised £50 for Anderson House by means of a sponsored run.

Computerised registration was introduced.

Obituary

'One of the sadder days in the life of a school,' wrote Jimmy Clelland, 'is when it loses one of its stalwarts. Such a day was Wednesday this week, when a number of us attended the funeral of Tommy Wardlaw, who was a janitor at the school until his retiral in 1980. Tommy was a great chap; he always had a cheery word for his many friends on the staff, and even in retirement he couldn't tear himself away completely from us. I visited Mrs Wardlaw late on Tuesday afternoon, and she recalled some of Tommy's associations with the school. "You know, Mr Clelland," she said, "Tommy was the kind of man who should never have retired. He loved that school." Even latterly, when failing health put a stop to his regular Friday visits, he kept himself informed about the school through his grandson, who is now in 1st Year.'

Both Julie Livingstone and Brenda Langford won second prize (in different sections) in the annual competition organised by the Bible Society of Scotland. Entrants were required to submit an essay, play, comic or newspaper-style article about the lives of Andrew and Jesus.

Sandra Lever, a flautist, won the Young Musician of the Year Competition sponsored by Motherwell District Council.

About 50% of the staff took part in a one-day strike as a protest against the government's latest proposals (these included school boards, opting out, national testing, league tables, teacher appraisal, TVEI compacts, and technology academies) - which the EIS claimed would 'destroy Scottish education'.

Duke of Edinburgh Awards Scheme

Under the supervision of May Kidd and Pat McGowan, ten senior pupils - Pamela Clarke, Eleanor Cowan, Lorna Dewar, Aonghas Morrison, Elaine Renwick, Louise Rodger, Martyn Turner, Gavin Tweedie, Richard Wolseley, and Ruth Wolseley - gained Bronze Awards. Three years later, David Nelson, Diane Douglas, Jill Gilliland, and Stephen Dewar gained Silver Awards.

ut et alios instruam

Drew Morrice wrote a series of articles for the *Wishaw Press* on educational matters.

An Open Day was held to enable parents of 1st Year pupils - and also parents of children who were scheduled to enrol at the school in August 1989 - to see what changes had taken place during the previous two or three years in the matter of exams, curricula, etc.

If there's one thing that sums up everything that's gone wrong since the War, it's Workshop.

Kingsley Amis, *Jake's Thing*

The following was the programme for the In-Service Day on 6 October:
9.00- 9.45: Workshop Sessions on A Curriculum Model for S1 / S2 chaired by the various elected mode representatives:

Mode	Chairperson	Venue
Language and Communication	*Miss Patrick*	*Room 9*
Scientific Studies	*Mr McDonald*	*Room 10*
Social and Environmental Studies	*Mr Robertson*	*Room 11*
Technological Activities	*Mrs Muir*	*Room 12*
Creative and Aesthetic Studies	*Mr Harvie*	*Room 6*
Religious and Moral Education	*Mr Bell*	*Room 5*
Physical Education	*Mr T. Young*	*Room 4*

9.45 - 10.30: Plenary Session in the hall.

Mr Amis and I rest our case.

Loco Locum

One morning, towards the end of the year, a stranger wandered into Jimmy Clelland's office. Since Jimmy had put in a request for a supply teacher to replace Liz Patrick, he jumped to the obvious conclusion: 'Are you the replacement English teacher?' 'Yes,' replied the stranger, so

Jimmy was more than happy to give him a timetable and direct him to the staffroom. Soon afterwards, a parent presented himself at the school - to warn Jimmy about a 'weird' man who had accosted several High School pupils in the Main Street. The police were summoned, and the new 'English teacher' was taken into custody. As a result of further inquiries, it was established that he was an absconder from some home or mental institution who had not been taking his medication.

Part of the school's war memorial

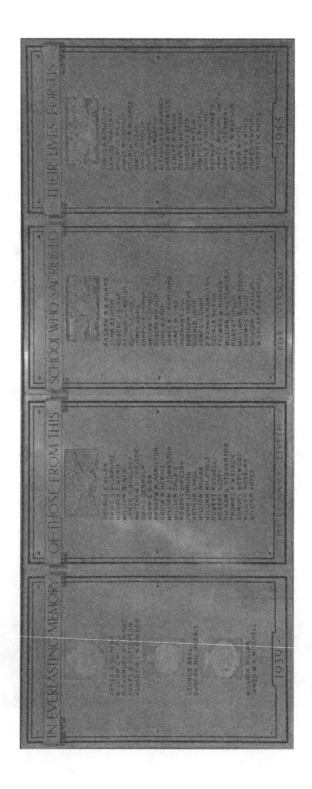

**Memorial name plaques from the school,
now displayed in Wishaw Old Parish Church.**

Helen Costley, long-serving secretary/Admin Assistant

Red Nose Day 1989

Matthew Bain, long-serving janitor

'The Bells of Bruges' Cast (1968)

501

Old Folks' Christmas Lunch

School Sports

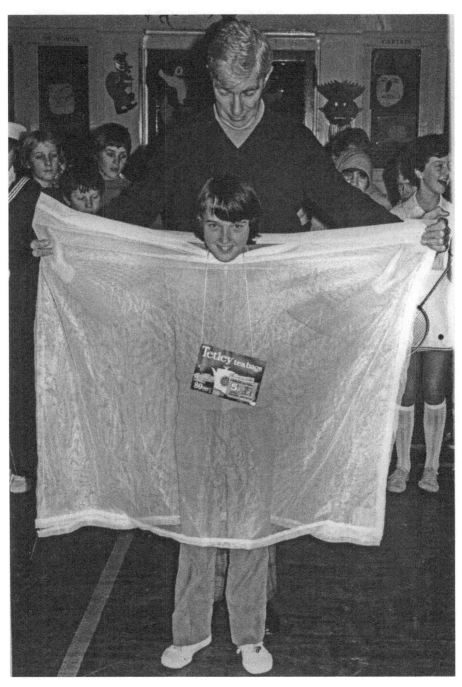

Hallowe'en Party

Third Year 'Musical Larks' (1947)

Junior Choir (early 1970s)

Senior Football Team in France (1971)

Horsa Huts at the rear of the school

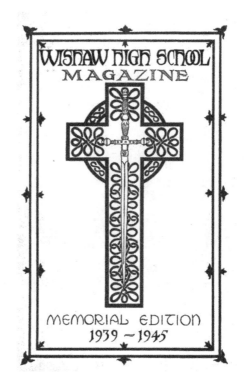

A selection of covers from the school magazine,
which was eventually entitled 'The Octagon'

506

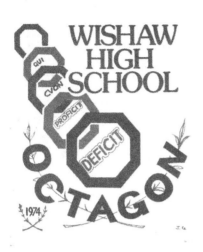

The Wishaw High School badge

Drama Club Rehersal (1962)

Girls at the school goldfish pond (1960s)

Linda Matthew, Neena Barr, Margaret Cleland, Marion Burrows

'Joseph and His Amazing Technicolour Dreamcoat' (1981)

The Mikado'(circa 1968)

Junior Choir (1977)

'Carousel' (1980)

School Choir (1980-81)

60

Sam Completes His Round

Sam retired in March 1988. To mark his retiral, the 6th Year presented him with a golf club, the perfect gift for someone who had previously told a reporter from the *Wishaw Press* that retirement would give him a chance to work on reducing his handicap. At the time, his handicap was 8, so he must have been a better than average golfer; however, we now have to ask the following (slightly more pertinent) question: 'How did he rate as a rector?'

'Sam had a lot of personal charm,' writes a former member of the Guidance staff. 'He was also a real "gentleman".

He was able to get on with practically everybody; he had no favourites and he was straight in his dealings with members of staff, refusing to talk about them behind their backs.

He had a great affection for the pupils, regarding them all as equally important; and also an amazing ability to put a name to every one of them, something that makes a child feel good.

He had quite remarkable tact and diplomacy: a school can be a minefield of prickly egos, but he was able to defuse potential explosions by handling every situation with kid gloves.

He had an infectious enthusiasm for everything to do with the school, and this rubbed off on the staff: enthusiasm seemed to breed enthusiasm.

He had tremendous humanity and kindness, and although he was not religious, I always thought of him as a really "good" man.

He had a great love of the English language, which showed itself in all sorts of ways: he was an excellent public speaker, for example, and he would read every report issued over his name (an onerous task) and correct, in a tactful way, errors of spelling and syntax. In addition, he always insisted on the comments in report forms being positive and constructive.

He was Rector at possibly the most difficult period in the school's history - the change from senior secondary to comprehensive status; and although he was, in my opinion, "a senior secondary type", he tried very hard to make the comprehensive system work.

The High School was a caring kind of place, where individuals - irrespective of their background - were regarded as being more important than academic results. In my time, I came into contact with many teachers from many schools in many different parts of Scotland, and I would say that in one respect - the humanity of its staff - the High School was pretty unique.'

Witness (Occasionally Hostile) for the Defence

It is beyond dispute that Sam had 'a lot of personal charm', and although he tended to be more popular, on the whole, with the ladies on the staff than with the men, I have spoken to very few people who have anything derogatory to say about him on a personal level.

I would question the notion that 'he had no favourites'. The sun was deemed to shine out of the Music Department's bassoons - and why not, since the choirs and the concert band were virtually the only groups to add any lustre to the school in the 1980s and 1990s.

Though he never seemed to take umbrage at anything, I'm sure that he must have been embarrassed or irritated by the behaviour of certain members of staff. I'm equally sure that he must have recorded the most egregious misdemeanours in the files all head teachers keep.

In many respects, Sam was very much a rector of the old school: he knew the names of all the pupils on the roll, and the abilities and personal qualities of many of them; he had a shrewd understanding of the strengths and weaknesses of individual members of staff; and he knew absolutely everything that went on in the school (whether or not he took action with regard to anything untoward that came to his notice is a different matter). He was most certainly not one of those managerial types (*Private Eye* calls them 'men in suits') with a striped tie and an aura of Old Spice who seem to be the flavour of the month with the educational establishment as far as headmasterships are concerned.

In the early years of his rectorship, he put in a regular appearance at different sporting fixtures on Saturday morning, and he took a particularly keen interest in the progress of the rugby team; he always presented the certificates on the Thursday evening of the Wiston week; and he always mucked in with the rest of the staff at the sports and the midsummer fête - indeed, on one occasion, I saw him lugging tables and chairs from the front lawn back into the school well after 4 o'clock. Incidentally (and sadly), it should be noted that not for the first, or the last, time such egalitarianism did not evoke unalloyed admiration in the ranks of the staff; for as he waltzed past Sam on his way to the nearest pub, Neil Jardine, a truculent geographer who refused to kowtow to anybody in authority, commented ironically that he (Sam) was 'doing a grand job'.

Sam was very considerate - and also very obliging - in his dealings with the staff, and requests for time off to attend a wedding, a funeral, or a course were never refused: in June 1972, for instance, I was given permission to attend a two-week coaching course arranged by the SFA.

Class, House and school trips, educational excursions, and holidays abroad (whether they were scheduled to take place during or outwith either the school day or the normal school terms)...they all benefited from the same accommodating style of management; nor was there ever any problem about getting a football, cricket, or hockey team away early. In view of Sam's helpful attitude with regard to all these, and many other, facets of school life, I always thought it was absolutely outrageous for the EIS members on the staff to work to rule on certain occasions.

Sam operated a bona fide 'open door' policy ('experto crede'): he was very supportive, to take a case in point, when I was shilly-shallying over a possible move to Whitburn Academy. On another occasion, Eddie Tweedlie Jnr. and I were planning to play golf at Turnberry during one of the midterm holidays, and we wanted to know if he could recommend a hotel or restaurant in Girvan that served a decent lunch at a reasonable price. When we went along to his room at five to four, he could not have been more helpful.

He may have insisted on the comments in report forms being 'positive and constructive', but what he got latterly from most teachers were permutations of several stock words and phrases.

It is difficult for a head teacher to preside over a major change (from senior secondary to comprehensive, for example) in the status of his school. Thanks to the zoning arrangements that were enacted in Wishaw, Sam had to preside over the conversion of a senior secondary school to a 'sink' school - for at no time during his rectorship was the High School a genuine six-year comprehensive (i.e. one with an acceptable social and intellectual mix). So the cards were well and truly stacked against him.

If, as many former members of staff have claimed, the High School was an exceptionally friendly and caring establishment (a claim that was confirmed by officialdom in an Information Pack, entitled "Teaching in Today's Lanarkshire", which was issued to trainee teachers in the mid-1970s: 'In the friendly atmosphere of Wishaw High School the young teacher can find much of lasting value'), Sam must surely take a lot of the credit - since the tone of a school is largely determined by its head teacher.

The Indictment

The academic reputation of the High School declined during his rectorship.

It is undeniable that fewer pupils achieved academic success during Sam's years as Rector; however, this was not due to his being Rector. What caused the decline was the double whammy of an outrageously unbalanced catchment area and the Parent's Charter. In any case, the High School had no divine right to remain a 'good' school *in perpetuum*: just as some cinemas are closed and some football clubs are relegated from the Premier League, some schools, in the nature of things, deteriorate and some schools are closed.

That would never have happened in my day.

Many former pupils were in the habit of comparing the High School in the 1940s, 1950s, and early 1960s with the High School in the 1970s and 1980s. They were not comparing like with like. In those earlier decades, the High School was only obliged to admit pupils who had some sort of academic potential (pupils, that is, who were deemed capable of eventually 'sitting their Highers'); latterly, the school was full of dead wood.

'Look at the state of the hall,' those FPs would say, looking for ammunition to support their unfavourable verdict on the school. However, the reality of the situation was that the hall was commandeered by the PE department on a daily basis (to supplement the hopelessly inadequate facilities they had at their disposal) and used for inappropriate purposes - as a badminton or volleyball court, for example.

That would never happen at Coltness High School.

In the local community, the High School was very often compared - to its disadvantage - with Garrion Academy and Coltness High School. Garrion Academy was the Alcatraz of educational establishments, a cold, soulless place, where the teachers were all yes-men and the pupils were merely ciphers. *Cui bono*? For twenty years, it managed to remain completely anonymous; and apart from its highly successful participation in the Duke of Edinburgh Awards Scheme, it is as difficult to find any noteworthy achievements in its brief history as it is to name three famous Belgians.

As for the pot-hunters of Coltness High School, what have they achieved apart from occasional triumphs on the football field and good results (with good pupils) in the SCE Examination? As in all hothouses, horticultural or academic, the atmosphere in that institution is suffocating.

**And he that strives to touch the stars,
Oft stumbles at a straw.**

Edmund Spenser, *The Shepherd's Calendar*

The High School may have 'stumbled at a straw' more often than Garrion Academy and Coltness High School (that was partly down to Sam), but it 'touched the stars' with much greater frequency - and that was primarily down to Sam, who fostered the sort of liberal atmosphere that encouraged people to do their own thing in many different spheres. The High School, consequently, produced some wonderfully eccentric characters, operettas and carol concerts, shambolic staff pantomimes, a brass band, 'the Wiston experience', and, above all, a unique ambience.

As far as comparisons with other schools are concerned, I am reminded of the following extract from the screenplay of *The Third Man*: *In Italy for thirty years, under the Borgias, they had warfare, terror, murder, and bloodshed; they produced Michelangelo, Leonardo da Vinci, and the Renaissance. In Switzerland they had brotherly love and five hundred years of democracy and peace; and what did they produce? The cuckoo clock.*

He should have been stricter with the pupils.

I don't think Sam was temperamentally suited to being a 'hard man' (in any case, the abolition of corporal punishment has led to 'hard men' becoming virtually an extinct species in Scottish schools), and his reaction to disciplinary problems was always fairly relaxed: 'suaviter in modo, suavissime in re' would have been the most appropriate motto for his coat of arms. However, apart from one or two unpleasant incidents, the High School was never out of control in the manner of The Ridings School in Halifax.

He should have been more assertive with the staff.

Sam didn't have an overbearing personality; and, on occasion, he seemed to be unwilling to muster the dogmatic obstinacy that might have enabled him to impose his ideas (and keep them imposed) on a staff that contained not only a lot of cynics but also a fair number of reactionaries who were set in their senior secondary ways. Leo Amery's comments about Asquith spring to mind:

For twenty years he has held a season ticket on the line of least resistance and has gone wherever the train of events has carried him, lucidly justifying his position at whatever point he has happened to find himself.

In the event, this insouciance had several beneficial consequences: it led, for example, to the visions he had of developing the High School in line with the educational philosophy of Jimmy Scobbie, the Rector of Dalziel High School, becoming blurred - and eventually evanescent. *Deo gratias.*

> **Damn with faint praise.....**
> **Willing to wound, and yet afraid to strike,**
> **Just hint a fault, and hesitate dislike.**

Alexander Pope, *An Epistle to Dr Arbuthnot*

Sam occasionally annoyed people by 'damning' them, or their efforts, with either 'faint praise' or praise considerably diminished by a throwaway codicil that 'hinted a fault':

This is what we at Wishaw High School call a concert. (This is what the rest of the civilised world calls an unmitigated shambles)

Mr Finlayson (HMI) inspected the Technical Department last Friday, and obviously enjoyed himself thoroughly. It would, however, be hard to say how much of this was due to what he found in the department, and how much to his evident delight at meeting colleagues with whom he had worked here nineteen years ago. (Mr Finlayson couldn't believe how much the Technical Department had deteriorated in the intervening years)

Never glad confident morning again

Robert Browning, *The Lost Leader*

Towards the end of his rectorship, he didn't display as much pizazz as in the 1960s and 1970s (I think he found it increasingly difficult to reconcile his complaisant style of leadership with the militant, work-to-rule mentality of most of the staff), and he tended to keep a low profile; in cricketing terms, he was content to play out time till close of play. And who can blame him? It would have been unrealistic to expect him to try and hit boundaries on a wicket that was deteriorating so rapidly and irreversibly - especially since he was being pressurised by a rather hostile field.

The Verdict

In most people's judgment, Sam was a nice man and/but a ....(for here the unanimity ends) rector. I don't think he was quite as nice as he appeared to be: for one thing, nobody reaches the top of the tree in politics, or the professions - or, indeed, in any field - by being nice all the time. On the other hand, he may have been too nice to be a head teacher; he was certainly very hesitant about exerting his authority.

'In a hierarchy,' according to the Peter Principle, 'every employee tends to rise to his level of incompetence.' Nowhere is this principle more likely to be validated than in schools, colleges, and other educational institutions - and the reason is quite simple: for the most part, teachers gain promotion because they have shown themselves to be skilled in the art of teaching, but the posts (above the level of principal teacher) to which they are promoted require the skills of a competent manager and administrator, rather than those of a brilliant teacher. A head teacher, for instance, 'must cope daily' (according to the Tupper Report) 'with mountains of distracting paperwork from a welter of official and semi-official sources, hardly any of which has relevance to the proper running of his school - and at the same time supervise staff, pupils and ancillaries, deal with the unexpected, cope with recalcitrant pupils without touching a hair on their heads, and entertain and be polite to parents, no matter how outrageous or rude. Above all, however, he must always be ready to pour forth the correct flannel to official visitors.'

By all accounts, Sam was an excellent classroom teacher, so the obvious question is: 'Should he have stayed there? Did he 'rise to his level of incompetence'? Should our final verdict on him as a rector replicate that of the Roman historian Tacitus on the Emperor Galba: 'maior privato visus dum privatus fuit et omnium consensu capax imperii nisi imperasset.'?'

The answer to these questions must be a definite 'No'. Paperwork was not his forte ('I have an instinct,' he said, 'for doing the thing that must be done at the last possible moment'), but he was a better organiser and administrator than he was given credit for by a lot of the staff.

He wasn't a control freak, and he allowed individual teachers and departments to get on with their day-to-day work with minimal interference on his part. He did, however, have a habit of appearing (for perfectly genuine reasons, it must be emphasised) in teachers' classrooms at the most inopportune moments - at the beginning or the end of a period, for example, when pupils tend to be particularly noisy and restless; or during a period when a teacher was engaged in mortal combat with the stroppiest class on his timetable. I don't know if the timing of these visits was deliberate...but it was the timing that made them so intensely irritating.

There was no danger whatsoever of Sam resorting to physical violence in his dealings with 'recalcitrant' pupils: whether he was confronted by pupils of that ilk, or 'rude' parents, or querulous members of staff, one word characterises his reaction - emollient.

Sam was in his element at parents' nights (in fact, he was in his element at school functions of every kind), and he deserves a pat on the back for his efforts as the High School's (unofficial) public relations officer.

He also had the ability to get on well with practically everybody; indeed, it was this aspect of his rectorship - forming and developing both working and personal relationships - that he found most rewarding. 'I think I should thank the people who have been with me,' he said on the eve of his retiral, 'because it has been the people, and not the job, who have made it so good.'

Although he was quite prepared to pay lip service to educational bureaucrats and their policies, he himself was no bureaucrat. He bent the rules and modified - or simply ignored - the edicts handed down from on high; and even when he did resort to unadulterated flannel to justify some crackpot scheme, I sometimes felt that his tongue was very much in his cheek.

520

'A school that is not a funfair,' according to A. S. Neill, 'is a bad school.' For the greater part of Sam's rectorship, the High School was a 'funfair'. So what sort of school did that make the High School? And what sort of rector did that make Sam? If A. J. C. Kerr, who 'bestrides' the history of the school 'like a Colossus', the modest and scholarly Dr Wilson, and Neil McKellar, the dour workaholic, were the Jack Nicklaus, Bobby Jones and Ben Hogan respectively of High School rectors, then Sam was the Walter Hagen of the foursome, a relaxed extrovert whose philosophy was: 'Never hurry, never worry, and always remember to smell the flowers on the way.'

61

Interregnum

Your mission, Jim, should you decide to accept it...

Jimmy Clelland was Acting Rector for exactly one year - from April 1988 till April 1989. During that period, nobody was appointed to any post on a permanent basis (the school's continued existence was still in the balance), and there were more people in 'acting' roles at the High School than in the cast of *Emmerdale Farm*.

Jimmy was described by Dick Loudon, one of the Assistant Directors of Education, as a 'couthie wee man'. He had no airs and graces (his choice of car bears witness to that), and in male company his language could sometimes be rather coarse; however, although he tried to hide it, he was a man of some sophistication.

> **This above all: to thine own self be true,**
> **And it must follow, as the night the day,**
> **Thou canst not then be false to any man.**

Shakespeare, *Hamlet*

During the great consortium wrangle, he was regarded by some union zealots as a fifth columnist in the service of Sam; and his popularity was further eroded among EIS members by his decision to opt out of all forms of industrial action in the early stages of the campaign for an independent review of teachers' salaries - so much so that he stopped frequenting the Admin staffroom, where he realised he was persona non grata. At the time, he claimed that it was against his principles to take part in a series of strikes; cynics, however, suggested that his unwillingness to toe the union line had less to do with principles than with a firm resolve not to jeopardise his prospects of becoming a head teacher - and in this instance their scepticism is supported by scientific fact. Apparently, the human brain evolved in such a way as to predispose it to lying, dissembling and self-deception, all three of these proclivities being conducive to good health, success in the workplace and harmonious relationships.

However, this revelation is double-edged: it certainly implies that other people are sometimes not completely straight with us; but since none of us are 'without sin' (on occasion, either publicly or in the privacy of our own minds, we are all less than honest about our motives for behaving in a certain way - as they do us very little credit), none of us have the right to 'cast the first stone' at Jimmy.

And now for something completely similar....

Jimmy made very few changes in the regime he inherited from Sam. As he was only Acting Rector, he probably felt that he didn't have the requisite authority, but since he had been an integral part of that regime for more than ten years, he may also have concluded that making numerous and / or drastic changes would be viewed as an admission of failure.

> **Be nice to people on your way up, because**
> **you'll meet 'em on your way down.**
>
> Wilson Mizner

Jimmy's relationship with the staff was very similar to Sam's. He avoided confrontation, setting great store by consulting them on every conceivable issue, and he was invariably tactful, considerate and good-humoured. These qualities are very often eschewed by the heads of large organisations, so why did Jimmy buck the trend? I believe he didn't want to alienate the staff by keeping them at arm's length both physically and emotionally, for if (as I think he may have suspected) he was not destined to be rector on a permanent basis, he would have to get along with those same teachers after his return to a lower echelon.

In the event, everybody gained from his sensitive and enlightened leadership. He himself was generally well liked (some members of staff were genuinely distressed, others enraged when he was replaced by an outsider); the staff were reassured by his willingness to lend an ear to any of them who had a personal problem or a grievance; and the atmosphere in the school was upbeat and friction-free.

General Peckem's attitude toward all the personnel in his command, officers and enlisted men, was marked by the same easy spirit of tolerance and permissiveness. He mentioned often that if the people who worked for him met him halfway, he would meet them more than halfway, with the result, as he always added with an astute chuckle, that there was never any meeting of the minds at all.

Joseph Heller, *Catch 22*

In his formal dealings with the staff as a whole, he was the epitome of patience and self-deprecation, as the following extracts from the *Staff Bulletin* illustrate:

I thought I might use the Staff Bulletin for an announcement about the In-Service Day on the 6th of October, in the hope that people will be more likely to read the Bulletin than one of my staff notices. (6.10.88)

I don't wish to sound churlish, but having just completed the collation of the 1st Year report forms that are about to be distributed to parents, I am amazed at the number of variations in the spelling of a name like 'Lynn'. Please remember that parents do take offence when we get children's names wrong. (27.5.88)

Last week I was mortified to note, on reading the Staff Bulletin, that I had wished people well to the point of being boring; in fact, I must have been in danger of running out of people. (2.9.88)

I begin this week with a plea - not a scold. Late arrival of registration returns is causing problems, so please try to get these down to the Front Office without fail and as soon as possible. (9.9.88).

I choose the Staff Bulletin rather than a staff notice for this gentle reminder, as I don't wish to sound carping. We have a wee problem. As you know, we qualify for external absence cover on Day 4 of an absence - or earlier, if an absence exceeding three days is notified in advance. To get this cover here in time, I really have to know fairly early on Day 3 - so that I can notify Staffing of our need in good time. I know it is not always easy to predict with certainty whether or not you will be fit to return the next day, but please do your best to phone early if you can, and remember that no phone call at all means that I can do nothing until the following morning. (4.11.88)

A word of complaint - just a little one really. When completing pupils' progress reports, would you please check with the official class lists distributed in August to ensure that all pupils' names are spelt correctly. It really does give offence to parents when we appear not to bother about getting a child's name right. Please bear this in mind for the next lot, which will be S3. (11.11.88)

Sorry, I'm carping again. Please, please, when you are writing progress reports on pupils, check the name - and in particular the spelling - against the class lists issued in August 1988. Matthew McCreaddie of S3, for example, did not have a matching pair out of six reports. As for the Stevens and the Alisons (or Allysons) – 'nough said. Please...this is important. (9.12.88)

'I wonder if anyone is born to obey,' said Isabel, 'and that may be why people command rather badly - they have no suitable material to work on.'

Dame Ivy Compton-Burnett, *Parents and Children*

Sam might or might not have drawn the staff's attention to their inconsistent spelling of pupils' names, but he certainly wouldn't have done so more than once; Jimmy, as we have just seen, raised this matter on at least three occasions. In both instances, the real and the hypothetical, the result was/would have been the same: nobody took/would have taken a blind bit of notice. Jimmy should have known (Sam undoubtedly did) that most teachers at the High School were immune to rectorial wheedling. Even so, he was a very competent administrator and an excellent public speaker; in my judgment, he was superior to Sam in both of these spheres.

With Jimmy as captain, the SS High School was still on the rocks and sinking fast, but at least the crew and passengers - and Jimmy himself - enjoyed themselves: he continued to play the organ, for example, at the Easter and Christmas services, and he participated with great gusto - and a red nose - in all the activities that took place on Comic Relief Day. Like Sam he was emotionally attached to the High School.

Jimmy was the last of a dying (now dead and buried) breed of paternalistic rectors who led from the front. Most of the present crop of head teachers would be unable to lead a queue outside a fish and chip shop. They wear sharp suits and striped ties. They are as oleaginous as Seth Pecksniff and "they didn't get where they are today" without keeping themselves au fait with the latest DEO-approved trends in educational theory and practice. They can talk the talk; but they aren't keen to walk the walk, as this would take them out their comfort zone - the private little world where they can devise mission statements, pore over computer printouts, and have a cup of tea with important visitors. Every week, they contrive to get their name and/or their picture in the local paper. They bask in the glory of their school's academic and sporting achievements. They react to bad publicity with the simulated candour, dubious statistics and unconvincing assurances that we associate with politicians:

I'm not going to hide behind a formal 'no comment'. Last Tuesday, one of our 3rd year pupils ran amok in the hall with a Black and Decker hedge trimmer. Admittedly (perhaps understandably), the incident occurred during a house assembly. Even so, I take a dim view of such irresponsible behaviour: not only does it contravene the strict disciplinary code all our pupils must observe, but it also detracts from the school's high standing in the local community. Having said that, I still think we should try to keep a sense of perspective: there was only one fatality (the individual in question had fallen asleep and was unable to defend himself); and in the last fortnight the number of teachers attacked with a gardening implement at school or house assemblies compares favourably with the national average. However, I am determined to prevent a repetition of last week's tragic events. Consequently, any pupil caught in possession of a hedge trimmer, machete, or telescopic ladder will be suspended forthwith; and I myself will be chairing an inter-school forum on Rhododendron Rage: How to recognise it and how to deal with it. Finally our thoughts are with the friends, relatives and pet tortoise of the deceased.

(For a fuller version of this cobblers visit www.SayNoToHedgeTrimmers.com)

To sum up, today's head teachers - plausible, chameleon-like and totally committed to the main chance - remind me very much of the Greek parvenus excoriated by the Roman satirist Juvenal:

> Ingenium velox, audacia perdita, sermo
> promptus et Isaeo torrentior. Ede, quid illum
> esse putes? Quem vis hominem secum attulit ad nos:
> grammaticus, rhetor, geometres, pictor, aliptes,
> augur, schoenobates, medicus, magus: omnia novit
> Graeculus esuriens; in caelum iusseris, ibit.

In some ways, as we shall see, the High School's next rector did not conform to this rather unattractive stereotype. He didn't radiate charisma, and there was very little prospect of his being asked to join the diplomatic corps or man a helpline for the Samaritans. Like Major Major in *Catch-22*, he 'inevitably stood out - even among men lacking all distinction - as a man lacking more distinction than all the rest, and people who met him were always impressed by how unimpressive he was'.

He wasn't smarmy, he didn't court popularity, and he certainly couldn't be described as a smooth talker. So far so good. Unfortunately, he also lacked two of the less objectionable qualities displayed by the new breed of head teachers - flexibility and approachability ('Call me Dick. My door is always open'). In practical terms, this meant that his relationship with the staff was very formal (Mr, Mrs and Miss were never supplanted by Christian names) and his management style was very formalistic.

Unsurprisingly, therefore, his efforts to halt the school's remorseless decline were not based on inspirational leadership (he lacked both the presence and the necessary eloquence) but on the formulation of less flexible (a High School euphemism for 'lax') administrative procedures and a more rigid disciplinary system. By opting for such a strategy, he ran the risk of destroying the atmosphere that was a major part of the school's raison d'être and went some way to counterbalancing its many shortcomings. I'm pretty certain, however that he was unaware of the risk he was taking, for he seemed to be equally unaware of the unique ambience he was jeopardising. Moreover, any inkling he may have had of that ambience certainly didn't lead him to believe that it would be of much practical use in the struggle to rescue the school from decline: so as it wasn't, in his judgement, part of the solution, it had to be part of the problem (decline) and was therefore expendable. On reflection, perhaps he was right. Perhaps my views on this issue have been distorted by nostalgia.

I end this digression, which has now pre-empted far too much of the main narrative, with a few less ambivalent assertions. Far from being the school's salvation, the changes initiated by the school's last rector amounted to no more than a rearrangement of the furniture on the deck of the *Titanic*. As he had just been appointed, he was more or less obliged to be proactive, but nothing and nobody could have saved the school, and euthanasia (voluntary or not) was already shaping up as the best possible outcome for all concerned.

62

Decline and Fall Part III - Somebody Up There Likes Us

Towards the end of 1988, Strathclyde Region set up a number of Area Review Groups to examine, *inter alia,* 'the future of non- denominational secondary provision' (i.e. to help it to decide how many secondary schools it could get away with closing) in certain parts of the region. Early in 1989, Jimmy Clelland submitted to the local ARG a school profile containing material which supported the proposition that the High School was 'a going concern'.

In March of that same year, the ARG visited the High School in order to inspect 'the nature and extent of the accommodation available at the school'. The weather was decidedly inclement, and the members of the ARG got extremely wet as they made their way round the hutted area and up to the annexe. According to the *Staff Bulletin*, they were more impressed by the annexe than by the main building; and, even more ominously, the one question that kept cropping up was: 'Why are there no pupils in this room?'

A week later, in the hall, there was a joint meeting of the ARG and all the personnel employed at the High School - teachers, janitors, cleaners, etc. By this time, most of the teaching staff were convinced that the school was going to be closed, and that the joint meeting would just be a matter of going through the motions; and even though Jimmy Clelland (who rose superbly to the occasion) managed to ruffle the equanimity of a saturnine member of the Divisional Education Department called Halliday by challenging some of the official statistics and raising the spectre of Coltness High School being overrun by the legions of the undead (i.e. technically brain-dead, but still animate) if the High School was closed, the general reaction to Jimmy's doughty efforts was: "C'est magnifique, mais ce n'est pas la guerre."

However, 'the age of miracles hadn't passed', for at the beginning of April the ARG recommended the retention of three non-denominational secondary schools in Wishaw; and this recommendation was confirmed by the Education Committee on the 26th of the same month. Perhaps, on reflection, such an outcome is not so surprising as it appeared to be at the time. Strathclyde Region was certainly determined to close a number of secondary schools, but the composition of the Area Review Groups (they included parents and representatives of the teachers' unions) was such that there was little likelihood of their coming up with the answers the Region wanted. Two years later, when the Region decided, for the second time, to bite the bullet with regard to school closures, it did not make the same mistake.

63

1989

Iain'll Fix It

Interviews for the post of Rector of Wishaw High School were held on 2 February. The short straw was drawn by Iain Murray, Depute Rector of Braidfield High School, Clydebank, who had previously taught, in different capacities, in the Science Departments of Paisley Grammar, Castlehead High School and Caldervale High School, and had also been an AHT at Vale of Leven Academy.

Murray was well versed in all the policies (Equal Opportunities, for example) that the Region wanted to implement in its schools; and since he was very much a team player (unlike Sam, who could be something of a maverick), the apparatchiks in the Education Department could be one hundred per cent certain that he would enforce those same policies with exemplary thoroughness - and that is just one of the many reasons why he was ideally suited for the post of Rector of the High School.

In the event, Murray was almost the first person to be appointed Rector (a designation that was soon to be replaced by the more politically correct 'head teacher') of a school that was closed before he entered on his rectorship therein. As it was, if the new supremo did try to get in touch with his new fiefdom by phone, he must have wondered if it really existed - since the phones were on the blink.

Read my lips...

Murray eventually took over at the helm of the High School on 10 April. One of his first pronouncements (to a reporter from the *Wishaw Press*) was the following:

There won't be any immediate changes. I want to take time to settle in at the school and find out about things first.

By the end of June, however, he was forced to admit to the staff that he had 'not kept to his statement in the *Wishaw Press*'. 'But I am sure,' he declared, 'that you will appreciate the need to introduce some changes before the start of the new session in August.'

Physics is fun.

A group of 3rd Year Physics pupils visited the nuclear power station at Torness.

Twelve High School pupils acted as litter marshals at the Royal Highland Show at Ingliston.

The school had begun to make greater use of the water sports facilities at Strathclyde Park, and six pupils - Margaret Gray, Gail Hughes, Ian Cleland, Sandy Kilgour, Jay Love, and Kenny Littlejohn - gained their One-Star Canoeing Certificate.

Lynsey Simkin won the 800 metres at the County Sports. Later in the year, she was invited to attend the one-day coaching course arranged for the Scottish Schools Athletics Association's under-17 squad at Grangemouth Stadium.

The Blue Shadows

Several senior pupils took part in a work shadowing project: Aonghas Morrison, for instance, 'shadowed' Iain Harris, manager of the Strip Mill at Ravenscraig. Work shadowing "allowed pupils to observe various working practices, and helped them to understand how contrasting personalities and points of view can blend in such a way as to produce something that meets customers' requirements".

The end of session entertainment took the form of a summer concert: *Memories of the 50s were evoked by the Junior Choir; the Senior Choir provided some haunting melodies from Phantom of the Opera; and the Concert Band played a wide range of pieces from its extensive repertoire, including music by Holst, Cimarosa, Tchaikovsky, and Acker Bilk.*

Pamela Clarke was selected to attend the Shell Expo Music School in Aberdeen during the summer holidays. Pamela played the clarinet in the High School's Concert Band, the Motherwell Concert Band, the Lanarkshire Youth Orchestra, and the Royal Scottish Academy of Music and Drama Junior Wind Band and Orchestra.

I have a cunning plan.

Murray's 'big idea' to boost the roll (and thus, hopefully, stave off the closure of the High School) was to encourage as many adults as possible to sign up for courses at the school. To kick-start this campaign, the following poster was produced:

Bored? Time on your hands?
Looking for new interests?
Want to learn new skills or upgrade qualifications?

Ever thought of...
Returning to school?

Painting for Pleasure	Keep Fit
Hostess Cookery	Computing
Typing	Cake Decoration
Dressmaking	Weight Training
Music Keyboard	Sports
Gardening	Graphic Art
Acoustic Guitar	Languages

An Adults' Open Day was also arranged, and this resulted in eighty enrolments.

Adults from the Edward Lawson Centre for the Mentally Handicapped began to visit the school on a regular basis, in order to participate in Art, Music, PE, and Home Economics classes.

The Scripture Union was very active from 1989 onwards; it organised such events as an indoor barbie, a craft sale, a games night, a *Mastermind* competition, and visits by missionaries who worked in Japan.

Twenty 3rd Year pupils attended a drama workshop (in the Museum of Transport in Glasgow), at which they 'assumed the personae of the women and children of Glasgow on the Home Front'.

Trojan Horse

Despite the misgivings of the EIS (which believed that the Secretary of State for Scotland had prescribed the creation of such boards in order to encourage schools to opt out of local authority control, a course of action that was likely to bring them under the sway of central government), every school in Scotland now had its own school board.

The members of the High School Board were: Mrs M Torrance, Mrs C. Pattison, Mrs E. Dunbar, Mr N. Littlejohn, Elspeth Banks, Janey Mauchline, and the Reverend Ian Coltart, who was elected interim chairman (a position he held until February 1990, when Les Dalrymple was elected permanent chairman); and the Board met for the first time on 22 October (thereafter, once a month). Among the matters it discussed were the requisition, staffing, study leave, and, latterly, the closure of the High School and its amalgamation with Garrion Academy. On the social side, the first event to be arranged was a Wine and Whist Night; and this was followed by the publication of a newsletter the Board hoped to bring out once a term, a fashion show, a Christmas raffle, and a tour of the school.

Eleanor Cowan was elected pupils' representative on the School Board.

A rugby team made up of pupils from the High School and Coltness High School played its first game - against Bellshill Academy.

At the Wishaw Schools' Swimming Gala, Stuart Thomson won four trophies: the Lawson Trophy (2 lengths freestyle); the Brochie Trophy (2 lengths breaststroke); the Davidson Shield (2 lengths backstroke); and the Bone, Connell and Baxter Trophy (best all-round swimmer). He was also a member of the relay team that won the British Service Trophy.

64

1990

I never promised you a rose garden.

Hannah Green

A Gardening Club was established by Neil Kerr. Its first project was to build a pond in one of the quadrangles.

A kindergarten? Now, that's a different matter.

A crèche was opened on the ground floor of the annexe under the supervision of Morag Costello and Carol Bence, assisted by several senior pupils. The crèche, which was free, was set up to assist adults (with children) who wished to attend classes at the High School; and by the end of the year there were fifty children on the register. To help with the financing of this innovation, Councillor John Donnelly, Chairman of the Lanark Division Community Development Committee, presented Murray with a cheque for £1000.

Senior pupils in the Art Department joined their counterparts at Dalziel High School on a weekend trip to Paris, where they visited the Louvre, the Pompidou Centre, and other less art-orientated tourist attractions.

Sandra Lever (first flute) and Pamela Clarke (bass clarinet) auditioned successfully for the Strathclyde Schools' Symphonic Wind Band.

PCs Rule OK

Everything was computerised during Murray's three years as head teacher. In addition, the main building was wired in such a way as to make it possible for every classroom to be connected to a computer network; and a new computer laboratory, equipped with Apple Mac computers and laser printers, became operational.

At the Lanark Division Secondary Schools' Cross-Country Championships, a 3rd Year girls' team (comprising, in this instance, Yvonne Anderson, Lee Carlyle, Lynsey Simkin, Helen Christie, Gillian Mason, and Carol Millar) from the High School was victorious for the third consecutive year.

The theatrical company T.A.G. presented *Sailmaker* before an audience of one hundred 4th Year pupils. Individual members of the company also talked to the pupils about props and other aspects of the theatre.

Two brass band concerts were held in conjunction with Lesmahagow High School.

Dave Taylor MBE gave a talk on 'Teenage Traffic Education' to 4th, 5th, and 6th Year pupils.

Not So Jolly Hockey Sticks

The inter-House hockey championship became a mixed event - or, as the *Wishaw Press* put it, 'the boys and girls from Belhaven and Murdostoun picked up sticks and started to take chunks out of each other'. Another game was described as 'very fierce, with many minor accidents'.

The High School began to partake of the myriad delights provided by Sky Television.

A soft drinks machine was installed in the main building.

The High School's Music Department was one of the first in Scotland to pilot the new Standard Grade Music Examination.

Nice one, Richard.

That's Entertainment featured the Concert Band and scenes from *Les Miserables*, *The Sound of Music*, and *West Side Story*. Richard Wolseley, who took part in the extract from *Les Miserables*, conducted the draw for the raffle prizes; one of the tickets he drew was his mother's.

During the summer holidays, the Concert Band toured Belgium. Concerts were staged in Ostend and Blankenberg, and the members of the band visited a theme park, several First World War battlefields, and the largest German (military) cemetery in the world.

Seven girls from the High School attended a coaching course run by the Scottish Schoolgirls and Youth Hockey Association (West District).

536

Sarah Brown received a special award for being the most improved player in the skills sessions.

> **For when the one Great Scorer comes to
> mark against your name,
> He writes – not that you won or lost – but
> how you played the game.**

Grantland Rice, *Alumnus Football*

Hockey was one of the few extra-curricular activities that were not affected adversely by the general decline of the school. The senior girls' hockey team was always well turned out, and the practice sessions organised by Janis Clark on Thursday afternoons (after school) were always well attended. In an article she wrote for the 1982 edition of *The Octagon*, Mandy Steven summed up the ethos of High School hockey teams as follows:

At Wishaw High School, hockey is played for the love and enjoyment of the game, and not for the rewards at the end of the season. In this respect, we are unbeatable.

It's never too late.

The number of adult students (which included mothers, housewives, the unemployed and even high-powered businessmen) climbed above the one hundred and twenty mark. "It's really marvellous," commented one of them, "to get an opportunity to return to school to gain extra qualifications or acquire new skills. Another asset for me is the crèche, the existence of which means that there is no excuse for not furthering your education, even if you have children of pre-school age." Students' fees were paid by Strathclyde Region, and the open learning packages on offer included SCOTVEC and CAST modules in English, history, modern studies and modern languages. Adult literacy classes were also available.

The Home Economics Department produced a cookbook entitled 'The Fast, Fun, Fabulous Recipe Book'.

David Pringle was elected pupils' representative on the School Board.

At the first meeting of the re-formed Parents' Association, Mrs Elizabeth Thomson was elected President. Two months later, the association held its first event - a whist drive.

The theatrical company 'Invisible Bouncers' performed *Too Much Punch for Judy* in the hall.

In an effort to raise money for the school library, the School Board held a fashion show in the Concert Hall at the Civic Centre.

'At Midsummer,' muttered Mr Squeers, resuming his complaint, 'I took down ten boys; ten twentys - two hundred pound. I go back at eight o'clock tomorrow morning, and have only got three; three oughts an ought, three twos six - sixty pound. What's become of all the boys? What's parents got in their heads? What does it all mean?'

Charles Dickens, *Nicholas Nickleby*

By the late 1980s, the roll had dipped well below 600 - primarily because, every year, a considerable number of the primary pupils (virtually all of P7 at Cambusnethan Primary, for instance, and two thirds of that same year group at Lammermoor Primary) who lived in the High School's catchment area opted, under the Parent's Charter, to attend Coltness High School. Murray made a big effort to reverse this trend, an effort that concentrated principally on establishing closer links between the High School and its feeder primaries. As part of this process, he himself and Elspeth Banks (followed, at a later date, by members of the Art, Music, Science, Computing, and Home Economics Departments) visited the primary schools in question in order to talk to parents of P7 pupils about the transition from primary to secondary education - and to pupils about what certain subjects in the secondary curriculum entailed. These visits were reinforced by a one-day visit to the High School by 135 P7 pupils, a Christmas party, a Primary Singing Day, a General Knowledge Competition (in February 1991), and a three-day visit to the High School (in June 1991). In the space of two years, as a result of this emphasis on primary-secondary liaison, there was a 15% increase in the 1st Year intake.

The school purchased a multi-gym, this new facility being used mainly by pupils in the PE Department.

Grant Law was first (out of sixteen) in the Higher Elementary Accordion Examinations held in Perth.

Joan Sandell, the new librarian, said that the library was 'nice and bright'.

It's good to talk.

A Health and Relationship module was inaugurated by Geraldine MacPhee, Principal Teacher of Home Economics. 5th and 6th Year pupils who did this module were encouraged to talk openly about the physical and emotional pressures associated with adolescence.

Classes 1A and IB, in conjunction with the Scottish Chamber Orchestra, performed a composition entitled 'Shipyard Blues' (a mixture of music and mime) at the Museum of Education in Glasgow.

A man of realities. A man of facts and calculations. A man who proceeds upon the principle that two and two are four, and nothing over, and who is not to be talked into allowing for anything over.

Charles Dickens, *Hard Times*

Murray ran a pretty tight ship, and nobody took any liberties. He also did everything by the book: so every time I went for a five- minute stroll up Waverley Drive, I had to inform his secretary.

On one occasion, the staff was divided into four or five seminar groups - so that they could discuss (it was assumed) the mechanics of the Region's campaign to stamp out racial discrimination in schools - and I found myself in the group chaired by Murray. There was very little discussion: he simply 'went round the class' half a dozen times, asking every member of the group his or her opinion on specific aspects of the policy document under consideration.

Murray was very focused: once he had decided to pursue a particular course of action, he concentrated on that course of action to the exclusion of everything - and everybody - else. However, this earnestness was occasionally lightened by a willingness to lend a sympathetic ear to members of staff with personal problems – though it was very obvious that he wasn't comfortable in the role of counsellor.

65

1991

The Beginning of the End

The painters and decorators arrived: so it was now absolutely inevitable that the High School would be closed.

The school said goodbye to Helen Leith (Senior Technician in the Science Department), who 'seemed to know the answer to just about every question she was asked - and my goodness, she was asked a lot'.

The Parents' Association organised a St Valentine's Disco.

Jennifer Hall won the senior section of a public speaking contest (for schools) held under the auspices of Wishaw Speakers' Club.

Steven Alexander won the Scottish Schools' Junior Badminton Championship. He was also Lanarkshire Champion.

A small group of 1st Year pupils, led by Lisa Paul and Cheryl Ann Thomson, who had organised a Bring and Buy Sale in aid of the Blue Peter Appeal for Romanian orphans, received the following letter from Lewis Bronze, Editor of *Blue Peter*:

Dear Class IA,

Thank you very much for your donation of £118 towards our Great Blue Peter Bring and Buy for Romania. It has made a valuable contribution to our appeal.

Your help, together with that of other Blue Peter viewers, will improve the lives of Romanian children living in orphanages.

With best wishes from Yvette, John, Diane, and all the rest of us on the programme.
Yours sincerely,
Lewis Bronze

A la recherche du temps perdu

'On a Saturday night towards the end of March,' wrote John Stewart, 'when everybody else was putting the clock back one hour, a group met in The Moorings in Motherwell to put the clock back twenty-five years. Fifty ex-pupils of Wishaw High School had been traced and had agreed to hold a reunion. They converged from Chingford, Buxted, Wales, and Wishaw - and even from Shotts. One FP, who is now in Germany, was delayed in the South of France setting up a computer exhibition - but he came anyway, a day late, and phoned a lot of the people he had missed the night before.

The FPs assembled, all of them sporting neat name badges (printed in large letters, in deference to the passing of time), to aid identification. People recognised the friends of yesteryear, some of them fatter of face, some thinner of hair, some unchanged. The characters had certainly remained as effervescent as ever, and the first problem for the chairman was how to make himself heard above the chatter in order to get everyone seated for the meal.

The girls' captain in session 1964-65, Margaret Harries (now Chairperson of the Welsh Social Workers' Association), and the boys' vice-captain, Peter Hughes (now Chairman of the Scottish Steelfounders' Association), gave short, humorous talks, reviving memories of our days together at the High School - and Graham Nichols got a special mention because he had turned up wearing his original school tie.

Most FPs had written short life histories; and when copies of these were distributed, we discovered that our class had spanned the world, from Canada to Australia, in jobs ranging from farming to finance. People exchanged reminiscences and chatted about their current lives, children, grandchildren, wives, husbands, and pets. There are six couples married to each other. One lady diffidently described herself as a housewife in Overtown, but further discussion revealed that she puts in more hours per week on charity work than many people do in their regular job.

Everyone declared the evening a great success, and voted to repeat the process in another twenty-five years - if a suitable retirement home can be found.'

Drama Students

Sixteen 5th Year pupils working on a module about the media went behind the scenes at the Citizens Theatre. They met the lighting crew, joiners, set designers, sound engineers, costume designers, seamstresses, stage managers, actors, and directors; they also visited the rehearsal rooms, examined props that had been used in previous productions, and were shown how various special effects were created.

Three displays were mounted in the school: one on France, one on fabrics and design, and one illustrating the harmful effects drugs, alcohol, and smoking can have on people's health.

The Scripture Union started collecting T-shirts for children on the streets of Lima.

Stuart Thomson won both a silver and a bronze medal at the Scottish Tae Kwon Do Championships. Jacqui Jamieson gained a black belt in that same martial art.

The Sewing Society produced various designs for Easter and Mother's Day.

The senior girls' hockey team were runners-up in the Tait Trophy competition.

Eleven 1st Year girls took part in a New Image Rugby Tournament at Cleland Estate. The girls were runners-up to Bellshill Academy and were awarded medals and a pennant.

In the competition (sponsored by British Coal) to find the best caretaker in Britain, Graham Sneddon, the head janitor, gained a Highly Commended Certificate. Graham was a droll character, with a dry - and sometimes dismissive - turn of phrase. The Direct Works Department, to take a case in point, was based at the High School (in the pavilion, actually), and Graham didn't have a very high regard for some of its operatives: 'These cunts couldnae hammer a nail through the centre of a doughnut,' he told me on one occasion. Graham had a dog called Jason, and whenever a football match was being played on Waverley, there was always a danger that it would cause havoc.

Julie Anderson's project for CSYS Biology - a behavioural study of black apes - was judged to be the best of the four hundred submitted to the Examination Board.

> **California here I come,**
> **Minnesota here I come,**
> **Pennsylvania.....**

Sales of the textbook (*The UK Political System*) written by John Wright and Sam Graham of the Modern Studies Department exceeded thirteen thousand. Wright was one of twenty-nine teachers from eighteen different countries who were invited to America to take part in a course for Modern Studies specialists sponsored by USIA. The course included lectures about various regions and field trips to such cities as Atlanta, San Francisco and Washington DC.

The High School forged close links with the Fairbridge Drake Trust (latterly, it was called simply Fairbridge), an organisation that aimed 'to build fair bridges out of the mental ghettos too many young people lived in, enabling them to walk into a constructive, purposeful future'. In 1991 and 1992, various groups of pupils (twenty 2nd Year pupils, for example, whose behaviour had been consistently good) were given the opportunity to take part in such outdoor activities as hillwalking, canoeing, and orienteering; and written appraisals of each pupil were later sent to the school.

At a regatta held at the Watersports Centre in Strathclyde Park, Stuart Hallford and Andrew McGregor won gold medals in sailing and canoeing respectively.

The Riding Club (it had eighteen members and was supervised by Lynn Veitch and Shirley Muir) attended classes at the Woodfoot Riding School in Larkhall.

First Impressions

The following comments - by 1st Year pupils, at the end of their first term at the High School - appeared in *High Times*:

> *The High School is not an easy place to find your way about.*
(Anon)

> *I like Wishaw High better than Primary because on the way to
> another class you can have a little talk to your pals.*
(David McKnight)

> *I hate carrying my bags about.*
(Cheryl Rodgers)

> *At Primary you get out early and get your dinner quickly.*
(Anon)

I would say my best thing is woodwork because you don't write anything.
(Thomas Bissett)

Wishaw High School is quite 'knackering' at first as you travel from the main building to the huts and the annexe.
(Richard Clark)

I like Wishaw High better than Primary because at the start of the year you can miss half the period by pretending you don't know where to go.
(Harry Hands)

A *Summer Serenade* included contributions from the Junior Choir, Julie Anderson (who 'brought the house down' with her renditions of 'The Power of Love' and 'I dreamed a dream'), the Concert Band, the Junior Band, the Senior Brass Group, the Woodwind Ensemble, the Guitar Ensemble, Grant Law (saxophone), and the Senior Girls' Ensemble, who sang 'One Hand One Heart', a song they later sang at the wedding of two FPs who met while they were members of the school choir.

At the Greengairs and District Horticultural Show, Aileen Barrie, Principal Teacher of Geography, won 1st Prize in the Blackcurrant Jam Section.

A group of 4th Year pupils went fishing at Lanark Loch with Jimmy Pringle.

Geraldine MacPhee, Principal Teacher of Home Economics, started a 'trim in' at lunchtime for the benefit of 6th Year pupils. There was a weekly charge, and the fines that were levied - if any of the pupils put on weight - were donated to a good cause at Christmas.

Andrew Loudon was victorious in a cross-country race (organised by Motherwell District Council) at Wishaw Sports Centre.

In November, an Astroturf pitch (suitable for both football and hockey) was opened in Houldsworth Park. The High School, the only secondary school in Wishaw to play competitive hockey, staged an exhibition game; and all the pupils who took part were presented with a commemorative pennant and a free pass for Wishaw Baths.

544

Two courses - Christmas Fayre Cookery and Crafty Christmas Fabrics - were on offer to returning adults. Each course lasted six weeks.

Mrs Cowie of the Home Economics Department baked twelve Christmas cakes in order to raise money for the Tear Fund.

Lorna Mitchell was a member of a group of pupils from Lanarkshire who visited the European Parliament in Strasbourg.

Born Losers

'At this point it is necessary to inform you,' according to a tongue-in-cheek intimation in the *Wishaw Press*, 'that parents are putting down their children's names for Wishaw High School (just as they do for Eton) before they are even born. One lady, whose baby is still "pending", has reserved a place for her son/daughter in the school crèche.'

Sisyphus Redux

One had to admire the doggedness with which Murray kept submitting requests to the officials in Lanark Division's Education Department that they should authorise certain improvements in the buildings and facilities at the High School. He could also be very decisive: after I had informed him that I had been granted early retirement, I don't think it took him more than ten seconds to decide that he was going to shut down the Classics Department.

66

Decline and Fall Part IV— 'Delenda est Carthago'

During the summer of 1990, two conflicting reports appeared in the *Wishaw Press*: 'a very reliable source' had told a member of the Forth (sic) Parents' Action Group that the High School was definitely going to be closed; and an equally 'reliable source' had stated that the High School was 'under consideration for a major upgrading programme'. The optimism engendered by the latter report only lasted a few months, for as a result of cuts in the Region's budget (which was published in November), the High School was not included in the capital building programme for 1990-91. 'We understand the present financial circumstances of Strathclyde Region,' Murray commented, 'and we accept that they are having to prioritise.'

In October 1991, the Education Committee approved the publication of a consultative document on the provision of non- denominational education in Central and South Wishaw and the neighbouring villages of Law, Overtown, Morningside, and Newmains. It was proposed in this document that all classes at the High School should be discontinued as from June 1992; that all pupils in attendance at the High School should be 'relocated' on the campus of Garrion Academy at the start of session 1992-93; and that all pupils in the High School's feeder primaries should in future transfer to Garrion Academy for the secondary stage of their education.

The reasons given to justify these proposals were as follows: the rolls of the High School and Garrion Academy had fallen well below those two schools' capacities; small rolls made it increasingly difficult to provide 'the full range of educational opportunities appropriate to a modern secondary education', and a merger was the best way to obviate this difficulty; and a combination of several factors - the respective capacities of the High School and Garrion Academy, the facilities that were available (or unavailable) at each of the two schools and, most importantly, the fact that it would cost £6.5 million to upgrade the High School (an option that was both 'economically unsound' and a logistical nightmare, since alternative accommodation would have to be found for 600-odd pupils for two years) - pointed clearly to the campus of Garrion Academy as the obvious site for such a merger.

Almost as an afterthought (and this may be of interest to those cynics who were convinced that the real objective of the proposed merger was to save, or even make, money for Strathclyde Region), the consultative document suggested that the buildings and grounds of the High School could be sold to private developers for more than a million pounds.

Les Dalrymple, Chairman of the School Board, criticised the consultative document for "reading like a lawyer's brief", and the pupils at the High School were reported to be 'very vociferous in their disapproval of the proposed merger'. On the other hand, the verbal reaction (to the document) of certain politicos was ominously evasive and obfuscatory; it sounded as if it had been crafted by Sir Humphrey Appleby, and it wouldn't have been out of place in a speech by Jim Hacker:

We certainly think that the future shape of education is very, very important, but we would want to comment after everyone has considered the position and all the arguments. It is not for us to prejudge the outcome. We can well understand people wanting to fight their corner, but equally we are living in hard times. At the end of the day, the Education Committee will need to look at the position having regard to the whole situation.

Unusually for an MP (on most contentious issues, local or otherwise, MPs normally nail their colours to the fence until opinion polls and focus groups persuade them that it would be expedient to adopt a particular stance), but no less worryingly (as far as the future of the High School was concerned), Dr Jeremy Bray was not as guarded about the recommendations of the consultative document as his local counterparts; in fact, he seemed to have come perilously close to making up his mind regarding the issue in question:

The creation and organisation of what would effectively be a new school (and the largest in Wishaw) could be an opportunity to reshape secondary education in Wishaw to meet the needs of children today.

Dr. Bray even came up with a name for the 'new' school - Wishaw Academy - justifying this rather crass suggestion with the even more witless assertion that he couldn't see why the name 'Wishaw Academy' would not be appropriate since 'there would be no confusion with Wishaw Academy Primary School'.

When a politician sticks his head so far above the parapet, it usually means that he knows something the general public doesn't; and in this instance it is not beyond the bounds of possibility that Dr Bray had heard through the political grapevine that the Labour Group on Strathclyde Regional Council had already targeted the High School for closure.

In my opinion, therefore, the political omens were far from favourable. The School Board, however, wasted no time in launching a campaign (based on the proposition: "It's not the Board who will save the school, but the people of Wishaw") to try and save the High School from closure; and to set the ball rolling, appeals for support were made (by letter) not only to nearly 500 parents but also to various political groups in the local community. For the most part, the campaign concentrated on the positive reasons for keeping the High School open, and steered clear of rubbishing Garrion Academy ("We don't wish to see it close either"); it did, however, include an element of scaremongering, insofar as it laid great stress on the 'facts' that if the High School was closed, not only would the building be demolished but all the pupils from its feeder primaries would have to attend the 'new' school at Gowkthrapple - since Coltness High School was full, and there were no plans to enlarge it.

Meanwhile, the consultation process was set in motion: fourteen public meetings were arranged, the most significant of which was the one held in the High School on 26 November. Feelings seem to have run very high at this 'packed and emotional' meeting, which was attended by more than 300 pupils, parents and members of staff, various politicians, and several officials from Lanark Division's Education Department. A pupil from the High School predicted continuous gang warfare at the 'new' school between the High School and Garrion Academy contingents; and, according to the *Wishaw Press*, he was accorded 'a roar of approval' when he fired the following (provocative) question at the DEO: 'Why should we go to Garrion and come home with a black eye just to save you money?'

The local councillors who were present expressed many worthy sentiments in support of the educational status quo in Wishaw. 'If I am given the choice,' declared Bill Irvine, 'between saving money and improving education in the area, then education will win every time.'

As for Dr Jeremy Bray, he was back where one normally expects to find politicians - sitting on the fence with both ears to the ground:
Both Garrion Academy and Wishaw High School have cause to be proud of their record in recent years, and they have both made real progress: so it is very natural that they should not wish to see all that effort thrown away. For every parent, the individual needs of his children are by far the most important consideration, and a big disruption in a child's

548

education (such as changing schools) can be stressful both before and after it takes place.

However, schools and the education authority have to consider the longer-term needs of all present and future pupils - and it is very difficult to balance these two.

After this public meeting - and a private meeting with officials from the Education Department - Les Dalrymple, Chairman of the School Board, declared: "I am more confident than ever that the school can be saved. It's definitely all there to play for."

The consultation process continued with the submission (to the DEO) of the views of various interested parties. These included Regional Councillors Irvine and Gibson; the School Boards and staff of the High School, Garrion Academy, Coltness High School, and their feeder primaries; EIS and SSTA members at the High School and Garrion Academy; Strathclyde Police; the Joint Wards of Wishaw Labour Party; Central Wishaw Community Council; and the supervisors of the crèche in the High School's annexe.

A barren superfluity of words

Sir Samuel Garth, *The Dispensary*

The ingeniousness of many of the arguments advanced in these submissions and the mechanical nature of the DEO's response ('Many of them were considered and coherent, but none of them by itself was fully convincing') have an air of unreality about them: they read like the transcript of a debate in the House of Commons whose outcome is a foregone conclusion since the Government can command a majority of 150.

However, one argument - that the existence of a school in the centre of Wishaw contributes to the economic well-being of the town - about which I was extremely sceptical at the time, has been fully validated by the derelict appearance (since the mid-1990s) of the bottom half of Wishaw Main Street, which is now a commercial wasteland.

Most of the other substantial arguments against the closure of the High School and its merger with Garrion Academy on the campus of the latter establishment focused on the respective locations of the two schools; the soundness or otherwise of their superstructures; the social, financial, and educational implications of the proposed closure and merger; the size of the 'new' school; and the significant role played by the High School in the social and cultural history of the local community.

Many of the submissions stressed the advantages of having a secondary school in the centre of Wishaw; these included easy access for pupils, parents, and returning adults if they were attending school on a daily basis or taking part in extra-curricular activities. Conversely, it would take pupils significantly longer to get to the 'new' school at Gowkthrapple; and some of them would have to change buses if they happened to be travelling by public transport after school or on a Saturday morning.

Great stress was also laid on the excellence of the main building at the High School and its place in the cultural heritage of the local community. Garrion Academy's superstructure, on the other hand, was described - with a hint of wishful thinking, perhaps - as lacking the solidity to cope with the wear and tear concomitant with a doubling of its roll.

In socially deprived areas, according to the School Board, small community schools like the High School, with its staffing 'enhancements' and small classes, could provide the supportive atmosphere that was particularly helpful to the many vulnerable children on its roll. Moreover, if the merger went ahead, there was the possibility of friction between pupils from two socially disparate communities, one of which was in essence an area of priority treatment.

Citing the cost of transporting pupils to the 'new' school, the Board also questioned the notion that the closure of the High School would save money in the long term. A more cost-effective strategy, it argued, would be to forget about closing the school, demolish the huts and the annexe, sell part of the land on which they were located, and spend some of the revenue from this sale on upgrading the main building.

The parents of pupils at the feeder primaries expressed concern about the effect a change of school might have on those High School pupils who were forced to transfer to another campus; and the School Board at Garrion Academy was worried by the possibility that the roll of the 'new' school would increase to unmanageable proportions.

And finally, many former pupils and teachers maintained that some consideration should be given to the fact that the High School had been in existence for almost ninety years, and that for most of this period it had been the only secondary school in the town.

The counter arguments of the DEO sounded equally plausible. It was conceded, of course, that the location of the 'new' school was neither as

550

central nor as readily accessible by public transport as that of the High School. No pupil, however, would have to travel more than 3½ miles to get to the 'new' school, and no pupil's journey would take longer than thirty minutes - such times and distances being deemed neither excessive nor in any way exceptional; pupils who lived more than two miles from the 'new' school would be provided with free transport; and bus passes would be available for those who stayed on after school to take part in extra-curricular activities.

A survey conducted by the Department of Architecture had certainly confirmed that the main building at the High School was structurally sound and would last for many years if properly maintained; however, the survey had delivered the same verdict about Garrion Academy's superstructure.

The DEO argued that small community schools in areas of deprivation might compound the social disadvantages they sought to remedy. In his judgment, reduced aspirations, more limited resources, and outdated buildings did not compensate for social deprivation - no matter how caring and supportive the staff in these schools might be.

Territorial and social tensions were always a possibility in a school that had been created as the result of a merger, but previous experience indicated that the problems were relatively short-lived, and could be overcome by good management and the creation of a distinctive school identity. Separate schools underlined differences between communities, whereas integration could help to obviate them.

The closure of the High School would save £70,000 per annum. These savings would continue indefinitely, and would only be marginally offset by the cost of transporting pupils to the 'new' school.

Pupils who were forced to change schools in the middle of their secondary careers were to be reassured by the expertise of the Education Department in merging the curricula of two separate schools with minimal disruption, a process that would be aided by enhanced staffing levels.

The roll of the 'new' school would only exceed its capacity if there was a total cessation of placing requests from the catchment areas of the High School and Garrion Academy - a highly unlikely eventuality, especially since Coltness High School would have spare capacity due to a decline in the number of pupils in its traditional catchment area.

There was no room for tradition in the 'brave new world' envisaged by the DEO. Education could not be a static or backward-looking process; it had to grow and change. Though its buildings might be demolished, the quintessential character of the High School would survive among its staff and pupils, enabling them to meet the challenges of tomorrow in a different setting.

Someone, somewhere, doesn't want a letter from you.

In addition to the written submissions, the DEO received the following: three petitions - one from the School Board at the High School with more than 300 signatures, one from a group of pupils at Garrion Academy with 380 signatures, and one from a pupil at one of the High School's feeder primaries with 47 signatures; 97 letters from individual members of the public; 10 standardised letters from 6th Year pupils at Garrion Academy; and 68 standardised letters from pupils, parents, and other interested parties associated with the High School. All these letters and petitions either supported the retention of the High School as one of three non-denominational secondary schools in Wishaw, or opposed the merger of the High School and Garrion Academy.

John Carlin, President of the Lanarkshire Association of the EIS, also issued the following statement:
The closure of Wishaw High School will be to the disadvantage of young people from Areas of Priority Treatment. There is a clear need for long-term investment in education, and our Association wishes to see existing schools retained and developed.

However, the scale of this negative response to the consultative document did not impress the DEO, who claimed that in his experience it was 'average and by no means overwhelming'.

We was robbed.

Joe Jacobs

Practically nobody was in favour of the closure of the High School and its merger with Garrion Academy, but that is what the DEO recommended to the Education Committee. 'It must be the force of argument,' he declared, 'that decides such issues. It is not enough to hold on to the status quo merely for the sake of it.'

If we take the first part of that statement at face value, then the arguments of those who opposed the closure of the High School were undoubtedly strong enough to gain, at the very least, 'a share of the points'. It is difficult, therefore, to avoid reaching the conclusion that Atropos had already cut the thread of the High School's existence; that the entire consultative process was a sham; and that the DEO was merely going through the (very cynical) motions. There seems to be little point in instituting a consultative process, if not a blind bit of notice is taken of the views of the consultees.

Deus ex (Party) Machina

All was not lost, however, for a week before the fateful meeting of the Education Committee Regional Councillor James Gibson proclaimed: 'Mr Irvine and I will pull out all the stops.' Alas and alack! Councillors Gibson and Irvine may have pulled out all the stops (short of voting against the party line), but they did not prevent the Education Committee from pulling the plug on the High School on 5 February 1992.

Infamy! Infamy! They've all got it in for me.

Carry on Cleo

The decision to close the High School was described as 'regrettable' by the Lanarkshire Association of the EIS; 'diabolical' by a spokesman for the Parents' Action Group; and 'very hard' by Councillor Gibson, who claimed that he and Councillor Irvine had done 'as much as they possibly could'. This claim was savaged in the correspondence columns of the *Wishaw Press*:

Two Labour councillors who promised to make representations against the closure, who openly professed their respect and affection for the High School (and confirmed these sentiments in private correspondence) ....voted for closure. Party before people, party before everything.

The two councillors who changed their minds and voted for closure should be run out of town. Mr Gibson's father-in-law must be turning in his grave.

In fairness to Councillors Gibson and Irvine, it should be pointed out that they may not have voted for the closure of the High School: they may have abstained.

Meanwhile, back in his beleaguered domain, Iain Murray was sad. "But we must look to the future," he said, "for it's the children who matter."

David Pringle, the pupils' representative on the School Board, was also sad - 'to see a good school go'.

Les Dalrymple, Chairman of the School Board, was angry: "It's not a democratic process when you listen to the people and then don't pay the slightest heed."

Drew Morrice, EIS rep at the High School, was disillusioned: 'A lot of good arguments were put forward by parents, teachers, the community and the EIS, and we feel that these arguments have not been properly addressed.'

Thomas Dalgleish, Chairman of Newmains Primary School Board, was displeased: "A lot of people don't want to send their children to Garrion."

Jean Jackson, one of the mature students enrolled at the High School, was disgusted: "The classes are great, the staff are very friendly, and you know that your children are safe in the crèche. I couldn't go to Garrion: it's too far to travel."

The less mature students at the High School were disgruntled: "I think it's terrible to close Wishaw High. It has a good spirit and good teachers." (Emma Henderson)

'Some parents have enough financial difficulties without having to fork out money for new school uniforms.' (Martin Tweedie)

'There could be fights between different groups of pupils.' (Kris Keene, who would probably have been in the thick of them)

A spokesman for Dalziel's Bakery in the Main Street was disappointed: "One of our most popular offers is the 'Kids' Special' (a drink, chips, and a cream ring for 60p), but obviously there won't be as big a demand for this from now on."

The reaction of Sam Love, Chairman of Central Wishaw Community Council, was more likely to discomfit local politicians and, consequently, more likely to bring about a reversal of the decisions taken by the Education Committee:

My phone hasn't stopped ringing - and people are angry. Strathclyde Regional Council are not carrying out the wishes of the people who elected them, and the public should make their feelings known at the next regional elections.

Roma locuta est; causa finita est.

St Augustine

Strathclyde Regional Council, however, was 'not for turning', and a spokesman for the Council defended the decision to close the High School by asserting that it was 'under-subscribed'. By the end of the week, it was slightly more 'under-subscribed', for a handful of the 'better' pupils in S3 decamped to Coltness High School.

A few days later, the School Board decided (unanimously) that opting out of regional control (the only course of action still open to the Board, if the High School was to be saved) was not 'a viable possibility' - since, in the words of Les Dalrymple, there was 'not really the will for opting out in Wishaw'.

According to Sam Love, the decision on whether or not the school should opt out of regional control should have been taken by parents - and not by the School Board; he also castigated the Board for 'not having fought at all' to save the school, and suggested that anybody connected with the High School (whether he was a teacher, or a cleaner, or a janitor, or a member of the School Board) who did not support opting out should resign. This uncompromising stance received a measure of support in a letter (written by James S. Taylor) that appeared in the *Wishaw Press*:

I, like many others, was particularly disappointed by the way in which the proposed closure of the High School was (apparently) so meekly accepted by parents in general and by the School Board in particular.

All I would venture to suggest on this issue (and the high- powered campaigns in the 1960s and 1970s to have Coltness High School converted into a six-year school and the zoning arrangements in North Wishaw distorted in its favour seem to validate such a suggestion) is that the Region would have had a hell of a fight on its hands if it had tried at any time to close that particular establishment.

This point is touched on by Sheila Sprot in the following pertinent (to some extent, possibly) comments about the closure of the High School:

Ultimately, what closed the High School was our political naivety: we should have had the politicians in our corner from the beginning, not just in the last couple of years when it was too late for anything but a rearguard action. I blame no one for this: we were all too busy getting on with the job to see the need for it. Other people were not so naive; and we could have learned a lot, for instance, from studying the political manoeuvres that led to Brandon High School moving from Motherwell to Coltness, the first nail in our coffin.

Good things happened at the High School, but they happened to the kind of inarticulate people who could not express in words what the school had done for them, or how it had helped them socially and educationally. That doesn't mean that they were not well taught or well cared for. The good we did was never publicised (as a matter of deliberate school policy), and this may have proved to be counterproductive in the end. In my opinion, we were always too modest about our achievements.

The powers that be always seem to respond to the people who stand up and say, 'Me, Me, Me', the people who draw attention to themselves vociferously. The humane, caring person is never very good at that kind of exhibitionism, and so he gets overlooked.

My own personal thoughts on the closure of the High School are as follows:

Given that Strathclyde Region was determined to close one of the three non-denominational secondary schools in Wishaw, it was obvious - in view of Coltness High School's great popularity with local parents and politicians - that the axe would fall on either the High School or Garrion Academy. Both these schools (especially the former) had seen better days, and neither of them had much political clout: so, in my judgment, what tipped the scales in Garrion's favour was the simple consideration that it was just not politically feasible to close a school that had been opened less than twenty years earlier. It may also, I suppose, have crossed the minds of some councillors (or, more likely, the minds of some of the officials in the Education Department) that if the High School was closed the Region would probably be able to make money from the sale of a prime site in the centre of Wishaw.

'We class schools, you see, into four grades: Leading School, First-rate School, Good School, and School. Frankly,' said Mr Levy, 'School is pretty bad.'

Evelyn Waugh, Decline and Fall

Whatever considerations may have influenced the Regional Councillors, their decision to close the High School was undoubtedly correct. For the first sixty years of its existence, the High School was a 'First-rate school'. However, from the late 1960s onwards - as a result of the Parent's Charter and the diabolical zoning arrangements that obtained in Wishaw – its status changed rapidly to 'Good School', and even more rapidly to 'School'. It did have several good features and it did experience, on occasion, a brief revival, but there were times when it could have been described as the anus of the educational world. Former members of staff still have nightmares about the 1st Year that infested the school in session 1991-92; and I myself couldn't get out of the High School and the teaching profession quickly enough after a series of horrendous experiences with the 3rd Year Latin class that appeared on my timetable the previous session. For three hours every week, I felt as though I had been thrown into a cage full of orang-utans with severe learning difficulties: some of the boys were so thick that they had to sing 'Happy Birthday' to themselves a couple of times before they could remember their name. In the words of Schiller, 'Mit der Dummheit kampfen Gotter selbst vergebens' (Against stupidity the gods themselves contend in vain).

67

1992

Infandum, regina, iubes renovare dolorem.

Virgil, *Aeneid*

A fish tank was set up in Room 21.

Kim Livingstone, 'a talented poet', represented the High School in a public speaking competition held under the auspices of Wishaw Speakers' Club. The following is one of her poems; its dark undertones are particularly striking:

Poor Old Joe

I'll tell you a story of long ago,
It's all about a man called Joe.
Firstly, let's get a couple of things straight:
Cats loathed him, and cats he did hate.
But his wife, whose name was Jane,
Thought her husband was a pain.
She loved cats, and cats loved her:
How she smiled to hear them purr.
So a kitten was bought, playful and smug,
A litter tray also, along with a rug.
A short time later another kitten was there,
And soon there were cats everywhere.
Joe mumbled and grumbled about the litter tray,
And how the cats were always in his way.
By this time the number of cats was just four,
But very soon Jane longed for more.
Two more were bought, along with others —
Unwanted kittens, craving for mothers.
Joe moaned and groaned, he could take no more:
Cats were arriving by the score,
Cats were taking over the house.
"At least," Jane reasoned, "we haven't a mouse."
That night, in their comfy bed,

Joe turned to Jane and finally said,
"It's either the cats or me, Jane,
You've got to choose.
Is it the cats you want to lose?"
"I'll think about it," Jane replied.
But overnight poor Joe died.
"It's the cats," the doctor said,
"That's the reason your husband's dead.
It's an allergy, and that is why
Poor old Joe just had to die."
The cremation was a sad affair:
Only Jane and the cats were there.
Jane had a brainwave the very next day:
"We can use his ashes for the litter tray."
So that's what happened to poor old Joe:
In the litter tray his ashes did go.
And that is why until this day
There are ashes in that litter tray.
Now poor old Joe will never be free,
For on him the cats tinkle with glee.

(Dedicated to my mum, stepdad, and our cats)

Alison Brown was runner-up in the under-14 singles at the Lanarkshire Schools' Badminton Championships; and she and her partner, Cheryl Rodgers, were runners-up in the under-15 doubles.

Pat McGowan, Acting Principal Teacher of English, was one of the judges at Morningside Primary's Burns Competition.

Hutchie Sneddon, a former pupil of the High School, was appointed Lord-Lieutenant of Lanarkshire. In the course of a distinguished career in local politics, he was Provost of the Burgh of Motherwell and Wishaw from 1971 till 1975, and Vice- President of the Confederation of Scottish Local Authorities from 1974 till 1976. He was awarded the OBE in 1968 and the CBE in 1983.

The interim Board of the 'new' school at Gowkthrapple held its first meeting.

A bulletin (entitled "The New School - What's in it for You") was published in order to keep all pupils at the High School and Garrion Academy up to date with the arrangements being made for the first session (1992-93) at the 'new' school. These arrangements were coordinated by Ruth Hodgson and Linda Johnstone, AHTs at the High School and Garrion Academy respectively.

Parturient montes, nascetur ridiculus mus.

Horace, *Ars Poetica*

Having assured pupils that the main building of the 'new' school would be re-roofed, the Merger Bulletin invited them to suggest an appropriate name and uniform for their prospective alma mater. Sixty different names were suggested, and pupils (and their parents) and teachers at the High School, Garrion Academy and their feeder primaries were asked to vote for one of the four most popular suggestions - Clyde Valley High School, Kirknethan High School, Craignethan High School, and Belhaven Academy. Clyde Valley High School topped the poll, an outcome that was welcomed by Councillor Bill Irvine: "I like the name; it's a name that is associated with quality." The High School's colours were represented in the uniform of the 'new' school by the mandatory light blue blouse or shirt.

At the morning assemblies, the Reverend Kenneth Armstrong of Wishaw Baptist Church gave a series of talks on a visit he had made to Romania. Another series of talks, on alcohol and drug abuse, was given by Billy Kennedy, a representative of the Scottish Band of Hope, to S1/2 Guidance classes.

Bibles were presented (for the last time) to 1st Year pupils by representatives of the Gideons' Bible Society.

As part of their 'options programme', fifty 2nd Year pupils visited the Careers 2000 Exhibition at the SEEC in Glasgow.

Jim Murray, Scottish Bantamweight Champion (and a former pupil of the High School), died as a result of the injuries he sustained during his attempt to win the British title.

Teachers and pupils from the High School visited Garrion Academy, as did the pupils' parents and returning adults. One of the parents, Mrs Evelyn Dunbar, expressed 'grave concern' about the inadequate heating, the state of the roof, and the general long-term neglect.

The Last Judgment

Murray made the following claims (in the school newspaper) about his years as head teacher of the High School:

I have noticed a steady improvement in the morale of pupils, staff, and parents as various aspects of the school have begun to improve. The main building has been repainted, and work is well in hand for the establishment of a fish pond in one of the quadrangles. The curriculum has been extended to include more courses, and class sizes have been reduced to the point where there are only a few teaching groups with more than twenty pupils. The wearing of school uniform and the attendance rate have improved.

The morale of pupils and their parents is such a nebulous entity that it is impossible to quantify it. As far as the morale of the staff was concerned, my morale definitely didn't improve in the late 1980s (it required almost superhuman willpower to drag myself out of my bed in the morning and face up to the prospect of another day at the chalkface); nor did that of any other teacher to whom I have spoken.

I have never understood why so many head teachers set such great store by their pupils wearing school uniform (they seem to regard this as the touchstone of their school's standing in the local community), and so I am pleased to record that Murray did not make a big thing of this issue.

Somehow or other, I have managed to acquire the absence sheet for 6 June 1992. The absence rates on that particular date were as follows: 1st Year - 28%; 2nd Year - 18%; 3rd Year - 22%; 4th Year - 72%; 5th Year - 50%.

Last Rites

A special Open Day was arranged to mark 'the end of an era', and Joan Sandell organised an exhibition of High School memorabilia in the library.

Strathclyde Regional Council gave an assurance that the war memorials and the boards listing the names of dux medallists would be preserved for future generations.

The last prize-giving took place on 25 June; and the last dux of the school was Fiona Dunbar. Regarding the closure of the High School, Fiona had this to say:

I have done most of my growing up at Wishaw High School, so it's quite sad. Almost everyone in Wishaw has had something to do with the school

561

at some time or other. I can't imagine what it will be like with the school not there.

Well done, thou good and faithful servants...

St Matthew ch. 25, v. 21 (adapted)

The following long-serving members of staff announced their retiral: Jimmy Clelland (Depute Rector), Harry Corbet (Technical Department), Helen Costley (Admin Assistant), Anne Donnelly (Principal Teacher of Guidance), Jack Harvie (Principal Teacher of Art), Ruth Hodgson (AHT), John McQueen (Principal Teacher of Chemistry), Hazel Morrison (Maths Department), Graham Sneddon (janitor), and Ina Ross (secretary), "the cheery voice on the High School's telephone service".

The Long Goodbye

On 30 June, the day on which the High School finally shut up shop, the staff received the following message from Ruth Hodgson and Linda Johnstone, the merger coordinators:

Sincere thanks to all of you for your cooperation and incredible cheerfulness in a seemingly never-ending and exhausting task over recent months.

You have packed and unpacked almost 3,000 boxes, using 360 rolls of vinyl sticky tape and almost 400 metres of bubble wrap; you have filled well over 1,000 white salvage bags with recyclable materials; you have filled almost 1,000 black rubbish bags and about ten skips; you have packed over 300 boxes of surplus paper and reading materials, which will go (thanks to Education Aid) to help with relief work in Albanian schools ... and all that was over and above your teaching.

Best wishes to all who are retiring, or who are taking up new positions elsewhere; special good wishes to those of you who as yet do not have a job; and all the best to the staff of the new Clyde Valley High School.

Have a good holiday everyone.

Tirez le rideau, la farce est jouée.

Rabelais

According to some of the survivors, the ship's band played on deck until the *Titanic* slipped beneath the icy waters of the Atlantic. In similar fashion ('si parva licet componere magnis') - and very appropriately, since it was the last in a long line of choirs and ensembles that had enriched the extra-curricular life of the school for more than eighty years, and had also kept on playing during the previous decade, impervious to all the disruption and uncertainty about the school's future - the Concert Band provided the background music as the High School 'sank unwept into oblivion'.

Perhaps not entirely 'unwept'; perhaps not 'into oblivion' - at least not right away.

Post war school trip to Clermand Ferrand (July 1952)
This is the official photo published in *La Montagne*

Certificate awarded to Wishaw High School (1991)

Class Picture (1930s)

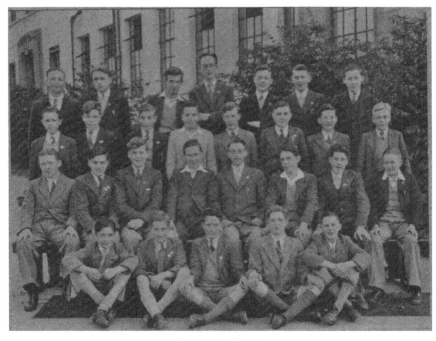

Class V-VI (1944)

Class picture from Coronation Year (1953)

Class 2D (1958)

Class 3C (1959)

Class picture (1960-61)

Class 1a1 (1960)

Class 1a1 (1962)

Class Photo (1963)

6th Year (1968)

4th Year Boys (1970)

4th Year Girls (1970)

Class picture (1971)

6th Year (1973)

Last day of school for 6th Year (1982)

6th Year (1985)

Class picture (1985)

Musical Director .... Mr S. LAIRD
Assistant Musical Director .... Mr T. AITKEN
Production Director .... THE RECTOR
Assistant Producer .... Mr J. MASON
Stage Manager .... Mr J. FLEMING
Assistant Stage Manager .... Mr A. LINDSAY
Business Manager .... Mr D. W. D. WINTON
Assistant Business Manager .... Miss M. L. YOUNG
Choreography .... Miss M. PARK
Scenery .... THE ART DEPARTMENT
                        THE TECHNICAL DEPARTMENT
Wardrobe .... Miss I. GIRDWOOD
Stage Electricians .... Dr. G. HUNTER
                        THOMAS GILCHRIST
                        ARTHUR CONNOR
                        WILLIAM HERBERT
Maquillage .... Under the Direction of
                        Mr J. H. SMITH
At the Electric Organ .... Mr MOFFAT RADCLIFFE
At the Drums .... Mr THOMAS PEW

★   ★   ★

Costumes of Principals and Chorus by
W. MUTRIE & SONS, EDINBURGH

★   ★   ★

SOFT DRINKS ON SALE
in the Foyer during interval

★   ★   ★

Buses will be available after the show

★   ★   ★

These programmes made possible through the
generosity of
COLIN P. BAIRD, Esq., O.B.E., Wishaw

★   ★   ★

The Rector wishes to acknowledge the School's
indebtedness to Mr R. H. F. Whiteside, Headmaster,
and to Mr Ross, Janitor, of Lammermoor P. School,
for many kindnesses, and to many other friends who
have given invaluable help in this production.

★   ★   ★

PROCEEDS IN AID OF
F.P. MEMORIAL PLAYING FIELDS FUND

WISHAW HIGH SENIOR
SECONDARY SCHOOL

presents

By permission of Bridget D'Oyly Carte

GILBERT AND SULLIVAN'S

THE GONDOLIERS

or

"THE KING OF BARATARIA"

in

LAMMERMOOR PRIMARY
SCHOOL HALL

JUNE 20, 21, 22, 23 and 24, 1961

Each evening at 7 p.m.

Programme for *The Gondoliers* (1961)

574

THE STORY OF THE OPERA

Act 1

Scene: The Piazetta, Venice, in the year 1750

The opera opens with a chorus of country girls who are excitedly awaiting the arrival of the principal gondoliers Marco and Giuseppe Palmieri, for these young blades are on this fair day to choose their brides from the girls. When Marco and Giuseppe arrive, the other gondoliers are rather jealous. Marco and Giuseppe choose Giannetta and Tessa for their wives during a rather contrived game of "blind man's buff." Escorted by the country girls and their reconciled swains they go off to be married.

Enter the Duke of Plaza-Toro, the Duchess, Casilda, and their suite (one drummer) just arrived from Spain. Casilda was wed in infancy to the child who is now King of Barataria. The Grand Inquisitor of Spain, already in Venice, will divulge the whereabouts of the King, so the Duchess to find the Grand Inquisitor. Left alone, Casilda rushes to the arms of the drummer, Luiz. They are secretly in love. Luiz knows Casilda's story because it was to his mother (Inez) that the Grand Inquisitor entrusted the infant prince.

When the Grand Inquisitor, Don Alhambra del Bolero, enters with the Duke and Duchess, he reveals that the final identity of the king can only be disclosed by Inez, who is being summoned.

The returning gondoliers and country girls congratulate the now married couples, and they are surprised when Don Alhambra re-enters to announce that either Marco or Giuseppe is rightfully King of Barataria, and that meanwhile they are to reign jointly. But their wives must be left behind. Giannetta and Tessa caution their departing husbands. The men embark and sail for Barataria.

Act 2

Scene: A pavilion in the Palace of Barataria, three months later.

At the court of Barataria Marco and Giuseppe are enthroned; their courtiers are enjoying themselves with out distinction of rank. The joint kings realise that they must work for their living.

And now, who should arrive but the country girls from Venice with the wives of the two kings, who announce, in celebration of the girls' arrival, a banquet and dance.

The dance is interrupted by the arrival of Don Alhambra, who is distressed by the disregard of rank that he sees. Re-enter Tessa and Giannetta. Don Alhambra explains that one of the kings is married already. Consternation! The Duke and Duchess of Plaza-Toro, now much more splendidly dressed, are ceremonially announced. The Duke is now enriched because he has made himself a limited company. When Marco and Giuseppe enter, the Duke reproaches them for their lack of courtly formality. He gives them a lesson in deportment. Finally, Inez, the baby prince's foster-mother, is brought in by Don Alhambra. She announces that the true prince is neither Marco nor Giuseppe; she had interchanged the babies and passed the prince off as her own son. He is, accordingly, Luiz! Sensation. Luiz enters crowned as king; he and Casilda embrace. All are pleased, and gondoliers and contadine prepare to return to Venice and resume their happy, carefree lives.

THE GONDOLIERS

OR

"THE KING OF BARATARIA"

* * *

Personaggi

The Duke of Plaza-Toro
(a Grandee of Spain) .... Alexander Robertson

Luiz (his attendant) .... Neil Hood

The Duchess of Plaza-Toro .... Marion Pomphrey

Casilda (her daughter) .... Anne Aikman

Don Alhambra del Bolero
(the Grand Inquisitor) .... Hugh Young

Marco Palmieri .... Ian McEwan

Giuseppe Palmieri .... Alistair Smith

Venetian Gondoliers—
   Antonio .... Alexander Kerr
   Francesco .... John Elder
   Giorgio .... Alexander Smith
   Annibale .... Eric Coskry

Contadine (country girls)—
   Giannetta .... Ann Nelson
   Tessa .... Joan Muir
   Fiammetta .... Joy Russell
   Vittoria .... Joyce McIvor
   Giulia .... Ann Bayliss

Inez (the King's foster-mother) .... Jean Guthrie

* * *

Chorus of Contadine

Sheena Anderson	Betty Miller
Margaret Carlton	Margaret Muir
Myra Carswell	Ruby Nicol
Sandra Galloway	Margaret Pettigrew
Margaret Graham	Maureen Shaw
Irene Hare	Wilma Shepherd
Barbara Hunter	Christine Stewart
Patricia Kelly	Muriel Telfer
Mary MacDonald	Irene Thorburn
Dorothy Maciver	Muriel Torrance
Valerie McLaren	Mary Watson
Margaret MacLeod	Elma Waugh

Chorus of Gondoliers, Men-at-Arms and Heralds

Kenneth Anderson	William Main
Ian Bill	Alexander Mauchline
Andrew Brown	John Moore
Robert George	Alistair Munro
John Higgins	George Pringle
Andrew Kerr	David Reid
Leslie Law	Alan Robertson
Kenneth Leitch	James Roy
James Littlejohn	John Sherwood
Archie McGregor	John Watt
Angus Mackay	

The Gondoliers Cast List and Scenario (1961)

575

School Dance (1947)

School Dance (circa 1976)

The Jeely Piece Song

I'm a skyescraper wean, I live on the 19th flair
An' I'm no gaun oot tae play ony mair,
For since we moved tae oor new hoose I'm wastin' away,
'Cos I'm gettin' wan less meal every day.

Refrain: Oh, ye canny fling pieces oot a twenty storey flat
         Seven hundred hungry weans will testify tae that.
         If it's butter, cheese or jeely, if the breid ispplain or pan,
         The odds against it reachin' earth are ninety-nine tae wan.

On the first day ma maw flung oot a dod o'malted broon
It went skitin' oot the windy an' went up instead o' doon.
Noo every twenty-seven hours it comes back intae sight
Cos my piece went intae orbit an' became a satelite.

On the next day ma maw flung me a piece oot wance again.
It went an' hit the pilot in a fast, low-flying plane,
He scraped it aff his goggles shouting through the intercom
" The Clydeside reds have got me wi' a breid an' jelly bomb".

On the third day ma maw thought she would try anither throw,
The Salvation Army baun was staunin' doon below,
For "Onward Christian Soldiers" wis the tune they should have played,
But the "oompah" man wis playin' a piece an' marmalade.

We've wrote away tae Oxfam tae try an' get some aid,
We've a' joined toegither an' formed a piece brigade,
We're gonny march tae London tae demand our Civil Rights
Like "Nae mair hooses ower piece flingin' heights".

Holy Ground

Fare Thee well my lovely Dinah
A thousand times adieu,
For we're going away from the
Holy Ground,
And the girls we all love true.
We will sail the south seas over
And we'll return for sure
To see again the girls we love
And the Holy Ground once more.

Chorus: Fine girls ye are,
        Yer the girl I do adore,
        And still I live in the hope
           to see
        The Holy Ground once more.

And now the storm is ragin'
And we are far from shore,
The good old ship is tossing about
And the rigging is all torn
But the secret of my mind, my love
You're the girl I do adore.
And still I live in hope to see
The Holy Ground once more.

Folk Club Song Sheet (1974-75)

The Octagon Committee (1964)

The Octagon Committee (1970)

Committees

EDITORIAL

Margaret Torrance
Audrey Johnston
Allister Alexander
Joan Dempsey
Norman Davidson
Jane Paterson
Ann Bramley
Craig Nicholson
Alan Watson

COVER
Graeme Sutton

PHOTOGRAPHS
Ronald Holden   George Price

BUSINESS

Dot Stewart
Hilary Mauchline
Kenneth Broadley
Aileen Spankie
Jim Hayburn
Robert Dougal
Agnes Tanner
Isobel Blakeway
Marion Nelson

17

The Octagon Committee (1977)

HIGH TIMES

Wishaw High School: ISSUE NO3 EASTER 1990

Happy Easter

Careers 2000

As part of their Careers Education programme fifty S.2 pupils, accompanied by five teachers travelled to the SECC on Thursday 22 February to visit the Careers 2000 Exhibition. This is an annual exhibition organised with the support of the Careers Service for schoolchildren. Information was available on a great variety of careers and many of the stands allowed pupils the opportunity of some practical involvement. Many of the boys found the Army display particularly interesting, while one of our girls returned to school with her hair newly fashioned in a French pleat, courtesy of a YTS hairdressing student.

On a more serious note, most of the pupils gained some benefit from the visit, either by speaking to specialists about a particular career which interests them, by taking home literature on a number of careers or simply by fixing their minds on thoughts of the future. As they approach their S.2 Course Options, any exercise which stimulates such thoughts must be of value.

A final word from the pupils, themselves:- "I thought it would be really boring but it was brilliant." "Everybody was really kind." "I got two posters, a calendar, three pens and six bugs." (The teachers who accompanied the pupils wish it to be known that the behaviour of all the pupils was excellent - ED)

I Got Rhythm

Rehearsals are now well under way for the Band's forthcoming joint concerts with Lesmahagow High School's Band. The dates for your diary are **Wednesday 21 March in Wishaw High** with a repeat performance for anyone double-booked for that evening, on **Thursday 22 March at Lesmahagow**. All Band members are looking forward to this joint venture and many members of staff will be able to renew acquaintance with Mr Gordon Currie, Principal Teacher of Music at Lesmahagow High

Keeping on Colour

On Friday 9 March more than thirty S.1 pupils proudly delivered home a letter praising their exceptionally good behaviour in school. This is the second occasion this session that such letters have been sent to parents and is a result of a scheme called "KEEP ON COLOUR", in which our S1 pupils are involved. KOC is a behaviour monitoring system, which logs period by period the behaviour of every First Year pupil. Teachers using a variety of coded letters fill information onto daily sheets, which are then collated at the end of each week. The results are displayed on a chart in each S1 register class, with well-behaved pupils being easily identified by the large, unbroken band of colour opposite their names.

Perhaps this explanation will go some way to explaining the rather cryptic comments at times overheard in the presence of First Year pupils "I got a "B" in Home Economics and a "W" in Science" can be taken to be the expression of a pupil's dismay at having failed to "KEEP ON COLOUR".

Ah dont like the colour oh him wan wee bit.

and a former pupil of Wishaw High, and Mr Ian Stirling, Headteacher at Lesmahagow, once Depute Head at Wishaw.

Fund-raising for the Band's trip to Belgium is progressing well. Money has been raised in all sorts of ingenious ways and in the process much fun has been had. Examples of this are the two very successful discos in February and the most enjoyable coffee morning, where parents, teachers and pupils, many of them with no connection with the band, worked together to raise

Comings & Goings.

High Times would like to extend a very warm welcome to two members of staff who have joined us since our last issue. Mr Bell, Principal Teacher of Mathematics made the short journey from Coltness High to return to the school he attended as a pupil, while Mrs Mc Phee a native of Motherwell, returned to the burgh to take up the post of Principal Teacher of Home Economics at Wishaw High. Both Teachers have settled in very quickly (Was it really only in January that they started?) and are already very much involved in the life of the school.

It is with very mixed feelings that we announce the departure of Mr Kay of the Art Department as he prepares to move to Coltness High as Principal Teacher of Art. Although we wish him well in his future career, we are sad to lose such a popular teacher and respected colleague. Wishaw High will miss him dearly, especially the editorial staff of High Times who now have a very large gap to fill.

No offence intended Ian. The "very large gap" refers to the contribution you make to this newspaper and not to your corporeal dimensions ! - ED>)

LITTLE PIGEON IN THE SKY

DROPPING THINGS FROM WAY ON HIGH

SAID THE FARMER WIPING HIS EYE

VERY GLAD THAT COWS CAN'T FLY

approximately £400. Well done, all who participated in whatever way.

Three members of the School Band have distinguished themselves by successfully auditioning for the Strathclyde Schools' Symphonic Windband. The girls, Fiona Dunbar (S.3), Lynn Findlay (S6) and Pamela Clarke (S.6) have already attended their first rehearsal and are looking forward to a week's residential course in the month of June.

High Times (1990)

580

Epilogue

The buildings in the grounds of the High School are declared surplus to educational requirements by the Education Committee.

March 1992

The Buildings and Properties Committee decides that the aforementioned buildings should be demolished: boarding them up and establishing a security patrol are deemed to be too costly.

Many Wishawtonians have suspected for some time that the Region intends to sell the buildings and playing fields at the High School to a property developer. Their suspicions seem to have been confirmed.

A spokesman for Wimpey Homes disclaims any interest in the site.

The Wishaw High Action Committee is formed, its basic remit being to organise a campaign to prevent the buildings in the grounds of the High School from being demolished. A campaign fund is also established and a series of public meetings arranged.

Gordon McNay, a former pupil with a wealth of experience in local government is asked to get involved. However, he declines:

All my years in local government taught me that trying to preserve buildings like the High School and put them to other uses is a recipe for pouring local taxpayers' money down the drain. Moreover, I am simply not prepared to be hypocritical, as I know perfectly well that if I had been the Chief Executive of the local authority in question and had been asked for my advice, my recommendation would have been that the building should be demolished, the land sold to the highest bidder and the money from the sale used to improve the educational infrastructure in Wishaw and district.

May 1992

Motherwell District Council admits that there is nothing it can do to prevent the demolition of the buildings in the grounds of the High School.

West Calder Community Holdings indicate that they are interested in these buildings as a possible location for a number of interconnected workshops and retail units.

The demolition of the buildings is scheduled to take place in the first week of July. As far as Strathclyde Region is concerned, time means money.

June 1992

"The people of Wishaw don't really give a damn about saving the buildings." (Reverend James Davidson of Wishaw Old Parish Church)

Strathclyde Police announce that the local constabulary will not be moving from Stewarton Street to the campus of the High School; nor will the DHSS or the Social Work Department.

A 24-hour School Watch Vigil is held outside the front gate of the High School. Two candles are lit - one to represent the main building at the High School, the other to represent the annexe (formerly Wishaw Public) - and extinguished 24 hours later.

6,000 Wishawtonians sign a petition opposing the demolition of the buildings in the grounds of the High School.

The demolition of the said buildings is postponed for three months, while a feasibility study (of public and private uses to which the buildings may be put) is carried out by a firm of chartered surveyors and property consultants - with input from Motherwell District Council, Strathclyde Regional Council, and the Lanarkshire Development Agency.

August 1992

'We are very interested in taking over the High School buildings.' (Bell College)

The demolition of the buildings is postponed again - till December.

"It is still the Region's intention to 'cleanse' the campus of the High School and put it on the market." (Morton Cadzow, Chairman of the Wishaw High Action Committee)

'The annexe of the High School is in extreme danger.' (Morton Cadzow)

The outbuildings of the annexe are demolished.

September 1992

The main building at the High School (but not its counterpart at the annexe) is accorded the status of a Category B Listed Building by Historic Scotland.

582

December 1992

The main building at the annexe is reduced to rubble. The site is destined to be occupied by a supermarket (Lidl).

Strathclyde Regional Council offers the main building at the High School to Bell College. If this offer is not taken up, the building and the rest of the campus are to be put up for sale on the open market.

April 1993

'Any idea of the main building at the High School becoming an annexe of Bell College is now "a dead duck". The £1 million price tag is too high.' (John Reid, Principal of Bell College)

'We are not allowed to accept less than the market value of the building, and we are hoping that it will go on the market in the summer.' (Spokesman for Strathclyde Regional Council)

'If the Region does not lease the building to Bell College, the people of Wishaw will not forgive them.'
(Morton Cadzow)

May 1993

The Wishaw High Action Committee asks Motherwell District Council to buy the building and lease it to Bell College.

'We cannot legally, morally, or financially purchase the building.'
(James Coyle, Director of Planning, Motherwell District Council)

August 1993

Both the main building and the playing fields at the High School are put up for sale on the open market. The site is described as 'suitable for residential development'.

September 1993

The Wishaw High Action Committee submits a nominal bid of £1 for the main building and playing fields at the High School.

October 1993

Strathclyde Region's Estates Department agrees to accept this bid provided that the Action Committee can, by the 14th of December, come up with a package that will ensure that the building is used for the benefit of the local community.

The Action Committee enters into talks with two major charities, and requests an extension of the December deadline.

December 1993

'We have given Wishaw High Action Committee every opportunity to buy the High School building, but it has been unable to comply with all the terms of the sale. We therefore have no option but to accept the bid of Miller Homes.' (Councillor Stan Gilmore, Chairman of Strathclyde Region's Buildings and Properties Committee)

'Given time, we would have put the necessary people and funds in place to make the High School a centre for charity and community activity.' (Spokesman for the Wishaw High Action Committee)

Miller Homes announce that the main building at the High School will be converted into flats.

January 1994

'The main thrust of our campaign must now be to ensure that the High School building keeps its facade and assembly hall.' (Morton Cadzow)

March 1994

Miller Homes seek planning permission to build 100 terraced and semi-detached houses in the area behind the High School building.

September 1994

A fire damages window seals in the High School building, and a number of leaks in the roof cause damage to the interior.

'The High School is a listed building and it is deteriorating.' (Stan Cook, Director of Planning, Motherwell District Council)

January 1996

Miller Partnerships apply to Motherwell District Council for permission to demolish the High School building. 'Experts,' they claim, 'have cast doubts on the structural integrity of the building, and the safety of the public and our customers comes before all other considerations.'

January 1997

North Lanarkshire Council agrees to grant Miller Partnerships permission to demolish the High School building. The final decision, however, rests with the Secretary of State for Scotland.

'I have written to Historic Scotland reminding them of their obligation to protect a Grade B Listed Building, and I hope that the Scottish Secretary will refuse the demolition order.' (Scott Dickson, a member of the Wishaw High Action Committee)

'This has been a story of manipulation and apathy: manipulation by Strathclyde Regional Council (whose Estates Department regarded the demolition of the school as a priority) and Miller Partnerships (whose word has certainly not been their bond); and apathy on the part of Motherwell District Council, especially the councillors representing Wishaw, who - with the exception of Councillor William Irvine - did little or nothing to save the last building of character in the town. It will never be replaced.' (Morton Cadzow)

August 1998

The roof of the High School building is badly damaged by a fire.

December 1998

Appendix A

Members of Staff

There are some discrepancies (with regard to dates and the correct spelling of names) between *The Octagon* and the files kept by Helen Costley, the Rector's secretary, so I can't guarantee the accuracy of every entry in this index. I have been able to establish the years in which some members of staff began and finished their period of service. As far as the others are concerned, the year that appears beside their name is in most cases the year in which, according to the school log, they were first appointed to a post at the School.

Subjects and posts have been abbreviated as follows:

A - Art; B - Biology; BS - Business Studies (formerly, Commercial); Ch - Chemistry; Cl - Classics; E - English; F - French; G - Geography; Ge - German; Gu - Guidance; H - History; HE - Home Economics (formerly, Domestic Science); L - Latin; M - Mathematics; ML - Modern Languages; MS - Modern Studies; Mu - Music; P - Physics; PC - Preparatory Classes; PE - Physical Education; Ru - Russian; RE - Religious Education; Rem - Remedial; S - Science; SD - Speech and Drama; TS - Technical Subjects; R - Rector; HT - Head Teacher; DR - Depute Rector; FA - First Assistant; AHT - Assistant Head Teacher; HLS - Head of the Lower School; HMS - Head of the Middle School; HUS - Head of the Upper School; WA - Woman Adviser; MM - Master of Method; AMM - Assistant Master of Method; PT - Principal Teacher; APT - Assistant Principal Teacher; SA - Special Assistant; SH - Senior Housemaster / Housemistress; H – Housemaster / Housemistress; AH – Assistant Housemaster / Housemistress; ST -Senior Teacher; FrA - French Assistant; GA - German Assistant; MI - Music Instructor; Lib - Librarian; AA - Admin Assistant; Sec - Secretary; J - Janitor; CS - Cook Supervisor; T - Technician; LT - Lab Technician; AVT - Audio-Visual Technician; NA - Nursing Auxiliary.

Adam, Mrs Linda - 1985; HE
Adams, David — 1974-77; Ch; Gu (H)
Adams, Westland — 1958; E
Ahmed, Syed — 1963; M; S

Aitken, Thomas — 1960; Mu
Alexander, David — 1983-85; G
Allan, Mrs Ann — 1981-87; PE
Allan, Miss Elizabeth — 1932; ML
Allan, John — 1959; M; P (PT)
Allan, Joseph – 1984-85; TS
Anderson, Alexander — 1945; E
Anderson, Miss Annette — 1958; E
Anderson, Tony — 1960; Cl
Anderson, David — 1969; M
Anderson, Miss Elizabeth — 1952; PC; E
Anderson, James — 1978-87; TS
Anderson, John — 1921-26; Cl; FA
Anderson, Miss May — 1986; MS
Anderson, William — 1967; G (PT)
Andrew, Miss Margo — 1987; A
Andrews, Mrs Isabella — 1975-77; BS (APT)
Andrews, Wilson — 1991; P
Anlauf, Peter — 1960; GA
Annand, George — 1964; Mu
Archibald, Miss Elizabeth — 1943; ML
Archibald, John — 1951; M; S
Archibald, Miss Marjorie — 1940; BS
Arneil, Helen — 1976-77; Mu
Arrighi, Josèphe — 1965; FrA
Arton, John — 1970-76; PE (PT)
Ash, Rattray — 1929; E; H
Auchinachie, Alexander — 1908; E

Baillie, William — 1932; M
Bain, Brian — 1979; PE
Bain, Matthew — 1923-55; J
Baird, Allan — 1981-91; TS (PT)
Baird, Miss Jane — 1986; H
Ballantyne, Miss Maggie — 1939; E
Banks, Mrs Elspeth — 1979-92; Mu (PT); AHT
Baradat, Michel — 1960; FrA
Barnard, Sam — 1966-88; R
Barnett, Miss E. — 1956; E
Barrie, Mrs Aileen — 1989-92; G (PT)

Barrie, Miss Janet — 1952-89; M (PT)
Barrie, Miss Jenny — 1946; E
Barrie, Miss Jill — 1984; TS
Beck, William — 1978-80; BS
Beddig, Karl — 1954; GA
Bell, David — 1977-92; TS; RE
Bell, Miss E.G. — 1963; BS
Bell, Miss Jean — 1949; M
Bell, Robert — 1972-83; E (APT)
Bell, William — 1990-92; M (PT)
Bellaton, M.B. — 1954; FrA
Bennet, Miss E. — 1920; PE
Benwick, Alan — 1964; S
Benwick, James — 1950; E
Bertrand, Gaston — 1929; FrA
Bhatti, Mrs Elizabeth — 1977-78; BS
Bickerton, Mrs Jean — 1980-85; HE
Binnie, Alexander — 1952; TS
Birnie, James — 1955; PC
Birse, Miss Isabel — 1946; A
Black, Archibald — 1933; Cl
Black, Donald — 1964; G
Black, Mrs Mary — 1907; ML
Blackburn, Richard — 1974-78; Ch; Gu (H)
Boa, Peter — 1974-77; ML (APT)
Boal, John — 1976-85; A
Bobkowski, Jakub — 1960; ML
Boissel, Pierre — 1947; FrA
Bonnar, Maurice — 1964-68; H
Bonnet, Francoise – 1982; Fra
Bonomy, John — 1948-79; PE (PT); Gu (SH)
Booth, Robert — 1912-27; Mu
Bowman, Arthur – 1970; T
Bowman, Martin – 1969; E
Boyd, Malcolm — 1961; BS (PT)
Boyd, Miss May — 1967; E
Boyle, Miss Agnes — 1956; Cl
Brash, Miss Jane — 1951; ML
Brebner, Mrs Eileen — 1957; ML

Bremner, Miss V. — 1957; E
Brodie, William — 1965; B
Brooks, Miss Angela — 1984; ML
Brown, Miss Ann — 1961; E
Brown, Miss Catherine — 1970; ML
Brown, Douglas — 1964; S
Brown, Miss Elizabeth — 1922; HE
Brown, Mrs Elsie — 1959; M
Brown, George — 1956-74; E (PT)
Brown, Mrs Isobel — 1987; A
Brown, Miss Margaret — 1953; BS
Brown, Miss Marion — 1959; E
Brown, Miss M.I. — 1954; M
Brown, Mrs Moira — 1969; E
Brown, Robert — 1939; M
Brown, Miss Rosaleen — 1989-90; Mu
Brownlee, Miss Rachel — 1948; E
Brownlie, Miss Annie — 1947; HE
Brownlie, Miss Mary — 1944; E
Brownlie, William — 1921; F; L
Bruce, Mrs Alison — 1981-83; ML
Bruce, George — 1911-20; S
Buchan, Mrs Barbara — 1973-75; ML
Buchanan, Mrs Elizabeth — 1982-89; B
Budge, James — 1953; E
Burns, Miss Margaret — 1923-59; L; F
Burnside, Paul — 1987; G (APT)

Cain, Patrick — 1986; E
Caldwell, Mrs Christine — 1979-82; G
Cameron, Miss Elizabeth — 1980; B (?); M (?)
Cameron, Miss E.E. — 1960; H
Cameron, James — 1928; S
Campbell, Miss Elizabeth — 1953; S
Campbell, Mrs Pauline — 1987-92; BS
Carle, Miss Jeanie — 1929; L; F
Carlin, Mrs Marion — 1987-90; H
Carmichael, David — 1974-78; Ch; Gu (AHT)
Carrier, Philippe — 1982; FrA
Carson, David — 1974; Mu (SA)

Cassells, Nancy — 1930; HE
Caulfield, Miss Elizabeth — 1988; H
Chalmers, George — 1949; Cl
Chambers, Kevin — 1984; M
Champey, Yolande — 1966; FrA
Cheyne, Miss L. — 1915; E (PT)
Chisolm, Robert — 1940; E; H
Christie, Miss M.A.M. — 1954; E
Cirot, Mlle. Raymonde — 1952; FrA
Clare, William — 1984; J
Clark, Mrs Alice — 1979-81; BS
Clark, Miss Ina — 1967; BS; Gu (AH)
Clark, Mrs Janis — 1978-92; PE
Clark, Mrs Jeanie — 1945; ML
Clark, Miss Margaret — 1943-48; E
Clark, William — 1938-64; S (PT)
Clarke, David — 1979-89; Ch
Clarke, Mrs Elizabeth — 1974-92; ML; Gu (PT)
Clarke, Robert — 1978-79; S
Clelland, James — 1976-92; Ch; HMS; DR
Coales, Mrs E. — 1972; Cl (PT)
Cochran, Kenneth — 1942-46; S (PT)
Cochrane, Miss Clare — 1991; Ch; M
Cockburn, Miss Agnes — 1943; E
Cocozza, Enrico — 1960; ML
Cook, David — 1955; Cl
Cooper, James — 1964; S
Copeland, Miss L.S. — 1965; G
Corbet, Henry — 1977-92; TS
Costley, Mrs Helen — 1962-92; AA
Coutts, Miss Deirdre — 1949; HE
Coutts, Miss Maggie — 1915-42; E (PT)
Cowie, Mrs Christina — 1986-92; HE
Craig, Colin — 1968; B
Craig, Robert — 1956; CL (PT)
Crawford, Barrie — 1988-92; ML (PT)
Crawford, David — 1971; LT
Cunningham, Mrs Elizabeth — 1973; E
Cunningham, Michael — 1988; G

Curran, John — 1950-51; M
Currie, Miss Dorothy — 1953; M

Dale, John — 1983; A
Dalzell, Robert — 1992; ML (PT)
Damon, Mlle. C. — 1957; FrA
Darling, Mrs Heather — 1986; A
Darling, Miss Margaret — 1946; E
Davidson, Miss Mary — 1945; E
Davies, David — 1951; H
Dawson, Miss Elizabeth — 1949; E; H
Dempsey, Harry — 1976; E
Dempsie, Joseph — 1939; BS
Dennis, Miss Christine — 1973; Mu
De Saintdo, Yves — 1958; FrA
Devlin, Hugh — 1987; LT
Devlin, John — 1984; M
Dewar, Mrs Margaret — 1969-91; HE
Dhesi, Parenjit — 1977-80; M
Dick, Angus — 1959; Ch (SA)
Dick, Thomas — 1952; Cl
Dickson, Mrs Anna — 1969-75; M
Dickson, Francis — 1920-43; S (PT)
Dickson, James — 1943-72; M (PT); DR
Dickson, Mrs Margaret — 1980-83; A
Dobbie, John — 1970; Mu (PT)
Donald, Miss L. — 1959; E
Donald, William — 1913; S
Donnelly, Miss Anne — 1961-92; E; Gu (PT)
Douglas, Mrs Jean — 1973; BS
Douglas, Mrs Ruth — 1974; ML; Gu (H)
Downes, Miss Elizabeth — 1917; E
Dreghorn, James — 1964; S
Drummond, David — 1956; E
Drummond, Miss Fiona — 1981; Ch
Drysdale, Bill — 1979-89; T
Dubber, Alf — 1930; E (PT)
Duncan, Ian — 1972; Ch; Gu (H)
Duncan, Miss Jeanie — 1950; PC
Dunn, Miss Margaret — 1956; E

Durignieuse, Jean — 1937; FrA
Duthart, Alex — 1980; MI
Dyet, Mrs Lorna — 1986; A
Dyke, Elizabeth — 1978; PE

Edward, Miss Mary — 1930-33; ML
Edwards, Mrs Louise — 1983; ML
Edwards, Miss R. — 1958; S
Egan, Kevin — 1987; P
Eisenberg, Christian — 1956; GA
Evans, Mhairi — 1991; E
Ewing, Mrs Elizabeth — 1985; E

Fagan, Mrs Jean — 1976-91; Rem
Fairservice, Miss Henrietta — 1961; HE
Fenton, Mrs Helen — 1987; M
Ferguson, Daniel — 1946; A
Ferguson, John — 1953; PE
Ferguson, William — 1926-42; S
Findlay, Mrs Christine — 1986; S
Finlayson, Mr A. — 1959; TS
Finlayson, Matthew — 1937; M
Fitzpatrick, Mrs Lorna — 1984; Rem
Fleming, Miss Davina — 1985; Rem
Fleming, James — 1960; ML; Gu (H)
Fleming, Miss Jane — 1956; Mu
Fletcher, Miss A.H. — 1960; M
Foote, Mrs Ann — 1978-80; Ch
Forrest, David — 1974-76; M; Gu (AH)
Forrest, James — 1957; E
Forrest, Miss Robina — 1950; BS
Forrest, Samuel — 1924-42; M (PT); FA
Forsyth, Tom – 1961; E (SA)
Frame, Robert — 1926-48; PE (PT)
Frame, Mrs Jane — 1975-77; HE
Fraser, Miss E.A. — 1964; M; S
Fraser, Mrs Mary — 1982-83; ML
Frew, Miss Mary — 1939; F
Frood, Miss C. — 1910-16; PE

Gaeta, Mrs Sylvia — 1986; A
Galbraith, William — 1973-84; P (PT)
Gallard, Paul — 1949; FrA
Galloway, Mrs Linda — 1978-81; Mu
Garanchet, Odile — 1971; FrA
Garrity, James — 1949; M
Gass, John — 1942; E
Gaudemer, Daniel — 1925; FrA
Gavin, Mrs Jessie — 1941; E
Gavin, Malcolm — 1932; M
Gerrard, John — 1915; S
Gibb, Clive — 1991-92; TS (PT)
Gibb, Miss Helen — 1944-47; ML
Gibbons, Fred — 1970; E; Gu (SH)
Gibson, Miss Marion — 1947-48; BS
Gilchrist, George — 1945; E
Gilchrist, Miss Pearl — 1932; E; L
Gilchrist, Robert — 1934; L; E
Gillies, Miss Mary — 1982-83; ML
Gillies, Miss Sheena — 1973; B
Girdwood, Miss Isabella — 1953-83; HE (PT)
Glegg, Miss Annie — 1932; ML
Glover, William — 1931-37; Mu
Gordon, Miss Grace — 1947; HE
Gordon, Miss Margaret — 1945; ML
Gordon, Robert — 1974; T
Govan, Clark — 1979-92; PE
Gow, Miss Annie — 1911; M
Gow, Miss Lizzie — 1911; ML
Gracie, Fraser — 1972-74; PE
Graham, Miss Agnes — 1944; E
Graham, James — 1970; T
Graham, John — 1983; G
Graham, Sam — 1975-92; MS; Gu (H)
Grant, Miss Elizabeth — 1912-15; M
Grant, Miss Jean — 1957; Mu
Gray, Miss C.C. — 1954; ML
Gray, Eric — 1952; ML
Gray, Miss Nora -1961; ML (APT)

Gray, William — 1947; M; S
Green, Mrs Margaret — 1974-79; Rem (PT)
Grierson, Miss Isobel — 1954; Cl (SA)
Guthrie, Dr A. — 1956; PC
Guy, Mrs Irene — 1980-81; ML
Gwyn-Davies, Mrs Pearl — 1958-85; AA

Haapa, William — 1975-77; E
Haines, Tom — 1982; A
Hair, David — 1930-49; M
Hale, Miss Anne — 1973; G
Halliday, Miss Margaret — 1969-75; BS
Hamilton, Mrs Diana — 1990; Mu (PT)
Hamilton, James — 1937; A
Hamilton, John — 1918; Cl
Hamilton, Miss Joyce — 1984-92; B (PT)
Hamilton, Miss Marion — 1946; L; F
Hamilton, Ronald — 1971-87; G (PT)
Hamilton, Miss S.L. — 1967-68; Mu
Hamilton, Thomas — 1929-46; S
Harkness, James — 1956; J
Harris, Mrs Maureen — 1986; H
Harvie, Miss Jessie — 1937; PC
Harvie, John — 1968-92; A (PT)
Harvie, Mrs Margaret — 1986-88; Cl
Hastie, Miss Mary — 1956; S
Hay Douglas — 1983-85; M
Hay, James — 1950; Cl
Heddig, K. — 1954; GA
Heeps, Miss Sandra — 1986; PE
Hefferman, Mrs Joyce — 1980-82; Ch
Heidet, Georges — 1927; FrA
Henderson, Miss Catriona — 1965; ML; Cl
Henderson, Miss Isabella — 1950-61; WA
Henderson, Peter — 1956; M
Hendry, Miss Lynn — 1987; HE
Hesse, W. — 1957; GA
Hitier, Pierre — 1934; FrA
Hobson, Miss Kathleen — 1967; E

Hodgson, Miss Ruth — 1974-92; Mu (PT); Gu (AHT)
Hogg, Miss Isabella — 1964; S
Hood, Mrs Anne — 1980-84; BS
Hood, Neil — 1964; G
Hope, Douglas — 1968; H
Howieson, Mrs Doreen — 1978-81; M
Hughes, James — 1946; M
Hughes, Mrs Mary — 1986; A
Humphries, Wilson — 1986; E
Hunter, Dr G. — 1960; S
Hunter, Miss M.L. — 1923; ML
Hunter, William — 1960; PE
Hutton, David — 1915; S
Hyslop, Miss Helen — 1938; BS
Hyslop, Miss Marion — 1965; G
Hyslop, Thomas — 1917; S

Jack, Andrew — 1950; PE
Jack, Mrs Karen — 1990-91; Mu
Jackson, John — 1911; AMM
Jackson, Mrs Mairi — 1974-78; PE; Gu (H)
Japp, Miss Myra — 1975-79; BS
Jardine, Neil — 1975-79; G
Jarvie, Miss Ann — 1954; S
Jeffrey, Miss Agnes — 1941; E
Jenkins, David — 1974-80; MI
Johnston, Alex — 1974; A
Johnston, Miss Annabelle — 1934; ML
Johnston, Miss Elizabeth — 1961; E
Johnston, Mrs Isobel — 1970-82; PE; Gu (SH)
Johnston, Peter — 1937; Mu (PT)
Johnston, Stewart — 1975-76; A
Johnstone, Miss Annie — 1916; PE (PT)
Johnstone, Miss Elizabeth — 1977; M
Johnstone, Mrs E. — 1987; HE
Johnstone, Graham — 1976-91; B (PT); HLS; AHT
Johnstone, Ian — 1957; TS
Johnstone, Mr R. — 1974; B (PT)
Jolas, Marcelle — 1945; FrA
Jope, James — 1950-58; M
596

Karne, Michael — 1989; M
Kay, Ian — 1976-90; A; ST
Keatings, Mrs Anne — 1988; ML
Kelly, Mr D.C. — 1957; S
Kelly, Mrs Kay — 1976-86; E
Kelman, John — 1925; S
Kerr, Andrew — 1966; Mu
Kerr; AJ.C. — 1906-37; R
Kerr, Miss Lesley — 1982-89; Lib
Kerr, Miss Lilly — 1929; PE
Kerr, Mrs Lynn — 1983-87; ML
Kerr, Neil — 1982-92; B
Kilpatrick, Mrs B.C. — 1956; BS
Kinnear, Mrs Elsa — 1975-86; Rem
Kirkwood, David — 1974; A
Koch, Gerhard — 1960; GA
Kozchuda, Franz — 1951; GA
Kydd, Mrs May — 1981-89; M
Kyle, Miss Linda — 1973; E

Lacaille, Gerard – 1976; FrA
Laird, David — 1971; M; Gu (SH)
Laird, Sid — 1957; M (PT)
Lammie, Robert — 1942; M
Lamond, Isabel — 1981-82; E
Latch, Archibald — 1935; M; E
Laurie, R.D.N. — 1942; M
Lawrence, Mrs Lorraine — 1982; LT
Lawson, Gavin — 1928; ML
Lawson, Miss Jean — 1918-49; M
Lawson, Thomas — 1948; G; E
Le Cam, Francette — 1963; FrA
Lees, David — 1932; E
Legge, Miss Esther — 1908-15; E; H (PT)
Leishman, Ian — 1949; E
Leitch, Archie — 1935; G (PT)
Leith, Mrs Helen — 1974-90; LT
Leonidas, Mlle. Catherine — 1987; FrA

Leslie, David — 1982; MS
Leslie, Miss Mabel — 1972-77; PE
Liddell, Robert — 1943; ML (PT); FA
Lind, Jack — 1984-92; P
Lindley, Mrs Dorothy — 1985; TS
Lindsay, Sandy — 1960; M
Lindsay, James — 1960-74; Cl (SA)
Lindsay, T.A. — 1913; S (PT)
Livingstone, Miss Joyce — 1977-79; B
Lochhead, Andrew — 1964; Cl
Logan, Mrs Margaret — 1975-80; ML (APT)
Logan, Mrs Mary — 1987; S
Loudon, Miss Abigail — 1921-55; PE; WA
Loudon, J.G. — 1954-56; S
Loudon, Miss Mamie — 1930; M
Lyall, William — 1907; S

McAllan, Miss A.D.A. — 1948; ML
McAllister, Miss Annie — 1935; HE
McArdle, Scott — 1970-80; TS (PT)
McAuslane, Miss Robina — 1944; BS
McBride, Donald — 1959; S; M
McBride, John — 1945; Cl
McBride, Mrs Mairi — 1948-79; A(SA)
McBroom, Mrs Elsie — 1948; M
McBroom, James — 1931-37; A
McCafferty, Mrs Linda — 1972; BS
McCann, Mrs Magda — 1983; S
McClelland, Mrs Edith — 1983; HE
McCall, Mrs Jean — 1966; BS
McConnell, R. — 1958; S
McCuish, Donald — 1972-76; P (PT)
McDade, D.F. — 1956; Cl
MacDonald, A. — 1959; S
MacDonald, Miss Agnes — 1966; E
MacDonald, Mr A.R. — 1962; Cl
McDonald, Miss Carolyn — 1982; A
MacDonald, Miss Daisy — 1908-43; ML (PT)
MacDonald, Duncan — 1940; BS
MacDonald, Miss Jean — 1938; BS
598

McDonald, Neil — 1985; P (PT)
MacDonald, R.S. — 1966; Ch (PT)
McDougall, Mrs Mary — 1984; BS (PT)
McDowall, Miss Janie — 1915; HE
McFarlane, Miss Beth — 1953; S
McFarlane, Mrs Elizabeth — 1974-75; E
McGarrity, James — 1949; M
McGeechan, William — 1981-86; P
McGibbon, G. — 1959; S
McGowan, Mrs Pat — 1984-92; E; ST
McGregor, Allan — 1947; H
McGregor, J.P. — 1956; PE
McGregor, Miss Janet — 1929; E; H
McGuire, John — 1980-83; P
McIntosh, Angus — 1950; G
McIntosh, Mrs Helen — 1967-89; E
McIntyre, Miss Anne — 1951; HE
McKay, Miss Catherine — 1938; BS
Mackay, David — 1952; G
Mackay, Miss J. — 1908; PE
Mackay, K. — 1957; PE
McKee, Miss Margaret — 1948; Mu
McKellar, Neil — 1953-66; R
McKenna, Charles — 1982; G
McKenzie, Miss E.B. — 1923; ML
McKenzie, Hugh — 1957; ML (SA)
McKenzie, Jean — 1981; Mu
MacKinnon, Miss E. — 1958; M
McLaren, Alex — 1986; E
McLaren, Miss Eleanor — 1987; BS
McLatchie, Mrs Margaret — 1980; MS
MacLean, Miss Katherine — 1908-40; M
MacLellan, Malcolm — 1958; S
McMahon, Archie — 1963-91; Cl (PT); Gu (AHM)
McManus, Mrs Frances — 1985; ML
McMillan, Miss Elspeth — 1959; E
McNaught, Malcolm — 1980-81; E
McNaughton, James — 1982; M
McPhail, Miss Mary — 1950; S

MacPhee, Miss Catriona — 1984; TS
MacPhee, Mrs Geraldine — 1990-92; HE (PT)
MacPherson, Mrs Mary — 1960; ML
McQueen, John — 1973-92; Ch (PT)

Mack, Mrs Ursula — 1971-85; ML
Malcolmson, Thomas — 1959; E
Marlin, Miss Elizabeth — 1927; E
Marshall, Miss Agnes — 1950; Mu
Marshall, Alan — 1973-76; TS; Gu (H)
Marshall, Mrs Carol — 1987-92; Sec
Marshall, Dick — 1957; A
Marshall, Miss Moira — 1924; E; H
Martin, Daniel — 1928-42; E
Martin, James — 1967; P
Mason, James — 1960; E
Mason, Mrs M. — 1977; BS
Mather, Robert — 1930; Cl
Matheson, John — 1991-92; Mu (PT)
Mauchline, Mrs Janey — 1977-92; E (APT)
Maxwell, Ian — 1973-92; M (APT)
Mays, Robert — 1937; M; S
Meehan, Mrs Siobhan — 1983; E
Millar, David — 1952; M
Millar, Miss Margaret — 1946; S
Miller, Miss Barbara — 1968; PE
Miller, Edward — 1955-57; E
Miller, Mrs Marlene — 1961; BS
Miller, Miss Olive — 1978-79; G
Miller, Tommy — 1961-73; J
Milliken, Margaret — 1973-78; MI
Milne, Douglas — 1961; E
Minto, Miss Mary — 1918; E
Mitchell, Gilbert — 1939; M
Mitchell, Mrs Harriet — 1985; HE
Mitchell, Mrs Margaret — 1975-79; Sec
Mitchell, Mrs Marion — 1985; E
Mitchell, Stanley — 1956; S
Moffat, Mrs Maureen — 1977; SD
Moingeon, Marielle — 1968; FrA

Moonie, Walter — 1946-49; Mu (PT)
Moreau, Pierre — 1936; FrA
Morrice, Drew — 1974-92; H; Gu (PT)
Morris, Mrs Diana — 1973-79; HE
Morris, Mrs Elaine — 1985; G
Morison, Miss Agnes — 1931; A
Morrison, David — 1970; S
Morrison, Miss Elizabeth — 1940; M
Morrison, Mrs Hazel — 1974-92; M
Morrison, John — 1953; M; S
Morrison, Miss Ruth — 1985; B
Muat, Norman — 1953; TS
Muir, Miss Catherine — 1934; F; E
Muir, Mrs Sandra — 1987; E
Muir, Mrs Shirley — 1981-92; BS (PT)
Muir, William — 1959; S
Munch, Adeline — 1963; GA
Murdoch, Miss Grace — 1954; Mu
Murray, Mrs Catherine — 1972-75; B (PT)
Murray, Mrs Evelyn — 1985; HE
Murray, Iain — 1989-92; HT

Nairn, Miss Ishbel — 1991-92; ML
Neil, Tom — 1965; M
Neilson, Mrs Elizabeth — 1983; HE
Nelson, Archie — 1944; S
Nelson, Mrs Elspeth — 1967-84; Ch (APT)
Nelson, Mrs N. — 1986; A
Nelson, William — 1939; BS
Nicholson, Evander — 1976-77; E
Nicol, Kenneth — 1974-87; Cl; Gu (APT)
Nicolas, Paul — 1933; FrA
Nimmo, Miss Aileen — 1970; S
Nimmo, Mrs Elizabeth — 1946; PG
Nimmo, Henry — 1921 -31; A
Noble, James — 1931-45; L; ML

O'Donnell, Mrs Catherine — 1990-91; B
O'Hare, Larry — 1988; G

Ohlraun, Helga — 1971; GA
O'Neill, Miss Elizabeth — 1988; B
Orr, Miss Janice — 1980-82; Lib
Orr, Jim — 1962; M
Oswald, Ernest — 1957; TS
Owens, Miss Carol — 1990-92; A
Owens, John — 1959; TS

Paquet, Robert — 1924; FrA
Parizot, Helene — 1964; FrA
Park, Miss Margaret — 1955; PE
Parker, Miss Rosina — 1950; E
Parton, John — 1945-81; TS (SA)
Paterson, Mrs Anna — 1975-76; H
Paterson, James — 1935-40; E; H
Paton, Miss Elma — 1956; E
Paton, Robert — 1957; Mu
Patrick, Miss Elizabeth — 1974-92; E (PT)
Patrick, Mrs Isobel — 1983-92; BS
Paul, Miss Jennifer — 1975-77; BS
Pearson, Mrs Eleanor — 1981; CS
Pearson, Miss Violet — 1950-89; HE (PT)
Phillips, Miss Maggie — 1926-30; E; L; H
Pollock, Miss Helen — 1930; M
Prentice, John — 1974-79; S; Gu
Prentice, Stoddart — 1937; M
Pringle, James — 1988-92; G (APT)

Quinn, Percy — 1945; E

Radcliffe, Charles — 1950; Mu
Ralston, John — 1971-87; H; HUS
Ramsauer, Ingelore — 1973; GA
Ramsay, Miss Mary — 1932; F
Ramsay, William — 1930; M
Randall, George — 1980-87; G
Rankin, Colin — 1968; G (SA)
Rankin, James — 1945; BS
Rankine, Mrs Beatrice — 1981-91; Sec
Reddick, Miss Annabelle — 1934; ML

Reekie, Miss Jemima — 1930-61; BS (PT)
Reid, Mrs Jane — 1982; G
Reid, Mrs Jenny — 1951; HE
Reid, Joseph — 1948; M; S
Richards, Miss M. J. — 1956; PC
Rice, William — 1946; M; S
Robb, David — 1954; E
Roberts, David — 1908-45; TS
Roberts, Miss Margaret — 1939; F; M
Robertson, David — 1949; ML
Robertson, David L. — 1930-38; S
Robertson, Mrs Eleanor — 1982; ML
Robertson, Mrs Jean — 1953; BS
Robertson, Robert — 1970-92; H (PT)
Robinson, Mrs B.M.T. — 1956; BS
Robinson, Mrs Elizabeth — 1966; PE; Gu (HM)
Rodger, Miss Marjory — 1975-80; B
Ronald, Miss Jenny — 1955; E
Roodhouse, Mrs Elizabeth — 1973; G
Ross, James — 1950; S
Ross, William — 1947-49; ML
Ross, W. S. — 1960-62; G
Ross, Mrs Williamina — 1979-92; Sec
Rousseau, Alfred — 1938; FrA
Roy, Ivor — 1975-84; B; HLS
Russell, Miss Anna — 1948; M
Russell, Mrs Elizabeth — 1971-86; Sec
Russell, J.C.K. — 1961; ML
Russell, Tom — 1973; Ch
Russell, William — 1935; A

Sadler, Miss Joan — 1969; E
Salines, Daniel — 1960; FrA
Sampais, John — 1987; ML
Samson, Mrs Margaret — 1966; E
Sandell, Miss Jane — 1990-92; Lib
Sandilands, Ian — 1951; M
Sauermann, Helmut — 1965; GA
Savage, Peter — 1982-92; Ch; ST

Schlutz, Rudolf – 1958; GA
Scott, Mrs Catherine — 1949; BS
Scott, Charlie — 1974; J
Scott, Miss Margaret — 1924; M
Scott, Miss M.A. — 1926; E; H
Scott, Miss M. — 1969; BS
Scott, R.W.A. — 1955; Mu
Scoular, Mrs Lydia — 1987; TS
Segger, Helmut — 1968; GA
Sellerbeck, Antje — 1966; GA
Shanks, Henry — 1975; T
Shanks, Miss Janet — 1933; F
Sharp, William — 1929; M; S
Sharp, W.A.C. — 1965; M
Shaw, Miss Annie — 1922; HE
Shaw, Douglas — 1965; Ch
Shedden, Ian — 1979; Rem (PT)
Sheriff, Miss Jane — 1922; E
Sheriff, Miss J.M. — 1957; ML
Sheriff, Miss Margaret — 1925-43; E
Simpson, Miss Avril — 1963; S
Simpson, Mrs Dorothy — 1989; M
Simpson, Miss Katherine — 1983; ML
Simpson, Miss Marion — 1911; ML (PT)
Simpson, William — 1933; L
Smith, Brian — 1975-77; E
Smith, GW. — 1966; Cl
Smith, Mrs Helen — 1985; BS
Smith, Miss I. — 1914-20; HE (PT)
Smith, James — 1972; M (PT)
Smith, John — 1942-68; A (PT)
Smith, Malcolm — 1967; G
Smith, Thomas — 1938; BS
Smith, Waddell — 1980-90; MI
Smyth, Anna — 1975; H
Sneddon, Miss Christine — 1936; E; H
Sneddon, Graham — 1984; J
Spankie, Mrs W — 1979-80; NA
Spence, Miss Jessie — 1976-80; ML
Spence, John — 1946; H (PT)

Sprot, Miss Sheila — 1964-88; M; Gu (PT)
Sproull, James — 1954; BS
Stalker, Donald — 1945-70; TS (PT)
Stalker, Mrs Donald — 1947; A
Stanier, John — 1974-77; B
Steel, Derek — 1982; E
Steele, Mrs Hazel — 1980-81; ML
Steven, William — 1966; E
Stevenson, Miss Ethel — 1911; HE
Stewart, A. — 1919; M
Stewart, Miss I.C. — 1918-61; HE (PT)
Stewart, Miss Lynn — 1982; ML
Stewart, William — 1947; E
Stewart, William L. — 1951; PC; M
Stirling, Ian — 1972-82; M; HMS; DR
Stirrat, Roy — 1949-53; E
Storie, Miss Moira — 1959; PE
Strachan, Mrs Blyth — 1982-88; E
Strang, Robert — 1946; H
Struthers, Miss Agnes — 1934-43; ML
Suckfull, Bernd — 1967; GA
Sutherland, Kenneth — 1963; G
Sutherland, Ronald — 1974-80; P
Syme, Miss Elsa — 1932-69; ML
Symon, Alexander — 1906-24; M; FA
Symon, Alexander Jnr. — 1915; S
Sweeney, John — 1984-85; B

Tait, David — 1912; Cl (PT); AMM
Taylor, Peter — 1981-84; TS
Telfer, Miss Audrey — 1961; ML
Telford, John — 1911-42: A (PT)
Thomasson, Raymond — 1955; H
Thomson, Miss Helen — 1932; A
Thomson, Miss Marabel — 1949; A
Thomson, Mrs Sandra — 1983; G
Thomson, Mrs Williamina — 1951; PC
Thorley, Mrs A. – 1974; G
Tomney, Andrew — 1929; PE

Torrance, Mrs Mary — 1981; E
Toulon, Bertrand — 1929; FrA
Trentin, Genevieve — 1967; FrA
Turkington, David — 1976; T
Turnbull, G.H. — 1954; E
Turner, Miss Laura — 1985; Mu
Turner, Mrs Sandra — 1987; E
Tweedlie, Edward — 1961-79; BS (PT)
Tweedlie, E.S. — 1970; E; Gu (AH)

Urquhart, Miss Jane — 1908; HE (PT)

Vass, Miss M. — 1936; E
Veitch, Mrs Lynne — 1977-92; A; Gu (APT)
Verth, Miss Jean — 1980-83; BS (PT)
Vetesse, Joseph — 1962; G
Villebonnet, Robert — 1951; FrA

Waddell, Miss Agnes — 1950; BS
Walker, Mrs Eleanor — 1984; E
Wallace, David — 1947-50; E
Wallace, Miss Janet — 1923; M; S
Wallace, Miss Linda — 1976-78; Mu
Wallace, Miss Margaret — 1962-69; E
Wardlaw, Tommy — 1980; J
Warren, Mrs Christine — 1978-79; Rem
Watson, Miss Agnes — 1930; ML
Watson, Dr David — 1955; S
Watt, Mrs Margaret — 1941; S
Watters, Mrs Janice — 1982; ML
Weir, Don — 1947; H (PT); HUS; DR
Weir, John — 1909-49; G (PT)
Weir, Miss Helen — 1941; ML
Weir, Robin — 1968; S
White, Mrs Elspeth — 1985; E
White, Miss Pat — 1979-82; B
White, Stanley — 1970; E
Whiteford, John — 1950-60; H
Whitelaw, Campbell — 1985; E
Wilkie, Mrs EJ. — 1958; E

Wilkie, Mrs June — 1981; HE
Willaime, Paul — 1926; FrA
Williams, Mrs Nessie — 1926-57; ML
Williamson, Mrs Sheena — 1975-78; G
Willis, Mrs Myra — 1969; A; Gu (H)
Wilson, Dr D.K. — 1937-53; R
Wilson, Miss Elizabeth — 1955; PE
Wilson, Miss Grace — 1951; A
Wilson, Ian — 1948; M
Wilson, J.T. — 1926; Cl (PT); FA
Wilson, Mrs Margaret — 1964; BS (SA)
Winton, Derek — 1957-88; ML (PT)
Woods, Alex — 1988; AVT
Wright, Miss Heather — 1984; Cl
Wright, Mrs Janette — 1976; Mu
Wright, John — 1974-92; MS (PT); HLS
Wright, Mrs M.B. — 1979; BS (PT)
Wyatt, Miss Joyce — 1955; S

Young, Colin — 1964; S
Young, D. — 1988; TS
Young, Edward — 1952; E
Young, Miss Helen — 1966-87; M (SA); Gu (PT)
Young, Mrs Jessie — 1963; BS
Young, Miss Margaret — 1929; F
Young, Miss M.L. — 1957; H; WA
Young, Robert — 1989; T
Young, Miss R.M. — 1954; ML
Young, Tom — 1976-92; PE (PT)
Young, William — 1981-89; Mu
Yuile, Jack — 1970; Ch (PT)
Yuill, Miss Margaret — 1962-69; ML (PT)

The following (whose Christian names I have been unable to ascertain) also served at the High School:

Aitkenhead, Miss — 1914; ML
Allan, Mrs — 1981; CS
Anderson, Miss — 1981; BS
Arthur, Mr — 1969; M

Baird, Miss — 1987; E
Barrie, Mrs — 1946; H
Baxter, Mrs — 1977; Ru
Bell, Miss — 1953; HE
Bell, Mrs — 1955; E
Bernardeau, Monsieur — 1931; FrA
Bond, Mr — 1969; M
Bradford, Miss — 1917; A
Brooks, Miss — 1991; E
Brown, Miss — 1962; BS
Brown, Mr — 1991; E
Browning, Mr — 1947; Mu

Calderhead, Mr — 1967; E
Campinchi, Monsieur — 1922; FrA
Camson, Mr — 1963; S
Chambers, Mrs — 1969; A
Choudhary, Mr — 1969; B
Cowan, Miss — 1917; HE
Craig, Mrs — 1957; Sec
Cunningham, Miss — 1987; A

Delagoutte, Monsieur — 1923; FrA
Deschamps, Mademoiselle — 1955; FrA
Devlin, Mrs — 1987; E
Dickinson, Mrs — 1973; BS
Dickson, Mrs — 1981; A

Edwards, Mr — 1963; S
Ewan, Miss — 1917; E
Fergie, Mr — 1963; S
Fife, Miss — 1955; Mu

Fordyce, Mr — 1944; E
Fullarton, Mr — 1916; TS
Gierthy, Miss — 1987; E
Glass, Miss — 1917; HE
Gordon, Miss — 1918; E
Gordon, Mr — 1909; AMM
Grangie, Monsieur — 1932; FrA
Green, Mr — 1925; PE
Griffin, Mr — 1963; G

Haddow, Mrs — 1937; E (PT)
Halliday, Miss — 1948; BS
Hamilton, Mrs — 1972; HE
Hamilton, Miss — 1981; ML
Harangee, Mrs — 1981; RE
Hausteck (?) / Hohnstedt (?), Herr — 1955; GA
Hill, Mrs — 1972; S
Hills, Miss — 1957; Sec
Hoffman, Herr — 1937; GA

Inglis, Mrs — 1968; Mu
Jack, Mr — 1921; E; H

Jackson, Mrs — 1985; M
Jamieson, Mr — 1963; M

Kilpatrick, Mr — 1946; E
Kilpatrick, Mr — 1963; M
Kirk, Miss — 1921; ML
Knox, Mrs — 1970; A

Lawrie, Mr — 1917; S
Layden, Mr — 1989; H

Mackay, Mrs — 1964; M
McColl, Miss — 1916; M
McCue, Mrs — 1963; Mu
McDonald, Miss — 1962; HE
McGeachy, Mr — 1974; MS

McGhee, Miss — 1977; MI
McIntyre, Mr — 1980; AVT
McKim, Mrs — 1953; BS
McLachlan, Mr — 1970; S
McLaren, Mr — 1962; TS
McLellan, Mrs — 1948; HE
McLeod, Miss — 1917; M
McNeil, Mrs — 1988; G
McPhee, Mr — 1988; TS
McRoberts, Mr — 1916; TS
McVean, Mr — 1963; S
Mackie, Miss — 1979; G
Marne, Mrs — 1977; BS
Meyer, Herr — 1938; GA
Millar, Dr — 1907; S
Moffat, Mrs – 1977; SD
Moir, Mrs — 1989; HE
Moore, Mrs — 1970; ML
Murray, Miss — 1918; E
Murray, Mrs — 1955; BS

Nimmo, Miss — 1918; G

Orr, Miss — 1982; HE
O'Neill, Miss — 1969; ML
O'Neill, Mrs — 1987; S
Owen, Miss — 1987; E

Patrick, Mr — 1945; BS
Prentice, Miss — 1957; Sec
Purcell. Miss — 1972; BS (APT)

Rankin, Miss — 1911; HE
Reid, Mrs — 1982; LT
Rocques, Monsieur — 1946; FrA

Stalker, Mrs — 1982; MI
Steele, Mrs — 1969; ML
Stephenson, Mr — 1963; TS
Stevenson, Miss — 1967; BS

Stewart, Mrs — 1960; Cl
Sommerville, Miss — 1939; BS
Stubbs, Mr — 1991; MU
Sykes, Mr — 1969; ML

Thomson, Miss — 1969; E

Waddell, Miss — 1916; PE
Walker, Miss — 1915; HE
Walker, Mr — 1943; TS
Weygandt, Herr — 1952; GA

I have not been able to establish what subjects the following (assuming they were on the teaching staff) taught:

Aitken, Mrs Jean
Ballantyne, Miss — 1968
Campbell, Hugh — 1988
Connelly, Miss Alice - AVT
Donaldson, Miss — 1972
Duguid, Miss Susan — 1908
Foote, David — 1907
Innes, Miss Yvonne — 1974
Keay, Maria — 1975-79
Kelly, Robert — 1988
McConnachie, Miss Jeanie — 1914
Melville, Miss — 1969
Pirie, Lorraine — 1982-86
Reid, Nancy — 1976
Ryan, Marie — 1978-79
Sandilands, Sandra — 1988
Smith, Mrs — 1972
Waddell, Mrs — 1988

Appendix B

Dux Medallists

1907	James McAlpin
1908	Robert P. Douglas
1909	James T. Wilson
1910	John Bell; Margaret McLeod
1911	Mary A.M. MacLean
1912	John C. Hunter
1913	Isabella S. Inglis; Annie B. Hunter; Agnes M. Leggate
1914	Janet Robertson
1915	Alexander Symon; Jeanie L. Brownlee
1916	John L.K. Gifford
1917	Marion Lindsay
1918	Christina R. Tudhope
1919	Margaret Phillips; Marion Tannahill
1920	Mary H. Brownlie
1921	George Thomson
1922	Jeanie Fraser
1923	Thomas S. Scott
1924	Agnes F. Watson
1925	Gina Jackson
1926	Pearl Gilchrist
1927	John Heugh
1928	Jenny Balmain
1929	Samuel Curran
1930	Ebenezer Loudon
1931	W. Walker Chambers
1932	Thomas Paterson
1933	Leonard J. Ash
1934	Robert Wilson
1935	Isobel F. Haddow
1936	Samuel A. Forrest
1937	Robert Dalziel
1938	Robert C. Curran
1939	Robert Deans
1940	I. Allan Brownlie
1941	Alexander McClelland

1942	George Sneddon
1943	Peter Nardone
1944	W. Orrock Stewart
1945	Robert Barrie
1946	Catherine Calder
1947	John Shields
1948	Jean Lawson
1949	Charles Black
1950	Thomas Russell; Robert Todd
1951	Christina Smellie
1952	William Wilson
1953	Francis Gardner
1954	Thomas Nardone; Robert I. Russell
1955	Jane D. Henry
1956	William J. Guthrie; George S. Halliday
1957	William H. Smith
1958	Ian Fraser
1959	Mary A. Swanson
1960	Norma H. Gill
1961	Wilma M. Shepherd
1962	Elspeth Chalmers; Ian Bill
1963	Margaret Stevenson
1964	Janet Cameron; Stephen Mearns
1965	Jean Crowe; Ronald Mackay
1966	Norman Lindsay
1967	Sandra Watt
1968	William McNeil
1969	William Muir
1970	Margaret Campbell
1971	Peter Melrose
1972	Kathleen Paton
1973	David Clarke
1974	Douglas Forrest; Wilbert Hall
1975	Janet Ferguson
1976	Andrew Herd
1977	Ronald Holden
1978	Moira Patrick; Evelyn Tweedlie
1979	David Dunbar
1980	Jamie Stevenson

1981	Avril Haddow
1982	Fiona Watson
1983	Sandra McCumisky
1984	Neil Robertson
1985	Angela Renwick
1986	Navid Sardar
1987	Gregor Dunlay
1988	Scott Dickson
1989	Eleanor Cowan
1990	Richard Wolseley
1991	Carol Millar
1992	Fiona Dunbar

Appendix C

School Captains

Boys' Captain

1927-28	William Rankin
1928-29	William Crockett
1929-30	Robert Russell
1930-31	William Wilson
1931-32	Robert Whitelaw
1932-33	John Young/Leonard Ash
1933-34	Douglas Reid
1934-35	George Lawrie
1935-36	Robert Syme
1936-37	George Henderson
1937-38	George Cowan
1938-39	David Denholm
1939-40	David Linning
1940-41	John McMinn
1941-42	John Archibald
1942-43	Peter Nardone
1943-44	Robert Osborne
1944-45	William Archibald
1945-46	Jack Cameron/Hunter Mackie
1946-47	John Shields
1947-48	Norman Muat
1948-49	John Allan
1949-50	Thomas Prentice
1950-51	James Robertson
1951-52	James Lumsden
1952-53	Derrick Marks
1953-54	Gordon Hunter
1954-55	James Murdoch
1955-56	William Hunter
1956-57	William Tennant
1957-58	William Ritchie
1958-59	William G. Anderson
1959-60	Andrew Hepburn

1960-61	Alexander Robertson
1961-62	John Moore
1962-63	Eric Barr
1963-64	Thomas Rae
1964-65	Edward Tweedlie
1965-66	Robert Wallace
1966-67	John Gillon
1967-68	George Watters
1968-69	Robert Thom
1969-70	Keith Gillon
1970-71	Gordon Kennedy
1971-72	Tom Costley
1972-73	Allan Henderson
1973-74	David Adam
1974-75	Hugh Gilchrist
1975-76	Peter Edment
1976-77	Ian Murray
1977-78	Alan Watson
1978-79	Ian Pickett
1979-80	Andrew MacLean
1980-81	Eric Graham
1981-82	Jim Hamilton
1982-83	Stuart Dick
1983-84	Robert MacLean
1985-86	John Moffat
1986-87	Navid Sardar
1991-92	David Pringle

Girls' Captain

1927-28	Megnon Westwood
1928-29	Jenny Balmain
1929-30	Nellie Preston
1930-31	Mary Hunter
1931-32	Maisie Wilson
1932-33	Cathie Grigor
1933-34	Margaret Archibald
1934-35	May Davidson
1935-36	Cathie Kerr
1936-37	Jean Sloan

1937-38	Chrissie Morrison
1938-39	Margaret Smith
1939-40	May Brownlie
1940-41	Margaret Napier/Nancy Marshall
1941-42	Margaret Chapman
1942-43	Margaret Fleming
1943-44	Essie Rogerson/Margaret King
1944-45	Jessie Whitehouse
1945-46	Anne Hunter
1946-47	Janet Barrie
1947-48	Cissie McPherson
1948-49	Margaret Murray
1949-50	Jeanette Taylor
1950-51	June Cleland
1951-52	Hazel Lyon
1952-53	Agnes Hepburn
1953-54	Lalla Weir
1954-55	Jane D. Henry
1955-56	Mary Beattie
1956-57	Margaret A. Clemenson
1957-58	Christine D. Irvine
1958-59	Mary A. Swanson
1959-60	Mary N. Hepburn
1960-61	Jean Guthrie
1961-62	Jennifer McComb
1962-63	Margaret Stevenson
1963-64	Janet Cameron
1964-65	Margaret Pearson
1965-66	Jennifer Mearns
1966-67	Ruth Robson
1967-68	Mary Tait
1968-69	Elizabeth Tweedlie
1969-70	Barbara Kirkland
1970-71	Anne Jarvie
1971-72	Grace Allison
1972-73	Linda Parker
1973-74	Frances Bell
1974-75	Margo McLean
1975-76	Ailie McPhail

1976-77	Aileen Spankie
1977-78	Moira Patrick
1978-79	Janis Cairns
1979-80	Ann Lennox
1980-81	Angela McMillan
1981-82	Carol Gray
1982-83	Deborah Johnstone
1983-84	June Sinclair
1985-86	Fiona McDonald
1986-87	Tracey Butler
1991-92	Lynsey Simkin

Appendix D

Sports Champions

Senior Boys

1925	Joseph Morrison
1927	Sam Curran; William Millar
1928	William Crockett
1929	Sam Curran
1930	Robert Gardiner
1931	Robert Gardiner
1932	Robert Gardiner
1933	Andrew Lawrence
1934	Andrew Lawrence
1935	Thomas Gardiner
1936	Andrew Lawrence
1937	Alex Rankin
1938	Andrew Vincent
1939	Harry Steele
1940	John Archibald
1943	William Archibald
1944	William Archibald
1945	William Archibald
1946	Kenneth McKenzie
1947	Spence Gray; Walter Hogg
1948	Peter Hill
1949	Hugh Jamieson
1950	Stanley Bruce; Ian Hunter
1951	Ian Hunter
1952	James Lumsden
1953	Gordon Hunter
1954	Gordon Hunter
1955	James Brownlie
1956	William Hunter
1957	William McLure
1958	Andrew Hepburn
1959	Andrew Hepburn
1960	Andrew Hepburn

1961	Alex Robertson
1962	Sam Francis
1963	Brian Harrison
1964	Roy Graham
1965	Tom Dale
1966	Ian Moir
1967	Ian Goodlet
1968	Derek McLeod
1969	Alex Hinshaw
1970	Alex Hinshaw
1971	Ian Philip
1972	John Paul
1973	Victor Topping
1974	Peter Irvine
1975	Donald Henderson
1976	Alan Patrick
1977	Jim Young
1978	Gordon Smith
1979	Peter MacLean
1980	Brian Muir
1981	Calum Currie
1982	Calum Currie
1984	Watson Borthwick
1985	Drew Clark
1988	David McKeown
1989	Greig Langford
1990	Matthew McCreadie
1991	Greig Langford

Senior Girls

1925	Margaret Grierson
1927	Margaret Grierson
1928	Nettie Murie
1929	Nettie Murie
1930	Nettie Murie
1931	Pearl Leggate
1932	Dorothy Maxwell
1933	Ella Chapman; Margaret Whitelaw
1934	Margaret Whitelaw

1935	May Davidson
1936	Isa May
1937	Jean Prentice; Margaret Watson
1938	Jessie Gill; Margaret Watson
1939	Edwina Craigmyle
1944	Nana Rodger
1945	Nana Rodger
1946	Margaret Cranston
1947	Margaret Cranston
1948	Betty Baxter
1949	Doris Weir
1950	Betty Laughlin
1951	Margaret Gilfillan; Jenny Tait
1952	Edith Anderson; Isobel Scott; Jemima O'Neil
1953	Betty Rodger
1954	Betty Rodger
1955	Betty Rodger
1956	Christine Irvine
1957	Christine Irvine
1958	Christine Irvine
1959	Olga Lithgow
1960	Ruby Nicol
1961	Ruby Nicol
1962	Mary Watson
1963	Evelyn Finlay
1964	Evelyn Finlay
1965	Jean Rae
1966	Marjorie Johnstone
1967	Christine Sloan
1968	Barbara Kirkland
1969	Barbara Kirkland
1970	Marion Parker
1971	Anne Hall
1972	Kitty Walker
1973	Anne Hall
1974	Ruth Fullarton
1975	Ruth Fullarton
1976	Jane Armit
1977	Margaret Torrance

1979	Moira Anderson
1980	Moira Anderson
1981	Moira Anderson
1982	Sandra Brown
1985	Michelle Allan
1987	Rebecca Murray
1988	Claire Dunlay
1989	Rebecca Murray
1990	Helen Christie

Intermediate Boys

1935	Alex Rankin
1936	Robert Curran
1937	Harry Steele
1938	William Jack
1939	John Archibald
1943	Alec Brown
1944	Kenneth McKenzie
1945	David Muircroft
1946	Robert Hunter
1947	Ian Hunter
1948	James Robertson
1949	Charles Broadley
1950	Arthur Reid
1951	William Hunter
1952	James Johnstone
1953	William Talbot
1954	Ian Johnstone
1955	David Leiper
1956	David Russell
1957	Tom Ashforth
1958	Alex Robertson
1959	Alex Robertson
1960	Brian Harrison
1961	James Gauld
1962	Alan Carson
1963	Eric Warren
1964	John McAra
1965	Kenneth McKinder

1966	Derek McLeod
1967	Norman Stevenson
1968	Jim Roberts
1969	Ian Philip
1970	Victor Topping
1971	Kenneth Smith
1972	Victor Topping
1973	Alan Fulton
1974	Gordon Fraser
1975	Alan Patrick
1976	Ronald Graham
1977	James Melville
1978	Calum Currie
1979	Jim McWhinnie
1980	Andrew Carse
1981	David Bradley
1982	Andrew Morrison
1983	Alan McRorie
1984	Drew Clark
1987	Ian Robertson

Intermediate Girls

1957	Ruby Nicol
1958	Irene Hare
1959	Isobel McNab
1960	Mary Watson
1961	Evelyn Finlay
1962	Elizabeth Johnstone; Patricia Thomson
1963	Jean Rae
1964	Marjorie Johnstone
1965	Elaine McNeil
1966	Janette Lewars
1967	Barbara Kirkland
1968	Isobel Teller
1969	Hazel Orr
1970	Anne Hall
1971	Jean Hastie
1972	Anne Hall

1973	Ruth Fullarton
1974	Jane Armit; Margaret Glover
1975	Elizabeth Bell
1976	Alison Watson
1977	Jane Hamilton
1978	Moira Anderson
1979	Margaret Ireland
1980	Angela Murdoch
1981	Sandra Brown
1982	Andrea Easton
1983	Christine Hall
1984	Tracey McCulloch
1987	Claire Dunlay

Junior Boys

1925	A. Roberts
1928	William Sneddon
1929	Hamilton Curran
1930	Adam Sommerville
1931	Robert Freeland
1932	James MacDonald
1993	Dick Steventon
1934	Alex McNay
1935	Robert Curran
1936	Harry Steele
1937	James Dunsmore
1938	John Archibald
1939	Bobby Rodger
1940	Sandy Muir
1941	William Archibald
1943	Robert Finlay
1944	James Boyle
1945	James Boyle
1946	James Robertson
1947	James Robertson
1948	James Lumsden
1949	Arthur Reid
1950	Donald Laird
1951	James Johnstone

1952	William Talbot
1953	Ian Johnstone
1954	David Leiper
1955	David Torrance; Frank McKenzie
1956	Tom Ashforth
1957	Alex Robertson
1958	Andrew Kerr
1959	Val Williams
1960	James Gauld
1961	Alan Carson
1962	Eric Warren
1963	John McAra
1964	Kenneth McKinder
1965	Peter Benzie
1966	Norman Stevenson
1967	Jim Roberts
1968	John Paul
1969	Alan Henderson
1970	Kenneth Smith
1971	Ian Morton
1972	Alex Higgins
1973	Iain McGillivray
1975	James Melville
1976	Gordon Smith
1977	Calum Currie
1978	Jim McWhinnie
1979	Andrew Carse
1980	Colin Airth
1981	Andrew Morrison
1982	Alistair McIntosh
1983	Kenneth Morrison
1984	Marcus Graham
1985	Marcus Graham
1987	Steven Alexander
1988	Steven Alexander
1989	Robert Cringles
1990	Arthur Calderwood
1991	Richard Graham

Junior Girls

1925	Margaret Baxter
1928	Maggie Phillips
1929	Katherine Douglas
1930	Pearl Leggate
1931	Agnes Glover
1932	May Greenhorn
1933	Mary Yates
1934	Margaret Watson
1935	Isobel Higgins
1936	Doris Hunter; Jessie Finlay
1937	Margaret Miller
1938	Margaret Adams
1939	Nancy Williamson
1940	Betty Rae
1941	Nan Welsh
1943	Jean Morrison
1944	Doris Docherty
1945	Jessie McCulloch
1946	Moira Russell
1947	Sandra Watt
1948	Margaret Gilfillan
1949	Betty Laughlin
1950	Gertrude Duncan
1951	Betty Rodger; Isobel Scott; Jemima O'Neil
1952	Betty Rodger
1953	Minnie Forrest
1954	Christine Irvine
1955	Nessie McInnes
1956	Isobel Gray; Ruby Nicol
1957	June Watson
1958	Margaret Simpson
1959	Margaret Hare
1960	Evelyn Finlay
1961	Ann Hitchcock; Pat Thomson
1962	Jean Rae
1963	Marjorie Johnstone
1964	Lee Marshall
1965	Barbara Howden
1966	Sandra Freel
1967	Isobel Telfer

1968	Hazel Orr
1969	Jennifer Muncie; Ann Hall
1970	Joyce Gladstone
1971	Moira Mathieson
1972	Lydia Milligan
1973	Jane Armit
1975	Alison Watson
1976	Jane Hamilton
1977	Moira Anderson
1978	Heather Robertson
1979	Angela Murdoch
1980	Laurie Kain
1981	Andrea Easton
1982	Gillian McDonald
1983	Michelle Allan
1984	Rebecca Murray
1985	Rebecca Murray
1987	Amanda Murray
1988	Helen Christie
1989	Jo Ann Murray
1990	Elizabeth Wardropper
1991	Deborah Tyrie

Appendix E

Representative Honours (Football)

Cambusnethan

1923	A. Young; G. Heron
1926	T. Liddell
1928	Lindsay; Sneddon; Wotherspoon
1929	A. Johnstone; R. Russell; J. Dykes; R. Nicol; J. Watt
1930	Kirk; Gibb
1932	J. Phillips; E. Tweedlie; J. Laurie; D. Steventon
1993	R. Skillen; J. McMillan; R. Finlayson; T. Brown; D. Steventon
1934	R. Skillen; R. Finlayson; McKay; Nicol; Watson; Fowler; Walker
1935	Russell; Johnston; Steele
1936	Murphy; Hunter; Clelland
1937	Murphy; Hunter; Clelland; J. Craig; W. Leitch; W. Jack
1938	J. Craig; W. Leitch; W. Jack; A. Park; J. McPherson; W. Williamson; A. Hunter
1948	J. Robertson; L. Bramley

Motherwell and Wishaw

1923	A. Young; G. Heron
1926	P. Paterson; A. Young
1949	Ross; Lumsden
1953	S. Reid; W. Reid
1960	I. Bill
1968	T. Costley; A. Merry; R. Nicholls

Lanarkshire

Under - 15

1917	G. Phillips; A. McGregor
1923	A. Wilson; G. Heron; W. Millar
1925	G. Heron; W. Semple

628

1926	W Crockett; W Millar; P. Paterson
1931	J. Dykes
1932	J. Dykes; T. Gardiner; R. Freeland
1934	McLachlan
1935	D. McKerrigan
1937	H. Steele
1942	T. Harris; W. Graham; A. Jack; J. Cameron; J. Rae
1943	J. Rae; J. Cameron; A. Bishop; R. Barrie
1947	J. Allen
1948	J. Robertson
1953	S. Reid; W. Reid
1956	D. McIntyre; R. Rodger
1958	J. Stevenson; F. McKenzie; A. Kerr
1959	J. Stevenson; F. McKenzie
1961	J. Moore; T. Rae; P. Hughes
1965	R. Wright
1968	R. Nicholls; A. Merry; T. Costley
1972	A. Keir; A. Armstrong; S. McEwan

Under – 16½

1966	R. Wright; J. Bissett
1967	R. Colquhoun; A. Pearson

Under - 18

1955	J. Brownlie
1960	A. Hepburn
1962	S. Francis; A. Mauchline; T. Rae
1964	I. Clelland; P. Hughes; D. Gilchrist
1965	P. Hughes
1966	D, McClair; R. Wright
1972	A. Merry; R. Wilson; T. Costley; L. Dalrymple

Rest of Scotland

1933	W. Gentleman
1942	J. Archibald; W. Jack; W. Leitch
1943	P. Nardone
1945	A. Jack

1951	J. Robertson
1958	R. Waugh
1960	A. Hepburn
1962	A. Kerr

Scottish Schools F.A. Select

| 1953 | W. Gibb; G. Hunter |

Appendix F

Golf Champions

Senior Boys

1933	John Kirk
1934	John Kirk
1935	Cochrane C. Cuthbert
1936	William Baxter
1937	William Baxter
1938	Robert Don
1940	John McMinn
1941	John McMinn
1942	Stanley Weir
1943	Douglas Harvie
1944	Thomas Baird
1945	Douglas Harvie
1946	James Haig
1947	James Jarvie
1948	Burns Yuill
1950	Robin Haston
1951	Tom Fraser
1952	Martin Shaw
1954	James Fuller
1955	Jack S. Brown
1958	William Chalmers
1959	William Cameron
1961	James B. Lithgow
1962	James B. Lithgow
1963	Alan Carson
1964	John D. Smith
1965	Robert McGregor
1968	William McNeil
1970	Jim Hamilton

Junior Boys

1957	Jim Tannahill
1958	Eric Barr
1960	Alex Nelson
1961	Alan Cater
1968	William Hamilton
1969	Jim Hamilton
1970	Jack Hamilton
1971	James Gibson

Junior Girls

1969	Anne Cuthbertson
1970	Anne Cuthbertson
1971	Elizabeth Masson

Appendix G

Swimming Champions

Senior Boys

1957	Robert Watt
1958	Robert Watt
1959	Cameron Morris
1960	Donald Gibson
1961	George Waddell
1962	George Barr; Donald Gibson
1963	Tom Rae
1964	Peter Meager
1965	John Bell
1967	James Coats
1968	James Thompson
1969	James Thompson
1970	Tim Eley; James Thompson
1971	Tim Eley
1972	Ian William Pettigrew
1973	Tim Eley
1975	Graeme Sutton
1976	Craig Hill
1977	Graeme Sutton
1978	William Mitchell
1979	John Lindsay
1980	David Birchall
1981	Gary Burns
1982	Alan Burns
1983	Alan Burns
1984	Craig O'Hara
1985	Marcus McLaughlan
1987	Andrew Stevenson
1988	David Thomson

Senior Girls

1957	Rita Brown
1958	Christine Stewart
1959	Christine Stewart
1960	Kay Littlejohn
1961	Mary Nicol
1962	Ann Torrance
1963	Ann Torrance
1964	Ann Torrance
1965	Janette Scott
1967	Ruth Robson
1968	Gillian Westlake
1969	Barbara Kirkland
1970	Elizabeth Bell; May Graham; Janice Gray
1971	Susan Delano
1973	Janice Isaac
1974	Helen Baird
1975	Anne Hinshelwood
1976	Isobel Blakeway
1977	Isobel Blakeway
1978	Elspeth Craig
1979	Allyson McClung
1980	Audrey White
1981	Audrey White
1982	Audrey White
1983	Karen Kennedy
1984	Kim Anderson
1985	Lorraine King
1987	Lorraine King
1988	Lorraine King

Intermediate Boys

1975	Craig Hill
1976	Colin Ferguson
1977	John Lindsay

Intermediate Girls

1975	Isobel Blakeway
1976	Margaret Craig
1977	Margaret Craig

Junior Boys

1957	Cameron Morris
1958	S. Francis
1959	Ian Wylie
1960	George Barr
1961	Wilson Struthers
1962	John Gillon
1963	James Coats
1964	Brian Pickering
1965	Ian Morris
1967	Richard Nicholls
1968	Ian Philip
1969	Ian Pettigrew
1970	Ian Pettigrew
1971	Ian Pettigrew
1973	Nelson Clark
1974	Graeme Sutton
1975	John Lindsay
1976	William Mitchell
1977	Gary Burns
1978	Gary Burns
1979	Scott Lennox
1980	Alan Burns
1981	Alan Burns
1982	Chris Glenn
1983	William Leitch
1984	Marcus McLaughlan
1985	George Wands
1987	Graham Donnelly; Stuart Thomson; John Clark
1988	Stuart Thomson

Junior Girls

1957	Christine Stewart
1958	M, Simpson
1959	Kay Littlejohn
1960	Susan Bell
1961	Ann Torrance
1962	Freda Stephenson
1963	Sheila Paterson
1964	Margaret Hamilton
1965	Ann Stevenson
1967	Sandra Clemenson
1968	Margaret Rafferty
1969	Maureen Clemenson
1970	Elizabeth McClure
1971	Jean Hamilton
1973	Helen Baird
1974	Anne Hinshelwood
1975	Margaret Craig
1976	Fiona Paterson
1977	Allyson McClung
1978	Allyson McClung
1979	Chelie Nicholls
1980	Chelie Nicholls
1981	Kim Anderson
1982	Gaynor Marr
1983	Lorraine King
1984	Lorraine King
1985	Karen Borthwick
1987	Gillian Dargavel
1988	Gillian Dargavel

The author would like to thank Jim Donnelly for supplying him with the photographs that appear on Page 586. He would also like to thank Vintage, Glen Telfer, Oxford University Press, Bloomsbury Publishing Plc, Peters Fraser and Dunlop Group Ltd., and Orion Publishing Group Ltd. for giving him permission to reproduce material from the following:

- *Catch 22*
- *Jock Stein – a Scots Life*
- *The Oxford Dictionary of Quotations*
- *The Bloomsbury Dictionary of Quotations*
- *Decline and Fall*
- *Lucky Jim*

If, through inadvertence (on the part of the author) or inaccessibility, any copywright holder has been overlooked, the publisher will be pleased to make the necessary arrangements at the first opportunity.

Nec me meminisse pigebit Elissae

Dum memor ipse mei, dum spiritus hos regit artus.

Virgil, *Aeneid*